Global Development Finance

External Debt of Developing Countries

Global Development Finance

External Debt of Developing Countries

2012

THE WORLD BANK
Washington, D.C.

1818 H Street NW
Washington DC 20433
Telephone: 202-473-1000
Internet: www.worldbank.org

1 2 3 4 14 13 12 11

ISBN (paper): 978-0-8213-8997-3
ISBN (electronic): 978-0-8213-9453-3
DOI: 10.1596/978-0-8213-8997-3

Table of Contents

Preface

The World Bank's Debtor Reporting System (DRS), from which the aggregates and country tables presented in this report are drawn, was established in 1951. The debt crisis of the 1980s brought increased attention to debt statistics and to the *World Debt Tables*, the predecessor to *Global Development Finance*. Now the global financial crisis has once again heightened awareness in developing countries of the importance of managing their external obligations. Central to this process is the measurement and monitoring of external debt stocks and flows in a coordinated and comprehensive way. The initial objective of the DRS was to support the World Bank's assessment of the creditworthiness of its borrowers. But it has grown as a tool to inform developing countries and the international community of trends in external financing and as a standard for the concepts and definitions on which countries can base their own debt management systems.

Over the years, the external financing options available to developing countries have evolved and expanded, and so too has the demand for timely and relevant data to measure the activity of public- and private-sector borrowers and creditors. Recurrent debt crises caused by adverse global economic conditions or poor economic management have demanded solutions, including debt restructuring and, in the case of the poorest, most highly indebted countries, outright debt forgiveness, formulated on the basis of detailed and robust information on external obligations.

Steps are continuously being taken to ensure that the data captured by the DRS mirror these developments and respond to the needs of debt managers and analysts. In this context, reporting requirements are periodically amended to reflect changes in borrowing patterns. Many developing countries increasingly rely on financing raised in domestic markets, so we are exploring ways to expand the coverage of public sector borrowing in domestic markets. At the same time, we are mindful that expanded coverage and efforts to enhance data accuracy and timeliness must be balanced against the reporting burden imposed on developing countries. Bringing modern technology to bear reduces reporting costs. In partnership with the major providers of debt data management systems to developing countries, the Commonwealth Secretariat (COMSEC) and the United Nations Conference on Trade and Development (UNCTAD), we have established standard code and system links that enable countries to provide their DRS reports electronically, in a seamless and automated data exchange process.

We recognize that robust debt data and good debt management go hand in hand, and the World Bank, together with its partners, is committed to improving the capacity of developing countries to manage their debt. We are also committed to maintaining the DRS as a rich source of information and welcome your comments and suggestions to ensure that it meets your needs.

Shaida Badiee
Director, Development Data Group

Acknowledgments

This volume and its companion volume, The Little Data Book on External Debt, were prepared by the Financial Data Team of the Development Data Group (DECDG), led by Ibrahim Levent under the supervision of Neil James Fantom, and comprising Nanasamudd Chhim, Akane Hanai, Wendy Huang, Hiroko Maeda, Gloria Moreno, Evis Rucaj, Yasue Sakuramoto, Rubena Sukaj, and Alagiriswamy Venkatesan, working closely with other teams in the Development Economics Vice Presidency's Development Data Group. The team was assisted by Awatif H. Abuzeid and Elysee Kiti. The system support team was led by Abdolreza Farivari. The Migration and Remittances unit provided worker remittances and compensation of employee data. The overview of current developments was prepared by Malvina Pollock and reviewed by Eric Swanson in consultation with the staff of DECDG; country economists reviewed the data tables. The work was carried out under the management of Shaida Badiee. Valuable advice was provided by Shahrokh Fardoust.

The production of this volume was managed by Azita Amjadi and Alison Kwong. The online database was prepared by Shelley Fu and William Prince, with technical support from Ramgopal Erabelly and Malarvizhi Veerappan. Mobile apps production was coordinated by Vilas K. Madlekar and Parastoo Oloumi. The cover was designed by Jomo Tariku. Staff members from External Affairs, Office of the Publisher, coordinated the publication and dissemination of the book.

Overview

The data and analysis presented in this edition of *Global Development Finance* are based on actual flows and debt related transactions for 2010 reported to the World Bank Debtor Reporting System (DRS) by 129 developing countries. The reports confirm that in 2010 international capital flows to developing countries surpassed preliminary estimates and returned to their pre-crisis level of $1.1 trillion, an increase of 68 percent over the comparable figure for 2009. Private capital flows surged in 2010 driven by a massive jump in short-term debt, a strong rebound in bonds and more moderate rise in equity flows. Debt related inflows jumped almost 200 percent compared to a 25 percent increase in net equity flows. The rebound in capital flows was concentrated in a small group of 10 middle income countries where net capital inflows rose by an average of nearly 80 percent in 2010, almost double the rate of increase (44 percent) recorded by other developing countries. These 10 countries accounted for 73 percent of developing countries GNI, and received 73 percent of total net capital flows to developing countries in 2010.

Developing Countries' Debt Stocks and Flows 2010

The combined stock of developing countries' external debt rose $437 billion to $4 trillion at end in 2010, reflecting net debt inflows of $495 billion, the downward effect of the year on year appreciation, vis-à-vis the US dollar, of foreign currencies in which around 30 percent of developing countries external debt is denominated, and debt forgiveness. Short term was the fastest growing component, rising by 34 percent in 2010 as compared to a 6 percent increase in the stock of outstanding long term external debt. Most short term debt was trade related and, measured against developing countries' imports it increased only marginally, to 17 percent compared to 16 percent in 2009. The stock of long term debt at end 2010 was fairly evenly divided between publicly guaranteed debt, 54 percent, and debt owed to private non-guaranteed borrowers, 46 percent, although the former rose twice as fast as the later in 2010, by 8 percent as compared to 4 percent. Developing countries' debt stock remained moderate, an average of 21 percent of gross national income (GNI) and 69 percent of export earnings and risks associated with the fact that short term debt constituted 25 percent of debt stock at end 2010 were mitigated by international reserves. The global economic crisis forced some developing countries to draw down international reserves but, in aggregate, developing countries recorded an accumulation of international reserves since the onset of the crisis: equivalent to 137 percent of external debt stock at end 2010 (table 1).

International capital flows rose by 68 percent to $1.1 trillion in 2010, equivalent to their 2007 pre-crisis level. Measured in relation to developing country gross national income (GNI), the increase in net capital flows was less striking: from 4.1 percent of GNI in 2009 to 5.8 percent in 2010 but well short of their 8.1 percent ratio in 2007. Debt flows from private creditors were close to five times their 2009 level, driven by a massive jump in short-term debt and a strong rebound in bond issuance by public and private sector borrowers. Foreign direct investment and portfolio flows were up by 27 percent and 18 percent, respectively, bringing total private equity flows to $635 billion in 2010, only slightly below their 2007 all-time

Table 1. External Debt Stock of Developing Countries and Select Ratios, 2005–10
$ billions

	2005	2006	2007	2008	2009	2010
Total External Debt Outstanding	**2,514.1**	**2,675.3**	**3,220.5**	**3,499.2**	**3,639.6**	**4,076.3**
Long-term (including IMF)	2,013.2	2,081.5	2,456.5	2,739.7	2,866.4	3,039.9
Public and publicly guaranteed (including IMF)	1,332.1	1,266.2	1,371.3	1,423.2	1,530.4	1,647.2
Private nonguaranteed	681.1	815.4	1,085.1	1,316.5	1,336.0	1,392.7
Short-term external debt	500.8	593.8	764.0	759.5	773.2	1,036.4
Ratios						
External debt outstanding to GNI (%)	26.6	23.9	23.2	21.0	22.4	21.0
External debt stocks to exports (%)	75.9	66.1	65.6	59.3	77.0	68.7
Reserves to external debt outstanding (%)	78.7	97.8	114.9	118.7	132.9	137.1
Short term debt to imports (%)	15.3	15.2	16.0	13.0	16.2	17.2

Sources: World Bank Debtor Reporting System and International Monetary Fund.

high of $667 billion. The net inflow of debt related financing from official creditors (excluding grants) declined by 11 percent, with those from the IMF down almost 50 percent from their 2009 level. By contrast, support from IBRD continued its upward trajectory with net inflows rising by a further 45 percent in 2010. Net inflows from other official creditors in 2010 held steady at their 2009 level (table 2).

The 2010 increase in net capital flows was accompanied by marked change in composition between equity and debt related flows. Over the past decade net equity flows to developing countries have consistently surpassed the level of debt related flows, reaching as high as 97 percent of aggregate net capital flows in 2002 and accounting for 75 percent of them ($509 billion) in 2009. However, periods of rapid increase in capital flows have often been marked by a reversal from equity to debt. For example, in 2007, when net capital flows increased by 65 percent, to $1,133 billion, the main driver was the 80 percent rise in debt related flows from private creditors (mostly to private sector corporate borrowers in developing countries) and not the more moderate, 35 percent rise in equity inflows. A similar pattern occurred in 2010 when net financing by private creditors, albeit largely of a short-term nature, fueled the rise in net capital flows (figure 1).

Capital flows to developing countries are heavily concentrated in the 10 middle-income countries, namely those with the largest external debt stock at end 2010, referred to hereafter as the top 10 borrowers. Over the past decade, the top 10 borrowers have commanded on average 70 percent of the annual aggregate net capital inflows to all developing countries and they have received a much larger share of net equity inflows than other developing countries (figure 2).

In 2010 net capital inflows to the top ten borrowers increased by an average of almost 80 percent compared to only 44 percent for all other developing countries combined. Net debt inflows rose to $359 billion, almost double the amount going to the other 119 developing countries and equity inflows increased by 30 percent compared to a 16 percent rise for other developing countries. China alone received 30 percent of the aggregate net capital inflows to all developing countries in 2010 while the combined share of the so-called BRICs (Brazil, the Russian Federation, India, and China) was 58 percent. Together the BRICs accounted for almost 40 percent, and the top ten borrowers for 64 percent of the end 2010 external debt stock owed by all developing countries (table 3).

At the regional level, East Asia and the Pacific saw the most pronounced rise in the net inflows in 2010: combined debt and equity flows increased by 90 percent, to $447 billion, dominated by the 52 percent rise in equity and 178 percent rise in debt flows to China. In Latin America and the Caribbean net capital inflows were up 83 percent over their 2009 level, underpinned by a rebound in FDI inflows and a threefold jump in debt related flows; the latter driven by a 20 percent rise in net inflows from official, largely multilateral, creditors, and a rapid rise in net medium- and short-term

Table 2. Net Capital Flows to Developing Countries, 2001–10
$ billions

	2001	2002	2003	2004	2005	2006	2007	2008	2009	2010
Net private and official inflows	212.6	168.4	261.7	347.3	519.7	686.5	1133.2	835.2	674.9	1129.7
Percent of GNI	3.7	2.9	3.9	4.4	5.5	6.1	8.1	5.0	4.1	5.8
Net equity inflows	165.5	163.3	179.2	245.5	382.0	495.2	667.1	570.7	508.7	634.5
Net FDI inflows	158.9	155.0	152.8	208.5	314.5	387.5	534.1	624.1	400.0	506.1
Net portfolio equity inflows	6.7	8.3	26.3	36.9	67.5	107.7	133.0	–53.4	108.8	128.4
Net debt flows	47.1	5.1	82.5	101.9	137.7	191.2	466.1	264.4	166.2	495.2
Official creditors	30.9	6.9	–12.0	–24.3	–64.3	–69.0	1.5	29.5	80.5	71.2
World Bank	7.4	–0.5	–2.6	2.4	2.6	–0.3	5.2	7.2	18.3	22.4
IMF	19.5	14.2	2.4	–14.7	–40.2	–26.7	–5.1	10.8	26.8	13.8
Other official	4.1	–6.7	–11.7	–11.9	–26.8	–42.0	1.5	11.5	35.4	35.0
Private creditors	16.1	–1.8	94.5	126.1	202.0	260.2	464.6	234.9	85.7	424.0
Net medium and long term debt flows	–3.5	–3.8	36.3	73.2	120.4	164.9	296.3	239.3	70.9	155.5
Bonds	15.7	11.1	23.1	33.9	49.4	34.3	91.7	26.7	51.1	111.4
Banks and other private	–19.2	–15.0	13.2	39.3	71.1	130.6	204.7	212.5	19.8	44.1
Net short term debt flows	19.6	2.0	58.2	52.9	81.6	95.3	168.3	–4.4	14.7	268.5
Change in reserves (– = increase)	–81.8	–165.4	–288.4	–395.7	–405.1	–636.9	–1085.3	–452.5	–681.9	–752.0
Memorandum items										
Official grants excluding tech cooperation	28.4	33.9	44.5	52.2	57.1	107.2	76.4	85.8	87.5	*90.0*
Workers remittances	90.1	108.2	134.6	155.6	187.0	221.6	276.4	322.9	306.3	319.6

Sources: World Bank Debtor Reporting System; International Monetary Fund; Bank for International Settlements; and Organization for Economic Co-operation and Development. Official grants data for 2010 are World Bank estimates.

Figure 1. Net Capital Flows to Developing Countries, Equity and Debt-Related Flows, 2001–10
percent

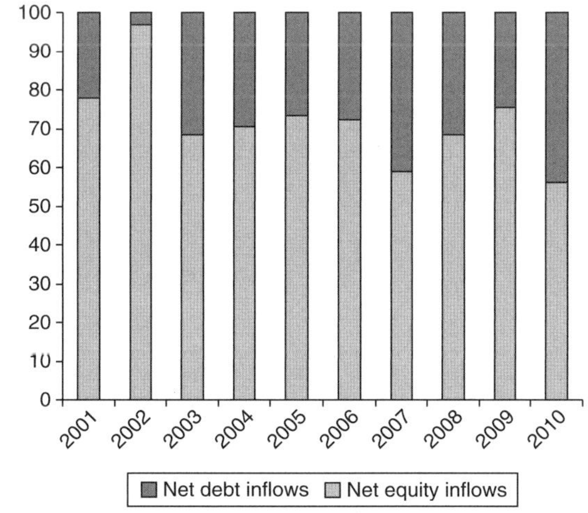

Sources: World Bank Debt Reporting System; International Monetary Fund; and World Bank estimates.

financing from private creditors to Brazil and Mexico. After a precipitous fall in 2009, net flows to countries in Europe and Central Asia bounced back, rising by 66 percent in 2010 on the back of higher short-term debt related flows from private creditors and bond issuance by public sector and corporate borrowers. Net inflows to countries in South Asia and Sub-Saharan Africa rose 30 percent and 15 percent, respectively, over the previous year. In South Asia, this was due to a rapid (92 percent) escalation in portfolio flows to India and net debt inflows of $35 billion from private creditors. In Sub-Saharan Africa, a 33 percent increase in net debt inflows on loans from official creditors and a resumption of short-term debt inflows, $1.5 billion in 2010 compared to an outflow of $10 billion in 2009, were in part offset by a 14 percent fall in net equity inflows. The Middle East and North Africa was the only developing region where net inflows declined in 2010 with increased bond issuance not enough to offset a halving of net debt inflows from official creditors and a 16 percent fall in equity flows (table 4). See the section entitled "Regional Developments and Trends" for a more extensive discussion on the composition of debt and equity flows to each region.

Figure 2. Aggregate Net Inflows to Top Ten Borrowers and Other Developing Countries, 2000–10

percent

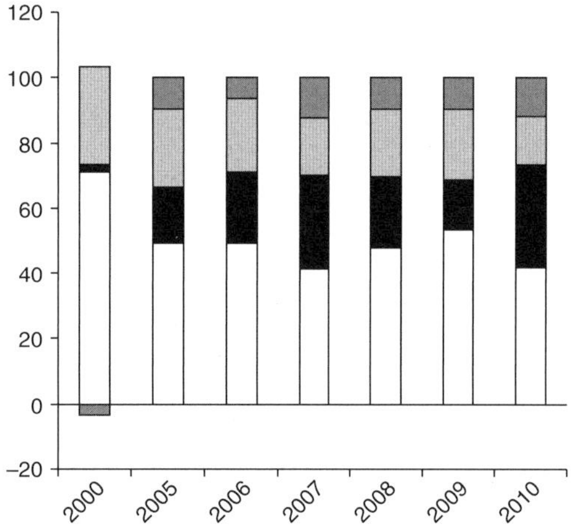

Source: World Bank Debtor Reporting System.

Recent Trends in Debt Flows

Net debt related flows soared in 2010, rising by close to 200 percent to $495 billion from $167 billion in 2009. In the process, the composition changed markedly in terms of both creditor and the category of borrowers to which flows were directed. In terms of creditor, financing from official creditors declined, largely as a consequence of the sharp fall in developing countries' purchases (equivalent to loan disbursements) from the IMF. Official creditors' share of total net debt related flows fell to 14 percent in 2010, compared to 49 percent in 2009. In contrast the net inflow from private creditors rose to $424 billion, close to five times its 2009 level (figure 3a). Viewed from the borrower perspective, it was private sector borrowers that saw net inflows rebound in 2010 to $353 billion, a ninefold increase from 2009. In contrast net inflows to public and publicly guaranteed borrowers rose only 12 percent in 2010 and their share of total net debt related flows fell to 29 percent from 76 percent in 2009 (figure 3b).

Slowdown in Financing from Official Bilateral and Multilateral Creditors

Net inflows of capital from official creditors in the form of concessional and non-concessional loans fell 11 percent in 2010 to $71 billion with a shift in composition between multilateral and bilateral creditors: the share of the former fell to 83 percent (from 92 percent in 2010) as the

Table 3. Top Ten Borrowers—External Debt Stock, 2010, and Net Inflows, 2009–10

$ billions

	External debt stock end 2010		Net inflow 2009			Net inflow 2010			% change in net flow 2010	% of total net flow 2010
Country	Amount	% of total	Total	Debt	Equity	Total	Debt	Equity		
China	548.6	13.5	185.9	43.5	142.4	337.3	120.9	216.4	81.4	29.9
Russian Federation	384.7	9.4	20.8	−19.1	39.9	52.1	14.0	38.1	150.5	4.6
Brazil	347.0	8.5	93.4	30.4	63.0	164.6	78.5	86.1	76.2	14.6
Turkey	293.9	7.2	−2.6	−13.8	11.2	40.4	27.7	12.7	−1653.8	3.6
India	290.3	7.1	75.1	18.4	56.7	102.7	38.6	64.1	36.8	9.1
Mexico	200.1	4.9	28.4	8.9	19.5	48.7	29.4	19.3	71.5	4.3
Indonesia	179.1	4.4	20.3	14.6	5.7	29.9	14.5	15.4	47.3	2.6
Argentina	127.9	3.1	1.5	−2.3	3.8	23.2	17.1	6.1	1446.7	2.1
Romania	121.5	3.0	17.9	13.0	4.9	13.7	10.2	3.5	−23.5	1.2
Kazakhstan	118.7	2.9	22.6	8.8	13.8	17.8	7.7	10.1	−21.2	1.6
Total top 10 borrowers	2611.8	64.1	463.1	102.3	360.8	830.4	358.5	471.9	79.3	73.5
Other developing countries	1464.5	35.9	211.8	63.9	147.9	299.3	136.7	162.6	41.3	26.5
All developing countries	4076.3	100.0	674.9	166.2	508.7	1129.7	495.2	634.5	67.4	100.0

Source: World Bank Debtor Reporting System.

Table 4. Net Capital Flows to Developing Regions, 2005–10
$ billions

	2005	2006	2007	2008	2009	2010
Net private and official inflows	519.7	686.5	1,133.2	835.2	674.9	1,129.7
by region:						
East Asia and the Pacific	209.0	238.6	301.6	211.7	235.3	447.1
Europe and Central Asia	135.3	248.9	424.1	313.0	104.0	172.8
Latin America and the Caribbean	93.8	68.7	208.3	181.9	173.7	318.6
Middle East and North Africa	19.4	14.5	29.6	21.0	29.2	26.2
South Asia	28.7	77.1	116.3	64.8	86.2	111.6
Sub-Saharan Africa	33.6	38.7	53.4	42.6	46.4	53.4

Sources: World Bank Debtor Reporting System.

net inflow from bilateral creditors continued its upward trajectory (table 5). For much of the past decade flows from bilateral creditors have been negative, a consequence of large payments, and in some instances pre-payments, by a number of middle-income countries on debt restructuring agreements concluded in prior years with Paris Club creditors. Additionally it reflects the fact that most OECD countries provide a large share of their bilateral assistance in the form of official grants, particularly to low-income countries with little or no access to market based financing. In 2009 the net inflow on loans from bilateral creditors turned sharply positive and they rose by a further 76 percent in 2010, driven by the emergence of a new, and important, group of bilateral creditors, in particular China. The 20 percent decline in the net inflow on loans from multilateral institutions in 2010 resulted almost entirely from the precipitous drop in developing countries' net new purchases from the IMF which more than offset the 45 percent rise in the net inflow on loans from IBRD. Although in aggregate net financing from the IMF in 2010 was broadly the same as in 2009, around SDR 20 billion, much of it was directed at high-income countries outside the scope of the World Bank Debtor Reporting System. When the IMF is excluded, net financing from multilateral institutions was down by only 3 percent from its 2009 level.

Since the onset of the most recent global economic crisis countries in Europe and Central Asia and Latin America and the Caribbean have commanded the lion's share of net loan inflows from official creditors. They received 39 percent and 25 percent, respectively, of the $181 billion in aggregate net inflows on loans from official creditors in 2008–10. South Asia and Sub-Saharan Africa each received around 15 percent of the total and only a negligible 5 percent went to countries in East Asia and the Pacific and the Middle East and North Africa.

Gross disbursements from multilateral institutions, (defined as IMF purchases and disbursements on loans from multilateral creditors) increased by 120 percent between 2007 and 2009. The dominant factor behind this rapid rise was member countries' purchases from the IMF; which rose fourteen fold to $27 billion in 2009 (from $2 billion in 2007). Disbursements from IBRD and IDA rose 73 percent over this period, and this pattern was mirrored in the increased level of lending by regional development banks—collectively their disbursements rose 59 percent from 2007 to 2009. In 2010 there was sharp reversal of the upward trend although IBRD registered a 19 percent increase in gross loan disbursements. (See Annex A for more information on IBRD and IDA financing in 2010). In contrast IMF purchases dropped 41 percent and gross disbursements from other multilateral institutions were down by 9 percent over the previous year. Gross disbursements on loans from bilateral creditors rose by 70 percent between 2007 and 2009 and, in contrast to multilateral flows, continued on an upward trend in 2010, rising by a further 23 percent to $34 billion, equivalent to almost 30 percent of 2010 gross flows from official creditors (figure 4). Intra-developing country lending, or so-called South-South flows have been a driving force behind the rise in lending by bilateral creditors and new commitments, a leading indicator of the level of future disbursements, suggests it continue to accelerate. Between 2007 and 2010 bilateral creditors signed

Figure 3. Net Debt Flows by Creditor and Borrower Type, 2001–10

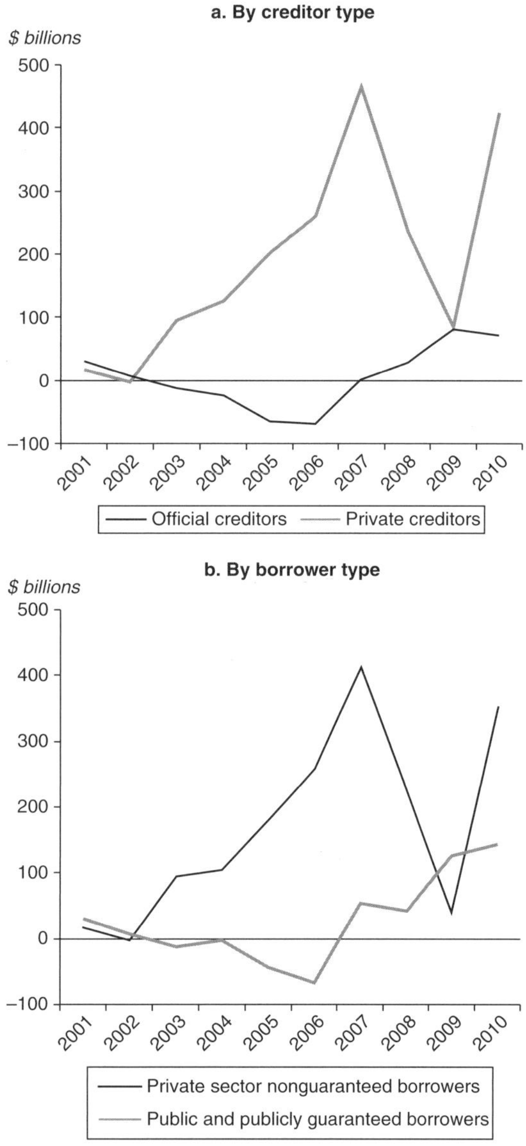

Source: World Bank Debtor Reporting System.

new loan agreements totaling around $135 billion of which China alone accounted for close to one third. Most bilateral loans are for the financing of large infrastructure projects.

Resurgence of Lending by Private Creditors in 2010

Net debt inflows from private creditors rose more rapidly than any other category of capital flows to developing countries in 2010. They surged to $424 billion, from $86 billion in 2009, only 10 percent below their pre-crisis peak in 2007. Net medium-term financing rose 119 percent in 2010, underpinned by strong inflows on bonds which more than doubled, to $111 billion, on the back of resurgence in new issuance by public and private sector borrowers. There were also several new entrants to the international capital market in 2010, including Albania, Belarus, Georgia, Jordan, Montenegro, and Vietnam. Net inflows from banks and other private institutions showed signs of recovery, rising by 123 percent, to $44.1 billion, albeit from a relatively low base, $19.8 billion in 2009. It was however, short-term, trade related, debt inflows that were dominant, accounting for 65 percent net inflows from private creditors in 2010. They soared to an all-time high of $269 billion, a massive jump over the $14 billion recorded in 2009 and 60 percent higher than their previous, pre-crisis high of $168 billion in 2007 (figure 5).

The rise in short term debt mirrored the upsurge in imports by developing countries which increased by 27 percent in US dollar terms in 2010 to $6 trillion, and closely correlated with the strong rebound in growth in the largest emerging markets. Short term inflow to the top ten borrowers was $220 billion, 80 percent of the total inflow of $269 billion in 2010: half of this went to China where imports rose 34 percent in US dollar terms in 2010. All regions recorded positive short term debt inflow in 2010, but the primary recipients were the East Asia and Pacific and Latin America and the Caribbean regions, which accounted for 53 percent and 25 percent respectively of total short-term debt inflows to developing countries in 2010. There was a marked turnaround in Europe and Central Asia, where net inflows rose to $46 billion, from an outflow of $38 billion in 2009, driven by renewed trade flows to Russia and Turkey and, to a lesser extent, Ukraine (table 6). China accounted for 75 percent of net short-term debt inflow to the East Asia and Pacific region, Argentina, Brazil, and Mexico for 86 percent of inflow to Latin America and the Caribbean, and Turkey for 62 percent of that to Europe and Central Asia.

Both public and private sector borrowers benefitted from the recovery in medium term financing from banks and other financial institutions, often export or project related financing benefitting from the guarantee of an export credit

Table 5. Net Official Loan Financing to Developing Countries, 2001–10
$ billions

	2001	2002	2003	2004	2005	2006	2007	2008	2009	2010
Total official creditors	30.9	6.9	–12.0	–24.3	–64.3	–69.0	1.5	29.5	80.5	71.2
Bilateral	–3.6	–8.2	–13.8	–12.2	–31.7	–45.8	–10.6	–1.9	6.7	11.9
Multilateral	34.5	15.2	1.8	–12.1	–32.6	–23.2	12.1	31.4	73.7	59.4
of which IBRD	2.4	–6.0	–7.7	–4.0	–3.0	–5.3	–0.4	2.7	11.8	17.1
IDA	5.0	5.5	5.0	6.4	5.6	5.0	5.5	4.6	6.5	5.3
IMF	19.5	14.2	2.4	–14.7	–40.2	–26.7	–5.1	10.8	26.8	13.8
Memorandum item:										
IDA grants	..	*0.3*	*0.4*	*1.1*	*1.2*	*1.2*	*1.9*	*2.1*	*2.5*	*2.2*

Sources: World Bank Debtor Reporting System and Organisation for Economic Co-operation and Development.

Figure 4. Gross Inflows from Bilateral and Multilateral Creditors to Developing Countries, 2005–10

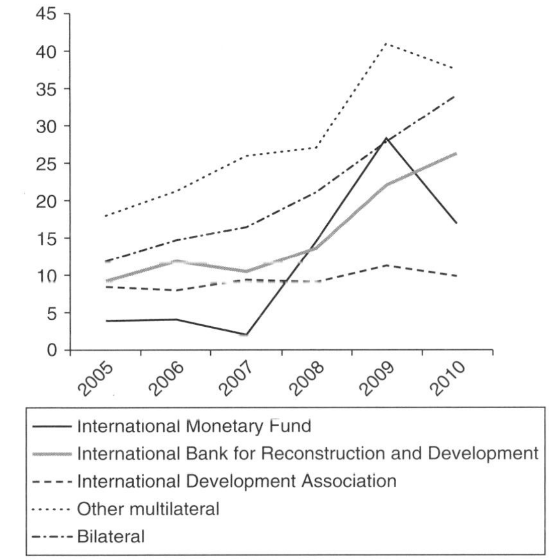

Source: World Bank Debtor Reporting System.

Figure 5. Net Private Debt Flows by Creditor Type, 2001–10

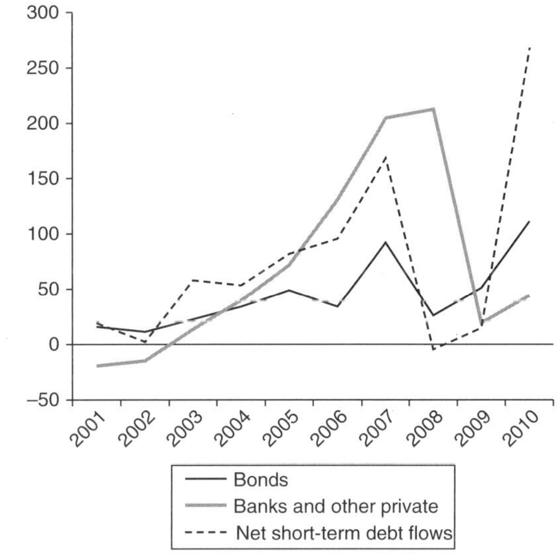

Source: World Bank Debtor Reporting System.

agency. Net inflow to public sector borrowers almost doubled in 2010, from $10 billion to $19.5 billion, while those to private sector borrowers, $21.6 billion, were 60 percent higher than in 2009, but still only around 20 percent of their peak 2007 level. The upturn in net inflow was fueled by a 20 percent rise in gross disbursements in 2010 to $350 billion, a marked turnaround from the 38 percent decline in comparable disbursements recorded in 2009. Consistent with the pattern of the past decade in volume terms gross disbursements to private sector borrowers far outweighed those to public sector borrowers: $300 billion, equivalent to 85 percent of the 2010 total. Maturities on medium-term bank loans typically average 5 years and, consequently, the large volume of gross disbursements to private sector borrowers has been accompanied by a rapid escalation in principal repayments. They increased to $276 billion in 2010 triple their 2000 level (figure 6).

A combination of favorable pricing conditions and investors' continued search for yield led to a record level of activity in international bond

Table 6. Net Short-Term Debt Flows to Developing Countries, 2007–10

$ billions

	2007	2008	2009	2010
East Asia and the Pacific	52.1	–11.4	63.5	141.5
Europe and Central Asia	72.5	–6.9	–38.5	45.5
Latin America and the Caribbean	23.0	5.7	–4.5	67.2
Middle East and North Africa	3.5	–4.2	1.6	1.1
South Asia	12.9	7.9	2.6	11.7
Sub-Saharan Africa	4.3	4.5	–9.9	1.5
All developing Countries	168.3	–4.4	14.7	268.5
Top ten borrowing countries	100.9	–13.9	27.1	220.3

Sources: World Bank Debtor Reporting System and Bank for International Settlements.

Figure 6. Gross Medium-Term Commercial Bank Flows to Developing Countries, 2000–10

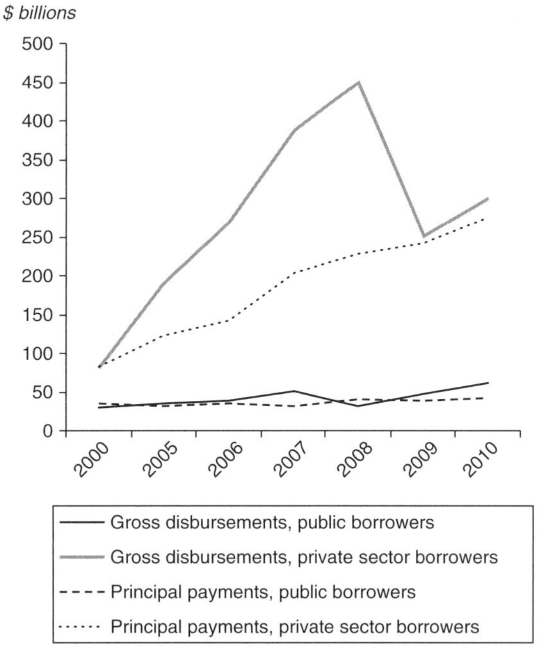

Source: World Bank Debtor Reporting System.

issuances by emerging markets in 2010. New issues by sovereigns, public sector, and corporate borrowers combined rose to $173 billion, an increase of 62 percent over 2009 and 8 percent above their 2007 pre-crisis level. The main driver was issuances by corporate borrowers in developing countries, which increased by 130 percent in 2010 and brought their share of total 2010 bond issuances to almost 50 percent, up from 35 percent in 2009 (table 7). Countries in Europe and Central Asia led the way in sovereign and public sector bond issues. They raised a total of $32 billion in international bond markets in 2010, more than double the $15 billion issued in 2009, including debut issues totaling $3.6 billion by Albania, Belarus, Georgia, Jordan and Montenegro. The Russian government returned to the markets for the first time since 1998 with a $5.5 billion 5 and 10 year note and Ukraine came back to the Eurobond market for the first time since 2007 with $1.5 billion 10 year note and a $0.5 billion 5 year issue.

Sovereign bond issuance jumped significantly in the Middle East and North Africa, where in addition to Lebanon, Egypt, Jordan, and Morocco came to the market in 2010. In South Asia public sector borrowers in India accounted for most of the sharp increase, but Sri Lanka returned to the market in October 2010 with a $1 billion 10 year sovereign bond issue. Latin America and the Caribbean region led corporate bond issuances, accounting for 62 percent of corporate bond issuances by all developing countries in 2010. The private sector in Brazil was the dominant player: with total issuances of $32 billion of which around half were placed by the financial sector and the other half by large Brazilian companies, including Telemar Norte Leste ($1.1 billion) and Vale ($1.8 billion) the world's largest exporter of iron ore. In Mexico corporate bond issuances rose to $11 billion (from $5 billion in 2009), while in

Table 7. Bond Issuances by Developing Countries, 2009–10

$ billions

	Sovereign borrowers		Corporate borrowers	
	2009	2010	2009	2010
East Asia and the Pacific	13.9	12.9	2.7	15.3
Europe and Central Asia	15.3	32.0	3.2	16.5
Latin America and the Caribbean	32.5	22.4	28.6	53.0
Middle East and North Africa	2.9	5.5	0.2	0.0
South Asia	2.3	12.1	2.5	1.3
Sub-Saharan Africa	2.2	2.0	0.0	0.0
All developing countries	69.1	86.9	37.2	86.1
Top ten borrowers	35.2	48.5	30.7	73.8

Source: World Bank Debtor Reporting System.

Peru they rose to $3 billion, three times the level of the previous year, with both Peruvian banks and companies active in the Eurobond markets. In East Asia and the Pacific region and Europe and Central Asia the major players were Chinese and Russian corporations, which each raised $12 billion in 2010. Power and construction companies were the big borrowers in China. In Russia blue chip companies like steelmaker Severstal, shipbuilder Sovcomflot, and banks like Alfa Bank led the way.

External Debt Burden of Developing Countries—Selected Indicators

Concomitant with the rise in debt related inflows in 2010 the combined stock of developing countries' external debt increased by 12 percent from $3,640 billion to $4,076 billion. At the regional level there were marked differences with the outstanding obligations of countries in East Asia and the Pacific rising by, on average, 21 percent, while those of countries in the Middle East and North Africa increased by only 2 percent over the prior year's level. Rising external debt stocks do not necessarily translate into an increased debt burden. That will also depend on the extent to which with the rate of growth of income and export earnings outpaces the accumulation of new external obligations.

Developing countries external debt indicators, measured in terms of gross national income (GNI) and export earnings, improved markedly from 2000 to 2008. Export earnings rose sharply due to increased export volume and the high international prices for primary commodities and the rotation of international capital flows from debt to equity and, in the case of low-income countries, large scale forgiveness of external debt obligations in the context of the HIPC and MDRI also played an important role in reducing external debt burdens. Total external debt outstanding for all developing countries reporting to the World Bank Debtor Reporting System measured as a ratio of exports, was 59.3 percent in 2008, less than half the 128.5 percent recorded in 2000. Measured against developing countries' GNI, it dropped from 37.8 percent to 21 percent over the same period. The past two years have been something of a roller-coaster. In 2009 sharply reduced developing countries' exports, down almost 20 percent from their 2008 level, combined with increased external borrowing to finance current account deficits and fiscal stimulus measures, pushed the ratio of total external debt outstanding to exports back up to 77 percent, its highest level since 2005. The ratio of outstanding external debt to GNI also rose, reflecting the 2 percent decline in developing countries' combined GNI. In 2010 the rapid rebound from the global economic crisis by many developing countries pushed GNI up by an average of 20 percent while their combined export earnings rose by 26 percent with concomitant improvement in the ratio of debt to GNI and to export earning to 21 percent and 69 percent, respectively, for all developing countries combined (figure 7).

At the regional level an improvement in the ratio of external debt to export earnings in 2010 was recorded by all six regions, but the ratio remains above its 2008 level. With the exception of East Asia and Pacific, all regions also saw an improvement in the ratio of external debt to GNI in 2010 and in two regions, Middle East and North Africa and South Asia, it was lower than in 2008. East Asia and Pacific has the lowest debt

Figure 7. Key Debt Indicators: Trend 2000–10

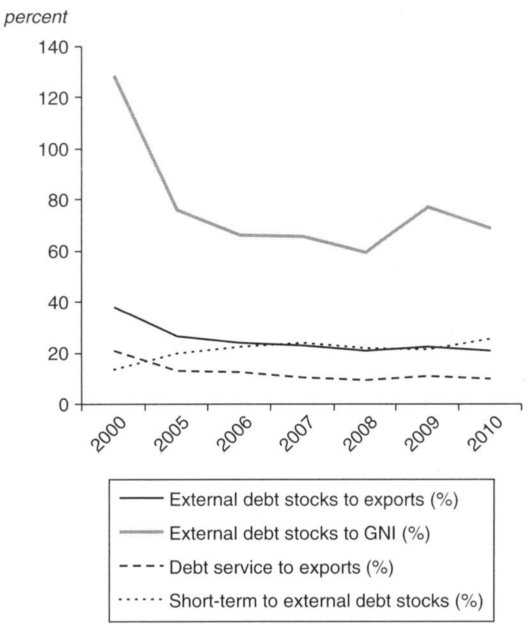

Sources: World Bank Debtor Reporting System and the International Monetary Fund.

burden measured against both GNI and export earnings, despite the sharp increase in debt outstanding in 2010. Countries in Europe and Central Asia are, on average, the most heavily indebted of all developing countries and were the ones severely impacted by the global economic crisis. This is reflected in the marked deterioration in the ratio of external debt to GNI and to export earnings in 2009: both ratios improved in 2010 to 43 percent and 122 percent, respectively, despite a moderate, 5 percent, increase in the stock of outstanding debt, but remained well above their 2008 level. The ratio of debt to exports for the top 10 borrowing countries combined is broadly the same as that for other developing countries, but they have a much lower debt burden measured in relation to GNI, an average of 18.4 percent in 2010 compared to an average of 27.9 percent for other developing countries (table 8).

Developing countries have seen a marked and almost continuous improvement in the sustainability of their external debt, measured by the ratio of external debt service to export earnings over the past decade. This held true in 2010, despite the 12 percent increase in developing countries' external debt obligations and parallel shift in the maturity composition and rise in short term debt, as a share of total outstanding external debt, to 25 percent, from 21 percent in 2009. The average debt service to export ratio for all developing countries combined was 9.8 percent, compared to 10.8 percent in 2009. The average debt service to export ratio for middle income countries in 2010 (10 percent) was below half its level in 2000 (21 percent). Even more striking is the improvement in low-income countries: their average debt service to export ratio has been reduced to 4.8 percent in 2010, from 17.2 percent in 1995 (figure 8). In part this is a consequence of increased exported earnings but also a direct outcome of debt restructuring and outright debt relief from official and private creditors in the context of the HIPC and MDRI (box 1).

Trends in Equity Flows 2010

Net equity inflows (direct investment and portfolio investment combined) in developing countries totaled $635 billion in 2010, up 25 percent from their level in 2009 and approaching their record level of $667 billion in 2007 (figure 9). Foreign direct investment at $506 billion remained the single largest component of capital flows to developing countries. However, it rose far less rapidly than debt related inflows, and its share of total net capital flows to developing countries fell from 59 percent in 2009 to 45 percent in 2010.

Table 8. Debt Indicators for Developing Country Regions
percent

	Debt Outstanding/GNI			Debt Outstanding/Exports		
Country group	2008	2009	2010	2008	2009	2010
East Asia and the Pacific	12.9	13.1	13.5	30.6	39.7	37.0
Europe and Central Asia	37.3	47.7	43.0	97.2	140.6	121.6
Latin America and the Caribbean	21.2	23.3	21.7	84.5	109.4	102.1
Middle East and North Africa	14.9	15.2	14.1	34.9	43.0	42.5
South Asia	21.0	20.7	19.2	84.3	107.7	94.3
Sub-Saharan Africa	21.2	22.4	20.0	48.8	66.1	54.0
Top ten borrowers	18.6	19.5	18.4	59.6	76.5	67.9
Other developing countries	27.1	29.7	27.9	58.8	77.8	70.0

Sources: World Bank Debtor Reporting System and International Monetary Fund.

Figure 8. Debt Service to Exports Ratio, 1995–10

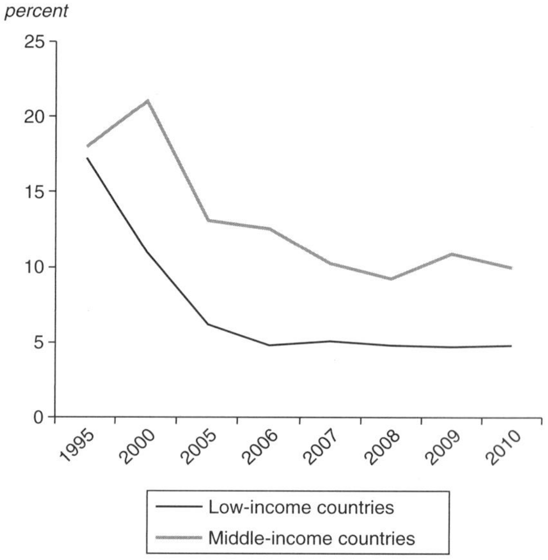

Sources: World Bank Debtor Reporting System and International Monetary Fund.

Box 1. Debt Restructuring with Paris Club Creditors, 2010

Developments in 2010

The Paris Club concluded debt restructuring agreements with seven countries reporting to the World Bank Debtor Reporting System in 2010, all of which were low-income countries eligible for the Heavily Indebted Poor Country (HIPC) Initiative. These agreements restructured a total of $13.2 billion (table B1.1).

Five countries, **Afghanistan, the Democratic Republic of the Congo, the Republic of Congo, Liberia, and Togo** reached the HIPC Completion Point in 2010 and concluded a stock of debt treatment that marked an exit from the Paris Club rescheduling process. Most of the debt treated by the Paris Club in 2010 related to claims on these countries. In aggregate $13 billion was restructured under these five, stock of debt, exit agreements of which $8.9 billion was cancelled. The share of debt cancelled for each debtor country was dictated by the common (debt) reduction factor: i.e. the effort required by each creditor to lower a country's external debt indicators to the levels set by the HIPC criteria. However, Paris Club creditors signaled their intension to cancel, on a bilateral basis, all of their remaining bilateral claims, thereby providing 100 percent debt relief to each country.

Comoros reached the HIPC Decision Point on June 29, 2010 and became eligible for debt relief on Cologne terms (90 percent net present value reduction). The agreement concluded in August 2010 topped up the 67 percent debt relief (in net present value) accorded under the agreement of November 2009 to 90 percent (in net present value). The 2009 agreement restructured a total of $13 billion in arrears of principal and interest as of June 30, 2009 and maturities falling due from July 2009 up to June 30, 2012.

Guinea-Bissau concluded an agreement in July 2010 to restructure a total of $171 million, following approval, in May 2010 of a new three year arrangement under the IMF Extended Credit Facility. Guinea-Bissau reached the HIPC Decision Point in December 2000. The agreement, concluded on Cologne terms (90 percent net present value reduction), restructured arrears of principal and interest as of December 31, 2009 and maturities falling due from January 1, 2010 to December 31, 2012. It cancelled $54 million and rescheduled $117 million over the three year consolidation period. Given the country's very limited payment capacity, creditors also agreed, on an exceptional basis, to defer the repayment of maturities and a significant share of arrears on short term and post-cut-off date debt (contracted after December 1986) and interest on restructured debt until after December, 2012. These measures reduced by 98 percent debt service due to Paris Club creditors between January 1, 2010 and December 31, 2012.

Table B1.1. Agreements with Paris Club Creditors, January 1, 2010–December 31, 2010

Country	Signature date (2010)	Cut-off date	Amount (millions of dollars) Total	Rescheduled	Cancelled	Concessionality (percent of npv)	Consolidation period Start	End
Afghanistan	17-Mar	Jun-99	1,027	585	442	90	stock	
Comoros	13-Aug	Jun-99	13	12	1	90	Jun-10	Jun-12
Congo, Dem. Rep.	25-Feb	Jun-83	2,957	1,647	1,310	90	Jul-09	Jun-12
Congo, Dem. Rep.	17-Nov	Jun-83	7,528	1,479	6,049	90	stock	
Congo, Rep.	18-Mar	Jan-86	2,474	1,493	981	90	stock	
Guinea-Bissau	06-Jul	Dec-86	171	117	54	90	Jan-10	Dec-12
Liberia	16-Sep	Jan-83	1,366	107	1,258	90	stock	
Togo	16-Dec	Jan-83	611	408	202	90	stock	

Source: Paris Club Secretariat.
Note: In 2010 Paris Club creditors also concluded an agreement with Antigua and Barbuda. Since this country does not borrow from the World Bank it is not required to report to the World Bank Debtor Reporting System.

The 2010 recovery in FDI inflows, following their 36 percent fall in 2009, was driven by improvements in the global investment environment, a revival in corporate earnings, and increased South-South investment, i.e. investment by one developing country in other. Much of the increase came from cross-border mergers and acquisitions (M&A), which typically react more

Figure 9. Net Equity Flows to Developing Countries, 2001–10

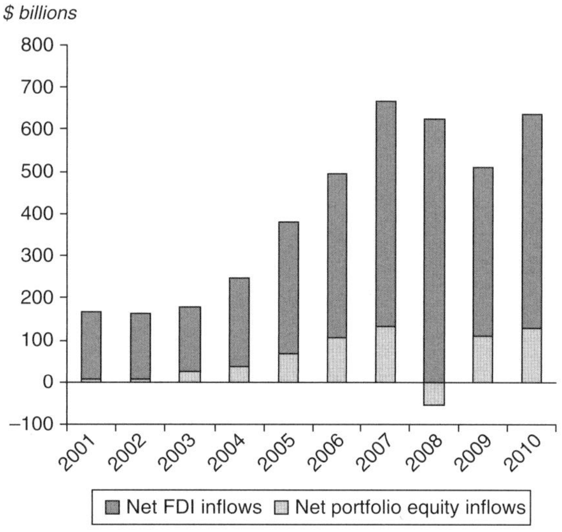

Sources: International Monetary Fund and World Bank estimates.

rapidly to changes in economic conditions than green field investment, and from higher reinvested earnings. The latter accounted for over one-third of FDI inflows in 2010. South-South investment, particularly from Asia, rose to an estimated 34 percent of total FDI inflows to developing countries in 2010, up from 25 percent in 2007. The increase in FDI inflows was broad based, with a large number of countries reporting higher FDI inflows, but the pace of recovery was less robust than the 30 percent increase in aggregate net FDI inflows in 2010 would seem to imply. This is because the overwhelming share of FDI inflows went to China, which rose by 62 percent to $185 billion. Excluding China, FDI inflows to developing countries rose by a more moderate 12 percent in 2010. China recently made important revisions to its official government statistics for 2005-2010 (box 2). According to the revised data, between 2005 and 2010 China received 30 percent of aggregate FDI inflows to the 129 developing countries reporting to the World Bank DRS. It is now the single largest recipient of FDI inflows among both developed and developing countries. China's manufacturing sector is the primary recipient of FDI inflows; it received $70 billion in 2010, a 50 percent increase over the comparable figure for 2009, while FDI inflows into the financial sector and real estate sector were up 300 percent and 78 percent to $12 billion and $21 billion, respectively.

Box 2. China—Revised Data Series for Foreign Direct Investment Inflows, 2005–10

In 2011 China's State Administration of Foreign Exchange (SAFE) significantly revised the official capital account statistics for 2005–10 following implementation of new accounting standards and methodology. The most important change was in respect of inflows of foreign direct investment which were subject to an upward revision of between 20–75 percent for the period 2005–10 (figure B2.1). According to SAFE, the primary reason for the revision was improved measurement of reinvested earnings by multinational corporations, hitherto not fully captured in government reports. According to the new data FDI inflows to China were $185 billion in 2010, equivalent to 37 percent of total FDI inflows to the 129 developing countries reporting to the World Bank Debtor Reporting System.

Figure B2.1. Revisions to China's FDI inflows, 2005–10

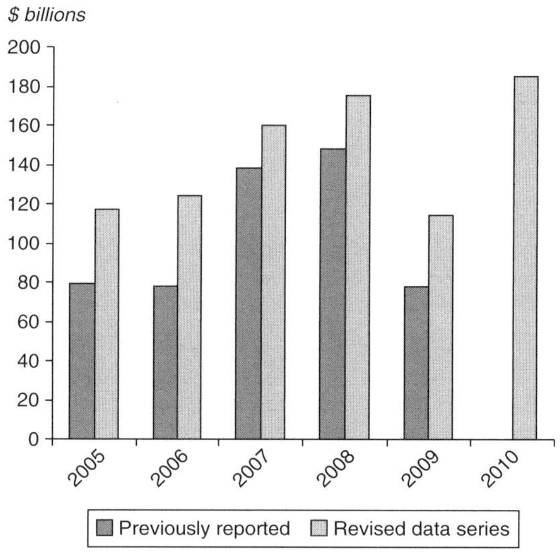

Source: China State Administration of Foreign Exchange.

All but two of the top ten developing country recipients of FDI registered increased inflows in 2010 (figure 10). Inflows to Brazil were up 87 percent on the back of the country's strong fundamentals while Indonesia's growth prospects, improved credit ratings, and large domestic

Figure 10. Net Foreign Direct Investment Inflows to Major Recipients, 2009–10
$ billions

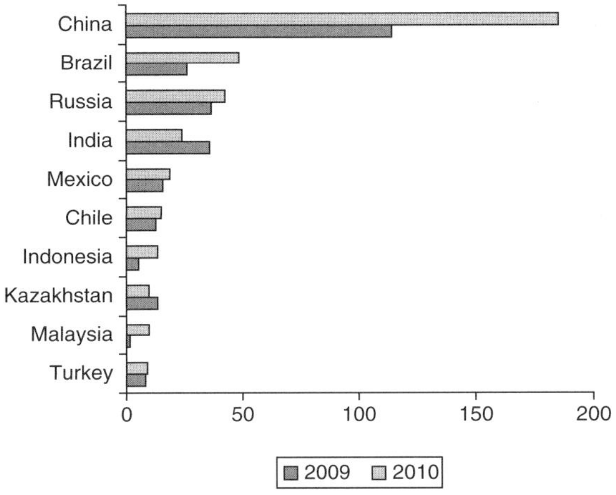

Sources: International Monetary Fund and World Bank estimates.

market proved an attractive draw. FDI increased by 173 percent over its 2009 level, directed primarily at transport and communications as well the more traditional mining sector. Malaysia recorded a fivefold increase in investment into its oil and gas and financial sectors in 2010. In sharp contrast FDI inflows to India continued on a downward path, falling by a further 32 percent, on top of the 18 percent decline registered in 2009. Policy and procedural issues, delays in opening the retail and insurance sectors to foreign investors, poor infrastructure, licensing issues, and a series of widely reported corruption cases are cited as factors behind investors' reticence to commit to new long-term investments. FDI inflows to Kazakhstan were also down sharply (27 percent) in 2010. The concentration of FDI inflows to developing countries increased further in 2010 with the top ten recipients increasing their share to 73 percent (from 67 percent in 2009). That said, a wide group of countries, particularly at the lower end of the income scale, reported increased FDI inflows in 2010. Low-income countries as a group saw FDI inflows increase by almost 40 percent in 2010 in largely part due to rising South-South investment in extractive industries and infrastructure development.

Portfolio equity flows are the most highly concentrated of all capital flows to developing countries. Between 2005 and 2010, investors provided $492 billion in portfolio equity inflows of which 99 percent went to 10 developing countries, but just 3 countries, China, Brazil and India, received 73 percent (table 9). Portfolio equity flows recovered rapidly from the impact of the global financial crisis, particularly in emerging markets viewed as having good growth prospects. Net inflows totaled $108 billion in 2009, a spectacular turnaround from the $53 billion outflow in 2008 and were up by an another 18 percent in 2010 to $128 billion as investor concerns about the severity of the impact of the global crisis on the corporate sector in emerging markets abated: stock markets in several emerging markets hit record levels in 2010. While the recovery in portfolio flows can be seen as beneficial there were concerns that a rapid surge may generate inflationary pressures and have the potential to destabilize currencies and domestic financial markets. Against this backdrop a number of countries took measures designed to slow the pace of portfolio equity inflows in 2010 and the aggregate pace of increase masks very disparate trends in individual countries. Among the top three recipients, inflows to Brazil were only marginally higher than in the previous year, and in China they slowed considerably, rising by only 10 percent, compared to their 225 percent rise in 2009. In sharp contrast portfolio equity flows to India surged to $40 billion, a 90 percent increase from 2009 with investors attracted by the country's strong growth and high rate of return on

Table 9. Net Inflow of Portfolio Equity, Top Ten Recipients, 2005–10
$ billions

	2005	2006	2007	2008	2009	2010
China	20.3	42.9	18.5	8.7	28.2	31.4
Brazil	6.5	7.7	26.2	–7.6	37.1	37.7
India	12.2	9.5	32.9	–15.0	21.1	40.0
South Africa	7.2	15.0	8.7	–4.7	9.4	5.8
Turkey	5.7	1.9	5.1	0.7	2.8	3.5
Thailand	5.1	5.2	4.3	–3.8	1.3	3.4
Vietnam	0.1	1.3	6.2	–0.6	0.1	2.4
Russia	–0.1	6.5	18.7	–15.0	3.4	–4.8
Indonesia	–0.2	1.9	3.6	0.3	0.8	2.1
Mexico	3.4	2.8	–0.5	–3.5	4.2	0.6
Top ten recipients	60.2	94.7	123.7	–40.5	108.4	122.1
Total all developing countries	67.5	107.7	133.0	–53.4	108.8	128.4

Sources: International Monetary Fund and World Bank estimates.

investments. When India is excluded, net portfolio equity flows to developing countries rose by only 1 percent in 2010. For other countries the story was mixed, with a net outflow of $5 billion from Russia and sharp falls in inflows to Mexico and South Africa offset by large increases to Nigeria and a number of Asian borrowers, including Indonesia, Thailand, and Vietnam.

Regional Developments and Trends

East Asia and the Pacific

Net capital flows to the region rose 90 percent in 2010 to a record high of $447 billion, almost 50 percent above their pre-crisis level although still below their peak in terms of GNI, 5.9 percent compared to 6.5 percent in 2007. The surge in inflows was driven by a sharp rebound in equity flows, particularly FDI, and a jump in short term, trade related, inflow to an unprecedented $142 billion, approaching three times its previous high in 2007 (table 10).

The stock of external debt rose 21 percent in 2010, but this was offset by a 30 percent increase in the dollar value of export earnings. The ratio of outstanding debt to export earnings improved to 37 percent from 40 percent in 2009 and remained the lowest of all six regions. Short term debt as a share of total debt is high, 46 percent, but risks are mitigated by the stock of international reserves: at end 2010 they were 333 percent of external debt stock.

Net debt inflows from private creditors soared to $176 billion, from $65 billion in 2009, on the back of a massive increase in net short term debt inflows and a rapid rise in medium term financing. Borrowers across the region reported net short term debt inflow, but China dominated the trend: its net short term debt inflow doubled in 2010 to $107 billion, equivalent to 76 percent of the regional total. Other countries reporting a sharp rise were Malaysia $11 billion (from $0.9 billion in 2009), Indonesia $7.2 billion (double the 2009 level), and the Philippines $2.3 billion (a marked turnaround from the net outflow of –$3 billion in 2009). Asian borrowers again took advantage of improved market conditions to issue $28 billion in bonds in 2010 of which 55 percent was issuance by private sector borrowers. Of this Chinese corporates, mainly power and construction

Table 10. Net Capital Inflows to East Asia and the Pacific, 2001–10

$ billions

Inflows	2001	2002	2003	2004	2005	2006	2007	2008	2009	2010
Net private and official inflows	81.6	49.6	75.9	127.0	209.0	238.6	301.6	211.7	235.3	447.1
Percent of GNI	4.6	2.5	3.4	4.8	6.9	6.5	6.5	3.6	3.7	5.9
Net equity inflows	50.7	63.2	69.3	89.7	168.1	207.9	234.0	206.8	166.3	268.2
Net FDI inflows	48.9	59.4	56.8	70.4	142.4	151.7	198.9	214.1	137.5	227.7
Net portfolio equity inflows	1.8	3.8	12.5	19.3	25.7	56.2	35.1	–7.3	28.9	40.5
Net debt flows	30.9	–13.6	6.6	37.3	40.9	30.7	67.6	4.9	69.0	178.9
Official creditors	3.1	–7.7	–7.2	–5.2	–3.3	–9.3	–3.4	–1.0	3.7	3.4
World Bank	0.9	–1.7	–1.5	–1.9	–0.6	–0.4	–0.3	1.2	2.2	2.7
IMF	–2.5	–2.7	–0.5	–1.6	–1.6	–8.5	0.0	0.0	0.1	0.0
Other official	4.7	–3.3	–5.2	–1.7	–1.1	–0.4	–3.1	–2.1	1.3	0.8
Private creditors	27.9	–5.9	13.8	42.5	44.2	40.0	71.0	5.9	65.3	175.5
Net medium and long term debt flows	–13.5	–12.3	–10.3	9.1	9.3	14.9	19.0	17.3	1.8	33.9
Bonds	0.4	0.1	1.7	9.6	10.1	4.0	1.2	1.2	8.4	20.8
Banks and other private	–13.9	–12.4	–12.0	–0.4	–0.7	10.9	17.8	16.1	–6.6	13.1
Net short term debt flows	41.4	6.5	24.1	33.4	34.8	25.1	52.1	–11.4	63.5	141.5
Change in reserves (- = increase)	–49.8	–92.8	–139.8	–237.1	–217.7	–295.4	–541.2	–432.2	–535.0	–551.0
Memorandum items										
Workers remittances	21.0	27.0	32.3	40.0	50.3	57.4	71.0	85.4	86.0	92.0

Sources: World Bank Debtor Reporting System; International Monetary Fund; Bank for International Settlements; and Organisation for Economic Co-operation and Development.

companies, accounted for three quarters. Corporates in the Philippines and Thailand raised $1 billion and $1.9 billion respectively. Amongst public sector borrowers the Philippines was the most active with total issuance of $6.6 billion, 21 percent higher than 2009 and Vietnam came to the market with a debut $1 billion sovereign bond. For most countries in the region financing from official creditors is limited. The exception is Vietnam, where gross disbursements from official creditors accounted for 72 percent of those to public sector borrowers in 2010. It was the third largest recipient of IDA disbursements in 2010 ($0.9 billion) and received disbursements of $0.7 billion from IBRD.

Net equity flows rose by 61 percent in 2010, underpinned by a 66 percent increase in FDI inflows and 40 percent rise in portfolio equity inflows. China dictated the trend, accounting for 81 percent of FDI inflows and 78 percent of portfolio equity inflows to the region in 2010. Indonesia's growth prospects, improved credit ratings, and large domestic market attracted investors and FDI increased 173 percent over its 2009 level to $13 billion, directed at transport, communications and the mining sector and FDI into Malaysia's oil and gas and financial sectors jumped to $10 billion from $1 billion in 2009. Net portfolio flows to China grew by a relatively moderate 11 percent, but those to the rest of the region surged to $9.1 billion ($0.7 billion in 2009) with Indonesia ($2.1 billion), Thailand ($3.4 billion) and Vietnam ($2.4 billion) the principal beneficiaries.

Europe and Central Asia

Net capital inflows increased 66 percent in 2010 to $173 billion, 5.8 percent of GNI, with debt inflows from private creditors both short-term debt and bond issuance more than offsetting the reduction in inflows from official creditors and continued declined in net equity flows. Despite this rebound net capital flows were only 40 percent of their pre-crisis level (table 11).

Countries in the region are, on average, the most heavily indebted of all developing countries, but the ratio of external debt stock to exports improved to 122 percent from 141 percent in 2009 as growth picked up and exports earnings rose 17 percent in dollar terms over their 2009 level. However, increased debt service payments, particular on debt contracted by private sector borrowers prior to the crisis keep the external debt service to export ratio unchanged at 24 percent.

Financing from official creditors slowed considerably in 2010 with gross disbursements down 30 percent from 2009. The primary factor was the reduction in purchases (disbursements) from the IMF by Romania and Ukraine which totaled $9.1 billion in 2010 compared to $15.6 billion in 2009. Gross disbursement by other multilateral creditors fell by 8 percent in 2010 although those from IBRD rose 8 percent to $5.4 billion, of which Turkey received just over half. Bond issuances by both public and private agencies soared to $49 billion from $18 billion in 2009. Issuance by public sector borrowers more than doubled from $15 billion in 2009 to $32 billion while that of private sector borrowers rose almost six fold from $3 billion in 2009 to $17 billion. Russia was the main driver, where issuance by its public sector borrowers totaled $16 billion in 2010, including a sovereign issue of $5.5 billion in 5 and 10 year notes, the first since 1998 and Russian corporate issuance totaled $12 billion. Ukraine came back to the Eurobond market for the first time since 2007 and there were debut sovereign issues by Albania, Belarus, Georgia and Montenegro. Most countries reported increased short term debt inflows in 2010, but they were heavily concentrated: Turkey accounted for 62 percent of the regional total. Russia and the Ukraine reported short term debt inflows of $6.8 billion and $6.4 billion, respectively in 2010 compared to outflows of $22.3 billion and $1.1 billion in 2009. Medium term flows from banks returned to negative territory in 2010 with an outflow of $7.9 billion, from an inflow of $16.4 billion in 2009. Gross disbursements increased 10 percent, but were offset by a 30 percent rise in principal repayments, notably by private sector borrowers in Russia and the Ukraine, on loans contracted prior to the global economic crisis.

FDI inflows to the region in 2010 were little changed from their 2009 level. Although they rose 20 percent in Russia, the third largest recipient of FDI among developing countries, to $45 billion they remained well below their 2008 level ($75 billion) and in Kazakhstan they fell 30 percent as investment into the hydro-carbon sector slowed and other investment in other sectors failed to take off. The 2009 resurgence in portfolio equity

Table 11. Net Capital Inflows to Europe and Central Asia, 2001–10
$ billions

Inflows	2001	2002	2003	2004	2005	2006	2007	2008	2009	2010
Net private and official inflows	21.4	38.1	82.9	104.1	135.3	248.9	424.1	313.0	104.0	172.8
Percent of GNI	3.1	4.8	8.3	7.9	8.1	12.3	16.1	9.7	4.1	5.8
Net equity inflows	14.6	17.1	25.6	44.4	58.6	106.6	163.2	146.9	92.3	85.4
Net FDI inflows	14.0	14.3	24.1	42.6	52.0	94.3	136.2	162.2	85.9	86.3
Net portfolio equity inflows	0.6	2.8	1.6	1.8	6.7	12.3	27.0	–15.3	6.4	–0.8
Net debt flows	6.7	21.0	57.3	59.7	76.6	142.2	260.9	166.0	11.7	87.4
Official creditors	6.6	3.9	–4.9	–7.6	–28.5	–30.4	–2.3	12.0	35.7	22.6
World Bank	2.0	1.0	–0.3	1.0	–0.7	0.2	0.2	0.7	3.0	3.5
IMF	6.1	4.8	–2.0	–5.9	–9.8	–5.8	–5.0	7.0	20.5	9.4
Other official	–1.5	–1.9	–2.5	–2.7	–18.0	–24.8	2.6	4.3	12.2	9.8
Private creditors	0.2	17.1	62.2	67.2	105.1	172.6	263.2	154.1	–24.0	64.8
Net medium and long term debt flows	0.6	14.7	34.2	53.5	84.4	128.4	190.7	160.9	14.5	19.2
Bonds	–0.4	3.1	7.3	14.6	16.8	34.0	60.0	16.4	–1.8	27.1
Banks and other private	1.0	11.6	27.0	38.9	67.6	94.4	130.7	144.5	16.4	–7.9
Net short term debt flows	–0.4	2.4	27.9	13.7	20.8	44.3	72.5	–6.9	–38.5	45.5
Change in reserves (– = increase)	–11.3	–28.8	–49.3	–69.3	–87.3	–174.0	–227.5	57.9	–26.6	–66.2
Memorandum items										
Workers remittances	8.7	8.8	9.1	12.7	19.7	24.9	38.7	45.0	36.1	36.0

Sources: World Bank Debtor Reporting System; International Monetary Fund; Bank for International Settlements; and Organisation for Economic Co-operation and Development.

inflows to the region was not repeated. Inflows to Turkey rose 25 percent to $3.5 billion, but this did little to offset the collapse in comparable flows to Russia (the only other country in the region where portfolio equity flows are significant) which turned sharply negative: –$4.8 billion as compared to an inflow of $3.4 billion in 2009.

Latin America and the Caribbean

Net capital flows to the region surged to $319 billion in 2010, 6.7 percent of GNI, well above their highest pre-crisis level. Driving this rebound was the fourfold increase in private capital flows, a rapid rise in net short term flows and turnaround in medium term bank financing, and a 44 percent increase in FDI inflows. The region was also one of only two (Sub-Saharan Africa the other) to record an increase in net debt inflows from official creditors in 2010 (table 12).

The 16 percent increase in external debt stock in 2010 outpaced the rise in export earnings and the ratio of external debt stock to exports deteriorated to 102 percent, from 85 percent in 2008, but external debt stock in relation to GNI remained moderate at 22 percent.

Net inflows from official creditors increased 20 percent over their 2009, much larger than to any other region, driven by higher gross disbursements from bilateral and multilateral creditors, including a tripling of purchases (disbursements) from the IMF under ongoing programs with the Dominican Republic, Haiti, Jamaica and Nicaragua. Gross disbursements from IBRD continued their upward trajectory, but rose only 3 percent in 2010, as compared to their spectacular, 90 percent jump in 2009, and remained highly concentrated with 69 percent going to Argentina, Brazil and Mexico. Bond issuance by public sector borrowers totaled $22 billion, down 31 percent from its 2009 level, but issuance by private sector borrowers skyrocketed to $53 billion, two and a half times its 2009 level, of which $32 billion was issued by Brazilian corporates: divided half and half between the financial sector and the country's largest companies, including Telemar Norte Leste and Vale. Corporate issuance in Mexico doubled to $11 billion and in Peru it tripled to $3 billion over 2009. Short term debt inflow soared to $67 billion, a record high and almost three times its pre-crisis level in 2007, but was highly concentrated with three countries, Argentina, Brazil and Mexico accounting for 86 percent of the regional total. Unlike most regions Latin America and the Caribbean also registered a sharp increase in the net inflow of medium term financing from commercial banks in 2010. These flows, which rose to $27 billion in 2010, from a

Table 12. Net Capital Inflows to Latin America and the Caribbean, 2001–10

$ billions

Inflows	2001	2002	2003	2004	2005	2006	2007	2008	2009	2010
Net private and official inflows	86.2	52.6	59.8	57.9	93.8	68.7	208.3	181.9	173.7	318.6
Percent of GNI	4.5	3.1	3.3	2.8	3.7	2.3	5.9	4.4	4.5	6.7
Net equity inflows	74.4	56.8	46.2	66.3	85.8	83.0	139.3	120.4	119.9	153.9
Net FDI inflows	71.8	55.3	42.9	66.8	73.5	72.0	110.4	130.0	78.3	112.6
Net portfolio equity inflows	2.5	1.4	3.3	–0.6	12.2	11.0	28.8	–9.7	41.6	41.3
Net debt flows	11.9	–4.2	13.5	–8.4	8.1	–14.3	69.0	61.6	53.8	164.7
Official creditors	20.6	12.4	4.7	–10.1	–31.3	–19.9	–1.1	6.5	17.9	21.4
World Bank	1.3	–0.6	–0.4	–1.0	–0.7	–3.4	–0.1	2.4	6.6	8.3
IMF	15.6	11.9	5.6	–6.3	–27.6	–12.1	0.0	0.0	0.4	1.3
Other official	3.8	1.1	–0.4	–2.9	–3.0	–4.4	–1.0	4.1	10.9	11.8
Private creditors	–8.8	–16.6	8.8	1.7	39.4	5.6	70.1	55.0	35.9	143.3
Net medium and long term debt flows	6.6	–10.4	7.5	1.1	19.0	5.1	47.1	49.4	40.4	76.2
Bonds	9.8	1.9	16.7	2.5	21.6	–11.2	12.6	9.0	40.7	48.8
Banks and other private	–3.3	–12.2	–9.2	–1.3	–2.6	16.3	34.6	40.4	–0.3	27.4
Net short term debt flows	–15.3	–6.2	1.3	0.6	20.4	0.5	23.0	5.7	–4.5	67.2
Change in reserves (– = increase)	–0.9	–2.6	–35.6	–25.4	–34.4	–55.5	–137.8	–50.1	–54.1	–90.2
Memorandum items										
Workers remittances	24.4	28.1	36.8	43.3	49.8	58.8	62.9	64.4	56.6	57.2

Sources: World Bank Debtor Reporting System; International Monetary Fund; Bank for International Settlements; and Organisation for Economic Co-operation and Development.

small outflow in 2009 went to both public and private sector borrowers, but were concentrated largely in Brazil and Mexico.

FDI inflows rose 44 percent in 2010 to $113 billion, above their 2007 level, but still 13 percent below their peak in 2008. With the exception of Venezuela all countries in the region reported rising FDI flows in 2010. The main driver was Brazil where inflows rose to $48 billion, close to double their 2009 level on the back of the country's very strong fundamentals. Mexico, the region's second largest recipient of FDI, reported inflows of $19 billion, up 22 percent over their 2009 level. Following the surge in 2009, portfolio equity inflows slowed as countries across the region took measures aimed at mitigating risks of volatility associated with these flows. Inflow to Brazil, $37.7 billion, was largely unchanged from 2009 while inflow to Mexico dropped to $0.6 billion in 2010 from $4.2 billion in 2009.

Middle East and North Africa

The region was the only one of the six regions to record a fall in net capital inflows in 2010. They fell 10 percent to $26.2 billion and 2.6 percent of GNI from 3.2 percent of GNI in 2009 on account of the decline in net equity flows. It was only partially offset by the rapid rise in net debt inflows. Although these rose by 84 percent they constituted only 13 percent of total net capital flows to the region in 2010 (table 13).

Debt indicators are moderate on account of the preponderance of equity in net capital flows to the region throughout the past decade and relatively robust export earnings. The ratio of debt stock to exports was 43 percent in 2010, lower than all other regions except East Asia and Pacific and international reserves are high in relation to external debt stock, 227 percent at end 2010.

Net debt flows from official creditors fell 50 percent in 2010 to $1.2 billion driven down by a slowdown in gross disbursements to Egypt and Morocco, including a 33 percent reduction in IBRD disbursements to Morocco. This was in part offset by an increase in IBRD disbursements to other countries, but overall they fell by 13 percent to the region in 2010. The net inflow from other official creditors also dropped sharply in 2010, due to lower disbursements and increased principal payments, but it remained positive. For much of the past decade net flows from bilateral creditors were negative on account of large principal payments on debt restructuring agreements concluded in the nineties with Paris Club and other bilateral

Table 13. Net Capital Inflows to Middle East and North Africa, 2001–10
$ billions

Inflows	2001	2002	2003	2004	2005	2006	2007	2008	2009	2010
Net private and official inflows	4.4	10.3	13.5	12.9	19.4	14.5	29.6	21.0	29.2	26.2
Percent of GNI	1.2	2.7	3.3	2.7	3.6	2.3	3.9	2.3	3.2	2.6
Net equity inflows	3.9	7.6	10.2	10.4	19.2	28.2	25.5	29.6	27.3	22.7
Net FDI inflows	4.0	8.1	10.0	9.7	16.8	27.2	27.6	29.2	26.1	22.7
Net portfolio equity inflows	0.0	–0.5	0.2	0.7	2.4	1.0	–2.1	0.4	1.2	0.0
Net debt flows	0.5	2.7	3.4	2.5	0.2	–13.7	4.1	–8.6	1.9	3.5
Official creditors	–1.4	–1.9	–2.0	–3.4	–3.2	–11.3	1.1	–1.8	2.4	1.2
World Bank	–0.1	–0.3	–0.3	–0.6	0.0	–0.8	1.0	–0.3	0.9	0.8
IMF	–0.1	–0.3	–0.6	–0.5	–0.7	–0.2	–0.1	–0.1	–0.1	0.0
Other official	–1.3	–1.4	–1.2	–2.3	–2.4	–10.3	0.2	–1.4	1.6	0.4
Private creditors	1.9	4.6	5.4	6.0	3.4	–2.5	3.0	–6.8	–0.5	2.3
Net medium and long term debt flows	4.9	5.3	0.8	2.7	3.1	–1.7	–0.5	–2.7	–2.0	1.2
Bonds	4.4	5.2	0.7	2.8	2.5	0.8	0.7	–0.8	0.1	3.2
Banks and other private	0.5	0.0	0.1	0.0	0.6	–2.5	–1.3	–1.8	–2.1	–1.9
Net short term debt flows	–3.0	–0.7	4.6	3.2	0.3	–0.8	3.5	–4.2	1.6	1.1
Change in reserves (– = increase)	–9.3	–12.6	–23.2	–14.7	–38.9	–37.8	–48.0	–43.4	–24.2	–24.1
Memorandum items										
Workers remittances	11.9	14.9	19.9	22.6	23.6	25.1	31.0	34.7	32.4	31.0

Sources: World Bank Debtor Reporting System; International Monetary Fund; Bank for International Settlements; and Organisation for Economic Co-operation and Development.

creditors by several countries, in particular Algeria, Egypt, and Morocco. Net debt inflows from private creditors turned positive in 2010 for the first time since 2007 to $2.3 billion on account of $5.5 billion in bond issuance including sovereign issues by Egypt ($1.5 billion), Morocco (€1 billion 10-year note; the country's first sovereign issue since 2007), and Jordan ($750 million 5-year, fixed-rate debut sovereign issue). Medium term inflows from commercial banks were little changed from 2009 and remained negative. The net inflow of short term debt fell, but there were divergent trends across the region. Short term inflows into Egypt returned to their 2008 level, $0.6 billion compared to an outflow of $0.3 billion in 2009 and Lebanon recorded an inflow of $0.4 billion compared zero short term debt flows in 2009. In contrast net short term flows to Iran contracted sharply to $0.2 billion (from $0.9 billion in 2009) and those to Morocco turned Morocco falling to –$0.4 billion compared to a positive inflow of $0.5 billion in 2009.

Net equity inflows declined 17 percent in 2010. Egypt and Lebanon, where portfolio equity flows are concentrated, saw flows dry up in 2010, compared to a net inflow of $1.2 billion in 2009. The 2010 story on FDI inflows was mixed. Egypt, the region's largest recipient of FDI, registered a 14 percent decline in FDI inflows to Lebanon were unchanged from their 2009 level and Iran saw FDI inflows, mainly to the oil and gas sector, increase by a further 20 percent, following their 87 percent surge in 2009. In Morocco FDI inflows were down 37 percent and those to Syria down 46 percent from their 2009 level.

South Asia

Net capital inflows to the region rose 29 percent in 2010 on the back of a 92 percent surge in net portfolio equity flows and more than doubling of net debt flows from private creditors, driven by both bond issuance and short term debt inflows. But at 5.5 percent of GNI net capital flows remained below their pre-crisis peak, 7.7 percent of GNI in 2007 (table 14).

The ratio of external debt stock, and debt service, to exports are low, on average 94 percent and 6 percent respectively, in 2010, but there are important differences between countries: for example India had an external debt stock to export ratio in 2010 of 81 percent while that of Pakistan was 199 percent. The comparable debt service-to-export

Table 14. Net Capital Inflows to South Asia, 2001–10
$ billions

Inflows	2001	2002	2003	2004	2005	2006	2007	2008	2009	2010
Net private and official inflows	8.1	7.5	14.5	21.3	28.7	77.1	116.3	64.8	86.2	111.6
Percent of GNI	1.3	1.1	1.9	2.3	2.7	6.5	7.7	4.2	5.1	5.3
Net equity inflows	8.9	7.9	13.5	16.8	23.6	36.5	66.7	35.2	59.9	67.4
Net FDI inflows	6.1	6.8	5.5	7.8	11.2	26.1	32.7	51.1	39.4	28.0
Net portfolio equity inflows	2.8	1.1	8.0	9.0	12.4	10.4	34.0	−15.8	20.5	39.4
Net debt flows	−0.9	−0.4	1.0	4.4	5.0	40.6	49.5	29.6	26.3	44.2
Official creditors	2.1	−2.3	−4.1	−0.2	2.9	3.6	4.4	8.8	11.0	9.6
World Bank	1.5	−1.0	−2.3	2.3	2.3	2.0	2.0	1.4	2.4	3.3
IMF	0.3	0.1	−0.1	−0.3	0.0	−0.1	−0.1	3.2	3.6	2.0
Other official	0.3	−1.3	−1.8	−2.3	0.6	1.7	2.5	4.2	5.0	4.4
Private creditors	−3.0	2.0	5.1	4.7	2.1	37.1	45.1	20.7	15.3	34.5
Net medium and long term debt flows	−2.1	0.1	3.1	4.0	−0.2	20.2	32.2	12.9	12.7	22.9
Bonds	−0.4	−0.7	−3.7	3.9	−2.8	6.4	10.7	1.7	1.9	10.1
Banks and other private	−1.6	0.8	6.8	0.1	2.7	13.9	21.5	11.2	10.8	12.8
Net short term debt flows	−0.9	1.8	2.0	0.7	2.3	16.8	12.9	7.9	2.6	11.7
Change in reserves (− = increase)	−10.2	−28.0	−36.9	−27.6	−6.8	−41.7	−103.8	26.3	−39.3	−22.3
Memorandum items										
Workers remittances	19.2	24.1	30.4	28.7	33.9	42.5	54.0	71.6	75.1	82.2

Sources: World Bank Debtor Reporting System; International Monetary Fund; Bank for International Settlements; and Organisation for Economic Co-operation and Development.

ratio was 6 percent and 15 percent, respectively. Reliance on multilateral creditors is high: the average share of public and publicly guaranteed debt owed to multilateral creditors (including the IMF) was 57 percent at end 2010.

Countries in South Asia are relatively poor and reliant, in large measure, on financing from official sources, including grants. Gross debt related flows from official creditors fell 4 percent in 2010 despite the more than twofold increase in disbursements by IBRD. Disbursements on IDA loans declined 33 percent and IMF purchases (disbursements) 42 percent with most of the downturn in Pakistan which saw net inflows from official creditors drop to $1.8 billion from $5.7 billion in 2009. In part this was due to prior year frontloading of budgetary and emergence support from IDA, but delays in implementing the IMF program approved in November 2008 and slowdown in lending by other bilateral and multilateral creditors, including the Asian Development Bank, compounded the problem. India was the principal beneficiary of increased IBRD financing to the region. It saw gross flows from official creditors rise by 44 percent to $8.6 billion in 2010, of which almost 40 percent came from IBRD. Net debt related flows from private creditors were evenly balanced between medium and short term financing from commercial banks and bond issuance, but 96 percent of these flows went to India. Bond issuance by public sector borrowers in India rose to $11 billion in 2010 from $1.8 billion in 2009. Sri Lanka returned to the markets in September 2010 with its third sovereign issue since 2007, a heavily oversubscribed $1 billion 10 year note for infrastructure and debt refinancing.

The 12 percent rise in net equity flows to the region in 2010 masked divergent trends in FDI and portfolio equity flows with the former down 29 percent, and the latter up 92 percent, in relation to their 2009 level. India totally dominated the regional picture: when India is excluded net equity flows to the region were unchanged from 2009 at $3.2 billion. FDI inflows to India fell a further 32 percent in 2010: policy and procedural issues, delays in opening the retail and insurance sectors to foreign investors, poor infrastructure, licensing issues, and a series of widely reported corruption cases are cited as factors behind investors' reticence to commit to new long term investments. In sharp contrast portfolio equity inflows to India surged to $40 billion, a 90 percent increase from 2009, driving not only the regional, but also the global trend.

Sub-Saharan Africa

Net capital flows to Sub-Saharan Africa rose 16 percent in 2010 driven by a 33 percent increase in net debt inflows on loans from official creditors and a resumption of short-term debt inflows. These were partially offset by a 14 percent fall in net equity inflows. Measured in terms of GNI net capital flows, at 5.2 percent, were unchanged from their 2009 level (table 15).

Debt indicators have improved significantly since 2000 due to economic reforms, a favorable external environment, increased aid, restructuring of debt, and outright debt forgiveness. When South Africa is excluded, the ratio of external debt stock to exports and to GNI was 58 percent and 24 percent respectively at end 2010, compared to 250 percent and 98 percent, respectively in 2000. Five more countries reached the HIPC Completion Point in 2010, bringing to 26 out of 33 eligible African countries that have completed the HIPC process and benefitted from HIPC and MDRI debt relief. Countries in the region restructured $13.2 billion owed to Paris Club creditors in 2010 of which $9 billion was forgiven (see box 1). On a bilateral basis Paris Club creditors committed to forgive an additional $4 billion.

Many countries in the region remain on the margin of international capital markets and dependent on financing from official credits, including grants. Net debt inflows from official creditors rose 33 percent in 2010 to $13 billion as a result of a sharp increase in gross disbursements by both multilateral and bilateral creditors. IDA, the single most important multilateral creditor to the region, disbursed $6 billion in 2010 (in loans and grants). IMF purchases fell by 45 percent from 2009, but twenty two countries received IMF financing in 2010 with Angola, the Democratic Republic of the Congo, Cote d'Ivoire, and Ghana among the largest recipients. Bilateral creditors, mostly non-OECD countries, notably China, are an increasing important source of financing particularly in mineral rich countries. Gross disbursements from bilateral creditors rose 83 percent in 2010 to $7.2 billion, only marginally less than the $7.4 billion in gross disbursements from multilateral creditors. South Africa was the only country in the region to tap the international bond markets in 2010 with a $2 billion heavily over-subscribed 10 year

Table 15. Net Capital Inflows to Sub-Saharan Africa, 2001–10

$ billions

Inflows	2001	2002	2003	2004	2005	2006	2007	2008	2009	2010
Net private and official inflows	10.9	10.4	15.0	24.2	33.6	38.7	53.4	42.6	46.4	53.4
Percent of GNI	3.5	3.2	3.6	4.7	5.6	5.4	6.6	4.6	5.2	5.2
Net equity inflows	13.0	10.7	14.3	17.8	26.6	33.0	38.4	31.8	43.0	36.8
Net FDI inflows	13.9	11.1	13.6	11.2	18.6	16.2	28.3	37.5	32.8	28.8
Net portfolio equity inflows	–0.9	–0.4	0.7	6.7	8.1	16.8	10.1	–5.7	10.2	8.0
Net debt flows	–2.1	–0.4	0.7	6.4	7.0	5.7	14.9	10.9	3.4	16.6
Official creditors	0.0	2.7	1.4	2.3	–0.9	–1.7	2.8	4.9	9.8	13.0
World Bank	1.8	2.2	2.2	2.5	2.4	2.2	2.4	1.9	3.1	4.0
IMF	0.1	0.5	0.0	–0.1	–0.4	–0.1	0.1	0.7	2.2	1.2
Other official	–1.9	0.1	–0.7	0.0	–2.9	–3.8	0.3	2.3	4.5	7.9
Private creditors	–2.1	–3.0	–0.8	4.0	7.9	7.4	12.1	6.0	–6.4	3.5
Net medium and long term debt flows	0.0	–1.2	0.9	2.7	4.9	–2.0	7.8	1.5	3.5	2.1
Bonds	1.9	1.5	0.4	0.6	1.3	0.3	6.5	–0.7	1.9	1.4
Banks and other private	–1.9	–2.7	0.5	2.1	3.5	–2.4	1.3	2.2	1.6	0.7
Net short term debt flows	–2.1	–1.8	–1.7	1.4	3.0	9.4	4.3	4.5	–9.9	1.5
Change in reserves (– = increase)	–0.2	–0.6	–3.6	–21.6	–20.0	–32.4	–26.9	–10.9	–2.7	1.8
Memorandum items										
Workers remittances	4.8	5.2	6.2	8.3	9.6	12.8	18.7	21.7	20.2	21.1

Sources: World Bank Debtor Reporting System; International Monetary Fund; Bank for International Settlements; and Organisation for Economic Co-operation and Development.

sovereign issue. It also recorded a net inflow of $1.0 billion in medium term bank financing compared to a net outflow of $0.3 billion from other countries in the region. In sharp contrast to the outflow of $9.9 billion outflow in 2009, short term debt turned positive in 2010 ($1.5 billion), but there were disparate trends at the country level: Angola, Nigeria and South Africa saw the largest outflow while Ethiopia, Ghana, and Zambia recorded the largest net inflow.

FDI into the region, directed mainly to the minerals and metals sector, constituted two-thirds of net capital flows (excluding grants) between 2001 and 2010. It fell by 12 percent in 2010 largely on account of lackluster performance of FDI inflows to South Africa, $1.5 billion compared to $5.4 billion the previous year, reflecting investor concerns over possible nationalization and power constraints. Excluding South Africa FDI to the region was up 7 percent in 2010 on account of increased South-South FDI particularly to the hydro-carbon sector and extractive industries. The 21 percent decline in net portfolio equity flows was also driven by the sharp drop in flows to South Africa which fell to $5.8 billion ($9.4 billion in 2009). This was partially offset by a rapid rise in portfolio equity flows to Nigeria which topped $2 billion in 2010 ($0.5 billion in 2009) where foreign investors are rebuilding their investment positions to pre-crisis levels.

Annex A. Trends in IBRD and IDA Financing to Developing Countries in 2010

Financing from IBRD and IDA is the most important source of multilateral financing to public sector borrowers in developing countries across the globe. In 2010 these two institutions of the World Bank Group extended $43 billion in new commitments and made disbursements (from 2010 commitments and the undisbursed pipeline of commitments made in prior years) of $34 billion. This was equivalent to 53 percent and 39 percent respectively of the commitments and disbursements from all multilateral institutions to public sector borrowers in 2010. The World Bank Group provides financial support in other forms to public and private sector borrowers and it is captured in several components of the data presented in Global Development Finance (box 3).

Trends in IBRD Financing

New IBRD loan commitments signed in 2010 totaled $32 billion, down 12 percent from their all-time high of $36 billion in 2009. Almost 40 percent of 2010 commitments went to countries in Latin America and the Caribbean, with Brazil the single largest recipient ($5.4 billion) among all IBRD borrowers, but overall commitments to this region were 9 percent below their 2009 level. Countries in the Middle East and North Africa and Sub-Saharan Africa recorded a sharp rise in IBRD commitments in 2010 driven primarily by an near doubling of lending to Egypt and Morocco and $3.8 billion extended to South Africa's power utility company, Eskom. In all other regions 2010 commitments were lower than the previous year with South Asia seeing the biggest

Box 3. World Bank Group Financing to Developing Countries in 2010

Financing from the World Bank Group takes a variety of forms: loans and guarantees from IBRD and loans, grants and guarantees from IDA to the public sector of the borrowing country; loans and equity financing from IFC to the private sector; and investment guarantees from MIGA.

Financing by the World Bank Group is captured in the data presented in *Global Development Finance* as follows:

- Loans from IBRD and IDA constitute part of the borrowing country's public and publicly guaranteed debt and are also separately identified by source.
- Grants provided by IDA are recorded in official grants.
- Loan financing from IFC is recorded as part of private non guaranteed debt.
- Equity financing from IFC and investments guaranteed by MIGA are recorded as part of foreign direct investment.

IBRD and IDA guarantees do not represent financing and are only recorded as a flow of funds if the guarantee is invoked.

fall as commitments to India fell back to $2 billion from their record $5.8 billion in 2009 when India was the single largest recipient of all IBRD borrowers. The concentration of IBRD commitments increased: 10 borrowers accounted for 85 percent of new IBRD loans in 2010 compared to 75 percent to the top ten borrowers in 2009.

Disbursements by IBRD from commitments made in 2010 and the undisbursed pipeline of commitments made in prior years continued their upward trajectory in 2010, but at a much slower pace than the previous year, rising by 16 percent to $26 billion, as compared to the 67 percent increase recorded in 2009. Disbursements to all regions rose with the exception of Middle East and North Africa. IBRD disbursements to countries in South Asia and East Asia rose by 127 percent and 21 percent respectively, driven by increased lending to India ($3.3 billion in 2010 up from $1.4 billion in 2009) and by disbursements of $0.7 billion under the new IBRD lending program to Vietnam. IBRD disbursements to Sub-Saharan Africa were almost three times those of 2009, albeit from a very low base, and concentrated largely in South Africa. IBRD disbursements to Latin American and the Caribbean and Europe and Central Asia rose moderately in 2010, but the combined share of aggregate IBRD disbursements to these regions increased to 63 percent from 50 percent in 2009 (figure 11).

IBRD disbursements remained heavily concentrated with 78 percent going to the top ten borrowers in 2010 (up from 76 percent in 2009). The top ten recipients were little changed from those of 2009: only Romania dropped from the list with Kazakhstan the new entrant (figure 12). The total amount of debt outstanding and disbursed to countries reporting to the World Bank Debtor Reporting System by IBRD stood at $125 billion at end 2010. Of this amount over half (57 percent) was owed by six borrowers: in order of importance, Brazil, China, Mexico, Turkey, India and Indonesia.

Figure 11. IBRD Disbursements, Regional Distribution, 2008–10

$ millions

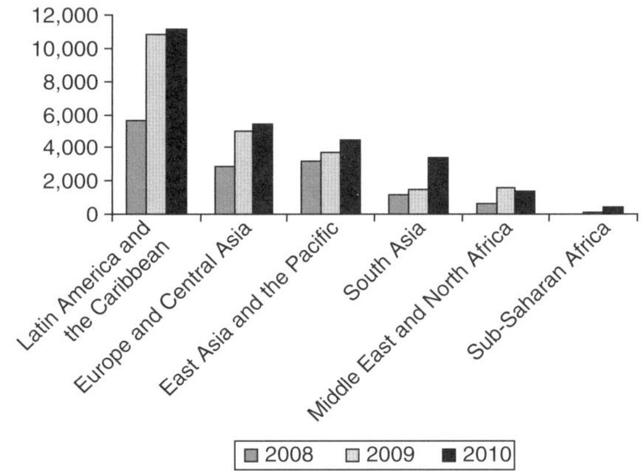

Source: World Bank Debtor Reporting System.

Figure 12. Top Ten Recipients of IBRD Disbursements, 2009 and 2010

$ millions

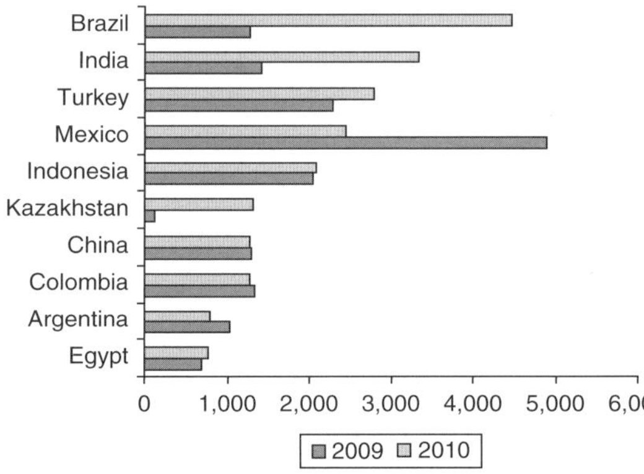

Source: World Bank Debtor Reporting System.

Trends in IDA Financing

IDA resources are reserved for the world's poorest countries, and its operations are concentrated primarily in South Asia and Sub-Saharan Africa. New loan commitments from IDA rose by 8 percent in 2010 to $11.3 billion, less than the 15 percent increase recorded in 2009. IDA resources are allocated to individual countries using a performance-based allocation system that also takes account of the size of the population and GNI per capita. IDA recipient countries in the top performance quintile receive around three times the commitment per capita as those in the lowest quintile. At the same time the distribution of IDA resources among the 79 IDA eligible countries is highly concentrated: four countries, in order of importance, India, Tanzania, Vietnam, and Bangladesh, absorbed almost half of new IDA loan commitments in 2010, and the top ten recipients accounted for 76 percent of the total.

Disbursements on IDA loans fell by 11.4 percent in 2010 to $7.7 billion and those on IDA grants slightly more, 11.9 percent, to $2.2 billion, but the downturn was not uniform across all regions. IDA disbursements (loans and grants) to countries in Sub-Saharan Africa rose by 5 percent and their share of aggregate IDA disbursements increased to 54 percent from 46 percent in 2009. IDA eligible countries in Europe and Central Asia, Latin America and the Caribbean and the Middle East and North Africa saw IDA disbursements increase by an average of 12 percent, driven in particular by higher IDA grant disbursements to Haiti and Yemen and increased IDA loan disbursements to Bosnia and Herzegovina and Moldova. However, the share of IDA resources going to these regions remained moderate. Only 10 percent of total IDA disbursements went to the three regions combined. South Asia, the second most important destination for IDA resources after Sub-Saharan Africa, saw IDA disbursements fall 34 percent in 2010, largely as a consequence of a precipitous drop in disbursements to Pakistan, which fell to around one third their 2009 level (to $371 million from $1,177 million in 2009), a consequence of prior year frontloading of fast disbursing development policy loans and emergency assistance, and a more moderate, 15 percent fall in disbursements to India. IDA disbursements to countries in East Asia and the Pacific region were also down 29 percent from their 2009 level due almost entirely to the 29 percent decline in disbursements to Vietnam (figure 13), a positive reflection of the country's creditworthiness and start of the transition to financing from IBRD and other market based sources.

Ten recipient countries received 60 percent of total IDA disbursements (loans and grants combined) compared to 65 percent in 2009. Only one of the top ten recipients in 2009, Afghanistan, dropped out of the group in 2010, with Ghana the new entrant. India was again the largest recipient of IDA disbursements, but its share of the total fell slightly to 10.8 percent (11.3 percent in 2009). By contrast, Nigeria rose to the second most important recipient of IDA in 2010, from sixth in 2009, increasing its share of total IDA disbursements, to 10.8 percent from 4.4 percent in 2009 (figure 14).

Figure 13. IDA Disbursements (Loans and Grants), Regional Distribution, 2008–10

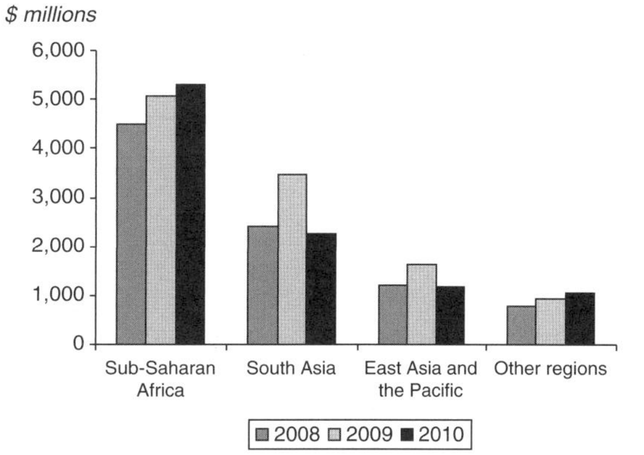

Source: World Bank Debtor Reporting System.

Figure 14. Top Ten Recipients of Gross IDA Disbursements (Loans and Grants), 2009 and 2010

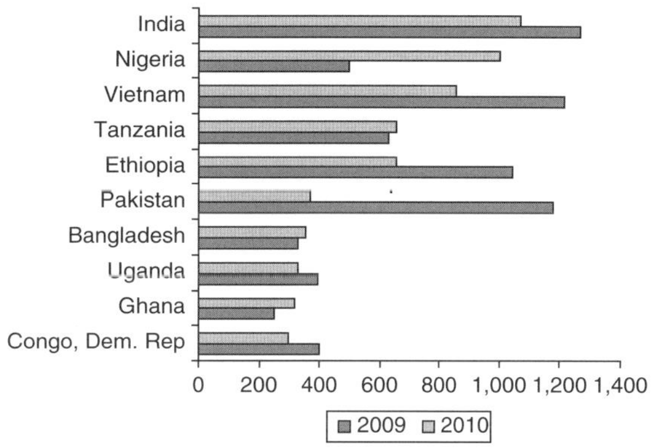

Source: World Bank Debtor Reporting System.

The outstanding IDA loan portfolio ($119 billion at end 2010) is heavily concentrated, with five East and South Asian countries accounting for a little over half of the total (53 percent). In order of importance they were India, Bangladesh, Pakistan, China, and Vietnam. This is in part a consequence of the fact that thirty-two countries, primarily in Sub-Saharan Africa, had reached the Highly Indebted Poor Countries (HIPC) Completion Point by end 2010 and benefited from debt relief from IDA under the HIPC and Multilateral Debt Relief Initiative (MDRI). African countries with the largest share of the outstanding IDA portfolio at end 2010 were Nigeria ($3.7 billion), Kenya ($3.2 billion) and Tanzania ($3.2 billion).

Notes

1. External loans to developing countries are extended by both official and private creditors. Loans contracted by public sector borrowers, or benefitting from a public sector guarantee, are categorized as public and publicly guaranteed debt. Loans contracted by private sector borrowers without any public sector guarantee constitute private non guaranteed debt.

2. Borrowers with outstanding obligations to IBRD classified as high-income countries and not included in the DRS are Barbados, Croatia, Estonia, Hungary, Republic of Korea, Poland, Slovak Republic, Slovenia, and Trinidad and Tobago.

Summary Tables

Summary Table 1. Key indebtedness indicators, 2008–10

Country	Total external debt, 2010 ($ millions)	Present value of debt, 2010 ($ millions)	Ratio of total external debt to exports of goods and services (%)	Ratio of present value of debt to exports of goods and services (%)	Ratio of total external debt to GNI (%)	Ratio of present value of debt to GNI (%)
Afghanistan	2,297	*721*	67	*21*	21	6
Albania	4,736	3,616	115	88	39	30
Algeria	5,276	4,687	6	5	3	3
Angola	18,562	15,787	26	22	26	22
Argentina	127,849	121,281	158	150	40	37
Armenia	6,103	4,687	238	183	60	46
Azerbaijan	6,974	3,894	25	14	16	9
Bangladesh	24,963	15,886	132	84	26	16
Belarus	25,726	23,088	83	75	47	42
Belize	1,045	784	129	96	84	63
Benin	1,221	*852*	101	*70*	18	*13*
Bhutan	898	714	109	87	69	55
Bolivia	5,267	*2,999*	72	*41*	31	*17*
Bosnia and Herzegovina	8,457	6,716	120	95	47	37
Botswana	1,709	1,141	28	19	13	9
Brazil	346,978	326,721	155	146	20	19
Bulgaria	48,077	44,915	170	159	102	95
Burkina Faso	2,053	*1,538*	225	*169*	25	*19*
Burundi	537	*194*	418	*151*	39	*14*
Cambodia	4,676	3,652	75	59	46	36
Cameroon	2,964	*1,194*	47	*19*	13	*5*
Cape Verde	857	455	136	72	56	29
Central African Republic	385	*246*	119	*76*	19	*12*
Chad	1,733	*1,845*	54	*57*	27	*28*
Chile	86,349	78,746	108	99	52	48
China	548,551	522,861	33	31	11	10
Colombia	63,064	92,182	145	212	26	38
Comoros	485	*163*	714	*240*	91	*31*
Congo, Dem. Rep.	5,774	*2,972*	151	*78*	52	*27*
Congo, Rep.	3,781	*1,577*	46	*19*	47	*20*
Costa Rica	8,849	8,090	65	59	29	27
Côte d'Ivoire	11,430	*10,597*	95	*88*	52	*48*
Djibouti	751	500	176	117	65	43
Dominica	267	202	163	124	74	56
Dominican Republic	13,045	10,906	107	89	28	24
Ecuador	14,815	12,770	75	64	26	22
Egypt, Arab Rep.	34,844	28,793	56	46	18	15
El Salvador	11,069	9,732	201	177	53	46
Eritrea	1,010	*597*	1,237	*732*	57	*34*
Ethiopia	7,147	*3,924*	194	*107*	24	*13*
Fiji	452	403	28	25	15	13
Gabon	2,331	2,126	18	16	21	19
Gambia, The	470	*217*	157	*73*	64	*29*
Georgia	9,238	7,536	225	184	80	65
Ghana	8,368	*4,956*	103	*61*	30	*18*
Grenada	576	631	309	338	96	106
Guatemala	14,340	12,115	139	118	37	32
Guinea	2,923	*2,007*	211	*145*	78	*54*
Guinea-Bissau	1,095	*124*	766	*87*	130	*15*
Guyana	1,354	*762*	131	*74*	57	*32*
Haiti	492	*282*	55	*32*	8	*4*
Honduras	4,168	*1,971*	57	*27*	30	*14*
India	290,282	252,804	91	79	20	18

(table continues on next page)

Summary Table 1. Key indebtedness indicators, 2008–10 (*continued*)

Country	Total external debt, 2010 ($ millions)	Present value of debt, 2010 ($ millions)	Ratio of total external debt to exports of goods and services (%)	Ratio of present value of debt to exports of goods and services (%)	Ratio of total external debt to GNI (%)	Ratio of present value of debt to GNI (%)
Indonesia	179,064	159,754	114	102	32	28
Iran, Islamic Rep.	12,570	10,954	—	—	4	3
Jamaica	13,865	13,246	232	221	107	102
Jordan	7,822	6,672	60	51	30	26
Kazakhstan	118,723	101,695	181	155	104	89
Kenya	8,400	5,912	102	72	28	20
Kosovo	342	241	35	25	6	4
Kyrgyz Republic	3,984	*1,750*	150	*66*	86	*38*
Lao PDR	5,559	3,959	296	211	92	65
Latvia	39,555	36,684	280	260	139	129
Lebanon	24,293	23,420	102	98	70	67
Lesotho	726	396	43	24	31	17
Liberia	228	*86*	37	*14*	31	*12*
Lithuania	29,602	27,225	116	107	75	69
Macedonia, FYR	5,804	5,289	130	118	63	57
Madagascar	2,295	*1,832*	75	*60*	26	*21*
Malawi	922	*717*	82	*63*	20	*16*
Malaysia	81,497	75,406	36	33	39	36
Maldives	1,229	1,020	129	107	95	79
Mali	2,326	*1,425*	94	*58*	27	*16*
Mauritania	2,461	*2,364*	131	*126*	71	*68*
Mauritius	1,076	803	20	15	11	8
Mexico	200,081	178,631	68	60	20	18
Moldova	4,615	4,076	154	136	74	65
Mongolia	2,444	1,697	83	58	48	33
Montenegro	1,554	1,331	71	60	37	31
Morocco	25,403	20,820	82	67	29	23
Mozambique	4,124	*1,980*	137	*66*	44	*21*
Myanmar	6,352	4,206	—	—	—	—
Nepal	3,702	*2,752*	203	*151*	27	*20*
Nicaragua	4,786	*2,249*	150	*71*	78	*37*
Niger	1,127	*561*	107	*53*	21	*10*
Nigeria	7,883	5,582	10	7	4	3
Pakistan	56,773	41,425	218	159	33	24
Panama	11,412	10,049	62	55	50	44
Papua New Guinea	5,822	4,580	101	79	70	55
Paraguay	4,938	4,298	55	48	30	26
Peru	36,271	32,384	100	89	28	25
Philippines	72,337	62,514	115	100	40	35
Romania	121,505	101,112	205	171	70	58
Russian Federation	384,740	347,210	80	72	27	25
Rwanda	795	*595*	137	*103*	15	*12*
Samoa	308	174	160	90	58	33
São Tomé and Principe	170	*49*	777	*224*	90	*26*
Senegal	3,677	*2,591*	95	*67*	28	*20*
Serbia	32,222	28,351	229	201	76	67
Seychelles	1,510	1,377	170	155	189	173
Sierra Leone	778	*432*	207	*115*	41	*23*
Solomon Islands	215	148	68	47	41	28
Somalia	2,942	3,656	—	—	—	—
South Africa	45,165	44,196	46	45	15	15
Sri Lanka	20,452	15,887	201	156	47	37
St. Kitts and Nevis	203	173	97	82	39	33
St. Lucia	464	390	81	68	53	44
St. Vincent and the Grenadines	261	191	127	93	47	35
Sudan	21,846	*37,205*	199	*339*	41	*70*
Swaziland	616	592	27	26	20	19
Syrian Arab Republic	4,729	4,294	25	23	9	8
Tajikistan	2,955	2,202	196	146	57	42

(table continues on next page)

Summary Table 1. Key indebtedness indicators, 2008–10 (*continued*)

Country	Total external debt, 2010 ($ millions)	Present value of debt, 2010 ($ millions)	Ratio of total external debt to exports of goods and services (%)	Ratio of present value of debt to exports of goods and services (%)	Ratio of total external debt to GNI (%)	Ratio of present value of debt to GNI (%)
Tanzania	8,664	*4,947*	148	*85*	40	*23*
Thailand	71,263	66,153	34	31	26	24
Togo	1,728	*392*	154	*35*	61	*14*
Tonga	144	92	260	167	41	26
Tunisia	21,584	19,307	86	77	53	47
Turkey	293,872	270,204	180	165	43	39
Turkmenistan	422	380	3	2	2	2
Uganda	2,994	*1,100*	90	*33*	19	*7*
Ukraine	117,128	107,452	157	144	82	75
Uruguay	11,347	10,234	113	102	34	31
Uzbekistan	7,404	5,972	56	45	22	18
Vanuatu	148	113	54	41	23	18
Venezuela, R.B.	55,572	55,591	70	70	16	16
Vietnam	35,139	26,565	49	37	38	29
Yemen, Rep.	6,324	3,971	71	44	24	15
Zambia	3,689	*1,561*	63	*27*	28	*12*
Zimbabwe	5,016	6,001	230	275	92	110

Source: World Bank data.
Note: GNI = gross national income; — = not available. For definitions of indicators, see the "About the data" section. Numbers in *italics* are based on the latest available Debt Sustainability Analysis for Low-Income Countries (LIC DSA) and include the effects of traditional relief, debt relief under the Heavily Indebted Poor Country (HIPC) Initiative, and relief under the Multilateral Debt Relief Initiative (MDRI). Under MDRI, the International Development Association (IDA), International Monetary Fund (IMF), and African Development Fund (AfDF) provide debt stock cancellation to post–completion point HIPCs on debt owed to the three institutions. The Inter-American Development Bank (IDB) provides similar debt stock cancellation under the IDB 2007 Debt Initiative. MDRI debt relief provides 100 percent stock cancellation on debt disbursed before end-2004 (for the IMF, AfDF, and IDB) or end-2003 (for IDA), and still outstanding at the time the country reaches the completion point under the HIPC Initiative. In line with the Debt Sustainability Framework for Low-Income Countries, only the conditional debt relief under the HIPC Initiative is included for countries in the interim period (between decision and completion point of the HIPC Initiative).

Summary Table 2. Composition of Total External Debt Stocks for 2010

$ millions

Country	Total external debt stocks	Total long-term external debt	Public and publicly guaranteed debt, multilateral	Public and publicly guaranteed debt, bilateral	Public and publicly guaranteed debt, bonds
Afghanistan	2,297	2,076	1,118	958	0
Albania	4,736	4,105	1,522	637	401
Algeria	5,276	3,498	10	1,795	0
Angola	18,562	15,440	436	7,716	0
Argentina	127,849	92,844	16,918	6,004	43,571
Armenia	6,103	4,744	1,513	1,042	0
Azerbaijan	6,974	6,050	1,745	920	0
Bangladesh	24,963	21,371	18,460	2,842	0
Belarus	25,726	10,251	295	5,587	1,802
Belize	1,045	1,031	256	150	21
Benin	1,221	1,134	927	207	0
Bhutan	898	892	332	561	0
Bolivia	5,267	5,164	2,259	523	0
Bosnia and Herzegovina	8,457	6,899	2,416	869	273
Botswana	1,709	1,352	1,222	129	0
Brazil	346,978	281,482	29,747	11,504	41,323
Bulgaria	48,077	32,704	2,330	823	1,301
Burkina Faso	2,053	1,925	1,600	307	0
Burundi	537	412	344	68	0
Cambodia	4,676	4,414	1,529	2,885	0
Cameroon	2,964	2,762	788	1,381	0
Cape Verde	857	847	597	197	0
Central African Republic	385	218	29	154	0
Chad	1,733	1,708	1,483	196	0
Chile	86,349	60,470	801	224	8,413
China	548,551	201,027	35,120	32,084	10,273
Colombia	63,064	54,855	15,786	432	17,686
Comoros	485	469	204	265	0
Congo, Dem. Rep.	5,774	4,957	2,571	2,279	0
Congo, Rep.	3,781	3,531	219	2,497	0
Costa Rica	8,849	6,418	1,709	430	1,435
Côte d'Ivoire	11,430	10,696	2,228	6,445	1,621
Djibouti	751	739	409	309	0
Dominica	267	216	116	55	40
Dominican Republic	13,045	9,958	3,074	3,091	1,721
Ecuador	14,815	14,446	5,171	2,404	868
Egypt, Arab Rep.	34,844	31,695	9,019	18,844	3,333
El Salvador	11,069	9,964	3,526	648	2,199
Eritrea	1,010	1,003	651	313	0
Ethiopia	7,147	6,545	2,812	1,825	0
Fiji	452	391	116	125	150
Gabon	2,331	2,158	384	521	879
Gambia, The	470	395	267	118	0
Georgia	9,238	7,224	1,802	588	750

Public and publicly guaranteed debt, commercial banks and other	Private nonguaranteed debt, bonds	Private nonguaranteed debt, commercial banks and other	IBRD (memo)	IDA (memo)	Use of IMF credit	Short-term debt
0	0	0	0	410	119	102
412	0	1,133	26	850	58	573
726	0	968	9	0	0	1,778
7,287	0	0	0	378	882	2,241
838	7,855	17,659	5,349	0	0	35,005
1	0	2,187	106	1,161	741	618
1,226	0	2,158	300	763	46	878
69	0	0	0	10,653	617	2,974
166	0	2,401	291	0	3,495	11,980
594	0	10	12	0	7	7
0	0	0	0	383	55	32
0	0	0	0	112	0	6
24	0	2,358	0	355	0	103
193	0	3,149	445	1,180	521	1,037
1	0	0	6	4	0	357
13,968	83,032	101,908	13,523	0	0	65,496
13	134	28,104	1,338	0	0	15,373
18	0	0	0	776	129	0
0	0	0	0	163	110	16
0	0	0	0	565	0	262
15	0	577	24	350	172	31
53	0	0	0	303	9	2
34	0	0	0	14	90	77
30	0	0	0	865	17	8
3,491	7,061	40,480	189	0	0	25,879
12,703	17,976	92,871	12,962	9,000	0	347,524
2,873	3,329	14,749	7,504	0	0	8,209
0	0	0	0	116	12	4
106	0	0	0	849	323	494
815	0	0	0	84	27	222
151	0	2,693	570	0	0	2,431
122	0	280	14	1,749	383	351
20	0	0	0	155	12	1
4	0	0	1	27	18	32
1,229	843	0	864	7	1,139	1,948
155	0	5,848	446	10	0	369
445	0	54	2,543	1,338	0	3,149
21	0	3,569	915	8	0	1,105
38	0	0	0	468	0	7
1,907	0	0	0	1,804	288	314
0	0	1	0	0	0	61
374	0	0	22	0	0	174
10	0	0	0	65	31	44
941	0	3,143	173	1,186	1,050	963

(table continues on next page)

Summary Table 2. Composition of Total External Debt Stocks for 2010 *(continued)*
$ millions

Country	Total external debt stocks	Total long-term external debt	Public and publicly guaranteed debt, multilateral	Public and publicly guaranteed debt, bilateral	Public and publicly guaranteed debt, bonds
Ghana	8,368	5,727	2,620	1,360	750
Grenada	576	495	190	89	210
Guatemala	14,340	12,745	4,213	359	955
Guinea	2,923	2,752	1,798	918	0
Guinea-Bissau	1,095	963	492	471	0
Guyana	1,354	888	502	365	0
Haiti	492	479	71	408	0
Honduras	4,168	3,740	1,891	823	50
India	290,282	233,834	46,531	26,111	20,430
Indonesia	179,064	147,809	22,567	43,917	16,990
Iran, Islamic Rep.	12,570	6,411	830	1,195	0
Jamaica	13,865	11,900	2,348	912	3,786
Jordan	7,822	6,504	2,528	2,892	914
Kazakhstan	118,723	109,686	2,785	1,057	0
Kenya	8,400	6,978	4,110	2,557	0
Kosovo	342	342	342	0	0
Kyrgyz Republic	3,984	3,612	1,296	1,146	0
Lao PDR	5,559	5,549	1,983	955	0
Latvia	39,555	25,319	5,246	11	1,069
Lebanon	24,293	20,713	1,320	906	17,422
Lesotho	726	698	623	61	0
Liberia	228	184	63	120	0
Lithuania	29,602	24,133	1,612	0	10,052
Macedonia, FYR	5,804	3,750	1,112	242	434
Madagascar	2,295	1,984	1,536	437	0
Malawi	922	715	576	139	0
Malaysia	81,497	46,421	237	3,513	15,575
Maldives	1,229	989	311	236	0
Mali	2,326	2,271	1,790	476	0
Mauritania	2,461	2,174	1,350	823	0
Mauritius	1,076	1,072	501	383	0
Mexico	200,081	161,068	21,112	4,542	63,519
Moldova	4,615	2,723	556	258	0
Mongolia	2,444	2,016	1,073	716	0
Montenegro	1,554	1,368	556	281	267
Morocco	25,403	23,603	10,149	7,085	1,336
Mozambique	4,124	2,960	2,205	657	0
Myanmar	6,352	4,395	1,415	2,574	0
Nepal	3,702	3,527	3,150	374	0
Nicaragua	4,786	3,922	1,637	1,028	0
Niger	1,127	972	720	251	0
Nigeria	7,883	4,686	4,304	289	0
Pakistan	56,773	45,746	24,614	16,789	1,550
Panama	11,412	11,412	1,814	314	8,071

Public and publicly guaranteed debt, commercial banks and other	Private nonguaranteed debt, bonds	Private nonguaranteed debt, commercial banks and other	IBRD (memo)	IDA (memo)	Use of IMF credit	Short-term debt
997	0	0	0	1,868	392	2,249
5	0	0	14	44	29	52
0	5	7,213	1,372	0	0	1,595
37	0	0	0	1,248	48	123
0	0	0	0	289	4	128
21	0	0	0	9	56	410
0	0	0	0	0	13	0
34	0	942	0	602	30	398
13,134	13,633	113,996	11,180	25,888	0	56,448
7,550	5,788	50,996	9,054	2,313	0	31,255
4,385	0	0	801	0	0	6,159
548	4,290	17	579	0	785	1,180
170	0	0	1,008	32	8	1,310
0	21,044	84,800	1,830	0	0	9,037
311	0	0	0	3,238	417	1,005
0	0	0	342	0	0	0
0	0	1,171	0	649	177	195
0	0	2,610	0	655	10	0
566	267	18,161	421	0	1,513	12,723
565	500	0	321	0	98	3,482
14	0	0	2	328	28	0
0	0	0	0	0	44	0
0	793	11,675	20	0	0	5,469
77	0	1,885	315	367	0	2,054
7	0	3	0	1,161	97	214
0	0	0	0	243	146	61
6,470	4,893	15,733	0	0	0	35,076
105	0	336	0	99	16	224
5	0	0	0	840	49	6
1	0	0	0	316	50	237
88	0	100	197	7	0	3
22,294	29,970	19,630	12,462	0	0	39,013
3	0	1,906	93	386	327	1,564
7	0	221	0	403	198	230
245	0	19	236	79	0	186
2,444	0	2,589	2,468	13	0	1,800
98	0	0	0	1,491	190	975
406	0	0	0	799	0	1,956
3	0	0	0	1,426	114	61
3	0	1,255	0	447	167	697
0	0	0	0	275	61	94
92	0	0	43	3,662	0	3,197
249	250	2,294	1,688	10,118	8,736	2,291
223	911	80	420	0	0	0

(table continues on next page)

Summary Table 2. Composition of Total External Debt Stocks for 2010 *(continued)*
$ millions

Country	Total external debt stocks	Total long-term external debt	Public and publicly guaranteed debt, multilateral	Public and publicly guaranteed debt, bilateral	Public and publicly guaranteed debt, bonds
Papua New Guinea	5,822	5,430	712	285	0
Paraguay	4,938	3,791	1,496	613	0
Peru	36,271	30,216	7,854	2,719	9,311
Philippines	72,337	66,042	8,372	14,826	20,221
Romania	121,505	81,383	13,373	860	1,670
Russian Federation	384,740	345,983	3,042	3,347	82,643
Rwanda	795	766	639	126	0
Samoa	308	299	219	80	0
São Tomé and Principe	170	145	37	108	0
Senegal	3,677	3,464	1,976	979	200
Serbia	32,222	27,389	4,848	3,296	0
Seychelles	1,510	498	74	174	169
Sierra Leone	778	661	371	79	0
Solomon Islands	215	202	106	20	0
Somalia	2,942	1,990	801	1,153	0
South Africa	45,165	32,860	1,139	0	11,065
Sri Lanka	20,452	17,368	6,079	7,524	2,000
St. Kitts and Nevis	203	198	99	34	24
St. Lucia	464	286	202	21	8
St. Vincent and the Grenadines	261	255	188	18	0
Sudan	21,846	14,444	3,342	8,474	0
Swaziland	616	385	240	123	0
Syrian Arab Republic	4,729	4,171	1,591	2,580	0
Tajikistan	2,955	2,733	945	861	0
Tanzania	8,664	6,795	4,382	1,077	0
Thailand	71,263	32,791	187	6,656	1,954
Togo	1,728	1,534	837	697	0
Tonga	144	144	71	72	0
Tunisia	21,584	16,605	6,664	3,494	3,819
Turkey	293,872	210,123	19,780	6,724	46,276
Turkmenistan	422	367	14	327	0
Uganda	2,994	2,671	2,416	255	0
Ukraine	116,808	76,104	4,392	1,397	9,148
Uruguay	11,347	9,797	3,495	117	6,021
Uzbekistan	7,404	7,167	1,175	1,998	0
Vanuatu	148	99	69	30	0
Venezuela, R.B.	55,572	40,146	4,014	942	29,762
Vietnam	35,139	28,145	12,262	12,993	2,020
Yemen, Rep.	6,324	5,933	3,283	2,647	0
Zambia	3,689	2,104	924	353	0
Zimbabwe	5,016	4,064	1,593	1,660	0
All developing countries	*4,076,298*	*2,975,259*	*483,841*	*338,734*	*527,752*

Public and publicly guaranteed debt, commercial banks and other	Private nonguaranteed debt, bonds	Private nonguaranteed debt, commercial banks and other	IBRD (memo)	IDA (memo)	Use of IMF credit	Short-term debt
33	0	4,400	139	86	0	392
260	0	1,421	257	13	0	1,147
143	7,298	2,891	2,965	0	0	6,055
1,221	1,651	19,751	2,567	171	0	6,295
4,654	0	60,826	2,830	0	15,092	25,029
73,891	73,329	109,730	2,618	0	0	38,756
0	0	0	0	259	15	14
0	0	0	0	99	9	0
0	0	0	0	14	5	20
0	0	308	0	1,017	213	0
1,332	165	17,747	1,818	681	2,034	2,798
82	0	0	17	0	31	980
211	0	0	0	155	113	4
0	0	77	0	42	10	4
37	0	0	0	443	172	780
5,549	5,471	9,636	384	0	0	12,305
847	0	919	0	2,531	1,311	1,773
41	0	0	10	1	3	1
55	0	0	21	59	11	167
49	0	0	5	21	6	0
2,629	0	0	0	1,290	390	7,012
23	0	0	2	2	0	231
0	0	0	0	15	0	558
0	0	927	0	377	101	122
113	0	1,224	0	3,248	354	1,515
2,561	4,570	16,864	73	56	0	38,471
0	0	0	0	554	133	61
1	0	0	0	24	0	0
632	0	1,996	1,381	18	0	4,979
20,308	8,502	108,533	11,563	42	5,627	78,123
18	0	7	11	0	0	55
0	0	0	0	1,682	9	314
1,308	5,114	54,744	3,212	0	14,245	26,459
72	93	0	1,055	0	0	1,550
252	0	3,741	259	114	0	238
0	0	0	0	12	0	49
2,368	3,060	0	0	0	0	15,426
870	0	0	700	7,010	45	6,949
3	0	0	0	2,180	78	313
33	0	794	0	430	395	1,191
432	0	378	463	513	110	843
232,259	*311,827*	*1,080,846*	*124,852*	*118,607*	*64,661*	*1,036,378*

(table continues on next page)

Summary Table 2. Composition of Total External Debt Stocks for 2010 *(continued)*
$ millions

Country	Total external debt stocks	Total long-term external debt	Public and publicly guaranteed debt, multilateral	Public and publicly guaranteed debt, bilateral	Public and publicly guaranteed debt, bonds
East Asia and the Pacific	1,013,971	545,176	86,037	121,732	67,184
Europe and Central Asia	1,273,418	994,159	72,697	32,271	156,088
Latin America and the Caribbean	1,038,725	828,184	130,489	38,770	238,992
Middle East and North Africa	143,595	119,872	35,803	41,747	26,825
South Asia	400,596	325,804	100,595	55,395	23,980
Sub-Saharan Africa	205,992	162,065	58,220	48,821	14,684
Low-income countries	116,593	99,631	63,201	28,856	0
Middle-income countries	3,959,705	2,875,628	420,640	309,878	527,752

Source: World Bank data.
Note: IBRD = International Bank for Reconstruction and Development; IDA = International Development Association; IMF = International Monetary Fund.

Public and publicly guaranteed debt, commercial banks and other	Private nonguaranteed debt, bonds	Private nonguaranteed debt, commercial banks and other	IBRD (memo)	IDA (memo)	Use of IMF credit	Short-term debt
31,822	34,878	203,524	25,494	21,234	271	468,525
105,607	109,348	518,148	28,251	7,835	45,027	234,232
49,464	147,747	222,723	48,533	1,606	2,265	208,277
9,391	500	5,606	8,532	3,751	195	23,528
14,407	13,883	117,545	12,868	51,238	10,913	63,879
21,568	5,471	13,301	1,175	32,943	5,991	37,936
3,871	0	3,703	463	36,019	4,156	12,806
228,387	311,827	1,077,144	124,389	82,589	60,505	1,023,572

Regional and Income Group Aggregate Tables

ALL DEVELOPING COUNTRIES

(US$ million, unless otherwise indicated)

	1995	2000	2005	2006	2007	2008	2009	2010
1. Summary external debt data								
External debt stocks	**1,860,622**	**2,126,351**	**2,514,065**	**2,675,295**	**3,220,517**	**3,499,172**	**3,639,595**	**4,076,298**
Long-term external debt	1,469,870	1,778,340	1,964,052	2,061,665	2,440,930	2,713,910	2,813,091	2,975,259
Public and publicly guaranteed	1,261,379	1,287,438	1,282,903	1,246,306	1,355,843	1,397,456	1,477,075	1,582,586
Private nonguaranteed	208,491	490,902	681,149	815,359	1,085,088	1,316,454	1,336,016	1,392,674
Use of IMF credit	59,881	58,266	49,179	19,859	15,540	25,740	53,298	64,661
Short-term external debt	330,871	289,745	500,834	593,771	764,046	759,522	773,206	1,036,378
interest arrears on long-term	44,516	31,741	28,423	26,027	27,637	27,495	26,428	21,090
Memorandum items								
Principal arrears on long-term	104,584	60,643	46,229	44,775	47,648	49,140	50,978	40,871
Long-term public sector debt	1,256,292	1,281,540	1,278,312	1,242,003	1,350,991	1,391,811	1,465,482	1,570,204
Long-term private sector debt	213,578	496,800	685,740	819,662	1,089,940	1,322,099	1,347,609	1,405,056
Public & publicly guaranteed commitments	140,659	145,910	159,300	143,401	194,324	185,948	247,087	250,764
External debt flows								
Disbursements	209,547	238,467	383,223	479,002	660,569	665,013	534,464	655,672
Long-term external debt	181,764	228,352	379,262	474,888	658,556	650,407	505,843	638,831
IMF purchases	27,783	10,114	3,961	4,113	2,013	14,607	28,621	16,842
Principal repayments	120,574	232,473	327,078	383,096	362,730	396,227	383,041	428,917
Long-term external debt	111,933	211,870	282,956	352,277	355,576	392,427	381,197	425,895
IMF repurchases	8,641	20,603	44,122	30,819	7,155	3,800	1,844	3,022
Net flows	143,080	-1,521	137,740	191,239	466,100	264,404	166,167	495,230
Long-term external debt	69,831	16,482	96,307	122,612	302,980	257,980	124,646	212,936
Short-term external debt	54,107	-7,515	81,594	95,333	168,261	-4,383	14,744	268,474
Interest payments	85,036	112,744	103,710	117,392	137,334	142,601	125,886	154,434
Long-term external debt	67,490	93,903	83,820	94,204	109,208	120,813	111,244	111,949
IMF charges	2,632	2,865	3,277	1,622	710	979	571	986
Short-term external debt	14,913	15,976	16,613	21,565	27,416	20,809	14,071	41,499
2. Other non-debt resource inflows								
Foreign direct investment	94,837	148,721	314,484	387,525	534,141	624,110	399,950	506,062
Portfolio equity	13,317	13,948	67,472	107,699	132,952	-53,363	108,756	128,413
3. Currency composition of public and publicly guaranteed debt (%)								
Euro	..	..	14.0	14.5	14.8	13.5	14.1	12.7
Japanese yen	13.0	11.9	10.1	9.9	8.9	10.6	10.1	10.4
Pound sterling	1.6	1.0	1.1	0.7	0.6	0.4	0.5	0.5
Swiss franc	1.1	0.5	0.6	0.6	0.6	0.5	0.5	0.4
U.S.dollars	48.2	63.0	66.0	66.7	67.6	67.8	67.9	69.4
4. Average terms of new commitments								
Official creditors								
Interest (%)	5.8	4.8	3.6	3.9	3.6	2.8	1.9	1.8
Maturity (years)	19.2	20.2	22.1	22.8	23.3	23.6	21.5	22.9
Grace period (years)	5.4	5.0	5.7	6.2	6.5	6.5	6.2	6.7
Private creditors								
Interest (%)	6.5	8.2	6.3	6.2	6.4	6.0	6.2	4.9
Maturity (years)	7.4	11.2	11.3	11.9	11.0	11.7	9.7	12.4
Grace period (years)	3.4	8.5	8.7	9.4	8.1	8.0	8.2	9.0
5. Major economic aggregates								
Gross national income (GNI)	4,797,416	5,628,860	9,436,088	11,209,853	13,910,950	16,633,250	16,264,212	19,437,081
Exports of goods, services & income	1,141,830	1,654,724	3,310,882	4,048,536	4,905,753	5,900,518	4,727,932	5,936,528
Worker remit. & comp. of employees	53,349	77,752	186,981	221,642	276,403	322,921	306,271	319,552
Imports of goods, services & income	1,301,854	1,706,988	3,271,139	3,896,346	4,773,434	5,834,427	4,764,531	6,033,022
Profit remittances on FDI	36,709	67,823	196,687	257,048	325,986	378,327	319,275	342,894
International reserves	439,401	642,754	1,979,073	2,615,959	3,701,232	4,153,683	4,835,610	5,587,636
6. Ratios								
External debt stocks to exports (%)	163.0	128.5	75.9	66.1	65.6	59.3	77.0	68.7
External debt stocks to GNI (%)	38.8	37.8	26.6	23.9	23.2	21.0	22.4	21.0
Debt service to exports (%)	18.0	20.9	13.0	12.4	10.2	9.1	10.8	9.8
Short-term to external debt stocks (%)	17.8	13.6	19.9	22.2	23.7	21.7	21.2	25.4
Multilateral to external debt stocks (%)	15.0	15.4	14.9	13.0	11.6	11.3	12.2	11.9
Reserves to external debt stocks (%)	23.6	30.2	78.7	97.8	114.9	118.7	132.9	137.1
Reserves to imports (months)	4.1	4.5	7.3	8.1	9.3	8.5	12.2	11.1

ALL DEVELOPING COUNTRIES

(US$ million, unless otherwise indicated)

	1995	*2000*	*2005*	*2006*	*2007*	*2008*	*2009*	*2010*
7. Long-term external debt								
Debt outstanding and disbursed	**1,469,870**	**1,778,340**	**1,964,052**	**2,061,665**	**2,440,930**	**2,713,910**	**2,813,091**	**2,975,259**
Public and publicly guaranteed	1,261,379	1,287,438	1,282,903	1,246,306	1,355,843	1,397,456	1,477,075	1,582,586
Official creditors	764,851	751,694	715,244	636,440	668,757	711,011	772,345	822,575
Multilateral	278,753	326,618	373,641	348,159	373,874	395,001	443,775	483,841
of which: IBRD	106,440	108,322	96,370	92,386	93,651	96,696	108,696	124,852
IDA	71,495	86,796	121,077	99,005	107,675	111,269	116,967	118,607
Bilateral	486,099	425,076	341,602	288,282	294,883	316,011	328,570	338,734
Private creditors	496,528	535,744	567,659	609,866	687,086	686,445	704,730	760,010
of which: Bonds	220,501	341,957	400,279	409,788	455,913	468,243	484,388	527,752
Commercial banks	146,863	125,803	125,950	163,807	198,841	190,359	189,535	202,652
Private nonguaranteed	208,491	490,902	681,149	815,359	1,085,088	1,316,454	1,336,016	1,392,674
of which: Bonds	51,018	89,492	155,162	192,861	250,265	241,846	256,961	311,827
Disbursements	**181,764**	**228,352**	**379,262**	**474,888**	**658,556**	**650,407**	**505,843**	**638,831**
Public and publicly guaranteed	128,269	137,193	142,619	151,919	186,837	174,672	217,405	253,309
Official creditors	64,895	52,387	46,076	54,722	60,069	68,706	100,215	105,448
Multilateral	31,117	34,261	34,253	40,007	43,714	47,599	72,435	71,390
of which: IBRD	12,545	12,969	9,180	11,934	10,498	13,608	22,703	26,246
IDA	5,474	5,219	7,207	6,771	7,358	6,864	8,712	7,688
Bilateral	33,778	18,126	11,823	14,715	16,355	21,107	27,780	34,059
Private creditors	63,374	84,806	96,543	97,197	126,768	105,966	117,190	147,860
of which: Bonds	22,036	55,784	61,066	57,988	75,318	73,523	69,052	86,861
Commercial banks	22,190	18,131	31,775	34,149	47,852	30,035	41,806	51,398
Private nonguaranteed	53,495	91,159	236,643	322,969	471,718	475,734	288,439	385,522
of which: Bonds	14,063	10,810	47,975	54,555	84,368	27,235	37,236	86,053
Principal repayments	**111,933**	**211,870**	**282,956**	**352,277**	**355,576**	**392,427**	**381,197**	**425,895**
Public and publicly guaranteed	86,015	113,674	145,932	191,849	127,648	143,529	117,318	124,527
Official creditors	42,587	47,540	70,215	97,008	53,409	49,992	46,498	48,021
Multilateral	19,653	22,591	26,691	36,471	26,490	26,982	25,467	25,854
of which: IBRD	11,364	9,418	12,130	17,188	10,866	10,947	10,860	9,165
IDA	542	948	1,621	1,779	1,836	2,296	2,252	2,342
Bilateral	22,934	24,949	43,524	60,536	26,920	23,010	21,031	22,167
Private creditors	43,428	66,134	75,717	94,841	74,239	93,537	70,820	76,506
of which: Bonds	11,091	31,454	44,589	60,257	43,145	53,897	32,705	35,031
Commercial banks	15,281	23,256	22,303	25,145	23,976	32,407	30,706	33,484
Private nonguaranteed	25,918	98,197	137,024	160,428	227,927	248,898	263,879	301,368
of which: Bonds	4,042	15,032	15,063	17,980	24,880	20,144	22,467	26,500
Interest payments	**67,490**	**93,903**	**83,820**	**94,204**	**109,208**	**120,813**	**111,244**	**111,949**
Public and publicly guaranteed	56,594	63,242	60,511	56,330	59,793	59,141	54,237	55,120
Official creditors	27,407	25,999	23,934	19,726	20,230	19,011	16,999	16,592
Multilateral	13,162	15,237	10,581	11,672	12,878	12,309	10,515	8,930
of which: IBRD	7,614	7,456	4,020	4,782	5,435	4,576	3,432	2,256
IDA	503	577	897	811	758	908	798	825
Bilateral	14,245	10,762	13,353	8,055	7,352	6,702	6,484	7,662
Private creditors	29,186	37,243	36,578	36,604	39,563	40,131	37,238	38,528
of which: Bonds	14,713	25,003	30,128	28,827	31,222	31,726	30,820	33,011
Commercial banks	7,822	8,561	4,919	6,256	6,539	6,706	5,180	4,349
Private nonguaranteed	10,897	30,662	23,309	37,874	49,415	61,671	57,006	56,829
of which: Bonds	3,172	7,776	8,861	14,076	16,282	15,893	16,400	18,110

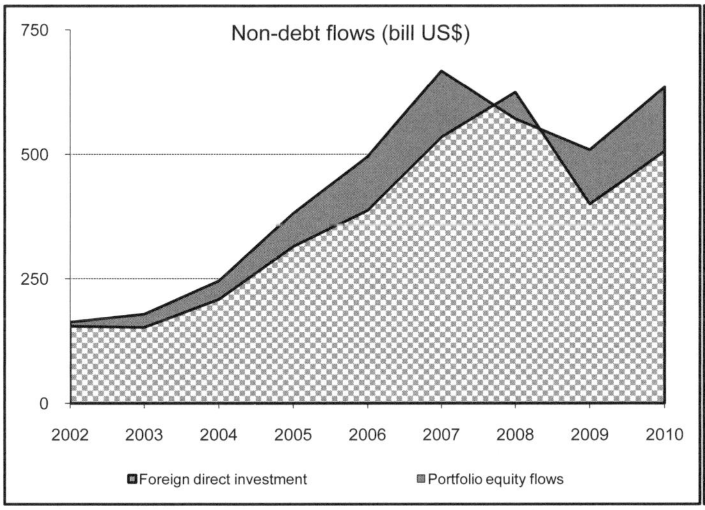

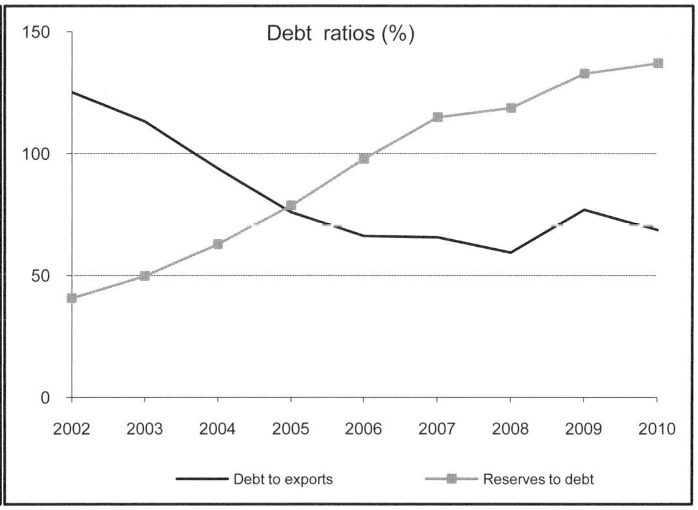

EAST ASIA AND PACIFIC

(US$ million, unless otherwise indicated)

	1995	2000	2005	2006	2007	2008	2009	2010
1. Summary external debt data								
External debt stocks	**455,520**	**496,193**	**613,430**	**646,167**	**722,828**	**754,725**	**833,821**	**1,013,971**
Long-term external debt	345,358	418,119	407,365	423,399	447,902	491,239	506,653	545,176
Public and publicly guaranteed	255,375	270,964	260,850	258,676	260,102	279,621	294,848	306,774
Private nonguaranteed	89,982	147,155	146,515	164,723	187,799	211,618	211,805	238,402
Use of IMF credit	1,337	16,452	8,545	239	215	162	291	271
Short-term external debt	108,826	61,621	197,521	222,529	274,712	263,325	326,877	468,525
interest arrears on long-term	2,952	5,336	1,090	994	1,125	1,155	1,226	1,338
Memorandum items								
Principal arrears on long-term	10,943	7,461	5,929	4,680	5,344	5,478	5,779	6,228
Long-term public sector debt	253,988	270,613	260,329	258,181	259,670	279,193	289,934	301,969
Long-term private sector debt	91,370	147,507	147,036	165,219	188,232	212,046	216,719	243,207
Public & publicly guaranteed commitments	46,429	26,963	24,975	20,367	19,086	28,871	42,584	41,977
External debt flows								
Disbursements	59,108	43,658	74,963	77,070	91,224	88,656	88,027	123,095
Long-term external debt	58,906	42,165	74,963	77,070	91,224	88,656	87,853	123,062
IMF purchases	203	1,493	0	0	0	0	174	33
Principal repayments	32,238	47,273	68,930	71,474	75,661	72,306	82,541	85,742
Long-term external debt	31,848	47,006	67,332	62,995	75,626	72,257	82,490	85,694
IMF repurchases	390	267	1,597	8,479	35	49	50	48
Net flows	54,090	-14,427	40,865	30,700	67,614	4,933	68,968	178,890
Long-term external debt	27,058	-4,841	7,631	14,075	15,598	16,399	5,363	37,368
Short-term external debt	27,220	-10,812	34,831	25,105	52,051	-11,417	63,481	141,537
Interest payments	20,622	25,234	17,861	21,999	25,492	23,024	18,701	47,087
Long-term external debt	15,538	20,430	12,844	14,244	17,456	16,909	14,303	18,042
IMF charges	69	793	336	308	3	1	2	2
Short-term external debt	5,014	4,011	4,682	7,446	8,033	6,114	4,397	29,042
2. Other non-debt resource inflows								
Foreign direct investment	50,796	45,168	142,435	151,673	198,905	214,135	137,453	227,709
Portfolio equity	3,746	6,589	25,684	56,191	35,094	-7,326	28,868	40,463
3. Currency composition of public and publicly guaranteed debt (%)								
Euro	..	..	8.4	9.0	9.2	7.5	6.6	5.7
Japanese yen	28.2	28.3	26.5	25.5	24.4	27.0	24.6	25.5
Pound sterling	0.4	0.4	0.7	0.6	0.6	0.4	0.3	0.3
Swiss franc	0.5	0.2	0.3	0.2	0.2	0.2	0.2	0.1
U.S.dollars	36.7	55.8	57.1	58.1	58.9	59.1	62.8	63.0
4. Average terms of new commitments								
Official creditors								
Interest (%)	5.3	3.8	3.1	4.2	3.3	2.3	1.5	1.3
Maturity (years)	22.0	26.9	24.9	25.1	25.5	24.9	24.7	24.8
Grace period (years)	5.6	6.3	6.7	6.5	7.3	7.1	6.3	7.4
Private creditors								
Interest (%)	6.4	6.6	5.6	6.6	5.2	5.2	6.8	5.5
Maturity (years)	9.6	13.0	11.1	15.7	16.2	13.0	11.1	15.2
Grace period (years)	4.4	5.0	8.3	11.4	11.9	8.5	8.7	7.6
5. Major economic aggregates								
Gross national income (GNI)	1,284,827	1,680,605	3,041,210	3,664,541	4,642,068	5,871,392	6,347,846	7,530,404
Exports of goods, services & income	416,035	636,015	1,379,914	1,705,206	2,108,699	2,462,617	2,101,318	2,741,865
Worker remit. & comp. of employees	8,918	15,799	50,286	57,409	71,009	85,446	85,963	91,959
Imports of goods, services & income	452,272	606,287	1,277,026	1,479,822	1,764,197	2,092,510	1,836,862	2,458,638
Profit remittances on FDI	15,893	31,671	73,892	77,104	91,664	104,299	117,556	122,031
International reserves	167,801	283,042	1,020,252	1,315,651	1,856,871	2,289,107	2,824,082	3,375,065
6. Ratios								
External debt stocks to exports (%)	109.5	78.0	44.5	37.9	34.3	30.6	39.7	37.0
External debt stocks to GNI (%)	35.5	29.5	20.2	17.6	15.6	12.9	13.1	13.5
Debt service to exports (%)	12.7	11.4	6.3	5.5	4.8	3.9	4.8	4.8
Short-term to external debt stocks (%)	23.9	12.4	32.2	34.4	38.0	34.9	39.2	46.2
Multilateral to external debt stocks (%)	11.8	13.3	10.5	10.3	9.6	9.8	9.7	8.5
Reserves to external debt stocks (%)	36.8	57.0	166.3	203.6	256.9	303.3	338.7	332.9
Reserves to imports (months)	4.5	5.6	9.6	10.7	12.6	13.1	18.4	16.5

EAST ASIA AND PACIFIC

(US$ million, unless otherwise indicated)

	1995	2000	2005	2006	2007	2008	2009	2010
7. Long-term external debt								
Debt outstanding and disbursed	**345,358**	**418,119**	**407,365**	**423,399**	**447,902**	**491,239**	**506,653**	**545,176**
Public and publicly guaranteed	255,375	270,964	260,850	258,676	260,102	279,621	294,848	306,774
Official creditors	159,571	171,436	172,445	172,494	177,954	194,122	201,669	207,769
Multilateral	53,607	65,756	64,368	66,424	69,641	73,617	80,671	86,037
of which: IBRD	27,912	30,476	23,331	22,550	21,693	22,275	23,383	25,494
IDA	9,692	12,520	16,498	17,683	19,086	19,683	20,921	21,234
Bilateral	105,964	105,680	108,076	106,069	108,313	120,505	120,998	121,732
Private creditors	95,804	99,529	88,405	86,182	82,148	85,498	93,179	99,005
of which: Bonds	23,690	35,834	52,285	54,913	55,340	57,220	60,812	67,184
Commercial banks	39,894	33,257	17,675	14,755	12,881	15,440	16,838	17,728
Private nonguaranteed	89,982	147,155	146,515	164,723	187,799	211,618	211,805	238,402
of which: Bonds	15,574	22,077	24,435	25,472	22,968	21,711	22,840	34,878
Disbursements	**58,906**	**42,165**	**74,963**	**77,070**	**91,224**	**88,656**	**87,853**	**123,062**
Public and publicly guaranteed	38,009	28,718	25,251	25,828	19,599	22,764	38,112	41,164
Official creditors	17,653	15,620	9,056	11,687	11,712	12,640	16,345	16,340
Multilateral	6,129	6,943	5,145	5,930	6,715	7,775	10,039	8,612
of which: IBRD	3,168	3,245	1,825	2,012	2,347	3,200	3,710	4,503
IDA	934	700	627	754	1,058	1,152	1,550	1,068
Bilateral	11,524	8,677	3,911	5,757	4,997	4,865	6,306	7,728
Private creditors	20,356	13,099	16,195	14,141	7,887	10,124	21,768	24,823
of which: Bonds	4,449	4,539	11,523	9,036	4,295	5,180	13,903	12,914
Commercial banks	8,785	2,535	3,034	1,912	1,207	3,411	3,701	5,869
Private nonguaranteed	20,897	13,446	49,711	51,241	71,625	65,893	49,740	81,898
of which: Bonds	5,731	1,106	4,981	3,444	1,701	368	2,733	15,328
Principal repayments	**31,848**	**47,006**	**67,332**	**62,995**	**75,626**	**72,257**	**82,490**	**85,694**
Public and publicly guaranteed	21,663	22,798	24,499	25,130	22,485	21,880	24,895	26,291
Official creditors	8,355	10,243	10,767	12,510	15,093	13,556	12,810	12,912
Multilateral	3,094	4,062	4,609	4,676	4,969	4,781	4,590	4,686
of which: IBRD	2,152	2,006	2,798	2,891	3,336	2,775	2,583	2,422
IDA	50	107	286	324	368	413	450	478
Bilateral	5,261	6,181	6,158	7,834	10,124	8,775	8,220	8,226
Private creditors	13,308	12,555	13,732	12,620	7,392	8,325	12,084	13,379
of which: Bonds	1,854	1,211	4,318	5,432	2,103	2,808	5,323	5,482
Commercial banks	5,320	7,160	5,471	2,684	2,606	1,675	2,629	2,993
Private nonguaranteed	10,185	24,208	42,833	37,865	53,141	50,377	57,596	59,403
of which: Bonds	120	5,168	2,115	3,022	2,719	1,533	2,929	1,947
Interest payments	**15,538**	**20,430**	**12,844**	**14,244**	**17,456**	**16,909**	**14,303**	**18,042**
Public and publicly guaranteed	12,045	12,891	8,633	9,262	10,583	10,174	9,419	10,524
Official creditors	6,283	7,237	4,043	4,470	5,113	4,664	3,947	4,578
Multilateral	3,051	3,833	2,018	2,245	2,492	2,282	1,726	1,408
of which: IBRD	1,999	2,146	1,028	1,168	1,298	1,085	734	524
IDA	69	87	133	131	134	146	139	146
Bilateral	3,232	3,404	2,025	2,225	2,621	2,382	2,221	3,170
Private creditors	5,763	5,654	4,590	4,793	5,470	5,510	5,473	5,947
of which: Bonds	1,238	2,288	3,217	3,658	3,952	4,064	4,380	4,928
Commercial banks	2,462	1,921	845	609	717	615	547	559
Private nonguaranteed	3,493	7,539	4,211	4,982	6,873	6,735	4,883	7,518
of which: Bonds	503	1,942	1,293	1,486	1,495	1,239	1,154	1,308

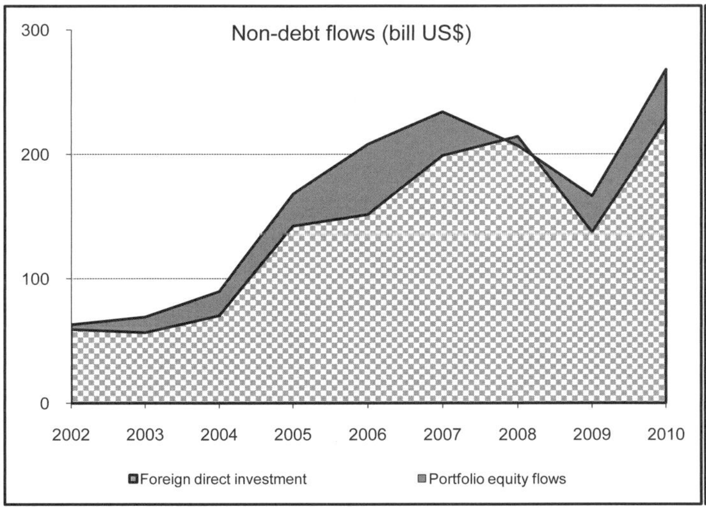

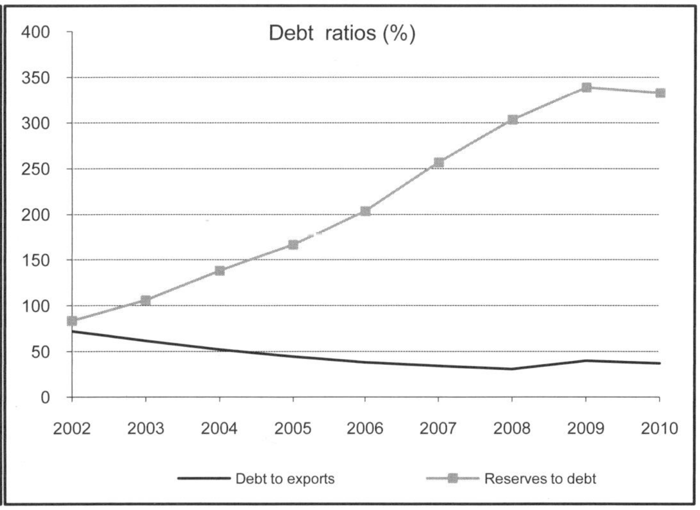

EUROPE AND CENTRAL ASIA

(US$ million, unless otherwise indicated)

	1995	2000	2005	2006	2007	2008	2009	2010
1. Summary external debt data								
External debt stocks	**246,643**	**367,800**	**613,601**	**751,739**	**1,047,612**	**1,206,210**	**1,212,410**	**1,273,418**
Long-term external debt	199,574	286,518	475,282	577,435	804,863	963,516	987,057	994,159
Public and publicly guaranteed	189,317	218,325	210,641	242,314	305,645	303,463	330,536	366,663
Private nonguaranteed	10,256	68,193	264,641	335,121	499,218	660,053	656,521	627,496
Use of IMF credit	15,788	21,773	18,810	13,088	8,550	15,158	36,222	45,027
Short-term external debt	31,282	59,508	119,508	161,216	234,199	227,536	189,131	234,232
interest arrears on long-term	7,818	8,508	4,098	1,538	1,586	1,773	1,890	1,461
Memorandum items								
Principal arrears on long-term	28,017	14,077	3,545	2,020	2,172	2,925	4,869	6,821
Long-term public sector debt	188,810	217,784	209,966	241,672	304,744	302,113	328,949	364,450
Long-term private sector debt	10,764	68,734	265,316	335,764	500,119	661,403	658,109	629,710
Public & publicly guaranteed commitments	14,658	21,526	31,207	35,572	73,011	49,376	51,691	62,533
External debt flows								
Disbursements	23,031	41,443	152,487	205,008	309,225	341,148	215,289	248,650
Long-term external debt	15,008	37,075	149,698	201,927	307,980	331,656	193,895	237,021
IMF purchases	8,024	4,369	2,789	3,081	1,245	9,492	21,394	11,629
Principal repayments	12,765	31,287	96,625	107,038	120,846	168,258	165,077	206,788
Long-term external debt	12,113	26,370	84,041	98,148	114,566	165,770	164,143	204,517
IMF repurchases	652	4,917	12,585	8,889	6,280	2,488	935	2,271
Net flows	14,234	19,521	76,638	142,238	260,909	166,040	11,689	87,393
Long-term external debt	2,895	10,705	65,657	103,778	193,414	165,887	29,753	32,505
Short-term external debt	3,968	9,365	20,776	44,268	72,530	-6,850	-38,523	45,531
Interest payments	9,256	16,753	25,483	32,919	44,026	55,227	49,767	46,433
Long-term external debt	7,589	12,716	20,298	26,396	35,376	47,473	44,530	40,530
IMF charges	558	1,064	1,125	905	623	429	454	818
Short-term external debt	1,109	2,973	4,060	5,618	8,027	7,326	4,784	5,085
2. Other non-debt resource inflows								
Foreign direct investment	5,778	9,798	51,962	94,338	136,152	162,200	85,927	86,268
Portfolio equity	248	986	6,680	12,301	27,002	-15,265	6,367	-846
3. Currency composition of public and publicly guaranteed debt (%)								
Euro	..	..	20.9	19.4	18.5	19.2	21.6	21.5
Japanese yen	8.2	5.2	3.3	2.9	2.4	3.1	2.9	2.9
Pound sterling	0.8	0.3	0.2	0.1	0.1	0.0	0.0	0.0
Swiss franc	2.7	0.3	0.5	1.1	1.0	1.0	0.4	0.3
U.S.dollars	47.6	64.1	70.9	73.2	75.7	74.6	73.0	73.1
4. Average terms of new commitments								
Official creditors								
Interest (%)	5.7	5.7	2.7	3.9	4.2	3.7	2.4	2.3
Maturity (years)	17.0	17.8	22.8	18.6	18.4	19.8	18.4	18.9
Grace period (years)	5.4	5.3	6.4	5.9	6.1	7.0	5.9	6.5
Private creditors								
Interest (%)	6.5	8.7	5.4	5.9	5.9	5.8	6.2	4.8
Maturity (years)	6.2	9.8	8.0	7.7	8.1	7.7	6.6	9.2
Grace period (years)	2.6	7.5	5.9	6.2	6.1	5.5	5.9	7.7
5. Major economic aggregates								
Gross national income (GNI)	758,617	694,348	1,662,717	2,028,818	2,630,779	3,234,326	2,540,148	2,963,163
Exports of goods, services & income	203,616	261,256	619,868	767,501	952,959	1,240,543	862,023	1,047,760
Worker remit. & comp. of employees	6,482	9,297	19,698	24,950	38,689	45,014	36,079	36,037
Imports of goods, services & income	223,651	249,262	619,371	792,315	1,047,340	1,324,445	908,808	1,098,640
Profit remittances on FDI	623	3,065	32,955	56,016	78,085	102,502	60,831	79,212
International reserves	43,240	68,091	314,138	488,160	715,709	657,825	684,441	750,644
6. Ratios								
External debt stocks to exports (%)	121.1	140.8	99.0	97.9	109.9	97.2	140.6	121.5
External debt stocks to GNI (%)	32.5	53.0	36.9	37.1	39.8	37.3	47.7	43.0
Debt service to exports (%)	10.8	18.4	19.7	18.2	17.3	18.0	24.9	24.2
Short-term to external debt stocks (%)	12.7	16.2	19.5	21.4	22.4	18.9	15.6	18.4
Multilateral to external debt stocks (%)	7.6	8.0	6.2	5.5	4.5	4.1	5.3	5.7
Reserves to external debt stocks (%)	17.5	18.5	51.2	64.9	68.3	54.5	56.5	58.9
Reserves to imports (months)	2.3	3.3	6.1	7.4	8.2	6.0	9.0	8.2

(US$ million, unless otherwise indicated)

	1995	2000	2005	2006	2007	2008	2009	2010
7. Long-term external debt								
Debt outstanding and disbursed	**199,574**	**286,518**	**475,282**	**577,435**	**804,863**	**963,516**	**987,057**	**994,159**
Public and publicly guaranteed	189,317	218,325	210,641	242,314	305,645	303,463	330,536	366,663
Official creditors	98,729	115,115	86,375	65,345	72,333	77,688	94,097	104,968
Multilateral	18,845	29,491	38,077	41,070	47,105	49,969	63,726	72,697
of which: IBRD	10,908	19,068	21,793	22,214	22,688	23,071	25,806	28,251
IDA	669	2,667	5,548	6,188	6,862	7,160	7,631	7,835
Bilateral	79,884	85,624	48,298	24,275	25,228	27,719	30,371	32,271
Private creditors	90,588	103,210	124,267	176,969	233,312	225,775	236,439	261,695
of which: Bonds	21,412	68,646	79,647	92,101	120,695	126,685	133,579	156,088
Commercial banks	35,523	24,725	39,474	80,400	109,250	96,314	100,424	103,376
Private nonguaranteed	10,256	68,193	264,641	335,121	499,218	660,053	656,521	627,496
of which: Bonds	149	3,333	46,448	70,958	108,189	115,941	108,733	109,348
Disbursements	**15,008**	**37,075**	**149,698**	**201,927**	**307,980**	**331,656**	**193,895**	**237,021**
Public and publicly guaranteed	12,803	21,250	26,150	42,406	70,578	41,161	63,105	73,519
Official creditors	5,327	6,925	5,190	6,338	9,349	11,270	21,064	19,296
Multilateral	3,418	4,373	4,251	5,184	6,481	7,479	16,575	15,344
of which: IBRD	2,166	2,655	1,816	2,477	2,153	2,825	4,968	5,383
IDA	370	351	420	412	468	423	509	439
Bilateral	1,909	2,552	940	1,154	2,868	3,792	4,488	3,952
Private creditors	7,476	14,325	20,960	36,068	61,229	29,891	42,041	54,223
of which: Bonds	2,419	7,907	7,787	15,553	31,685	18,488	15,267	31,975
Commercial banks	1,579	5,337	12,953	20,382	29,381	11,233	26,625	22,004
Private nonguaranteed	2,205	15,824	123,548	159,520	237,402	290,496	130,790	163,502
of which: Bonds	0	566	21,619	25,562	42,353	16,253	3,225	16,456
Principal repayments	**12,113**	**26,370**	**84,041**	**98,148**	**114,566**	**165,770**	**164,143**	**204,517**
Public and publicly guaranteed	10,940	12,747	39,062	43,566	23,010	37,243	28,047	31,622
Official creditors	3,652	5,804	23,887	30,935	6,624	6,304	5,856	6,019
Multilateral	1,987	2,270	4,034	3,757	3,817	4,018	3,830	3,828
of which: IBRD	901	961	2,932	2,654	2,411	2,472	2,336	2,261
IDA	6	6	23	38	56	75	92	105
Bilateral	1,665	3,534	19,853	27,179	2,807	2,286	2,026	2,191
Private creditors	7,289	6,943	15,175	12,630	16,386	30,938	22,191	25,603
of which: Bonds	2,765	2,241	10,660	5,614	7,283	10,602	9,620	7,667
Commercial banks	1,829	2,425	3,000	6,040	7,905	19,581	12,031	17,500
Private nonguaranteed	1,172	13,623	44,979	54,583	91,556	128,527	136,096	172,895
of which: Bonds	0	930	1,982	1,530	6,794	7,746	10,697	13,673
Interest payments	**7,589**	**12,716**	**20,298**	**26,396**	**35,376**	**47,473**	**44,530**	**40,530**
Public and publicly guaranteed	7,214	9,058	12,323	12,589	13,232	14,856	13,414	13,455
Official creditors	3,096	3,004	4,043	3,534	2,652	2,684	2,330	1,940
Multilateral	1,027	1,566	1,442	1,583	1,901	1,916	1,679	1,302
of which: IBRD	591	1,080	872	1,071	1,217	1,083	848	399
IDA	3	19	45	47	50	54	53	56
Bilateral	2,068	1,437	2,601	1,951	751	768	651	637
Private creditors	4,118	6,054	8,280	9,055	10,580	12,171	11,085	11,515
of which: Bonds	1,616	4,292	6,457	6,468	7,684	8,798	8,999	9,424
Commercial banks	1,402	1,247	1,530	2,337	2,667	3,182	1,944	1,981
Private nonguaranteed	375	3,658	7,975	13,807	22,143	32,617	31,115	27,076
of which: Bonds	13	312	2,732	4,544	7,017	7,904	8,073	7,369

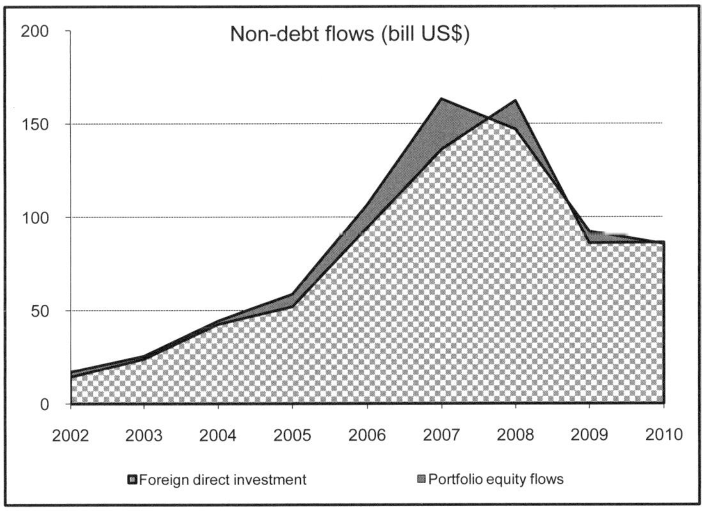

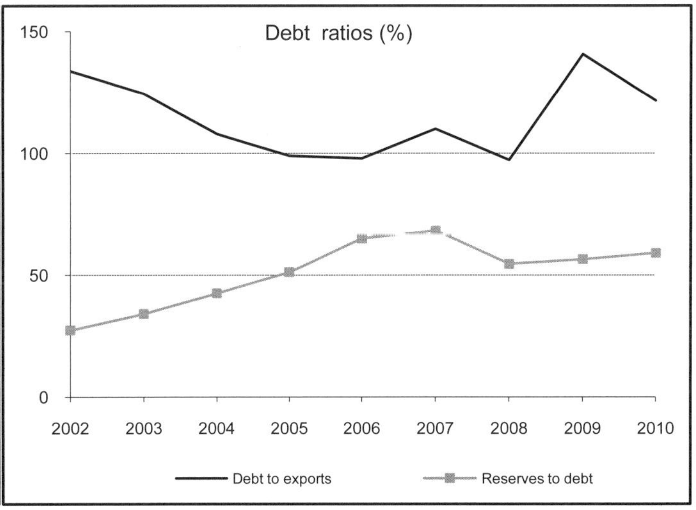

LATIN AMERICA AND CARIBBEAN

(US$ million, unless otherwise indicated)

	1995	2000	2005	2006	2007	2008	2009	2010
1. Summary external debt data								
External debt stocks	**608,673**	**751,068**	**738,623**	**736,981**	**824,828**	**882,341**	**899,103**	**1,038,725**
Long-term external debt	459,185	631,256	606,510	617,331	680,098	731,327	751,466	828,184
Public and publicly guaranteed	371,882	389,534	410,027	392,670	404,130	417,621	429,963	457,714
Private nonguaranteed	87,303	241,722	196,483	224,661	275,968	313,706	321,503	370,470
Use of IMF credit	26,632	8,846	13,122	737	804	824	1,243	2,265
Short-term external debt	122,856	110,966	118,991	118,913	143,927	150,190	146,393	208,277
interest arrears on long-term	10,303	1,674	8,904	8,321	10,367	10,943	11,672	6,374
Memorandum items								
Principal arrears on long-term	15,834	3,510	12,361	13,126	16,955	19,264	20,449	9,959
Long-term public sector debt	369,917	386,575	407,550	390,442	401,931	415,034	426,100	453,530
Long-term private sector debt	89,269	244,681	198,959	226,889	278,167	316,292	325,366	374,654
Public & publicly guaranteed commitments	49,943	66,072	55,281	49,936	52,159	62,140	88,341	74,870
External debt flows								
Disbursements	89,784	119,832	100,122	132,640	149,257	158,864	155,204	193,616
Long-term external debt	74,013	116,322	99,530	132,077	149,008	158,651	154,754	192,157
IMF purchases	15,772	3,510	593	564	249	213	450	1,459
Principal repayments	43,123	124,162	112,476	147,474	103,180	102,976	96,857	96,088
Long-term external debt	40,291	109,925	84,303	134,791	102,960	102,804	96,804	95,937
IMF repurchases	2,832	14,237	28,172	12,683	220	173	53	151
Net flows	61,053	-5,247	8,060	-14,329	69,045	61,576	53,821	164,709
Long-term external debt	33,722	6,397	15,226	-2,714	46,048	55,848	57,951	96,220
Short-term external debt	14,392	-917	20,413	504	22,968	5,688	-4,526	67,182
Interest payments	35,905	54,789	40,709	45,828	47,720	44,884	41,265	44,157
Long-term external debt	28,411	47,273	33,347	39,605	40,635	40,740	38,344	38,914
IMF charges	1,100	777	1,732	330	35	26	9	17
Short-term external debt	6,393	6,739	5,630	5,894	7,050	4,117	2,912	5,227
2. Other non-debt resource inflows								
Foreign direct investment	30,201	79,052	73,544	72,003	110,437	130,026	78,321	112,626
Portfolio equity	4,754	-561	12,209	11,047	28,837	-9,658	41,582	41,300
3. Currency composition of public and publicly guaranteed debt (%)								
Euro	..	..	9.5	10.7	11.4	10.2	11.1	8.9
Japanese yen	8.2	6.6	3.4	3.0	2.8	3.2	4.0	4.4
Pound sterling	1.1	0.6	0.2	0.3	0.2	0.1	0.4	0.4
Swiss franc	0.6	0.3	0.2	0.1	0.1	0.1	0.2	0.3
U.S.dollars	62.1	73.4	82.0	81.6	82.2	83.6	82.1	84.5
4. Average terms of new commitments								
Official creditors								
Interest (%)	7.6	5.9	4.4	5.4	5.2	3.5	2.1	1.8
Maturity (years)	14.2	12.5	18.8	18.9	18.3	20.6	18.8	19.6
Grace period (years)	4.1	2.8	4.9	5.4	5.0	5.3	6.4	6.0
Private creditors								
Interest (%)	6.8	9.4	7.3	6.2	7.2	6.5	5.9	5.3
Maturity (years)	4.1	12.6	14.5	14.9	16.3	15.9	11.1	14.3
Grace period (years)	2.9	11.6	12.0	12.7	12.5	11.3	9.8	12.6
5. Major economic aggregates								
Gross national income (GNI)	1,698,096	1,967,875	2,545,138	2,992,656	3,554,140	4,153,365	3,866,338	4,786,771
Exports of goods, services & income	289,620	442,911	666,610	798,414	911,867	1,044,003	821,954	1,017,266
Worker remit. & comp. of employees	13,318	20,164	49,795	58,840	62,874	64,414	56,572	57,245
Imports of goods, services & income	343,890	512,714	686,106	817,863	968,269	1,146,839	901,707	1,137,215
Profit remittances on FDI	14,909	22,785	53,525	76,782	90,487	94,352	77,457	88,845
International reserves	138,616	158,413	257,309	312,791	450,589	500,720	554,850	645,038
6. Ratios								
External debt stocks to exports (%)	210.2	169.6	110.8	92.3	90.5	84.5	109.4	102.1
External debt stocks to GNI (%)	35.8	38.2	29.0	24.6	23.2	21.2	23.3	21.7
Debt service to exports (%)	27.3	40.4	23.0	24.6	16.6	14.2	16.8	13.8
Short-term to external debt stocks (%)	20.2	14.8	16.1	16.1	17.4	17.0	16.3	20.1
Multilateral to external debt stocks (%)	11.9	12.3	14.0	13.0	11.6	11.5	12.8	12.6
Reserves to external debt stocks (%)	22.8	21.1	34.8	42.4	54.6	56.7	61.7	62.1
Reserves to imports (months)	4.8	3.7	4.5	4.6	5.6	5.2	7.4	6.8

(US$ million, unless otherwise indicated)

7. Long-term external debt

	1995	2000	2005	2006	2007	2008	2009	2010
Debt outstanding and disbursed	**459,185**	**631,256**	**606,510**	**617,331**	**680,098**	**731,327**	**751,466**	**828,184**
Public and publicly guaranteed	371,882	389,534	410,027	392,670	404,130	417,621	429,963	457,714
Official creditors	159,022	139,658	134,217	123,807	121,353	130,632	149,159	169,259
Multilateral	72,134	92,652	103,248	95,870	95,349	101,372	115,092	130,489
of which: IBRD	36,299	37,429	34,958	31,528	31,534	33,857	40,439	48,533
IDA	2,186	3,387	5,049	1,529	1,692	1,778	1,468	1,606
Bilateral	86,888	47,005	30,969	27,937	26,004	29,260	34,067	38,770
Private creditors	212,860	249,877	275,810	268,863	282,776	286,989	280,804	288,456
of which: Bonds	165,105	210,023	232,945	226,132	235,342	240,986	240,414	238,992
Commercial banks	34,360	31,394	38,479	39,594	43,340	42,633	36,222	44,181
Private nonguaranteed	87,303	241,722	196,483	224,661	275,968	313,706	321,503	370,470
of which: Bonds	33,829	60,325	75,499	82,939	95,586	82,025	102,493	147,747
Disbursements	**74,013**	**116,322**	**99,530**	**132,077**	**149,008**	**158,651**	**154,754**	**192,157**
Public and publicly guaranteed	46,483	58,420	54,860	48,843	44,789	63,410	68,601	75,403
Official creditors	23,663	16,176	12,897	16,745	14,762	19,361	31,008	34,447
Multilateral	9,893	13,297	10,528	14,673	13,064	15,772	24,282	25,954
of which: IBRD	4,624	5,595	3,550	5,570	3,067	5,679	10,790	11,151
IDA	277	202	306	178	129	114	157	210
Bilateral	13,771	2,879	2,369	2,072	1,698	3,589	6,726	8,493
Private creditors	22,819	42,244	41,963	32,098	30,027	44,049	37,593	40,956
of which: Bonds	13,654	35,022	35,298	24,272	23,538	36,092	32,523	22,420
Commercial banks	7,427	6,476	6,168	7,229	6,155	7,798	4,405	16,083
Private nonguaranteed	27,530	57,903	44,670	83,233	104,220	95,242	86,153	116,754
of which: Bonds	7,412	8,312	16,018	20,751	26,935	10,020	28,605	52,980
Principal repayments	**40,291**	**109,925**	**84,303**	**134,791**	**102,960**	**102,804**	**96,804**	**95,937**
Public and publicly guaranteed	27,594	51,901	43,873	78,880	47,743	47,501	36,765	41,193
Official creditors	14,493	16,788	16,655	24,553	15,859	12,871	13,463	14,380
Multilateral	8,309	9,787	10,920	19,237	10,818	10,496	9,778	10,199
of which: IBRD	4,974	3,798	4,561	9,143	3,311	3,407	4,301	3,061
IDA	21	18	39	29	14	24	20	46
Bilateral	6,185	7,000	5,735	5,317	5,042	2,375	3,685	4,181
Private creditors	13,101	35,114	27,218	54,326	31,884	34,630	23,302	26,813
of which: Bonds	5,833	26,575	19,163	43,062	24,603	27,881	13,358	18,944
Commercial banks	4,240	6,934	7,270	10,111	6,501	6,117	8,755	6,541
Private nonguaranteed	12,696	58,024	40,430	55,911	55,217	55,303	60,039	54,745
of which: Bonds	3,922	8,849	10,583	13,165	13,292	9,228	7,062	7,680
Interest payments	**28,411**	**47,273**	**33,347**	**39,605**	**40,635**	**40,740**	**38,344**	**38,914**
Public and publicly guaranteed	22,582	29,249	24,140	24,600	25,257	23,626	21,952	22,102
Official creditors	8,831	8,531	5,590	5,994	5,996	5,464	5,035	4,685
Multilateral	4,850	6,323	4,452	4,985	5,020	4,658	4,085	3,751
of which: IBRD	2,651	2,801	1,507	1,813	1,781	1,545	1,302	1,050
IDA	23	17	37	23	12	14	12	11
Bilateral	3,981	2,209	1,138	1,009	976	806	950	934
Private creditors	13,751	20,717	18,550	18,606	19,260	18,162	16,917	17,417
of which: Bonds	11,254	17,194	16,721	16,496	17,245	16,275	14,864	15,959
Commercial banks	1,568	2,715	1,629	1,934	1,710	1,630	1,756	1,205
Private nonguaranteed	5,829	18,024	9,208	15,004	15,378	17,114	16,392	16,811
of which: Bonds	2,597	5,185	4,534	7,607	7,177	6,123	6,543	7,905

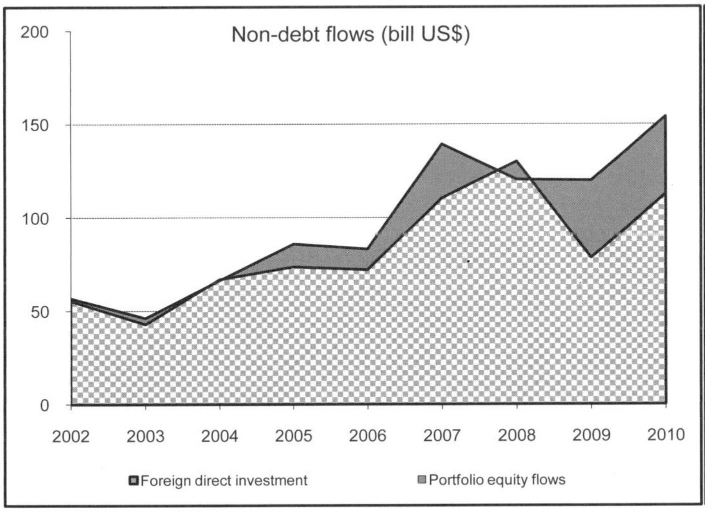

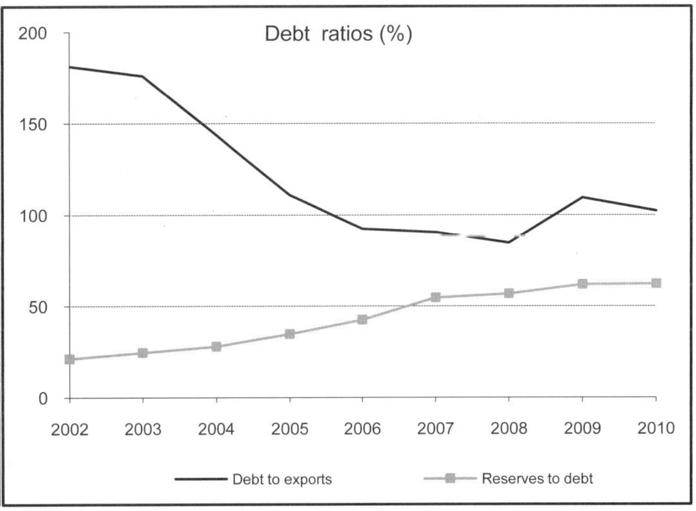

MIDDLE EAST AND NORTH AFRICA

(US$ million, unless otherwise indicated)

	1995	2000	2005	2006	2007	2008	2009	2010
1. Summary external debt data								
External debt stocks	**161,736**	**139,233**	**145,387**	**136,869**	**148,268**	**137,931**	**141,010**	**143,595**
Long-term external debt	141,183	116,545	122,593	114,967	122,977	116,905	118,411	119,872
Public and publicly guaranteed	140,296	112,575	115,831	108,351	116,355	110,248	112,261	113,766
Private nonguaranteed	887	3,970	6,762	6,616	6,623	6,657	6,150	6,106
Use of IMF credit	2,177	2,542	547	423	353	258	200	195
Short-term external debt	18,375	20,145	22,247	21,479	24,937	20,768	22,400	23,528
interest arrears on long-term	2,673	2,629	298	307	256	259	326	342
Memorandum items								
Principal arrears on long-term	8,720	9,977	509	482	442	419	418	424
Long-term public sector debt	139,868	112,209	115,183	107,601	115,197	109,180	111,253	112,832
Long-term private sector debt	1,315	4,336	7,410	7,367	7,780	7,725	7,158	7,040
Public & publicly guaranteed commitments	12,036	10,177	13,605	12,061	10,585	9,759	11,733	15,337
External debt flows								
Disbursements	11,547	9,241	14,795	11,938	14,913	11,879	13,668	14,586
Long-term external debt	10,958	9,218	14,795	11,938	14,835	11,833	13,666	14,533
IMF purchases	590	24	0	0	78	46	2	53
Principal repayments	11,418	10,936	14,879	24,884	14,365	16,303	13,283	12,189
Long-term external debt	11,029	10,698	14,133	24,734	14,199	16,168	13,220	12,135
IMF repurchases	390	238	745	150	166	135	64	54
Net flows	3,702	-3,022	178	-13,724	4,057	-8,595	1,949	3,509
Long-term external debt	-71	-1,480	662	-12,796	636	-4,335	446	2,398
Short-term external debt	3,573	-1,327	261	-777	3,509	-4,171	1,564	1,112
Interest payments	7,393	5,867	6,010	5,971	5,840	5,399	4,961	4,927
Long-term external debt	6,311	4,888	4,794	4,784	4,740	4,775	4,361	4,263
IMF charges	112	130	32	14	12	7	3	2
Short-term external debt	970	849	1,184	1,172	1,088	617	597	662
2. Other non-debt resource inflows								
Foreign direct investment	870	3,878	16,763	27,228	27,601	29,219	26,079	22,670
Portfolio equity	32	252	2,410	963	-2,096	422	1,200	36
3. Currency composition of public and publicly guaranteed debt (%)								
Euro	..	..	29.5	31.0	33.3	31.4	32.2	30.5
Japanese yen	9.5	10.2	8.3	7.9	7.3	9.0	8.4	8.8
Pound sterling	1.1	0.9	1.7	1.7	1.6	0.6	0.6	0.6
Swiss franc	1.0	1.1	1.5	1.5	1.3	1.2	1.4	1.3
U.S.dollars	44.0	51.2	46.3	44.6	42.5	42.5	41.5	42.5
4. Average terms of new commitments								
Official creditors								
Interest (%)	5.2	4.6	3.8	3.8	3.6	3.4	2.2	1.7
Maturity (years)	17.3	19.5	19.1	22.5	19.4	21.2	20.5	21.5
Grace period (years)	5.2	5.5	5.7	6.9	5.9	5.6	5.7	5.8
Private creditors								
Interest (%)	7.2	7.5	5.7	6.8	6.0	8.6	7.8	4.7
Maturity (years)	9.7	7.4	7.4	10.9	7.8	5.8	7.0	14.5
Grace period (years)	3.3	3.5	5.3	7.9	5.4	5.7	6.5	10.8
5. Major economic aggregates								
Gross national income (GNI)	273,332	362,754	539,427	624,057	761,728	926,597	926,767	1,018,299
Exports of goods, services & income	89,138	117,615	216,120	265,310	312,740	395,622	328,128	337,575
Worker remit. & comp. of employees	11,468	10,460	23,647	25,125	31,041	34,699	32,412	31,016
Imports of goods, services & income	91,459	105,104	204,805	228,686	280,391	357,489	337,205	352,389
Profit remittances on FDI	941	1,721	8,245	9,342	9,208	10,410	11,355	3,595
International reserves	38,387	49,482	148,207	186,054	234,053	277,486	301,670	325,791
6. Ratios								
External debt stocks to exports (%)	181.4	118.4	67.3	51.6	47.4	34.9	43.0	42.5
External debt stocks to GNI (%)	59.2	38.4	27.0	21.9	19.5	14.9	15.2	14.1
Debt service to exports (%)	21.1	14.3	9.7	11.6	6.5	5.5	5.6	5.1
Short-term to external debt stocks (%)	11.4	14.5	15.3	15.7	16.8	15.1	15.9	16.4
Multilateral to external debt stocks (%)	14.1	16.6	17.8	18.8	20.6	22.4	24.5	24.9
Reserves to external debt stocks (%)	23.7	35.5	101.9	135.9	157.9	201.2	213.9	226.9
Reserves to imports (months)	5.0	5.6	8.7	9.8	10.0	9.3	10.7	11.1

(US$ million, unless otherwise indicated)

	1995	2000	2005	2006	2007	2008	2009	2010
7. Long-term external debt								
Debt outstanding and disbursed	**141,183**	**116,545**	**122,593**	**114,967**	**122,977**	**116,905**	**118,411**	**119,872**
Public and publicly guaranteed	140,296	112,575	115,831	108,351	116,355	110,248	112,261	113,766
Official creditors	105,107	88,163	77,471	70,215	76,497	74,278	77,734	77,550
Multilateral	22,871	23,099	25,834	25,701	30,476	30,836	34,602	35,803
of which: IBRD	10,646	7,664	6,757	6,144	7,447	7,123	8,016	8,532
IDA	2,105	2,685	3,344	3,616	3,795	3,802	3,831	3,751
Bilateral	82,236	65,064	51,637	44,514	46,022	43,441	43,132	41,747
Private creditors	35,189	24,412	38,361	38,136	39,857	35,970	34,527	36,216
of which: Bonds	2,036	7,375	22,142	23,179	24,579	23,907	23,544	26,825
Commercial banks	10,340	8,412	8,718	8,067	8,961	7,632	7,384	6,559
Private nonguaranteed	887	3,970	6,762	6,616	6,623	6,657	6,150	6,106
of which: Bonds	50	836	1,011	805	530	470	670	500
Disbursements	**10,958**	**9,218**	**14,795**	**11,938**	**14,835**	**11,833**	**13,666**	**14,533**
Public and publicly guaranteed	10,775	7,937	12,875	10,741	13,080	9,724	12,071	13,236
Official creditors	5,986	3,407	5,421	5,088	7,051	6,266	8,101	7,070
Multilateral	3,503	1,942	3,813	3,434	5,490	3,670	5,750	4,852
of which: IBRD	1,455	532	895	739	1,723	684	1,625	1,409
IDA	128	118	202	225	145	126	110	84
Bilateral	2,483	1,465	1,608	1,654	1,562	2,597	2,351	2,218
Private creditors	4,790	4,530	7,454	5,653	6,029	3,458	3,970	6,166
of which: Bonds	888	2,031	4,144	3,799	3,635	2,257	2,894	5,502
Commercial banks	874	1,092	2,264	1,444	2,076	1,027	1,010	640
Private nonguaranteed	183	1,281	1,920	1,197	1,755	2,108	1,595	1,297
of which: Bonds	50	115	530	0	0	0	200	0
Principal repayments	**11,029**	**10,698**	**14,133**	**24,734**	**14,199**	**16,168**	**13,220**	**12,135**
Public and publicly guaranteed	10,902	10,461	13,324	23,078	11,788	14,185	10,990	10,304
Official creditors	7,349	5,915	7,855	16,195	5,877	7,938	5,609	5,903
Multilateral	2,021	2,014	3,407	4,762	2,634	2,608	2,337	2,451
of which: IBRD	1,109	869	1,030	1,673	771	986	731	572
IDA	28	45	76	82	90	98	103	108
Bilateral	5,328	3,900	4,449	11,433	3,243	5,330	3,272	3,452
Private creditors	3,553	4,547	5,469	6,883	5,911	6,247	5,381	4,401
of which: Bonds	278	896	1,883	2,810	2,620	3,021	3,022	2,168
Commercial banks	629	1,425	1,764	2,470	1,913	1,722	1,347	1,404
Private nonguaranteed	127	237	809	1,656	2,411	1,983	2,230	1,831
of which: Bonds	0	50	265	206	275	60	0	170
Interest payments	**6,311**	**4,888**	**4,794**	**4,784**	**4,740**	**4,775**	**4,361**	**4,263**
Public and publicly guaranteed	6,278	4,734	4,504	4,480	4,466	4,515	4,100	4,048
Official creditors	4,258	3,127	2,498	2,267	2,136	2,226	2,022	2,112
Multilateral	1,361	1,305	1,014	1,030	1,085	1,191	1,071	976
of which: IBRD	748	602	308	296	329	352	260	161
IDA	15	20	28	27	28	30	28	28
Bilateral	2,897	1,822	1,484	1,237	1,051	1,034	951	1,136
Private creditors	2,020	1,607	2,006	2,213	2,330	2,290	2,077	1,936
of which: Bonds	88	458	1,366	1,499	1,591	1,623	1,669	1,662
Commercial banks	617	569	320	399	430	401	267	191
Private nonguaranteed	33	154	290	304	274	260	262	215
of which: Bonds	0	69	90	74	57	40	43	51

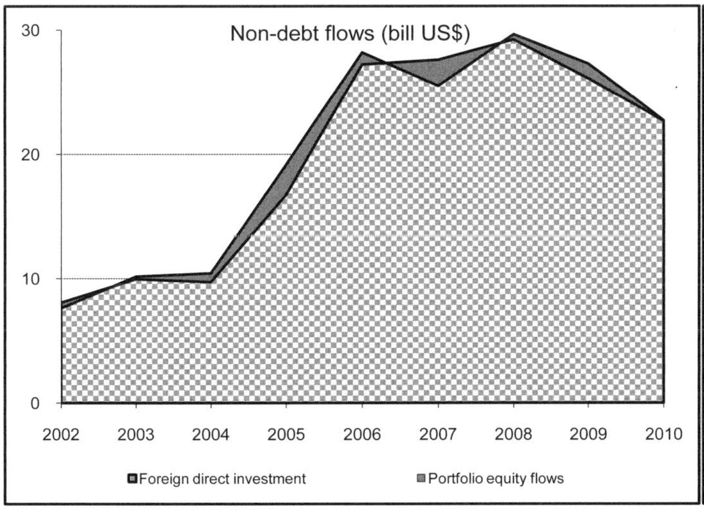

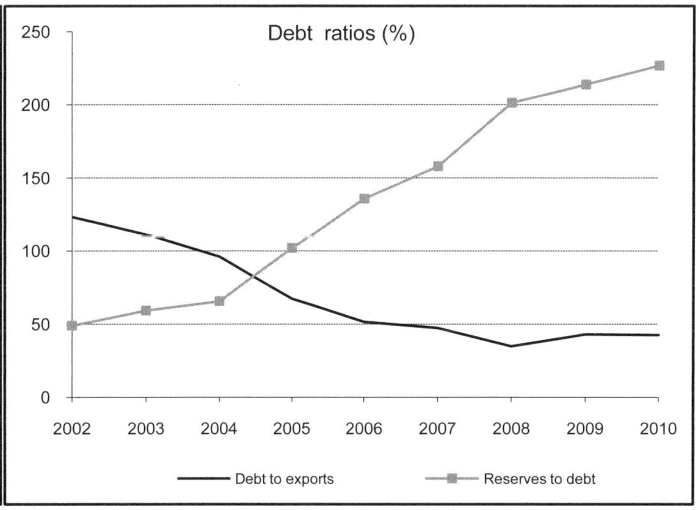

SOUTH ASIA

(US$ million, unless otherwise indicated)

	1995	2000	2005	2006	2007	2008	2009	2010
1. Summary external debt data								
External debt stocks	**152,282**	**161,043**	**188,531**	**232,851**	**287,534**	**321,146**	**353,417**	**400,596**
Long-term external debt	137,937	153,065	174,473	201,953	243,649	266,288	292,199	325,804
Public and publicly guaranteed	129,636	134,552	116,372	126,998	144,428	156,023	169,387	194,376
Private nonguaranteed	8,301	18,514	58,101	74,956	99,221	110,265	122,812	131,428
Use of IMF credit	5,293	1,918	2,208	2,232	2,277	5,374	9,081	10,913
Short-term external debt	9,051	6,059	11,851	28,665	41,607	49,483	52,137	63,879
interest arrears on long-term	59	120	30	18	36	33	47	100
Memorandum items								
Principal arrears on long-term	81	276	68	90	150	86	141	159
Long-term public sector debt	128,962	133,778	116,200	126,847	144,293	155,829	169,184	194,142
Long-term private sector debt	8,975	19,287	58,273	75,107	99,356	110,459	123,014	131,662
Public & publicly guaranteed commitments	8,435	12,817	10,443	12,965	20,635	17,483	22,817	24,912
External debt flows								
Disbursements	12,071	14,190	24,777	38,957	71,730	49,093	39,248	52,398
Long-term external debt	11,869	13,995	24,521	38,785	71,642	45,650	35,271	50,074
IMF purchases	202	195	256	171	88	3,443	3,978	2,325
Principal repayments	11,610	9,798	22,038	15,150	35,110	27,408	15,585	19,891
Long-term external debt	9,605	9,315	21,763	14,889	34,953	27,140	15,228	19,541
IMF repurchases	2,006	483	275	261	157	268	356	349
Net flows	2,497	3,454	5,023	40,633	49,544	29,565	26,304	44,161
Long-term external debt	2,264	4,680	2,759	23,896	36,689	18,510	20,043	30,532
Short-term external debt	2,037	-938	2,284	16,826	12,924	7,880	2,640	11,653
Interest payments	6,524	5,659	5,685	6,374	9,013	9,069	7,223	7,469
Long-term external debt	5,666	5,277	5,214	5,755	6,941	7,336	6,460	6,493
IMF charges	234	58	26	26	23	23	76	140
Short-term external debt	624	323	446	592	2,049	1,710	687	836
2. Other non-debt resource inflows								
Foreign direct investment	2,931	4,368	11,229	26,087	32,742	51,071	39,404	27,960
Portfolio equity	1,585	2,518	12,406	10,388	33,970	-15,836	20,541	39,447
3. Currency composition of public and publicly guaranteed debt (%)								
Euro	..	..	7.5	7.5	7.2	6.3	6.0	4.9
Japanese yen	17.0	15.3	19.1	18.3	17.1	20.1	18.3	18.4
Pound sterling	3.6	2.8	2.2	1.9	1.5	1.3	1.1	0.9
Swiss franc	0.7	0.3	0.3	0.2	0.2	0.2	0.1	0.1
U.S.dollars	46.0	56.6	54.4	55.6	56.7	55.0	57.7	60.4
4. Average terms of new commitments								
Official creditors								
Interest (%)	3.7	5.1	2.0	3.1	3.4	1.9	1.4	1.8
Maturity (years)	25.8	23.4	27.7	26.2	26.1	26.8	25.6	27.9
Grace period (years)	7.7	6.4	7.9	6.2	6.9	6.5	6.6	7.9
Private creditors								
Interest (%)	5.8	4.4	4.7	4.7	6.7	4.1	4.3	2.9
Maturity (years)	6.0	5.3	6.1	7.9	9.2	9.0	4.0	7.2
Grace period (years)	3.9	4.6	4.1	6.8	4.6	2.7	3.0	4.5
5. Major economic aggregates								
Gross national income (GNI)	473,560	603,668	1,043,978	1,186,944	1,511,378	1,525,991	1,705,510	2,090,779
Exports of goods, services & income	61,117	88,739	201,532	248,253	304,933	380,860	328,149	424,897
Worker remit. & comp. of employees	10,005	17,206	33,924	42,525	54,044	71,638	75,063	82,209
Imports of goods, services & income	86,693	116,954	258,918	316,030	384,182	508,643	436,818	565,989
Profit remittances on FDI	392	721	7,979	11,542	15,236	16,583	16,197	17,147
International reserves	30,704	47,221	156,716	198,417	302,183	275,859	315,151	337,472
6. Ratios								
External debt stocks to exports (%)	249.2	181.5	93.5	93.8	94.3	84.3	107.7	94.3
External debt stocks to GNI (%)	32.2	26.7	18.1	19.6	19.0	21.0	20.7	19.2
Debt service to exports (%)	29.7	17.4	13.8	8.7	14.5	9.6	7.0	6.4
Short-term to external debt stocks (%)	5.9	3.8	6.3	12.3	14.5	15.4	14.8	15.9
Multilateral to external debt stocks (%)	37.3	37.9	36.9	32.6	29.0	27.7	26.9	25.1
Reserves to external debt stocks (%)	20.2	29.3	83.1	85.2	105.1	85.9	89.2	84.2
Reserves to imports (months)	4.3	4.8	7.3	7.5	9.4	6.5	8.7	7.2

(US$ million, unless otherwise indicated)

7. Long-term external debt

	1995	2000	2005	2006	2007	2008	2009	2010
Debt outstanding and disbursed	**137,937**	**153,065**	**174,473**	**201,953**	**243,649**	**266,288**	**292,199**	**325,804**
Public and publicly guaranteed	129,636	134,552	116,372	126,998	144,428	156,023	169,387	194,376
Official creditors	104,110	101,864	109,589	116,638	127,148	137,669	145,635	155,989
Multilateral	56,867	61,051	69,604	75,950	83,312	89,008	95,071	100,595
of which: IBRD	13,035	10,209	7,514	8,151	8,766	9,376	10,151	12,868
IDA	29,001	31,963	42,193	45,803	48,915	49,529	51,505	51,238
Bilateral	47,243	40,812	39,984	40,688	43,836	48,661	50,565	55,395
Private creditors	25,526	32,688	6,783	10,360	17,280	18,354	23,751	38,387
of which: Bonds	3,474	10,928	2,525	4,178	7,879	7,670	12,671	23,980
Commercial banks	14,176	19,576	3,768	5,482	8,581	9,904	10,395	13,760
Private nonguaranteed	8,301	18,514	58,101	74,956	99,221	110,265	122,812	131,428
of which: Bonds	1,065	1,560	6,461	11,204	16,277	15,682	16,176	13,883
Disbursements	**11,869**	**13,995**	**24,521**	**38,785**	**71,642**	**45,650**	**35,271**	**50,074**
Public and publicly guaranteed	9,935	13,409	10,987	14,197	22,203	24,635	17,874	30,691
Official creditors	6,392	6,119	7,405	8,291	9,298	11,233	12,783	13,692
Multilateral	3,972	4,347	5,728	6,244	6,989	7,937	8,799	9,211
of which: IBRD	860	866	1,081	1,134	1,178	1,176	1,498	3,395
IDA	1,374	1,655	2,709	2,452	2,572	2,151	2,944	1,944
Bilateral	2,420	1,772	1,677	2,047	2,309	3,296	3,984	4,481
Private creditors	3,542	7,290	3,582	5,905	12,905	13,401	5,092	16,999
of which: Bonds	85	5,520	2,314	3,252	8,639	11,507	2,265	12,050
Commercial banks	1,901	940	1,245	2,368	4,128	1,862	2,819	4,948
Private nonguaranteed	1,934	586	13,534	24,589	49,439	21,015	17,396	19,382
of which: Bonds	520	0	3,520	4,799	7,793	594	2,473	1,288
Principal repayments	**9,605**	**9,315**	**21,763**	**14,889**	**34,953**	**27,140**	**15,228**	**19,541**
Public and publicly guaranteed	9,107	8,607	14,496	6,987	11,362	16,339	8,713	8,876
Official creditors	5,763	5,351	4,461	4,643	4,809	5,586	5,413	6,049
Multilateral	2,227	2,827	2,166	2,485	2,517	3,080	3,164	3,409
of which: IBRD	1,173	1,231	523	543	631	687	707	726
IDA	318	548	949	1,069	1,112	1,223	1,321	1,349
Bilateral	3,537	2,524	2,295	2,158	2,292	2,506	2,248	2,640
Private creditors	3,343	3,256	10,035	2,344	6,553	10,753	3,301	2,827
of which: Bonds	320	50	8,565	1,597	5,313	9,533	1,088	748
Commercial banks	2,002	2,868	1,274	670	1,199	1,145	2,139	2,009
Private nonguaranteed	498	707	7,266	7,902	23,591	10,801	6,515	10,665
of which: Bonds	0	35	117	57	409	880	1,779	2,451
Interest payments	**5,666**	**5,277**	**5,214**	**5,755**	**6,941**	**7,336**	**6,460**	**6,493**
Public and publicly guaranteed	5,004	4,396	3,940	2,415	2,735	2,947	2,688	2,767
Official creditors	2,934	2,274	1,904	2,053	2,249	2,306	2,142	2,077
Multilateral	1,640	1,366	899	1,135	1,327	1,333	1,092	879
of which: IBRD	995	613	252	387	470	401	266	104
IDA	215	236	342	343	355	388	371	380
Bilateral	1,294	907	1,005	919	922	973	1,050	1,199
Private creditors	2,070	2,122	2,036	362	486	641	545	689
of which: Bonds	196	210	1,849	154	211	290	259	232
Commercial banks	1,317	1,806	171	198	264	330	269	255
Private nonguaranteed	663	881	1,274	3,340	4,206	4,389	3,772	3,726
of which: Bonds	58	227	151	276	404	345	346	451

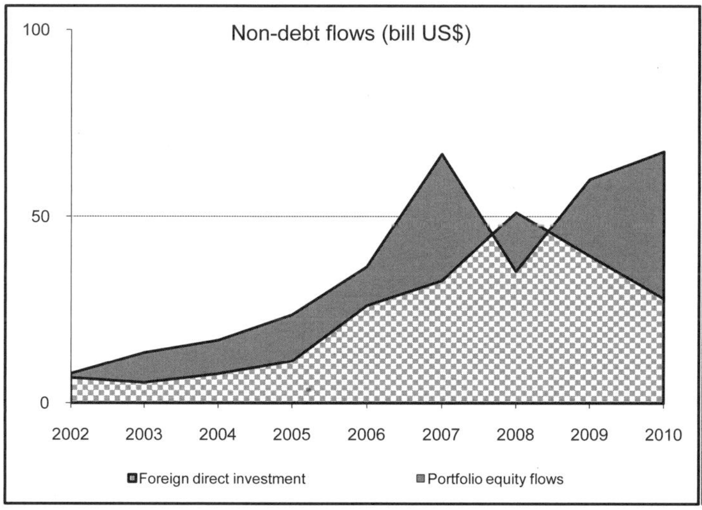

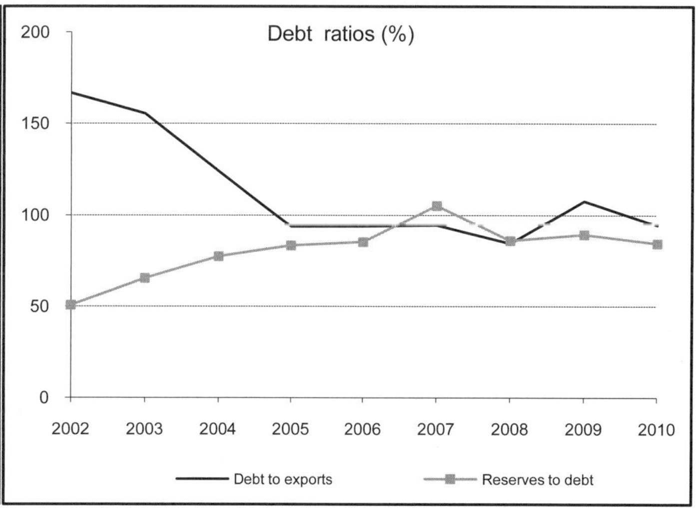

SUB-SAHARAN AFRICA

(US$ million, unless otherwise indicated)

	1995	2000	2005	2006	2007	2008	2009	2010
1. Summary external debt data								
External debt stocks	**235,768**	**211,015**	**214,493**	**170,688**	**189,447**	**196,819**	**199,834**	**205,992**
Long-term external debt	186,633	172,835	177,830	126,578	141,442	144,635	157,305	162,065
Public and publicly guaranteed	174,873	161,487	169,182	117,297	125,183	130,480	140,080	143,293
Private nonguaranteed	11,760	11,348	8,648	9,281	16,259	14,155	17,224	18,772
Use of IMF credit	8,654	6,734	5,947	3,140	3,341	3,963	6,261	5,991
Short-term external debt	40,481	31,445	30,716	40,969	44,665	48,221	36,269	37,936
interest arrears on long-term	20,712	13,473	14,003	14,849	14,266	13,334	11,266	11,474
Memorandum items								
Principal arrears on long-term	40,990	25,343	23,817	24,376	22,585	20,969	19,322	17,278
Long-term public sector debt	174,747	160,580	169,084	117,261	125,156	130,461	140,062	143,281
Long-term private sector debt	11,886	12,255	8,746	9,318	16,286	14,174	17,243	18,784
Public & publicly guaranteed commitments	9,157	8,355	23,790	12,501	18,846	18,320	29,920	31,136
External debt flows								
Disbursements	14,005	10,102	16,078	13,389	24,220	15,372	23,027	23,327
Long-term external debt	11,011	9,578	15,755	13,092	23,867	13,960	20,404	21,983
IMF purchases	2,994	525	323	298	354	1,413	2,623	1,344
Principal repayments	9,419	9,016	12,131	17,076	13,569	8,976	9,698	8,219
Long-term external debt	7,048	8,557	11,384	16,719	13,272	8,289	9,313	8,070
IMF repurchases	2,371	460	747	357	296	687	385	149
Net flows	7,502	-1,799	6,976	5,721	14,930	10,885	3,437	16,568
Long-term external debt	3,963	1,021	4,372	-3,627	10,594	5,671	11,091	13,913
Short-term external debt	2,917	-2,886	3,028	9,407	4,279	4,488	-9,893	1,460
Interest payments	5,337	4,443	7,961	4,302	5,244	4,998	3,968	4,362
Long-term external debt	3,975	3,319	7,323	3,421	4,061	3,580	3,246	3,707
IMF charges	559	43	27	39	14	494	28	8
Short-term external debt	803	1,081	612	842	1,169	925	694	647
2. Other non-debt resource inflows								
Foreign direct investment	4,259	6,458	18,551	16,196	28,304	37,459	32,765	28,828
Portfolio equity	2,952	4,164	8,083	16,808	10,146	-5,700	10,198	8,014
3. Currency composition of public and publicly guaranteed debt (%)								
Euro	..	..	19.8	22.8	21.8	19.4	18.9	15.1
Japanese yen	5.5	4.1	3.6	3.2	2.8	3.8	3.2	2.4
Pound sterling	3.8	2.1	4.2	1.7	1.5	1.0	1.1	0.7
Swiss franc	2.1	1.5	1.9	2.5	2.5	2.5	2.5	2.8
U.S.dollars	40.7	61.4	55.0	51.8	52.1	54.0	54.0	56.8
4. Average terms of new commitments								
Official creditors								
Interest (%)	1.8	1.1	4.3	1.5	1.4	1.8	1.6	1.7
Maturity (years)	31.7	36.3	21.4	29.3	31.1	29.2	23.8	25.6
Grace period (years)	8.7	9.1	4.5	7.2	7.8	7.7	6.1	6.7
Private creditors								
Interest (%)	5.7	5.8	5.6	6.8	6.7	4.3	6.0	3.0
Maturity (years)	12.4	7.7	7.2	11.2	8.8	6.7	8.1	13.8
Grace period (years)	1.9	2.1	1.9	4.9	5.3	1.0	4.5	5.7
5. Major economic aggregates								
Gross national income (GNI)	310,011	319,885	605,039	714,969	813,792	927,613	891,648	1,030,221
Exports of goods, services & income	90,831	114,029	239,831	279,331	333,944	403,588	302,503	381,517
Worker remit. & comp. of employees	3,159	4,825	9,630	12,794	18,746	21,710	20,183	21,087
Imports of goods, services & income	111,296	117,777	242,210	287,361	367,782	454,698	373,032	449,772
Profit remittances on FDI	3,952	7,860	17,650	23,931	39,134	47,127	33,276	32,065
International reserves	20,652	36,505	82,452	114,886	141,827	152,687	155,416	153,626
6. Ratios								
External debt stocks to exports (%)	259.6	185.1	89.4	61.1	56.7	48.8	66.1	54.0
External debt stocks to GNI (%)	76.1	66.0	35.5	23.9	23.3	21.2	22.4	20.0
Debt service to exports (%)	16.2	11.8	8.4	7.7	5.6	3.5	4.5	3.3
Short-term to external debt stocks (%)	17.2	14.9	14.3	24.0	23.6	24.5	18.1	18.4
Multilateral to external debt stocks (%)	23.1	25.9	33.8	25.3	25.3	25.5	27.3	28.3
Reserves to external debt stocks (%)	8.8	17.3	38.4	67.3	74.9	77.6	77.8	74.6
Reserves to imports (months)	2.2	3.7	4.1	4.8	4.6	4.0	5.0	4.1

SUB-SAHARAN AFRICA

(US$ million, unless otherwise indicated)

	1995	*2000*	*2005*	*2006*	*2007*	*2008*	*2009*	*2010*
7. Long-term external debt								
Debt outstanding and disbursed	**186,633**	**172,835**	**177,830**	**126,578**	**141,442**	**144,635**	**157,305**	**162,065**
Public and publicly guaranteed	174,873	161,487	169,182	117,297	125,183	130,480	140,080	143,293
Official creditors	138,312	135,459	135,148	87,942	93,471	96,623	104,051	107,041
Multilateral	54,428	54,568	72,511	43,144	47,991	50,199	54,614	58,220
of which: IBRD	7,641	3,477	2,015	1,799	1,524	994	900	1,175
IDA	27,842	33,574	48,444	24,187	27,325	29,318	31,612	32,943
Bilateral	83,884	80,891	62,638	44,798	45,480	46,424	49,436	48,821
Private creditors	36,561	26,029	34,034	29,355	31,712	33,858	36,030	36,252
of which: Bonds	4,784	9,150	10,734	9,285	12,078	11,775	13,368	14,684
Commercial banks	12,568	8,439	17,836	15,509	15,829	18,436	18,272	17,048
Private nonguaranteed	11,760	11,348	8,648	9,281	16,259	14,155	17,224	18,772
of which: Bonds	350	1,360	1,307	1,484	6,715	6,017	6,049	5,471
Disbursements	**11,011**	**9,578**	**15,755**	**13,092**	**23,867**	**13,960**	**20,404**	**21,983**
Public and publicly guaranteed	10,264	7,459	12,496	9,903	16,589	12,979	17,640	19,294
Official creditors	5,873	4,141	6,107	6,572	7,897	7,935	10,915	14,603
Multilateral	4,202	3,359	4,789	4,542	4,976	4,967	6,989	7,416
of which: IBRD	274	75	14	1	31	45	113	405
IDA	2,390	2,193	2,943	2,749	2,987	2,898	3,444	3,943
Bilateral	1,671	782	1,318	2,029	2,921	2,968	3,926	7,186
Private creditors	4,390	3,318	6,389	3,331	8,692	5,044	6,725	4,692
of which: Bonds	541	765	0	2,076	3,525	0	2,200	2,000
Commercial banks	1,623	1,752	6,112	814	4,905	4,704	3,246	1,854
Private nonguaranteed	747	2,119	3,260	3,189	7,278	980	2,764	2,689
of which: Bonds	350	712	1,307	0	5,587	0	0	0
Principal repayments	**7,048**	**8,557**	**11,384**	**16,719**	**13,272**	**8,289**	**9,313**	**8,070**
Public and publicly guaranteed	5,808	7,159	10,677	14,207	11,260	6,382	7,908	6,240
Official creditors	2,975	3,440	6,588	8,170	5,147	3,737	3,347	2,758
Multilateral	2,016	1,630	1,554	1,555	1,736	1,999	1,768	1,282
of which: IBRD	1,056	552	286	284	406	620	202	123
IDA	120	225	248	238	195	463	266	255
Bilateral	959	1,811	5,034	6,615	3,411	1,738	1,579	1,477
Private creditors	2,834	3,719	4,089	6,037	6,113	2,644	4,561	3,482
of which: Bonds	40	480	1	1,742	1,222	52	294	23
Commercial banks	1,261	2,444	3,523	3,169	3,853	2,167	3,804	3,038
Private nonguaranteed	1,240	1,398	706	2,511	2,012	1,907	1,405	1,830
of which: Bonds	0	0	0	0	1,390	698	0	578
Interest payments	**3,975**	**3,319**	**7,323**	**3,421**	**4,061**	**3,580**	**3,246**	**3,707**
Public and publicly guaranteed	3,471	2,915	6,971	2,983	3,520	3,023	2,664	2,225
Official creditors	2,006	1,826	5,856	1,408	2,084	1,666	1,523	1,201
Multilateral	1,234	843	757	694	1,053	927	861	614
of which: IBRD	630	213	53	47	339	109	22	19
IDA	178	199	313	240	179	277	196	204
Bilateral	772	983	5,099	713	1,031	739	662	587
Private creditors	1,465	1,089	1,115	1,575	1,436	1,357	1,141	1,024
of which: Bonds	322	561	517	552	539	677	649	807
Commercial banks	457	303	425	778	750	548	398	158
Private nonguaranteed	504	405	352	438	541	556	582	1,483
of which: Bonds	0	41	61	89	132	241	241	1,027

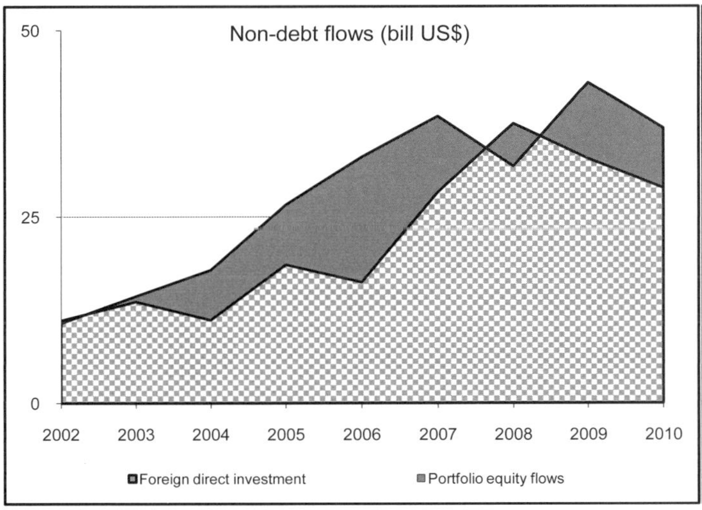

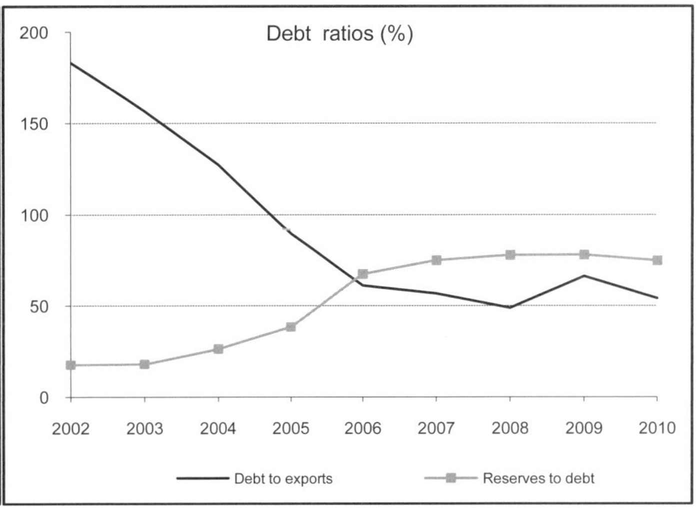

LOW-INCOME COUNTRIES

(US$ million, unless otherwise indicated)

	1995	2000	2005	2006	2007	2008	2009	2010
1. Summary external debt data								
External debt stocks	**113,033**	**108,371**	**117,997**	**99,743**	**109,232**	**115,451**	**119,669**	**116,593**
Long-term external debt	98,419	92,872	103,423	84,975	92,919	98,250	103,185	99,631
Public and publicly guaranteed	95,691	90,326	102,613	84,032	91,660	95,379	100,165	95,929
Private nonguaranteed	2,728	2,546	811	943	1,259	2,871	3,019	3,703
Use of IMF credit	4,710	4,037	4,324	2,852	3,151	4,047	5,304	4,156
Short-term external debt	9,904	11,461	10,250	11,916	13,162	13,153	11,181	12,806
interest arrears on long-term	7,452	7,639	6,843	7,202	7,237	6,286	5,292	5,651
Memorandum items								
Principal arrears on long-term	17,967	15,441	13,620	14,179	15,128	14,081	15,053	14,078
Long-term public sector debt	95,227	90,029	102,452	83,923	91,535	95,255	100,032	95,895
Long-term private sector debt	3,192	2,843	971	1,051	1,383	2,996	3,152	3,736
Public & publicly guaranteed commitments	3,851	4,217	6,210	7,906	9,075	9,301	10,240	13,158
External debt flows								
Disbursements	5,347	3,991	5,641	5,744	6,490	9,384	11,278	10,664
Long-term external debt	4,890	3,602	5,239	5,419	6,117	7,775	9,774	9,919
IMF purchases	457	389	402	324	373	1,610	1,505	745
Principal repayments	2,901	2,393	2,492	2,140	2,615	3,005	3,041	4,064
Long-term external debt	2,599	1,999	2,036	1,900	2,405	2,396	2,747	3,870
IMF repurchases	302	394	456	241	210	609	293	194
Net flows	2,775	1,246	2,574	4,912	5,085	7,321	7,259	7,832
Long-term external debt	2,291	1,603	3,202	3,520	3,711	5,378	7,026	6,049
Short-term external debt	329	-353	-575	1,308	1,211	942	-979	1,232
Interest payments	1,438	1,116	1,039	1,102	1,601	1,819	1,187	1,137
Long-term external debt	1,249	827	854	838	1,339	1,163	1,047	1,008
IMF charges	60	37	17	37	12	495	31	5
Short-term external debt	129	251	168	227	250	161	110	125
2. Other non-debt resource inflows								
Foreign direct investment	1,233	2,385	4,471	5,390	9,935	10,522	9,231	12,716
Portfolio equity	-10	0	49	70	139	-25	-2	-52
3. Currency composition of public and publicly guaranteed debt (%)								
Euro	..	..	8.8	11.1	11.3	10.0	9.3	6.7
Japanese yen	11.7	10.8	9.3	10.7	10.0	10.5	9.7	8.2
Pound sterling	2.6	2.3	1.7	1.4	1.3	1.0	1.0	0.9
Swiss franc	1.0	0.7	0.6	0.7	0.5	0.4	0.3	0.3
U.S.dollars	41.3	51.5	54.2	49.9	49.1	49.4	49.7	50.2
4. Average terms of new commitments								
Official creditors								
Interest (%)	1.7	1.2	1.2	1.5	1.4	1.3	1.3	1.0
Maturity (years)	34.3	36.4	35.2	33.5	34.6	34.2	31.4	33.4
Grace period (years)	9.3	9.3	8.8	8.5	8.8	9.0	7.9	9.2
Private creditors								
Interest (%)	3.4	5.2	3.9	6.3	4.2	4.1	4.0	1.8
Maturity (years)	5.7	11.5	14.3	16.6	10.9	7.8	9.3	17.8
Grace period (years)	1.1	3.2	3.6	3.2	2.5	2.7	2.9	3.9
5. Major economic aggregates								
Gross national income (GNI)	135,122	160,215	232,472	254,435	301,279	356,119	378,964	409,271
Exports of goods, services & income	25,183	31,867	57,025	68,142	83,364	101,175	89,830	108,306
Worker remit. & comp. of employees	2,125	4,078	9,860	12,737	16,382	21,748	22,555	24,553
Imports of goods, services & income	41,832	45,124	78,719	91,793	115,044	146,728	131,988	156,562
Profit remittances on FDI	252	653	3,605	3,687	3,265	3,126	2,799	2,134
International reserves	9,744	10,917	19,345	22,491	28,804	29,773	41,985	42,464
6. Ratios								
External debt stocks to exports (%)	448.9	340.1	206.9	146.4	131.0	114.1	133.2	107.7
External debt stocks to GNI (%)	83.7	67.6	50.8	39.2	36.3	32.4	31.6	28.5
Debt service to exports (%)	17.2	11.0	6.2	4.8	5.1	4.8	4.7	4.8
Short-term to external debt stocks (%)	8.8	10.6	8.7	11.9	12.0	11.4	9.3	11.0
Multilateral to external debt stocks (%)	39.4	45.9	58.6	50.7	51.3	51.3	52.0	54.2
Reserves to external debt stocks (%)	8.6	10.1	16.4	22.5	26.4	25.8	35.1	36.4
Reserves to imports (months)	2.8	2.9	2.9	2.9	3.0	2.4	3.8	3.3

(US$ million, unless otherwise indicated)

	1995	2000	2005	2006	2007	2008	2009	2010
7. Long-term external debt								
Debt outstanding and disbursed	**98,419**	**92,872**	**103,423**	**84,975**	**92,919**	**98,250**	**103,185**	**99,631**
Public and publicly guaranteed	95,691	90,326	102,613	84,032	91,660	95,379	100,165	95,929
Official creditors	91,045	86,996	99,243	80,729	88,307	92,249	96,110	92,057
Multilateral	44,589	49,743	69,133	50,520	55,994	59,284	62,224	63,201
of which: IBRD	1,458	718	618	622	480	464	463	463
IDA	27,443	31,597	45,650	30,255	33,318	35,147	36,116	36,019
Bilateral	46,456	37,253	30,110	30,209	32,313	32,965	33,886	28,856
Private creditors	4,646	3,330	3,369	3,303	3,353	3,131	4,056	3,871
of which: Bonds	129	7	1	1	0	0	0	0
Commercial banks	1,517	1,659	1,628	1,587	1,624	1,568	1,419	1,142
Private nonguaranteed	2,728	2,546	811	943	1,259	2,871	3,019	3,703
of which: Bonds	0	0	0	0	0	0	0	0
Disbursements	**4,890**	**3,602**	**5,239**	**5,419**	**6,117**	**7,775**	**9,774**	**9,919**
Public and publicly guaranteed	4,624	3,547	5,179	5,235	5,822	6,846	8,993	8,189
Official creditors	4,173	3,364	4,991	5,197	5,792	6,790	7,858	7,333
Multilateral	3,156	2,911	4,429	4,117	4,731	5,197	5,924	5,011
of which: IBRD	32	19	1	0	0	0	0	0
IDA	1,837	1,925	2,710	2,363	2,831	2,905	2,767	2,662
Bilateral	1,017	453	561	1,079	1,061	1,593	1,934	2,321
Private creditors	451	183	188	38	30	56	1,135	857
of which: Bonds	0	0	0	0	0	0	0	0
Commercial banks	149	108	57	18	9	6	7	385
Private nonguaranteed	265	55	60	185	295	928	781	1,730
of which: Bonds	0	0	0	0	0	0	0	0
Principal repayments	**2,599**	**1,999**	**2,036**	**1,900**	**2,405**	**2,396**	**2,747**	**3,870**
Public and publicly guaranteed	2,396	1,776	1,922	1,847	2,266	2,087	2,057	2,705
Official creditors	1,743	1,539	1,776	1,691	2,180	2,005	1,942	2,017
Multilateral	824	786	1,106	1,130	1,382	1,321	1,232	1,221
of which: IBRD	218	104	5	5	167	26	0	0
IDA	160	270	374	406	393	590	487	507
Bilateral	918	753	670	560	798	684	710	796
Private creditors	653	237	146	157	85	82	115	688
of which: Bonds	30	0	1	0	0	0	0	0
Commercial banks	284	129	82	74	18	19	37	576
Private nonguaranteed	203	223	114	52	140	309	690	1,165
of which: Bonds	0	0	0	0	0	0	0	0
Interest payments	**1,249**	**827**	**854**	**838**	**1,339**	**1,163**	**1,047**	**1,008**
Public and publicly guaranteed	1,174	732	836	826	1,325	1,125	977	885
Official creditors	1,018	668	812	791	1,296	1,099	948	848
Multilateral	546	423	602	568	947	737	617	594
of which: IBRD	110	36	2	2	294	1	0	0
IDA	196	194	314	272	228	274	239	234
Bilateral	472	245	209	223	349	362	331	254
Private creditors	156	64	25	35	29	26	29	37
of which: Bonds	6	0	0	0	0	0	0	0
Commercial banks	86	36	9	12	9	8	14	19
Private nonguaranteed	74	96	17	12	14	38	69	123
of which: Bonds	0	0	0	0	0	0	0	0

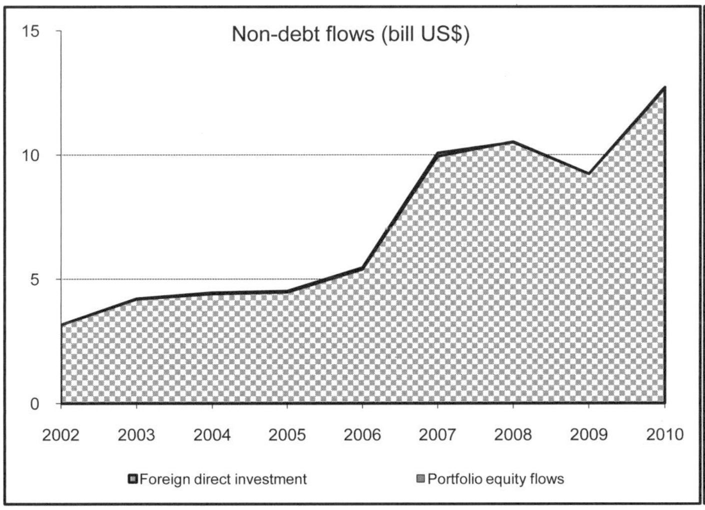

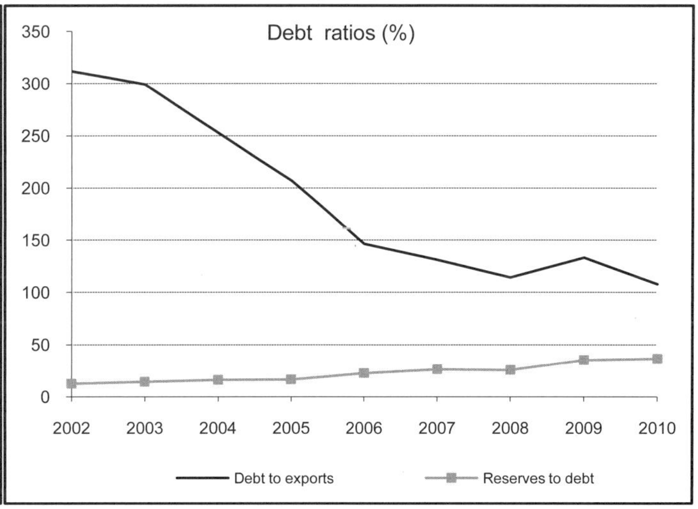

MIDDLE-INCOME COUNTRIES

(US$ million, unless otherwise indicated)

	1995	2000	2005	2006	2007	2008	2009	2010
1. Summary external debt data								
External debt stocks	**1,747,589**	**2,017,980**	**2,396,068**	**2,575,552**	**3,111,285**	**3,383,722**	**3,519,926**	**3,959,705**
Long-term external debt	1,371,451	1,685,468	1,860,628	1,976,690	2,348,012	2,615,660	2,709,906	2,875,628
Public and publicly guaranteed	1,165,689	1,197,112	1,180,290	1,162,274	1,264,183	1,302,077	1,376,910	1,486,657
Private nonguaranteed	205,762	488,356	680,338	814,416	1,083,829	1,313,583	1,332,997	1,388,971
Use of IMF credit	55,172	54,229	44,855	17,007	12,389	21,693	47,994	60,505
Short-term external debt	320,967	278,284	490,584	581,855	750,884	746,369	762,026	1,023,572
interest arrears on long-term	37,064	24,102	21,580	18,825	20,399	21,209	21,136	15,439
Memorandum items								
Principal arrears on long-term	86,617	45,202	32,609	30,595	32,520	35,059	35,924	26,792
Long-term public sector debt	1,161,065	1,191,511	1,175,860	1,158,079	1,259,455	1,296,556	1,365,449	1,474,309
Long-term private sector debt	210,386	493,957	684,769	818,611	1,088,556	1,319,104	1,344,457	1,401,319
Public & publicly guaranteed commitments	136,808	141,693	153,089	135,495	185,248	176,647	236,847	237,606
External debt flows								
Disbursements	204,200	234,476	377,582	473,258	654,080	655,629	523,186	645,008
Long-term external debt	176,874	224,750	374,024	469,469	652,439	642,632	496,070	628,912
IMF purchases	27,326	9,725	3,559	3,789	1,640	12,997	27,117	16,097
Principal repayments	117,673	230,080	324,585	380,956	360,115	393,222	380,000	424,853
Long-term external debt	109,334	209,872	280,919	350,377	353,170	390,031	378,450	422,024
IMF repurchases	8,339	20,209	43,666	30,579	6,945	3,191	1,550	2,829
Net flows	140,304	-2,766	135,166	186,327	461,014	257,083	158,908	487,398
Long-term external debt	67,540	14,879	93,104	119,092	299,269	252,601	117,620	206,887
Short-term external debt	53,778	-7,162	82,169	94,025	167,050	-5,325	15,723	267,243
Interest payments	83,597	111,628	102,671	116,290	135,733	140,782	124,699	153,298
Long-term external debt	66,242	93,076	82,966	93,367	107,870	119,650	110,197	110,942
IMF charges	2,571	2,827	3,260	1,585	698	484	541	982
Short-term external debt	14,784	15,724	16,445	21,338	27,165	20,648	13,961	41,374
2. Other non-debt resource inflows								
Foreign direct investment	93,604	146,336	310,013	382,135	524,206	613,587	390,719	493,345
Portfolio equity	13,327	13,948	67,423	107,629	132,814	-53,338	108,757	128,465
3. Currency composition of public and publicly guaranteed debt (%)								
Euro	..	..	14.4	14.7	15.1	13.8	14.5	13.0
Japanese yen	13.1	12.0	10.1	9.8	8.9	10.6	10.1	10.5
Pound sterling	1.5	0.9	1.0	0.7	0.6	0.4	0.4	0.4
Swiss franc	1.1	0.4	0.6	0.6	0.6	0.6	0.5	0.5
U.S.dollars	48.7	63.9	67.1	67.9	69.0	69.2	69.2	70.7
4. Average terms of new commitments								
Official creditors								
Interest (%)	6.0	5.1	3.8	4.2	4.0	2.9	1.9	1.9
Maturity (years)	18.5	18.7	20.8	21.5	21.7	22.4	20.8	21.7
Grace period (years)	5.2	4.7	5.4	5.9	6.1	6.2	6.1	6.4
Private creditors								
Interest (%)	6.5	8.2	6.3	6.2	6.4	6.0	6.2	4.9
Maturity (years)	7.4	11.2	11.3	11.8	11.0	11.7	9.7	12.3
Grace period (years)	3.4	8.5	8.7	9.5	8.1	8.0	8.2	9.1
5. Major economic aggregates								
Gross national income (GNI)	4,660,936	5,467,289	9,197,759	10,946,254	13,596,825	16,261,351	15,873,869	19,009,329
Exports of goods, services & income	1,117,625	1,623,451	3,253,909	3,980,218	4,822,353	5,799,505	4,640,317	5,829,275
Worker remit. & comp. of employees	51,224	73,674	177,120	208,905	260,020	301,173	283,716	294,999
Imports of goods, services & income	1,260,596	1,661,458	3,190,879	3,802,615	4,656,274	5,685,743	4,632,376	5,873,025
Profit remittances on FDI	36,457	67,170	193,082	253,361	322,721	375,200	316,476	340,760
International reserves	429,657	631,836	1,959,728	2,593,468	3,672,428	4,123,910	4,793,625	5,545,172
6. Ratios								
External debt stocks to exports (%)	156.4	124.3	73.6	64.7	64.5	58.3	75.9	67.9
External debt stocks to GNI (%)	37.5	36.9	26.1	23.5	22.9	20.8	22.2	20.8
Debt service to exports (%)	18.0	21.0	13.1	12.6	10.3	9.2	10.9	9.9
Short-term to external debt stocks (%)	18.4	13.8	20.5	22.6	24.1	22.1	21.6	25.8
Multilateral to external debt stocks (%)	13.4	13.7	12.7	11.6	10.2	9.9	10.8	10.6
Reserves to external debt stocks (%)	24.6	31.3	81.8	100.7	118.0	121.9	136.2	140.0
Reserves to imports (months)	4.1	4.6	7.4	8.2	9.5	8.7	12.4	11.3

(US$ million, unless otherwise indicated)

7. Long-term external debt

	1995	2000	2005	2006	2007	2008	2009	2010
Debt outstanding and disbursed	**1,371,451**	**1,685,468**	**1,860,628**	**1,976,690**	**2,348,012**	**2,615,660**	**2,709,906**	**2,875,628**
Public and publicly guaranteed	1,165,689	1,197,112	1,180,290	1,162,274	1,264,183	1,302,077	1,376,910	1,486,657
Official creditors	673,806	664,698	616,000	555,711	580,450	618,763	676,235	730,518
Multilateral	234,164	276,875	304,508	297,638	317,881	335,717	381,551	420,640
of which: IBRD	104,982	107,604	95,752	91,764	93,171	96,232	108,233	124,389
IDA	44,052	55,199	75,427	68,750	74,356	76,122	80,851	82,589
Bilateral	439,642	387,823	311,492	258,073	262,570	283,046	294,684	309,878
Private creditors	491,882	532,414	564,290	606,562	683,733	683,314	700,675	756,139
of which: Bonds	220,372	341,950	400,278	409,787	455,913	468,243	484,388	527,752
Commercial banks	145,345	124,144	124,322	162,220	197,217	188,792	188,116	201,509
Private nonguaranteed	205,762	488,356	680,338	814,416	1,083,829	1,313,583	1,332,997	1,388,971
of which: Bonds	51,018	89,492	155,162	192,861	250,265	241,846	256,961	311,827
Disbursements	**176,874**	**224,750**	**374,024**	**469,469**	**652,439**	**642,632**	**496,070**	**628,912**
Public and publicly guaranteed	123,644	133,646	137,440	146,684	181,015	167,826	208,412	245,119
Official creditors	60,721	49,023	41,086	49,525	54,277	61,916	92,357	98,116
Multilateral	27,961	31,350	29,824	35,890	38,983	42,402	66,510	66,379
of which: IBRD	12,514	12,951	9,180	11,934	10,498	13,608	22,703	26,246
IDA	3,636	3,295	4,497	4,408	4,527	3,959	5,945	5,026
Bilateral	32,761	17,673	11,262	13,635	15,294	19,513	25,847	31,737
Private creditors	62,923	84,623	96,355	97,159	126,738	105,910	116,054	147,003
of which: Bonds	22,036	55,784	61,066	57,988	75,318	73,523	69,052	86,861
Commercial banks	22,041	18,023	31,718	34,131	47,843	30,030	41,799	51,014
Private nonguaranteed	53,230	91,104	236,583	322,784	471,424	474,806	287,658	383,792
of which: Bonds	14,063	10,810	47,975	54,555	84,368	27,235	37,236	86,053
Principal repayments	**109,334**	**209,872**	**280,919**	**350,377**	**353,170**	**390,031**	**378,450**	**422,024**
Public and publicly guaranteed	83,619	111,898	144,010	190,001	125,383	141,441	115,261	121,822
Official creditors	40,844	46,001	68,438	95,317	51,229	47,987	44,556	46,004
Multilateral	18,829	21,805	25,585	35,341	25,108	25,661	24,235	24,633
of which: IBRD	11,146	9,314	12,125	17,183	10,699	10,922	10,860	9,164
IDA	382	679	1,247	1,373	1,443	1,706	1,765	1,835
Bilateral	22,015	24,196	42,853	59,976	26,121	22,326	20,321	21,371
Private creditors	42,774	65,897	75,571	94,685	74,154	93,455	70,705	75,818
of which: Bonds	11,061	31,454	44,588	60,257	43,145	53,897	32,705	35,031
Commercial banks	14,996	23,127	22,221	25,071	23,958	32,388	30,669	32,909
Private nonguaranteed	25,715	97,974	136,910	160,376	227,788	248,589	263,189	300,202
of which: Bonds	4,042	15,032	15,063	17,980	24,880	20,144	22,467	26,500
Interest payments	**66,242**	**93,076**	**82,966**	**93,367**	**107,870**	**119,650**	**110,197**	**110,942**
Public and publicly guaranteed	55,419	62,510	59,675	55,504	58,468	58,017	53,260	54,235
Official creditors	26,389	25,331	23,122	18,935	18,935	17,912	16,051	15,744
Multilateral	12,616	14,814	9,979	11,104	11,931	11,572	9,898	8,336
of which: IBRD	7,504	7,421	4,017	4,780	5,141	4,575	3,432	2,256
IDA	307	384	583	539	530	634	559	591
Bilateral	13,773	10,516	13,143	7,832	7,003	6,340	6,153	7,408
Private creditors	29,030	37,179	36,553	36,569	39,534	40,105	37,209	38,492
of which: Bonds	14,707	25,003	30,128	28,827	31,222	31,726	30,820	33,011
Commercial banks	7,736	8,525	4,910	6,244	6,530	6,698	5,167	4,330
Private nonguaranteed	10,822	30,566	23,291	37,863	49,401	61,633	56,937	56,706
of which: Bonds	3,172	7,776	8,861	14,076	16,282	15,893	16,400	18,110

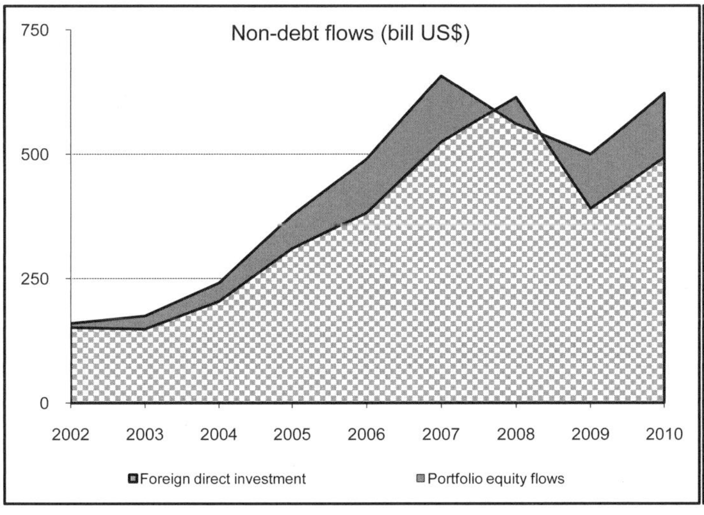

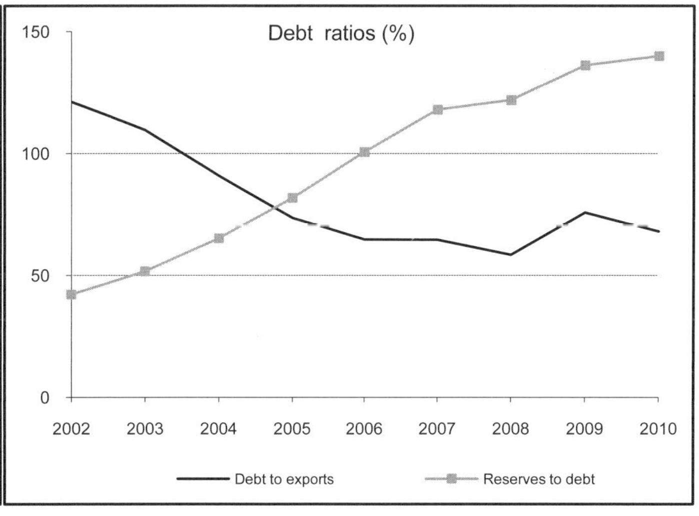

Country Tables

AFGHANISTAN

(US$ million, unless otherwise indicated)

	1995	2000	2005	2006	2007	2008	2009	2010
1. Summary external debt data								
External debt stocks	..	..	..	**929**	**1,974**	**2,089**	**2,223**	**2,297**
Long-term external debt	..	..	..	911	1,894	1,985	2,097	2,076
Public and publicly guaranteed	..	..	..	911	1,894	1,985	2,097	2,076
Private nonguaranteed	..	..	..	0	0	0	0	0
Use of IMF credit	0	0	0	0	59	87	106	119
Short-term external debt	..	..	..	18	21	17	20	102
interest arrears on long-term	..	..	..	18	21	17	20	67
Memorandum items								
Principal arrears on long-term	..	..	..	87	89	56	54	54
Long-term public sector debt	..	..	..	911	1,894	1,985	2,097	2,076
Long-term private sector debt	..	..	..	0	0	0	0	0
Public & publicly guaranteed commitments	..	..	..	130	37	58	0	0
External debt flows								
Disbursements	..	..	..	146	202	132	126	87
Long-term external debt	..	..	..	146	147	96	109	79
IMF purchases	0	0	0	0	55	36	17	9
Principal repayments	..	..	..	3	1	1	3	1
Long-term external debt	..	..	..	3	1	1	3	1
IMF repurchases	0	0	0	0	0	0	0	0
Net flows	..	..	..	143	201	131	123	86
Long-term external debt	..	..	..	143	146	95	106	78
Short-term external debt	..	..	..	0	0	0	0	0
Interest payments	..	..	..	6	3	6	7	8
Long-term external debt	..	..	..	6	3	6	7	7
IMF charges	0	0	0	0	0	0	1	0
Short-term external debt	..	..	..	0	0	0	0	1
2. Other non-debt resource inflows								
Foreign direct investment	..	..	..	238	243	300	185	76
Portfolio equity	..	..	..	..	..	..	..	..
3. Currency composition of public and publicly guaranteed debt (%)								
Euro	..	..	..	0.0	0.0	0.0	0.0	0.0
Japanese yen	..	..	..	0.0	0.0	0.0	0.0	0.0
Pound sterling	..	..	..	2.8	1.3	0.0	0.0	0.0
Swiss franc	..	..	..	0.0	0.0	0.0	0.0	0.0
U.S.dollars	..	..	..	63.3	74.5	73.0	69.1	59.8
4. Average terms of new commitments								
Official creditors								
Interest (%)	..	..	..	1.2	1.4	0.5	0.0	0.0
Maturity (years)	..	..	..	39.8	31.6	34.6	0.0	0.0
Grace period (years)	..	..	..	10.3	8.1	10.0	0.0	0.0
Private creditors								
Interest (%)	..	..	..	0.0	0.0	0.0	0.0	0.0
Maturity (years)	..	..	..	0.0	0.0	0.0	0.0	0.0
Grace period (years)	..	..	..	0.0	0.0	0.0	0.0	0.0
5. Major economic aggregates								
Gross national income (GNI)	..	..	..	8,209	10,184	10,644	..	..
Exports of goods, services & income	..	..	..	..	..	..	..	..
Worker remit. & comp. of employees	..	..	..	..	..	..	..	..
Imports of goods, services & income	..	..	..	..	..	..	..	..
Profit remittances on FDI	..	..	..	..	..	..	..	..
Current account balance	..	..	..	..	..	..	..	..
International reserves	..	..	..	..	..	..	..	..
6. Ratios								
External debt stocks to exports (%)	..	..	..	..	..	..	..	..
External debt stocks to GNI (%)	..	..	..	11.3	19.4	19.6	..	..
Debt service to exports (%)	..	..	..	..	..	..	..	..
Short-term to external debt stocks (%)	..	..	..	2.0	1.1	0.8	0.9	4.4
Multilateral to external debt stocks (%)	..	..	..	70.4	41.5	43.3	45.7	48.7
Reserves to external debt stocks (%)	..	..	..	..	..	..	..	..
Reserves to imports (months)	..	..	..	..	..	..	..	..

(US$ million, unless otherwise indicated)

	1995	2000	2005	2006	2007	2008	2009	2010
7. Long-term external debt								
Debt outstanding and disbursed	..	..	..	**911**	**1,894**	**1,985**	**2,097**	**2,076**
Public and publicly guaranteed	..	..	..	911	1,894	1,985	2,097	2,076
Official creditors	..	..	..	910	1,893	1,984	2,096	2,076
Multilateral	..	..	..	654	819	903	1,016	1,118
of which: IBRD	0	0	0	0	0	0	0	0
IDA	0	0	294	343	399	438	466	410
Bilateral	..	..	..	257	1,074	1,081	1,080	958
Private creditors	..	..	..	0	0	0	0	0
of which: Bonds	..	..	..	0	0	0	0	0
Commercial banks	..	..	..	0	0	0	0	0
Private nonguaranteed	..	..	..	0	0	0	0	0
of which: Bonds	..	..	..	0	0	0	0	0
Disbursements	..	..	..	**146**	**147**	**96**	**109**	**79**
Public and publicly guaranteed	..	..	..	146	147	96	109	79
Official creditors	..	..	..	146	147	96	109	79
Multilateral	..	..	..	107	140	96	109	79
of which: IBRD	0	0	0	0	0	0	0	0
IDA	0	0	84	39	44	44	27	8
Bilateral	..	..	..	40	7	1	0	0
Private creditors	..	..	..	0	0	0	0	0
of which: Bonds	..	..	..	0	0	0	0	0
Commercial banks	..	..	..	0	0	0	0	0
Private nonguaranteed	..	..	..	0	0	0	0	0
of which: Bonds	..	..	..	0	0	0	0	0
Principal repayments	..	..	..	**3**	**1**	**1**	**3**	**1**
Public and publicly guaranteed	..	..	..	3	1	1	3	1
Official creditors	..	..	..	3	1	1	3	1
Multilateral	..	..	..	3	1	1	1	1
of which: IBRD	0	0	0	0	0	0	0	0
IDA	0	0	3	3	0	0	0	0
Bilateral	..	..	..	0	0	0	2	0
Private creditors	..	..	..	0	0	0	0	0
of which: Bonds	..	..	..	0	0	0	0	0
Commercial banks	..	..	..	0	0	0	0	0
Private nonguaranteed	..	..	..	0	0	0	0	0
of which: Bonds	..	..	..	0	0	0	0	0
Interest payments	..	..	..	**6**	**3**	**6**	**7**	**7**
Public and publicly guaranteed	..	..	..	6	3	6	7	7
Official creditors	..	..	..	6	3	6	7	7
Multilateral	..	..	..	6	3	6	7	7
of which: IBRD	0	0	0	0	0	0	0	0
IDA	0	0	3	3	0	2	2	2
Bilateral	..	..	..	0	0	0	0	0
Private creditors	..	..	..	0	0	0	0	0
of which: Bonds	..	..	..	0	0	0	0	0
Commercial banks	..	..	..	0	0	0	0	0
Private nonguaranteed	..	..	..	0	0	0	0	0
of which: Bonds	..	..	..	0	0	0	0	0
8. Debt stock-flow reconciliation								
Total change in external debt stocks	..	..	..	229	1,045	115	134	75
Net flows on external debt	..	..	..	143	201	131	123	86
9. Debt restructurings								
Total amount rescheduled	..	..	..	95	842	52	1	0
Total amount forgiven	..	..	..	0	21	52	4	204
Debt buyback	..	..	..	0	0	0	0	0

10. Contractual obligations on outstanding long-term external debt

	2011	2012	2013	2014	2015	2016	2017	2018
Official creditors								
Principal	12	24	36	87	97	102	94	86
Interest	12	18	18	60	56	55	51	47
Private creditors								
Principal	0	0	0	0	0	0	0	0
Interest	0	0	0	0	0	0	0	0

Notes:

Data for 2010 include the effects of Paris Club debt restructuring agreements signed in 2010 and of MDRI and HIPC debt reliefs in the amount of $72.9 million.

ALBANIA

(US$ million, unless otherwise indicated)

	1995	2000	2005	2006	2007	2008	2009	2010
1. Summary external debt data								
External debt stocks	**459**	**1,070**	**2,054**	**2,422**	**2,854**	**3,904**	**4,693**	**4,736**
Long-term external debt	332	945	1,808	1,943	2,253	2,894	3,786	4,105
Public and publicly guaranteed	332	930	1,381	1,584	1,796	2,225	2,803	2,972
Private nonguaranteed	0	15	426	359	458	668	983	1,133
Use of IMF credit	65	88	92	93	90	80	71	58
Short-term external debt	62	37	155	386	511	930	835	573
interest arrears on long-term	2	3	1	1	1	0	0	0
Memorandum items								
Principal arrears on long-term	27	271	16	16	17	1	0	0
Long-term public sector debt	332	929	1,381	1,584	1,796	2,225	2,803	2,972
Long-term private sector debt	0	16	426	359	458	668	983	1,133
Public & publicly guaranteed commitments	193	176	224	311	280	610	544	653
External debt flows								
Disbursements	83	139	506	191	300	813	753	825
Long-term external debt	72	120	494	184	293	806	750	825
IMF purchases	11	19	12	7	7	8	4	0
Principal repayments	2	17	51	159	92	96	135	379
Long-term external debt	0	10	41	147	78	80	121	367
IMF repurchases	1	7	9	11	14	15	14	12
Net flows	-97	130	609	264	332	1,138	523	184
Long-term external debt	72	110	452	36	215	725	628	458
Short-term external debt	-178	8	154	231	124	420	-95	-262
Interest payments	9	11	30	47	61	68	91	85
Long-term external debt	5	9	25	29	34	50	80	77
IMF charges	1	1	0	1	1	1	1	0
Short-term external debt	3	2	4	17	26	17	11	8
2. Other non-debt resource inflows								
Foreign direct investment	70	143	262	325	662	959	964	1,110
Portfolio equity	..	..	..	..	..	23	3	8
3. Currency composition of public and publicly guaranteed debt (%)								
Euro	..	..	28.2	31.2	35.3	47.3	54.9	57.0
Japanese yen	2.5	3.1	3.9	3.4	3.0	2.8	2.1	2.2
Pound sterling	0.0	0.0	0.0	0.0	0.0	0.0	0.0	0.0
Swiss franc	0.0	0.0	0.0	0.0	0.0	0.0	0.0	0.0
U.S.dollars	60.2	71.8	58.3	54.9	51.0	40.0	33.6	30.8
4. Average terms of new commitments								
Official creditors								
Interest (%)	3.3	3.5	2.0	3.4	4.3	1.8	3.0	3.5
Maturity (years)	25.2	29.7	19.5	20.2	20.7	28.3	19.3	16.5
Grace period (years)	7.3	10.5	6.7	6.6	5.3	8.3	5.8	4.0
Private creditors								
Interest (%)	3.0	0.5	0.0	0.3	5.3	6.2	11.0	7.0
Maturity (years)	22.7	-2,000.4	0.0	29.9	11.2	15.4	3.3	5.8
Grace period (years)	11.7	24.8	0.0	18.8	1.7	6.0	3.0	4.8
5. Major economic aggregates								
Gross national income (GNI)	2,468	3,790	8,541	9,347	11,006	13,135	11,936	11,681
Exports of goods, services & income	376	819	2,048	2,629	3,407	4,307	3,908	4,169
Worker remit. & comp. of employees	427	598	1,290	1,359	1,468	1,495	1,317	1,156
Imports of goods, services & income	865	1,509	3,913	4,569	5,989	7,705	7,053	6,794
Profit remittances on FDI	4	0	2	5	9	301	436	362
Current account balance	-12	-156	-571	-671	-1,151	-2,019	-1,838	-1,404
International reserves	265	646	1,440	1,813	2,162	2,364	2,369	2,541
6. Ratios								
External debt stocks to exports (%)	122.1	130.5	100.3	92.1	83.8	90.6	120.1	113.6
External debt stocks to GNI (%)	18.6	28.2	24.1	25.9	25.9	29.7	39.3	40.5
Debt service to exports (%)	2.8	3.4	3.9	7.8	4.5	3.8	5.8	11.1
Short-term to external debt stocks (%)	13.6	3.4	7.5	16.0	17.9	23.8	17.8	12.1
Multilateral to external debt stocks (%)	25.0	39.8	42.3	41.8	41.3	33.2	31.3	32.1
Reserves to external debt stocks (%)	57.8	60.4	70.1	74.8	75.7	60.6	50.5	53.6
Reserves to imports (months)	3.7	5.1	4.4	4.8	4.3	3.7	4.0	4.5

ALBANIA

(US$ million, unless otherwise indicated)

	1995	2000	2005	2006	2007	2008	2009	2010
7. Long-term external debt								
Debt outstanding and disbursed	**332**	**945**	**1,808**	**1,943**	**2,253**	**2,894**	**3,786**	**4,105**
Public and publicly guaranteed	332	930	1,381	1,584	1,796	2,225	2,803	2,972
Official creditors	307	908	1,357	1,558	1,770	1,879	2,132	2,159
Multilateral	115	426	869	1,013	1,179	1,295	1,469	1,522
of which: IBRD	0	0	0	0	6	17	24	26
IDA	109	346	655	729	803	817	849	850
Bilateral	192	482	488	545	591	584	664	637
Private creditors	25	22	24	27	25	346	671	813
of which: Bonds	0	0	0	0	0	0	0	401
Commercial banks	0	0	2	3	4	331	635	336
Private nonguaranteed	0	15	426	359	458	668	983	1,133
of which: Bonds	0	0	0	0	0	0	0	0
Disbursements	**72**	**120**	**494**	**184**	**293**	**806**	**750**	**825**
Public and publicly guaranteed	72	120	117	168	164	567	559	631
Official creditors	72	120	116	168	163	210	256	184
Multilateral	48	101	83	115	130	171	190	149
of which: IBRD	0	0	0	0	5	12	7	3
IDA	43	64	34	46	48	27	34	26
Bilateral	24	19	34	53	32	39	66	35
Private creditors	0	0	0	0	1	356	303	447
of which: Bonds	0	0	0	0	0	0	0	398
Commercial banks	0	0	0	0	0	345	284	6
Private nonguaranteed	0	0	377	15	128	239	191	194
of which: Bonds	0	0	0	0	0	0	0	0
Principal repayments	**0**	**10**	**41**	**147**	**78**	**80**	**121**	**367**
Public and publicly guaranteed	0	10	40	58	56	58	80	346
Official creditors	0	9	40	55	52	58	80	88
Multilateral	0	2	18	24	26	27	40	46
of which: IBRD	0	0	0	0	0	0	0	0
IDA	0	0	4	5	6	7	9	11
Bilateral	0	6	22	31	26	30	40	42
Private creditors	0	1	1	3	4	0	1	257
of which: Bonds	0	0	0	0	0	0	0	0
Commercial banks	0	0	0	0	0	0	0	257
Private nonguaranteed	0	0	1	90	22	23	41	21
of which: Bonds	0	0	0	0	0	0	0	0
Interest payments	**5**	**9**	**25**	**29**	**34**	**50**	**80**	**77**
Public and publicly guaranteed	5	8	23	25	31	44	69	65
Official creditors	4	7	23	25	31	35	36	31
Multilateral	1	4	14	14	18	24	24	22
of which: IBRD	0	0	0	0	0	1	1	0
IDA	1	2	5	6	6	6	6	6
Bilateral	3	3	10	11	13	11	12	9
Private creditors	1	0	0	0	0	9	33	34
of which: Bonds	0	0	0	0	0	0	0	0
Commercial banks	0	0	0	0	0	9	33	34
Private nonguaranteed	0	1	2	4	3	6	10	12
of which: Bonds	0	0	0	0	0	0	0	0
8. Debt stock-flow reconciliation								
Total change in external debt stocks	-424	351	498	368	432	1,049	789	43
Net flows on external debt	-97	130	609	264	332	1,138	523	184
9. Debt restructurings								
Total amount rescheduled	6	28	10	9	0	8	41	0
Total amount forgiven	116	0	0	2	0	0	0	0
Debt buyback	30	0	0	0	0	0	0	0

10. Contractual obligations on outstanding long-term external debt

	2011	2012	2013	2014	2015	2016	2017	2018
Official creditors								
Principal	123	132	148	153	175	164	168	171
Interest	38	42	43	43	41	38	35	31
Private creditors								
Principal	225	226	191	208	538	114	122	100
Interest	65	58	53	49	45	12	9	6

Notes:

Short-term debt is based on reports provided by the Central Bank.

ALGERIA

(US$ million, unless otherwise indicated)

	1995	2000	2005	2006	2007	2008	2009	2010
1. Summary external debt data								
External debt stocks	**33,052**	**25,388**	**16,871**	**5,721**	**5,908**	**5,935**	**5,424**	**5,276**
Long-term external debt	31,313	23,448	16,355	5,180	5,158	4,631	3,932	3,498
Public and publicly guaranteed	31,313	23,448	15,489	3,876	4,009	3,187	2,950	2,530
Private nonguaranteed	0	0	866	1,304	1,148	1,444	982	968
Use of IMF credit	1,478	1,718	0	0	0	0	0	0
Short-term external debt	261	222	516	541	750	1,304	1,492	1,778
interest arrears on long-term	3	0	0	0	0	0	0	0
Memorandum items								
Principal arrears on long-term	1	0	0	0	0	0	0	0
Long-term public sector debt	31,225	23,327	15,315	3,816	3,787	2,991	2,762	2,381
Long-term private sector debt	89	122	1,040	1,364	1,371	1,640	1,170	1,117
Public & publicly guaranteed commitments	2,427	1,419	445	212	94	0	5	5
External debt flows								
Disbursements	4,157	1,215	1,239	853	585	580	194	30
Long-term external debt	3,683	1,215	1,239	853	585	580	194	30
IMF purchases	475	0	0	0	0	0	0	0
Principal repayments	2,419	2,813	5,057	12,791	1,122	1,058	879	573
Long-term external debt	2,248	2,721	4,445	12,791	1,122	1,058	879	573
IMF repurchases	171	93	612	0	0	0	0	0
Net flows	1,361	-1,572	-3,733	-11,914	-328	76	-496	-257
Long-term external debt	1,435	-1,506	-3,207	-11,939	-537	-478	-685	-543
Short-term external debt	-378	27	85	25	209	554	189	286
Interest payments	1,832	1,655	921	626	224	191	139	111
Long-term external debt	1,741	1,552	888	610	202	160	121	93
IMF charges	69	92	18	1	0	0	0	0
Short-term external debt	22	10	15	15	22	31	18	18
2. Other non-debt resource inflows								
Foreign direct investment	..	438	1,081	1,796	1,662	2,595	2,760	2,291
Portfolio equity	..	..	..	..	..	..	..	..
3. Currency composition of public and publicly guaranteed debt (%)								
Euro	..	..	40.5	58.4	60.1	58.7	59.7	57.3
Japanese yen	13.1	14.4	8.2	6.1	4.7	5.2	4.4	4.9
Pound sterling	0.9	1.0	1.4	0.0	0.0	0.0	0.0	0.0
Swiss franc	0.7	0.5	0.8	0.1	0.1	0.0	0.0	0.0
U.S.dollars	38.0	44.5	40.9	30.0	28.9	30.2	30.1	31.6
4. Average terms of new commitments								
Official creditors								
Interest (%)	6.2	6.2	3.2	0.5	0.9	0.0	2.0	0.5
Maturity (years)	11.7	15.0	12.9	17.5	14.7	0.0	21.8	11.5
Grace period (years)	3.3	4.1	3.6	3.4	7.7	0.0	6.7	6.5
Private creditors								
Interest (%)	7.2	6.2	0.8	3.5	4.6	0.0	0.0	0.0
Maturity (years)	8.9	7.4	11.2	12.0	6.0	0.0	0.0	0.0
Grace period (years)	1.9	1.9	4.0	3.1	0.9	0.0	0.0	0.0
5. Major economic aggregates								
Gross national income (GNI)	39,574	52,080	97,259	112,669	134,004	169,689	139,577	155,538
Exports of goods, services & income	..	..	50,268	59,721	67,230	87,212	52,917	65,400
Worker remit. & comp. of employees	1,120	790	2,060	1,610	2,120	2,202	2,059	2,044
Imports of goods, services & income	..	..	31,154	32,409	38,818	55,546	55,147	55,280
Profit remittances on FDI	..	..	5,485	6,295	5,405	6,206	5,892	..
Current account balance	..	..	21,181	28,923	30,631	34,440	402	12,760
International reserves	4,164	13,556	59,167	81,463	114,972	148,099	155,112	170,461
6. Ratios								
External debt stocks to exports (%)	..	..	33.6	9.6	8.8	6.8	10.2	8.1
External debt stocks to GNI (%)	83.5	48.7	17.3	5.1	4.4	3.5	3.9	3.4
Debt service to exports (%)	..	..	11.9	22.5	2.0	1.4	1.9	1.0
Short-term to external debt stocks (%)	0.8	0.9	3.1	9.5	12.7	22.0	27.5	33.7
Multilateral to external debt stocks (%)	11.8	16.2	14.5	2.5	2.3	0.2	0.2	0.2
Reserves to external debt stocks (%)	12.6	53.4	350.7	1,423.9	1,946.2	2,495.5	2,859.7	3,230.9
Reserves to imports (months)	..	..	22.8	30.2	35.5	32.0	33.8	37.0

(US$ million, unless otherwise indicated)

	1995	2000	2005	2006	2007	2008	2009	2010
7. Long-term external debt								
Debt outstanding and disbursed	**31,313**	**23,448**	**16,355**	**5,180**	**5,158**	**4,631**	**3,932**	**3,498**
Public and publicly guaranteed	31,313	23,448	15,489	3,876	4,009	3,187	2,950	2,530
Official creditors	15,695	17,597	12,462	2,171	2,317	2,066	2,020	1,805
Multilateral	3,915	4,123	2,443	144	136	13	11	10
of which: IBRD	2,049	1,425	779	119	113	11	10	9
IDA	0	0	0	0	0	0	0	0
Bilateral	11,780	13,473	10,020	2,026	2,182	2,053	2,009	1,795
Private creditors	15,618	5,851	3,027	1,706	1,692	1,121	930	726
of which: Bonds	0	0	0	0	0	0	0	0
Commercial banks	4,529	2,508	1,038	59	76	60	54	42
Private nonguaranteed	0	0	866	1,304	1,148	1,444	982	968
of which: Bonds	0	0	0	0	0	0	0	0
Disbursements	**3,683**	**1,215**	**1,239**	**853**	**585**	**580**	**194**	**30**
Public and publicly guaranteed	3,683	1,215	776	401	282	173	71	28
Official creditors	1,596	795	445	263	109	157	70	27
Multilateral	932	349	358	54	6	5	0	0
of which: IBRD	554	58	31	16	6	5	0	0
IDA	0	0	0	0	0	0	0	0
Bilateral	664	446	87	209	103	152	70	27
Private creditors	2,087	420	331	138	173	16	1	1
of which: Bonds	0	0	0	0	0	0	0	0
Commercial banks	222	0	8	34	20	0	0	1
Private nonguaranteed	0	0	463	451	304	407	123	2
of which: Bonds	0	0	0	0	0	0	0	0
Principal repayments	**2,248**	**2,721**	**4,445**	**12,791**	**1,122**	**1,058**	**879**	**573**
Public and publicly guaranteed	2,248	2,721	4,217	12,640	590	914	357	339
Official creditors	671	1,055	3,012	10,976	199	370	148	171
Multilateral	454	351	1,190	2,396	16	127	1	2
of which: IBRD	260	172	156	677	12	107	1	1
IDA	0	0	0	0	0	0	0	0
Bilateral	217	704	1,821	8,579	183	243	147	169
Private creditors	1,577	1,666	1,205	1,664	391	544	209	168
of which: Bonds	278	0	0	0	0	0	0	0
Commercial banks	220	439	348	1,029	11	13	8	9
Private nonguaranteed	0	0	229	151	532	144	522	234
of which: Bonds	0	0	0	0	0	0	0	0
Interest payments	**1,741**	**1,552**	**888**	**610**	**202**	**160**	**121**	**93**
Public and publicly guaranteed	1,741	1,552	863	557	145	113	72	62
Official creditors	823	1,131	718	442	61	49	33	34
Multilateral	251	297	163	118	7	12	1	1
of which: IBRD	137	128	46	21	6	12	1	1
IDA	0	0	0	0	0	0	0	0
Bilateral	572	834	555	324	53	37	32	33
Private creditors	917	421	145	115	84	63	39	28
of which: Bonds	13	0	0	0	0	0	0	0
Commercial banks	251	146	34	30	3	2	2	1
Private nonguaranteed	0	0	25	53	57	48	49	31
of which: Bonds	0	0	0	0	0	0	0	0
8. Debt stock-flow reconciliation								
Total change in external debt stocks	2,810	-2,618	-5,314	-11,150	187	27	-511	-148
Net flows on external debt	1,361	-1,572	-3,733	-11,914	-328	76	-496	-257
9. Debt restructurings								
Total amount rescheduled	5,096	0	0	0	0	0	0	0
Total amount forgiven	0	0	0	0	0	0	0	0
Debt buyback	0	0	0	0	0	0	0	0

10. Contractual obligations on outstanding long-term external debt

	2011	2012	2013	2014	2015	2016	2017	2018
Official creditors								
Principal	294	262	231	224	181	151	138	85
Interest	40	36	31	27	22	19	16	13
Private creditors								
Principal	295	361	224	168	412	96	67	41
Interest	42	34	32	18	35	11	6	3

Notes:

Short-term debt data are reported by the country.

ANGOLA

(US$ million, unless otherwise indicated)

	1995	2000	2005	2006	2007	2008	2009	2010
1. Summary external debt data								
External debt stocks	**11,500**	**9,408**	**11,834**	**9,473**	**11,492**	**15,100**	**16,616**	**18,562**
Long-term external debt	9,543	8,085	9,518	7,341	9,223	12,683	13,629	15,440
Public and publicly guaranteed	9,543	8,085	9,518	7,341	9,223	12,683	13,629	15,440
Private nonguaranteed	0	0	0	0	0	0	0	0
Use of IMF credit	0	0	0	0	0	0	359	882
Short-term external debt	1,958	1,323	2,316	2,132	2,270	2,418	2,629	2,241
interest arrears on long-term	1,232	874	577	161	89	70	85	68
Memorandum items								
Principal arrears on long-term	4,190	2,853	1,877	700	327	254	308	213
Long-term public sector debt	9,513	8,059	9,506	7,334	9,221	12,682	13,628	15,439
Long-term private sector debt	29	26	12	7	2	1	0	0
Public & publicly guaranteed commitments	420	1,033	14,150	2,036	4,378	4,188	5,705	5,464
External debt flows								
Disbursements	550	1,045	3,676	1,222	5,647	4,621	4,146	4,454
Long-term external debt	550	1,045	3,676	1,222	5,647	4,621	3,793	3,930
IMF purchases	0	0	0	0	0	0	353	524
Principal repayments	332	1,530	2,289	3,514	3,779	1,129	3,130	2,109
Long-term external debt	332	1,530	2,289	3,514	3,779	1,129	3,130	2,109
IMF repurchases	0	0	0	0	0	0	0	0
Net flows	-90	-733	2,603	-2,060	2,078	3,659	1,212	1,974
Long-term external debt	218	-485	1,387	-2,292	1,868	3,492	662	1,821
Short-term external debt	-308	-248	1,216	232	210	167	196	-371
Interest payments	132	175	313	908	683	511	423	200
Long-term external debt	79	149	257	824	579	443	392	164
IMF charges	0	0	0	0	0	0	0	6
Short-term external debt	53	26	57	83	104	68	31	30
2. Other non-debt resource inflows								
Foreign direct investment	472	879	-1,304	-38	-893	1,679	2,205	..
Portfolio equity	..	..	..	..	..	..	..	..
3. Currency composition of public and publicly guaranteed debt (%)								
Euro	..	..	8.2	6.2	6.4	7.7	9.7	8.6
Japanese yen	0.3	0.5	0.3	0.0	0.0	0.0	0.0	0.0
Pound sterling	0.9	1.0	0.9	0.2	0.2	0.1	0.1	0.1
Swiss franc	0.1	0.1	0.0	0.0	0.0	0.0	0.0	0.0
U.S.dollars	81.0	86.3	87.8	90.5	91.1	90.6	88.5	89.9
4. Average terms of new commitments								
Official creditors								
Interest (%)	8.1	0.8	6.5	1.1	0.4	0.6	3.4	3.8
Maturity (years)	9.9	39.8	13.8	10.9	12.1	43.4	8.7	9.2
Grace period (years)	0.4	10.3	2.0	1.5	2.7	10.4	1.7	0.9
Private creditors								
Interest (%)	8.1	5.0	6.6	8.0	6.3	4.5	6.5	4.6
Maturity (years)	8.6	3.1	7.7	9.0	6.8	7.4	5.3	9.7
Grace period (years)	0.4	1.3	1.3	0.8	1.0	0.8	1.2	2.1
5. Major economic aggregates								
Gross national income (GNI)	3,688	7,449	26,601	39,679	51,674	70,461	68,671	75,516
Exports of goods, services & income	3,852	8,222	24,312	33,492	45,329	64,666	41,582	51,375
Worker remit. & comp. of employees	..	..	..	..	..	82	..	..
Imports of goods, services & income	4,302	7,454	19,201	22,612	34,526	57,261	48,784	43,900
Profit remittances on FDI	386	929	3,406	5,278	7,268	13,185	6,130	..
Current account balance	-295	796	5,138	10,690	10,581	7,194	-7,572	7,127
International reserves	213	1,198	3,197	8,599	11,197	17,869	13,664	19,749
6. Ratios								
External debt stocks to exports (%)	298.6	114.4	48.7	28.3	25.4	23.4	40.0	36.1
External debt stocks to GNI (%)	311.9	126.3	44.5	23.9	22.2	21.4	24.2	24.6
Debt service to exports (%)	12.0	20.7	10.7	13.2	9.8	2.5	8.5	4.5
Short-term to external debt stocks (%)	17.0	14.1	19.6	22.5	19.7	16.0	15.8	12.1
Multilateral to external debt stocks (%)	1.7	3.1	3.1	4.2	3.6	2.8	2.7	2.3
Reserves to external debt stocks (%)	1.9	12.7	27.0	90.8	97.4	118.3	82.2	106.4
Reserves to imports (months)	0.6	1.9	2.0	4.6	3.9	3.7	3.4	5.4

ANGOLA

(US$ million, unless otherwise indicated)

	1995	2000	2005	2006	2007	2008	2009	2010
7. Long-term external debt								
Debt outstanding and disbursed	**9,543**	**8,085**	**9,518**	**7,341**	**9,223**	**12,683**	**13,629**	**15,440**
Public and publicly guaranteed	9,543	8,085	9,518	7,341	9,223	12,683	13,629	15,440
Official creditors	2,226	2,703	3,174	2,581	3,202	4,001	4,814	8,152
Multilateral	191	294	371	396	416	421	441	436
of which: IBRD	0	0	0	0	0	0	0	0
IDA	81	226	319	347	365	369	385	378
Bilateral	2,035	2,409	2,803	2,186	2,786	3,580	4,373	7,716
Private creditors	7,316	5,382	6,344	4,760	6,021	8,682	8,814	7,287
of which: Bonds	0	0	0	0	0	0	0	0
Commercial banks	873	2,625	5,062	3,928	5,248	7,790	7,939	6,241
Private nonguaranteed	0	0	0	0	0	0	0	0
of which: Bonds	0	0	0	0	0	0	0	0
Disbursements	**550**	**1,045**	**3,676**	**1,222**	**5,647**	**4,621**	**3,793**	**3,930**
Public and publicly guaranteed	550	1,045	3,676	1,222	5,647	4,621	3,793	3,930
Official creditors	119	34	321	505	951	1,100	1,111	3,656
Multilateral	30	24	34	21	9	16	23	10
of which: IBRD	0	0	0	0	0	0	0	0
IDA	30	24	30	18	8	12	19	6
Bilateral	89	10	287	485	942	1,084	1,088	3,646
Private creditors	431	1,011	3,355	717	4,695	3,521	2,682	274
of which: Bonds	0	0	0	0	0	0	0	0
Commercial banks	396	1,010	3,236	573	4,562	3,276	2,542	24
Private nonguaranteed	0	0	0	0	0	0	0	0
of which: Bonds	0	0	0	0	0	0	0	0
Principal repayments	**332**	**1,530**	**2,289**	**3,514**	**3,779**	**1,129**	**3,130**	**2,109**
Public and publicly guaranteed	332	1,530	2,289	3,514	3,779	1,129	3,130	2,109
Official creditors	24	268	505	1,207	352	275	310	282
Multilateral	2	27	8	15	7	8	8	9
of which: IBRD	0	0	0	0	0	0	0	0
IDA	0	0	5	5	5	6	6	7
Bilateral	22	241	497	1,192	345	267	302	273
Private creditors	308	1,262	1,784	2,307	3,427	854	2,821	1,827
of which: Bonds	0	0	0	0	0	0	0	0
Commercial banks	108	1,149	1,654	1,713	3,253	715	2,663	1,784
Private nonguaranteed	0	0	0	0	0	0	0	0
of which: Bonds	0	0	0	0	0	0	0	0
Interest payments	**79**	**149**	**257**	**824**	**579**	**443**	**392**	**164**
Public and publicly guaranteed	79	149	257	824	579	443	392	164
Official creditors	12	36	61	364	162	118	143	114
Multilateral	1	28	4	7	3	4	4	5
of which: IBRD	0	0	0	0	0	0	0	0
IDA	0	2	3	3	2	3	3	4
Bilateral	12	8	57	357	159	115	139	109
Private creditors	67	113	195	460	416	325	250	50
of which: Bonds	0	0	0	0	0	0	0	0
Commercial banks	33	93	160	330	352	260	218	40
Private nonguaranteed	0	0	0	0	0	0	0	0
of which: Bonds	0	0	0	0	0	0	0	0
8. Debt stock-flow reconciliation								
Total change in external debt stocks	207	-891	2,472	-2,361	2,019	3,608	1,516	1,946
Net flows on external debt	-90	-733	2,603	-2,060	2,078	3,659	1,212	1,974
9. Debt restructurings								
Total amount rescheduled	437	0	0	2	21	67	0	0
Total amount forgiven	0	0	122	400	72	25	18	18
Debt buyback	0	0	0	0	0	0	0	0

10. Contractual obligations on outstanding long-term external debt

	2011	2012	2013	2014	2015	2016	2017	2018
Official creditors								
Principal	2,498	2,730	2,738	2,710	2,685	2,681	2,490	1,896
Interest	227	301	316	288	240	186	126	70
Private creditors								
Principal	2,959	2,413	1,644	1,153	496	195	194	139
Interest	210	174	123	86	56	38	24	11

ARGENTINA

(US$ million, unless otherwise indicated)

	1995	2000	2005	2006	2007	2008	2009	2010
1. Summary external debt data								
External debt stocks	**98,465**	**140,914**	**124,939**	**115,863**	**117,317**	**118,902**	**120,283**	**127,849**
Long-term external debt	70,979	107,543	80,586	87,564	98,058	98,925	100,651	92,844
Public and publicly guaranteed	54,913	81,633	54,225	60,754	68,029	68,627	72,927	67,331
Private nonguaranteed	16,066	25,909	26,361	26,811	30,028	30,298	27,723	25,514
Use of IMF credit	6,131	5,056	9,513	0	0	0	0	0
Short-term external debt	21,355	28,315	34,841	28,299	19,260	19,977	19,632	35,005
interest arrears on long-term	0	0	7,735	7,452	9,452	10,003	10,760	5,457
Memorandum items								
Principal arrears on long-term	0	0	11,193	12,125	16,157	18,466	19,637	9,156
Long-term public sector debt	54,891	81,582	54,205	60,655	67,935	68,539	72,866	67,283
Long-term private sector debt	16,088	25,961	26,381	26,909	30,123	30,386	27,785	25,561
Public & publicly guaranteed commitments	8,381	11,985	2,462	5,747	7,522	4,969	3,375	1,156
External debt flows								
Disbursements	11,319	20,853	4,690	8,789	9,089	7,037	7,537	6,845
Long-term external debt	8,954	18,759	4,690	8,789	9,089	7,037	7,537	6,845
IMF purchases	2,365	2,094	0	0	0	0	0	0
Principal repayments	3,532	15,679	7,009	14,819	5,171	4,635	8,784	10,444
Long-term external debt	3,048	14,400	3,438	5,026	5,171	4,635	8,784	10,444
IMF repurchases	484	1,280	3,571	9,793	0	0	0	0
Net flows	21,972	4,074	14,787	-12,289	-7,121	2,568	-2,350	17,078
Long-term external debt	5,906	4,359	1,252	3,763	3,918	2,402	-1,248	-3,599
Short-term external debt	14,185	-1,100	17,106	-6,259	-11,039	166	-1,102	20,676
Interest payments	5,322	11,163	2,962	3,979	3,774	3,089	3,343	3,596
Long-term external debt	4,320	9,236	2,108	2,959	2,900	2,849	3,222	3,426
IMF charges	274	195	510	83	0	0	0	0
Short-term external debt	727	1,732	344	937	874	240	121	170
2. Other non-debt resource inflows								
Foreign direct investment	5,609	10,418	5,265	5,537	6,473	9,726	4,017	6,337
Portfolio equity	1,091	-3,227	-48	707	1,785	-531	-212	-208
3. Currency composition of public and publicly guaranteed debt (%)								
Euro	..	..	36.6	36.6	39.1	36.9	36.0	31.2
Japanese yen	9.2	6.2	2.7	2.5	2.3	2.9	2.7	3.1
Pound sterling	0.2	0.6	0.1	0.1	0.1	0.1	0.1	0.0
Swiss franc	1.6	0.4	0.4	0.4	0.4	0.4	0.4	0.4
U.S.dollars	57.5	61.0	54.4	55.9	54.7	57.0	58.8	63.8
4. Average terms of new commitments								
Official creditors								
Interest (%)	6.5	7.2	4.2	5.5	6.1	3.3	1.9	1.2
Maturity (years)	16.3	18.2	17.3	20.3	18.9	18.4	26.3	24.8
Grace period (years)	4.7	4.8	4.6	5.0	4.8	3.6	3.9	4.0
Private creditors								
Interest (%)	7.4	10.0	5.0	5.7	6.6	6.8	5.4	2.9
Maturity (years)	4.8	11.6	8.4	11.1	13.7	12.8	28.5	28.5
Grace period (years)	4.6	11.6	3.7	6.0	11.5	11.3	19.0	19.0
5. Major economic aggregates								
Gross national income (GNI)	253,396	276,656	176,575	208,884	255,510	319,508	297,639	353,713
Exports of goods, services & income	29,356	38,697	51,334	60,254	72,968	87,794	70,254	84,079
Worker remit. & comp. of employees	64	86	432	541	606	698	621	641
Imports of goods, services & income	35,070	48,076	46,543	52,947	65,967	81,209	61,896	80,638
Profit remittances on FDI	2,129	3,086	5,456	7,112	7,283	7,902	8,360	8,516
Current account balance	-5,118	-8,981	5,275	7,767	7,354	6,755	8,405	3,082
International reserves	15,979	25,152	28,082	32,022	46,149	46,385	48,007	52,208
6. Ratios								
External debt stocks to exports (%)	335.4	364.1	243.4	192.3	160.8	135.4	171.2	152.1
External debt stocks to GNI (%)	38.9	50.9	70.8	55.5	45.9	37.2	40.4	36.1
Debt service to exports (%)	30.2	69.4	19.4	36.2	12.3	8.8	17.3	16.7
Short-term to external debt stocks (%)	21.7	20.1	27.9	24.4	16.4	16.8	16.3	27.4
Multilateral to external debt stocks (%)	9.5	11.5	12.5	12.9	12.7	12.4	13.4	13.2
Reserves to external debt stocks (%)	16.2	17.8	22.5	27.6	39.3	39.0	39.9	40.8
Reserves to imports (months)	5.5	6.3	7.2	7.3	8.4	6.9	9.3	7.8

(US$ million, unless otherwise indicated)

	1995	2000	2005	2006	2007	2008	2009	2010
7. Long-term external debt								
Debt outstanding and disbursed	**70,979**	**107,543**	**80,586**	**87,564**	**98,058**	**98,925**	**100,651**	**92,844**
Public and publicly guaranteed	54,913	81,633	54,225	60,754	68,029	68,627	72,927	67,331
Official creditors	20,658	20,484	20,344	20,184	20,443	20,575	22,333	22,922
Multilateral	9,373	16,235	15,571	14,984	14,909	14,780	16,157	16,918
of which: IBRD	4,913	8,789	6,881	6,206	5,674	5,069	5,305	5,349
IDA	0	0	0	0	0	0	0	0
Bilateral	11,285	4,249	4,774	5,200	5,535	5,794	6,176	6,004
Private creditors	34,255	61,149	33,881	40,569	47,586	48,052	50,595	44,409
of which: Bonds	32,670	60,622	33,373	40,018	46,589	47,088	49,670	43,571
Commercial banks	793	294	171	201	211	205	208	201
Private nonguaranteed	16,066	25,909	26,361	26,811	30,028	30,298	27,723	25,514
of which: Bonds	7,582	11,138	8,772	10,138	12,073	7,921	6,850	7,855
Disbursements	**8,954**	**18,759**	**4,690**	**8,789**	**9,089**	**7,037**	**7,537**	**6,845**
Public and publicly guaranteed	6,604	14,277	3,183	3,893	5,647	4,047	3,591	2,545
Official creditors	2,804	1,937	989	1,666	2,385	2,022	3,498	2,455
Multilateral	1,936	1,923	985	1,662	2,373	2,000	3,070	2,437
of which: IBRD	941	1,019	362	459	505	332	1,028	787
IDA	0	0	0	0	0	0	0	0
Bilateral	868	13	4	4	12	22	429	18
Private creditors	3,800	12,340	2,194	2,227	3,263	2,025	93	90
of which: Bonds	3,630	12,338	2,194	2,227	3,263	2,025	93	90
Commercial banks	105	2	0	0	0	0	0	0
Private nonguaranteed	2,350	4,482	1,507	4,896	3,441	2,990	3,946	4,300
of which: Bonds	834	1,408	540	2,896	2,241	0	476	2,037
Principal repayments	**3,048**	**14,400**	**3,438**	**5,026**	**5,171**	**4,635**	**8,784**	**10,444**
Public and publicly guaranteed	1,783	8,896	1,672	2,539	3,230	2,367	3,071	4,789
Official creditors	1,356	1,837	1,489	2,362	2,676	2,363	1,783	1,917
Multilateral	512	825	1,462	2,354	2,568	2,253	1,637	1,648
of which: IBRD	259	538	928	1,134	1,037	936	793	741
IDA	0	0	0	0	0	0	0	0
Bilateral	844	1,012	27	9	108	111	146	268
Private creditors	427	7,059	183	177	554	3	1,287	2,872
of which: Bonds	128	6,842	182	175	554	3	1,232	2,818
Commercial banks	158	162	0	1	0	0	0	0
Private nonguaranteed	1,265	5,503	1,766	2,487	1,941	2,268	5,714	5,655
of which: Bonds	631	2,309	680	1,303	606	2,009	430	969
Interest payments	**4,320**	**9,236**	**2,108**	**2,959**	**2,900**	**2,849**	**3,222**	**3,426**
Public and publicly guaranteed	3,435	7,196	1,392	1,309	1,618	1,644	1,887	2,337
Official creditors	1,374	1,589	751	842	868	763	656	613
Multilateral	617	1,256	747	838	864	719	581	552
of which: IBRD	306	701	288	346	350	258	169	147
IDA	0	0	0	0	0	0	0	0
Bilateral	757	334	5	4	4	44	76	60
Private creditors	2,062	5,606	641	467	750	881	1,231	1,725
of which: Bonds	1,960	5,465	640	466	750	881	1,195	1,695
Commercial banks	56	121	0	0	0	0	0	0
Private nonguaranteed	885	2,041	716	1,650	1,282	1,206	1,335	1,089
of which: Bonds	641	1,109	585	1,135	759	710	562	567
8. Debt stock-flow reconciliation								
Total change in external debt stocks	23,646	570	-37,439	-9,076	1,454	1,585	1,381	7,567
Net flows on external debt	21,972	4,074	14,787	-12,289	-7,121	2,568	-2,350	17,078
9. Debt restructurings								
Total amount rescheduled	248	0	20,136	2,096	983	0	0	8,115
Total amount forgiven	863	689	40,333	3	0	0	10	9,347
Debt buyback	0	2,745	0	0	0	0	0	0

10. Contractual obligations on outstanding long-term external debt

	2011	2012	2013	2014	2015	2016	2017	2018
Official creditors								
Principal	2,131	2,287	1,984	1,965	1,930	1,782	1,560	1,438
Interest	478	442	396	349	300	254	215	183
Private creditors								
Principal	5,558	5,180	4,422	1,847	4,940	2,186	6,219	1,344
Interest	4,010	3,696	3,374	3,142	2,996	2,618	2,299	1,903

Notes:

Long-term private nonguaranteed debt data for 2010 are reported by the country for the second time. Historical data are World Bank staff estimates. Short-term debt data are revised from 2007 to 2009 based on BIS data and 2010 based on country data. Long-term provincial debt data are World Bank staff estimates.

ARMENIA

(US$ million, unless otherwise indicated)

	1995	2000	2005	2006	2007	2008	2009	2010
1. Summary external debt data								
External debt stocks	**371**	**916**	**1,842**	**2,004**	**2,898**	**3,406**	**4,886**	**6,103**
Long-term external debt	298	697	1,368	1,533	2,281	2,818	3,778	4,744
Public and publicly guaranteed	298	675	923	1,037	1,282	1,446	2,376	2,557
Private nonguaranteed	0	21	446	496	999	1,373	1,401	2,187
Use of IMF credit	70	175	176	164	158	135	587	741
Short-term external debt	2	44	298	307	459	453	521	618
interest arrears on long-term	1	6	0	0	0	0	0	0
Memorandum items								
Principal arrears on long-term	75	4	0	0	0	0	0	0
Long-term public sector debt	298	675	923	1,037	1,282	1,446	2,376	2,557
Long-term private sector debt	0	21	446	496	999	1,373	1,401	2,187
Public & publicly guaranteed commitments	131	74	251	65	203	201	898	248
External debt flows								
Disbursements	148	84	177	175	761	783	1,713	1,919
Long-term external debt	102	84	168	165	751	776	1,247	1,734
IMF purchases	46	0	10	10	10	7	466	184
Principal repayments	3	31	104	80	82	280	323	879
Long-term external debt	3	15	69	49	58	253	300	857
IMF repurchases	0	16	34	31	24	27	23	22
Net flows	147	42	-38	104	831	497	1,458	1,137
Long-term external debt	100	69	98	116	693	523	947	877
Short-term external debt	1	-11	-112	9	152	-6	68	97
Interest payments	8	15	35	70	107	85	100	89
Long-term external debt	7	9	23	59	91	70	79	60
IMF charges	2	3	1	1	1	1	4	8
Short-term external debt	0	2	11	11	15	15	17	21
2. Other non-debt resource inflows								
Foreign direct investment	25	104	239	453	699	935	777	570
Portfolio equity	0	0	1	-1	0	-1	1	0
3. Currency composition of public and publicly guaranteed debt (%)								
Euro	..	..	8.0	8.8	9.0	8.7	6.3	5.8
Japanese yen	0.0	0.0	0.2	0.4	7.0	12.1	11.3	14.6
Pound sterling	0.0	0.0	0.0	0.0	0.0	0.0	0.0	0.0
Swiss franc	0.0	0.0	0.0	0.0	0.0	0.0	0.0	0.0
U.S.dollars	62.6	93.3	86.3	82.6	71.2	62.9	66.0	62.8
4. Average terms of new commitments								
Official creditors								
Interest (%)	1.3	0.8	0.8	0.8	1.5	1.2	2.9	1.9
Maturity (years)	32.6	35.7	39.6	32.2	24.4	32.1	19.7	20.6
Grace period (years)	9.2	10.2	10.0	10.3	8.7	8.8	5.9	5.8
Private creditors								
Interest (%)	0.0	0.0	0.0	0.0	0.0	0.0	0.0	0.7
Maturity (years)	0.0	0.0	0.0	0.0	0.0	0.0	0.0	14.4
Grace period (years)	0.0	0.0	0.0	0.0	0.0	0.0	0.0	3.9
5. Major economic aggregates								
Gross national income (GNI)	1,466	1,964	5,033	6,600	9,485	12,133	8,708	9,424
Exports of goods, services & income	354	551	1,873	2,134	2,588	2,751	2,054	2,897
Worker remit. & comp. of employees	65	87	498	658	846	1,062	769	996
Imports of goods, services & income	741	1,017	2,449	2,946	4,122	5,272	4,237	4,833
Profit remittances on FDI	..	22	170	244	332	279	332	364
Current account balance	-218	-278	-52	-117	-590	-1,383	-1,369	-1,373
International reserves	111	314	669	1,072	1,659	1,407	2,004	1,866
6. Ratios								
External debt stocks to exports (%)	104.7	166.4	98.3	93.9	112.0	123.8	237.9	210.7
External debt stocks to GNI (%)	25.3	46.6	36.6	30.4	30.6	28.1	56.1	64.8
Debt service to exports (%)	3.2	8.3	7.4	7.0	7.3	13.3	20.6	33.4
Short-term to external debt stocks (%)	0.6	4.8	16.2	15.3	15.8	13.3	10.7	10.1
Multilateral to external debt stocks (%)	56.1	52.9	43.9	45.1	35.9	32.6	29.2	24.8
Reserves to external debt stocks (%)	30.0	34.3	36.3	53.5	57.2	41.3	41.0	30.6
Reserves to imports (months)	1.8	3.7	3.3	4.4	4.8	3.2	5.7	4.6

ARMENIA

(US$ million, unless otherwise indicated)

	1995	2000	2005	2006	2007	2008	2009	2010
7. Long-term external debt								
Debt outstanding and disbursed	**298**	**697**	**1,368**	**1,533**	**2,281**	**2,818**	**3,778**	**4,744**
Public and publicly guaranteed	298	675	923	1,037	1,282	1,446	2,376	2,557
Official creditors	298	658	921	1,036	1,281	1,444	2,375	2,556
Multilateral	208	485	808	905	1,041	1,111	1,427	1,513
of which: IBRD	5	8	6	6	5	5	53	106
IDA	91	388	746	841	965	1,025	1,161	1,161
Bilateral	90	173	113	131	240	333	948	1,042
Private creditors	0	17	1	1	1	1	1	1
of which: Bonds	0	0	0	0	0	0	0	0
Commercial banks	0	5	0	0	0	0	0	0
Private nonguaranteed	0	21	446	496	999	1,373	1,401	2,187
of which: Bonds	0	0	0	0	0	0	0	0
Disbursements	**102**	**84**	**168**	**165**	**751**	**776**	**1,247**	**1,734**
Public and publicly guaranteed	102	63	50	83	207	164	941	198
Official creditors	102	62	50	83	207	164	941	198
Multilateral	102	58	37	72	110	92	324	127
of which: IBRD	3	0	0	0	0	0	49	53
IDA	88	54	34	64	93	80	142	36
Bilateral	0	4	14	11	97	72	617	71
Private creditors	0	1	0	0	0	0	0	0
of which: Bonds	0	0	0	0	0	0	0	0
Commercial banks	0	0	0	0	0	0	0	0
Private nonguaranteed	0	21	117	82	544	612	306	1,536
of which: Bonds	0	0	0	0	0	0	0	0
Principal repayments	**3**	**15**	**69**	**49**	**58**	**253**	**300**	**857**
Public and publicly guaranteed	3	15	16	17	17	15	21	24
Official creditors	3	13	16	17	17	15	21	24
Multilateral	0	8	14	15	15	13	15	18
of which: IBRD	0	0	1	1	1	1	1	1
IDA	0	0	3	6	7	11	14	15
Bilateral	3	5	2	2	2	2	6	6
Private creditors	0	2	0	0	0	0	0	0
of which: Bonds	0	0	0	0	0	0	0	0
Commercial banks	0	0	0	0	0	0	0	0
Private nonguaranteed	0	0	53	32	42	238	279	833
of which: Bonds	0	0	0	0	0	0	0	0
Interest payments	**7**	**9**	**23**	**59**	**91**	**70**	**79**	**60**
Public and publicly guaranteed	7	9	9	9	10	11	23	35
Official creditors	7	9	9	9	10	11	23	35
Multilateral	7	8	8	8	8	9	9	12
of which: IBRD	0	0	0	0	0	0	0	1
IDA	0	3	6	6	7	8	8	8
Bilateral	0	1	2	2	2	2	14	23
Private creditors	0	0	0	0	0	0	0	0
of which: Bonds	0	0	0	0	0	0	0	0
Commercial banks	0	0	0	0	0	0	0	0
Private nonguaranteed	0	0	14	49	81	58	56	25
of which: Bonds	0	0	0	0	0	0	0	0
8. Debt stock-flow reconciliation								
Total change in external debt stocks	156	15	-127	162	894	508	1,480	1,217
Net flows on external debt	147	42	-38	104	831	497	1,458	1,137
9. Debt restructurings								
Total amount rescheduled	0	14	0	0	0	0	0	0
Total amount forgiven	0	0	0	0	0	0	0	0
Debt buyback	0	0	0	0	0	0	0	0

10. Contractual obligations on outstanding long-term external debt

	2011	2012	2013	2014	2015	2016	2017	2018
Official creditors								
Principal	28	30	81	98	111	120	134	144
Interest	36	38	38	37	36	34	32	30
Private creditors								
Principal	560	416	366	239	184	140	113	90
Interest	95	71	49	36	25	17	10	5

Notes:

Short-term debt is based on reports provided by the country.

AZERBAIJAN

(US$ million, unless otherwise indicated)

	1995	2000	2005	2006	2007	2008	2009	2010
1. Summary external debt data								
External debt stocks	**321**	**1,384**	**1,941**	**2,492**	**3,521**	**4,263**	**4,531**	**6,974**
Long-term external debt	206	892	1,591	1,838	2,375	3,014	3,660	6,050
Public and publicly guaranteed	206	794	1,404	1,734	2,232	2,687	3,346	3,892
Private nonguaranteed	0	99	187	104	143	327	314	2,158
Use of IMF credit	101	336	164	134	103	79	62	46
Short-term external debt	14	156	186	520	1,043	1,169	810	878
interest arrears on long-term	6	0	0	0	0	0	0	0
Memorandum items								
Principal arrears on long-term	36	0	0	0	0	0	0	0
Long-term public sector debt	206	794	1,404	1,734	2,232	2,687	3,346	3,892
Long-term private sector debt	0	99	187	104	143	327	314	2,158
Public & publicly guaranteed commitments	188	202	1,387	412	723	1,928	1,627	823
External debt flows								
Disbursements	205	306	449	468	490	741	870	2,780
Long-term external debt	102	306	430	468	490	741	870	2,780
IMF purchases	103	0	19	0	0	0	0	0
Principal repayments	0	74	200	206	90	174	264	315
Long-term external debt	0	22	152	169	53	152	246	300
IMF repurchases	0	51	48	37	37	22	19	15
Net flows	207	360	298	596	923	694	247	2,532
Long-term external debt	102	284	279	299	437	589	624	2,479
Short-term external debt	2	127	48	334	523	126	-359	68
Interest payments	10	56	35	55	97	122	83	95
Long-term external debt	9	37	26	39	78	88	64	75
IMF charges	1	14	2	2	1	1	0	0
Short-term external debt	0	5	6	15	18	33	19	20
2. Other non-debt resource inflows								
Foreign direct investment	330	130	1,680	-584	-4,749	15	473	563
Portfolio equity	0	0	0	1	2	0	0	1
3. Currency composition of public and publicly guaranteed debt (%)								
Euro	..	..	13.6	19.6	22.3	21.1	27.0	28.9
Japanese yen	0.0	19.3	26.6	20.9	17.1	17.6	12.7	13.8
Pound sterling	0.0	0.0	0.0	0.0	0.0	0.0	0.0	0.0
Swiss franc	0.0	12.1	3.3	2.3	1.7	1.4	1.0	0.6
U.S.dollars	51.4	61.1	51.9	50.9	51.0	51.6	51.3	49.4
4. Average terms of new commitments								
Official creditors								
Interest (%)	1.4	4.3	2.3	4.3	4.9	2.7	1.4	1.5
Maturity (years)	32.2	22.6	28.8	24.7	20.1	21.5	25.2	17.6
Grace period (years)	9.4	4.7	7.7	8.0	4.2	4.8	6.6	4.7
Private creditors								
Interest (%)	0.0	8.2	3.5	6.0	6.6	4.8	4.5	3.0
Maturity (years)	0.0	11.4	13.3	12.0	9.8	13.0	14.0	10.0
Grace period (years)	0.0	1.1	3.0	0.5	1.3	5.0	3.5	2.5
5. Major economic aggregates								
Gross national income (GNI)	3,039	4,987	11,599	18,302	27,970	40,992	40,255	46,870
Exports of goods, services & income	795	2,174	8,534	14,235	22,845	32,728	23,398	29,216
Worker remit. & comp. of employees	3	57	693	813	1,287	1,554	1,274	1,432
Imports of goods, services & income	1,306	2,415	8,850	11,093	14,831	17,325	13,942	14,686
Profit remittances on FDI	0	317	1,582	2,624	4,995	5,401	3,664	3,815
Current account balance	-401	-168	167	3,708	9,019	16,454	10,178	15,040
International reserves	121	680	1,178	2,500	4,273	6,467	5,364	6,409
6. Ratios								
External debt stocks to exports (%)	40.4	63.7	22.7	17.5	15.4	13.0	19.4	23.9
External debt stocks to GNI (%)	10.6	27.8	16.7	13.6	12.6	10.4	11.3	14.9
Debt service to exports (%)	1.3	6.0	2.8	1.8	0.8	0.9	1.5	1.4
Short-term to external debt stocks (%)	4.4	11.3	9.6	20.9	29.6	27.4	17.9	12.6
Multilateral to external debt stocks (%)	30.8	23.3	32.5	29.5	27.4	26.7	32.3	25.0
Reserves to external debt stocks (%)	37.7	49.1	60.7	100.3	121.3	151.7	118.4	91.9
Reserves to imports (months)	1.1	3.4	1.6	2.7	3.5	4.5	4.6	5.2

(US$ million, unless otherwise indicated)

	1995	2000	2005	2006	2007	2008	2009	2010
7. Long-term external debt								
Debt outstanding and disbursed	**206**	**892**	**1,591**	**1,838**	**2,375**	**3,014**	**3,660**	**6,050**
Public and publicly guaranteed	206	794	1,404	1,734	2,232	2,687	3,346	3,892
Official creditors	206	656	1,130	1,277	1,539	1,858	2,178	2,665
Multilateral	99	323	630	735	963	1,140	1,461	1,745
of which: IBRD	0	0	0	5	21	78	199	300
IDA	30	216	501	583	660	698	739	763
Bilateral	107	333	500	542	576	719	717	920
Private creditors	0	138	274	457	693	829	1,168	1,226
of which: Bonds	0	0	0	0	0	0	0	0
Commercial banks	0	113	274	403	552	634	949	1,023
Private nonguaranteed	0	99	187	104	143	327	314	2,158
of which: Bonds	0	0	0	0	0	0	0	0
Disbursements	**102**	**306**	**430**	**468**	**490**	**741**	**870**	**2,780**
Public and publicly guaranteed	102	300	306	443	443	526	820	866
Official creditors	102	213	70	266	233	283	431	559
Multilateral	90	56	57	211	219	213	367	353
of which: IBRD	0	0	0	5	16	56	122	101
IDA	30	27	48	60	58	50	45	46
Bilateral	13	157	13	55	14	70	64	206
Private creditors	0	88	236	177	210	242	389	307
of which: Bonds	0	0	0	0	0	0	0	0
Commercial banks	0	84	236	121	119	167	346	296
Private nonguaranteed	0	6	124	25	47	216	50	1,914
of which: Bonds	0	0	0	0	0	0	0	0
Principal repayments	**0**	**22**	**152**	**169**	**53**	**152**	**246**	**300**
Public and publicly guaranteed	0	15	55	53	43	129	193	228
Official creditors	0	13	38	34	26	49	115	101
Multilateral	0	9	18	17	21	29	54	42
of which: IBRD	0	0	0	0	0	0	0	0
IDA	0	0	2	4	6	8	9	10
Bilateral	0	4	21	17	5	20	61	58
Private creditors	0	2	16	19	16	80	78	128
of which: Bonds	0	0	0	0	0	0	0	0
Commercial banks	0	0	16	17	13	59	59	101
Private nonguaranteed	0	7	97	116	11	23	53	72
of which: Bonds	0	0	0	0	0	0	0	0
Interest payments	**9**	**37**	**26**	**39**	**78**	**88**	**64**	**75**
Public and publicly guaranteed	9	32	19	32	71	77	52	62
Official creditors	9	31	16	18	34	29	31	27
Multilateral	2	7	9	11	26	21	22	19
of which: IBRD	0	0	0	1	1	3	5	4
IDA	0	2	4	4	5	5	5	6
Bilateral	7	24	7	7	8	8	9	9
Private creditors	0	1	4	14	37	48	21	35
of which: Bonds	0	0	0	0	0	0	0	0
Commercial banks	0	0	4	13	24	35	15	32
Private nonguaranteed	0	5	7	7	7	11	12	13
of which: Bonds	0	0	0	0	0	0	0	0
8. Debt stock-flow reconciliation								
Total change in external debt stocks	208	306	94	551	1,030	741	269	2,442
Net flows on external debt	207	360	298	596	923	694	247	2,532
9. Debt restructurings								
Total amount rescheduled	0	0	0	0	0	0	0	0
Total amount forgiven	0	0	0	0	0	0	0	0
Debt buyback	0	0	0	0	0	0	0	0

10. Contractual obligations on outstanding long-term external debt

	2011	2012	2013	2014	2015	2016	2017	2018
Official creditors								
Principal	135	199	249	299	312	350	351	355
Interest	46	52	54	59	58	55	51	47
Private creditors								
Principal	183	203	278	256	245	225	207	182
Interest	48	48	45	38	32	26	21	16

Notes:

Long-term private nonguaranteed debt data cover European Bank for Reconstruction and Development and other private creditors.

BANGLADESH

(US$ million, unless otherwise indicated)

	1995	2000	2005	2006	2007	2008	2009	2010
1. Summary external debt data								
External debt stocks	**15,726**	**15,535**	**18,381**	**20,035**	**21,298**	**22,880**	**23,802**	**24,963**
Long-term external debt	14,905	14,985	17,385	18,380	19,428	20,300	21,187	21,371
Public and publicly guaranteed	14,905	14,985	17,385	18,380	19,428	20,300	21,187	21,371
Private nonguaranteed	0	0	0	0	0	0	0	0
Use of IMF credit	622	216	308	476	501	686	675	617
Short-term external debt	199	334	688	1,178	1,370	1,894	1,940	2,974
interest arrears on long-term	15	0	16	0	4	1	1	2
Memorandum items								
Principal arrears on long-term	13	4	1	3	53	11	7	22
Long-term public sector debt	14,905	14,985	17,385	18,380	19,428	20,300	21,187	21,371
Long-term private sector debt	0	0	0	0	0	0	0	0
Public & publicly guaranteed commitments	716	588	1,106	1,322	1,997	2,751	1,796	2,007
External debt flows								
Disbursements	757	861	976	1,213	1,080	1,939	1,499	963
Long-term external debt	757	861	878	1,063	1,080	1,732	1,499	963
IMF purchases	0	0	97	150	0	206	0	0
Principal repayments	574	572	566	482	735	640	727	780
Long-term external debt	513	487	566	482	735	632	703	734
IMF repurchases	61	86	0	0	0	8	23	46
Net flows	182	368	370	1,237	532	1,826	818	1,216
Long-term external debt	244	374	312	581	344	1,100	795	229
Short-term external debt	-1	80	-40	506	188	527	46	1,033
Interest payments	180	194	233	228	255	249	228	233
Long-term external debt	167	165	197	167	180	203	197	199
IMF charges	3	7	1	2	2	7	6	3
Short-term external debt	10	22	35	59	72	39	25	32
2. Other non-debt resource inflows								
Foreign direct investment	2	280	813	697	653	1,010	713	968
Portfolio equity	-15	1	20	31	153	-48	-153	..
3. Currency composition of public and publicly guaranteed debt (%)								
Euro	..	..	0.7	0.8	0.9	0.7	0.6	0.5
Japanese yen	25.6	20.3	14.2	12.5	10.4	10.0	9.0	9.8
Pound sterling	3.5	3.0	2.1	1.9	1.7	1.5	1.4	1.2
Swiss franc	0.0	0.0	0.0	0.0	0.0	0.0	0.0	0.0
U.S.dollars	41.7	44.3	50.7	52.3	51.9	52.4	53.5	52.7
4. Average terms of new commitments								
Official creditors								
Interest (%)	1.9	2.4	1.5	2.0	2.1	1.2	2.0	0.9
Maturity (years)	38.2	28.4	35.2	33.6	32.4	37.6	25.4	35.8
Grace period (years)	10.0	7.4	9.2	8.7	8.2	9.5	7.3	9.3
Private creditors								
Interest (%)	0.0	3.0	0.0	0.0	0.0	0.0	0.0	0.0
Maturity (years)	0.0	12.7	0.0	0.0	0.0	0.0	0.0	0.0
Grace period (years)	0.0	3.2	0.0	0.0	0.0	0.0	0.0	0.0
5. Major economic aggregates								
Gross national income (GNI)	39,097	48,857	63,355	65,952	73,523	86,607	97,485	109,438
Exports of goods, services & income	4,702	7,293	10,668	13,065	14,335	17,690	17,098	21,765
Worker remit. & comp. of employees	1,202	1,968	4,315	5,428	6,562	8,941	10,521	10,852
Imports of goods, services & income	7,790	10,018	15,618	17,802	20,766	26,382	24,522	30,595
Profit remittances on FDI	0	149	661	765	903	840	1,105	1,164
Current account balance	-824	-306	-176	1,196	857	926	3,556	2,502
International reserves	2,376	1,516	2,825	3,877	5,277	5,787	10,342	11,175
6. Ratios								
External debt stocks to exports (%)	334.5	213.0	172.3	153.3	148.6	129.3	139.2	114.7
External debt stocks to GNI (%)	40.2	31.8	29.0	30.4	29.0	26.4	24.4	22.8
Debt service to exports (%)	16.1	10.5	7.5	5.4	6.9	5.0	5.6	4.7
Short-term to external debt stocks (%)	1.3	2.2	3.7	5.9	6.4	8.3	8.2	11.9
Multilateral to external debt stocks (%)	61.5	70.8	76.4	74.6	76.6	75.6	77.2	74.0
Reserves to external debt stocks (%)	15.1	9.8	15.4	19.4	24.8	25.3	43.4	44.8
Reserves to imports (months)	3.7	1.8	2.2	2.6	3.0	2.6	5.1	4.4

BANGLADESH

(US$ million, unless otherwise indicated)

	1995	2000	2005	2006	2007	2008	2009	2010
7. Long-term external debt								
Debt outstanding and disbursed	**14,905**	**14,985**	**17,385**	**18,380**	**19,428**	**20,300**	**21,187**	**21,371**
Public and publicly guaranteed	14,905	14,985	17,385	18,380	19,428	20,300	21,187	21,371
Official creditors	14,727	14,809	17,201	18,217	19,280	20,202	21,103	21,303
Multilateral	9,669	10,998	14,044	14,947	16,315	17,296	18,376	18,460
of which: IBRD	55	24	0	0	0	0	0	0
IDA	5,638	6,431	8,688	9,297	10,077	10,613	10,746	10,653
Bilateral	5,057	3,810	3,157	3,270	2,965	2,907	2,726	2,842
Private creditors	179	176	184	163	148	98	84	69
of which: Bonds	0	0	0	0	0	0	0	0
Commercial banks	12	15	32	30	26	18	15	10
Private nonguaranteed	0	0	0	0	0	0	0	0
of which: Bonds	0	0	0	0	0	0	0	0
Disbursements	**757**	**861**	**878**	**1,063**	**1,080**	**1,732**	**1,499**	**963**
Public and publicly guaranteed	757	861	878	1,063	1,080	1,732	1,499	963
Official creditors	677	794	878	1,063	1,080	1,706	1,499	963
Multilateral	494	650	814	742	1,008	1,451	1,430	850
of which: IBRD	0	0	0	0	0	0	0	0
IDA	198	357	547	398	602	820	297	326
Bilateral	183	145	64	321	71	255	69	113
Private creditors	79	67	0	0	0	27	0	0
of which: Bonds	0	0	0	0	0	0	0	0
Commercial banks	0	15	0	0	0	0	0	0
Private nonguaranteed	0	0	0	0	0	0	0	0
of which: Bonds	0	0	0	0	0	0	0	0
Principal repayments	**513**	**487**	**566**	**482**	**735**	**632**	**703**	**734**
Public and publicly guaranteed	513	487	566	482	735	632	703	734
Official creditors	414	465	551	459	719	612	690	723
Multilateral	104	168	290	328	383	434	477	498
of which: IBRD	5	5	0	0	0	0	0	0
IDA	41	82	153	172	193	213	234	243
Bilateral	310	297	260	131	335	178	214	225
Private creditors	99	22	16	24	17	20	13	11
of which: Bonds	0	0	0	0	0	0	0	0
Commercial banks	2	0	5	5	5	5	3	5
Private nonguaranteed	0	0	0	0	0	0	0	0
of which: Bonds	0	0	0	0	0	0	0	0
Interest payments	**167**	**165**	**197**	**167**	**180**	**203**	**197**	**199**
Public and publicly guaranteed	167	165	197	167	180	203	197	199
Official creditors	162	156	195	166	178	199	195	197
Multilateral	87	93	133	137	144	161	157	160
of which: IBRD	4	2	0	0	0	0	0	0
IDA	42	47	70	70	72	77	79	78
Bilateral	75	63	62	29	34	38	38	37
Private creditors	5	9	2	2	2	3	2	2
of which: Bonds	0	0	0	0	0	0	0	0
Commercial banks	0	0	0	1	1	1	0	0
Private nonguaranteed	0	0	0	0	0	0	0	0
of which: Bonds	0	0	0	0	0	0	0	0
8. Debt stock-flow reconciliation								
Total change in external debt stocks	244	-845	-1,205	1,653	1,263	1,582	922	1,161
Net flows on external debt	182	368	370	1,237	532	1,826	818	1,216
9. Debt restructurings								
Total amount rescheduled	0	0	0	0	0	0	0	0
Total amount forgiven	0	0	0	83	158	533	0	0
Debt buyback	0	0	0	0	0	0	0	0

10. Contractual obligations on outstanding long-term external debt

	2011	2012	2013	2014	2015	2016	2017	2018
Official creditors								
Principal	798	837	1,130	1,151	949	1,005	1,051	1,105
Interest	236	242	244	237	229	227	221	218
Private creditors								
Principal	23	20	15	15	2	2	2	2
Interest	2	2	1	1	0	0	0	0

BELARUS

(US$ million, unless otherwise indicated)

	1995	2000	2005	2006	2007	2008	2009	2010
1. Summary external debt data								
External debt stocks	**1,694**	**2,140**	**4,737**	**5,352**	**10,341**	**12,266**	**17,490**	**25,726**
Long-term external debt	1,302	787	1,233	1,697	3,463	5,308	6,594	10,251
Public and publicly guaranteed	1,301	689	786	842	2,338	3,719	4,823	7,850
Private nonguaranteed	0	98	448	855	1,125	1,589	1,772	2,401
Use of IMF credit	283	114	0	0	0	0	2,871	3,495
Short-term external debt	110	1,239	3,503	3,654	6,878	6,959	8,024	11,980
interest arrears on long-term	19	14	1	4	2	2	3	0
Memorandum items								
Principal arrears on long-term	140	29	37	22	10	4	19	0
Long-term public sector debt	1,301	689	777	837	2,336	3,719	4,823	7,850
Long-term private sector debt	0	98	456	860	1,127	1,589	1,772	2,401
Public & publicly guaranteed commitments	145	136	412	174	1,639	1,961	1,492	3,582
External debt flows								
Disbursements	441	249	648	747	2,532	2,709	4,980	5,675
Long-term external debt	258	249	648	747	2,532	2,709	2,154	5,007
IMF purchases	182	0	0	0	0	0	2,825	668
Principal repayments	108	261	519	483	757	858	866	905
Long-term external debt	108	206	510	483	757	858	866	905
IMF repurchases	0	56	9	0	0	0	0	0
Net flows	369	-89	695	412	5,000	1,932	5,178	8,729
Long-term external debt	150	43	138	264	1,775	1,851	1,289	4,102
Short-term external debt	36	-76	566	148	3,225	82	1,064	3,959
Interest payments	74	107	161	250	322	349	313	506
Long-term external debt	59	39	51	72	81	232	172	239
IMF charges	10	7	0	0	0	0	13	66
Short-term external debt	4	61	111	178	241	117	128	201
2. Other non-debt resource inflows								
Foreign direct investment	15	119	305	354	1,785	2,181	1,884	1,403
Portfolio equity	0	1	1	-1	5	1	1	1
3. Currency composition of public and publicly guaranteed debt (%)								
Euro	..	..	14.4	26.0	9.9	4.1	7.7	15.8
Japanese yen	2.3	2.2	1.1	0.7	0.1	0.0	0.0	0.2
Pound sterling	0.0	0.0	0.0	0.0	0.0	0.0	0.0	0.0
Swiss franc	0.7	0.1	0.0	0.0	0.0	0.0	0.0	0.0
U.S.dollars	50.8	48.9	71.8	61.1	85.5	93.3	89.4	70.5
4. Average terms of new commitments								
Official creditors								
Interest (%)	5.1	6.8	5.0	5.9	4.6	6.1	4.1	6.9
Maturity (years)	16.0	5.9	7.6	16.9	14.9	12.1	13.4	4.9
Grace period (years)	5.6	2.4	1.4	5.4	5.4	4.2	4.7	2.7
Private creditors								
Interest (%)	8.1	7.2	8.9	7.2	4.8	0.0	3.2	8.8
Maturity (years)	5.8	2.5	1.1	2.3	3.0	0.0	9.0	5.1
Grace period (years)	1.6	1.0	1.1	1.3	1.0	0.0	2.3	5.1
5. Major economic aggregates								
Gross national income (GNI)	13,922	12,690	30,266	37,206	45,546	61,149	49,507	54,989
Exports of goods, services & income	5,271	7,667	18,350	22,482	27,901	37,696	25,341	30,400
Worker remit. & comp. of employees	29	139	255	340	354	443	358	376
Imports of goods, services & income	5,805	8,160	18,079	24,134	31,124	42,855	31,793	39,021
Profit remittances on FDI	0	5	135	236	435	682	872	1,039
Current account balance	-458	-338	436	-1,448	-3,032	-4,988	-6,178	-8,317
International reserves	377	350	1,342	1,386	4,179	3,063	5,640	5,025
6. Ratios								
External debt stocks to exports (%)	32.1	27.9	25.8	23.8	37.1	32.5	69.0	84.6
External debt stocks to GNI (%)	12.2	16.9	15.6	14.4	22.7	20.1	35.3	46.8
Debt service to exports (%)	3.4	4.8	3.7	3.3	3.9	3.2	4.7	4.6
Short-term to external debt stocks (%)	6.5	57.9	74.0	68.3	66.5	56.7	45.9	46.6
Multilateral to external debt stocks (%)	11.1	10.1	1.7	1.2	0.5	0.4	1.5	1.1
Reserves to external debt stocks (%)	22.3	16.4	28.3	25.9	40.4	25.0	32.2	19.5
Reserves to imports (months)	0.8	0.5	0.9	0.7	1.6	0.9	2.1	1.5

(US$ million, unless otherwise indicated)

	1995	2000	2005	2006	2007	2008	2009	2010
7. Long-term external debt								
Debt outstanding and disbursed	**1,302**	**787**	**1,233**	**1,697**	**3,463**	**5,308**	**6,594**	**10,251**
Public and publicly guaranteed	1,301	689	786	842	2,338	3,719	4,823	7,850
Official creditors	769	400	566	571	2,076	3,547	4,694	5,882
Multilateral	188	217	81	65	52	50	261	295
of which: IBRD	116	105	59	50	42	42	256	291
IDA	0	0	0	0	0	0	0	0
Bilateral	582	183	485	506	2,023	3,497	4,433	5,587
Private creditors	532	289	219	271	262	172	128	1,968
of which: Bonds	0	0	0	0	0	0	0	1,802
Commercial banks	46	56	57	102	107	68	46	110
Private nonguaranteed	0	98	448	855	1,125	1,589	1,772	2,401
of which: Bonds	0	0	0	0	19	19	19	0
Disbursements	**258**	**249**	**648**	**747**	**2,532**	**2,709**	**2,154**	**5,007**
Public and publicly guaranteed	258	143	254	207	1,717	1,568	1,265	3,628
Official creditors	131	25	188	74	1,596	1,563	1,254	1,733
Multilateral	77	25	7	5	7	16	216	37
of which: IBRD	11	6	7	5	7	16	216	37
IDA	0	0	0	0	0	0	0	0
Bilateral	54	0	181	69	1,589	1,547	1,038	1,696
Private creditors	127	118	66	133	121	5	11	1,895
of which: Bonds	0	0	0	0	0	0	0	1,796
Commercial banks	20	48	34	83	96	0	10	99
Private nonguaranteed	0	106	395	540	815	1,141	889	1,379
of which: Bonds	0	0	0	0	19	0	0	0
Principal repayments	**108**	**206**	**510**	**483**	**757**	**858**	**866**	**905**
Public and publicly guaranteed	108	134	177	171	253	183	158	163
Official creditors	84	52	94	73	98	97	99	110
Multilateral	70	49	42	23	21	19	5	3
of which: IBRD	0	14	16	15	16	17	3	1
IDA	0	0	0	0	0	0	0	0
Bilateral	15	4	52	50	77	78	95	107
Private creditors	24	82	83	98	155	86	59	53
of which: Bonds	0	0	0	0	0	0	0	0
Commercial banks	0	28	12	42	101	35	33	32
Private nonguaranteed	0	71	333	311	505	675	708	742
of which: Bonds	0	0	0	0	0	0	0	19
Interest payments	**59**	**39**	**51**	**72**	**81**	**232**	**172**	**239**
Public and publicly guaranteed	59	38	39	45	49	176	105	154
Official creditors	32	18	17	28	30	159	97	114
Multilateral	23	17	5	4	4	3	2	2
of which: IBRD	8	6	3	3	3	2	2	2
IDA	0	0	0	0	0	0	0	0
Bilateral	10	2	12	24	26	156	94	112
Private creditors	26	19	22	16	19	17	8	40
of which: Bonds	0	0	0	0	0	0	0	37
Commercial banks	1	4	4	6	8	8	4	2
Private nonguaranteed	0	1	12	27	33	56	67	85
of which: Bonds	0	0	0	0	1	2	2	1
8. Debt stock-flow reconciliation								
Total change in external debt stocks	398	-122	708	615	4,989	1,926	5,224	8,236
Net flows on external debt	369	-89	695	412	5,000	1,932	5,178	8,729
9. Debt restructurings								
Total amount rescheduled	0	50	0	0	0	0	0	0
Total amount forgiven	0	0	0	0	0	0	15	0
Debt buyback	0	0	0	0	0	0	0	0

10. Contractual obligations on outstanding long-term external debt

	2011	2012	2013	2014	2015	2016	2017	2018
Official creditors								
Principal	190	1,216	456	601	584	509	519	496
Interest	239	236	139	119	96	77	63	49
Private creditors								
Principal	652	607	376	293	1,015	163	131	131
Interest	210	194	184	176	91	8	4	1

Notes:

Short-term debt is based on reports provided by the National Bank.

BELIZE

(US$ million, unless otherwise indicated)

	1995	*2000*	*2005*	*2006*	*2007*	*2008*	*2009*	*2010*
1. Summary external debt data								
External debt stocks	**255**	**615**	**1,021**	**1,046**	**1,060**	**1,044**	**1,071**	**1,045**
Long-term external debt	219	565	1,014	1,038	1,053	1,036	1,054	1,031
Public and publicly guaranteed	219	557	989	1,018	1,039	1,020	1,040	1,021
Private nonguaranteed	0	8	25	20	14	16	14	10
Use of IMF credit	0	0	0	0	0	0	7	7
Short-term external debt	36	50	7	8	7	7	10	7
interest arrears on long-term	1	0	7	8	7	7	10	7
Memorandum items								
Principal arrears on long-term	1	0	2	0	1	1	1	1
Long-term public sector debt	219	557	989	1,018	1,038	1,020	1,035	1,017
Long-term private sector debt	0	8	25	20	15	16	19	14
Public & publicly guaranteed commitments	29	224	199	106	581	28	90	71
External debt flows								
Disbursements	31	223	213	100	604	41	78	31
Long-term external debt	31	223	213	100	604	41	71	31
IMF purchases	0	0	0	0	0	0	7	0
Principal repayments	25	41	157	77	591	56	53	53
Long-term external debt	25	41	157	77	591	56	53	53
IMF repurchases	0	0	0	0	0	0	0	0
Net flows	27	181	55	23	13	-15	25	-22
Long-term external debt	6	182	55	23	13	-15	18	-22
Short-term external debt	21	-1	0	0	0	0	0	0
Interest payments	11	35	74	65	64	49	46	48
Long-term external debt	10	32	74	65	64	49	46	48
IMF charges	0	0	0	0	0	0	0	0
Short-term external debt	1	3	0	0	0	0	0	0
2. Other non-debt resource inflows								
Foreign direct investment	21	23	127	109	140	170	109	96
Portfolio equity	..	..	..	4	..	2	..	..
3. Currency composition of public and publicly guaranteed debt (%)								
Euro	..	..	1.6	1.7	1.6	1.1	1.5	1.3
Japanese yen	0.0	0.0	0.0	0.0	0.0	0.0	0.0	0.0
Pound sterling	10.0	1.8	0.4	0.4	0.2	0.1	0.1	0.1
Swiss franc	0.1	0.0	0.0	0.0	0.0	0.0	0.0	0.0
U.S.dollars	62.7	92.6	96.5	96.6	96.8	97.5	97.2	97.5
4. Average terms of new commitments								
Official creditors								
Interest (%)	5.9	6.3	0.0	2.9	5.1	3.8	1.9	2.0
Maturity (years)	17.9	21.1	28.4	10.5	21.6	18.9	22.2	22.5
Grace period (years)	3.9	5.3	1.0	2.4	5.4	4.3	4.6	5.3
Private creditors								
Interest (%)	8.6	9.5	4.7	0.0	4.2	4.3	0.0	0.0
Maturity (years)	4.8	8.1	7.1	0.0	22.0	22.0	0.0	0.0
Grace period (years)	0.3	3.0	1.6	0.0	12.5	12.5	0.0	0.0
5. Major economic aggregates								
Gross national income (GNI)	599	775	1,000	1,088	1,118	1,197	1,236	1,303
Exports of goods, services & income	300	441	634	800	831	872	733	834
Worker remit. & comp. of employees	14	26	46	65	75	78	80	80
Imports of goods, services & income	351	663	836	899	976	1,129	895	972
Profit remittances on FDI	8	31	35	52	87	107	56	102
Current account balance	-17	-156	-151	-25	-52	-145	-83	-46
International reserves	38	123	71	114	109	166	214	218
6. Ratios								
External debt stocks to exports (%)	85.0	139.3	161.1	130.7	127.6	119.6	146.1	125.3
External debt stocks to GNI (%)	42.6	79.3	102.0	96.2	94.8	87.2	86.6	80.3
Debt service to exports (%)	12.2	17.3	36.5	17.8	78.9	12.1	13.5	12.1
Short-term to external debt stocks (%)	14.0	8.1	0.7	0.7	0.7	0.7	0.9	0.7
Multilateral to external debt stocks (%)	35.1	22.6	22.0	21.8	23.0	22.1	23.8	24.5
Reserves to external debt stocks (%)	14.7	20.0	7.0	10.9	10.2	15.9	20.0	20.9
Reserves to imports (months)	1.3	2.2	1.0	1.5	1.3	1.8	2.9	2.7

(US$ million, unless otherwise indicated)

	1995	2000	2005	2006	2007	2008	2009	2010
7. Long-term external debt								
Debt outstanding and disbursed	**219**	**565**	**1,014**	**1,038**	**1,053**	**1,036**	**1,054**	**1,031**
Public and publicly guaranteed	219	557	989	1,018	1,039	1,020	1,040	1,021
Official creditors	175	228	348	415	391	386	417	406
Multilateral	89	139	225	228	243	230	254	256
of which: IBRD	30	40	35	30	25	21	16	12
IDA	0	0	0	0	0	0	0	0
Bilateral	86	89	124	188	148	156	162	150
Private creditors	44	328	641	603	648	635	624	615
of which: Bonds	0	75	482	466	24	22	21	21
Commercial banks	39	245	149	129	619	610	603	594
Private nonguaranteed	0	8	25	20	14	16	14	10
of which: Bonds	0	0	0	0	0	0	0	0
Disbursements	**31**	**223**	**213**	**100**	**604**	**41**	**71**	**31**
Public and publicly guaranteed	31	218	213	100	604	41	71	31
Official creditors	26	27	48	97	63	40	70	31
Multilateral	12	22	14	17	36	16	40	21
of which: IBRD	6	2	1	0	0	0	0	0
IDA	0	0	0	0	0	0	0	0
Bilateral	13	4	34	80	26	24	30	10
Private creditors	5	192	165	3	541	2	1	0
of which: Bonds	0	86	143	0	0	0	0	0
Commercial banks	5	96	12	3	541	2	1	0
Private nonguaranteed	0	5	0	0	0	0	0	0
of which: Bonds	0	0	0	0	0	0	0	0
Principal repayments	**25**	**41**	**157**	**77**	**591**	**56**	**53**	**53**
Public and publicly guaranteed	25	41	155	73	585	52	51	49
Official creditors	18	20	21	31	88	38	39	41
Multilateral	7	9	14	16	22	22	17	18
of which: IBRD	2	4	4	5	5	5	4	4
IDA	0	0	0	0	0	0	0	0
Bilateral	11	11	6	15	66	16	23	23
Private creditors	8	22	135	42	497	15	12	8
of which: Bonds	0	11	36	16	441	2	1	0
Commercial banks	5	9	98	22	52	10	8	8
Private nonguaranteed	0	0	2	5	6	4	2	4
of which: Bonds	0	0	0	0	0	0	0	0
Interest payments	**10**	**32**	**74**	**65**	**64**	**49**	**46**	**48**
Public and publicly guaranteed	10	32	73	64	64	49	45	47
Official creditors	8	12	15	17	19	17	15	13
Multilateral	4	7	10	10	11	10	8	8
of which: IBRD	2	3	2	2	2	1	1	0
IDA	0	0	0	0	0	0	0	0
Bilateral	4	4	5	7	8	7	7	5
Private creditors	2	20	58	47	45	31	30	34
of which: Bonds	0	1	41	36	23	2	2	2
Commercial banks	2	18	16	10	21	29	28	32
Private nonguaranteed	0	0	1	1	0	0	0	1
of which: Bonds	0	0	0	0	0	0	0	0
8. Debt stock-flow reconciliation								
Total change in external debt stocks	56	219	51	25	14	-16	27	-25
Net flows on external debt	27	181	55	23	13	-15	25	-22
9. Debt restructurings								
Total amount rescheduled	0	0	0	0	0	7	0	0
Total amount forgiven	0	0	0	0	0	0	0	0
Debt buyback	0	0	0	0	0	0	0	0

10. Contractual obligations on outstanding long-term external debt

	2011	2012	2013	2014	2015	2016	2017	2018
Official creditors								
Principal	39	31	31	34	34	42	33	31
Interest	12	12	11	11	10	9	8	7
Private creditors								
Principal	12	31	9	9	8	5	5	4
Interest	29	27	26	25	24	24	23	23

Notes:

Long-term private nonguaranteed debt data are World Bank staff estimates.

BENIN

(US$ million, unless otherwise indicated)

	1995	*2000*	*2005*	*2006*	*2007*	*2008*	*2009*	*2010*
1. Summary external debt data								
External debt stocks	**1,397**	**1,388**	**1,538**	**641**	**764**	**917**	**1,072**	**1,221**
Long-term external debt	1,265	1,238	1,444	597	755	857	990	1,134
Public and publicly guaranteed	1,265	1,238	1,444	597	755	857	990	1,134
Private nonguaranteed	0	0	0	0	0	0	0	0
Use of IMF credit	84	84	53	3	4	22	39	55
Short-term external debt	47	66	41	41	5	37	44	32
interest arrears on long-term	8	1	2	2	5	4	32	25
Memorandum items								
Principal arrears on long-term	71	2	6	8	9	13	36	41
Long-term public sector debt	1,265	1,238	1,444	597	755	857	990	1,134
Long-term private sector debt	0	0	0	0	0	0	0	0
Public & publicly guaranteed commitments	113	140	266	91	228	147	232	284
External debt flows								
Disbursements	104	48	98	162	160	162	166	209
Long-term external debt	90	39	97	161	158	143	150	193
IMF purchases	14	9	1	1	1	19	16	16
Principal repayments	25	53	31	27	18	17	25	30
Long-term external debt	23	43	24	27	18	17	25	30
IMF repurchases	2	11	7	0	0	0	0	0
Net flows	95	-54	82	135	102	178	120	175
Long-term external debt	67	-4	73	134	140	127	125	163
Short-term external debt	16	-48	15	0	-39	33	-21	-5
Interest payments	23	21	16	14	11	42	12	13
Long-term external debt	21	16	14	12	10	41	12	13
IMF charges	0	0	0	0	0	0	0	0
Short-term external debt	2	4	2	2	1	0	0	0
2. Other non-debt resource inflows								
Foreign direct investment	13	60	53	53	255	170	134	111
Portfolio equity	0	0	2	0	5	-2	9	..
3. Currency composition of public and publicly guaranteed debt (%)								
Euro	..	..	4.4	4.9	3.8	3.2	5.3	9.7
Japanese yen	0.0	2.6	0.0	0.0	0.0	0.0	0.0	0.0
Pound sterling	0.5	0.3	0.0	0.0	0.0	0.0	0.0	0.0
Swiss franc	0.0	0.0	0.0	0.0	0.0	0.0	0.0	0.0
U.S.dollars	45.0	54.7	50.6	27.0	27.8	24.3	21.5	19.9
4. Average terms of new commitments								
Official creditors								
Interest (%)	1.7	1.9	1.3	1.2	1.5	1.5	1.3	1.0
Maturity (years)	32.4	32.7	30.4	32.6	32.5	30.1	36.8	31.5
Grace period (years)	8.9	8.3	9.3	8.3	8.4	8.0	8.9	9.4
Private creditors								
Interest (%)	0.0	0.0	0.0	0.0	0.0	0.0	0.0	0.0
Maturity (years)	0.0	0.0	0.0	0.0	0.0	0.0	0.0	0.0
Grace period (years)	0.0	0.0	0.0	0.0	0.0	0.0	0.0	0.0
5. Major economic aggregates								
Gross national income (GNI)	1,965	2,243	4,259	4,623	5,428	6,672	6,605	6,633
Exports of goods, services & income	638	552	797	976	1,386	1,675	..	..
Worker remit. & comp. of employees	100	87	173	224	282	251	251	248
Imports of goods, services & income	926	744	1,188	1,452	2,189	2,456	2,310	..
Profit remittances on FDI	6	1	9	15	53	30	32	..
Current account balance	-167	-81	-226	-217	-534	-536	-649	..
International reserves	198	459	655	912	1,209	1,263	1,230	1,200
6. Ratios								
External debt stocks to exports (%)	219.0	251.5	192.8	65.6	55.1	54.7	..	..
External debt stocks to GNI (%)	71.1	61.9	36.1	13.9	14.1	13.7	16.2	18.4
Debt service to exports (%)	7.5	13.5	5.9	4.2	2.1	3.5	..	..
Short-term to external debt stocks (%)	3.4	4.8	2.7	6.4	0.6	4.1	4.1	2.7
Multilateral to external debt stocks (%)	63.2	69.8	88.2	72.2	78.1	75.5	74.7	75.9
Reserves to external debt stocks (%)	14.2	33.1	42.6	142.4	158.2	137.8	114.7	98.3
Reserves to imports (months)	2.6	7.4	6.6	7.5	6.6	6.2	6.4	..

(US$ million, unless otherwise indicated)

	1995	2000	2005	2006	2007	2008	2009	2010
7. Long-term external debt								
Debt outstanding and disbursed	**1,265**	**1,238**	**1,444**	**597**	**755**	**857**	**990**	**1,134**
Public and publicly guaranteed	1,265	1,238	1,444	597	755	857	990	1,134
Official creditors	1,261	1,235	1,444	597	755	857	990	1,134
Multilateral	882	969	1,356	463	597	692	801	927
of which: IBRD	0	0	0	0	0	0	0	0
IDA	498	578	771	126	176	255	309	383
Bilateral	379	266	88	134	159	165	188	207
Private creditors	4	3	0	0	0	0	0	0
of which: Bonds	0	0	0	0	0	0	0	0
Commercial banks	0	0	0	0	0	0	0	0
Private nonguaranteed	0	0	0	0	0	0	0	0
of which: Bonds	0	0	0	0	0	0	0	0
Disbursements	**90**	**39**	**97**	**161**	**158**	**143**	**150**	**193**
Public and publicly guaranteed	90	39	97	161	158	143	150	193
Official creditors	90	39	97	161	158	143	150	193
Multilateral	80	27	92	85	138	138	117	166
of which: IBRD	0	0	0	0	0	0	0	0
IDA	31	36	49	32	43	84	51	79
Bilateral	10	12	4	75	21	5	33	27
Private creditors	0	0	0	0	0	0	0	0
of which: Bonds	0	0	0	0	0	0	0	0
Commercial banks	0	0	0	0	0	0	0	0
Private nonguaranteed	0	0	0	0	0	0	0	0
of which: Bonds	0	0	0	0	0	0	0	0
Principal repayments	**23**	**43**	**24**	**27**	**18**	**17**	**25**	**30**
Public and publicly guaranteed	23	43	24	27	18	17	25	30
Official creditors	23	43	20	27	18	17	25	30
Multilateral	16	14	20	21	17	14	17	21
of which: IBRD	0	0	0	0	0	0	0	0
IDA	3	4	6	3	0	0	0	0
Bilateral	7	28	1	6	2	3	8	8
Private creditors	0	0	4	0	0	0	0	0
of which: Bonds	0	0	0	0	0	0	0	0
Commercial banks	0	0	0	0	0	0	0	0
Private nonguaranteed	0	0	0	0	0	0	0	0
of which: Bonds	0	0	0	0	0	0	0	0
Interest payments	**21**	**16**	**14**	**12**	**10**	**41**	**12**	**13**
Public and publicly guaranteed	21	16	14	12	10	41	12	13
Official creditors	21	16	14	12	10	41	12	13
Multilateral	8	11	13	12	10	24	10	11
of which: IBRD	0	0	0	0	0	0	0	0
IDA	4	4	6	4	1	2	2	2
Bilateral	12	5	1	1	1	17	2	2
Private creditors	0	0	0	0	0	0	0	0
of which: Bonds	0	0	0	0	0	0	0	0
Commercial banks	0	0	0	0	0	0	0	0
Private nonguaranteed	0	0	0	0	0	0	0	0
of which: Bonds	0	0	0	0	0	0	0	0
8. Debt stock-flow reconciliation								
Total change in external debt stocks	14	-88	-60	-897	123	153	156	149
Net flows on external debt	95	-54	82	135	102	178	120	175
9. Debt restructurings								
Total amount rescheduled	5	53	0	0	0	0	0	0
Total amount forgiven	139	7	15	1,076	0	6	0	0
Debt buyback	0	0	0	0	0	0	0	0

10. Contractual obligations on outstanding long-term external debt

	2011	2012	2013	2014	2015	2016	2017	2018
Official creditors								
Principal	49	52	58	60	63	60	61	61
Interest	15	17	18	18	17	16	15	14
Private creditors								
Principal	0	0	0	0	0	0	0	0
Interest	0	0	0	0	0	0	0	0

Notes:

Benin was granted debt relief effective in 2006 under MDRI.

BHUTAN

(US$ million, unless otherwise indicated)

	1995	*2000*	*2005*	*2006*	*2007*	*2008*	*2009*	*2010*
1. Summary external debt data								
External debt stocks	**105.8**	**203.8**	**649.2**	**713.3**	**793.0**	**685.5**	**751.9**	**898.2**
Long-term external debt	105.2	202.2	636.7	697.3	775.0	677.5	746.9	892.2
Public and publicly guaranteed	105.2	202.2	636.7	697.3	775.0	677.5	746.9	892.2
Private nonguaranteed	0.0	0.0	0.0	0.0	0.0	0.0	0.0	0.0
Use of IMF credit	0.0	0.0	0.0	0.0	0.0	0.0	0.0	0.0
Short-term external debt	0.6	1.5	12.5	16.0	18.0	8.0	5.0	6.0
interest arrears on long-term	0.6	0.0	4.5	0.0	0.0	0.0	0.0	0.0
Memorandum items								
Principal arrears on long-term	0.2	0.0	4.1	0.0	0.0	0.0	0.0	0.0
Long-term public sector debt	105.2	202.2	636.7	697.3	775.0	677.5	746.9	892.2
Long-term private sector debt	0.0	0.0	0.0	0.0	0.0	0.0	0.0	0.0
Public & publicly guaranteed commitments	24.0	85.1	60.3	25.0	556.0	0.0	175.8	1045.2
External debt flows								
Disbursements	9.9	34.8	81.9	45.2	31.9	31.7	91.9	177.8
Long-term external debt	9.9	34.8	81.9	45.2	31.9	31.7	91.9	177.8
IMF purchases	0.0	0.0	0.0	0.0	0.0	0.0	0.0	0.0
Principal repayments	7.2	4.7	4.6	5.9	23.9	43.5	41.1	46.6
Long-term external debt	7.2	4.7	4.6	5.9	23.9	43.5	41.1	46.6
IMF repurchases	0.0	0.0	0.0	0.0	0.0	0.0	0.0	0.0
Net flows	2.7	29.6	85.3	47.3	10.0	-21.8	47.8	132.2
Long-term external debt	2.7	30.1	77.3	39.3	8.0	-11.8	50.8	131.2
Short-term external debt	0.0	-0.5	8.0	8.0	2.0	-10.0	-3.0	1.0
Interest payments	2.6	2.0	2.2	4.4	7.9	38.0	34.4	37.6
Long-term external debt	2.6	1.8	2.0	3.4	6.9	38.0	34.4	37.5
IMF charges	0.0	0.0	0.0	0.0	0.0	0.0	0.0	0.0
Short-term external debt	0.0	0.2	0.2	1.0	1.0	0.0	0.0	0.1
2. Other non-debt resource inflows								
Foreign direct investment	..	..	9.0	6.1	73.8	28.7	17.6	11.7
Portfolio equity	..	..	..	..	..	..	..	..
3. Currency composition of public and publicly guaranteed debt (%)								
Euro	..	..	9.6	10.9	11.1	11.6	11.5	10.1
Japanese yen	0.0	0.0	0.0	0.0	0.0	0.0	0.0	3.3
Pound sterling	0.0	0.0	0.0	0.0	0.0	0.0	0.0	0.0
Swiss franc	0.0	0.0	0.0	0.0	0.0	0.0	0.0	0.0
U.S.dollars	28.6	17.7	18.2	19.2	19.0	22.9	24.0	22.3
4. Average terms of new commitments								
Official creditors								
Interest (%)	1.3	3.6	0.8	1.4	9.2	0.8	4.3	9.8
Maturity (years)	33.4	32.1	28.6	32.0	19.9	38.9	24.7	22.4
Grace period (years)	11.2	10.5	7.1	8.5	7.7	9.4	6.1	8.0
Private creditors								
Interest (%)	0.0	0.0	0.0	0.0	0.0	0.0	0.0	0.0
Maturity (years)	0.0	0.0	0.0	0.0	0.0	0.0	0.0	0.0
Grace period (years)	0.0	0.0	0.0	0.0	0.0	0.0	0.0	0.0
5. Major economic aggregates								
Gross national income (GNI)	291.6	418.7	806.6	899.9	1190.9	1231.4	1229.6	1419.7
Exports of goods, services & income	..	..	..	381.9	658.0	688.6	534.8	..
Worker remit. & comp. of employees	..	..	..	2.2	2.9	3.6	4.8	4.8
Imports of goods, services & income	..	..	..	565.8	610.2	832.2	733.4	..
Profit remittances on FDI	..	..	..	0.4	1.1	1.9	1.1	..
Current account balance	..	..	..	-79.1	143.4	-26.8	-112.9	..
International reserves	130.5	317.6	467.4	545.3	699.0	764.8	890.9	1002.1
6. Ratios								
External debt stocks to exports (%)	..	..	..	186.8	120.5	99.5	140.6	..
External debt stocks to GNI (%)	36.3	48.7	80.5	79.3	66.6	55.7	61.2	63.3
Debt service to exports (%)	..	..	..	2.7	4.8	11.8	14.1	..
Short-term to external debt stocks (%)	0.5	0.8	1.9	2.2	2.3	1.2	0.7	0.7
Multilateral to external debt stocks (%)	64.5	49.4	27.3	27.4	28.2	34.7	38.0	36.9
Reserves to external debt stocks (%)	123.3	155.9	72.0	76.5	88.1	111.6	118.5	111.6
Reserves to imports (months)	..	..	..	11.6	13.7	11.0	14.6	..

	1995	2000	2005	2006	2007	2008	2009	2010
7. Long-term external debt								
Debt outstanding and disbursed	**105.2**	**202.2**	**636.7**	**697.3**	**775.0**	**677.5**	**746.9**	**892.2**
Public and publicly guaranteed	105.2	202.2	636.7	697.3	775.0	677.5	746.9	892.2
Official creditors	98.4	202.2	636.7	697.3	775.0	677.5	746.9	892.2
Multilateral	68.2	100.6	177.1	195.8	223.7	238.1	286.0	331.6
of which: IBRD	0.0	0.0	0.0	0.0	0.0	0.0	0.0	0.0
IDA	22.5	26.1	63.3	76.0	87.5	94.3	113.9	112.3
Bilateral	30.2	101.6	459.6	501.5	551.4	439.4	460.9	560.6
Private creditors	6.8	0.0	0.0	0.0	0.0	0.0	0.0	0.0
of which: Bonds	0.0	0.0	0.0	0.0	0.0	0.0	0.0	0.0
Commercial banks	0.0	0.0	0.0	0.0	0.0	0.0	0.0	0.0
Private nonguaranteed	0.0	0.0	0.0	0.0	0.0	0.0	0.0	0.0
of which: Bonds	0.0	0.0	0.0	0.0	0.0	0.0	0.0	0.0
Disbursements	**9.9**	**34.8**	**81.9**	**45.2**	**31.9**	**31.7**	**91.9**	**177.8**
Public and publicly guaranteed	9.9	34.8	81.9	45.2	31.9	31.7	91.9	177.8
Official creditors	9.9	34.8	81.9	45.2	31.9	31.7	91.9	177.8
Multilateral	5.8	11.8	22.1	15.1	21.4	14.7	51.3	50.1
of which: IBRD	0.0	0.0	0.0	0.0	0.0	0.0	0.0	0.0
IDA	1.2	3.6	8.4	10.3	8.8	8.6	19.9	2.1
Bilateral	4.1	23.0	59.9	30.1	10.5	16.9	40.6	127.8
Private creditors	0.0	0.0	0.0	0.0	0.0	0.0	0.0	0.0
of which: Bonds	0.0	0.0	0.0	0.0	0.0	0.0	0.0	0.0
Commercial banks	0.0	0.0	0.0	0.0	0.0	0.0	0.0	0.0
Private nonguaranteed	0.0	0.0	0.0	0.0	0.0	0.0	0.0	0.0
of which: Bonds	0.0	0.0	0.0	0.0	0.0	0.0	0.0	0.0
Principal repayments	**7.2**	**4.7**	**4.6**	**5.9**	**23.9**	**43.5**	**41.1**	**46.6**
Public and publicly guaranteed	7.2	4.7	4.6	5.9	23.9	43.5	41.1	46.6
Official creditors	4.9	4.7	4.6	5.9	23.9	43.5	41.1	46.6
Multilateral	0.6	1.3	2.2	2.5	2.7	3.7	5.3	6.4
of which: IBRD	0.0	0.0	0.0	0.0	0.0	0.0	0.0	0.0
IDA	0.1	0.3	0.7	0.8	0.8	1.0	1.2	1.7
Bilateral	4.3	3.4	2.5	3.4	21.2	39.8	35.7	40.2
Private creditors	2.3	0.0	0.0	0.0	0.0	0.0	0.0	0.0
of which: Bonds	0.0	0.0	0.0	0.0	0.0	0.0	0.0	0.0
Commercial banks	0.0	0.0	0.0	0.0	0.0	0.0	0.0	0.0
Private nonguaranteed	0.0	0.0	0.0	0.0	0.0	0.0	0.0	0.0
of which: Bonds	0.0	0.0	0.0	0.0	0.0	0.0	0.0	0.0
Interest payments	**2.6**	**1.8**	**2.0**	**3.4**	**6.9**	**38.0**	**34.4**	**37.5**
Public and publicly guaranteed	2.6	1.8	2.0	3.4	6.9	38.0	34.4	37.5
Official creditors	2.0	1.8	2.0	3.4	6.9	38.0	34.4	37.5
Multilateral	0.6	0.9	1.6	1.8	1.8	2.1	2.2	3.0
of which: IBRD	0.0	0.0	0.0	0.0	0.0	0.0	0.0	0.0
IDA	0.2	0.2	0.6	0.6	0.6	0.7	0.7	0.8
Bilateral	1.4	0.9	0.4	1.6	5.1	35.9	32.2	34.5
Private creditors	0.6	0.0	0.0	0.0	0.0	0.0	0.0	0.0
of which: Bonds	0.0	0.0	0.0	0.0	0.0	0.0	0.0	0.0
Commercial banks	0.0	0.0	0.0	0.0	0.0	0.0	0.0	0.0
Private nonguaranteed	0.0	0.0	0.0	0.0	0.0	0.0	0.0	0.0
of which: Bonds	0.0	0.0	0.0	0.0	0.0	0.0	0.0	0.0
8. Debt stock-flow reconciliation								
Total change in external debt stocks	1.3	20.0	55.9	64.1	79.7	-107.5	66.4	146.3
Net flows on external debt	2.7	29.6	85.3	47.3	10.0	-21.8	47.8	132.2
9. Debt restructurings								
Total amount rescheduled	0.0	0.0	0.0	0.0	0.0	0.0	0.0	0.0
Total amount forgiven	0.0	0.0	0.0	0.0	0.0	0.0	0.0	0.0
Debt buyback	0.0	0.0	0.0	0.0	0.0	0.0	0.0	0.0

10. Contractual obligations on outstanding long-term external debt

	2011	2012	2013	2014	2015	2016	2017	2018
Official creditors								
Principal	72.2	72.7	77.6	81.3	122.8	94.8	86.1	122.2
Interest	35.4	30.7	25.8	20.3	60.9	51.7	76.7	121.2
Private creditors								
Principal	0.0	0.0	0.0	0.0	0.0	0.0	0.0	0.0
Interest	0.0	0.0	0.0	0.0	0.0	0.0	0.0	0.0

BOLIVIA, PLURINATIONAL STATE OF

(US$ million, unless otherwise indicated)

	1995	*2000*	*2005*	*2006*	*2007*	*2008*	*2009*	*2010*
1. Summary external debt data								
External debt stocks	**5,272**	**5,785**	**6,908**	**5,798**	**4,992**	**5,528**	**5,743**	**5,267**
Long-term external debt	4,698	5,163	6,482	5,563	4,815	5,370	5,189	5,164
Public and publicly guaranteed	4,459	4,137	4,568	3,175	2,194	2,401	2,542	2,806
Private nonguaranteed	239	1,026	1,914	2,388	2,621	2,969	2,647	2,358
Use of IMF credit	268	220	244	15	0	0	0	0
Short-term external debt	307	402	182	220	177	158	554	103
interest arrears on long-term	20	2	0	0	0	0	0	0
Memorandum items								
Principal arrears on long-term	30	19	0	0	0	0	0	0
Long-term public sector debt	4,459	3,759	4,545	3,157	2,184	2,392	2,533	2,795
Long-term private sector debt	239	1,403	1,937	2,406	2,631	2,978	2,656	2,368
Public & publicly guaranteed commitments	684	180	551	185	1,059	1,173	1,156	881
External debt flows								
Disbursements	520	759	895	364	912	1,263	512	552
Long-term external debt	494	744	880	364	912	1,263	512	552
IMF purchases	26	15	14	0	0	0	0	0
Principal repayments	199	454	355	208	539	767	453	567
Long-term external debt	173	434	315	208	525	767	453	567
IMF repurchases	26	20	40	0	15	0	0	0
Net flows	341	294	449	194	329	477	455	-467
Long-term external debt	321	309	565	155	387	496	59	-16
Short-term external debt	20	-10	-91	38	-43	-19	396	-451
Interest payments	173	180	174	215	202	179	138	79
Long-term external debt	155	159	159	203	194	175	119	76
IMF charges	1	1	6	2	1	0	0	0
Short-term external debt	17	20	10	10	7	4	19	4
2. Other non-debt resource inflows								
Foreign direct investment	393	736	-239	281	366	512	423	622
Portfolio equity	0	0	0	0	0	0	0	0
3. Currency composition of public and publicly guaranteed debt (%)								
Euro	..	..	1.5	2.6	4.2	3.6	3.1	2.7
Japanese yen	13.2	12.3	0.0	0.0	0.0	0.0	0.0	0.0
Pound sterling	0.7	0.2	0.0	0.0	0.0	0.0	0.0	0.0
Swiss franc	0.0	0.0	0.0	0.0	0.0	0.0	0.0	0.0
U.S.dollars	32.7	45.0	75.3	66.2	76.5	79.7	82.0	84.8
4. Average terms of new commitments								
Official creditors								
Interest (%)	3.8	4.3	4.9	4.1	2.7	3.6	3.4	2.1
Maturity (years)	29.1	28.1	21.6	24.9	22.8	19.9	22.3	20.7
Grace period (years)	7.8	7.8	5.6	5.8	5.2	5.3	5.2	4.6
Private creditors								
Interest (%)	6.7	1.8	0.0	0.0	5.0	4.8	2.2	0.1
Maturity (years)	5.6	34.3	0.0	0.0	2.0	2.7	15.0	35.7
Grace period (years)	1.0	8.6	0.0	0.0	2.0	2.0	4.5	26.8
5. Major economic aggregates								
Gross national income (GNI)	6,494	8,172	9,173	11,054	12,631	16,139	16,666	18,926
Exports of goods, services & income	1,262	1,610	3,401	4,587	5,327	7,373	5,666	6,922
Worker remit. & comp. of employees	7	127	346	612	1,065	1,144	1,069	1,088
Imports of goods, services & income	1,809	2,443	3,363	4,091	5,002	6,664	6,065	7,129
Profit remittances on FDI	24	148	271	392	644	681	769	863
Current account balance	-303	-446	622	1,317	1,591	1,993	814	874
International reserves	1,005	1,184	1,795	3,194	5,314	7,720	8,575	9,731
6. Ratios								
External debt stocks to exports (%)	417.7	359.4	203.1	126.4	93.7	75.0	101.4	76.1
External debt stocks to GNI (%)	81.2	70.8	75.3	52.4	39.5	34.3	34.5	27.8
Debt service to exports (%)	29.5	39.4	15.6	9.2	13.9	12.8	10.4	9.3
Short-term to external debt stocks (%)	5.8	7.0	2.6	3.8	3.5	2.9	9.6	2.0
Multilateral to external debt stocks (%)	48.9	48.5	60.9	47.5	33.9	32.6	34.3	42.9
Reserves to external debt stocks (%)	19.1	20.5	26.0	55.1	106.4	139.7	149.3	184.8
Reserves to imports (months)	6.7	5.8	6.4	9.4	12.7	13.9	17.0	16.4

(US$ million, unless otherwise indicated)

	1995	2000	2005	2006	2007	2008	2009	2010
7. Long-term external debt								
Debt outstanding and disbursed	**4,698**	**5,163**	**6,482**	**5,563**	**4,815**	**5,370**	**5,189**	**5,164**
Public and publicly guaranteed	4,459	4,137	4,568	3,175	2,194	2,401	2,542	2,806
Official creditors	4,396	4,103	4,541	3,148	2,158	2,304	2,451	2,782
Multilateral	2,579	2,803	4,206	2,754	1,690	1,803	1,971	2,259
of which: IBRD	95	0	0	0	0	0	0	0
IDA	770	1,096	1,673	233	259	281	316	355
Bilateral	1,817	1,300	336	393	468	502	480	523
Private creditors	63	33	27	28	36	97	92	24
of which: Bonds	17	0	0	0	10	10	0	0
Commercial banks	9	3	5	8	8	74	81	14
Private nonguaranteed	239	1,026	1,914	2,388	2,621	2,969	2,647	2,358
of which: Bonds	0	0	0	0	0	0	0	0
Disbursements	**494**	**744**	**880**	**364**	**912**	**1,263**	**512**	**552**
Public and publicly guaranteed	427	276	434	259	319	590	415	522
Official creditors	427	263	429	255	308	524	408	519
Multilateral	383	238	346	183	222	458	330	436
of which: IBRD	0	0	0	0	0	0	0	0
IDA	113	61	71	34	16	25	34	46
Bilateral	45	25	83	72	86	66	79	84
Private creditors	0	13	4	4	10	67	7	3
of which: Bonds	0	0	0	0	10	0	0	0
Commercial banks	0	0	4	3	0	66	7	0
Private nonguaranteed	67	468	447	105	593	673	97	30
of which: Bonds	0	0	0	0	0	0	0	0
Principal repayments	**173**	**434**	**315**	**208**	**525**	**767**	**453**	**567**
Public and publicly guaranteed	155	153	184	200	165	375	196	246
Official creditors	147	149	182	196	161	370	184	176
Multilateral	120	118	169	181	145	351	166	138
of which: IBRD	26	12	0	0	0	0	0	0
IDA	2	0	8	5	0	1	2	2
Bilateral	27	32	13	14	16	19	18	38
Private creditors	8	4	2	4	4	5	13	70
of which: Bonds	0	0	0	0	0	0	10	0
Commercial banks	4	1	1	1	0	0	0	66
Private nonguaranteed	18	281	131	8	360	392	257	322
of which: Bonds	0	0	0	0	0	0	0	0
Interest payments	**155**	**159**	**159**	**203**	**194**	**175**	**119**	**76**
Public and publicly guaranteed	137	112	100	111	103	98	71	53
Official creditors	133	111	99	111	103	98	67	50
Multilateral	100	82	94	101	92	88	57	42
of which: IBRD	9	1	0	0	0	0	0	0
IDA	6	1	12	6	2	2	2	2
Bilateral	33	29	5	10	11	10	10	8
Private creditors	4	1	0	0	0	1	4	4
of which: Bonds	0	0	0	0	0	0	0	0
Commercial banks	1	0	0	0	0	0	3	4
Private nonguaranteed	19	47	59	92	91	77	48	22
of which: Bonds	0	0	0	0	0	0	0	0
8. Debt stock-flow reconciliation								
Total change in external debt stocks	396	237	686	-1,110	-805	536	215	-476
Net flows on external debt	341	294	449	194	329	477	455	-467
9. Debt restructurings								
Total amount rescheduled	196	0	0	0	0	0	0	0
Total amount forgiven	82	64	65	1,787	1,182	17	87	0
Debt buyback	0	0	0	0	0	0	0	0

10. Contractual obligations on outstanding long-term external debt

	2011	2012	2013	2014	2015	2016	2017	2018
Official creditors								
Principal	185	190	236	279	313	315	320	314
Interest	68	77	84	86	83	78	74	67
Private creditors								
Principal	578	514	634	220	207	103	68	202
Interest	86	63	48	17	14	11	9	13

BOSNIA AND HERZEGOVINA

(US$ million, unless otherwise indicated)

	1995	2000	2005	2006	2007	2008	2009	2010
1. Summary external debt data								
External debt stocks	**..**	**2,773**	**6,222**	**7,242**	**8,823**	**8,303**	**9,625**	**8,457**
Long-term external debt	..	2,619	5,323	6,051	7,133	7,398	7,662	6,899
Public and publicly guaranteed	..	1,957	2,556	2,716	2,958	3,000	3,570	3,751
Private nonguaranteed	..	663	2,767	3,335	4,175	4,398	4,091	3,149
Use of IMF credit	48	105	62	20	2	0	286	521
Short-term external debt	..	49	837	1,171	1,687	905	1,677	1,037
interest arrears on long-term	..	1	0	0	0	0	0	0
Memorandum items								
Principal arrears on long-term	..	1	0	0	0	0	0	0
Long-term public sector debt	..	1,957	2,556	2,716	2,958	3,000	3,570	3,751
Long-term private sector debt	..	663	2,767	3,335	4,175	4,398	4,091	3,149
Public & publicly guaranteed commitments	..	197	120	616	231	302	375	656
External debt flows								
Disbursements	..	138	536	754	1,022	471	683	771
Long-term external debt	..	103	536	754	1,022	471	401	534
IMF purchases	46	36	0	0	0	0	282	237
Principal repayments	..	190	134	188	145	139	510	1,128
Long-term external debt	..	170	95	144	127	137	510	1,128
IMF repurchases	28	20	39	44	18	2	0	0
Net flows	..	-41	879	899	1,392	-450	945	-997
Long-term external debt	..	-68	441	609	895	335	-109	-594
Short-term external debt	..	11	477	334	516	-782	772	-640
Interest payments	..	127	151	183	290	307	290	231
Long-term external debt	..	119	136	176	217	256	217	177
IMF charges	5	5	3	2	1	0	1	5
Short-term external debt	..	3	12	4	73	50	72	49
2. Other non-debt resource inflows								
Foreign direct investment	..	146	608	768	2,071	982	240	232
Portfolio equity	..	0	0	0	0	0	0	0
3. Currency composition of public and publicly guaranteed debt (%)								
Euro	..	..	33.9	35.7	38.0	38.9	48.6	51.0
Japanese yen	..	0.0	1.2	1.3	1.2	1.5	1.2	1.3
Pound sterling	..	0.0	0.0	0.0	0.0	0.0	0.0	0.0
Swiss franc	..	2.3	1.7	1.2	1.2	1.2	1.1	1.0
U.S.dollars	..	27.6	41.3	40.9	40.1	39.1	32.8	30.8
4. Average terms of new commitments								
Official creditors								
Interest (%)	..	3.7	1.9	3.1	3.9	4.7	1.7	0.9
Maturity (years)	..	23.3	17.1	20.6	22.3	16.2	16.1	22.1
Grace period (years)	..	6.7	5.9	6.9	6.1	4.3	4.8	7.4
Private creditors								
Interest (%)	..	0.0	0.0	2.9	4.2	1.2	1.0	1.4
Maturity (years)	..	0.0	0.0	12.1	15.1	13.4	13.5	13.0
Grace period (years)	..	0.0	0.0	2.9	6.9	6.0	4.5	3.5
5. Major economic aggregates								
Gross national income (GNI)	..	6,096	11,216	12,717	15,722	19,131	17,630	17,317
Exports of goods, services & income	..	2,247	4,227	5,254	6,728	8,041	6,360	6,819
Worker remit. & comp. of employees	..	1,607	2,043	2,157	2,700	2,735	2,133	1,905
Imports of goods, services & income	..	4,234	8,103	8,486	11,093	13,486	9,738	10,086
Profit remittances on FDI	..	0	97	175	344	187	-70	27
Current account balance	..	-396	-1,844	-998	-1,648	-2,605	-1,075	-1,008
International reserves	..	497	2,548	3,655	5,002	4,464	4,548	4,383
6. Ratios								
External debt stocks to exports (%)	..	123.4	147.2	137.8	131.1	103.3	151.3	124.0
External debt stocks to GNI (%)	..	45.5	55.5	57.0	56.1	43.4	54.6	48.8
Debt service to exports (%)	..	14.2	6.8	7.1	6.5	5.5	12.6	19.9
Short-term to external debt stocks (%)	..	1.8	13.5	16.2	19.1	10.9	17.4	12.3
Multilateral to external debt stocks (%)	..	45.6	27.5	24.9	22.0	23.9	22.8	28.6
Reserves to external debt stocks (%)	..	17.9	40.9	50.5	56.7	53.8	47.3	51.8
Reserves to imports (months)	..	1.4	3.8	5.2	5.4	4.0	5.6	5.2

BOSNIA AND HERZEGOVINA

(US$ million, unless otherwise indicated)

	1995	2000	2005	2006	2007	2008	2009	2010
7. Long-term external debt								
Debt outstanding and disbursed	..	**2,619**	**5,323**	**6,051**	**7,133**	**7,398**	**7,662**	**6,899**
Public and publicly guaranteed	..	1,957	2,556	2,716	2,958	3,000	3,570	3,751
Official creditors	..	1,832	2,401	2,547	2,764	2,800	3,043	3,285
Multilateral	..	1,266	1,712	1,802	1,942	1,984	2,198	2,416
of which: IBRD	472	562	481	466	453	443	417	445
IDA	0	398	921	983	1,068	1,077	1,102	1,180
Bilateral	..	566	689	744	821	816	845	869
Private creditors	..	125	155	169	195	200	527	466
of which: Bonds	..	0	0	0	0	0	322	273
Commercial banks	..	125	155	169	195	200	206	193
Private nonguaranteed	..	663	2,767	3,335	4,175	4,398	4,091	3,149
of which: Bonds	..	0	0	0	0	0	0	0
Disbursements	..	**103**	**536**	**754**	**1,022**	**471**	**401**	**534**
Public and publicly guaranteed	..	98	150	125	149	189	329	464
Official creditors	..	98	150	125	137	163	316	450
Multilateral	..	90	133	94	118	128	271	372
of which: IBRD	..	0	0	0	0	0	0	50
IDA	..	44	56	27	57	29	33	115
Bilateral	..	8	17	32	19	35	46	78
Private creditors	..	0	0	0	12	26	12	14
of which: Bonds	..	0	0	0	0	0	0	0
Commercial banks	..	0	0	0	12	26	12	14
Private nonguaranteed	..	5	386	628	873	282	73	69
of which: Bonds	..	0	0	0	0	0	0	0
Principal repayments	..	**170**	**95**	**144**	**127**	**137**	**510**	**1,128**
Public and publicly guaranteed	..	170	54	67	79	91	109	145
Official creditors	..	170	51	63	72	82	96	107
Multilateral	..	166	44	56	63	71	84	94
of which: IBRD	..	0	24	24	24	25	25	25
IDA	..	0	0	4	9	12	15	18
Bilateral	..	3	7	8	9	11	12	13
Private creditors	..	0	3	3	7	9	13	37
of which: Bonds	..	0	0	0	0	0	0	25
Commercial banks	..	0	3	3	7	9	13	13
Private nonguaranteed	..	1	41	78	48	46	401	984
of which: Bonds	..	0	0	0	0	0	0	0
Interest payments	..	**119**	**136**	**176**	**217**	**256**	**217**	**177**
Public and publicly guaranteed	..	89	53	61	70	80	63	55
Official creditors	..	86	48	56	63	70	56	47
Multilateral	..	74	35	43	49	54	41	32
of which: IBRD	..	33	17	23	26	26	17	8
IDA	..	3	7	8	8	8	8	8
Bilateral	..	13	13	13	14	16	14	15
Private creditors	..	2	6	6	6	10	8	9
of which: Bonds	..	0	0	0	0	0	0	5
Commercial banks	..	2	6	6	6	10	8	3
Private nonguaranteed	..	30	83	114	147	176	153	121
of which: Bonds	..	0	0	0	0	0	0	0
8. Debt stock-flow reconciliation								
Total change in external debt stocks	..	397	633	1,020	1,580	-520	1,322	-1,168
Net flows on external debt	..	-41	879	899	1,392	-450	945	-997
9. Debt restructurings								
Total amount rescheduled	..	4	0	0	0	0	0	0
Total amount forgiven	..	0	0	0	0	0	28	0
Debt buyback	..	0	0	0	0	0	0	0

10. Contractual obligations on outstanding long-term external debt

	2011	2012	2013	2014	2015	2016	2017	2018
Official creditors								
Principal	176	173	198	225	233	236	247	253
Interest	60	60	59	57	53	49	45	41
Private creditors								
Principal	884	678	611	368	295	229	196	147
Interest	128	94	70	48	35	25	17	11

Notes:

Data on long-term private nonguaranteed debt from 2005 are World Bank staff estimates.

BOTSWANA

(US$ million, unless otherwise indicated)

	1995	2000	2005	2006	2007	2008	2009	2010
1. Summary external debt data								
External debt stocks	**717**	**453**	**447**	**382**	**413**	**434**	**1,617**	**1,709**
Long-term external debt	707	438	412	358	391	391	1,388	1,352
Public and publicly guaranteed	707	438	412	358	391	391	1,388	1,352
Private nonguaranteed	0	0	0	0	0	0	0	0
Use of IMF credit	0	0	0	0	0	0	0	0
Short-term external debt	10	15	35	24	22	43	229	357
interest arrears on long-term	6	0	0	0	0	0	0	0
Memorandum items								
Principal arrears on long-term	9	1	0	0	0	0	0	0
Long-term public sector debt	676	432	412	358	391	391	1,388	1,352
Long-term private sector debt	31	5	0	0	0	0	0	0
Public & publicly guaranteed commitments	0	0	0	75	50	0	1,777	341
External debt flows								
Disbursements	67	28	11	4	50	54	1,006	17
Long-term external debt	67	28	11	4	50	54	1,006	17
IMF purchases	0	0	0	0	0	0	0	0
Principal repayments	64	52	40	45	37	61	36	56
Long-term external debt	64	52	40	45	37	61	36	56
IMF repurchases	0	0	0	0	0	0	0	0
Net flows	4	-29	-17	-51	11	15	1,156	89
Long-term external debt	3	-24	-30	-40	13	-6	970	-39
Short-term external debt	1	-5	13	-11	-2	21	186	128
Interest payments	27	17	13	12	10	8	11	19
Long-term external debt	27	15	12	10	9	7	9	16
IMF charges	0	0	0	0	0	0	0	0
Short-term external debt	0	1	1	2	1	1	2	4
2. Other non-debt resource inflows								
Foreign direct investment	70	57	492	751	647	895	252	529
Portfolio equity	6	-6	27	36	9	-37	18	0
3. Currency composition of public and publicly guaranteed debt (%)								
Euro	..	..	6.9	8.2	8.0	7.2	2.0	0.3
Japanese yen	11.1	11.4	17.1	10.4	13.3	13.9	3.5	3.6
Pound sterling	3.8	2.3	5.2	6.1	5.5	3.6	1.0	0.8
Swiss franc	0.1	0.1	0.1	0.0	0.0	0.0	0.0	0.0
U.S.dollars	13.4	18.0	20.5	20.8	18.3	24.9	7.7	8.1
4. Average terms of new commitments								
Official creditors								
Interest (%)	0.0	0.0	0.0	4.6	3.3	0.0	0.8	1.0
Maturity (years)	0.0	0.0	0.0	18.2	20.9	0.0	20.7	23.4
Grace period (years)	0.0	0.0	0.0	5.2	5.9	0.0	5.8	4.5
Private creditors								
Interest (%)	0.0	0.0	0.0	0.0	0.0	0.0	0.0	0.0
Maturity (years)	0.0	0.0	0.0	0.0	0.0	0.0	0.0	0.0
Grace period (years)	0.0	0.0	0.0	0.0	0.0	0.0	0.0	0.0
5. Major economic aggregates								
Gross national income (GNI)	4,741	5,280	9,416	10,483	11,638	12,841	11,514	14,771
Exports of goods, services & income	2,904	3,378	5,740	5,821	6,339	6,147	4,531	5,094
Worker remit. & comp. of employees	59	26	131	116	105	114	88	100
Imports of goods, services & income	2,565	3,050	4,851	4,755	5,649	6,719	5,935	6,383
Profit remittances on FDI	416	658	1,066	1,043	989	1,057	727	..
Current account balance	300	545	1,562	1,938	1,796	468	-526	-754
International reserves	4,695	6,318	6,309	7,992	9,790	9,119	8,704	7,885
6. Ratios								
External debt stocks to exports (%)	24.7	13.4	7.8	6.6	6.5	7.1	35.7	33.5
External debt stocks to GNI (%)	15.1	8.6	4.8	3.6	3.5	3.4	14.0	11.6
Debt service to exports (%)	3.1	2.0	0.9	1.0	0.7	1.1	1.0	1.5
Short-term to external debt stocks (%)	1.4	3.3	7.8	6.3	5.3	9.9	14.2	20.9
Multilateral to external debt stocks (%)	70.1	65.7	58.6	64.2	58.2	57.1	77.4	71.5
Reserves to external debt stocks (%)	654.7	1,395.5	1,410.5	2,091.3	2,369.9	2,102.1	538.2	461.5
Reserves to imports (months)	22.0	24.9	15.6	20.2	20.8	16.3	17.6	14.8

(US$ million, unless otherwise indicated)

	1995	2000	2005	2006	2007	2008	2009	2010
7. Long-term external debt								
Debt outstanding and disbursed	**707**	**438**	**412**	**358**	**391**	**391**	**1,388**	**1,352**
Public and publicly guaranteed	707	438	412	358	391	391	1,388	1,352
Official creditors	660	410	401	349	384	389	1,387	1,351
Multilateral	503	297	262	245	240	248	1,252	1,222
of which: IBRD	96	16	2	1	0	0	0	6
IDA	12	9	7	6	6	5	5	4
Bilateral	157	112	139	104	144	141	135	129
Private creditors	47	28	12	9	7	2	2	1
of which: Bonds	0	0	0	0	0	0	0	0
Commercial banks	33	20	7	5	4	0	0	0
Private nonguaranteed	0	0	0	0	0	0	0	0
of which: Bonds	0	0	0	0	0	0	0	0
Disbursements	**67**	**28**	**11**	**4**	**50**	**54**	**1,006**	**17**
Public and publicly guaranteed	67	28	11	4	50	54	1,006	17
Official creditors	67	24	11	4	50	54	1,006	17
Multilateral	23	8	0	2	8	44	997	16
of which: IBRD	1	0	0	0	0	0	0	6
IDA	0	0	0	0	0	0	0	0
Bilateral	44	16	11	3	43	11	9	1
Private creditors	0	4	0	0	0	0	0	0
of which: Bonds	0	0	0	0	0	0	0	0
Commercial banks	0	4	0	0	0	0	0	0
Private nonguaranteed	0	0	0	0	0	0	0	0
of which: Bonds	0	0	0	0	0	0	0	0
Principal repayments	**64**	**52**	**40**	**45**	**37**	**61**	**36**	**56**
Public and publicly guaranteed	64	52	40	45	37	61	36	56
Official creditors	58	45	38	42	35	56	35	55
Multilateral	48	33	28	30	25	26	21	41
of which: IBRD	24	7	1	1	1	0	0	0
IDA	0	0	0	0	0	0	0	0
Bilateral	9	12	10	12	10	30	14	14
Private creditors	6	7	2	2	2	5	1	1
of which: Bonds	0	0	0	0	0	0	0	0
Commercial banks	5	6	2	2	2	4	0	0
Private nonguaranteed	0	0	0	0	0	0	0	0
of which: Bonds	0	0	0	0	0	0	0	0
Interest payments	**27**	**15**	**12**	**10**	**9**	**7**	**9**	**16**
Public and publicly guaranteed	27	15	12	10	9	7	9	16
Official creditors	24	14	11	10	9	7	9	16
Multilateral	21	11	8	7	6	5	5	12
of which: IBRD	9	1	0	0	0	0	0	1
IDA	0	0	0	0	0	0	0	0
Bilateral	3	3	4	3	3	3	3	3
Private creditors	3	1	0	0	0	0	0	0
of which: Bonds	0	0	0	0	0	0	0	0
Commercial banks	2	1	0	0	0	0	0	0
Private nonguaranteed	0	0	0	0	0	0	0	0
of which: Bonds	0	0	0	0	0	0	0	0
8. Debt stock-flow reconciliation								
Total change in external debt stocks	17	-51	-63	-65	31	21	1,184	91
Net flows on external debt	4	-29	-17	-51	11	15	1,156	89
9. Debt restructurings								
Total amount rescheduled	0	0	0	0	0	0	0	0
Total amount forgiven	0	0	0	28	0	0	0	0
Debt buyback	0	0	0	0	0	0	0	0

10. Contractual obligations on outstanding long-term external debt

	2011	2012	2013	2014	2015	2016	2017	2018
Official creditors								
Principal	53	34	33	35	143	147	152	155
Interest	12	13	13	13	13	13	12	11
Private creditors								
Principal	1	1	0	0	0	0	0	0
Interest	0	0	0	0	0	0	0	0

BRAZIL

(US$ million, unless otherwise indicated)

	1995	2000	2005	2006	2007	2008	2009	2010
1. Summary external debt data								
External debt stocks	**160,469**	**241,550**	**187,526**	**193,458**	**237,605**	**262,151**	**276,910**	**346,978**
Long-term external debt	129,090	208,809	163,533	173,133	198,357	225,500	237,121	281,482
Public and publicly guaranteed	98,260	96,127	94,028	84,245	79,595	79,658	87,295	96,542
Private nonguaranteed	30,830	112,682	69,505	88,889	118,762	145,842	149,826	184,940
Use of IMF credit	142	1,768	0	0	0	0	0	0
Short-term external debt	31,238	30,973	23,993	20,325	39,248	36,652	39,789	65,496
interest arrears on long-term	1,546	176	0	2	2	8	3	4
Memorandum items								
Principal arrears on long-term	3,936	1,821	18	3	6	5	9	4
Long-term public sector debt	97,392	95,681	92,677	83,044	78,374	78,408	84,686	93,444
Long-term private sector debt	31,698	113,127	70,855	90,089	119,983	147,092	152,435	188,038
Public & publicly guaranteed commitments	7,606	30,607	12,659	9,248	11,070	12,812	25,693	15,703
External debt flows								
Disbursements	20,207	44,051	27,402	52,622	59,904	69,505	57,670	84,723
Long-term external debt	20,207	44,051	27,402	52,622	59,904	69,505	57,670	84,723
IMF purchases	0	0	0	0	0	0	0	0
Principal repayments	11,051	47,733	49,561	47,388	40,422	40,285	30,425	31,972
Long-term external debt	11,002	41,040	25,751	47,388	40,422	40,285	30,425	31,972
IMF repurchases	49	6,693	23,810	0	0	0	0	0
Net flows	8,797	-1,851	-23,433	1,564	38,405	26,618	30,386	78,458
Long-term external debt	9,205	3,011	1,651	5,234	19,482	29,220	27,244	52,752
Short-term external debt	-359	1,831	-1,274	-3,670	18,923	-2,602	3,142	25,706
Interest payments	10,522	17,111	13,282	14,785	14,514	16,175	14,165	13,835
Long-term external debt	8,719	15,280	10,303	13,150	13,025	15,037	13,675	13,150
IMF charges	10	336	1,079	109	0	0	0	0
Short-term external debt	1,792	1,494	1,900	1,526	1,489	1,138	489	684
2. Other non-debt resource inflows								
Foreign direct investment	4,859	32,779	15,066	18,782	34,585	45,058	25,949	48,438
Portfolio equity	2,775	3,076	6,451	7,716	26,217	-7,565	37,071	37,684
3. Currency composition of public and publicly guaranteed debt (%)								
Euro	..	..	9.4	10.4	9.8	9.0	7.2	6.1
Japanese yen	8.7	7.4	6.1	5.4	4.7	5.9	5.0	5.0
Pound sterling	1.8	1.0	0.2	0.3	0.0	0.1	0.1	0.1
Swiss franc	0.3	0.3	0.1	0.0	0.0	0.0	0.0	0.0
U.S.dollars	68.3	70.4	79.3	79.0	80.7	80.6	84.2	86.0
4. Average terms of new commitments								
Official creditors								
Interest (%)	5.9	5.7	4.7	6.0	4.6	3.6	2.4	0.8
Maturity (years)	19.9	8.6	18.5	17.1	16.7	23.6	15.2	25.3
Grace period (years)	4.9	1.3	4.3	4.4	3.9	3.8	5.0	4.6
Private creditors								
Interest (%)	7.7	9.9	8.7	7.5	8.5	5.4	5.6	5.0
Maturity (years)	3.3	15.5	14.5	15.1	13.7	14.1	11.2	10.4
Grace period (years)	2.1	14.2	14.0	15.0	9.4	13.6	9.0	10.1
5. Major economic aggregates								
Gross national income (GNI)	757,886	626,768	856,883	1,061,994	1,337,851	1,613,509	1,562,412	2,049,172
Exports of goods, services & income	56,098	68,205	137,550	163,708	196,096	240,904	189,549	241,089
Worker remit. & comp. of employees	3,315	1,649	3,540	4,253	4,382	5,089	4,234	4,000
Imports of goods, services & income	77,855	93,950	127,123	154,393	198,574	273,320	217,189	291,242
Profit remittances on FDI	2,814	4,238	11,035	13,884	19,692	28,773	21,029	26,584
Current account balance	-18,136	-24,225	13,985	13,621	1,551	-28,192	-24,302	-47,365
International reserves	51,477	33,015	53,799	85,843	180,334	193,783	238,539	288,575
6. Ratios								
External debt stocks to exports (%)	286.1	354.2	136.3	118.2	121.2	108.8	146.1	143.9
External debt stocks to GNI (%)	21.2	38.5	21.9	18.2	17.8	16.2	17.7	16.9
Debt service to exports (%)	38.5	95.1	45.7	38.0	28.0	23.4	23.5	19.0
Short-term to external debt stocks (%)	19.5	12.8	12.8	10.5	16.5	14.0	14.4	18.9
Multilateral to external debt stocks (%)	5.8	7.6	10.3	11.3	9.6	9.3	8.9	8.6
Reserves to external debt stocks (%)	32.1	13.7	28.7	44.4	75.9	73.9	86.1	83.2
Reserves to imports (months)	7.9	4.2	5.1	6.7	10.9	8.5	13.2	11.9

BRAZIL

(US$ million, unless otherwise indicated)

	1995	2000	2005	2006	2007	2008	2009	2010
7. Long-term external debt								
Debt outstanding and disbursed	**129,090**	**208,809**	**163,533**	**173,133**	**198,357**	**225,500**	**237,121**	**281,482**
Public and publicly guaranteed	98,260	96,127	94,028	84,245	79,595	79,658	87,295	96,542
Official creditors	27,837	29,351	25,843	25,382	26,148	29,026	32,385	41,251
Multilateral	9,366	18,330	19,356	21,929	22,721	24,358	24,754	29,747
of which: IBRD	6,038	7,377	8,083	9,694	9,676	10,671	10,065	13,523
IDA	0	0	0	0	0	0	0	0
Bilateral	18,471	11,021	6,487	3,454	3,427	4,668	7,632	11,504
Private creditors	70,423	66,776	68,185	58,862	53,447	50,632	54,910	55,290
of which: Bonds	54,615	54,096	59,077	49,173	45,441	42,035	47,107	41,323
Commercial banks	12,158	11,478	8,331	9,575	7,719	8,389	7,621	13,738
Private nonguaranteed	30,830	112,682	69,505	88,889	118,762	145,842	149,826	184,940
of which: Bonds	11,290	16,846	35,969	38,764	45,311	37,855	53,342	83,032
Disbursements	**20,207**	**44,051**	**27,402**	**52,622**	**59,904**	**69,505**	**57,670**	**84,723**
Public and publicly guaranteed	8,111	19,636	13,195	11,122	6,273	16,642	13,727	19,301
Official creditors	2,005	5,244	3,326	4,249	2,063	4,319	6,845	11,306
Multilateral	1,257	4,478	2,326	3,865	1,986	2,965	3,270	6,999
of which: IBRD	838	1,692	773	2,203	606	1,726	1,274	4,472
IDA	0	0	0	0	0	0	0	0
Bilateral	747	766	1,001	384	78	1,354	3,575	4,307
Private creditors	6,107	14,391	9,868	6,873	4,210	12,323	6,882	7,995
of which: Bonds	1,661	10,836	8,252	5,614	2,977	10,254	6,100	0
Commercial banks	4,340	3,532	1,608	1,240	1,182	2,061	724	7,869
Private nonguaranteed	12,096	24,415	14,207	41,500	53,630	52,863	43,943	65,422
of which: Bonds	4,563	2,886	6,579	9,832	13,930	6,754	17,015	32,384
Principal repayments	**11,002**	**41,040**	**25,751**	**47,388**	**40,422**	**40,285**	**30,425**	**31,972**
Public and publicly guaranteed	6,522	17,226	9,444	24,474	14,079	16,282	7,740	9,573
Official creditors	3,719	7,045	3,300	4,534	2,263	2,352	3,413	2,621
Multilateral	1,683	4,309	1,774	1,512	1,679	1,734	2,835	1,929
of which: IBRD	1,377	887	1,029	743	805	812	1,872	960
IDA	0	0	0	0	0	0	0	0
Bilateral	2,035	2,736	1,526	3,022	584	618	577	692
Private creditors	2,804	10,181	6,145	19,941	11,816	13,931	4,327	6,952
of which: Bonds	919	8,397	4,187	17,885	8,110	11,952	2,673	5,642
Commercial banks	1,051	1,546	1,923	2,015	3,612	1,897	1,572	1,236
Private nonguaranteed	4,480	23,813	16,306	22,914	26,343	24,002	22,685	22,398
of which: Bonds	2,670	2,773	7,063	3,479	8,471	2,420	1,383	2,636
Interest payments	**8,719**	**15,280**	**10,303**	**13,150**	**13,025**	**15,037**	**13,675**	**13,150**
Public and publicly guaranteed	6,624	6,926	6,689	7,136	7,069	6,048	5,778	5,166
Official creditors	1,567	1,915	1,047	1,224	1,352	1,283	1,205	961
Multilateral	750	1,407	807	973	1,174	1,111	919	634
of which: IBRD	491	464	307	432	548	498	359	180
IDA	0	0	0	0	0	0	0	0
Bilateral	817	508	240	251	178	172	286	327
Private creditors	5,056	5,010	5,642	5,911	5,717	4,765	4,573	4,205
of which: Bonds	4,416	4,212	5,033	5,012	4,959	4,272	4,025	3,777
Commercial banks	376	759	602	891	742	480	531	418
Private nonguaranteed	2,095	8,355	3,614	6,014	5,956	8,989	7,898	7,985
of which: Bonds	837	1,562	2,161	3,799	3,454	2,842	2,936	4,207
8. Debt stock-flow reconciliation								
Total change in external debt stocks	8,075	-2,558	-32,260	5,933	44,147	24,546	14,758	70,068
Net flows on external debt	8,797	-1,851	-23,433	1,564	38,405	26,618	30,386	78,458
9. Debt restructurings								
Total amount rescheduled	234	0	4,271	0	28	265	4	78
Total amount forgiven	0	137	0	0	0	56	0	0
Debt buyback	0	6,342	0	0	0	0	0	0

10. Contractual obligations on outstanding long-term external debt

	2011	2012	2013	2014	2015	2016	2017	2018
Official creditors								
Principal	3,360	3,530	3,123	2,915	5,031	4,851	4,680	4,260
Interest	905	845	781	739	663	553	442	335
Private creditors								
Principal	23,068	21,489	21,052	14,985	26,030	14,585	18,100	11,126
Interest	15,049	13,884	13,036	11,801	10,478	8,982	7,919	7,478

Notes:

Short-term debt for 2010 is based on reports provided by the country.

BULGARIA

(US$ million, unless otherwise indicated)

	1995	2000	2005	2006	2007	2008	2009	2010
1. Summary external debt data								
External debt stocks	**10,379**	**11,212**	**15,700**	**20,990**	**32,967**	**48,603**	**53,499**	**48,077**
Long-term external debt	9,150	8,440	10,597	12,609	18,930	30,268	34,921	32,704
Public and publicly guaranteed	8,808	7,671	5,075	5,066	5,242	4,397	4,772	4,466
Private nonguaranteed	342	769	5,522	7,543	13,689	25,871	30,148	28,238
Use of IMF credit	717	1,322	660	341	0	0	0	0
Short-term external debt	512	1,450	4,442	8,040	14,036	18,334	18,578	15,373
interest arrears on long-term	74	0	0	0	0	0	0	0
Memorandum items								
Principal arrears on long-term	227	1	0	0	0	0	0	0
Long-term public sector debt	8,808	7,671	5,075	5,066	5,242	4,397	4,772	4,466
Long-term private sector debt	342	769	5,522	7,543	13,689	25,871	30,148	28,238
Public & publicly guaranteed commitments	678	700	266	104	455	732	280	274
External debt flows								
Disbursements	259	995	3,710	3,616	7,740	15,545	8,191	1,499
Long-term external debt	259	719	3,710	3,616	7,740	15,545	8,191	1,499
IMF purchases	0	276	0	0	0	0	0	0
Principal repayments	565	712	3,352	1,992	3,033	3,765	3,694	3,381
Long-term external debt	319	573	2,909	1,645	2,686	3,765	3,694	3,381
IMF repurchases	246	139	443	346	347	0	0	0
Net flows	-194	465	1,564	5,222	10,704	16,078	4,740	-5,087
Long-term external debt	-61	145	801	1,970	5,054	11,780	4,496	-1,881
Short-term external debt	113	183	1,206	3,598	5,996	4,298	244	-3,205
Interest payments	575	584	613	744	1,164	1,610	1,516	634
Long-term external debt	501	456	445	489	603	858	773	568
IMF charges	50	63	37	24	9	0	0	0
Short-term external debt	24	65	130	230	552	752	743	66
2. Other non-debt resource inflows								
Foreign direct investment	90	1,002	4,312	7,758	13,215	9,979	3,389	2,168
Portfolio equity	0	5	449	148	89	-106	8	9
3. Currency composition of public and publicly guaranteed debt (%)								
Euro	..	..	48.4	50.7	52.4	51.7	56.8	56.1
Japanese yen	9.0	5.5	5.1	6.5	7.4	12.9	12.4	14.4
Pound sterling	0.2	0.1	0.0	0.0	0.0	0.0	0.0	0.0
Swiss franc	1.1	0.3	0.0	0.0	0.0	0.0	0.0	0.0
U.S.dollars	66.1	80.1	44.9	41.7	39.3	34.6	30.4	29.2
4. Average terms of new commitments								
Official creditors								
Interest (%)	5.9	6.2	3.0	3.7	4.9	2.3	2.0	2.3
Maturity (years)	17.3	16.7	16.2	16.1	16.6	20.7	17.6	20.1
Grace period (years)	5.4	4.4	4.7	2.6	4.5	5.1	5.3	5.9
Private creditors								
Interest (%)	3.4	7.6	4.2	5.0	0.0	2.0	0.0	0.0
Maturity (years)	4.7	16.0	9.4	10.0	0.0	29.2	0.0	0.0
Grace period (years)	3.2	4.9	1.9	0.5	0.0	9.2	0.0	0.0
5. Major economic aggregates								
Gross national income (GNI)	12,637	12,580	28,979	32,358	38,878	49,256	46,900	45,871
Exports of goods, services & income	6,926	7,321	17,674	21,972	27,487	31,925	24,392	28,358
Worker remit. & comp. of employees	..	58	1,613	1,716	1,694	1,919	1,592	1,387
Imports of goods, services & income	7,084	8,314	22,034	28,680	39,909	45,094	29,975	30,972
Profit remittances on FDI	0	107	912	1,857	3,742	2,722	1,822	1,964
Current account balance	-26	-703	-3,347	-5,863	-11,437	-11,846	-4,258	-578
International reserves	1,635	3,507	8,697	11,756	17,545	17,930	18,522	17,223
6. Ratios								
External debt stocks to exports (%)	149.9	153.2	88.8	95.5	119.9	152.2	219.3	169.5
External debt stocks to GNI (%)	82.1	89.1	54.2	64.9	84.8	98.7	114.1	104.8
Debt service to exports (%)	16.5	17.7	22.4	12.4	15.3	16.8	21.4	14.2
Short-term to external debt stocks (%)	4.9	12.9	28.3	38.3	42.6	37.7	34.7	32.0
Multilateral to external debt stocks (%)	11.9	13.8	15.7	11.4	8.1	4.5	4.7	4.8
Reserves to external debt stocks (%)	15.8	31.3	55.4	56.0	53.2	36.9	34.6	35.8
Reserves to imports (months)	2.8	5.1	4.7	4.9	5.3	4.8	7.4	6.7

BULGARIA

(US$ million, unless otherwise indicated)

	1995	2000	2005	2006	2007	2008	2009	2010
7. Long-term external debt								
Debt outstanding and disbursed	**9,150**	**8,440**	**10,597**	**12,609**	**18,930**	**30,268**	**34,921**	**32,704**
Public and publicly guaranteed	8,808	7,671	5,075	5,066	5,242	4,397	4,772	4,466
Official creditors	2,950	2,603	3,045	3,012	3,362	3,019	3,322	3,152
Multilateral	1,230	1,542	2,457	2,392	2,674	2,198	2,507	2,330
of which: IBRD	444	824	1,453	1,331	1,604	1,207	1,509	1,338
IDA	0	0	0	0	0	0	0	0
Bilateral	1,720	1,061	587	620	688	821	815	823
Private creditors	5,857	5,068	2,030	2,054	1,880	1,378	1,450	1,314
of which: Bonds	5,412	4,982	1,920	1,937	1,792	1,342	1,430	1,301
Commercial banks	394	26	111	116	86	34	19	12
Private nonguaranteed	342	769	5,522	7,543	13,689	25,871	30,148	28,238
of which: Bonds	0	0	526	736	855	522	146	134
Disbursements	**259**	**719**	**3,710**	**3,616**	**7,740**	**15,545**	**8,191**	**1,499**
Public and publicly guaranteed	259	405	402	260	368	370	520	200
Official creditors	129	381	383	243	361	362	520	200
Multilateral	38	156	328	150	293	227	446	176
of which: IBRD	15	71	200	38	201	56	370	20
IDA	0	0	0	0	0	0	0	0
Bilateral	91	225	55	93	68	136	74	23
Private creditors	129	24	19	17	7	8	0	0
of which: Bonds	33	0	0	0	0	0	0	0
Commercial banks	96	24	19	16	7	8	0	0
Private nonguaranteed	0	313	3,308	3,355	7,372	15,175	7,671	1,299
of which: Bonds	0	0	249	215	0	0	0	0
Principal repayments	**319**	**573**	**2,909**	**1,645**	**2,686**	**3,765**	**3,694**	**3,381**
Public and publicly guaranteed	319	345	1,761	515	404	858	281	268
Official creditors	92	297	255	502	299	715	266	261
Multilateral	25	58	214	430	253	658	187	185
of which: IBRD	0	27	85	276	65	462	85	90
IDA	0	0	0	0	0	0	0	0
Bilateral	67	239	41	73	47	57	79	76
Private creditors	228	48	1,507	13	105	143	15	7
of which: Bonds	39	46	1,496	0	87	124	0	0
Commercial banks	182	1	11	13	18	19	15	7
Private nonguaranteed	0	229	1,147	1,130	2,282	2,908	3,413	3,113
of which: Bonds	0	0	10	49	0	287	372	0
Interest payments	**501**	**456**	**445**	**489**	**603**	**858**	**773**	**568**
Public and publicly guaranteed	501	424	327	352	285	286	211	160
Official creditors	178	139	93	100	129	148	106	71
Multilateral	61	81	75	82	110	124	84	49
of which: IBRD	31	49	40	44	62	72	43	17
IDA	0	0	0	0	0	0	0	0
Bilateral	118	58	18	19	19	24	22	22
Private creditors	323	285	234	252	156	139	105	89
of which: Bonds	315	284	229	245	149	133	104	89
Commercial banks	7	0	5	7	7	5	1	0
Private nonguaranteed	0	32	118	137	318	572	562	408
of which: Bonds	0	0	30	44	55	36	29	11
8. Debt stock-flow reconciliation								
Total change in external debt stocks	550	192	33	5,290	11,977	15,636	4,896	-5,422
Net flows on external debt	-194	465	1,564	5,222	10,704	16,078	4,740	-5,087
9. Debt restructurings								
Total amount rescheduled	84	0	0	0	0	0	0	0
Total amount forgiven	0	12	72	14	20	83	0	0
Debt buyback	0	0	0	0	0	127	0	0

10. Contractual obligations on outstanding long-term external debt

	2011	2012	2013	2014	2015	2016	2017	2018
Official creditors								
Principal	328	338	272	285	296	303	310	285
Interest	83	73	65	59	52	46	39	33
Private creditors								
Principal	7,582	5,328	5,327	2,838	3,033	1,718	1,442	1,154
Interest	1,325	1,006	724	516	351	219	135	68

Notes:

Data on long-term private nonguaranteed debt from 2008 are World Bank staff estimates based on reports provided by the country. The data may include long-term public and publicly guaranteed debt owed by the state-owned railway. Short-term debt data are based on the Central Bank data.

BURKINA FASO

(US$ million, unless otherwise indicated)

	1995	2000	2005	2006	2007	2008	2009	2010
1. Summary external debt data								
External debt stocks	**1,271**	**1,422**	**1,994**	**1,123**	**1,450**	**1,670**	**1,822**	**2,053**
Long-term external debt	1,140	1,226	1,868	999	1,257	1,505	1,711	1,925
Public and publicly guaranteed	1,140	1,226	1,868	999	1,257	1,505	1,711	1,925
Private nonguaranteed	0	0	0	0	0	0	0	0
Use of IMF credit	75	112	104	35	37	54	110	129
Short-term external debt	56	84	22	89	155	110	0	0
interest arrears on long-term	12	5	0	0	0	0	0	0
Memorandum items								
Principal arrears on long-term	37	42	36	39	37	34	34	35
Long-term public sector debt	1,140	1,226	1,868	999	1,257	1,505	1,711	1,925
Long-term private sector debt	0	0	0	0	0	0	0	0
Public & publicly guaranteed commitments	37	53	232	294	389	405	48	57
External debt flows								
Disbursements	139	99	218	300	226	312	266	296
Long-term external debt	112	91	203	281	225	294	212	274
IMF purchases	27	7	15	19	1	18	54	21
Principal repayments	28	33	28	27	25	27	27	33
Long-term external debt	28	26	24	27	25	27	27	32
IMF repurchases	0	7	4	0	0	0	0	1
Net flows	124	47	188	341	267	240	129	263
Long-term external debt	83	65	179	255	200	266	185	242
Short-term external debt	14	-19	-2	67	66	-45	-110	0
Interest payments	20	14	17	17	17	18	15	18
Long-term external debt	18	12	16	15	12	14	15	18
IMF charges	0	1	0	0	0	0	0	0
Short-term external debt	2	1	1	2	5	3	0	0
2. Other non-debt resource inflows								
Foreign direct investment	10	23	32	74	370	152	105	37
Portfolio equity	..	-3	-4	1	-1	-2	..	..
3. Currency composition of public and publicly guaranteed debt (%)								
Euro	..	..	1.7	6.2	6.7	13.0	12.6	12.2
Japanese yen	0.0	0.0	0.0	0.0	0.0	0.0	0.0	0.0
Pound sterling	0.3	0.1	0.0	0.0	0.0	0.0	0.0	0.0
Swiss franc	0.0	0.0	0.0	0.0	0.0	0.0	0.0	0.0
U.S.dollars	55.5	59.4	56.5	40.3	39.4	36.2	35.4	33.6
4. Average terms of new commitments								
Official creditors								
Interest (%)	0.8	1.4	0.9	0.8	1.3	1.1	0.8	0.8
Maturity (years)	39.9	37.1	35.8	40.9	32.6	35.5	49.9	41.3
Grace period (years)	10.4	7.8	8.8	10.1	8.5	9.1	10.4	9.4
Private creditors								
Interest (%)	0.0	0.0	4.2	0.0	0.0	0.0	0.0	0.0
Maturity (years)	0.0	0.0	11.2	0.0	0.0	0.0	0.0	0.0
Grace period (years)	0.0	0.0	1.7	0.0	0.0	0.0	0.0	0.0
5. Major economic aggregates								
Gross national income (GNI)	2,369	2,606	5,411	5,756	6,752	7,932	8,019	8,810
Exports of goods, services & income	..	251	589	732	811	1,069	1,140	..
Worker remit. & comp. of employees	78	67	57	68	84	99	99	95
Imports of goods, services & income	..	691	1,458	1,515	1,775	2,442	2,035	..
Profit remittances on FDI	..	3	7	7	11	38	35	..
Current account balance	..	-319	-634	-543	-560	-963	-380	..
International reserves	347	243	438	555	1,029	928	1,296	1,068
6. Ratios								
External debt stocks to exports (%)	..	567.6	338.6	153.5	178.6	156.2	159.7	..
External debt stocks to GNI (%)	53.6	54.6	36.9	19.5	21.5	21.1	22.7	23.3
Debt service to exports (%)	..	18.6	7.7	6.0	5.1	4.2	3.7	..
Short-term to external debt stocks (%)	4.4	5.9	1.1	7.9	10.7	6.6	..	..
Multilateral to external debt stocks (%)	77.2	72.0	85.2	69.8	67.5	71.5	76.5	77.9
Reserves to external debt stocks (%)	27.3	17.1	22.0	49.4	71.0	55.5	71.1	52.0
Reserves to imports (months)	..	4.2	3.6	4.4	7.0	4.6	7.6	..

(US$ million, unless otherwise indicated)

	1995	2000	2005	2006	2007	2008	2009	2010
7. Long-term external debt								
Debt outstanding and disbursed	**1,140**	**1,226**	**1,868**	**999**	**1,257**	**1,505**	**1,711**	**1,925**
Public and publicly guaranteed	1,140	1,226	1,868	999	1,257	1,505	1,711	1,925
Official creditors	1,135	1,222	1,868	987	1,232	1,484	1,690	1,907
Multilateral	981	1,024	1,699	784	979	1,193	1,394	1,600
of which: IBRD	0	0	0	0	0	0	0	0
IDA	608	593	1,043	371	468	626	721	776
Bilateral	154	198	169	202	252	291	296	307
Private creditors	5	3	0	12	26	22	22	18
of which: Bonds	0	0	0	0	0	0	0	0
Commercial banks	0	0	0	0	0	0	0	0
Private nonguaranteed	0	0	0	0	0	0	0	0
of which: Bonds	0	0	0	0	0	0	0	0
Disbursements	**112**	**91**	**203**	**281**	**225**	**294**	**212**	**274**
Public and publicly guaranteed	112	91	203	281	225	294	212	274
Official creditors	112	91	203	270	211	294	212	274
Multilateral	106	76	191	232	161	239	195	247
of which: IBRD	0	0	0	0	0	0	0	0
IDA	85	38	107	125	80	160	90	67
Bilateral	6	16	13	38	50	55	17	28
Private creditors	0	0	0	12	14	0	0	0
of which: Bonds	0	0	0	0	0	0	0	0
Commercial banks	0	0	0	0	0	0	0	0
Private nonguaranteed	0	0	0	0	0	0	0	0
of which: Bonds	0	0	0	0	0	0	0	0
Principal repayments	**28**	**26**	**24**	**27**	**25**	**27**	**27**	**32**
Public and publicly guaranteed	28	26	24	27	25	27	27	32
Official creditors	28	26	24	27	22	25	27	29
Multilateral	24	20	17	18	11	15	16	18
of which: IBRD	0	0	0	0	0	0	0	0
IDA	4	1	5	3	0	0	0	0
Bilateral	4	6	8	9	11	9	10	11
Private creditors	0	0	0	0	3	3	0	2
of which: Bonds	0	0	0	0	0	0	0	0
Commercial banks	0	0	0	0	0	0	0	0
Private nonguaranteed	0	0	0	0	0	0	0	0
of which: Bonds	0	0	0	0	0	0	0	0
Interest payments	**18**	**12**	**16**	**15**	**12**	**14**	**15**	**18**
Public and publicly guaranteed	18	12	16	15	12	14	15	18
Official creditors	18	12	16	15	12	14	15	18
Multilateral	11	9	14	13	9	11	11	13
of which: IBRD	0	0	0	0	0	0	0	0
IDA	4	4	8	5	4	4	5	5
Bilateral	6	2	2	3	3	3	3	5
Private creditors	0	0	0	0	0	0	0	0
of which: Bonds	0	0	0	0	0	0	0	0
Commercial banks	0	0	0	0	0	0	0	0
Private nonguaranteed	0	0	0	0	0	0	0	0
of which: Bonds	0	0	0	0	0	0	0	0
8. Debt stock-flow reconciliation								
Total change in external debt stocks	139	-161	5	-871	327	220	152	232
Net flows on external debt	124	47	188	341	267	240	129	263
9. Debt restructurings								
Total amount rescheduled	0	17	1	4	0	1	0	1
Total amount forgiven	15	81	45	1,290	3	7	3	6
Debt buyback	0	92	0	0	0	0	0	0

10. Contractual obligations on outstanding long-term external debt

	2011	2012	2013	2014	2015	2016	2017	2018
Official creditors								
Principal	55	55	65	73	77	83	93	97
Interest	23	23	23	23	22	22	21	20
Private creditors								
Principal	3	3	3	3	3	3	0	0
Interest	1	1	0	0	0	0	0	0

Notes:

Burkina Faso was granted debt relief effective in 2006 under MDRI.

BURUNDI

(US$ million, unless otherwise indicated)

	1995	2000	2005	2006	2007	2008	2009	2010
1. Summary external debt data								
External debt stocks	**1162.0**	**1108.0**	**1321.8**	**1411.8**	**1455.7**	**1438.2**	**512.7**	**537.1**
Long-term external debt	1099.3	1036.0	1229.6	1291.4	1343.7	1303.2	414.7	411.7
Public and publicly guaranteed	1099.3	1036.0	1229.6	1291.4	1343.7	1303.2	414.7	411.7
Private nonguaranteed	0.0	0.0	0.0	0.0	0.0	0.0	0.0	0.0
Use of IMF credit	47.8	7.0	58.2	82.7	98.2	116.9	90.9	109.6
Short-term external debt	14.9	65.0	34.1	37.6	13.8	18.1	7.1	15.8
interest arrears on long-term	2.0	19.7	33.1	36.6	12.8	4.1	0.1	0.8
Memorandum items								
Principal arrears on long-term	3.0	82.1	75.2	76.4	60.2	64.6	19.8	18.8
Long-term public sector debt	1099.3	1036.0	1229.6	1291.4	1343.7	1303.2	414.7	411.7
Long-term private sector debt	0.0	0.0	0.0	0.0	0.0	0.0	0.0	0.0
Public & publicly guaranteed commitments	38.8	50.3	39.2	3.8	2.4	37.0	8.0	5.1
External debt flows								
Disbursements	44.8	41.3	63.3	60.4	42.2	46.6	43.9	55.8
Long-term external debt	44.8	41.3	42.1	39.4	31.3	24.8	23.6	35.6
IMF purchases	0.0	0.0	21.1	21.0	10.9	21.7	20.4	20.1
Principal repayments	26.8	14.0	27.1	12.9	11.2	11.3	15.3	1.8
Long-term external debt	17.8	9.4	27.1	12.9	11.2	11.3	8.4	1.8
IMF repurchases	9.1	4.5	0.0	0.0	0.0	0.0	6.9	0.0
Net flows	26.3	18.4	34.2	47.5	31.0	48.3	21.6	62.0
Long-term external debt	27.1	31.8	15.0	26.5	20.1	13.5	15.2	33.9
Short-term external debt	8.3	-8.9	-2.0	0.0	0.0	13.0	-7.0	8.0
Interest payments	11.8	7.9	12.2	5.5	7.8	8.2	4.1	1.6
Long-term external debt	11.0	4.5	11.9	5.1	7.3	7.4	3.6	1.4
IMF charges	0.3	0.1	0.2	0.3	0.5	0.6	0.4	0.0
Short-term external debt	0.5	3.3	0.1	0.1	0.0	0.2	0.1	0.1
2. Other non-debt resource inflows								
Foreign direct investment	2.0	11.7	0.6	0.0	0.5	3.8	0.3	0.8
Portfolio equity	0.0	0.0	0.0	0.0	0.0	0.0	0.0	0.0
3. Currency composition of public and publicly guaranteed debt (%)								
Euro	..	..	11.1	11.4	11.9	9.9	17.1	9.3
Japanese yen	2.9	2.8	1.4	0.7	0.7	1.0	3.0	3.0
Pound sterling	0.0	0.0	0.0	0.0	0.0	0.0	0.0	0.0
Swiss franc	0.0	0.0	0.0	0.0	0.0	0.0	0.0	0.0
U.S.dollars	55.1	59.4	61.8	61.3	60.4	60.5	34.1	37.2
4. Average terms of new commitments								
Official creditors								
Interest (%)	0.8	1.7	0.8	0.0	1.5	1.0	1.0	1.0
Maturity (years)	38.0	31.3	47.8	19.6	22.5	19.5	28.5	19.6
Grace period (years)	9.8	8.2	10.2	10.1	4.7	6.4	10.0	8.0
Private creditors								
Interest (%)	0.0	0.0	0.0	0.0	0.0	0.0	0.0	0.0
Maturity (years)	0.0	0.0	0.0	0.0	0.0	0.0	0.0	0.0
Grace period (years)	0.0	0.0	0.0	0.0	0.0	0.0	0.0	0.0
5. Major economic aggregates								
Gross national income (GNI)	988.0	723.4	776.2	910.0	973.9	1164.6	1331.3	1589.0
Exports of goods, services & income	139.7	55.4	98.7	97.3	98.3	163.9	117.3	..
Worker remit. & comp. of employees	..	..	0.1	0.0	0.2	3.6	28.2	28.2
Imports of goods, services & income	281.8	165.0	343.9	460.4	447.5	609.4	538.0	..
Profit remittances on FDI	3.1	0.4	2.1	3.4	4.8	5.3	8.1	10.1
Current account balance	10.4	-50.2	-5.7	-133.5	-108.0	-259.4	-163.6	-300.9
International reserves	216.1	37.6	100.6	131.1	177.1	266.5	323.1	332.1
6. Ratios								
External debt stocks to exports (%)	831.6	1999.7	1338.6	1450.6	1480.8	877.7	437.0	..
External debt stocks to GNI (%)	117.6	153.2	170.3	155.1	149.5	123.5	38.5	33.8
Debt service to exports (%)	27.6	39.4	39.8	18.9	19.4	11.9	16.6	..
Short-term to external debt stocks (%)	1.3	5.9	2.6	2.7	0.9	1.3	1.4	2.9
Multilateral to external debt stocks (%)	80.1	80.4	80.3	79.6	80.9	80.6	61.9	64.0
Reserves to external debt stocks (%)	18.6	3.4	7.6	9.3	12.2	18.5	63.0	61.8
Reserves to imports (months)	9.2	2.7	3.5	3.4	4.7	5.2	7.2	..

BURUNDI

(US$ million, unless otherwise indicated)

	1995	2000	2005	2006	2007	2008	2009	2010
7. Long-term external debt								
Debt outstanding and disbursed	**1099.3**	**1036.0**	**1229.6**	**1291.4**	**1343.7**	**1303.2**	**414.7**	**411.7**
Public and publicly guaranteed	1099.3	1036.0	1229.6	1291.4	1343.7	1303.2	414.7	411.7
Official creditors	1097.6	1032.0	1227.5	1290.8	1342.9	1303.2	414.7	411.7
Multilateral	930.5	890.4	1061.8	1124.0	1177.0	1159.5	317.2	343.8
of which: IBRD	0.0	0.0	0.0	0.0	0.0	0.0	0.0	0.0
IDA	591.4	600.5	750.8	797.0	830.1	818.5	147.2	162.7
Bilateral	167.1	141.6	165.7	166.9	165.9	143.7	97.4	67.9
Private creditors	1.6	4.0	2.1	0.6	0.7	0.0	0.0	0.0
of which: Bonds	0.0	0.0	0.0	0.0	0.0	0.0	0.0	0.0
Commercial banks	0.0	0.0	0.0	0.0	0.0	0.0	0.0	0.0
Private nonguaranteed	0.0	0.0	0.0	0.0	0.0	0.0	0.0	0.0
of which: Bonds	0.0	0.0	0.0	0.0	0.0	0.0	0.0	0.0
Disbursements	**44.8**	**41.3**	**42.1**	**39.4**	**31.3**	**24.8**	**23.6**	**35.6**
Public and publicly guaranteed	44.8	41.3	42.1	39.4	31.3	24.8	23.6	35.6
Official creditors	44.8	38.2	42.1	36.9	31.3	24.8	23.6	35.6
Multilateral	40.6	38.2	42.1	36.9	29.8	24.3	23.6	35.6
of which: IBRD	0.0	0.0	0.0	0.0	0.0	0.0	0.0	0.0
IDA	27.3	36.4	27.4	28.9	19.2	13.8	8.7	17.8
Bilateral	4.2	0.0	0.0	0.0	1.5	0.5	0.0	0.0
Private creditors	0.0	3.0	0.0	2.5	0.0	0.0	0.0	0.0
of which: Bonds	0.0	0.0	0.0	0.0	0.0	0.0	0.0	0.0
Commercial banks	0.0	0.0	0.0	0.0	0.0	0.0	0.0	0.0
Private nonguaranteed	0.0	0.0	0.0	0.0	0.0	0.0	0.0	0.0
of which: Bonds	0.0	0.0	0.0	0.0	0.0	0.0	0.0	0.0
Principal repayments	**17.8**	**9.4**	**27.1**	**12.9**	**11.2**	**11.3**	**8.4**	**1.8**
Public and publicly guaranteed	17.8	9.4	27.1	12.9	11.2	11.3	8.4	1.8
Official creditors	16.9	9.4	22.5	8.9	11.2	11.3	8.4	1.8
Multilateral	11.8	9.4	22.3	8.9	10.7	10.0	8.4	1.8
of which: IBRD	0.0	0.0	0.0	0.0	0.0	0.0	0.0	0.0
IDA	2.9	8.8	8.5	0.0	0.0	0.1	0.1	0.0
Bilateral	5.1	0.0	0.2	0.0	0.6	1.3	0.0	0.0
Private creditors	0.9	0.0	4.6	4.0	0.0	0.0	0.0	0.0
of which: Bonds	0.0	0.0	0.0	0.0	0.0	0.0	0.0	0.0
Commercial banks	0.0	0.0	0.0	0.0	0.0	0.0	0.0	0.0
Private nonguaranteed	0.0	0.0	0.0	0.0	0.0	0.0	0.0	0.0
of which: Bonds	0.0	0.0	0.0	0.0	0.0	0.0	0.0	0.0
Interest payments	**11.0**	**4.5**	**11.9**	**5.1**	**7.3**	**7.4**	**3.6**	**1.4**
Public and publicly guaranteed	11.0	4.5	11.9	5.1	7.3	7.4	3.6	1.4
Official creditors	10.9	4.5	11.9	5.1	7.3	7.4	3.6	1.4
Multilateral	8.5	4.5	11.7	4.5	5.6	6.2	3.1	1.3
of which: IBRD	0.0	0.0	0.0	0.0	0.0	0.0	0.0	0.0
IDA	4.6	4.4	4.3	1.7	2.4	3.7	1.0	0.8
Bilateral	2.4	0.0	0.2	0.6	1.7	1.2	0.5	0.1
Private creditors	0.1	0.0	0.0	0.0	0.0	0.0	0.0	0.0
of which: Bonds	0.0	0.0	0.0	0.0	0.0	0.0	0.0	0.0
Commercial banks	0.0	0.0	0.0	0.0	0.0	0.0	0.0	0.0
Private nonguaranteed	0.0	0.0	0.0	0.0	0.0	0.0	0.0	0.0
of which: Bonds	0.0	0.0	0.0	0.0	0.0	0.0	0.0	0.0
8. Debt stock-flow reconciliation								
Total change in external debt stocks	34.6	-26.9	-68.5	90.0	43.9	-17.5	-925.5	24.4
Net flows on external debt	26.3	18.4	34.2	47.5	31.0	48.3	21.6	62.0
9. Debt restructurings								
Total amount rescheduled	0.0	0.0	0.0	3.9	3.3	0.0	71.4	3.4
Total amount forgiven	16.7	0.0	11.5	28.2	22.4	53.2	821.0	1.8
Debt buyback	0.0	0.0	0.0	0.0	0.0	0.0	0.0	0.0

10. Contractual obligations on outstanding long-term external debt

	2011	2012	2013	2014	2015	2016	2017	2018
Official creditors								
Principal	13.0	13.1	14.7	14.2	16.2	16.3	15.7	17.0
Interest	3.3	3.4	3.4	3.3	3.2	3.1	3.0	2.8
Private creditors								
Principal	0.0	0.0	0.0	0.0	0.0	0.0	0.0	0.0
Interest	0.0	0.0	0.0	0.0	0.0	0.0	0.0	0.0

Notes:

Data for 2010 include the effects of MDRI and HIPC debt reliefs in the amount of $325 thousand.

CAMBODIA

(US$ million, unless otherwise indicated)

	1995	2000	2005	2006	2007	2008	2009	2010
1. Summary external debt data								
External debt stocks	**2,284**	**2,628**	**3,515**	**3,527**	**3,761**	**4,215**	**4,364**	**4,676**
Long-term external debt	2,110	2,328	3,155	3,318	3,537	3,892	4,099	4,414
Public and publicly guaranteed	2,110	2,328	3,155	3,318	3,537	3,892	4,099	4,414
Private nonguaranteed	0	0	0	0	0	0	0	0
Use of IMF credit	72	73	81	0	0	0	0	0
Short-term external debt	102	227	279	209	224	323	265	262
interest arrears on long-term	90	131	243	173	164	197	208	215
Memorandum items								
Principal arrears on long-term	653	1,275	1,485	1,508	1,545	1,599	1,613	1,646
Long-term public sector debt	2,110	2,328	3,155	3,318	3,537	3,892	4,099	4,414
Long-term private sector debt	0	0	0	0	0	0	0	0
Public & publicly guaranteed commitments	161	185	208	149	390	305	727	488
External debt flows								
Disbursements	123	90	168	153	154	383	211	347
Long-term external debt	80	79	168	153	154	383	211	347
IMF purchases	42	11	0	0	0	0	0	0
Principal repayments	5	14	16	15	13	19	26	33
Long-term external debt	5	7	8	15	13	19	26	33
IMF repurchases	0	7	9	0	0	0	0	0
Net flows	100	128	154	138	165	430	116	303
Long-term external debt	75	72	160	138	141	364	185	313
Short-term external debt	-18	52	2	0	24	66	-69	-10
Interest payments	3	18	15	15	18	23	23	29
Long-term external debt	1	12	12	13	15	21	22	28
IMF charges	1	1	0	0	0	0	0	0
Short-term external debt	1	5	2	2	3	2	1	1
2. Other non-debt resource inflows								
Foreign direct investment	151	149	381	483	867	815	530	783
Portfolio equity	0	0	0	0	0	0	0	..
3. Currency composition of public and publicly guaranteed debt (%)								
Euro	..	..	0.8	0.8	0.9	0.9	0.9	0.8
Japanese yen	0.4	0.3	1.1	1.2	1.5	2.0	2.4	2.8
Pound sterling	0.0	0.0	0.0	0.0	0.0	0.0	0.0	0.0
Swiss franc	0.0	0.0	0.0	0.0	0.0	0.0	0.0	0.0
U.S.dollars	27.2	30.2	39.4	39.0	39.0	40.1	40.6	41.2
4. Average terms of new commitments								
Official creditors								
Interest (%)	1.8	1.3	1.4	1.0	1.5	1.2	1.3	1.5
Maturity (years)	37.5	30.3	26.9	26.2	23.6	29.4	25.4	25.0
Grace period (years)	9.7	8.2	9.2	9.8	7.7	8.6	3.3	8.4
Private creditors								
Interest (%)	0.0	0.0	0.0	0.0	0.0	0.0	0.0	0.0
Maturity (years)	0.0	0.0	0.0	0.0	0.0	0.0	0.0	0.0
Grace period (years)	0.0	0.0	0.0	0.0	0.0	0.0	0.0	0.0
5. Major economic aggregates								
Gross national income (GNI)	3,380	3,534	6,006	6,969	8,263	9,831	9,962	10,779
Exports of goods, services & income	979	1,893	4,096	5,079	5,748	6,462	5,982	..
Worker remit. & comp. of employees	12	121	200	297	353	325	338	369
Imports of goods, services & income	1,442	2,453	4,923	5,971	6,830	8,127	7,422	..
Profit remittances on FDI	4	123	227	270	353	403	349	..
Current account balance	-186	-136	-307	-262	-488	-1,051	-866	..
International reserves	192	611	1,158	1,411	2,140	2,639	3,286	3,817
6. Ratios								
External debt stocks to exports (%)	233.3	138.8	85.8	69.4	65.4	65.2	72.9	..
External debt stocks to GNI (%)	67.6	74.4	58.5	50.6	45.5	42.9	43.8	43.4
Debt service to exports (%)	0.7	1.7	0.8	0.6	0.5	0.7	0.8	..
Short-term to external debt stocks (%)	4.5	8.6	7.9	5.9	6.0	7.7	6.1	5.6
Multilateral to external debt stocks (%)	5.2	14.5	30.1	33.1	34.5	33.7	34.4	32.7
Reserves to external debt stocks (%)	8.4	23.3	32.9	40.0	56.9	62.6	75.3	81.6
Reserves to imports (months)	1.6	3.0	2.8	2.8	3.8	3.9	5.3	..

CAMBODIA

(US$ million, unless otherwise indicated)

	1995	2000	2005	2006	2007	2008	2009	2010
7. Long-term external debt								
Debt outstanding and disbursed	**2,110**	**2,328**	**3,155**	**3,318**	**3,537**	**3,892**	**4,099**	**4,414**
Public and publicly guaranteed	2,110	2,328	3,155	3,318	3,537	3,892	4,099	4,414
Official creditors	2,097	2,328	3,155	3,318	3,537	3,892	4,099	4,414
Multilateral	118	381	1,059	1,168	1,298	1,420	1,501	1,529
of which: IBRD	0	0	0	0	0	0	0	0
IDA	65	207	462	500	535	545	566	565
Bilateral	1,979	1,947	2,096	2,150	2,239	2,472	2,598	2,885
Private creditors	13	0	0	0	0	0	0	0
of which: Bonds	0	0	0	0	0	0	0	0
Commercial banks	0	0	0	0	0	0	0	0
Private nonguaranteed	0	0	0	0	0	0	0	0
of which: Bonds	0	0	0	0	0	0	0	0
Disbursements	**80**	**79**	**168**	**153**	**154**	**383**	**211**	**347**
Public and publicly guaranteed	80	79	168	153	154	383	211	347
Official creditors	64	79	168	153	154	383	211	347
Multilateral	61	78	130	79	78	145	92	80
of which: IBRD	0	0	0	0	0	0	0	0
IDA	25	37	36	19	18	20	23	17
Bilateral	4	1	38	74	76	238	119	267
Private creditors	16	0	0	0	0	0	0	0
of which: Bonds	0	0	0	0	0	0	0	0
Commercial banks	0	0	0	0	0	0	0	0
Private nonguaranteed	0	0	0	0	0	0	0	0
of which: Bonds	0	0	0	0	0	0	0	0
Principal repayments	**5**	**7**	**8**	**15**	**13**	**19**	**26**	**33**
Public and publicly guaranteed	5	7	8	15	13	19	26	33
Official creditors	2	7	8	15	13	19	26	33
Multilateral	0	0	5	9	11	17	23	29
of which: IBRD	0	0	0	0	0	0	0	0
IDA	0	0	2	4	5	6	6	8
Bilateral	2	7	2	6	2	2	3	5
Private creditors	3	0	0	0	0	0	0	0
of which: Bonds	0	0	0	0	0	0	0	0
Commercial banks	0	0	0	0	0	0	0	0
Private nonguaranteed	0	0	0	0	0	0	0	0
of which: Bonds	0	0	0	0	0	0	0	0
Interest payments	**1**	**12**	**12**	**13**	**15**	**21**	**22**	**28**
Public and publicly guaranteed	1	12	12	13	15	21	22	28
Official creditors	1	12	12	13	15	21	22	28
Multilateral	1	3	10	10	11	13	13	14
of which: IBRD	0	0	0	0	0	0	0	0
IDA	0	1	4	4	4	4	4	4
Bilateral	0	9	3	3	4	8	9	14
Private creditors	0	0	0	0	0	0	0	0
of which: Bonds	0	0	0	0	0	0	0	0
Commercial banks	0	0	0	0	0	0	0	0
Private nonguaranteed	0	0	0	0	0	0	0	0
of which: Bonds	0	0	0	0	0	0	0	0
8. Debt stock-flow reconciliation								
Total change in external debt stocks	375	111	76	11	234	454	149	312
Net flows on external debt	100	128	154	138	165	430	116	303
9. Debt restructurings								
Total amount rescheduled	224	0	0	0	1	0	0	0
Total amount forgiven	13	0	0	106	0	0	0	4
Debt buyback	0	0	0	0	0	0	0	0

10. Contractual obligations on outstanding long-term external debt

	2011	2012	2013	2014	2015	2016	2017	2018
Official creditors								
Principal	63	74	86	113	123	131	149	176
Interest	40	41	42	42	41	40	39	37
Private creditors								
Principal	0	0	0	0	0	0	0	0
Interest	0	0	0	0	0	0	0	0

Notes:

Cambodia was granted debt relief effective in 2006 under MDRI.

CAMEROON

(US$ million, unless otherwise indicated)

	1995	2000	2005	2006	2007	2008	2009	2010
1. Summary external debt data								
External debt stocks	**10,950**	**10,323**	**7,273**	**3,243**	**3,004**	**2,756**	**2,946**	**2,964**
Long-term external debt	9,908	8,864	6,667	2,733	2,749	2,690	2,748	2,762
Public and publicly guaranteed	9,620	8,547	6,075	2,243	2,113	2,055	2,132	2,185
Private nonguaranteed	288	317	592	489	636	636	615	577
Use of IMF credit	51	235	272	8	17	24	175	172
Short-term external debt	991	1,224	334	502	238	41	23	31
interest arrears on long-term	349	205	280	434	39	41	23	31
Memorandum items								
Principal arrears on long-term	474	322	51	91	1	19	68	134
Long-term public sector debt	9,543	8,500	6,075	2,243	2,113	2,055	2,132	2,185
Long-term private sector debt	365	364	592	489	636	636	615	577
Public & publicly guaranteed commitments	197	100	47	41	453	149	628	492
External debt flows								
Disbursements	174	354	231	162	270	287	491	278
Long-term external debt	161	286	227	158	262	279	344	278
IMF purchases	13	69	4	4	8	8	147	0
Principal repayments	217	270	576	376	369	358	336	155
Long-term external debt	211	253	537	355	369	358	336	155
IMF repurchases	6	17	39	21	0	0	0	0
Net flows	117	-21	-683	-200	32	-270	155	122
Long-term external debt	-50	33	-310	-197	-107	-79	8	122
Short-term external debt	160	-105	-339	14	131	-199	0	0
Interest payments	214	288	245	140	143	119	59	53
Long-term external debt	173	215	231	135	135	115	58	53
IMF charges	2	2	1	0	0	0	0	0
Short-term external debt	38	72	12	4	8	5	0	0
2. Other non-debt resource inflows								
Foreign direct investment	7	159	234	16	191	-24	668	-1
Portfolio equity	0	0	-4	-6	-14	-1	0	0
3. Currency composition of public and publicly guaranteed debt (%)								
Euro	..	..	65.9	76.9	72.7	65.7	63.5	54.8
Japanese yen	0.3	0.5	1.3	0.0	0.0	0.0	0.0	0.3
Pound sterling	1.2	2.0	1.7	0.0	0.0	0.0	0.0	0.0
Swiss franc	1.1	0.7	0.6	0.4	0.3	0.3	0.3	0.3
U.S.dollars	9.6	24.4	20.8	10.5	12.6	14.2	14.2	18.7
4. Average terms of new commitments								
Official creditors								
Interest (%)	2.6	0.9	0.4	1.4	0.9	0.7	1.3	0.9
Maturity (years)	23.3	38.6	30.7	24.3	37.1	36.7	29.0	31.8
Grace period (years)	7.7	9.5	9.2	5.6	8.6	9.3	7.7	8.9
Private creditors								
Interest (%)	0.0	0.0	0.0	0.0	0.0	0.0	5.2	0.0
Maturity (years)	0.0	0.0	0.0	0.0	0.0	0.0	11.9	0.0
Grace period (years)	0.0	0.0	0.0	0.0	0.0	0.0	2.4	0.0
5. Major economic aggregates								
Gross national income (GNI)	8,205	9,464	16,126	17,706	20,608	23,407	22,059	22,030
Exports of goods, services & income	2,053	2,602	4,280	4,911	6,393	7,439	5,550	5,738
Worker remit. & comp. of employees	11	30	77	130	167	167	192	195
Imports of goods, services & income	2,032	2,960	5,010	5,031	6,552	8,487	6,947	6,740
Profit remittances on FDI	21	41	289	10	385	165	436	166
Current account balance	90	-249	-493	193	286	-450	-1,119	-856
International reserves	15	220	965	1,735	2,932	3,113	3,676	3,643
6. Ratios								
External debt stocks to exports (%)	533.4	396.7	169.9	66.0	47.0	37.0	53.1	51.7
External debt stocks to GNI (%)	133.4	109.1	45.1	18.3	14.6	11.8	13.4	13.5
Debt service to exports (%)	21.0	21.5	19.2	10.5	8.0	6.4	7.1	3.6
Short-term to external debt stocks (%)	9.0	11.9	4.6	15.5	7.9	1.5	0.8	1.0
Multilateral to external debt stocks (%)	15.4	13.7	21.8	15.7	18.7	22.4	23.2	26.6
Reserves to external debt stocks (%)	0.1	2.1	13.3	53.5	97.6	113.0	124.8	122.9
Reserves to imports (months)	0.1	0.9	2.3	4.1	5.4	4.4	6.3	6.5

CAMEROON

(US$ million, unless otherwise indicated)

	1995	2000	2005	2006	2007	2008	2009	2010
7. Long-term external debt								
Debt outstanding and disbursed	**9,908**	**8,864**	**6,667**	**2,733**	**2,749**	**2,690**	**2,748**	**2,762**
Public and publicly guaranteed	9,620	8,547	6,075	2,243	2,113	2,055	2,132	2,185
Official creditors	8,737	8,230	5,992	2,180	2,112	2,053	2,122	2,169
Multilateral	1,684	1,419	1,585	510	562	618	682	788
of which: IBRD	639	218	84	46	40	35	30	24
IDA	443	769	1,032	170	198	225	273	350
Bilateral	7,052	6,811	4,407	1,669	1,550	1,435	1,440	1,381
Private creditors	883	317	83	64	2	2	10	15
of which: Bonds	0	0	0	0	0	0	0	0
Commercial banks	298	172	40	45	2	2	10	15
Private nonguaranteed	288	317	592	489	636	636	615	577
of which: Bonds	0	0	0	0	0	0	0	0
Disbursements	**161**	**286**	**227**	**158**	**262**	**279**	**344**	**278**
Public and publicly guaranteed	161	247	130	119	180	192	135	278
Official creditors	161	247	130	118	180	192	127	271
Multilateral	81	115	68	84	83	106	93	141
of which: IBRD	6	0	0	0	0	0	0	0
IDA	35	55	31	29	20	29	48	82
Bilateral	80	133	62	34	97	86	33	131
Private creditors	0	0	0	1	0	0	8	6
of which: Bonds	0	0	0	0	0	0	0	0
Commercial banks	0	0	0	1	0	0	8	6
Private nonguaranteed	0	39	98	39	82	87	209	0
of which: Bonds	0	0	0	0	0	0	0	0
Principal repayments	**211**	**253**	**537**	**355**	**369**	**358**	**336**	**155**
Public and publicly guaranteed	183	166	396	194	186	166	107	117
Official creditors	146	162	396	194	167	166	107	117
Multilateral	130	97	92	86	40	41	39	21
of which: IBRD	91	53	32	39	5	5	5	5
IDA	4	7	12	6	0	1	2	2
Bilateral	16	66	303	108	127	125	68	96
Private creditors	36	4	0	0	19	0	0	0
of which: Bonds	0	0	0	0	0	0	0	0
Commercial banks	25	4	0	0	16	0	0	0
Private nonguaranteed	28	86	141	161	183	192	229	38
of which: Bonds	0	0	0	0	0	0	0	0
Interest payments	**173**	**215**	**231**	**135**	**135**	**115**	**58**	**53**
Public and publicly guaranteed	163	198	181	79	93	70	27	38
Official creditors	152	198	180	79	70	70	27	37
Multilateral	80	48	27	20	16	14	11	8
of which: IBRD	56	22	5	4	2	2	2	1
IDA	3	5	8	5	2	2	2	2
Bilateral	72	149	153	59	54	56	16	29
Private creditors	10	1	1	0	23	0	0	0
of which: Bonds	0	0	0	0	0	0	0	0
Commercial banks	5	1	0	0	23	0	0	0
Private nonguaranteed	11	17	51	57	42	44	31	15
of which: Bonds	0	0	0	0	0	0	0	0
8. Debt stock-flow reconciliation								
Total change in external debt stocks	1,687	-239	-3,025	-4,030	-239	-248	190	19
Net flows on external debt	117	-21	-683	-200	32	-270	155	122
9. Debt restructurings								
Total amount rescheduled	1,070	206	68	20	4	0	0	0
Total amount forgiven	0	7	166	4,292	144	16	3	9
Debt buyback	0	0	0	0	0	0	0	0

10. Contractual obligations on outstanding long-term external debt

	2011	2012	2013	2014	2015	2016	2017	2018
Official creditors								
Principal	157	132	132	139	154	142	137	138
Interest	51	51	50	49	46	43	41	39
Private creditors								
Principal	54	55	55	55	55	55	55	55
Interest	8	8	7	6	5	4	3	3

Notes:

Cameroon was granted debt relief effective in 2006 under MDRI.

CAPE VERDE

(US$ million, unless otherwise indicated)

	1995	2000	2005	2006	2007	2008	2009	2010
1. Summary external debt data								
External debt stocks	**214.1**	**318.9**	**476.6**	**523.2**	**579.6**	**625.2**	**706.8**	**857.3**
Long-term external debt	184.9	315.0	463.3	509.5	564.9	611.4	694.3	847.3
Public and publicly guaranteed	184.9	315.0	463.3	509.5	564.9	611.4	694.3	847.3
Private nonguaranteed	0.0	0.0	0.0	0.0	0.0	0.0	0.0	0.0
Use of IMF credit	0.0	0.0	12.3	13.0	13.5	12.4	11.0	8.6
Short-term external debt	29.2	3.9	0.9	0.7	1.3	1.4	1.5	1.5
interest arrears on long-term	4.6	3.9	0.9	0.7	1.3	1.4	1.5	1.5
Memorandum items								
Principal arrears on long-term	19.6	32.2	3.2	2.4	2.4	2.4	2.4	2.4
Long-term public sector debt	184.9	315.0	463.3	509.5	564.9	611.4	694.3	847.3
Long-term private sector debt	0.0	0.0	0.0	0.0	0.0	0.0	0.0	0.0
Public & publicly guaranteed commitments	11.5	33.9	88.8	27.4	209.9	361.0	267.4	386.7
External debt flows								
Disbursements	21.7	29.0	77.9	48.9	51.1	74.8	97.3	192.1
Long-term external debt	21.7	29.0	74.3	48.9	51.1	74.8	97.3	192.1
IMF purchases	0.0	0.0	3.7	0.0	0.0	0.0	0.0	0.0
Principal repayments	5.6	11.3	28.8	25.2	23.0	24.7	26.9	27.9
Long-term external debt	5.6	11.3	28.8	25.2	22.8	23.9	25.4	25.6
IMF repurchases	0.0	0.0	0.0	0.0	0.2	0.8	1.5	2.3
Net flows	34.7	2.0	49.1	23.7	28.1	50.1	70.4	164.3
Long-term external debt	16.1	17.7	45.4	23.7	28.3	50.9	71.9	166.5
Short-term external debt	18.7	-15.7	0.0	0.0	0.0	0.0	0.0	0.0
Interest payments	4.1	4.8	6.8	6.3	6.5	6.6	7.0	7.9
Long-term external debt	3.4	4.8	6.8	6.3	6.4	6.6	6.9	7.9
IMF charges	0.0	0.0	0.1	0.1	0.1	0.1	0.1	0.0
Short-term external debt	0.8	0.0	0.0	0.0	0.0	0.0	0.0	0.0
2. Other non-debt resource inflows								
Foreign direct investment	26.0	33.4	80.4	131.8	191.9	211.3	119.8	111.4
Portfolio equity	0.0	0.0	0.0	0.3	2.2	0.0	1.8	0.0
3. Currency composition of public and publicly guaranteed debt (%)								
Euro	..	..	13.4	15.0	16.1	18.1	19.0	25.7
Japanese yen	0.0	0.0	0.0	0.0	0.0	0.0	0.2	1.0
Pound sterling	0.0	0.0	0.0	0.0	0.0	0.0	0.0	0.0
Swiss franc	0.0	0.0	0.0	0.0	0.0	0.0	0.0	0.0
U.S.dollars	35.4	56.2	54.3	53.4	49.7	48.5	43.4	38.3
4. Average terms of new commitments								
Official creditors								
Interest (%)	0.8	2.0	3.5	2.9	1.3	1.9	1.6	0.9
Maturity (years)	39.8	31.3	32.5	38.1	25.7	27.2	25.8	27.4
Grace period (years)	10.3	10.4	8.4	9.0	8.2	6.8	7.0	8.8
Private creditors								
Interest (%)	0.0	5.7	0.0	0.0	0.0	0.0	1.7	1.7
Maturity (years)	0.0	10.6	0.0	0.0	0.0	0.0	33.0	32.1
Grace period (years)	0.0	2.2	0.0	0.0	0.0	0.0	12.8	12.7
5. Major economic aggregates								
Gross national income (GNI)	485.3	520.0	965.7	1062.9	1299.8	1503.5	1543.6	1578.9
Exports of goods, services & income	87.5	150.9	377.5	497.0	599.4	744.6	603.0	668.8
Worker remit. & comp. of employees	105.9	86.9	136.6	136.6	138.9	155.1	138.1	138.6
Imports of goods, services & income	300.7	343.6	699.0	868.8	1099.0	1265.2	1155.4	1112.6
Profit remittances on FDI	0.5	5.1	10.9	24.1	28.2	38.2	26.3	..
Current account balance	-61.6	-58.0	-40.7	-82.7	-198.3	-205.5	-239.3	..
International reserves	36.9	28.3	174.0	254.5	364.5	361.5	397.9	382.2
6. Ratios								
External debt stocks to exports (%)	244.8	211.3	126.3	105.3	96.7	84.0	117.2	128.2
External debt stocks to GNI (%)	44.1	61.3	49.4	49.2	44.6	41.6	45.8	54.3
Debt service to exports (%)	11.2	10.7	9.5	6.3	4.9	4.2	5.6	5.3
Short-term to external debt stocks (%)	13.6	1.2	0.2	0.1	0.2	0.2	0.2	0.2
Multilateral to external debt stocks (%)	67.4	72.6	78.9	78.9	78.6	77.3	75.5	69.7
Reserves to external debt stocks (%)	17.2	8.9	36.5	48.6	62.9	57.8	56.3	44.6
Reserves to imports (months)	1.5	1.0	3.0	3.5	4.0	3.4	4.1	4.1

CAPE VERDE

(US$ million, unless otherwise indicated)

	1995	2000	2005	2006	2007	2008	2009	2010
7. Long-term external debt								
Debt outstanding and disbursed	**184.9**	**315.0**	**463.3**	**509.5**	**564.9**	**611.4**	**694.3**	**847.3**
Public and publicly guaranteed	184.9	315.0	463.3	509.5	564.9	611.4	694.3	847.3
Official creditors	178.5	307.5	441.7	492.2	550.0	601.5	687.8	794.8
Multilateral	144.3	231.6	376.0	413.0	455.7	483.6	533.4	597.3
of which: IBRD	0.0	0.0	0.0	0.0	0.0	0.0	0.0	0.0
IDA	33.0	97.9	205.1	235.9	267.4	283.8	286.4	303.1
Bilateral	34.2	75.9	65.6	79.3	94.3	117.9	154.4	197.4
Private creditors	6.4	7.5	21.6	17.3	14.8	9.9	6.5	52.5
of which: Bonds	0.0	0.0	0.0	0.0	0.0	0.0	0.0	0.0
Commercial banks	0.0	0.0	1.8	1.5	1.0	0.3	0.2	0.0
Private nonguaranteed	0.0	0.0	0.0	0.0	0.0	0.0	0.0	0.0
of which: Bonds	0.0	0.0	0.0	0.0	0.0	0.0	0.0	0.0
Disbursements	**21.7**	**29.0**	**74.3**	**48.9**	**51.1**	**74.8**	**97.3**	**192.1**
Public and publicly guaranteed	21.7	29.0	74.3	48.9	51.1	74.8	97.3	192.1
Official creditors	17.5	29.0	64.9	48.8	51.1	74.8	97.3	142.5
Multilateral	15.2	23.7	48.8	30.0	34.5	36.6	58.6	85.2
of which: IBRD	0.0	0.0	0.0	0.0	0.0	0.0	0.0	0.0
IDA	6.0	10.4	27.2	22.1	22.7	20.8	3.8	25.4
Bilateral	2.2	5.3	16.1	18.7	16.6	38.2	38.7	57.2
Private creditors	4.2	0.0	9.4	0.1	0.0	0.0	0.0	49.7
of which: Bonds	0.0	0.0	0.0	0.0	0.0	0.0	0.0	0.0
Commercial banks	0.0	0.0	0.9	0.1	0.0	0.0	0.0	0.0
Private nonguaranteed	0.0	0.0	0.0	0.0	0.0	0.0	0.0	0.0
of which: Bonds	0.0	0.0	0.0	0.0	0.0	0.0	0.0	0.0
Principal repayments	**5.6**	**11.3**	**28.8**	**25.2**	**22.8**	**23.9**	**25.4**	**25.6**
Public and publicly guaranteed	5.6	11.3	28.8	25.2	22.8	23.9	25.4	25.6
Official creditors	5.6	9.5	23.4	18.7	18.6	19.6	21.7	22.1
Multilateral	4.8	6.3	12.5	8.8	9.6	10.6	13.3	14.7
of which: IBRD	0.0	0.0	0.0	0.0	0.0	0.0	0.0	0.0
IDA	0.1	0.3	1.4	1.5	1.8	2.6	3.3	3.7
Bilateral	0.8	3.2	11.0	9.9	9.0	9.0	8.5	7.4
Private creditors	0.0	1.8	5.4	6.5	4.2	4.3	3.6	3.5
of which: Bonds	0.0	0.0	0.0	0.0	0.0	0.0	0.0	0.0
Commercial banks	0.0	0.0	1.4	0.6	0.6	0.7	0.1	0.1
Private nonguaranteed	0.0	0.0	0.0	0.0	0.0	0.0	0.0	0.0
of which: Bonds	0.0	0.0	0.0	0.0	0.0	0.0	0.0	0.0
Interest payments	**3.4**	**4.8**	**6.8**	**6.3**	**6.4**	**6.6**	**6.9**	**7.9**
Public and publicly guaranteed	3.4	4.8	6.8	6.3	6.4	6.6	6.9	7.9
Official creditors	3.4	3.9	5.8	5.8	6.1	6.3	6.8	7.8
Multilateral	3.3	2.8	4.2	4.2	4.4	4.7	4.9	5.5
of which: IBRD	0.0	0.0	0.0	0.0	0.0	0.0	0.0	0.0
IDA	0.2	0.7	1.6	1.7	1.8	2.1	2.0	2.1
Bilateral	0.1	1.1	1.6	1.6	1.8	1.6	1.9	2.4
Private creditors	0.0	0.9	1.0	0.5	0.3	0.3	0.2	0.1
of which: Bonds	0.0	0.0	0.0	0.0	0.0	0.0	0.0	0.0
Commercial banks	0.0	0.0	0.5	0.1	0.1	0.0	0.0	0.0
Private nonguaranteed	0.0	0.0	0.0	0.0	0.0	0.0	0.0	0.0
of which: Bonds	0.0	0.0	0.0	0.0	0.0	0.0	0.0	0.0
8. Debt stock-flow reconciliation								
Total change in external debt stocks	38.2	-8.8	13.4	46.7	56.4	45.6	81.6	150.5
Net flows on external debt	34.7	2.0	49.1	23.7	28.1	50.1	70.4	164.3
9. Debt restructurings								
Total amount rescheduled	0.0	0.0	0.0	0.0	0.0	0.0	0.0	0.0
Total amount forgiven	0.0	0.0	0.0	0.0	0.0	0.0	0.0	0.0
Debt buyback	0.0	0.0	0.0	0.0	0.0	0.0	0.0	0.0

10. Contractual obligations on outstanding long-term external debt

	2011	2012	2013	2014	2015	2016	2017	2018
Official creditors								
Principal	25.3	23.7	40.0	43.3	46.6	46.4	47.6	50.7
Interest	12.0	13.6	14.2	14.4	14.0	13.5	12.9	12.2
Private creditors								
Principal	2.0	0.5	0.0	0.0	0.0	0.0	0.0	0.0
Interest	2.7	5.4	6.4	6.8	6.9	6.9	6.9	6.9

CENTRAL AFRICAN REPUBLIC

(US$ million, unless otherwise indicated)

	1995	2000	2005	2006	2007	2008	2009	2010
1. Summary external debt data								
External debt stocks	**946.0**	**860.0**	**1019.6**	**1009.6**	**959.8**	**954.0**	**394.1**	**384.8**
Long-term external debt	853.9	797.3	877.2	867.8	840.6	808.0	236.7	217.8
Public and publicly guaranteed	853.9	797.3	877.2	867.8	840.6	808.0	236.7	217.8
Private nonguaranteed	0.0	0.0	0.0	0.0	0.0	0.0	0.0	0.0
Use of IMF credit	34.9	21.5	35.9	42.1	49.4	63.0	78.4	90.4
Short-term external debt	57.1	41.2	106.6	99.6	69.8	83.0	79.0	76.6
interest arrears on long-term	35.7	26.1	97.6	90.6	69.8	71.0	75.0	74.6
Memorandum items								
Principal arrears on long-term	74.2	97.7	227.1	218.7	163.4	152.1	148.9	129.7
Long-term public sector debt	853.7	796.3	875.8	866.4	838.9	808.0	236.7	217.8
Long-term private sector debt	0.3	1.0	1.3	1.5	1.6	0.0	0.0	0.0
Public & publicly guaranteed commitments	16.6	28.0	0.0	0.0	3.3	23.5	0.0	33.6
External debt flows								
Disbursements	32.6	16.1	0.0	10.2	34.9	24.9	44.4	19.3
Long-term external debt	32.6	16.1	0.0	0.0	3.2	1.9	4.8	6.0
IMF purchases	0.0	0.0	0.0	10.2	31.7	23.0	39.6	13.2
Principal repayments	10.0	8.3	5.6	53.0	69.1	19.1	27.7	1.0
Long-term external debt	2.6	7.5	0.7	47.0	42.4	11.3	8.4	1.0
IMF repurchases	7.4	0.8	4.9	6.0	26.7	7.7	19.4	0.0
Net flows	25.1	-13.8	-5.6	-42.8	-43.2	17.9	8.7	16.2
Long-term external debt	30.0	8.6	-0.7	-47.0	-39.2	-9.4	-3.6	5.0
Short-term external debt	2.4	-21.6	0.0	0.0	-9.0	12.0	-8.0	-2.0
Interest payments	5.7	5.9	0.9	17.8	20.3	6.6	3.4	1.3
Long-term external debt	3.5	4.3	0.2	16.5	19.6	6.1	3.0	1.2
IMF charges	1.0	0.1	0.4	0.9	0.4	0.3	0.3	0.0
Short-term external debt	1.2	1.4	0.3	0.3	0.2	0.2	0.1	0.0
2. Other non-debt resource inflows								
Foreign direct investment	6.2	0.8	32.4	34.6	56.7	117.1	42.3	72.0
Portfolio equity	..	..	..	..	..	..	..	..
3. Currency composition of public and publicly guaranteed debt (%)								
Euro	..	..	5.9	6.3	3.8	3.4	4.0	3.9
Japanese yen	0.7	0.7	0.6	0.6	0.3	0.4	0.0	0.0
Pound sterling	0.0	0.1	0.1	0.1	0.1	0.1	0.0	0.0
Swiss franc	2.8	2.2	2.5	2.7	2.2	2.3	5.0	5.9
U.S.dollars	56.2	61.2	59.6	57.6	62.5	64.0	61.2	68.3
4. Average terms of new commitments								
Official creditors								
Interest (%)	0.8	0.8	0.0	0.0	1.0	1.8	0.0	0.5
Maturity (years)	39.7	39.8	0.0	0.0	32.6	20.4	0.0	26.6
Grace period (years)	10.2	10.3	0.0	0.0	3.1	5.9	0.0	5.8
Private creditors								
Interest (%)	0.0	0.0	0.0	0.0	0.0	0.0	0.0	0.0
Maturity (years)	0.0	0.0	0.0	0.0	0.0	0.0	0.0	0.0
Grace period (years)	0.0	0.0	0.0	0.0	0.0	0.0	0.0	0.0
5. Major economic aggregates								
Gross national income (GNI)	1100.9	946.8	1348.0	1472.9	1685.7	1960.7	1974.4	2008.8
Exports of goods, services & income	..	..	..	..	..	..	..	..
Worker remit. & comp. of employees	..	..	..	..	..	..	..	..
Imports of goods, services & income	..	..	..	..	..	..	..	..
Profit remittances on FDI	..	..	..	..	..	..	..	..
Current account balance	..	..	..	..	..	..	..	..
International reserves	237.9	136.3	144.9	132.4	91.9	131.5	210.6	181.2
6. Ratios								
External debt stocks to exports (%)	..	..	..	..	..	..	..	..
External debt stocks to GNI (%)	85.9	90.8	75.6	68.5	56.9	48.7	20.0	19.2
Debt service to exports (%)	..	..	..	..	..	..	..	..
Short-term to external debt stocks (%)	6.0	4.8	10.5	9.9	7.3	8.7	20.0	19.9
Multilateral to external debt stocks (%)	67.3	67.8	61.6	60.6	62.8	59.9	12.6	7.6
Reserves to external debt stocks (%)	25.2	15.9	14.2	13.1	9.6	13.8	53.4	47.1
Reserves to imports (months)	..	..	..	..	..	..	..	..

(US$ million, unless otherwise indicated)

	1995	2000	2005	2006	2007	2008	2009	2010
7. Long-term external debt								
Debt outstanding and disbursed	**853.9**	**797.3**	**877.2**	**867.8**	**840.6**	**808.0**	**236.7**	**217.8**
Public and publicly guaranteed	853.9	797.3	877.2	867.8	840.6	808.0	236.7	217.8
Official creditors	835.6	764.8	843.1	833.5	805.9	773.5	202.3	183.6
Multilateral	636.2	583.3	628.3	612.1	602.5	571.3	49.8	29.4
of which: IBRD	0.0	0.0	0.0	0.0	0.0	0.0	0.0	0.0
IDA	414.0	391.3	422.7	395.1	402.8	389.9	9.0	13.9
Bilateral	199.4	181.5	214.8	221.4	203.4	202.2	152.6	154.2
Private creditors	18.4	32.6	34.1	34.4	34.7	34.5	34.4	34.2
of which: Bonds	0.0	0.0	0.0	0.0	0.0	0.0	0.0	0.0
Commercial banks	0.0	0.0	0.0	0.0	0.0	0.0	0.0	0.0
Private nonguaranteed	0.0	0.0	0.0	0.0	0.0	0.0	0.0	0.0
of which: Bonds	0.0	0.0	0.0	0.0	0.0	0.0	0.0	0.0
Disbursements	**32.6**	**16.1**	**0.0**	**0.0**	**3.2**	**1.9**	**4.8**	**6.0**
Public and publicly guaranteed	32.6	16.1	0.0	0.0	3.2	1.9	4.8	6.0
Official creditors	32.6	16.1	0.0	0.0	3.2	1.9	4.8	6.0
Multilateral	32.6	16.1	0.0	0.0	3.2	1.9	3.8	5.1
of which: IBRD	0.0	0.0	0.0	0.0	0.0	0.0	0.0	0.0
IDA	29.8	12.9	0.0	0.0	3.2	1.9	3.8	5.0
Bilateral	0.0	0.0	0.0	0.0	0.0	0.0	1.0	1.0
Private creditors	0.0	0.0	0.0	0.0	0.0	0.0	0.0	0.0
of which: Bonds	0.0	0.0	0.0	0.0	0.0	0.0	0.0	0.0
Commercial banks	0.0	0.0	0.0	0.0	0.0	0.0	0.0	0.0
Private nonguaranteed	0.0	0.0	0.0	0.0	0.0	0.0	0.0	0.0
of which: Bonds	0.0	0.0	0.0	0.0	0.0	0.0	0.0	0.0
Principal repayments	**2.6**	**7.5**	**0.7**	**47.0**	**42.4**	**11.3**	**8.4**	**1.0**
Public and publicly guaranteed	2.6	7.5	0.7	47.0	42.4	11.3	8.4	1.0
Official creditors	2.6	7.4	0.7	47.0	42.4	11.3	8.4	1.0
Multilateral	2.6	6.9	0.7	47.0	42.4	9.5	6.0	0.0
of which: IBRD	0.0	0.0	0.0	0.0	0.0	0.0	0.0	0.0
IDA	1.3	5.7	0.0	46.7	9.6	3.1	1.7	0.0
Bilateral	0.0	0.5	0.0	0.0	0.0	1.8	2.4	1.0
Private creditors	0.0	0.0	0.0	0.0	0.0	0.0	0.0	0.0
of which: Bonds	0.0	0.0	0.0	0.0	0.0	0.0	0.0	0.0
Commercial banks	0.0	0.0	0.0	0.0	0.0	0.0	0.0	0.0
Private nonguaranteed	0.0	0.0	0.0	0.0	0.0	0.0	0.0	0.0
of which: Bonds	0.0	0.0	0.0	0.0	0.0	0.0	0.0	0.0
Interest payments	**3.5**	**4.3**	**0.2**	**16.5**	**19.6**	**6.1**	**3.0**	**1.2**
Public and publicly guaranteed	3.5	4.3	0.2	16.5	19.6	6.1	3.0	1.2
Official creditors	3.5	4.3	0.2	16.5	19.6	6.1	3.0	1.2
Multilateral	3.5	3.4	0.2	16.5	19.6	4.4	2.4	0.1
of which: IBRD	0.0	0.0	0.0	0.0	0.0	0.0	0.0	0.0
IDA	2.9	3.2	0.0	16.5	3.3	3.1	1.6	0.1
Bilateral	0.0	0.9	0.0	0.0	0.0	1.7	0.7	1.1
Private creditors	0.0	0.0	0.0	0.0	0.0	0.0	0.0	0.0
of which: Bonds	0.0	0.0	0.0	0.0	0.0	0.0	0.0	0.0
Commercial banks	0.0	0.0	0.0	0.0	0.0	0.0	0.0	0.0
Private nonguaranteed	0.0	0.0	0.0	0.0	0.0	0.0	0.0	0.0
of which: Bonds	0.0	0.0	0.0	0.0	0.0	0.0	0.0	0.0
8. Debt stock-flow reconciliation								
Total change in external debt stocks	57.9	-51.4	-59.2	-10.1	-49.8	-5.8	-559.9	-9.3
Net flows on external debt	25.1	-13.8	-5.6	-42.8	-43.2	17.9	8.7	16.2
9. Debt restructurings								
Total amount rescheduled	7.6	2.9	0.0	0.0	20.8	3.2	0.0	0.0
Total amount forgiven	1.3	0.7	0.0	0.0	8.2	14.1	519.5	22.1
Debt buyback	0.0	0.0	0.0	0.0	0.0	0.0	0.0	0.0

10. Contractual obligations on outstanding long-term external debt

	2011	2012	2013	2014	2015	2016	2017	2018
Official creditors								
Principal	2.8	2.9	2.9	4.0	6.2	6.5	6.6	6.5
Interest	1.6	1.6	1.7	1.7	1.7	1.6	1.5	1.4
Private creditors								
Principal	0.0	0.0	0.0	0.0	0.0	0.0	0.0	0.0
Interest	0.0	0.0	0.0	0.0	0.0	0.0	0.0	0.0

Notes:

Data on long-term public debt for 2010 are World Bank staff estimates.

CHAD

(US$ million, unless otherwise indicated)

	1995	2000	2005	2006	2007	2008	2009	2010
1. Summary external debt data								
External debt stocks	**842**	**1,088**	**1,584**	**1,706**	**1,797**	**1,750**	**1,746**	**1,733**
Long-term external debt	776	986	1,494	1,627	1,712	1,705	1,714	1,708
Public and publicly guaranteed	776	986	1,494	1,627	1,712	1,705	1,714	1,708
Private nonguaranteed	0	0	0	0	0	0	0	0
Use of IMF credit	49	78	79	68	56	41	29	17
Short-term external debt	17	25	11	12	29	4	4	8
interest arrears on long-term	9	10	6	8	6	4	4	7
Memorandum items								
Principal arrears on long-term	36	52	26	24	22	30	30	39
Long-term public sector debt	776	986	1,494	1,627	1,712	1,705	1,714	1,708
Long-term private sector debt	0	0	0	0	0	0	0	0
Public & publicly guaranteed commitments	116	178	139	7	141	15	15	21
External debt flows								
Disbursements	73	59	116	102	50	97	38	57
Long-term external debt	61	46	110	102	50	97	38	57
IMF purchases	13	14	6	0	0	0	0	0
Principal repayments	10	14	37	40	49	119	55	57
Long-term external debt	3	13	24	24	34	105	43	46
IMF repurchases	7	1	13	16	15	14	13	11
Net flows	63	44	75	61	21	-44	-17	2
Long-term external debt	57	33	85	78	17	-7	-5	12
Short-term external debt	0	-2	-3	-1	19	-23	0	1
Interest payments	5	10	17	17	19	19	23	17
Long-term external debt	4	9	16	16	19	18	23	17
IMF charges	1	0	0	0	0	0	0	0
Short-term external debt	1	1	0	0	1	0	0	0
2. Other non-debt resource inflows								
Foreign direct investment	33	115	-99	-279	-69	234	462	781
Portfolio equity	0	..	..	..	..	..	..	..
3. Currency composition of public and publicly guaranteed debt (%)								
Euro	..	..	3.3	3.8	3.6	3.3	3.3	3.2
Japanese yen	0.0	0.0	0.0	0.0	0.0	0.0	0.0	0.0
Pound sterling	0.0	0.0	0.0	0.0	0.0	0.0	0.0	0.0
Swiss franc	0.0	0.0	0.0	0.0	0.0	0.0	0.0	0.0
U.S.dollars	54.9	58.7	66.1	65.1	64.4	60.2	59.8	58.3
4. Average terms of new commitments								
Official creditors								
Interest (%)	1.0	0.7	1.6	0.0	1.3	0.6	5.7	5.1
Maturity (years)	38.0	40.5	23.7	28.6	19.9	22.7	13.9	10.5
Grace period (years)	8.7	10.1	6.5	9.1	6.9	6.0	4.3	2.0
Private creditors								
Interest (%)	0.0	0.0	0.0	0.0	0.0	0.0	0.0	0.0
Maturity (years)	0.0	0.0	0.0	0.0	0.0	0.0	0.0	0.0
Grace period (years)	0.0	0.0	0.0	0.0	0.0	0.0	0.0	0.0
5. Major economic aggregates								
Gross national income (GNI)	1,441	1,368	4,277	4,888	5,817	6,687	6,124	6,734
Exports of goods, services & income	..	..	..	..	..	..	..	..
Worker remit. & comp. of employees	..	..	..	..	..	..	..	..
Imports of goods, services & income	..	..	..	..	..	..	..	..
Profit remittances on FDI	..	..	..	..	..	..	..	..
Current account balance	..	..	..	..	..	..	..	..
International reserves	147	114	231	632	964	1,355	617	632
6. Ratios								
External debt stocks to exports (%)	..	..	..	..	..	..	..	..
External debt stocks to GNI (%)	58.4	79.6	37.0	34.9	30.9	26.2	28.5	25.7
Debt service to exports (%)	..	..	..	..	..	..	..	..
Short-term to external debt stocks (%)	2.0	2.3	0.7	0.7	1.6	0.2	0.2	0.5
Multilateral to external debt stocks (%)	76.6	76.7	84.6	85.0	85.0	84.0	84.9	85.5
Reserves to external debt stocks (%)	17.4	10.5	14.6	37.0	53.7	77.4	35.3	36.5
Reserves to imports (months)	..	..	..	..	..	..	..	..

CHAD

(US$ million, unless otherwise indicated)

	1995	2000	2005	2006	2007	2008	2009	2010
7. Long-term external debt								
Debt outstanding and disbursed	**776**	**986**	**1,494**	**1,627**	**1,712**	**1,705**	**1,714**	**1,708**
Public and publicly guaranteed	776	986	1,494	1,627	1,712	1,705	1,714	1,708
Official creditors	774	971	1,462	1,594	1,679	1,672	1,682	1,679
Multilateral	645	834	1,340	1,450	1,527	1,469	1,482	1,483
of which: IBRD	0	0	35	30	26	0	0	0
IDA	379	515	864	925	968	905	896	865
Bilateral	129	137	122	144	152	203	200	196
Private creditors	2	15	32	33	33	33	32	30
of which: Bonds	0	0	0	0	0	0	0	0
Commercial banks	0	0	0	0	0	0	0	0
Private nonguaranteed	0	0	0	0	0	0	0	0
of which: Bonds	0	0	0	0	0	0	0	0
Disbursements	**61**	**46**	**110**	**102**	**50**	**97**	**38**	**57**
Public and publicly guaranteed	61	46	110	102	50	97	38	57
Official creditors	61	46	110	102	50	97	38	57
Multilateral	61	36	108	71	39	38	34	56
of which: IBRD	0	0	1	0	0	0	0	0
IDA	42	18	64	31	16	5	3	3
Bilateral	0	10	2	31	12	59	4	2
Private creditors	0	0	0	0	0	0	0	0
of which: Bonds	0	0	0	0	0	0	0	0
Commercial banks	0	0	0	0	0	0	0	0
Private nonguaranteed	0	0	0	0	0	0	0	0
of which: Bonds	0	0	0	0	0	0	0	0
Principal repayments	**3**	**13**	**24**	**24**	**34**	**105**	**43**	**46**
Public and publicly guaranteed	3	13	24	24	34	105	43	46
Official creditors	3	13	23	24	33	105	42	44
Multilateral	3	10	17	18	28	100	36	38
of which: IBRD	0	0	2	5	5	26	0	0
IDA	1	4	4	5	7	62	17	19
Bilateral	1	3	5	6	5	5	5	6
Private creditors	0	1	1	1	1	0	1	2
of which: Bonds	0	0	0	0	0	0	0	0
Commercial banks	0	0	0	0	0	0	0	0
Private nonguaranteed	0	0	0	0	0	0	0	0
of which: Bonds	0	0	0	0	0	0	0	0
Interest payments	**4**	**9**	**16**	**16**	**19**	**18**	**23**	**17**
Public and publicly guaranteed	4	9	16	16	19	18	23	17
Official creditors	4	9	16	16	18	18	23	17
Multilateral	3	6	14	13	15	15	19	12
of which: IBRD	0	0	1	2	2	1	0	0
IDA	3	3	6	6	7	8	7	6
Bilateral	0	3	2	3	3	3	4	5
Private creditors	0	0	0	0	0	0	0	0
of which: Bonds	0	0	0	0	0	0	0	0
Commercial banks	0	0	0	0	0	0	0	0
Private nonguaranteed	0	0	0	0	0	0	0	0
of which: Bonds	0	0	0	0	0	0	0	0
8. Debt stock-flow reconciliation								
Total change in external debt stocks	58	-8	-56	122	90	-47	-4	-13
Net flows on external debt	63	44	75	61	21	-44	-17	2
9. Debt restructurings								
Total amount rescheduled	45	0	12	0	0	0	0	0
Total amount forgiven	62	0	18	22	5	4	5	0
Debt buyback	0	0	0	0	0	0	0	0

10. Contractual obligations on outstanding long-term external debt

	2011	2012	2013	2014	2015	2016	2017	2018
Official creditors								
Principal	65	71	73	82	88	85	86	82
Interest	19	19	19	18	17	15	14	13
Private creditors								
Principal	2	2	2	2	2	1	0	0
Interest	0	0	0	0	0	0	0	0

CHILE

(US$ million, unless otherwise indicated)

	1995	*2000*	*2005*	*2006*	*2007*	*2008*	*2009*	*2010*
1. Summary external debt data								
External debt stocks	**22,038**	**37,239**	**45,434**	**50,195**	**56,191**	**65,419**	**73,145**	**86,349**
Long-term external debt	18,607	31,067	38,345	38,725	42,626	47,570	51,507	60,470
Public and publicly guaranteed	7,179	5,205	9,161	9,380	9,317	8,777	9,262	12,929
Private nonguaranteed	11,429	25,861	29,184	29,344	33,308	38,793	42,245	47,541
Use of IMF credit	0	0	0	0	0	0	0	0
Short-term external debt	3,431	6,172	7,089	11,470	13,565	17,849	21,638	25,879
interest arrears on long-term	0	0	0	0	0	0	0	0
Memorandum items								
Principal arrears on long-term	0	0	0	0	0	0	0	0
Long-term public sector debt	7,179	5,125	9,158	9,368	9,306	8,769	9,256	12,925
Long-term private sector debt	11,429	25,941	29,188	29,357	33,319	38,801	42,251	47,545
Public & publicly guaranteed commitments	314	264	995	1,423	894	1,063	1,979	3,862
External debt flows								
Disbursements	3,821	4,943	9,156	12,620	13,795	18,995	19,343	19,677
Long-term external debt	3,821	4,943	9,156	12,620	13,795	18,995	19,343	19,677
IMF purchases	0	0	0	0	0	0	0	0
Principal repayments	3,671	3,938	6,073	12,551	9,749	14,278	15,574	11,005
Long-term external debt	3,369	3,938	6,073	12,551	9,749	14,278	15,574	11,005
IMF repurchases	303	0	0	0	0	0	0	0
Net flows	-284	2,860	2,720	4,450	6,140	9,001	7,558	12,914
Long-term external debt	452	1,005	3,083	69	4,045	4,717	3,769	8,672
Short-term external debt	-434	1,855	-363	4,381	2,095	4,284	3,789	4,241
Interest payments	1,293	2,235	1,510	1,992	2,149	1,937	1,843	2,388
Long-term external debt	1,114	2,081	1,289	1,655	1,597	1,547	1,389	1,733
IMF charges	13	0	0	0	0	0	0	0
Short-term external debt	165	154	221	338	553	389	454	655
2. Other non-debt resource inflows								
Foreign direct investment	2,957	4,860	6,984	7,298	12,534	15,150	12,874	15,095
Portfolio equity	-249	-427	1,571	-124	388	1,948	328	1,748
3. Currency composition of public and publicly guaranteed debt (%)								
Euro	..	..	1.0	1.1	1.2	1.1	1.0	0.7
Japanese yen	9.5	5.0	0.4	2.5	2.2	0.0	0.0	0.0
Pound sterling	2.9	0.2	0.0	0.0	0.0	0.0	0.0	0.0
Swiss franc	0.9	0.1	0.0	0.0	0.0	0.0	0.0	0.0
U.S.dollars	42.0	84.1	98.0	95.8	96.0	98.2	98.5	98.9
4. Average terms of new commitments								
Official creditors								
Interest (%)	6.1	1.0	4.2	5.2	5.1	2.9	2.9	1.7
Maturity (years)	19.5	17.0	13.1	13.1	15.7	9.8	12.1	19.6
Grace period (years)	5.8	1.5	4.7	6.0	5.5	5.7	5.6	4.3
Private creditors								
Interest (%)	6.8	6.9	5.1	5.8	5.6	4.7	4.5	3.6
Maturity (years)	10.9	5.5	19.2	15.7	6.4	5.6	6.5	8.9
Grace period (years)	3.0	3.0	18.2	13.0	5.0	2.2	5.9	8.9
5. Major economic aggregates								
Gross national income (GNI)	68,637	72,333	107,763	128,372	145,641	157,560	149,316	188,032
Exports of goods, services & income	20,226	24,891	50,853	69,885	83,259	83,010	67,984	87,820
Worker remit. & comp. of employees	..	13	13	3	3	3	4	3
Imports of goods, services & income	21,883	26,346	51,187	66,137	78,930	89,247	66,977	88,409
Profit remittances on FDI	2,178	2,539	11,416	19,913	22,832	17,430	14,801	18,956
Current account balance	-1,350	-898	1,449	7,154	7,458	-3,307	2,570	3,802
International reserves	14,860	15,055	16,933	19,397	16,843	23,079	25,292	27,827
6. Ratios								
External debt stocks to exports (%)	109.0	149.6	89.3	71.8	67.5	78.8	107.6	98.3
External debt stocks to GNI (%)	32.1	51.5	42.2	39.1	38.6	41.5	49.0	45.9
Debt service to exports (%)	24.5	24.8	14.9	20.8	14.3	19.5	25.6	15.2
Short-term to external debt stocks (%)	15.6	16.6	15.6	22.9	24.1	27.3	29.6	30.0
Multilateral to external debt stocks (%)	13.0	3.8	1.8	1.8	1.6	1.2	1.2	0.9
Reserves to external debt stocks (%)	67.4	40.4	37.3	38.6	30.0	35.3	34.6	32.2
Reserves to imports (months)	8.1	6.9	4.0	3.5	2.6	3.1	4.5	3.8

CHILE

(US$ million, unless otherwise indicated)

	1995	2000	2005	2006	2007	2008	2009	2010
7. Long-term external debt								
Debt outstanding and disbursed	**18,607**	**31,067**	**38,345**	**38,725**	**42,626**	**47,570**	**51,507**	**60,470**
Public and publicly guaranteed	7,179	5,205	9,161	9,380	9,317	8,777	9,262	12,929
Official creditors	3,583	1,887	1,089	1,151	1,136	1,004	1,041	1,025
Multilateral	2,871	1,406	827	897	907	793	848	801
of which: IBRD	1,372	808	289	346	354	200	215	189
IDA	11	7	4	3	2	2	1	0
Bilateral	712	481	262	254	229	211	193	224
Private creditors	3,596	3,318	8,072	8,229	8,182	7,773	8,221	11,904
of which: Bonds	0	0	5,406	5,938	5,401	4,513	5,413	8,413
Commercial banks	3,509	3,250	2,666	2,291	2,781	3,260	2,808	3,241
Private nonguaranteed	11,429	25,861	29,184	29,344	33,308	38,793	42,245	47,541
of which: Bonds	866	6,339	4,761	4,779	3,631	4,296	5,126	7,061
Disbursements	**3,821**	**4,943**	**9,156**	**12,620**	**13,795**	**18,995**	**19,343**	**19,677**
Public and publicly guaranteed	342	346	1,197	1,186	689	1,030	2,385	4,010
Official creditors	194	147	176	112	64	132	109	111
Multilateral	146	113	162	92	47	126	109	51
of which: IBRD	83	48	55	62	14	53	29	32
IDA	0	0	0	0	0	0	0	0
Bilateral	48	34	14	20	16	6	0	60
Private creditors	148	199	1,022	1,074	626	899	2,276	3,900
of which: Bonds	0	0	500	650	0	0	900	3,000
Commercial banks	141	199	522	424	626	899	1,376	650
Private nonguaranteed	3,479	4,597	7,959	11,434	13,105	17,965	16,958	15,667
of which: Bonds	500	672	700	813	843	1,680	2,184	2,695
Principal repayments	**3,369**	**3,938**	**6,073**	**12,551**	**9,749**	**14,278**	**15,574**	**11,005**
Public and publicly guaranteed	2,277	757	1,362	973	740	1,590	1,903	336
Official creditors	2,003	277	371	61	58	261	75	119
Multilateral	1,884	177	345	23	40	243	54	96
of which: IBRD	704	115	206	5	6	207	14	58
IDA	1	1	1	1	1	1	1	1
Bilateral	119	100	26	38	18	17	21	23
Private creditors	273	480	990	912	682	1,329	1,828	217
of which: Bonds	0	0	422	118	537	888	0	0
Commercial banks	240	479	544	794	145	441	1,828	217
Private nonguaranteed	1,092	3,181	4,711	11,578	9,010	12,689	13,671	10,669
of which: Bonds	11	0	193	763	1,103	1,002	1,327	828
Interest payments	**1,114**	**2,081**	**1,289**	**1,655**	**1,597**	**1,547**	**1,389**	**1,733**
Public and publicly guaranteed	653	377	460	495	529	529	422	418
Official creditors	387	138	49	49	55	46	40	27
Multilateral	348	112	43	43	50	42	31	23
of which: IBRD	137	70	16	17	20	13	6	2
IDA	0	0	0	0	0	0	0	0
Bilateral	39	26	6	6	5	5	9	4
Private creditors	266	239	411	446	474	482	383	392
of which: Bonds	0	0	299	313	336	249	281	337
Commercial banks	258	234	112	133	138	234	101	55
Private nonguaranteed	461	1,704	829	1,160	1,068	1,018	966	1,314
of which: Bonds	26	440	347	359	345	326	404	440
8. Debt stock-flow reconciliation								
Total change in external debt stocks	-117	2,444	1,675	4,760	5,996	9,228	7,727	13,204
Net flows on external debt	-284	2,860	2,720	4,450	6,140	9,001	7,558	12,914
9. Debt restructurings								
Total amount rescheduled	0	0	0	0	0	0	0	0
Total amount forgiven	145	0	0	0	0	0	0	0
Debt buyback	0	0	0	0	0	0	0	0

10. Contractual obligations on outstanding long-term external debt

	2011	2012	2013	2014	2015	2016	2017	2018
Official creditors								
Principal	130	83	106	160	166	165	158	107
Interest	25	24	24	23	22	20	18	15
Private creditors								
Principal	11,276	10,528	6,121	4,300	4,688	1,616	1,365	770
Interest	1,879	1,775	1,324	1,264	1,123	973	1,098	742

Notes:

Short-term debt is based on reports provided by the country.

CHINA

(US$ million, unless otherwise indicated)

	1995	2000	2005	2006	2007	2008	2009	2010
1. Summary external debt data								
External debt stocks	**118,090**	**145,339**	**282,955**	**322,761**	**373,083**	**379,800**	**432,197**	**548,551**
Long-term external debt	95,764	132,259	134,688	149,384	169,385	192,612	191,688	201,027
Public and publicly guaranteed	94,674	94,470	84,196	85,718	87,101	90,838	94,038	90,180
Private nonguaranteed	1,090	37,789	50,492	63,666	82,284	101,774	97,650	110,847
Use of IMF credit	0	0	0	0	0	0	0	0
Short-term external debt	22,325	13,080	148,267	173,377	203,698	187,188	240,509	347,524
interest arrears on long-term	0	0	0	0	0	0	0	0
Memorandum items								
Principal arrears on long-term	0	0	0	0	0	0	0	0
Long-term public sector debt	93,573	94,470	83,937	85,474	86,929	90,680	93,896	90,051
Long-term private sector debt	2,192	37,789	50,751	63,910	82,456	101,932	97,793	110,976
Public & publicly guaranteed commitments	22,812	10,702	10,233	6,275	6,927	6,010	7,238	11,758
External debt flows								
Disbursements	21,985	19,006	29,228	26,524	36,907	38,188	23,648	42,423
Long-term external debt	21,985	19,006	29,228	26,524	36,907	38,188	23,648	42,423
IMF purchases	0	0	0	0	0	0	0	0
Principal repayments	9,070	19,362	20,936	18,120	20,405	23,959	33,448	28,539
Long-term external debt	9,070	19,362	20,936	18,120	20,405	23,959	33,448	28,539
IMF repurchases	0	0	0	0	0	0	0	0
Net flows	17,758	-2,457	40,789	33,514	46,823	-2,280	43,521	120,899
Long-term external debt	12,915	-357	8,292	8,404	16,502	14,230	-9,800	13,884
Short-term external debt	4,842	-2,100	32,497	25,110	30,321	-16,510	53,321	107,015
Interest payments	5,996	7,231	6,519	9,361	11,406	9,298	6,330	34,071
Long-term external debt	4,657	6,064	3,218	3,820	5,464	4,812	3,122	6,269
IMF charges	0	0	0	0	0	0	0	0
Short-term external debt	1,340	1,168	3,302	5,541	5,942	4,486	3,208	27,802
2. Other non-debt resource inflows								
Foreign direct investment	35,849	38,399	117,208	124,082	160,052	175,148	114,215	185,081
Portfolio equity	0	6,912	20,346	42,861	18,510	8,721	28,161	31,357
3. Currency composition of public and publicly guaranteed debt (%)								
Euro	..	..	8.3	8.9	8.4	6.8	6.4	6.9
Japanese yen	20.7	17.0	13.6	12.4	8.5	9.0	7.8	7.3
Pound sterling	0.2	0.1	0.1	0.1	0.1	0.0	0.0	0.0
Swiss franc	0.0	0.1	0.1	0.1	0.0	0.0	0.0	0.0
U.S.dollars	58.1	71.3	74.1	75.3	80.2	81.7	83.7	84.0
4. Average terms of new commitments								
Official creditors								
Interest (%)	6.8	7.2	4.3	5.4	5.4	3.5	1.7	1.9
Maturity (years)	18.3	21.1	22.5	22.7	21.8	23.0	25.9	24.1
Grace period (years)	3.7	4.9	5.5	5.7	5.4	5.8	5.8	6.2
Private creditors								
Interest (%)	6.3	5.9	4.6	5.0	4.1	4.6	5.0	10.5
Maturity (years)	7.3	17.0	10.4	14.4	9.6	13.6	14.4	30.1
Grace period (years)	2.4	3.0	5.4	0.9	2.1	1.1	0.9	5.1
5. Major economic aggregates								
Gross national income (GNI)	716,233	1,183,815	2,267,538	2,728,108	3,519,744	4,553,265	5,034,545	5,906,327
Exports of goods, services & income	152,431	292,111	875,847	1,116,323	1,425,236	1,683,328	1,441,928	1,897,242
Worker remit. & comp. of employees	878	5,237	24,102	27,954	38,791	48,524	48,729	51,300
Imports of goods, services & income	152,248	277,904	767,150	912,776	1,109,907	1,316,763	1,214,556	1,634,801
Profit remittances on FDI	9,953	20,198	47,776	49,758	61,547	72,609	90,805	103,476
Current account balance	1,618	20,518	134,082	232,746	353,996	412,364	261,120	305,374
International reserves	80,288	171,763	831,410	1,080,756	1,546,365	1,966,037	2,452,899	2,913,712
6. Ratios								
External debt stocks to exports (%)	77.5	49.8	32.3	28.9	26.2	22.6	30.0	28.9
External debt stocks to GNI (%)	16.5	12.3	12.5	11.8	10.6	8.3	8.6	9.3
Debt service to exports (%)	9.9	9.1	3.1	2.5	2.2	2.0	2.8	3.3
Short-term to external debt stocks (%)	18.9	9.0	52.4	53.7	54.6	49.3	55.6	63.4
Multilateral to external debt stocks (%)	13.8	17.8	9.3	8.6	7.8	8.1	7.7	6.4
Reserves to external debt stocks (%)	68.0	118.2	293.8	334.8	414.5	517.7	567.5	531.2
Reserves to imports (months)	6.3	7.4	13.0	14.2	16.7	17.9	24.2	21.4

CHINA

(US$ million, unless otherwise indicated)

	1995	2000	2005	2006	2007	2008	2009	2010
7. Long-term external debt								
Debt outstanding and disbursed	**95,764**	**132,259**	**134,688**	**149,384**	**169,385**	**192,612**	**191,688**	**201,027**
Public and publicly guaranteed	94,674	94,470	84,196	85,718	87,101	90,838	94,038	90,180
Official creditors	36,982	50,374	52,421	54,334	58,323	63,349	68,358	67,204
Multilateral	16,302	25,811	26,413	27,738	29,258	30,655	33,207	35,120
of which: IBRD	7,209	11,118	11,140	11,415	11,762	12,464	12,756	12,962
IDA	7,038	8,771	9,741	9,997	10,151	9,786	9,521	9,000
Bilateral	20,680	24,563	26,008	26,596	29,066	32,693	35,151	32,084
Private creditors	57,693	44,096	31,775	31,384	28,778	27,489	25,681	22,976
of which: Bonds	10,684	11,371	16,039	16,342	16,526	15,728	11,626	10,273
Commercial banks	23,869	10,619	3,247	3,763	3,030	2,868	2,735	2,202
Private nonguaranteed	1,090	37,789	50,492	63,666	82,284	101,774	97,650	110,847
of which: Bonds	1,090	1,068	3,574	5,279	6,018	5,970	7,020	17,976
Disbursements	**21,985**	**19,006**	**29,228**	**26,524**	**36,907**	**38,188**	**23,648**	**42,423**
Public and publicly guaranteed	21,441	11,924	9,776	6,278	7,130	5,449	6,481	10,125
Official creditors	9,073	5,790	2,170	3,588	3,403	3,893	3,310	4,348
Multilateral	2,838	3,303	2,010	2,153	2,425	2,870	2,657	2,623
of which: IBRD	1,457	1,528	1,061	1,134	1,194	1,604	1,290	1,282
IDA	812	379	70	34	14	9	1	0
Bilateral	6,235	2,487	159	1,434	978	1,023	653	1,725
Private creditors	12,368	6,133	7,606	2,690	3,727	1,556	3,171	5,777
of which: Bonds	1,224	848	4,208	0	1,456	0	0	0
Commercial banks	4,977	131	2,161	17	215	27	46	673
Private nonguaranteed	544	7,082	19,452	20,246	29,777	32,739	17,167	32,298
of which: Bonds	544	390	1,622	1,945	740	0	925	11,821
Principal repayments	**9,070**	**19,362**	**20,936**	**18,120**	**20,405**	**23,959**	**33,448**	**28,539**
Public and publicly guaranteed	9,070	10,235	6,659	6,520	5,342	6,750	6,473	8,831
Official creditors	1,171	4,270	1,413	2,684	2,949	2,809	2,594	3,643
Multilateral	420	1,400	1,195	1,333	1,397	1,520	1,602	1,795
of which: IBRD	350	578	787	901	908	971	992	1,086
IDA	14	66	217	243	276	309	331	349
Bilateral	751	2,870	217	1,351	1,552	1,289	993	1,848
Private creditors	7,899	5,965	5,246	3,836	2,393	3,940	3,878	5,188
of which: Bonds	1,451	443	550	0	0	742	500	431
Commercial banks	2,645	2,016	1,936	149	676	264	200	372
Private nonguaranteed	0	9,127	14,277	11,600	15,063	17,209	26,976	19,708
of which: Bonds	0	534	370	240	0	350	464	277
Interest payments	**4,657**	**6,064**	**3,218**	**3,820**	**5,464**	**4,812**	**3,122**	**6,269**
Public and publicly guaranteed	4,623	4,140	2,201	2,306	3,237	2,591	2,108	2,626
Official creditors	1,288	2,386	1,375	1,429	1,701	1,407	1,090	1,844
Multilateral	619	1,518	680	935	1,105	1,009	733	522
of which: IBRD	460	713	351	542	653	553	363	143
IDA	49	65	79	74	74	79	69	67
Bilateral	669	867	695	493	596	398	358	1,321
Private creditors	3,335	1,754	826	877	1,537	1,184	1,017	783
of which: Bonds	594	521	430	502	778	497	557	393
Commercial banks	1,333	222	71	80	182	33	42	32
Private nonguaranteed	33	1,924	1,017	1,514	2,227	2,220	1,015	3,643
of which: Bonds	33	93	248	343	445	431	445	672
8. Debt stock-flow reconciliation								
Total change in external debt stocks	17,633	-2,900	37,412	39,806	50,322	6,717	52,397	116,354
Net flows on external debt	17,758	-2,457	40,789	33,514	46,823	-2,280	43,521	120,899
9. Debt restructurings								
Total amount rescheduled	0	0	0	0	0	0	0	0
Total amount forgiven	0	0	0	0	0	0	0	0
Debt buyback	0	0	0	0	0	0	0	0

10. Contractual obligations on outstanding long-term external debt

	2011	2012	2013	2014	2015	2016	2017	2018
Official creditors								
Principal	6,537	6,588	6,117	6,095	5,961	5,747	5,640	5,392
Interest	2,002	1,792	1,590	1,404	1,221	1,048	879	714
Private creditors								
Principal	34,044	28,478	18,370	14,249	16,642	6,428	7,053	4,445
Interest	5,557	4,225	3,339	2,689	1,955	1,079	691	394

Notes:

Data on long-term public and publicly guaranteed, long-term private nonguaranteed and short-term debt for 2010 are World Bank staff estimates based on aggregate information provided by the authority.

COLOMBIA

(US$ million, unless otherwise indicated)

	1995	2000	2005	2006	2007	2008	2009	2010
1. Summary external debt data								
External debt stocks	**25,044**	**33,937**	**37,744**	**38,048**	**43,697**	**46,428**	**52,120**	**63,064**
Long-term external debt	19,499	31,066	31,568	33,285	38,536	40,795	48,107	54,855
Public and publicly guaranteed	13,946	20,806	22,579	24,744	27,424	28,983	35,358	36,777
Private nonguaranteed	5,553	10,259	8,989	8,541	11,112	11,812	12,749	18,078
Use of IMF credit	0	0	0	0	0	0	0	0
Short-term external debt	5,545	2,871	6,176	4,763	5,161	5,633	4,013	8,209
interest arrears on long-term	2	0	0	0	0	0	0	0
Memorandum items								
Principal arrears on long-term	177	8	0	0	0	0	0	0
Long-term public sector debt	13,945	20,805	22,578	24,743	27,423	28,506	34,831	36,274
Long-term private sector debt	5,555	10,261	8,990	8,542	11,113	12,289	13,276	18,581
Public & publicly guaranteed commitments	1,792	3,782	4,879	4,916	4,647	5,106	7,971	2,917
External debt flows								
Disbursements	4,179	3,803	6,521	8,943	8,860	7,094	13,146	12,840
Long-term external debt	4,179	3,803	6,521	8,943	8,860	7,094	13,146	12,840
IMF purchases	0	0	0	0	0	0	0	0
Principal repayments	2,347	2,900	7,403	7,769	5,642	4,877	5,914	6,553
Long-term external debt	2,347	2,900	7,403	7,769	5,642	4,877	5,914	6,553
IMF repurchases	0	0	0	0	0	0	0	0
Net flows	2,894	-191	174	-240	3,616	2,690	5,611	10,483
Long-term external debt	1,832	903	-883	1,173	3,218	2,218	7,232	6,287
Short-term external debt	1,062	-1,094	1,056	-1,413	398	472	-1,620	4,196
Interest payments	1,998	2,204	2,838	2,579	2,993	3,028	2,912	3,227
Long-term external debt	1,687	2,032	2,585	2,359	2,749	2,764	2,723	2,842
IMF charges	0	0	0	0	0	0	0	0
Short-term external debt	311	172	254	220	244	265	189	386
2. Other non-debt resource inflows								
Foreign direct investment	968	2,436	10,252	6,656	9,049	10,596	7,137	6,765
Portfolio equity	165	17	86	-30	790	-86	67	1,351
3. Currency composition of public and publicly guaranteed debt (%)								
Euro	..	..	4.2	3.5	3.5	1.4	1.1	1.0
Japanese yen	5.6	3.6	1.6	1.3	1.1	1.1	2.2	2.3
Pound sterling	0.1	0.8	0.8	0.8	0.8	0.0	0.0	0.0
Swiss franc	0.2	0.0	0.0	0.0	0.0	0.0	0.0	0.0
U.S.dollars	49.9	74.4	85.2	88.1	89.8	93.7	94.3	94.9
4. Average terms of new commitments								
Official creditors								
Interest (%)	6.4	8.8	5.1	5.5	5.7	3.4	1.6	1.7
Maturity (years)	20.4	12.1	15.9	17.7	12.3	23.1	23.9	22.1
Grace period (years)	4.8	3.1	6.0	5.3	4.8	7.1	7.0	5.8
Private creditors								
Interest (%)	3.8	7.6	8.0	7.5	9.2	6.8	6.6	7.5
Maturity (years)	6.1	10.2	11.4	18.3	13.4	14.5	14.0	12.0
Grace period (years)	4.0	7.5	10.2	17.9	13.2	13.7	13.6	11.2
5. Major economic aggregates								
Gross national income (GNI)	90,928	98,048	141,110	156,873	199,409	234,312	226,344	276,093
Exports of goods, services & income	12,971	16,850	25,467	30,077	36,067	44,416	39,517	46,593
Worker remit. & comp. of employees	815	1,610	3,346	3,928	4,523	4,884	4,180	4,058
Imports of goods, services & income	18,286	17,728	31,435	37,808	47,273	56,851	49,286	60,100
Profit remittances on FDI	359	655	3,565	4,591	6,598	8,706	7,628	9,983
Current account balance	-4,516	795	-1,886	-2,989	-5,977	-6,923	-5,157	-9,032
International reserves	8,452	9,006	14,955	15,437	20,951	23,671	24,987	28,076
6. Ratios								
External debt stocks to exports (%)	193.1	201.4	148.2	126.5	121.2	104.5	131.9	135.4
External debt stocks to GNI (%)	27.5	34.6	26.7	24.3	21.9	19.8	23.0	22.8
Debt service to exports (%)	33.5	30.3	40.2	34.4	23.9	17.8	22.3	21.0
Short-term to external debt stocks (%)	22.1	8.5	16.4	12.5	11.8	12.1	7.7	13.0
Multilateral to external debt stocks (%)	21.2	18.5	25.5	28.5	25.8	28.2	28.2	25.0
Reserves to external debt stocks (%)	33.7	26.5	39.6	40.6	47.9	51.0	47.9	44.5
Reserves to imports (months)	5.5	6.1	5.7	4.9	5.3	5.0	6.1	5.6

COLOMBIA

(US$ million, unless otherwise indicated)

	1995	2000	2005	2006	2007	2008	2009	2010
7. Long-term external debt								
Debt outstanding and disbursed	**19,499**	**31,066**	**31,568**	**33,285**	**38,536**	**40,795**	**48,107**	**54,855**
Public and publicly guaranteed	13,946	20,806	22,579	24,744	27,424	28,983	35,358	36,777
Official creditors	7,063	7,722	10,568	11,657	11,993	13,739	15,211	16,218
Multilateral	5,316	6,274	9,615	10,841	11,277	13,114	14,695	15,786
of which: IBRD	2,548	1,920	3,896	4,563	4,756	5,438	6,570	7,504
IDA	11	7	4	3	2	2	1	0
Bilateral	1,747	1,448	954	816	717	626	515	432
Private creditors	6,883	13,084	12,011	13,087	15,431	15,244	20,148	20,559
of which: Bonds	1,733	8,201	10,927	12,162	12,354	12,280	17,159	17,686
Commercial banks	4,163	4,252	824	777	2,246	2,225	2,214	2,094
Private nonguaranteed	5,553	10,259	8,989	8,541	11,112	11,812	12,749	18,078
of which: Bonds	717	762	370	540	809	809	2,709	3,329
Disbursements	**4,179**	**3,803**	**6,521**	**8,943**	**8,860**	**7,094**	**13,146**	**12,840**
Public and publicly guaranteed	1,569	2,939	4,400	5,578	4,494	3,862	8,105	3,499
Official creditors	685	660	1,467	2,237	1,585	2,567	2,413	2,124
Multilateral	394	508	1,467	2,219	1,581	2,546	2,398	2,123
of which: IBRD	238	266	705	942	564	847	1,331	1,279
IDA	0	0	0	0	0	0	0	0
Bilateral	290	152	0	18	4	21	15	1
Private creditors	885	2,279	2,932	3,341	2,909	1,296	5,691	1,375
of which: Bonds	535	1,804	2,304	2,696	1,293	1,000	5,491	1,335
Commercial banks	257	469	616	645	1,615	296	200	40
Private nonguaranteed	2,610	865	2,121	3,364	4,366	3,232	5,041	9,340
of which: Bonds	592	0	0	170	469	0	1,900	620
Principal repayments	**2,347**	**2,900**	**7,403**	**7,769**	**5,642**	**4,877**	**5,914**	**6,553**
Public and publicly guaranteed	2,200	2,068	4,712	3,863	2,915	2,172	1,789	2,306
Official creditors	1,110	557	2,223	1,177	1,364	883	939	1,112
Multilateral	647	440	2,072	1,005	1,248	755	811	1,029
of which: IBRD	414	242	218	259	432	158	216	342
IDA	1	1	1	1	1	1	1	1
Bilateral	463	116	151	171	117	128	128	83
Private creditors	1,090	1,511	2,488	2,687	1,551	1,289	850	1,194
of which: Bonds	119	469	1,723	1,879	1,353	953	623	983
Commercial banks	723	838	680	693	152	316	211	196
Private nonguaranteed	147	832	2,692	3,906	2,727	2,705	4,126	4,248
of which: Bonds	0	110	0	0	200	0	0	0
Interest payments	**1,687**	**2,032**	**2,585**	**2,359**	**2,749**	**2,764**	**2,723**	**2,842**
Public and publicly guaranteed	962	1,414	1,948	1,652	1,949	2,107	2,005	2,135
Official creditors	505	541	574	580	681	656	602	557
Multilateral	388	470	529	543	648	629	582	542
of which: IBRD	190	126	174	210	256	241	242	249
IDA	0	0	0	0	0	0	0	0
Bilateral	118	71	44	37	33	27	20	15
Private creditors	457	873	1,374	1,072	1,267	1,451	1,403	1,577
of which: Bonds	58	515	1,284	1,005	1,058	1,112	1,073	1,282
Commercial banks	310	298	70	53	49	184	170	125
Private nonguaranteed	725	618	637	707	800	656	718	707
of which: Bonds	15	84	36	43	75	68	129	221
8. Debt stock-flow reconciliation								
Total change in external debt stocks	3,106	-490	-167	303	5,649	2,731	5,692	10,944
Net flows on external debt	2,894	-191	174	-240	3,616	2,690	5,611	10,483
9. Debt restructurings								
Total amount rescheduled	0	0	0	0	0	0	0	0
Total amount forgiven	0	0	0	0	0	0	0	0
Debt buyback	0	0	0	0	0	0	0	0

10. Contractual obligations on outstanding long-term external debt

	2011	2012	2013	2014	2015	2016	2017	2018
Official creditors								
Principal	1,055	1,093	1,071	1,328	1,203	1,149	1,038	1,157
Interest	322	300	281	258	233	210	189	170
Private creditors								
Principal	3,631	3,164	1,664	3,581	5,139	1,273	3,206	1,453
Interest	13,281	11,042	9,444	8,560	7,060	3,847	3,321	2,827

Notes:

Short-term debt is based on the Central Bank data.

COMOROS

(US$ million, unless otherwise indicated)

	1995	2000	2005	2006	2007	2008	2009	2010
1. Summary external debt data								
External debt stocks	**211.2**	**226.1**	**278.8**	**282.3**	**286.7**	**279.4**	**277.6**	**485.4**
Long-term external debt	201.2	206.9	258.0	260.3	279.5	270.6	263.4	469.3
Public and publicly guaranteed	201.2	206.9	258.0	260.3	279.5	270.6	263.4	469.3
Private nonguaranteed	0.0	0.0	0.0	0.0	0.0	0.0	0.0	0.0
Use of IMF credit	3.3	1.5	0.0	0.0	0.0	5.1	10.1	12.3
Short-term external debt	6.7	17.6	20.8	22.0	7.2	3.6	4.0	3.8
interest arrears on long-term	4.7	8.6	17.8	18.0	3.2	3.6	4.0	3.8
Memorandum items								
Principal arrears on long-term	21.4	41.9	58.3	61.2	19.9	21.5	21.7	17.2
Long-term public sector debt	201.2	206.9	258.0	260.3	279.5	270.6	263.4	469.3
Long-term private sector debt	0.0	0.0	0.0	0.0	0.0	0.0	0.0	0.0
Public & publicly guaranteed commitments	4.7	0.0	0.6	0.0	0.0	0.0	0.0	215.0
External debt flows								
Disbursements	9.6	2.1	3.3	3.0	4.8	6.7	6.9	217.4
Long-term external debt	9.6	2.1	3.3	3.0	4.8	1.4	0.3	215.0
IMF purchases	0.0	0.0	0.0	0.0	0.0	5.3	6.5	2.4
Principal repayments	0.4	1.8	2.6	2.4	12.8	8.1	8.9	3.1
Long-term external debt	0.4	1.2	2.6	2.4	12.8	8.1	7.2	3.1
IMF repurchases	0.0	0.6	0.0	0.0	0.0	0.0	1.7	0.0
Net flows	11.2	2.3	0.7	1.6	-8.0	-5.5	-2.1	214.3
Long-term external debt	9.2	0.9	0.7	0.6	-8.0	-6.7	-6.9	211.9
Short-term external debt	2.0	2.0	0.0	1.0	0.0	-4.0	0.0	0.0
Interest payments	0.6	1.4	1.4	1.4	13.3	4.2	2.9	1.1
Long-term external debt	0.5	0.8	1.3	1.2	13.1	4.2	2.9	1.1
IMF charges	0.0	0.0	0.0	0.0	0.0	0.0	0.0	0.0
Short-term external debt	0.1	0.6	0.2	0.2	0.2	0.0	0.0	0.0
2. Other non-debt resource inflows								
Foreign direct investment	0.9	0.1	0.6	0.6	7.5	7.5	9.1	9.4
Portfolio equity	0.0	..	..	..	..	..	..	..
3. Currency composition of public and publicly guaranteed debt (%)								
Euro	..	..	12.4	12.3	11.6	11.4	11.4	6.2
Japanese yen	0.0	0.0	0.0	0.0	0.0	0.0	0.0	0.0
Pound sterling	0.0	0.0	0.0	0.0	0.0	0.0	0.0	0.0
Swiss franc	0.0	0.0	0.0	0.0	0.0	0.0	0.0	0.0
U.S.dollars	27.2	31.9	40.6	41.3	42.6	43.2	43.8	69.9
4. Average terms of new commitments								
Official creditors								
Interest (%)	0.9	0.0	1.0	0.0	0.0	0.0	0.0	0.0
Maturity (years)	37.7	0.0	39.7	0.0	0.0	0.0	0.0	25.8
Grace period (years)	10.4	0.0	10.2	0.0	0.0	0.0	0.0	5.3
Private creditors								
Interest (%)	0.0	0.0	0.0	0.0	0.0	0.0	0.0	0.0
Maturity (years)	0.0	0.0	0.0	0.0	0.0	0.0	0.0	0.0
Grace period (years)	0.0	0.0	0.0	0.0	0.0	0.0	0.0	0.0
5. Major economic aggregates								
Gross national income (GNI)	232.9	202.2	385.9	403.6	466.9	530.3	534.6	538.8
Exports of goods, services & income	49.2	..	59.5	63.5	69.7	81.1	79.7	..
Worker remit. & comp. of employees	12.2	..	..	..	..	..	..	..
Imports of goods, services & income	105.7	..	138.3	155.7	174.7	254.8	245.4	..
Profit remittances on FDI	0.2	..	..	..	..	..	..	..
Current account balance	-19.0	..	-26.8	-22.5	-29.5	-68.8	-45.9	..
International reserves	44.9	43.4	86.1	93.9	117.6	112.7	150.9	146.1
6. Ratios								
External debt stocks to exports (%)	429.0	..	468.5	444.6	411.6	344.4	348.3	..
External debt stocks to GNI (%)	90.7	111.8	72.2	70.0	61.4	52.7	51.9	90.1
Debt service to exports (%)	2.0	..	6.7	5.9	37.5	15.2	14.8	..
Short-term to external debt stocks (%)	3.2	7.8	7.4	7.8	2.5	1.3	1.5	0.8
Multilateral to external debt stocks (%)	74.1	73.4	74.4	76.8	79.6	78.5	77.3	42.0
Reserves to external debt stocks (%)	21.2	19.2	30.9	33.3	41.0	40.3	54.4	30.1
Reserves to imports (months)	5.1	..	7.5	7.2	8.1	5.3	7.4	..

COMOROS

(US$ million, unless otherwise indicated)

	1995	2000	2005	2006	2007	2008	2009	2010
7. Long-term external debt								
Debt outstanding and disbursed	**201.2**	**206.9**	**258.0**	**260.3**	**279.5**	**270.6**	**263.4**	**469.3**
Public and publicly guaranteed	201.2	206.9	258.0	260.3	279.5	270.6	263.4	469.3
Official creditors	201.2	206.9	258.0	260.3	279.5	270.6	263.4	469.3
Multilateral	156.5	165.9	207.3	216.9	228.1	219.4	214.6	204.1
of which: IBRD	0.0	0.0	0.0	0.0	0.0	0.0	0.0	0.0
IDA	64.1	70.8	111.1	117.1	124.4	122.3	120.4	115.5
Bilateral	44.7	41.1	50.7	43.5	51.4	51.2	48.8	265.2
Private creditors	0.0	0.0	0.0	0.0	0.0	0.0	0.0	0.0
of which: Bonds	0.0	0.0	0.0	0.0	0.0	0.0	0.0	0.0
Commercial banks	0.0	0.0	0.0	0.0	0.0	0.0	0.0	0.0
Private nonguaranteed	0.0	0.0	0.0	0.0	0.0	0.0	0.0	0.0
of which: Bonds	0.0	0.0	0.0	0.0	0.0	0.0	0.0	0.0
Disbursements	**9.6**	**2.1**	**3.3**	**3.0**	**4.8**	**1.4**	**0.3**	**215.0**
Public and publicly guaranteed	9.6	2.1	3.3	3.0	4.8	1.4	0.3	215.0
Official creditors	9.6	2.1	3.3	3.0	4.8	1.4	0.3	215.0
Multilateral	9.6	2.1	3.3	3.0	4.8	1.4	0.3	0.0
of which: IBRD	0.0	0.0	0.0	0.0	0.0	0.0	0.0	0.0
IDA	9.6	2.1	2.7	3.0	4.8	1.4	0.3	0.0
Bilateral	0.0	0.0	0.0	0.0	0.0	0.0	0.0	215.0
Private creditors	0.0	0.0	0.0	0.0	0.0	0.0	0.0	0.0
of which: Bonds	0.0	0.0	0.0	0.0	0.0	0.0	0.0	0.0
Commercial banks	0.0	0.0	0.0	0.0	0.0	0.0	0.0	0.0
Private nonguaranteed	0.0	0.0	0.0	0.0	0.0	0.0	0.0	0.0
of which: Bonds	0.0	0.0	0.0	0.0	0.0	0.0	0.0	0.0
Principal repayments	**0.4**	**1.2**	**2.6**	**2.4**	**12.8**	**8.1**	**7.2**	**3.1**
Public and publicly guaranteed	0.4	1.2	2.6	2.4	12.8	8.1	7.2	3.1
Official creditors	0.4	1.2	2.6	2.4	12.8	8.1	7.2	3.1
Multilateral	0.4	1.2	2.6	2.4	12.8	8.1	7.2	3.1
of which: IBRD	0.0	0.0	0.0	0.0	0.0	0.0	0.0	0.0
IDA	0.4	0.8	2.0	2.0	2.3	2.6	3.1	1.7
Bilateral	0.0	0.0	0.0	0.0	0.0	0.0	0.0	0.0
Private creditors	0.0	0.0	0.0	0.0	0.0	0.0	0.0	0.0
of which: Bonds	0.0	0.0	0.0	0.0	0.0	0.0	0.0	0.0
Commercial banks	0.0	0.0	0.0	0.0	0.0	0.0	0.0	0.0
Private nonguaranteed	0.0	0.0	0.0	0.0	0.0	0.0	0.0	0.0
of which: Bonds	0.0	0.0	0.0	0.0	0.0	0.0	0.0	0.0
Interest payments	**0.5**	**0.8**	**1.3**	**1.2**	**13.1**	**4.2**	**2.9**	**1.1**
Public and publicly guaranteed	0.5	0.8	1.3	1.2	13.1	4.2	2.9	1.1
Official creditors	0.5	0.8	1.3	1.2	13.1	4.2	2.9	1.1
Multilateral	0.5	0.8	1.3	1.2	12.9	3.9	2.6	1.1
of which: IBRD	0.0	0.0	0.0	0.0	0.0	0.0	0.0	0.0
IDA	0.4	0.8	0.9	0.9	0.9	0.8	1.1	0.7
Bilateral	0.0	0.0	0.0	0.0	0.2	0.3	0.3	0.0
Private creditors	0.0	0.0	0.0	0.0	0.0	0.0	0.0	0.0
of which: Bonds	0.0	0.0	0.0	0.0	0.0	0.0	0.0	0.0
Commercial banks	0.0	0.0	0.0	0.0	0.0	0.0	0.0	0.0
Private nonguaranteed	0.0	0.0	0.0	0.0	0.0	0.0	0.0	0.0
of which: Bonds	0.0	0.0	0.0	0.0	0.0	0.0	0.0	0.0
8. Debt stock-flow reconciliation								
Total change in external debt stocks	8.5	-2.7	-15.1	3.6	4.4	-7.4	-1.8	207.8
Net flows on external debt	11.2	2.3	0.7	1.6	-8.0	-5.5	-2.1	214.3
9. Debt restructurings								
Total amount rescheduled	2.0	0.0	0.0	0.0	68.6	0.0	0.0	29.1
Total amount forgiven	0.4	0.0	0.0	0.0	0.0	0.0	0.0	1.7
Debt buyback	0.0	0.0	0.0	0.0	0.0	0.0	0.0	0.0

10. Contractual obligations on outstanding long-term external debt

	2011	2012	2013	2014	2015	2016	2017	2018
Official creditors								
Principal	6.7	7.0	6.5	6.8	7.2	17.5	17.5	18.5
Interest	1.6	1.6	1.6	1.5	1.5	1.4	1.4	1.4
Private creditors								
Principal	0.0	0.0	0.0	0.0	0.0	0.0	0.0	0.0
Interest	0.0	0.0	0.0	0.0	0.0	0.0	0.0	0.0

Notes:

Data for 2010 include the effects of Paris Club debt restructuring agreements signed in 2010 and of Enhanced HIPC Initiative in the amount of $1.2 million.

CONGO, DEMOCRATIC REPUBLIC OF

(US$ million, unless otherwise indicated)

	1995	2000	2005	2006	2007	2008	2009	2010
1. Summary external debt data								
External debt stocks	**13,239**	**11,692**	**10,600**	**11,244**	**12,365**	**12,210**	**12,276**	**5,774**
Long-term external debt	9,636	7,880	9,412	9,891	10,931	10,880	10,869	4,957
Public and publicly guaranteed	9,636	7,880	9,412	9,891	10,931	10,880	10,869	4,957
Private nonguaranteed	0	0	0	0	0	0	0	0
Use of IMF credit	485	391	791	833	808	654	800	323
Short-term external debt	3,118	3,421	397	520	626	677	607	494
interest arrears on long-term	2,937	3,042	359	378	446	471	493	280
Memorandum items								
Principal arrears on long-term	4,569	4,949	1,186	1,279	1,533	1,684	2,249	748
Long-term public sector debt	9,621	7,867	9,412	9,891	10,931	10,880	10,869	4,957
Long-term private sector debt	15	13	0	0	0	0	0	0
Public & publicly guaranteed commitments	14	0	45	45	0	0	0	0
External debt flows								
Disbursements	0	0	288	182	116	100	387	116
Long-term external debt	0	0	249	182	116	100	105	40
IMF purchases	0	0	39	0	0	0	282	76
Principal repayments	1	0	112	142	219	307	376	140
Long-term external debt	0	0	112	142	155	170	226	83
IMF repurchases	1	0	0	0	64	137	150	57
Net flows	61	20	95	144	-65	-181	-81	76
Long-term external debt	0	0	137	40	-39	-70	-121	-43
Short-term external debt	63	20	-81	104	38	26	-92	100
Interest payments	24	25	102	143	277	285	247	128
Long-term external debt	0	0	97	134	267	275	241	125
IMF charges	16	0	2	4	4	4	4	0
Short-term external debt	8	25	3	5	6	6	2	2
2. Other non-debt resource inflows								
Foreign direct investment	-22	72	..	256	1,808	1,727	664	2,939
Portfolio equity	..	..	..	..	..	..	..	..
3. Currency composition of public and publicly guaranteed debt (%)								
Euro	..	..	30.1	31.3	31.0	28.8	29.2	7.3
Japanese yen	3.7	4.8	7.3	6.8	6.3	7.9	7.7	0.0
Pound sterling	0.9	1.1	1.2	1.3	1.2	0.9	1.0	0.0
Swiss franc	0.3	0.2	0.3	0.3	0.3	0.3	0.2	0.1
U.S.dollars	40.8	44.6	46.0	45.2	41.8	42.0	41.6	48.7
4. Average terms of new commitments								
Official creditors								
Interest (%)	2.5	0.0	1.5	2.2	0.0	0.0	0.0	0.0
Maturity (years)	19.9	0.0	30.3	27.8	0.0	0.0	0.0	0.0
Grace period (years)	4.4	0.0	6.7	1.7	0.0	0.0	0.0	0.0
Private creditors								
Interest (%)	0.0	0.0	0.0	0.0	0.0	0.0	0.0	0.0
Maturity (years)	0.0	0.0	0.0	1.3	0.0	0.0	0.0	0.0
Grace period (years)	0.0	0.0	0.0	0.2	0.0	0.0	0.0	0.0
5. Major economic aggregates								
Gross national income (GNI)	4,878	3,918	6,760	8,143	9,621	10,337	10,425	12,263
Exports of goods, services & income	..	..	2,755	3,155	6,566	7,716	5,047	7,125
Worker remit. & comp. of employees	..	..	..	..	..	..	..	..
Imports of goods, services & income	..	..	3,924	4,272	7,562	9,761	7,571	10,542
Profit remittances on FDI	..	..	..	..	..	..	..	..
Current account balance	..	..	..	-395	-134	-1,050	-1,123	-2,529
International reserves	157	83	131	155	181	78	1,615	1,841
6. Ratios								
External debt stocks to exports (%)	..	..	384.7	356.4	188.3	158.3	243.2	81.0
External debt stocks to GNI (%)	271.4	298.4	156.8	138.1	128.5	118.1	117.8	47.1
Debt service to exports (%)	..	..	7.8	9.0	7.6	7.7	12.3	3.8
Short-term to external debt stocks (%)	23.6	29.3	3.7	4.6	5.1	5.5	4.9	8.6
Multilateral to external debt stocks (%)	18.0	18.5	28.8	29.2	32.8	34.0	34.1	44.5
Reserves to external debt stocks (%)	1.2	0.7	1.2	1.4	1.5	0.6	13.2	31.9
Reserves to imports (months)	..	..	0.4	0.4	0.3	0.1	2.6	2.1

(US$ million, unless otherwise indicated)

	1995	2000	2005	2006	2007	2008	2009	2010
7. Long-term external debt								
Debt outstanding and disbursed	**9,636**	**7,880**	**9,412**	**9,891**	**10,931**	**10,880**	**10,869**	**4,957**
Public and publicly guaranteed	9,636	7,880	9,412	9,891	10,931	10,880	10,869	4,957
Official creditors	8,758	7,384	9,042	9,524	10,574	10,528	10,538	4,850
Multilateral	2,382	2,164	3,050	3,280	4,056	4,150	4,187	2,571
of which: IBRD	92	81	0	0	0	0	0	0
IDA	1,321	1,188	2,050	2,251	2,402	2,437	2,497	849
Bilateral	6,376	5,220	5,992	6,244	6,518	6,379	6,351	2,279
Private creditors	878	496	370	367	357	351	332	106
of which: Bonds	5	3	1	1	0	0	0	0
Commercial banks	117	81	1	1	1	0	0	0
Private nonguaranteed	0	0	0	0	0	0	0	0
of which: Bonds	0	0	0	0	0	0	0	0
Disbursements	**0**	**0**	**249**	**182**	**116**	**100**	**105**	**40**
Public and publicly guaranteed	0	0	249	182	116	100	105	40
Official creditors	0	0	249	182	116	100	105	40
Multilateral	0	0	249	143	105	100	105	40
of which: IBRD	0	0	0	0	0	0	0	0
IDA	0	0	226	138	99	92	85	19
Bilateral	0	0	0	39	10	0	0	0
Private creditors	0	0	0	0	1	0	0	0
of which: Bonds	0	0	0	0	0	0	0	0
Commercial banks	0	0	0	0	0	0	0	0
Private nonguaranteed	0	0	0	0	0	0	0	0
of which: Bonds	0	0	0	0	0	0	0	0
Principal repayments	**0**	**0**	**112**	**142**	**155**	**170**	**226**	**83**
Public and publicly guaranteed	0	0	112	142	155	170	226	83
Official creditors	0	0	110	136	150	163	205	80
Multilateral	0	0	11	19	40	58	69	56
of which: IBRD	0	0	0	0	0	0	0	0
IDA	0	0	0	1	1	3	7	1
Bilateral	0	0	98	116	111	105	136	24
Private creditors	0	0	2	6	5	7	21	4
of which: Bonds	0	0	1	0	0	0	0	0
Commercial banks	0	0	0	0	0	0	0	0
Private nonguaranteed	0	0	0	0	0	0	0	0
of which: Bonds	0	0	0	0	0	0	0	0
Interest payments	**0**	**0**	**97**	**134**	**267**	**275**	**241**	**125**
Public and publicly guaranteed	0	0	97	134	267	275	241	125
Official creditors	0	0	95	132	264	272	239	125
Multilateral	0	0	52	62	113	126	125	120
of which: IBRD	0	0	0	0	0	0	0	0
IDA	0	0	12	12	14	15	16	12
Bilateral	0	0	43	70	151	145	115	4
Private creditors	0	0	1	2	2	3	2	0
of which: Bonds	0	0	0	0	0	0	0	0
Commercial banks	0	0	0	0	0	0	0	0
Private nonguaranteed	0	0	0	0	0	0	0	0
of which: Bonds	0	0	0	0	0	0	0	0
8. Debt stock-flow reconciliation								
Total change in external debt stocks	918	-356	-834	643	1,122	-155	66	-6,502
Net flows on external debt	61	20	95	144	-65	-181	-81	76
9. Debt restructurings								
Total amount rescheduled	0	0	34	0	0	0	0	1,479
Total amount forgiven	0	0	95	37	40	161	37	6,603
Debt buyback	0	0	0	0	0	0	0	0

10. Contractual obligations on outstanding long-term external debt

	2011	2012	2013	2014	2015	2016	2017	2018
Official creditors								
Principal	135	139	146	148	137	135	185	154
Interest	22	87	86	85	84	83	82	81
Private creditors								
Principal	4	4	4	3	0	0	0	0
Interest	0	0	0	0	0	0	0	0

Notes:

Data on long-term public and publicly guaranteed debt for 2010 are World Bank staff estimates. Data for 2008, 2009, and 2010 include the effects of MDRI and HIPC debt relief, in the amount of $42,477 thousand, $37,364 thousand, $1,642,856 thousand respectively. Data also include the effects of Paris Club debt restructuring agreements signed in 2010.

CONGO, REPUBLIC OF

(US$ million, unless otherwise indicated)

	1995	2000	2005	2006	2007	2008	2009	2010
1. Summary external debt data								
External debt stocks	**5,887**	**4,782**	**6,144**	**6,560**	**5,648**	**5,932**	**4,903**	**3,781**
Long-term external debt	4,867	3,682	5,404	5,749	5,246	5,505	4,684	3,531
Public and publicly guaranteed	4,867	3,682	5,404	5,749	5,246	5,505	4,684	3,531
Private nonguaranteed	0	0	0	0	0	0	0	0
Use of IMF credit	19	41	26	35	37	38	43	27
Short-term external debt	1,002	1,059	714	776	364	389	176	222
interest arrears on long-term	412	638	703	713	259	252	107	105
Memorandum items								
Principal arrears on long-term	950	1,727	2,511	2,564	1,008	979	410	353
Long-term public sector debt	4,867	3,682	5,404	5,749	5,246	5,505	4,684	3,531
Long-term private sector debt	0	0	0	0	0	0	0	0
Public & publicly guaranteed commitments	31	24	640	17	10	13	394	79
External debt flows								
Disbursements	15	15	232	163	28	21	10	75
Long-term external debt	15	1	220	152	28	19	7	73
IMF purchases	0	14	12	12	0	2	4	2
Principal repayments	88	6	77	54	74	112	86	151
Long-term external debt	85	6	65	50	74	112	86	151
IMF repurchases	2	0	12	4	0	0	0	0
Net flows	163	-52	166	162	-4	-60	-144	-28
Long-term external debt	-70	-5	155	102	-46	-94	-80	-78
Short-term external debt	236	-61	11	52	42	32	-68	48
Interest payments	99	38	35	33	34	70	77	45
Long-term external debt	62	7	34	31	29	64	75	42
IMF charges	1	1	0	0	0	0	0	0
Short-term external debt	35	30	0	2	4	5	2	3
2. Other non-debt resource inflows								
Foreign direct investment	125	166	514	1,488	2,638	2,483	2,083	2,816
Portfolio equity	0	0	..	..	..	..	..	..
3. Currency composition of public and publicly guaranteed debt (%)								
Euro	..	..	35.9	36.0	41.9	40.3	43.5	12.7
Japanese yen	0.2	0.2	0.1	0.1	0.2	0.2	0.0	0.0
Pound sterling	3.5	4.9	5.3	6.4	6.3	4.4	5.5	0.0
Swiss franc	0.5	0.3	0.2	0.2	0.3	0.3	0.3	0.0
U.S.dollars	24.1	29.9	52.6	51.4	43.9	47.9	43.6	78.9
4. Average terms of new commitments								
Official creditors								
Interest (%)	2.2	2.0	0.6	2.4	1.0	2.8	0.9	3.2
Maturity (years)	31.8	15.0	16.6	39.5	19.7	19.5	19.5	16.0
Grace period (years)	9.0	7.0	4.8	10.4	5.2	4.8	5.2	6.1
Private creditors								
Interest (%)	0.0	0.0	0.0	0.0	0.0	4.0	0.0	4.0
Maturity (years)	0.0	0.0	0.0	0.0	0.0	9.8	0.0	7.8
Grace period (years)	0.0	0.0	0.0	0.0	0.0	0.2	0.0	0.3
5. Major economic aggregates								
Gross national income (GNI)	1,228	2,275	4,039	5,105	5,747	8,728	6,878	8,619
Exports of goods, services & income	1,383	2,642	4,983	6,352	6,151	..	..	..
Worker remit. & comp. of employees	4	10	11	13	15	15	15	15
Imports of goods, services & income	2,050	2,013	4,318	6,202	8,294	..	..	..
Profit remittances on FDI	326	466	1,296	1,403	1,651	..	..	..
Current account balance	-625	648	696	124	-2,181	..	..	..
International reserves	64	225	738	1,848	2,184	3,881	3,806	4,447
6. Ratios								
External debt stocks to exports (%)	425.8	181.0	123.3	103.3	91.8	..	..	..
External debt stocks to GNI (%)	479.3	210.2	152.1	128.5	98.3	68.0	71.3	43.9
Debt service to exports (%)	13.5	1.7	2.2	1.4	1.7	..	..	..
Short-term to external debt stocks (%)	17.0	22.1	11.6	11.8	6.4	6.6	3.6	5.9
Multilateral to external debt stocks (%)	10.7	10.4	8.3	7.9	8.9	8.0	9.4	5.8
Reserves to external debt stocks (%)	1.1	4.7	12.0	28.2	38.7	65.4	77.6	117.6
Reserves to imports (months)	0.4	1.3	2.0	3.6	3.2	..	..	..

CONGO, REPUBLIC OF

(US$ million, unless otherwise indicated)

	1995	2000	2005	2006	2007	2008	2009	2010
7. Long-term external debt								
Debt outstanding and disbursed	**4,867**	**3,682**	**5,404**	**5,749**	**5,246**	**5,505**	**4,684**	**3,531**
Public and publicly guaranteed	4,867	3,682	5,404	5,749	5,246	5,505	4,684	3,531
Official creditors	3,947	2,920	3,293	3,608	3,863	4,150	3,840	2,716
Multilateral	631	499	512	517	500	476	463	219
of which: IBRD	105	65	0	0	0	0	0	0
IDA	174	159	280	295	303	299	298	84
Bilateral	3,316	2,421	2,780	3,091	3,363	3,674	3,377	2,497
Private creditors	920	762	2,111	2,140	1,383	1,355	844	815
of which: Bonds	0	0	0	0	0	0	0	0
Commercial banks	778	686	2,017	2,037	1,281	1,261	779	756
Private nonguaranteed	0	0	0	0	0	0	0	0
of which: Bonds	0	0	0	0	0	0	0	0
Disbursements	**15**	**1**	**220**	**152**	**28**	**19**	**7**	**73**
Public and publicly guaranteed	15	1	220	152	28	19	7	73
Official creditors	15	1	220	152	28	14	7	73
Multilateral	1	0	85	18	14	9	5	12
of which: IBRD	1	0	0	0	0	0	0	0
IDA	0	0	35	8	2	3	3	2
Bilateral	15	1	135	134	14	4	1	62
Private creditors	0	0	0	0	0	5	0	0
of which: Bonds	0	0	0	0	0	0	0	0
Commercial banks	0	0	0	0	0	0	0	0
Private nonguaranteed	0	0	0	0	0	0	0	0
of which: Bonds	0	0	0	0	0	0	0	0
Principal repayments	**85**	**6**	**65**	**50**	**74**	**112**	**86**	**151**
Public and publicly guaranteed	85	6	65	50	74	112	86	151
Official creditors	33	6	65	50	72	84	86	127
Multilateral	20	6	47	31	23	21	22	23
of which: IBRD	18	2	0	0	0	0	0	0
IDA	1	1	5	3	2	2	2	1
Bilateral	12	0	19	19	49	64	64	104
Private creditors	53	0	0	0	1	28	1	24
of which: Bonds	0	0	0	0	0	0	0	0
Commercial banks	46	0	0	0	0	24	0	24
Private nonguaranteed	0	0	0	0	0	0	0	0
of which: Bonds	0	0	0	0	0	0	0	0
Interest payments	**62**	**7**	**34**	**31**	**29**	**64**	**75**	**42**
Public and publicly guaranteed	62	7	34	31	29	64	75	42
Official creditors	20	7	34	31	29	59	57	30
Multilateral	11	7	26	14	11	9	8	7
of which: IBRD	10	1	0	0	0	0	0	0
IDA	1	1	2	2	2	2	2	1
Bilateral	9	0	8	17	19	50	49	23
Private creditors	42	0	0	0	0	5	18	12
of which: Bonds	0	0	0	0	0	0	0	0
Commercial banks	39	0	0	0	0	5	18	12
Private nonguaranteed	0	0	0	0	0	0	0	0
of which: Bonds	0	0	0	0	0	0	0	0
8. Debt stock-flow reconciliation								
Total change in external debt stocks	586	-138	-420	416	-912	285	-1,030	-1,122
Net flows on external debt	163	-52	166	162	-4	-60	-144	-28
9. Debt restructurings								
Total amount rescheduled	108	0	86	124	616	312	53	1,536
Total amount forgiven	24	0	141	152	1,282	114	766	1,147
Debt buyback	0	0	0	0	0	0	0	0

10. Contractual obligations on outstanding long-term external debt

	2011	2012	2013	2014	2015	2016	2017	2018
Official creditors								
Principal	224	215	111	140	156	179	178	179
Interest	24	52	50	51	50	47	44	43
Private creditors								
Principal	24	28	32	32	32	32	32	31
Interest	11	11	10	9	9	8	10	9

Notes:

Data on long-term public debt for 2010 are World Bank staff estimates. Data include the effects of London Club debt restructuring agreement signed in 2007 and Paris Club debt restructuring agreement signed in 2008 and 2010. However, data for 2010 does not reflect the $1.4 billion of debt relief that Paris Club creditors have committed to bilaterally. Data for 2008, 2009, and 2010 include the effects of MDRI and HIPC debt relief, in the amount of $3,596 thousand, $3,576 thousand, and $210,763 thousand respectively.

COSTA RICA

(US$ million, unless otherwise indicated)

	1995	2000	2005	2006	2007	2008	2009	2010
1. Summary external debt data								
External debt stocks	**3,766**	**4,636**	**6,489**	**6,996**	**8,406**	**9,196**	**7,978**	**8,849**
Long-term external debt	3,312	3,688	4,392	4,640	5,171	5,207	5,735	6,418
Public and publicly guaranteed	3,097	3,452	3,161	3,315	3,650	3,174	3,197	3,725
Private nonguaranteed	214	236	1,231	1,325	1,521	2,033	2,538	2,693
Use of IMF credit	24	0	0	0	0	0	0	0
Short-term external debt	430	948	2,097	2,355	3,234	3,989	2,243	2,431
interest arrears on long-term	32	12	2	2	0	0	0	0
Memorandum items								
Principal arrears on long-term	98	29	0	0	0	0	0	0
Long-term public sector debt	3,095	3,451	3,161	3,315	3,650	3,174	3,197	3,725
Long-term private sector debt	216	237	1,231	1,325	1,521	2,033	2,538	2,693
Public & publicly guaranteed commitments	25	824	358	416	149	446	1,850	50
External debt flows								
Disbursements	211	758	986	458	610	1,115	1,322	1,504
Long-term external debt	211	758	986	458	610	1,115	1,322	1,504
IMF purchases	0	0	0	0	0	0	0	0
Principal repayments	401	388	569	498	559	1,112	795	653
Long-term external debt	357	388	569	498	559	1,112	795	653
IMF repurchases	44	0	0	0	0	0	0	0
Net flows	-148	549	841	218	931	758	-1,218	1,038
Long-term external debt	-146	370	416	-40	51	3	527	851
Short-term external debt	42	179	425	258	880	755	-1,745	188
Interest payments	251	262	274	294	347	462	428	429
Long-term external debt	225	206	180	176	207	352	367	362
IMF charges	3	0	0	0	0	0	0	0
Short-term external debt	23	56	94	118	140	110	62	67
2. Other non-debt resource inflows								
Foreign direct investment	337	409	861	1,469	1,896	2,078	1,347	1,466
Portfolio equity	..	..	..	..	..	..	..	..
3. Currency composition of public and publicly guaranteed debt (%)								
Euro	..	..	1.7	1.6	1.7	1.8	1.7	1.3
Japanese yen	8.2	4.0	2.7	2.1	2.3	3.8	5.1	5.9
Pound sterling	0.1	0.0	0.0	0.0	0.0	0.0	0.0	0.0
Swiss franc	0.0	0.0	0.0	0.0	0.0	0.0	0.0	0.0
U.S.dollars	49.1	69.9	77.1	80.2	83.0	87.9	87.9	89.1
4. Average terms of new commitments								
Official creditors								
Interest (%)	2.2	6.3	5.7	4.8	6.2	4.5	3.1	0.0
Maturity (years)	7.3	4.3	17.5	15.1	14.8	17.3	19.6	0.0
Grace period (years)	1.2	1.8	4.0	3.9	3.8	4.0	4.1	0.0
Private creditors								
Interest (%)	6.9	8.3	8.2	6.9	6.0	0.0	5.1	3.3
Maturity (years)	6.0	17.3	12.1	10.3	1.4	0.0	7.2	3.0
Grace period (years)	1.5	17.3	0.5	10.3	0.3	0.0	5.6	0.5
5. Major economic aggregates								
Gross national income (GNI)	11,497	14,697	19,174	21,788	25,468	28,935	28,767	33,001
Exports of goods, services & income	4,597	7,992	10,528	12,208	13,559	14,400	12,718	13,969
Worker remit. & comp. of employees	123	136	420	513	618	605	513	552
Imports of goods, services & income	5,089	8,793	11,779	13,580	15,675	17,565	13,585	15,670
Profit remittances on FDI	109	1,141	743	853	1,131	749	986	606
Current account balance	-358	-707	-981	-1,023	-1,646	-2,787	-576	-1,439
International reserves	1,060	1,318	2,314	3,117	4,115	3,801	4,068	4,630
6. Ratios								
External debt stocks to exports (%)	81.9	58.0	61.6	57.3	62.0	63.9	62.7	63.3
External debt stocks to GNI (%)	32.8	31.5	33.8	32.1	33.0	31.8	27.7	26.8
Debt service to exports (%)	14.2	8.1	8.0	6.5	6.7	10.9	9.6	7.7
Short-term to external debt stocks (%)	11.4	20.4	32.3	33.7	38.5	43.4	28.1	27.5
Multilateral to external debt stocks (%)	36.6	28.1	18.1	18.0	14.2	11.3	14.8	19.3
Reserves to external debt stocks (%)	28.1	28.4	35.7	44.6	49.0	41.3	51.0	52.3
Reserves to imports (months)	2.5	1.8	2.4	2.8	3.2	2.6	3.6	3.5

COSTA RICA

(US$ million, unless otherwise indicated)

	1995	2000	2005	2006	2007	2008	2009	2010
7. Long-term external debt								
Debt outstanding and disbursed	**3,312**	**3,688**	**4,392**	**4,640**	**5,171**	**5,207**	**5,735**	**6,418**
Public and publicly guaranteed	3,097	3,452	3,161	3,315	3,650	3,174	3,197	3,725
Official creditors	2,486	1,861	1,370	1,452	1,476	1,362	1,577	2,139
Multilateral	1,380	1,305	1,176	1,260	1,195	1,039	1,179	1,709
of which: IBRD	300	121	59	53	45	41	57	570
IDA	3	2	1	1	1	0	0	0
Bilateral	1,106	556	194	192	281	322	398	430
Private creditors	611	1,591	1,791	1,864	2,174	1,812	1,620	1,586
of which: Bonds	572	1,542	1,669	1,685	1,900	1,660	1,435	1,435
Commercial banks	3	23	102	161	257	137	172	138
Private nonguaranteed	214	236	1,231	1,325	1,521	2,033	2,538	2,693
of which: Bonds	0	0	0	0	0	0	0	0
Disbursements	**211**	**758**	**986**	**458**	**610**	**1,115**	**1,322**	**1,504**
Public and publicly guaranteed	201	749	75	142	118	320	523	770
Official creditors	200	249	75	92	118	309	380	767
Multilateral	183	130	69	77	102	245	258	706
of which: IBRD	16	6	5	5	1	4	24	521
IDA	0	0	0	0	0	0	0	0
Bilateral	18	118	6	15	16	63	122	61
Private creditors	0	500	0	50	0	11	143	2
of which: Bonds	0	500	0	50	0	0	75	0
Commercial banks	0	0	0	0	0	11	68	0
Private nonguaranteed	10	9	910	316	492	795	799	734
of which: Bonds	0	0	0	0	0	0	0	0
Principal repayments	**357**	**388**	**569**	**498**	**559**	**1,112**	**795**	**653**
Public and publicly guaranteed	333	371	365	276	263	829	500	266
Official creditors	323	334	306	230	221	456	165	230
Multilateral	176	154	276	213	192	413	119	179
of which: IBRD	55	33	17	11	9	8	7	9
IDA	0	0	0	0	0	0	0	0
Bilateral	146	180	31	18	30	43	47	51
Private creditors	10	37	59	45	42	373	335	36
of which: Bonds	4	30	41	34	35	240	300	0
Commercial banks	2	4	17	11	7	130	33	34
Private nonguaranteed	24	17	204	222	296	283	294	387
of which: Bonds	0	0	0	0	0	0	0	0
Interest payments	**225**	**206**	**180**	**176**	**207**	**352**	**367**	**362**
Public and publicly guaranteed	204	190	105	96	115	246	215	207
Official creditors	163	104	63	53	42	78	73	81
Multilateral	95	84	57	50	39	68	63	70
of which: IBRD	27	12	3	3	3	3	2	3
IDA	0	0	0	0	0	0	0	0
Bilateral	67	20	5	3	3	10	10	11
Private creditors	42	86	43	42	73	168	142	126
of which: Bonds	37	80	39	37	68	152	131	116
Commercial banks	0	2	3	5	4	14	10	8
Private nonguaranteed	21	16	74	80	92	106	152	155
of which: Bonds	0	0	0	0	0	0	0	0
8. Debt stock-flow reconciliation								
Total change in external debt stocks	-110	490	773	507	1,410	790	-1,217	870
Net flows on external debt	-148	549	841	218	931	758	-1,218	1,038
9. Debt restructurings								
Total amount rescheduled	0	0	0	0	0	0	0	0
Total amount forgiven	3	0	0	0	0	0	0	0
Debt buyback	0	0	0	0	0	0	0	0

10. Contractual obligations on outstanding long-term external debt

	2011	2012	2013	2014	2015	2016	2017	2018
Official creditors								
Principal	258	232	253	231	218	182	173	165
Interest	71	62	53	45	37	32	27	24
Private creditors								
Principal	969	802	741	603	238	309	159	121
Interest	229	188	130	100	68	54	41	34

Notes:

Data on long-term private nonguaranteed debt are World Bank staff estimates. Short-term debt is based on reports provided by the country.

COTE D'IVOIRE

(US$ million, unless otherwise indicated)

	1995	2000	2005	2006	2007	2008	2009	2010
1. Summary external debt data								
External debt stocks	**18,899**	**12,138**	**11,912**	**12,764**	**13,865**	**12,568**	**11,702**	**11,430**
Long-term external debt	14,562	10,546	10,866	11,605	12,237	11,036	11,251	10,696
Public and publicly guaranteed	11,902	9,063	9,965	10,823	11,646	10,622	10,980	10,416
Private nonguaranteed	2,660	1,482	900	782	591	414	271	280
Use of IMF credit	427	549	198	150	173	188	352	383
Short-term external debt	3,910	1,043	848	1,010	1,455	1,344	99	351
interest arrears on long-term	1,020	79	848	1,010	1,455	1,344	99	44
Memorandum items								
Principal arrears on long-term	2,686	169	1,499	2,033	2,497	2,218	183	122
Long-term public sector debt	11,901	9,063	9,965	10,823	11,646	10,622	10,980	10,416
Long-term private sector debt	2,661	1,482	900	782	591	414	271	280
Public & publicly guaranteed commitments	716	72	40	58	162	73	144	0
External debt flows								
Disbursements	924	148	55	116	140	118	359	127
Long-term external debt	743	148	55	116	77	54	58	72
IMF purchases	181	0	0	0	62	64	301	55
Principal repayments	625	481	255	217	345	829	841	258
Long-term external debt	539	442	164	160	298	784	697	248
IMF repurchases	86	39	91	57	47	44	143	10
Net flows	935	-617	-308	-101	-206	-711	-482	176
Long-term external debt	204	-294	-109	-44	-221	-731	-639	-176
Short-term external debt	636	-283	-108	0	0	0	0	307
Interest payments	421	539	50	50	84	221	266	124
Long-term external debt	390	462	46	49	82	216	264	122
IMF charges	8	3	1	1	1	5	2	0
Short-term external debt	23	74	3	0	0	0	0	2
2. Other non-debt resource inflows								
Foreign direct investment	211	235	312	319	427	446	381	418
Portfolio equity	1	1	14	2	2	2	-9	..
3. Currency composition of public and publicly guaranteed debt (%)								
Euro	..	..	51.9	53.4	55.6	56.2	58.6	57.6
Japanese yen	1.4	1.4	1.3	1.2	1.1	1.6	2.0	2.3
Pound sterling	0.9	0.6	0.4	0.4	0.4	0.3	0.4	0.4
Swiss franc	0.5	0.2	0.2	0.2	0.2	0.2	0.0	0.0
U.S.dollars	22.0	53.7	37.7	35.9	34.1	33.0	34.0	35.2
4. Average terms of new commitments								
Official creditors								
Interest (%)	1.9	0.8	1.7	0.2	4.8	1.7	3.7	0.0
Maturity (years)	29.8	46.2	20.0	7.8	15.3	20.5	21.3	0.0
Grace period (years)	8.5	9.6	5.7	1.7	4.4	5.7	6.6	0.0
Private creditors								
Interest (%)	14.5	0.0	0.0	0.0	0.5	0.0	0.0	0.0
Maturity (years)	19.6	0.0	0.0	0.0	11.7	0.0	0.0	0.0
Grace period (years)	0.1	0.0	0.0	0.0	3.7	0.0	0.0	0.0
5. Major economic aggregates								
Gross national income (GNI)	10,013	9,715	15,643	16,589	18,913	22,434	22,078	21,729
Exports of goods, services & income	4,526	4,512	8,724	9,518	9,820	11,651	11,702	..
Worker remit. & comp. of employees	151	119	163	167	185	199	185	179
Imports of goods, services & income	4,782	4,423	8,222	8,508	9,616	10,867	9,917	..
Profit remittances on FDI	204	284	370	478	531	581	..	..
Current account balance	-492	-241	40	479	-139	452	1,670	..
International reserves	529	674	1,367	1,798	2,519	2,253	3,267	3,624
6. Ratios								
External debt stocks to exports (%)	417.5	269.0	136.5	134.1	141.2	107.9	100.0	..
External debt stocks to GNI (%)	188.7	124.9	76.2	76.9	73.3	56.0	53.0	52.6
Debt service to exports (%)	23.1	22.6	3.5	2.8	4.4	9.0	9.5	..
Short-term to external debt stocks (%)	20.7	8.6	7.1	7.9	10.5	10.7	0.8	3.1
Multilateral to external debt stocks (%)	20.6	24.4	25.9	26.1	25.0	23.0	20.3	19.5
Reserves to external debt stocks (%)	2.8	5.6	11.5	14.1	18.2	17.9	27.9	31.7
Reserves to imports (months)	1.3	1.8	2.0	2.5	3.1	2.5	4.0	..

COTE D'IVOIRE

(US$ million, unless otherwise indicated)

	1995	2000	2005	2006	2007	2008	2009	2010
7. Long-term external debt								
Debt outstanding and disbursed	**14,562**	**10,546**	**10,866**	**11,605**	**12,237**	**11,036**	**11,251**	**10,696**
Public and publicly guaranteed	11,902	9,063	9,965	10,823	11,646	10,622	10,980	10,416
Official creditors	9,217	6,669	7,673	8,384	9,062	8,123	8,914	8,673
Multilateral	3,900	2,958	3,087	3,330	3,471	2,892	2,374	2,228
of which: IBRD	1,573	599	423	456	479	117	42	14
IDA	813	1,366	1,763	1,847	1,909	1,797	1,781	1,749
Bilateral	5,317	3,711	4,586	5,054	5,591	5,232	6,540	6,445
Private creditors	2,685	2,394	2,292	2,439	2,584	2,499	2,066	1,743
of which: Bonds	0	2,343	2,159	2,293	2,425	2,346	1,931	1,621
Commercial banks	2,630	14	133	146	160	152	135	118
Private nonguaranteed	2,660	1,482	900	782	591	414	271	280
of which: Bonds	0	0	0	0	0	0	0	0
Disbursements	**743**	**148**	**55**	**116**	**77**	**54**	**58**	**72**
Public and publicly guaranteed	670	148	21	88	57	35	36	49
Official creditors	669	148	21	88	57	35	36	48
Multilateral	340	148	11	71	35	24	23	45
of which: IBRD	19	0	0	0	0	0	0	0
IDA	226	76	0	0	0	13	13	40
Bilateral	329	0	10	17	22	10	13	3
Private creditors	1	0	0	0	0	0	0	0
of which: Bonds	0	0	0	0	0	0	0	0
Commercial banks	1	0	0	0	0	0	0	0
Private nonguaranteed	73	0	34	28	20	19	22	24
of which: Bonds	0	0	0	0	0	0	0	0
Principal repayments	**539**	**442**	**164**	**160**	**298**	**784**	**697**	**248**
Public and publicly guaranteed	514	329	21	14	112	588	532	168
Official creditors	479	283	21	13	112	588	532	166
Multilateral	286	143	20	12	106	587	504	127
of which: IBRD	199	57	0	0	30	377	73	25
IDA	0	0	0	0	16	117	41	41
Bilateral	193	140	0	1	6	1	28	39
Private creditors	36	46	0	0	0	0	0	2
of which: Bonds	0	46	0	0	0	0	0	0
Commercial banks	5	0	0	0	0	0	0	2
Private nonguaranteed	25	113	143	146	187	196	165	80
of which: Bonds	0	0	0	0	0	0	0	0
Interest payments	**390**	**462**	**46**	**49**	**82**	**216**	**264**	**122**
Public and publicly guaranteed	257	342	3	2	41	183	241	107
Official creditors	252	189	3	2	41	183	241	105
Multilateral	172	78	3	2	41	183	238	24
of which: IBRD	135	32	0	0	10	83	6	1
IDA	5	8	0	0	8	61	14	13
Bilateral	81	111	0	0	1	1	3	81
Private creditors	5	153	0	0	0	0	0	2
of which: Bonds	0	153	0	0	0	0	0	0
Commercial banks	1	0	0	0	0	0	0	2
Private nonguaranteed	133	120	43	47	41	33	23	15
of which: Bonds	0	0	0	0	0	0	0	0
8. Debt stock-flow reconciliation								
Total change in external debt stocks	1,503	-1,032	-1,287	852	1,101	-1,297	-866	-272
Net flows on external debt	935	-617	-308	-101	-206	-711	-482	176
9. Debt restructurings								
Total amount rescheduled	381	72	0	0	0	0	3,078	530
Total amount forgiven	322	29	0	0	0	0	1,103	180
Debt buyback	0	0	0	0	0	0	0	0

10. Contractual obligations on outstanding long-term external debt

	2011	2012	2013	2014	2015	2016	2017	2018
Official creditors								
Principal	1,393	761	529	531	533	535	524	776
Interest	242	244	240	225	208	191	173	155
Private creditors								
Principal	303	289	262	254	246	242	237	134
Interest	23	19	15	12	10	7	5	3

Notes:

Data on long-term public debt for 2010 are World Bank staff estimates.

DJIBOUTI

(US$ million, unless otherwise indicated)

	1995	2000	2005	2006	2007	2008	2009	2010
1. Summary external debt data								
External debt stocks	**272.4**	**258.1**	**406.4**	**469.2**	**675.3**	**698.5**	**755.3**	**751.3**
Long-term external debt	268.9	238.3	378.9	441.2	653.4	680.4	737.2	738.7
Public and publicly guaranteed	268.9	238.3	378.9	441.2	653.4	680.4	737.2	738.7
Private nonguaranteed	0.0	0.0	0.0	0.0	0.0	0.0	0.0	0.0
Use of IMF credit	0.0	13.4	18.7	18.0	16.1	17.4	15.8	12.1
Short-term external debt	3.5	6.4	8.9	10.0	5.8	0.7	2.3	0.5
interest arrears on long-term	3.5	6.4	8.9	10.0	5.8	0.7	2.3	0.5
Memorandum items								
Principal arrears on long-term	13.1	22.4	21.3	26.3	40.2	2.2	6.9	2.2
Long-term public sector debt	268.9	238.3	378.9	441.2	653.4	680.4	737.2	738.7
Long-term private sector debt	0.0	0.0	0.0	0.0	0.0	0.0	0.0	0.0
Public & publicly guaranteed commitments	0.0	48.6	87.6	41.1	22.7	38.4	24.3	48.8
External debt flows								
Disbursements	18.4	11.3	26.5	63.7	39.0	52.0	69.6	37.3
Long-term external debt	18.4	7.7	26.5	63.7	39.0	45.9	67.4	37.3
IMF purchases	0.0	3.6	0.0	0.0	0.0	6.1	2.3	0.0
Principal repayments	9.2	10.7	11.9	18.5	17.1	21.8	26.7	25.7
Long-term external debt	9.2	8.4	11.0	16.9	14.3	17.5	22.5	22.4
IMF repurchases	0.0	2.3	0.8	1.6	2.8	4.3	4.2	3.3
Net flows	9.2	0.7	14.7	45.2	22.0	30.2	42.9	11.5
Long-term external debt	9.2	-0.7	15.5	46.8	24.7	28.4	44.9	14.9
Short-term external debt	0.0	0.0	0.0	0.0	0.0	0.0	0.0	0.0
Interest payments	2.0	2.6	3.8	5.0	6.6	7.8	8.3	8.2
Long-term external debt	2.0	2.2	3.7	4.9	6.5	7.7	8.2	8.2
IMF charges	0.0	0.4	0.1	0.1	0.1	0.1	0.1	0.0
Short-term external debt	0.0	0.0	0.0	0.0	0.0	0.0	0.0	0.0
2. Other non-debt resource inflows								
Foreign direct investment	3.2	3.3	22.2	108.3	195.4	227.7	96.9	26.8
Portfolio equity	0.0	0.0	0.0	0.0	0.0	0.0	0.0	0.0
3. Currency composition of public and publicly guaranteed debt (%)								
Euro	..	..	13.1	16.8	33.9	31.6	30.5	28.3
Japanese yen	0.0	0.0	0.0	0.0	0.0	0.0	0.0	0.0
Pound sterling	0.0	0.0	0.0	0.0	0.0	0.0	0.0	0.0
Swiss franc	0.0	0.0	0.0	0.0	0.0	0.0	0.0	0.0
U.S.dollars	12.4	16.2	34.2	32.7	25.8	25.5	24.7	24.7
4. Average terms of new commitments								
Official creditors								
Interest (%)	0.0	2.3	1.3	1.8	3.9	2.9	2.5	1.9
Maturity (years)	0.0	29.9	38.0	10.9	24.8	20.8	26.3	24.2
Grace period (years)	0.0	6.9	9.0	6.5	5.8	5.0	7.3	6.0
Private creditors								
Interest (%)	0.0	0.0	6.9	0.0	0.0	0.0	0.0	0.0
Maturity (years)	0.0	0.0	11.5	0.0	0.0	0.0	0.0	0.0
Grace period (years)	0.0	0.0	2.0	0.0	0.0	0.0	0.0	0.0
5. Major economic aggregates								
Gross national income (GNI)	515.0	567.0	775.8	853.9	935.9	1072.5	1120.1	..
Exports of goods, services & income	220.7	218.4	319.8	341.5	341.7	411.3	436.4	453.6
Worker remit. & comp. of employees	11.9	12.3	25.8	28.5	28.6	30.3	32.5	32.7
Imports of goods, services & income	263.5	287.1	372.3	436.8	592.3	716.5	593.6	498.3
Profit remittances on FDI	4.6	4.2	5.9	5.9	4.2	5.0	6.5	0.0
Current account balance	17.5	-19.0	20.1	-16.6	-171.4	-225.4	-71.1	50.5
International reserves	72.2	67.8	89.3	120.3	132.1	175.5	241.8	249.0
6. Ratios								
External debt stocks to exports (%)	123.4	118.1	127.1	137.4	197.6	169.8	173.1	165.6
External debt stocks to GNI (%)	52.9	45.5	52.4	54.9	72.2	65.1	67.4	..
Debt service to exports (%)	5.0	6.1	4.9	6.9	6.9	7.2	8.0	7.5
Short-term to external debt stocks (%)	1.3	2.5	2.2	2.1	0.9	0.1	0.3	0.1
Multilateral to external debt stocks (%)	50.1	53.6	66.1	65.2	51.4	51.9	52.9	54.5
Reserves to external debt stocks (%)	26.5	26.3	22.0	25.6	19.6	25.1	32.0	33.1
Reserves to imports (months)	3.3	2.8	2.9	3.3	2.7	2.9	4.9	6.0

DJIBOUTI

(US$ million, unless otherwise indicated)

	1995	2000	2005	2006	2007	2008	2009	2010
7. Long-term external debt								
Debt outstanding and disbursed	**268.9**	**238.3**	**378.9**	**441.2**	**653.4**	**680.4**	**737.2**	**738.7**
Public and publicly guaranteed	268.9	238.3	378.9	441.2	653.4	680.4	737.2	738.7
Official creditors	268.9	238.3	373.3	418.0	622.6	653.0	713.0	718.3
Multilateral	136.4	138.3	268.7	305.7	347.0	362.8	399.4	409.3
of which: IBRD	0.0	0.0	0.0	0.0	0.0	0.0	0.0	0.0
IDA	46.2	49.9	120.3	133.3	147.2	151.6	158.4	154.7
Bilateral	132.5	100.0	104.6	112.3	275.6	290.2	313.6	308.9
Private creditors	0.0	0.0	5.6	23.2	30.8	27.4	24.2	20.4
of which: Bonds	0.0	0.0	0.0	0.0	0.0	0.0	0.0	0.0
Commercial banks	0.0	0.0	5.6	5.6	12.3	13.5	15.2	14.2
Private nonguaranteed	0.0	0.0	0.0	0.0	0.0	0.0	0.0	0.0
of which: Bonds	0.0	0.0	0.0	0.0	0.0	0.0	0.0	0.0
Disbursements	**18.4**	**7.7**	**26.5**	**63.7**	**39.0**	**45.9**	**67.4**	**37.3**
Public and publicly guaranteed	18.4	7.7	26.5	63.7	39.0	45.9	67.4	37.3
Official creditors	18.4	7.7	26.5	44.5	39.0	45.9	67.4	37.3
Multilateral	10.0	7.7	16.2	34.2	29.6	24.0	44.8	20.7
of which: IBRD	0.0	0.0	0.0	0.0	0.0	0.0	0.0	0.0
IDA	2.8	3.9	4.7	8.2	9.7	7.2	7.4	1.4
Bilateral	8.4	0.0	10.3	10.4	9.4	21.9	22.6	16.5
Private creditors	0.0	0.0	0.0	19.1	0.0	0.0	0.0	0.0
of which: Bonds	0.0	0.0	0.0	0.0	0.0	0.0	0.0	0.0
Commercial banks	0.0	0.0	0.0	0.0	0.0	0.0	0.0	0.0
Private nonguaranteed	0.0	0.0	0.0	0.0	0.0	0.0	0.0	0.0
of which: Bonds	0.0	0.0	0.0	0.0	0.0	0.0	0.0	0.0
Principal repayments	**9.2**	**8.4**	**11.0**	**16.9**	**14.3**	**17.5**	**22.5**	**22.4**
Public and publicly guaranteed	9.2	8.4	11.0	16.9	14.3	17.5	22.5	22.4
Official creditors	9.2	8.4	11.0	14.5	13.2	13.6	17.4	20.0
Multilateral	4.4	4.0	5.1	8.2	7.9	8.7	9.7	11.0
of which: IBRD	0.0	0.0	0.0	0.0	0.0	0.0	0.0	0.0
IDA	0.3	0.5	1.4	1.2	1.8	1.6	1.8	2.3
Bilateral	4.8	4.4	6.0	6.3	5.3	5.0	7.7	9.0
Private creditors	0.0	0.0	0.0	2.4	1.1	3.9	5.1	2.4
of which: Bonds	0.0	0.0	0.0	0.0	0.0	0.0	0.0	0.0
Commercial banks	0.0	0.0	0.0	0.0	0.0	0.0	0.0	0.2
Private nonguaranteed	0.0	0.0	0.0	0.0	0.0	0.0	0.0	0.0
of which: Bonds	0.0	0.0	0.0	0.0	0.0	0.0	0.0	0.0
Interest payments	**2.0**	**2.2**	**3.7**	**4.9**	**6.5**	**7.7**	**8.2**	**8.2**
Public and publicly guaranteed	2.0	2.2	3.7	4.9	6.5	7.7	8.2	8.2
Official creditors	2.0	2.2	3.7	4.9	6.5	7.2	7.6	7.6
Multilateral	0.9	1.4	2.7	3.9	4.6	5.2	5.0	5.2
of which: IBRD	0.0	0.0	0.0	0.0	0.0	0.0	0.0	0.0
IDA	0.3	0.4	1.0	0.8	1.1	1.3	1.1	1.1
Bilateral	1.1	0.8	1.0	1.1	1.9	2.0	2.6	2.4
Private creditors	0.0	0.0	0.0	0.0	0.0	0.5	0.6	0.6
of which: Bonds	0.0	0.0	0.0	0.0	0.0	0.0	0.0	0.0
Commercial banks	0.0	0.0	0.0	0.0	0.0	0.0	0.0	0.1
Private nonguaranteed	0.0	0.0	0.0	0.0	0.0	0.0	0.0	0.0
of which: Bonds	0.0	0.0	0.0	0.0	0.0	0.0	0.0	0.0
8. Debt stock-flow reconciliation								
Total change in external debt stocks	14.8	-9.6	-13.4	62.8	206.1	23.2	56.7	-3.9
Net flows on external debt	9.2	0.7	14.7	45.2	22.0	30.2	42.9	11.5
9. Debt restructurings								
Total amount rescheduled	0.0	2.1	0.0	0.0	0.0	58.2	8.7	17.0
Total amount forgiven	0.0	0.0	0.6	2.1	0.0	0.0	0.0	0.0
Debt buyback	0.0	0.0	0.0	0.0	0.0	0.0	0.0	0.0

10. Contractual obligations on outstanding long-term external debt

	2011	2012	2013	2014	2015	2016	2017	2018
Official creditors								
Principal	29.3	48.2	29.3	26.6	26.9	32.3	33.0	33.7
Interest	8.6	10.1	9.6	9.4	9.2	8.8	8.3	7.8
Private creditors								
Principal	5.5	5.5	1.2	1.2	1.2	1.2	0.1	0.3
Interest	0.6	0.4	0.3	0.2	0.2	0.1	0.0	0.0

Notes:

Data on long-term public and publicly guaranteed debt include the effects of Paris Club debt restructuring agreement signed in 2008.

DOMINICA

(US$ million, unless otherwise indicated)

	1995	2000	2005	2006	2007	2008	2009	2010
1. Summary external debt data								
External debt stocks	**103.3**	**164.8**	**273.7**	**253.3**	**289.2**	**301.2**	**256.3**	**266.7**
Long-term external debt	94.9	145.8	221.6	217.3	214.0	203.2	198.7	216.0
Public and publicly guaranteed	94.9	145.8	221.6	217.3	214.0	203.2	198.7	216.0
Private nonguaranteed	0.0	0.0	0.0	0.0	0.0	0.0	0.0	0.0
Use of IMF credit	1.7	0.0	11.6	14.0	12.1	15.0	19.6	18.2
Short-term external debt	6.7	19.0	40.6	22.0	63.0	83.0	37.9	32.5
interest arrears on long-term	0.2	0.0	8.6	11.0	14.0	17.0	17.9	1.5
Memorandum items								
Principal arrears on long-term	1.8	0.3	6.5	6.0	11.2	10.2	10.7	19.3
Long-term public sector debt	94.9	145.8	221.6	217.3	214.0	203.2	198.7	216.0
Long-term private sector debt	0.0	0.0	0.0	0.0	0.0	0.0	0.0	0.0
Public & publicly guaranteed commitments	5.1	57.3	25.8	0.0	6.0	5.6	13.7	20.1
External debt flows								
Disbursements	9.5	56.2	8.0	6.5	4.9	11.1	13.4	29.4
Long-term external debt	9.5	56.2	4.5	3.1	4.9	7.9	8.3	29.4
IMF purchases	0.0	0.0	3.5	3.4	0.0	3.2	5.1	0.0
Principal repayments	4.4	6.7	10.0	11.2	13.0	12.9	15.7	11.1
Long-term external debt	3.6	6.7	9.6	9.6	10.5	12.9	14.9	10.0
IMF repurchases	0.9	0.0	0.4	1.6	2.5	0.0	0.8	1.1
Net flows	4.6	49.7	-37.0	-25.7	29.9	15.2	-48.3	29.4
Long-term external debt	5.9	49.5	-5.2	-6.4	-5.6	-5.0	-6.6	19.5
Short-term external debt	-0.5	0.2	-35.0	-21.0	38.0	17.0	-46.0	11.0
Interest payments	2.4	4.1	6.2	6.8	6.6	6.2	5.1	4.5
Long-term external debt	2.0	3.0	4.6	5.5	4.9	4.3	4.4	4.1
IMF charges	0.0	0.0	0.2	0.2	0.1	0.2	0.1	0.0
Short-term external debt	0.4	1.1	1.5	1.1	1.6	1.7	0.6	0.3
2. Other non-debt resource inflows								
Foreign direct investment	54.1	17.6	19.2	25.9	40.5	56.5	41.3	30.8
Portfolio equity	..	..	..	..	..	..	..	..
3. Currency composition of public and publicly guaranteed debt (%)								
Euro	..	..	5.4	4.0	3.4	2.7	3.4	3.0
Japanese yen	1.1	0.4	0.0	0.0	0.0	0.0	0.0	0.0
Pound sterling	13.3	2.8	0.0	0.0	0.0	0.0	0.0	0.0
Swiss franc	0.0	0.0	0.0	0.0	0.0	0.0	0.0	0.0
U.S.dollars	60.8	81.1	86.0	87.3	86.8	86.9	85.1	80.6
4. Average terms of new commitments								
Official creditors								
Interest (%)	2.6	5.2	2.4	0.0	0.8	1.2	2.1	2.6
Maturity (years)	26.4	21.3	21.9	0.0	34.5	31.1	26.8	18.5
Grace period (years)	8.8	6.9	7.6	0.0	10.0	8.4	8.6	5.1
Private creditors								
Interest (%)	0.0	1.9	0.0	0.0	0.0	3.5	0.0	0.0
Maturity (years)	0.0	9.2	0.0	0.0	0.0	15.6	0.0	0.0
Grace period (years)	0.0	2.3	0.0	0.0	0.0	2.6	0.0	0.0
5. Major economic aggregates								
Gross national income (GNI)	210.7	231.8	270.3	300.7	324.8	353.7	359.8	364.4
Exports of goods, services & income	110.7	149.2	135.3	150.6	156.4	170.7	161.2	158.7
Worker remit. & comp. of employees	13.4	16.3	25.0	25.4	25.9	26.1	25.4	26.2
Imports of goods, services & income	158.9	227.1	231.0	220.0	264.5	314.1	282.3	275.4
Profit remittances on FDI	12.2	33.0	22.7	7.4	13.0	12.5	13.4	11.4
Current account balance	-40.2	-59.8	-76.1	-49.9	-86.9	-124.3	-101.9	-96.8
International reserves	22.1	29.4	49.2	63.0	60.5	55.2	75.5	76.1
6. Ratios								
External debt stocks to exports (%)	93.3	110.5	202.3	168.2	184.9	176.4	159.0	168.0
External debt stocks to GNI (%)	49.0	71.1	101.3	84.2	89.0	85.2	71.2	73.2
Debt service to exports (%)	6.1	7.2	12.0	11.9	12.5	11.2	12.9	9.8
Short-term to external debt stocks (%)	6.5	11.5	14.8	8.7	21.8	27.6	14.8	12.2
Multilateral to external debt stocks (%)	62.2	50.6	46.0	47.9	41.8	38.9	46.0	43.6
Reserves to external debt stocks (%)	21.4	17.8	18.0	24.9	20.9	18.3	29.4	28.5
Reserves to imports (months)	1.7	1.6	2.6	3.4	2.7	2.1	3.2	3.3

(US$ million, unless otherwise indicated)

	1995	2000	2005	2006	2007	2008	2009	2010
7. Long-term external debt								
Debt outstanding and disbursed	**94.9**	**145.8**	**221.6**	**217.3**	**214.0**	**203.2**	**198.7**	**216.0**
Public and publicly guaranteed	94.9	145.8	221.6	217.3	214.0	203.2	198.7	216.0
Official creditors	94.9	114.2	172.0	167.7	164.4	156.8	154.2	171.5
Multilateral	64.3	83.4	126.0	121.4	121.0	117.1	117.8	116.1
of which: IBRD	0.0	2.4	3.9	3.3	2.5	1.8	1.2	0.8
IDA	12.2	13.6	21.7	22.5	25.4	26.5	27.5	27.0
Bilateral	30.6	30.8	46.0	46.3	43.4	39.7	36.4	55.4
Private creditors	0.0	31.6	49.6	49.6	49.6	46.4	44.5	44.5
of which: Bonds	0.0	31.6	47.1	47.1	47.1	42.2	40.3	40.3
Commercial banks	0.0	0.0	0.0	0.0	0.0	1.7	1.7	1.7
Private nonguaranteed	0.0	0.0	0.0	0.0	0.0	0.0	0.0	0.0
of which: Bonds	0.0	0.0	0.0	0.0	0.0	0.0	0.0	0.0
Disbursements	**9.5**	**56.2**	**4.5**	**3.1**	**4.9**	**7.9**	**8.3**	**29.4**
Public and publicly guaranteed	9.5	56.2	4.5	3.1	4.9	7.9	8.3	29.4
Official creditors	9.5	25.7	4.5	3.1	4.9	6.2	8.3	29.4
Multilateral	3.5	19.3	3.9	2.6	4.7	6.2	6.0	7.4
of which: IBRD	0.0	0.7	0.3	0.0	0.0	0.0	0.0	0.0
IDA	0.1	-0.1	0.5	0.1	2.3	1.8	1.4	0.5
Bilateral	6.0	6.3	0.6	0.5	0.1	0.0	2.3	22.1
Private creditors	0.0	30.5	0.0	0.0	0.0	1.7	0.0	0.0
of which: Bonds	0.0	30.5	0.0	0.0	0.0	0.0	0.0	0.0
Commercial banks	0.0	0.0	0.0	0.0	0.0	1.7	0.0	0.0
Private nonguaranteed	0.0	0.0	0.0	0.0	0.0	0.0	0.0	0.0
of which: Bonds	0.0	0.0	0.0	0.0	0.0	0.0	0.0	0.0
Principal repayments	**3.6**	**6.7**	**9.6**	**9.6**	**10.5**	**12.9**	**14.9**	**10.0**
Public and publicly guaranteed	3.6	6.7	9.6	9.6	10.5	12.9	14.9	10.0
Official creditors	3.6	6.7	9.6	9.6	10.5	12.9	13.0	10.0
Multilateral	2.0	3.9	7.9	8.0	6.9	9.3	7.8	6.6
of which: IBRD	0.0	0.0	0.4	0.6	0.8	0.8	0.6	0.4
IDA	0.1	0.1	0.3	0.3	0.4	0.5	0.5	0.5
Bilateral	1.5	2.8	1.7	1.6	3.6	3.6	5.2	3.4
Private creditors	0.0	0.0	0.0	0.0	0.0	0.0	1.9	0.0
of which: Bonds	0.0	0.0	0.0	0.0	0.0	0.0	1.9	0.0
Commercial banks	0.0	0.0	0.0	0.0	0.0	0.0	0.0	0.0
Private nonguaranteed	0.0	0.0	0.0	0.0	0.0	0.0	0.0	0.0
of which: Bonds	0.0	0.0	0.0	0.0	0.0	0.0	0.0	0.0
Interest payments	**2.0**	**3.0**	**4.6**	**5.5**	**4.9**	**4.3**	**4.4**	**4.1**
Public and publicly guaranteed	2.0	3.0	4.6	5.5	4.9	4.3	4.4	4.1
Official creditors	2.0	2.9	4.2	4.9	4.4	4.1	3.9	3.8
Multilateral	1.6	1.9	3.2	3.2	3.1	2.8	2.8	2.6
of which: IBRD	0.0	0.1	0.2	0.2	0.2	0.1	0.1	0.0
IDA	0.1	0.1	0.2	0.2	0.2	0.2	0.2	0.2
Bilateral	0.4	1.0	1.0	1.7	1.3	1.3	1.2	1.2
Private creditors	0.0	0.1	0.3	0.6	0.4	0.2	0.5	0.3
of which: Bonds	0.0	0.1	0.3	0.6	0.4	0.2	0.2	0.3
Commercial banks	0.0	0.0	0.0	0.0	0.0	0.0	0.3	0.1
Private nonguaranteed	0.0	0.0	0.0	0.0	0.0	0.0	0.0	0.0
of which: Bonds	0.0	0.0	0.0	0.0	0.0	0.0	0.0	0.0
8. Debt stock-flow reconciliation								
Total change in external debt stocks	5.2	49.3	-30.7	-20.5	35.9	12.1	-44.9	10.4
Net flows on external debt	4.6	49.7	-37.0	-25.7	29.9	15.2	-48.3	29.4
9. Debt restructurings								
Total amount rescheduled	0.0	0.0	14.6	11.5	0.0	0.0	0.0	0.0
Total amount forgiven	0.0	0.0	0.1	0.0	0.0	0.0	0.0	0.0
Debt buyback	0.0	0.0	0.0	0.0	0.0	0.0	0.0	0.0

10. Contractual obligations on outstanding long-term external debt

	2011	2012	2013	2014	2015	2016	2017	2018
Official creditors								
Principal	10.8	7.7	9.1	9.5	9.2	9.7	9.6	8.5
Interest	3.5	3.3	3.2	3.0	2.8	2.6	2.4	2.2
Private creditors								
Principal	0.1	0.1	0.1	30.7	0.1	0.1	0.1	0.1
Interest	3.0	3.0	3.0	3.0	0.2	0.2	0.2	0.2

DOMINICAN REPUBLIC

(US$ million, unless otherwise indicated)

	1995	2000	2005	2006	2007	2008	2009	2010
1. Summary external debt data								
External debt stocks	**4,447**	**4,541**	**7,072**	**8,553**	**10,142**	**10,119**	**11,046**	**13,045**
Long-term external debt	3,672	3,311	5,770	6,634	7,118	7,689	8,600	9,958
Public and publicly guaranteed	3,653	3,311	5,769	6,221	6,273	6,846	7,757	9,115
Private nonguaranteed	19	0	2	414	845	843	843	843
Use of IMF credit	160	52	400	459	548	492	767	1,139
Short-term external debt	616	1,178	901	1,459	2,476	1,938	1,679	1,948
interest arrears on long-term	214	28	20	8	9	3	0	0
Memorandum items								
Principal arrears on long-term	320	56	144	32	13	15	0	0
Long-term public sector debt	3,626	3,299	5,761	6,214	6,268	6,841	7,753	9,111
Long-term private sector debt	46	13	9	420	851	848	847	846
Public & publicly guaranteed commitments	167	469	811	1,336	343	1,028	2,935	1,826
External debt flows								
Disbursements	195	303	894	1,701	1,427	1,420	1,700	2,591
Long-term external debt	195	303	674	1,560	1,250	1,298	1,391	2,061
IMF purchases	0	0	220	142	177	122	308	530
Principal repayments	234	257	763	1,023	927	863	817	817
Long-term external debt	200	257	763	918	813	699	770	670
IMF repurchases	34	0	0	105	114	164	47	147
Net flows	105	311	96	1,249	1,516	25	627	2,044
Long-term external debt	-5	46	-88	642	437	600	622	1,392
Short-term external debt	143	265	-36	570	1,016	-532	-256	269
Interest payments	175	263	248	320	453	547	505	521
Long-term external debt	145	211	211	255	327	446	431	443
IMF charges	10	3	9	22	26	24	7	10
Short-term external debt	20	50	27	42	100	78	67	68
2. Other non-debt resource inflows								
Foreign direct investment	414	953	1,123	1,085	1,667	2,870	2,067	1,626
Portfolio equity	..	..	..	..	..	..	..	..
3. Currency composition of public and publicly guaranteed debt (%)								
Euro	..	..	2.8	3.4	6.2	7.7	8.6	6.4
Japanese yen	7.7	5.0	2.8	2.1	1.8	2.0	1.9	1.6
Pound sterling	0.0	0.0	0.0	0.0	0.0	0.0	0.0	0.0
Swiss franc	0.0	0.0	0.0	0.0	0.0	0.0	0.0	0.0
U.S.dollars	63.7	73.8	86.9	88.0	85.9	85.4	85.4	88.9
4. Average terms of new commitments								
Official creditors								
Interest (%)	6.6	6.5	1.7	4.1	3.7	2.6	2.7	1.5
Maturity (years)	20.2	14.4	21.5	21.5	21.2	22.5	17.1	20.7
Grace period (years)	5.2	1.8	4.1	4.5	4.1	3.4	4.9	5.8
Private creditors								
Interest (%)	8.4	6.5	3.2	6.6	6.5	6.0	4.8	6.6
Maturity (years)	9.5	10.3	4.1	13.5	9.2	7.1	10.7	10.8
Grace period (years)	2.0	2.7	1.2	8.7	2.2	2.6	2.9	7.2
5. Major economic aggregates								
Gross national income (GNI)	15,589	22,955	32,102	34,100	39,234	43,684	44,829	49,789
Exports of goods, services & income	5,859	9,264	10,498	11,877	12,797	12,411	10,918	12,171
Worker remit. & comp. of employees	839	1,839	2,719	3,084	3,427	3,667	3,467	3,369
Imports of goods, services & income	7,034	12,193	13,668	16,309	18,364	20,443	16,382	19,724
Profit remittances on FDI	624	1,068	1,765	1,932	2,194	1,669	1,577	0
Current account balance	-183	-1,027	-473	-1,287	-2,166	-4,519	-2,159	-4,435
International reserves	373	632	1,853	2,127	2,562	2,288	2,905	3,501
6. Ratios								
External debt stocks to exports (%)	75.9	49.0	67.4	72.0	79.3	81.5	101.2	107.2
External debt stocks to GNI (%)	28.5	19.8	22.0	25.1	25.8	23.2	24.6	26.2
Debt service to exports (%)	7.0	5.6	9.6	11.3	10.8	11.4	12.1	11.0
Short-term to external debt stocks (%)	13.8	25.9	12.7	17.1	24.4	19.1	15.2	14.9
Multilateral to external debt stocks (%)	23.2	24.9	25.6	22.2	18.6	18.6	23.6	23.6
Reserves to external debt stocks (%)	8.4	13.9	26.2	24.9	25.3	22.6	26.3	26.8
Reserves to imports (months)	0.6	0.6	1.6	1.6	1.7	1.3	2.1	2.1

DOMINICAN REPUBLIC

(US$ million, unless otherwise indicated)

	1995	2000	2005	2006	2007	2008	2009	2010
7. Long-term external debt								
Debt outstanding and disbursed	**3,672**	**3,311**	**5,770**	**6,634**	**7,118**	**7,689**	**8,600**	**9,958**
Public and publicly guaranteed	3,653	3,311	5,769	6,221	6,273	6,846	7,757	9,115
Official creditors	2,996	2,565	3,146	3,497	3,626	4,353	5,327	6,165
Multilateral	1,033	1,132	1,807	1,901	1,886	1,883	2,608	3,074
of which: IBRD	282	292	405	438	472	449	748	864
IDA	17	14	11	10	9	9	8	7
Bilateral	1,962	1,433	1,339	1,596	1,741	2,469	2,718	3,091
Private creditors	657	746	2,623	2,724	2,646	2,493	2,431	2,950
of which: Bonds	520	506	1,147	1,452	1,326	1,201	1,076	1,721
Commercial banks	33	121	980	1,106	1,194	1,200	1,276	1,155
Private nonguaranteed	19	0	2	414	845	843	843	843
of which: Bonds	0	0	0	412	844	843	843	843
Disbursements	**195**	**303**	**674**	**1,560**	**1,250**	**1,298**	**1,391**	**2,061**
Public and publicly guaranteed	195	303	673	1,148	820	1,298	1,391	2,061
Official creditors	187	147	402	613	454	1,023	1,302	1,127
Multilateral	157	100	199	187	184	213	904	622
of which: IBRD	36	39	64	67	73	20	352	175
IDA	0	0	0	0	0	0	0	0
Bilateral	30	46	204	426	270	810	399	505
Private creditors	8	156	271	534	366	275	89	935
of which: Bonds	0	0	0	324	0	0	0	750
Commercial banks	8	90	227	193	357	272	85	170
Private nonguaranteed	0	0	2	412	431	0	0	0
of which: Bonds	0	0	0	412	431	0	0	0
Principal repayments	**200**	**257**	**763**	**918**	**813**	**699**	**770**	**670**
Public and publicly guaranteed	184	257	763	918	813	698	769	670
Official creditors	161	217	171	373	353	294	338	295
Multilateral	79	63	110	113	215	215	191	151
of which: IBRD	40	21	38	34	39	43	54	59
IDA	1	1	1	1	1	1	1	1
Bilateral	82	154	61	261	137	80	147	143
Private creditors	23	40	592	544	460	404	432	375
of which: Bonds	0	4	336	20	125	125	125	105
Commercial banks	3	18	163	173	291	242	288	252
Private nonguaranteed	16	0	0	0	0	1	0	0
of which: Bonds	0	0	0	0	0	0	0	0
Interest payments	**145**	**211**	**211**	**255**	**327**	**446**	**431**	**443**
Public and publicly guaranteed	143	211	211	253	271	337	323	334
Official creditors	120	158	108	142	147	136	150	155
Multilateral	51	58	82	90	98	87	83	91
of which: IBRD	20	22	21	23	25	24	22	30
IDA	0	0	0	0	0	0	0	0
Bilateral	69	100	26	52	50	48	67	64
Private creditors	23	53	103	112	123	202	173	179
of which: Bonds	13	38	16	45	56	125	113	134
Commercial banks	3	7	37	56	61	70	56	42
Private nonguaranteed	2	0	0	2	57	108	108	108
of which: Bonds	0	0	0	2	57	108	108	108
8. Debt stock-flow reconciliation								
Total change in external debt stocks	173	-145	-53	1,481	1,589	-22	926	1,999
Net flows on external debt	105	311	96	1,249	1,516	25	627	2,044
9. Debt restructurings								
Total amount rescheduled	2	0	1,209	203	0	0	0	0
Total amount forgiven	0	1	0	0	0	0	0	0
Debt buyback	0	0	316	0	0	0	0	0

10. Contractual obligations on outstanding long-term external debt

	2011	2012	2013	2014	2015	2016	2017	2018
Official creditors								
Principal	638	531	696	866	504	483	422	399
Interest	134	128	121	101	80	71	63	55
Private creditors								
Principal	499	858	699	352	272	207	142	692
Interest	297	263	212	191	182	172	167	136

Notes:

Data include the effects of Paris Club debt restructuring agreement signed in 2005. Long-term private nonguaranteed debt data only cover Inter-American Development Bank and Bonds.

ECUADOR

(US$ million, unless otherwise indicated)

	1995	2000	2005	2006	2007	2008	2009	2010
1. Summary external debt data								
External debt stocks	**13,877**	**13,254**	**17,316**	**17,296**	**17,797**	**17,379**	**14,130**	**14,815**
Long-term external debt	12,391	12,310	15,519	15,284	15,902	15,694	12,735	14,446
Public and publicly guaranteed	11,951	10,875	10,850	10,304	10,719	10,053	6,920	8,598
Private nonguaranteed	440	1,435	4,668	4,980	5,183	5,642	5,815	5,848
Use of IMF credit	173	148	78	23	0	0	0	0
Short-term external debt	1,312	797	1,719	1,990	1,894	1,685	1,396	369
interest arrears on long-term	12	3	1	0	0	31	37	37
Memorandum items								
Principal arrears on long-term	10	6	5	0	0	1	1	1
Long-term public sector debt	11,951	10,875	10,850	10,304	10,715	10,036	6,894	8,569
Long-term private sector debt	440	1,435	4,668	4,980	5,188	5,659	5,841	5,877
Public & publicly guaranteed commitments	1,162	404	1,328	1,303	1,248	17	166	4,890
External debt flows								
Disbursements	1,028	1,125	3,154	2,638	3,048	1,776	1,419	3,059
Long-term external debt	1,028	976	3,154	2,638	3,048	1,776	1,419	3,059
IMF purchases	0	150	0	0	0	0	0	0
Principal repayments	750	1,065	3,242	2,935	2,362	1,704	4,388	1,351
Long-term external debt	721	1,065	3,047	2,877	2,339	1,704	4,388	1,351
IMF repurchases	29	0	195	58	23	0	0	0
Net flows	-173	-194	-234	-27	591	-168	-3,264	681
Long-term external debt	307	-89	106	-239	709	72	-2,969	1,708
Short-term external debt	-451	-254	-145	271	-95	-240	-295	-1,027
Interest payments	656	813	957	1,271	1,325	1,009	642	498
Long-term external debt	565	708	842	1,175	1,227	926	578	484
IMF charges	10	4	7	3	1	0	0	0
Short-term external debt	81	102	107	93	97	84	64	14
2. Other non-debt resource inflows								
Foreign direct investment	452	-23	493	271	194	1,001	316	167
Portfolio equity	13	0	2	0	0	1	2	..
3. Currency composition of public and publicly guaranteed debt (%)								
Euro	..	..	3.4	3.5	3.4	3.0	4.1	2.8
Japanese yen	4.1	4.5	3.5	3.4	3.1	2.6	3.3	2.6
Pound sterling	0.7	0.8	0.7	0.8	0.7	0.5	0.8	0.6
Swiss franc	0.0	0.0	0.0	0.0	0.0	0.0	0.0	0.0
U.S.dollars	71.2	83.3	87.4	87.7	88.7	90.0	86.7	90.3
4. Average terms of new commitments								
Official creditors								
Interest (%)	6.2	6.9	6.6	6.7	5.4	3.0	3.3	5.1
Maturity (years)	16.4	17.2	8.1	16.7	20.9	18.7	23.2	12.0
Grace period (years)	6.0	5.2	2.9	4.5	4.2	2.2	5.6	3.7
Private creditors								
Interest (%)	7.9	7.5	9.3	6.0	0.0	6.3	0.0	0.0
Maturity (years)	12.0	9.9	10.0	10.7	0.0	12.6	0.0	0.0
Grace period (years)	2.5	2.5	9.8	1.9	0.0	3.1	0.0	0.0
5. Major economic aggregates								
Gross national income (GNI)	19,281	14,530	35,245	39,813	43,742	53,088	56,091	64,195
Exports of goods, services & income	5,295	5,976	11,566	14,378	16,329	20,647	15,607	19,686
Worker remit. & comp. of employees	386	1,322	2,460	2,934	3,094	2,828	2,502	2,569
Imports of goods, services & income	6,736	6,403	13,880	15,863	17,924	22,506	18,372	23,790
Profit remittances on FDI	144	329	1,004	977	1,160	787	822	..
Current account balance	-1,000	926	347	1,618	1,588	1,087	-268	-1,794
International reserves	1,788	1,179	2,148	2,026	3,521	4,473	3,792	2,622
6. Ratios								
External debt stocks to exports (%)	262.1	221.8	149.7	120.3	109.0	84.2	90.5	75.3
External debt stocks to GNI (%)	72.0	91.2	49.1	43.4	40.7	32.7	25.2	23.1
Debt service to exports (%)	26.6	31.4	36.3	29.3	22.6	13.1	32.2	9.4
Short-term to external debt stocks (%)	9.5	6.0	9.9	11.5	10.6	9.7	9.9	2.5
Multilateral to external debt stocks (%)	21.9	27.7	20.8	23.1	26.2	24.7	30.8	34.9
Reserves to external debt stocks (%)	12.9	8.9	12.4	11.7	19.8	25.7	26.8	17.7
Reserves to imports (months)	3.2	2.2	1.9	1.5	2.4	2.4	2.5	1.3

ECUADOR

(US$ million, unless otherwise indicated)

	1995	2000	2005	2006	2007	2008	2009	2010
7. Long-term external debt								
Debt outstanding and disbursed	**12,391**	**12,310**	**15,519**	**15,284**	**15,902**	**15,694**	**12,735**	**14,446**
Public and publicly guaranteed	11,951	10,875	10,850	10,304	10,719	10,053	6,920	8,598
Official creditors	5,210	5,881	5,948	6,136	6,592	5,964	5,855	7,575
Multilateral	3,044	3,670	3,609	3,988	4,658	4,293	4,346	5,171
of which: IBRD	1,082	840	799	746	684	612	532	446
IDA	26	21	15	14	13	12	11	10
Bilateral	2,165	2,212	2,339	2,147	1,934	1,672	1,509	2,404
Private creditors	6,742	4,993	4,902	4,168	4,128	4,088	1,065	1,023
of which: Bonds	5,999	3,950	4,600	3,860	3,860	3,860	873	868
Commercial banks	385	910	241	212	194	163	134	105
Private nonguaranteed	440	1,435	4,668	4,980	5,183	5,642	5,815	5,848
of which: Bonds	10	0	0	0	0	0	0	0
Disbursements	**1,028**	**976**	**3,154**	**2,638**	**3,048**	**1,776**	**1,419**	**3,059**
Public and publicly guaranteed	818	595	991	928	1,357	353	384	2,307
Official creditors	733	524	318	844	1,333	343	382	2,305
Multilateral	593	446	316	840	1,323	339	377	1,229
of which: IBRD	319	69	39	21	8	5	0	3
IDA	0	0	0	0	0	0	0	0
Bilateral	141	78	2	4	9	5	5	1,076
Private creditors	85	71	674	83	24	10	2	2
of which: Bonds	0	0	650	0	0	0	0	0
Commercial banks	57	71	24	22	24	10	2	2
Private nonguaranteed	210	381	2,162	1,710	1,691	1,423	1,035	752
of which: Bonds	10	0	0	0	0	0	0	0
Principal repayments	**721**	**1,065**	**3,047**	**2,877**	**2,339**	**1,704**	**4,388**	**1,351**
Public and publicly guaranteed	711	548	922	1,585	1,028	962	3,526	633
Official creditors	486	397	802	772	963	914	501	589
Multilateral	235	324	409	481	685	733	321	403
of which: IBRD	98	89	74	74	70	77	81	89
IDA	1	1	1	1	1	1	1	1
Bilateral	252	73	393	291	277	180	180	185
Private creditors	225	151	120	813	65	49	3,025	44
of which: Bonds	10	0	0	740	0	0	2,987	6
Commercial banks	59	119	101	51	42	41	31	31
Private nonguaranteed	10	517	2,125	1,292	1,311	741	862	718
of which: Bonds	0	0	0	0	0	0	0	0
Interest payments	**565**	**708**	**842**	**1,175**	**1,227**	**926**	**578**	**484**
Public and publicly guaranteed	563	535	657	749	736	655	329	325
Official creditors	321	295	275	317	327	311	226	254
Multilateral	173	264	171	220	238	246	177	173
of which: IBRD	69	74	32	40	42	33	23	17
IDA	0	0	0	0	0	0	0	0
Bilateral	148	31	104	97	89	64	49	82
Private creditors	242	240	383	432	409	345	103	71
of which: Bonds	147	140	367	410	392	331	91	61
Commercial banks	50	89	12	16	10	9	7	6
Private nonguaranteed	1	172	185	426	492	270	248	159
of which: Bonds	0	0	0	0	0	0	0	0
8. Debt stock-flow reconciliation								
Total change in external debt stocks	-1,084	-2,740	-133	-19	501	-418	-3,249	685
Net flows on external debt	-173	-194	-234	-27	591	-168	-3,264	681
9. Debt restructurings								
Total amount rescheduled	5,818	4,674	0	0	0	0	0	0
Total amount forgiven	1,180	2,522	2	1	4	3	5	6
Debt buyback	0	0	0	0	0	0	2,987	0

10. Contractual obligations on outstanding long-term external debt

	2011	2012	2013	2014	2015	2016	2017	2018
Official creditors								
Principal	987	1,158	925	866	584	644	714	674
Interest	270	297	281	255	230	214	187	159
Private creditors								
Principal	1,219	1,611	691	452	1,261	381	450	241
Interest	274	322	227	182	178	88	109	45

Notes:

Short-term debt data from 2007 are based on reports provided by the country.

EGYPT, ARAB REPUBLIC OF

(US$ million, unless otherwise indicated)

	1995	*2000*	*2005*	*2006*	*2007*	*2008*	*2009*	*2010*
1. Summary external debt data								
External debt stocks	**33,475**	**29,010**	**30,184**	**30,556**	**33,998**	**33,365**	**33,308**	**34,844**
Long-term external debt	31,000	24,906	28,529	28,837	31,762	30,522	30,746	31,695
Public and publicly guaranteed	30,687	24,333	28,436	28,756	31,742	30,442	30,672	31,641
Private nonguaranteed	313	573	93	81	21	80	74	54
Use of IMF credit	103	0	0	0	0	0	0	0
Short-term external debt	2,372	4,104	1,656	1,720	2,236	2,842	2,561	3,149
interest arrears on long-term	4	0	2	1	1	0	0	0
Memorandum items								
Principal arrears on long-term	148	14	8	2	2	2	2	0
Long-term public sector debt	30,684	24,332	28,150	28,316	31,136	29,908	30,232	31,281
Long-term private sector debt	316	574	379	520	626	614	514	414
Public & publicly guaranteed commitments	207	981	3,053	2,369	1,437	2,650	2,185	3,846
External debt flows								
Disbursements	642	569	3,020	791	3,152	1,124	2,071	3,382
Long-term external debt	642	569	3,020	791	3,152	1,124	2,071	3,382
IMF purchases	0	0	0	0	0	0	0	0
Principal repayments	988	1,100	1,573	1,626	2,014	2,311	2,040	2,106
Long-term external debt	894	1,100	1,573	1,626	2,014	2,311	2,040	2,106
IMF repurchases	94	0	0	0	0	0	0	0
Net flows	92	-720	1,383	-770	1,654	-579	-250	1,864
Long-term external debt	-251	-530	1,447	-835	1,138	-1,186	31	1,276
Short-term external debt	438	-189	-64	65	516	607	-281	588
Interest payments	1,393	733	699	840	907	934	870	867
Long-term external debt	1,252	619	616	744	795	821	767	741
IMF charges	9	0	0	0	0	0	0	0
Short-term external debt	132	113	83	96	112	113	102	126
2. Other non-debt resource inflows								
Foreign direct investment	598	1,235	5,376	10,043	11,578	9,495	6,712	6,386
Portfolio equity	0	269	729	502	-3,199	-674	393	..
3. Currency composition of public and publicly guaranteed debt (%)								
Euro	..	..	32.6	35.1	35.5	34.3	35.4	31.2
Japanese yen	13.1	13.8	12.5	12.1	10.6	13.3	12.7	13.1
Pound sterling	1.4	1.2	1.9	2.0	1.8	1.3	1.3	1.1
Swiss franc	2.7	2.1	1.8	1.9	1.7	1.8	1.7	1.7
U.S.dollars	34.5	39.8	38.1	35.8	36.1	35.1	34.1	38.3
4. Average terms of new commitments								
Official creditors								
Interest (%)	3.1	4.7	5.2	4.5	2.2	3.0	1.4	0.9
Maturity (years)	22.0	21.7	18.8	21.3	16.5	21.6	21.3	25.7
Grace period (years)	6.6	5.9	7.6	7.1	6.5	6.0	7.0	6.7
Private creditors								
Interest (%)	6.5	5.8	4.4	2.2	6.4	1.3	5.1	6.0
Maturity (years)	4.3	4.3	7.6	5.3	6.6	3.7	6.4	16.6
Grace period (years)	2.4	3.1	7.1	3.1	4.8	2.4	1.4	16.4
5. Major economic aggregates								
Gross national income (GNI)	60,300	100,770	89,432	108,015	131,650	164,178	189,138	214,548
Exports of goods, services & income	14,838	18,735	32,141	39,241	47,707	57,826	45,601	49,365
Worker remit. & comp. of employees	3,226	2,852	5,017	5,330	7,656	8,694	7,150	7,725
Imports of goods, services & income	19,123	23,878	35,787	42,375	55,618	68,999	56,910	66,239
Profit remittances on FDI	228	92	647	915	1,015	680	2,101	..
Current account balance	-254	-971	2,103	2,635	412	-1,415	-3,349	-4,435
International reserves	17,122	13,785	21,857	26,007	32,214	34,331	34,897	37,029
6. Ratios								
External debt stocks to exports (%)	225.6	154.8	93.9	77.9	71.3	57.7	73.0	70.6
External debt stocks to GNI (%)	55.5	28.8	33.8	28.3	25.8	20.3	17.6	16.2
Debt service to exports (%)	16.0	9.8	7.1	6.3	6.1	5.6	6.4	6.0
Short-term to external debt stocks (%)	7.1	14.1	5.5	5.6	6.6	8.5	7.7	9.0
Multilateral to external debt stocks (%)	12.0	13.5	16.8	18.1	21.9	22.3	25.3	25.9
Reserves to external debt stocks (%)	51.1	47.5	72.4	85.1	94.8	102.9	104.8	106.3
Reserves to imports (months)	10.7	6.9	7.3	7.4	7.0	6.0	7.4	6.7

(US$ million, unless otherwise indicated)

	1995	2000	2005	2006	2007	2008	2009	2010
7. Long-term external debt								
Debt outstanding and disbursed	**31,000**	**24,906**	**28,529**	**28,837**	**31,762**	**30,522**	**30,746**	**31,695**
Public and publicly guaranteed	30,687	24,333	28,436	28,756	31,742	30,442	30,672	31,641
Official creditors	28,934	23,794	25,662	26,437	28,772	27,855	28,372	27,863
Multilateral	4,022	3,915	5,076	5,536	7,443	7,446	8,412	9,019
of which: IBRD	1,320	639	492	544	1,181	1,255	1,850	2,543
IDA	1,035	1,266	1,420	1,481	1,490	1,444	1,400	1,338
Bilateral	24,912	19,879	20,585	20,901	21,328	20,409	19,959	18,844
Private creditors	1,753	540	2,774	2,318	2,970	2,588	2,301	3,778
of which: Bonds	0	0	1,829	1,576	2,199	2,184	1,883	3,333
Commercial banks	560	317	798	608	665	314	333	374
Private nonguaranteed	313	573	93	81	21	80	74	54
of which: Bonds	0	100	0	0	0	0	0	0
Disbursements	**642**	**569**	**3,020**	**791**	**3,152**	**1,124**	**2,071**	**3,382**
Public and publicly guaranteed	642	362	3,020	791	3,151	1,054	2,062	3,377
Official creditors	602	218	1,061	729	2,414	957	1,965	1,772
Multilateral	392	168	873	578	2,230	686	1,513	1,362
of which: IBRD	42	6	97	108	723	143	684	777
IDA	83	49	69	57	13	11	2	10
Bilateral	209	50	188	151	183	271	452	410
Private creditors	40	144	1,958	62	738	97	97	1,605
of which: Bonds	0	0	1,250	0	643	0	0	1,500
Commercial banks	31	132	707	60	83	93	97	104
Private nonguaranteed	0	207	0	0	0	70	9	5
of which: Bonds	0	0	0	0	0	0	0	0
Principal repayments	**894**	**1,100**	**1,573**	**1,626**	**2,014**	**2,311**	**2,040**	**2,106**
Public and publicly guaranteed	832	984	1,573	1,625	1,953	2,300	2,021	2,080
Official creditors	542	863	1,346	1,354	1,869	1,831	1,909	2,014
Multilateral	310	298	427	370	669	573	619	589
of which: IBRD	198	87	77	66	97	77	89	83
IDA	14	23	41	42	47	50	52	54
Bilateral	232	564	919	984	1,199	1,259	1,290	1,425
Private creditors	290	121	227	271	84	469	112	66
of which: Bonds	0	0	0	0	0	0	0	0
Commercial banks	91	57	201	254	36	437	86	46
Private nonguaranteed	62	116	0	1	61	11	20	25
of which: Bonds	0	0	0	0	0	0	0	0
Interest payments	**1,252**	**619**	**616**	**744**	**795**	**821**	**767**	**741**
Public and publicly guaranteed	1,228	603	612	725	793	818	765	740
Official creditors	1,121	573	545	581	673	705	645	572
Multilateral	232	147	136	174	229	259	230	200
of which: IBRD	114	41	21	27	47	58	55	41
IDA	7	9	11	11	11	11	10	10
Bilateral	889	425	409	406	444	446	414	372
Private creditors	106	31	68	145	120	112	120	168
of which: Bonds	0	0	51	106	84	85	112	157
Commercial banks	44	16	12	35	34	24	7	8
Private nonguaranteed	24	16	4	19	2	3	2	1
of which: Bonds	0	12	0	0	0	0	0	0
8. Debt stock-flow reconciliation								
Total change in external debt stocks	976	-1,875	-854	372	3,442	-633	-57	1,536
Net flows on external debt	92	-720	1,383	-770	1,654	-579	-250	1,864
9. Debt restructurings								
Total amount rescheduled	309	22	1	1	1	0	0	0
Total amount forgiven	54	25	0	0	0	0	0	0
Debt buyback	0	0	0	0	0	0	0	0

10. Contractual obligations on outstanding long-term external debt

	2011	2012	2013	2014	2015	2016	2017	2018
Official creditors								
Principal	3,111	3,714	3,430	3,047	3,021	2,735	1,585	1,625
Interest	599	550	490	424	362	310	267	234
Private creditors								
Principal	323	506	60	57	1,304	50	40	34
Interest	317	275	240	209	152	95	94	93

Notes:

Short-term debt is based on the Central Bank data from 2001. Data on long-term private nonguaranteed debt are revised based on reports provided by the country.

EL SALVADOR

(US$ million, unless otherwise indicated)

	1995	2000	2005	2006	2007	2008	2009	2010
1. Summary external debt data								
External debt stocks	**2,509**	**4,467**	**9,265**	**10,168**	**9,807**	**10,601**	**10,102**	**11,069**
Long-term external debt	1,984	2,822	7,409	8,878	8,515	9,059	9,239	9,964
Public and publicly guaranteed	1,979	2,710	4,786	5,589	5,435	5,743	6,100	6,394
Private nonguaranteed	5	111	2,622	3,289	3,079	3,316	3,139	3,569
Use of IMF credit	0	0	0	0	0	0	0	0
Short-term external debt	525	1,645	1,856	1,289	1,292	1,542	863	1,105
interest arrears on long-term	3	0	0	0	0	0	0	0
Memorandum items								
Principal arrears on long-term	6	0	0	0	0	0	0	0
Long-term public sector debt	1,972	2,705	4,782	5,585	5,432	5,739	6,097	6,392
Long-term private sector debt	11	117	2,626	3,293	3,083	3,319	3,142	3,572
Public & publicly guaranteed commitments	832	347	693	1,146	251	1,068	810	943
External debt flows								
Disbursements	206	371	1,222	1,643	251	1,042	1,216	1,055
Long-term external debt	206	371	1,222	1,643	251	1,042	1,216	1,055
IMF purchases	0	0	0	0	0	0	0	0
Principal repayments	160	157	405	671	550	488	685	602
Long-term external debt	160	157	405	671	550	488	685	602
IMF repurchases	0	0	0	0	0	0	0	0
Net flows	383	807	894	405	-296	804	-148	694
Long-term external debt	46	214	817	972	-299	554	531	452
Short-term external debt	337	592	77	-567	3	250	-679	242
Interest payments	120	212	445	564	539	518	491	477
Long-term external debt	98	139	344	464	466	484	475	464
IMF charges	0	0	0	0	0	0	0	0
Short-term external debt	22	73	101	100	74	34	15	13
2. Other non-debt resource inflows								
Foreign direct investment	38	173	55	18	105	371	231	-6
Portfolio equity	0	0	..	..	..	..	..	..
3. Currency composition of public and publicly guaranteed debt (%)								
Euro	..	..	3.5	3.3	3.8	3.4	3.2	2.8
Japanese yen	1.8	6.7	4.9	4.3	4.7	5.9	5.2	5.2
Pound sterling	0.0	0.0	0.0	0.0	0.0	0.0	0.0	0.0
Swiss franc	0.0	0.0	0.0	0.0	0.0	0.0	0.0	0.0
U.S.dollars	46.7	68.3	81.5	84.1	83.2	83.5	85.3	86.5
4. Average terms of new commitments								
Official creditors								
Interest (%)	6.5	7.2	5.1	6.0	5.6	5.5	2.5	2.2
Maturity (years)	22.3	18.6	18.8	18.3	21.9	10.7	24.8	19.8
Grace period (years)	5.2	4.0	2.2	4.0	3.3	3.3	4.9	3.9
Private creditors								
Interest (%)	6.1	9.6	7.7	7.6	0.0	4.1	0.0	0.0
Maturity (years)	26.3	9.2	30.4	27.9	0.0	2.0	0.0	0.0
Grace period (years)	5.8	2.3	30.4	27.9	0.0	2.0	0.0	0.0
5. Major economic aggregates								
Gross national income (GNI)	9,404	12,881	16,491	18,123	19,801	21,571	20,437	20,815
Exports of goods, services & income	2,094	3,803	4,585	5,033	5,512	5,940	4,869	5,672
Worker remit. & comp. of employees	1,064	1,765	3,030	3,485	3,712	3,758	3,405	3,449
Imports of goods, services & income	3,744	6,031	8,242	9,270	10,474	11,219	8,615	9,759
Profit remittances on FDI	0	60	181	91	159	39	172	102
Current account balance	-262	-431	-622	-766	-1,217	-1,532	-304	-488
International reserves	940	1,901	1,890	1,963	2,304	2,646	3,122	2,897
6. Ratios								
External debt stocks to exports (%)	119.8	117.5	202.1	202.0	177.9	178.5	207.5	195.1
External debt stocks to GNI (%)	26.7	34.7	56.2	56.1	49.5	49.1	49.4	53.2
Debt service to exports (%)	13.4	9.7	18.5	24.5	19.8	16.9	24.1	19.0
Short-term to external debt stocks (%)	20.9	36.8	20.0	12.7	13.2	14.5	8.5	10.0
Multilateral to external debt stocks (%)	54.7	42.5	26.2	24.7	25.6	26.1	31.4	31.9
Reserves to external debt stocks (%)	37.5	42.6	20.4	19.3	23.5	25.0	30.9	26.2
Reserves to imports (months)	3.0	3.8	2.8	2.5	2.6	2.8	4.3	3.6

(US$ million, unless otherwise indicated)

	1995	2000	2005	2006	2007	2008	2009	2010
7. Long-term external debt								
Debt outstanding and disbursed	**1,984**	**2,822**	**7,409**	**8,878**	**8,515**	**9,059**	**9,239**	**9,964**
Public and publicly guaranteed	1,979	2,710	4,786	5,589	5,435	5,743	6,100	6,394
Official creditors	1,870	2,505	3,067	3,141	3,160	3,475	3,836	4,175
Multilateral	1,374	1,900	2,431	2,507	2,507	2,770	3,170	3,526
of which: IBRD	307	309	436	417	401	400	569	915
IDA	20	16	12	11	10	9	9	8
Bilateral	496	605	636	633	653	705	666	648
Private creditors	109	205	1,719	2,448	2,275	2,267	2,264	2,220
of which: Bonds	0	82	1,636	2,344	2,242	2,174	2,174	2,199
Commercial banks	74	102	58	78	5	68	66	0
Private nonguaranteed	5	111	2,622	3,289	3,079	3,316	3,139	3,569
of which: Bonds	0	0	0	0	0	0	0	0
Disbursements	**206**	**371**	**1,222**	**1,643**	**251**	**1,042**	**1,216**	**1,055**
Public and publicly guaranteed	206	321	682	998	251	666	910	707
Official creditors	201	200	337	373	250	601	910	707
Multilateral	165	159	308	347	226	563	905	707
of which: IBRD	26	34	129	25	35	52	228	408
IDA	0	0	0	0	0	0	0	0
Bilateral	35	41	28	25	24	38	5	0
Private creditors	5	120	345	625	0	65	0	0
of which: Bonds	0	32	343	625	0	0	0	0
Commercial banks	5	87	0	0	0	65	0	0
Private nonguaranteed	0	51	540	645	0	376	306	348
of which: Bonds	0	0	0	0	0	0	0	0
Principal repayments	**160**	**157**	**405**	**671**	**550**	**488**	**685**	**602**
Public and publicly guaranteed	157	124	244	457	340	349	557	453
Official creditors	123	120	228	330	280	346	554	386
Multilateral	78	87	184	287	241	305	508	341
of which: IBRD	21	17	40	44	51	53	59	63
IDA	1	1	1	1	1	1	1	1
Bilateral	45	33	44	43	39	41	45	44
Private creditors	33	4	16	127	60	4	4	68
of which: Bonds	0	0	0	121	30	0	0	0
Commercial banks	25	4	14	5	28	2	2	66
Private nonguaranteed	3	33	160	214	210	139	127	149
of which: Bonds	0	0	0	0	0	0	0	0
Interest payments	**98**	**139**	**344**	**464**	**466**	**484**	**475**	**464**
Public and publicly guaranteed	98	132	257	334	348	368	373	349
Official creditors	89	123	118	126	137	136	139	117
Multilateral	62	103	101	111	123	121	124	101
of which: IBRD	22	24	14	22	24	19	16	13
IDA	0	0	0	0	0	0	0	0
Bilateral	27	19	17	16	14	15	15	15
Private creditors	9	9	139	207	211	232	235	233
of which: Bonds	0	8	133	206	209	232	232	232
Commercial banks	7	1	6	1	2	0	3	1
Private nonguaranteed	0	7	87	131	117	116	102	115
of which: Bonds	0	0	0	0	0	0	0	0
8. Debt stock-flow reconciliation								
Total change in external debt stocks	412	778	748	903	-361	794	-499	967
Net flows on external debt	383	807	894	405	-296	804	-148	694
9. Debt restructurings								
Total amount rescheduled	0	0	0	0	0	0	0	0
Total amount forgiven	0	17	0	0	0	3	0	0
Debt buyback	0	0	0	0	0	0	0	0

10. Contractual obligations on outstanding long-term external debt

	2011	2012	2013	2014	2015	2016	2017	2018
Official creditors								
Principal	478	392	268	274	282	289	281	268
Interest	137	122	109	98	89	79	70	61
Private creditors								
Principal	1,176	679	605	359	289	219	184	145
Interest	330	271	235	214	197	184	173	164

Notes:

Data on long-term private nonguaranteed debt for 2010 are World Bank staff estimates based on reports provided by the country.

ERITREA

(US$ million, unless otherwise indicated)

	1995	2000	2005	2006	2007	2008	2009	2010
1. Summary external debt data								
External debt stocks	**37**	**300**	**725**	**785**	**859**	**961**	**1,019**	**1,010**
Long-term external debt	37	298	723	781	856	957	1,013	1,003
Public and publicly guaranteed	37	298	723	781	856	957	1,013	1,003
Private nonguaranteed	0	0	0	0	0	0	0	0
Use of IMF credit	0	0	0	0	0	0	0	0
Short-term external debt	0	2	2	4	4	4	6	7
interest arrears on long-term	0	2	2	4	4	4	6	7
Memorandum items								
Principal arrears on long-term	0	5	14	21	18	8	13	21
Long-term public sector debt	37	298	723	781	856	957	1,013	1,003
Long-term private sector debt	0	0	0	0	0	0	0	0
Public & publicly guaranteed commitments	111	174	0	39	46	80	49	0
External debt flows								
Disbursements	7	51	71	38	42	105	58	8
Long-term external debt	7	51	71	38	42	105	58	8
IMF purchases	0	0	0	0	0	0	0	0
Principal repayments	0	0	12	6	2	7	11	12
Long-term external debt	0	0	12	6	2	7	11	12
IMF repurchases	0	0	0	0	0	0	0	0
Net flows	7	50	59	32	40	98	46	-4
Long-term external debt	7	50	59	32	40	98	46	-4
Short-term external debt	0	0	0	0	0	0	0	0
Interest payments	0	2	8	6	4	9	10	10
Long-term external debt	0	2	8	6	4	9	10	10
IMF charges	0	0	0	0	0	0	0	0
Short-term external debt	0	0	0	0	0	0	0	0
2. Other non-debt resource inflows								
Foreign direct investment	..	28	-1	0	0	0	0	..
Portfolio equity	..	..	..	..	..	..	..	..
3. Currency composition of public and publicly guaranteed debt (%)								
Euro	..	..	5.3	5.4	5.5	4.7	4.4	4.0
Japanese yen	0.0	0.0	0.0	0.0	0.0	0.0	0.0	0.0
Pound sterling	0.0	0.0	0.0	0.0	0.0	0.0	0.0	0.0
Swiss franc	0.0	0.0	0.0	0.0	0.0	0.0	0.0	0.0
U.S.dollars	66.3	57.0	68.5	68.1	67.9	66.6	67.8	67.4
4. Average terms of new commitments								
Official creditors								
Interest (%)	2.0	0.7	0.0	2.0	2.0	5.5	1.7	0.0
Maturity (years)	23.9	39.7	0.0	22.9	17.6	5.5	18.2	0.0
Grace period (years)	5.6	10.4	0.0	6.3	3.1	3.0	5.0	0.0
Private creditors								
Interest (%)	0.0	0.0	0.0	0.0	0.0	0.0	0.0	0.0
Maturity (years)	0.0	0.0	0.0	0.0	0.0	0.0	0.0	0.0
Grace period (years)	0.0	0.0	0.0	0.0	0.0	0.0	0.0	0.0
5. Major economic aggregates								
Gross national income (GNI)	586	634	1,089	1,202	1,311	1,368	1,839	2,097
Exports of goods, services & income	142	107	..	..	..	..	..	..
Worker remit. & comp. of employees	..	3	..	..	..	..	..	..
Imports of goods, services & income	498	510	..	..	..	..	..	..
Profit remittances on FDI	0	4	..	..	..	..	..	..
Current account balance	-31	-105	..	..	..	..	..	..
International reserves	40	36	28	25	34	58	90	114
6. Ratios								
External debt stocks to exports (%)	25.8	280.7	..	..	..	..	..	..
External debt stocks to GNI (%)	6.3	47.3	66.5	65.3	65.6	70.3	55.4	48.2
Debt service to exports (%)	0.1	2.8	..	..	..	..	..	..
Short-term to external debt stocks (%)	..	0.7	0.2	0.5	0.4	0.5	0.6	0.7
Multilateral to external debt stocks (%)	66.3	50.6	70.4	71.6	71.3	66.9	64.5	64.5
Reserves to external debt stocks (%)	110.4	12.0	3.9	3.2	4.0	6.0	8.8	11.3
Reserves to imports (months)	1.0	0.8	..	..	..	..	..	..

ERITREA

(US$ million, unless otherwise indicated)

	1995	2000	2005	2006	2007	2008	2009	2010
7. Long-term external debt								
Debt outstanding and disbursed	**37**	**298**	**723**	**781**	**856**	**957**	**1,013**	**1,003**
Public and publicly guaranteed	37	298	723	781	856	957	1,013	1,003
Official creditors	37	298	690	745	815	917	972	965
Multilateral	24	152	510	562	613	644	658	651
of which: IBRD	0	0	0	0	0	0	0	0
IDA	24	84	381	419	457	473	477	468
Bilateral	12	146	180	183	201	274	315	313
Private creditors	0	0	33	37	41	40	41	38
of which: Bonds	0	0	0	0	0	0	0	0
Commercial banks	0	0	0	0	0	0	0	0
Private nonguaranteed	0	0	0	0	0	0	0	0
of which: Bonds	0	0	0	0	0	0	0	0
Disbursements	**7**	**51**	**71**	**38**	**42**	**105**	**58**	**8**
Public and publicly guaranteed	7	51	71	38	42	105	58	8
Official creditors	7	51	71	37	42	104	58	8
Multilateral	5	39	70	33	28	32	12	8
of which: IBRD	0	0	0	0	0	0	0	0
IDA	5	32	57	20	21	23	4	4
Bilateral	2	12	1	4	14	72	46	0
Private creditors	0	0	0	0	0	1	0	0
of which: Bonds	0	0	0	0	0	0	0	0
Commercial banks	0	0	0	0	0	0	0	0
Private nonguaranteed	0	0	0	0	0	0	0	0
of which: Bonds	0	0	0	0	0	0	0	0
Principal repayments	**0**	**0**	**12**	**6**	**2**	**7**	**11**	**12**
Public and publicly guaranteed	0	0	12	6	2	7	11	12
Official creditors	0	0	12	6	2	7	11	12
Multilateral	0	0	7	4	1	5	7	8
of which: IBRD	0	0	0	0	0	0	0	0
IDA	0	0	1	1	1	3	3	4
Bilateral	0	0	5	2	0	1	4	4
Private creditors	0	0	0	0	0	0	0	0
of which: Bonds	0	0	0	0	0	0	0	0
Commercial banks	0	0	0	0	0	0	0	0
Private nonguaranteed	0	0	0	0	0	0	0	0
of which: Bonds	0	0	0	0	0	0	0	0
Interest payments	**0**	**2**	**8**	**6**	**4**	**9**	**10**	**10**
Public and publicly guaranteed	0	2	8	6	4	9	10	10
Official creditors	0	2	8	6	4	9	10	10
Multilateral	0	1	6	5	4	5	5	5
of which: IBRD	0	0	0	0	0	0	0	0
IDA	0	0	3	4	3	3	3	4
Bilateral	0	1	3	1	0	4	5	5
Private creditors	0	0	0	0	0	0	0	0
of which: Bonds	0	0	0	0	0	0	0	0
Commercial banks	0	0	0	0	0	0	0	0
Private nonguaranteed	0	0	0	0	0	0	0	0
of which: Bonds	0	0	0	0	0	0	0	0
8. Debt stock-flow reconciliation								
Total change in external debt stocks	8	47	19	60	74	102	57	-9
Net flows on external debt	7	50	59	32	40	98	46	-4
9. Debt restructurings								
Total amount rescheduled	0	0	0	0	17	21	5	0
Total amount forgiven	0	0	0	0	6	0	0	0
Debt buyback	0	0	0	0	0	0	0	0

10. Contractual obligations on outstanding long-term external debt

	2011	2012	2013	2014	2015	2016	2017	2018
Official creditors								
Principal	72	72	71	46	39	35	36	34
Interest	12	10	9	8	7	7	6	6
Private creditors								
Principal	0	0	0	0	0	0	0	0
Interest	0	0	0	0	0	0	0	0

Notes:

Data on long-term public and publicly guaranteed debt for 2010 are World Bank staff estimates.

ETHIOPIA

(US$ million, unless otherwise indicated)

	1995	*2000*	*2005*	*2006*	*2007*	*2008*	*2009*	*2010*
1. Summary external debt data								
External debt stocks	**10,322**	**5,495**	**6,208**	**2,277**	**2,620**	**2,879**	**5,030**	**7,147**
Long-term external debt	9,788	5,339	5,928	2,201	2,571	2,829	4,817	6,545
Public and publicly guaranteed	9,788	5,339	5,928	2,201	2,571	2,829	4,817	6,545
Private nonguaranteed	0	0	0	0	0	0	0	0
Use of IMF credit	73	77	160	0	0	0	168	288
Short-term external debt	460	79	120	76	49	50	45	314
interest arrears on long-term	437	65	36	36	32	32	32	30
Memorandum items								
Principal arrears on long-term	3,628	652	508	374	373	373	373	364
Long-term public sector debt	9,788	5,339	5,928	2,201	2,571	2,829	4,817	6,545
Long-term private sector debt	0	0	0	0	0	0	0	0
Public & publicly guaranteed commitments	170	500	748	1,904	992	1,234	1,539	2,619
External debt flows								
Disbursements	232	185	527	370	376	379	2,310	1,882
Long-term external debt	232	185	527	370	376	379	2,145	1,760
IMF purchases	0	0	0	0	0	0	165	122
Principal repayments	92	85	40	89	88	72	62	130
Long-term external debt	92	72	36	89	88	72	62	130
IMF repurchases	0	13	4	0	0	0	0	0
Net flows	133	90	478	237	265	309	2,244	2,023
Long-term external debt	140	114	491	281	289	307	2,084	1,630
Short-term external debt	-8	-11	-9	-44	-23	1	-5	271
Interest payments	63	53	54	49	45	40	42	62
Long-term external debt	61	52	49	47	44	39	40	50
IMF charges	0	0	1	0	0	0	0	0
Short-term external debt	1	1	3	3	1	1	1	13
2. Other non-debt resource inflows								
Foreign direct investment	14	135	265	545	222	109	221	184
Portfolio equity	..	..	..	..	..	..	..	..
3. Currency composition of public and publicly guaranteed debt (%)								
Euro	..	..	5.6	14.9	17.5	16.9	8.5	10.1
Japanese yen	0.4	0.3	0.2	0.1	0.1	0.1	0.0	0.0
Pound sterling	0.2	0.3	0.0	0.0	0.0	0.0	0.0	0.0
Swiss franc	0.1	0.1	0.0	0.0	0.0	0.0	0.0	0.0
U.S.dollars	29.0	75.8	72.4	63.6	58.3	55.3	68.8	70.3
4. Average terms of new commitments								
Official creditors								
Interest (%)	1.0	0.8	0.9	1.1	0.9	2.8	1.3	1.7
Maturity (years)	36.3	38.4	32.3	34.9	39.5	25.5	31.4	27.3
Grace period (years)	9.3	10.0	6.3	8.9	9.6	6.2	8.7	8.0
Private creditors								
Interest (%)	0.0	0.0	0.0	6.4	5.2	4.7	4.5	2.0
Maturity (years)	0.0	0.0	0.0	16.8	7.5	6.6	10.2	13.3
Grace period (years)	0.0	0.0	0.0	3.3	2.9	2.9	2.9	1.0
5. Major economic aggregates								
Gross national income (GNI)	7,545	8,119	12,271	15,126	19,567	26,662	31,921	29,625
Exports of goods, services & income	836	1,008	1,973	2,254	2,729	3,552	3,440	..
Worker remit. & comp. of employees	27	53	174	172	358	387	262	225
Imports of goods, services & income	1,533	1,673	4,943	5,314	6,945	9,653	9,089	..
Profit remittances on FDI	0	9	21	24	18	17	18	..
Current account balance	39	13	-1,568	-1,786	-828	-1,806	-2,191	..
International reserves	815	363	1,043	867	1,290	871	1,781	..
6. Ratios								
External debt stocks to exports (%)	1,234.8	544.9	314.7	101.0	96.0	81.1	146.2	..
External debt stocks to GNI (%)	136.8	67.7	50.6	15.1	13.4	10.8	15.8	24.1
Debt service to exports (%)	18.5	13.7	4.7	6.2	4.9	3.1	3.0	..
Short-term to external debt stocks (%)	4.5	1.4	1.9	3.3	1.9	1.7	0.9	4.4
Multilateral to external debt stocks (%)	22.8	50.1	75.8	47.5	52.5	55.7	46.0	39.3
Reserves to external debt stocks (%)	7.9	6.6	16.8	38.1	49.2	30.2	35.4	..
Reserves to imports (months)	6.4	2.6	2.5	2.0	2.2	1.1	2.4	..

ETHIOPIA

(US$ million, unless otherwise indicated)

	1995	2000	2005	2006	2007	2008	2009	2010
7. Long-term external debt								
Debt outstanding and disbursed	**9,788**	**5,339**	**5,928**	**2,201**	**2,571**	**2,829**	**4,817**	**6,545**
Public and publicly guaranteed	9,788	5,339	5,928	2,201	2,571	2,829	4,817	6,545
Official creditors	9,198	5,226	5,564	1,885	2,299	2,590	3,556	4,638
Multilateral	2,354	2,752	4,703	1,082	1,376	1,603	2,313	2,812
of which: IBRD	0	0	0	0	0	0	0	0
IDA	1,470	1,779	3,359	553	711	859	1,422	1,804
Bilateral	6,844	2,473	861	803	923	987	1,243	1,825
Private creditors	590	113	364	316	272	239	1,260	1,907
of which: Bonds	0	0	0	0	0	0	0	0
Commercial banks	253	12	1	0	0	0	0	300
Private nonguaranteed	0	0	0	0	0	0	0	0
of which: Bonds	0	0	0	0	0	0	0	0
Disbursements	**232**	**185**	**527**	**370**	**376**	**379**	**2,145**	**1,760**
Public and publicly guaranteed	232	185	527	370	376	379	2,145	1,760
Official creditors	232	184	400	370	376	379	1,098	1,021
Multilateral	209	181	323	290	272	285	756	504
of which: IBRD	0	0	0	0	0	0	0	0
IDA	84	137	162	179	132	160	553	389
Bilateral	23	3	76	80	104	95	341	518
Private creditors	0	2	127	0	0	0	1,048	739
of which: Bonds	0	0	0	0	0	0	0	0
Commercial banks	0	0	0	0	0	0	0	305
Private nonguaranteed	0	0	0	0	0	0	0	0
of which: Bonds	0	0	0	0	0	0	0	0
Principal repayments	**92**	**72**	**36**	**89**	**88**	**72**	**62**	**130**
Public and publicly guaranteed	92	72	36	89	88	72	62	130
Official creditors	44	62	25	44	44	39	34	39
Multilateral	40	56	15	34	34	30	28	32
of which: IBRD	4	0	0	0	0	0	0	0
IDA	12	21	0	0	0	3	4	4
Bilateral	3	6	10	10	9	8	6	7
Private creditors	48	10	11	45	44	33	27	91
of which: Bonds	0	0	0	0	0	0	0	0
Commercial banks	39	4	0	1	0	0	0	5
Private nonguaranteed	0	0	0	0	0	0	0	0
of which: Bonds	0	0	0	0	0	0	0	0
Interest payments	**61**	**52**	**49**	**47**	**44**	**39**	**40**	**50**
Public and publicly guaranteed	61	52	49	47	44	39	40	50
Official creditors	32	48	40	30	29	27	33	35
Multilateral	24	34	29	25	17	19	19	23
of which: IBRD	0	0	0	0	0	0	0	0
IDA	11	13	15	9	6	7	8	11
Bilateral	9	14	11	5	12	8	14	12
Private creditors	29	4	10	17	15	11	8	15
of which: Bonds	0	0	0	0	0	0	0	0
Commercial banks	27	1	0	0	0	0	0	1
Private nonguaranteed	0	0	0	0	0	0	0	0
of which: Bonds	0	0	0	0	0	0	0	0
8. Debt stock-flow reconciliation								
Total change in external debt stocks	244	-62	-455	-3,931	343	259	2,151	2,118
Net flows on external debt	133	90	478	237	265	309	2,244	2,023
9. Debt restructurings								
Total amount rescheduled	30	0	168	0	0	0	0	0
Total amount forgiven	8	0	452	4,357	13	31	0	11
Debt buyback	0	0	0	0	0	0	0	0

10. Contractual obligations on outstanding long-term external debt

	2011	2012	2013	2014	2015	2016	2017	2018
Official creditors								
Principal	130	142	162	207	281	303	342	354
Interest	68	77	82	86	86	83	79	74
Private creditors								
Principal	231	236	252	246	230	209	185	185
Interest	35	35	32	29	24	19	16	13

Notes:

Ethiopia was granted debt relief effective in 2006 under MDRI.

FIJI

(US$ million, unless otherwise indicated)

	1995	2000	2005	2006	2007	2008	2009	2010
1. Summary external debt data								
External debt stocks	**178.2**	**172.6**	**185.7**	**354.2**	**369.3**	**379.9**	**431.7**	**452.2**
Long-term external debt	163.2	172.4	185.4	342.2	347.0	360.5	361.6	391.1
Public and publicly guaranteed	163.2	172.4	185.4	342.2	347.0	360.1	361.0	390.6
Private nonguaranteed	0.0	0.0	0.0	0.0	0.0	0.4	0.5	0.5
Use of IMF credit	0.0	0.0	0.0	0.0	0.0	0.0	0.0	0.0
Short-term external debt	15.0	0.2	0.4	12.0	22.3	19.4	70.1	61.1
interest arrears on long-term	0.1	0.2	0.4	1.0	0.3	0.4	0.1	0.1
Memorandum items								
Principal arrears on long-term	0.0	0.0	0.0	2.0	1.5	2.2	0.0	0.0
Long-term public sector debt	163.2	99.5	112.5	269.3	274.1	287.2	288.1	317.7
Long-term private sector debt	0.0	72.9	72.9	72.9	72.9	73.3	73.4	73.4
Public & publicly guaranteed commitments	10.5	0.0	25.0	170.7	0.0	0.0	17.6	131.2
External debt flows								
Disbursements	15.2	7.1	14.1	162.8	12.6	13.4	15.2	32.6
Long-term external debt	15.2	7.1	14.1	162.8	12.6	13.4	15.2	32.6
IMF purchases	0.0	0.0	0.0	0.0	0.0	0.0	0.0	0.0
Principal repayments	31.2	16.9	8.5	7.6	10.4	7.8	9.8	7.6
Long-term external debt	31.2	16.9	8.5	7.6	10.4	7.8	9.8	7.6
IMF repurchases	0.0	0.0	0.0	0.0	0.0	0.0	0.0	0.0
Net flows	-17.1	-9.8	-47.5	166.2	13.2	2.6	56.5	15.9
Long-term external debt	-16.0	-9.8	5.5	155.2	2.2	5.6	5.5	24.9
Short-term external debt	-1.1	0.0	-53.0	11.0	11.0	-3.0	51.0	-9.0
Interest payments	11.2	7.7	5.5	6.2	16.9	16.1	15.0	14.2
Long-term external debt	10.3	7.7	5.5	5.7	16.1	15.8	14.4	13.3
IMF charges	0.0	0.0	0.0	0.0	0.0	0.0	0.0	0.0
Short-term external debt	0.9	0.0	0.0	0.6	0.8	0.3	0.6	0.9
2. Other non-debt resource inflows								
Foreign direct investment	70.0	0.6	155.7	412.4	337.8	309.4	56.1	128.9
Portfolio equity	0.0	0.0	1.7	-3.0	4.2	1.4	-1.1	..
3. Currency composition of public and publicly guaranteed debt (%)								
Euro	..	..	2.3	1.3	1.3	1.1	0.6	0.5
Japanese yen	0.0	0.8	9.7	4.9	4.8	5.4	4.9	4.8
Pound sterling	3.3	0.0	0.0	0.0	0.0	0.0	0.0	0.0
Swiss franc	0.0	0.0	0.0	0.0	0.0	0.0	0.0	0.0
U.S.dollars	0.8	49.0	64.2	81.2	83.4	82.7	83.3	80.6
4. Average terms of new commitments								
Official creditors								
Interest (%)	4.5	0.0	4.3	2.0	0.0	0.0	0.7	1.0
Maturity (years)	12.0	0.0	24.7	20.4	0.0	0.0	31.6	15.3
Grace period (years)	4.5	0.0	5.2	0.4	0.0	0.0	8.1	3.8
Private creditors								
Interest (%)	0.0	0.0	0.0	6.9	0.0	0.0	0.0	0.0
Maturity (years)	0.0	0.0	0.0	5.0	0.0	0.0	0.0	0.0
Grace period (years)	0.0	0.0	0.0	5.0	0.0	0.0	0.0	0.0
5. Major economic aggregates								
Gross national income (GNI)	1931.1	1717.4	3050.1	2982.2	3304.9	3537.2	2829.1	2983.4
Exports of goods, services & income	1139.1	1023.2	1615.3	1546.6	1653.0	1922.3	1393.5	..
Worker remit. & comp. of employees	32.9	44.0	185.1	184.7	160.5	123.4	153.8	183.3
Imports of goods, services & income	1254.7	..	2088.3	2343.1	2316.6	2749.6	1809.8	..
Profit remittances on FDI	83.7	0.0	114.7	162.5	116.9	56.9	30.3	..
Current account balance	-112.7	..	-299.8	-599.0	-482.0	-644.8	-236.0	..
International reserves	349.3	412.0	321.3	313.3	528.3	322.2	570.0	720.5
6. Ratios								
External debt stocks to exports (%)	15.6	16.9	11.5	22.9	22.3	19.8	31.0	..
External debt stocks to GNI (%)	9.2	10.1	6.1	11.9	11.2	10.7	15.3	15.2
Debt service to exports (%)	3.7	2.4	0.9	0.9	1.6	1.2	1.8	..
Short-term to external debt stocks (%)	8.4	0.1	0.2	3.4	6.0	5.1	16.2	13.5
Multilateral to external debt stocks (%)	84.0	51.4	49.5	27.3	27.5	28.6	24.0	25.6
Reserves to external debt stocks (%)	196.0	238.7	173.0	88.5	143.1	84.8	132.0	159.3
Reserves to imports (months)	3.3	..	1.8	1.6	2.7	1.4	3.8	..

(US$ million, unless otherwise indicated)

	1995	2000	2005	2006	2007	2008	2009	2010
7. Long-term external debt								
Debt outstanding and disbursed	**163.2**	**172.4**	**185.4**	**342.2**	**347.0**	**360.5**	**361.6**	**391.1**
Public and publicly guaranteed	163.2	172.4	185.4	342.2	347.0	360.1	361.0	390.6
Official creditors	162.7	172.4	185.4	192.2	197.0	210.1	211.0	240.6
Multilateral	149.7	88.8	91.8	96.7	101.6	108.6	103.6	115.6
of which: IBRD	35.3	19.7	6.3	4.3	2.6	1.5	0.0	0.0
IDA	0.0	0.0	0.0	0.0	0.0	0.0	0.0	0.0
Bilateral	13.0	83.6	93.5	95.5	95.4	101.4	107.5	125.0
Private creditors	0.6	0.0	0.0	150.0	150.0	150.0	150.0	150.0
of which: Bonds	0.0	0.0	0.0	150.0	150.0	150.0	150.0	150.0
Commercial banks	0.4	0.0	0.0	0.0	0.0	0.0	0.0	0.0
Private nonguaranteed	0.0	0.0	0.0	0.0	0.0	0.4	0.5	0.5
of which: Bonds	0.0	0.0	0.0	0.0	0.0	0.0	0.0	0.0
Disbursements	**15.2**	**7.1**	**14.1**	**162.8**	**12.6**	**13.4**	**15.2**	**32.6**
Public and publicly guaranteed	15.2	7.1	14.1	162.8	12.6	13.2	15.0	32.6
Official creditors	15.2	7.1	14.1	12.8	12.6	13.2	15.0	32.6
Multilateral	15.2	5.6	14.1	9.7	12.6	10.0	5.3	16.7
of which: IBRD	5.6	1.0	0.0	0.0	0.0	0.0	0.0	0.0
IDA	0.0	0.0	0.0	0.0	0.0	0.0	0.0	0.0
Bilateral	0.0	1.5	0.0	3.1	0.0	3.3	9.7	15.9
Private creditors	0.0	0.0	0.0	150.0	0.0	0.0	0.0	0.0
of which: Bonds	0.0	0.0	0.0	150.0	0.0	0.0	0.0	0.0
Commercial banks	0.0	0.0	0.0	0.0	0.0	0.0	0.0	0.0
Private nonguaranteed	0.0	0.0	0.0	0.0	0.0	0.2	0.3	0.0
of which: Bonds	0.0	0.0	0.0	0.0	0.0	0.0	0.0	0.0
Principal repayments	**31.2**	**16.9**	**8.5**	**7.6**	**10.4**	**7.8**	**9.8**	**7.6**
Public and publicly guaranteed	31.2	16.9	8.5	7.6	10.4	7.7	9.7	7.6
Official creditors	30.2	16.9	8.5	7.6	10.4	7.7	9.7	7.6
Multilateral	28.2	14.8	6.5	6.3	9.1	6.3	6.3	6.2
of which: IBRD	11.5	7.7	2.3	2.2	1.8	1.3	1.4	0.0
IDA	0.0	0.0	0.0	0.0	0.0	0.0	0.0	0.0
Bilateral	2.0	2.1	2.0	1.3	1.3	1.4	3.4	1.4
Private creditors	1.0	0.0	0.0	0.0	0.0	0.0	0.0	0.0
of which: Bonds	0.0	0.0	0.0	0.0	0.0	0.0	0.0	0.0
Commercial banks	0.2	0.0	0.0	0.0	0.0	0.0	0.0	0.0
Private nonguaranteed	0.0	0.0	0.0	0.0	0.0	0.0	0.0	0.0
of which: Bonds	0.0	0.0	0.0	0.0	0.0	0.0	0.0	0.0
Interest payments	**10.3**	**7.7**	**5.5**	**5.7**	**16.1**	**15.8**	**14.4**	**13.3**
Public and publicly guaranteed	10.3	7.7	5.5	5.7	16.1	15.8	14.4	13.3
Official creditors	10.2	7.7	5.5	5.7	5.8	5.5	4.1	3.0
Multilateral	9.5	5.2	3.2	3.8	4.1	3.8	2.5	1.2
of which: IBRD	3.0	1.4	0.4	0.3	0.2	0.1	0.0	0.0
IDA	0.0	0.0	0.0	0.0	0.0	0.0	0.0	0.0
Bilateral	0.7	2.5	2.3	1.9	1.6	1.7	1.5	1.8
Private creditors	0.1	0.0	0.0	0.0	10.3	10.3	10.3	10.3
of which: Bonds	0.0	0.0	0.0	0.0	10.3	10.3	10.3	10.3
Commercial banks	0.1	0.0	0.0	0.0	0.0	0.0	0.0	0.0
Private nonguaranteed	0.0	0.0	0.0	0.0	0.0	0.0	0.0	0.0
of which: Bonds	0.0	0.0	0.0	0.0	0.0	0.0	0.0	0.0
8. Debt stock-flow reconciliation								
Total change in external debt stocks	-12.8	-19.0	-60.2	168.5	15.1	10.6	51.8	20.5
Net flows on external debt	-17.1	-9.8	-47.5	166.2	13.2	2.6	56.5	15.9
9. Debt restructurings								
Total amount rescheduled	0.0	0.0	0.0	0.0	0.0	0.0	0.0	0.0
Total amount forgiven	0.0	0.0	0.0	0.0	2.2	0.0	4.1	0.0
Debt buyback	0.0	0.0	0.0	0.0	0.0	0.0	0.0	0.0

10. Contractual obligations on outstanding long-term external debt

	2011	2012	2013	2014	2015	2016	2017	2018
Official creditors								
Principal	87.8	15.1	18.1	18.2	19.6	25.3	24.7	23.9
Interest	5.7	4.1	3.9	3.7	3.5	3.2	2.8	2.5
Private creditors								
Principal	150.1	0.1	0.1	0.1	0.1	0.0	0.0	0.0
Interest	10.3	0.0	0.0	0.0	0.0	0.0	0.0	0.0

GABON

(US$ million, unless otherwise indicated)

	1995	2000	2005	2006	2007	2008	2009	2010
1. Summary external debt data								
External debt stocks	**4,361**	**3,902**	**3,877**	**4,187**	**2,845**	**2,173**	**2,130**	**2,331**
Long-term external debt	3,977	3,457	3,562	3,697	2,599	2,055	2,022	2,158
Public and publicly guaranteed	3,977	3,457	3,562	3,697	2,599	2,055	2,022	2,158
Private nonguaranteed	0	0	0	0	0	0	0	0
Use of IMF credit	97	89	68	57	25	0	0	0
Short-term external debt	287	355	247	434	221	118	108	174
interest arrears on long-term	0	63	187	344	6	10	5	6
Memorandum items								
Principal arrears on long-term	26	118	341	773	38	28	9	9
Long-term public sector debt	3,977	3,457	3,562	3,697	2,599	2,055	2,022	2,158
Long-term private sector debt	0	0	0	0	0	0	0	0
Public & publicly guaranteed commitments	89	20	142	40	1,946	641	420	702
External debt flows								
Disbursements	279	51	18	87	1,089	108	260	482
Long-term external debt	222	34	18	87	1,089	108	260	482
IMF purchases	57	17	0	0	0	0	0	0
Principal repayments	216	198	136	128	2,280	642	315	307
Long-term external debt	165	188	111	114	2,246	617	315	307
IMF repurchases	52	10	25	14	34	25	0	0
Net flows	14	-363	-58	-11	-1,066	-641	-60	240
Long-term external debt	57	-154	-93	-27	-1,157	-509	-55	175
Short-term external debt	-49	-216	60	30	125	-107	-5	65
Interest payments	240	154	57	42	386	228	148	138
Long-term external debt	217	124	52	36	377	224	144	133
IMF charges	5	4	3	3	3	1	0	0
Short-term external debt	17	26	2	3	6	4	4	5
2. Other non-debt resource inflows								
Foreign direct investment	-315	-43	242	268	269	209	33	170
Portfolio equity	0	0	0	0	0	0	0	0
3. Currency composition of public and publicly guaranteed debt (%)								
Euro	..	..	47.5	48.9	35.1	26.4	24.5	26.1
Japanese yen	0.9	0.8	0.5	0.5	0.4	0.5	0.2	0.2
Pound sterling	5.0	4.6	4.4	4.9	4.6	0.9	0.7	0.4
Swiss franc	0.8	0.5	0.2	0.2	0.2	0.0	0.0	0.0
U.S.dollars	11.5	29.1	36.2	34.6	44.7	54.4	55.1	54.7
4. Average terms of new commitments								
Official creditors								
Interest (%)	4.7	0.0	1.4	4.2	4.9	2.5	0.0	1.3
Maturity (years)	13.0	9.7	16.8	14.4	19.4	18.1	19.9	18.7
Grace period (years)	5.9	0.7	4.3	2.9	5.3	6.1	10.0	6.5
Private creditors								
Interest (%)	0.0	0.0	2.6	0.0	7.3	4.9	3.1	2.7
Maturity (years)	0.0	0.0	5.8	0.0	10.6	7.8	6.3	8.7
Grace period (years)	0.0	0.0	2.7	0.0	7.1	2.3	1.6	2.1
5. Major economic aggregates								
Gross national income (GNI)	4,293	4,289	7,708	8,187	10,082	12,684	9,874	11,467
Exports of goods, services & income	2,980	3,547	5,647	..	..	..	..	..
Worker remit. & comp. of employees	4	6	11	..	..	..	..	..
Imports of goods, services & income	2,423	2,483	3,395	..	..	..	..	..
Profit remittances on FDI	236	473	765	..	..	..	..	..
Current account balance	515	1,001	1,983	..	..	..	..	..
International reserves	153	194	675	1,122	1,238	1,935	1,993	1,736
6. Ratios								
External debt stocks to exports (%)	146.3	110.0	68.7	..	..	..	..	..
External debt stocks to GNI (%)	101.6	91.0	50.3	51.1	28.2	17.1	21.6	20.3
Debt service to exports (%)	15.3	9.9	3.4	..	..	..	..	..
Short-term to external debt stocks (%)	6.6	9.1	6.4	10.4	7.8	5.4	5.1	7.5
Multilateral to external debt stocks (%)	13.5	12.0	10.1	9.7	14.3	17.5	18.8	16.5
Reserves to external debt stocks (%)	3.5	5.0	17.4	26.8	43.5	89.0	93.6	74.5
Reserves to imports (months)	0.8	0.9	2.4	..	..	..	..	..

GABON

(US$ million, unless otherwise indicated)

	1995	2000	2005	2006	2007	2008	2009	2010
7. Long-term external debt								
Debt outstanding and disbursed	**3,977**	**3,457**	**3,562**	**3,697**	**2,599**	**2,055**	**2,022**	**2,158**
Public and publicly guaranteed	3,977	3,457	3,562	3,697	2,599	2,055	2,022	2,158
Official creditors	3,778	3,338	3,443	3,576	1,464	994	926	905
Multilateral	588	468	393	408	406	381	401	384
of which: IBRD	110	64	30	19	12	20	18	22
IDA	0	0	0	0	0	0	0	0
Bilateral	3,190	2,871	3,050	3,168	1,058	613	525	521
Private creditors	199	119	119	121	1,135	1,062	1,096	1,253
of which: Bonds	0	0	0	0	1,000	946	901	879
Commercial banks	148	103	39	29	60	79	168	356
Private nonguaranteed	0	0	0	0	0	0	0	0
of which: Bonds	0	0	0	0	0	0	0	0
Disbursements	**222**	**34**	**18**	**87**	**1,089**	**108**	**260**	**482**
Public and publicly guaranteed	222	34	18	87	1,089	108	260	482
Official creditors	222	13	18	61	41	62	147	195
Multilateral	150	11	15	57	37	17	74	67
of which: IBRD	4	9	0	0	0	12	4	7
IDA	0	0	0	0	0	0	0	0
Bilateral	72	2	3	4	4	45	73	128
Private creditors	0	21	0	26	1,048	45	113	287
of which: Bonds	0	0	0	0	1,000	0	0	0
Commercial banks	0	21	0	0	37	45	107	236
Private nonguaranteed	0	0	0	0	0	0	0	0
of which: Bonds	0	0	0	0	0	0	0	0
Principal repayments	**165**	**188**	**111**	**114**	**2,246**	**617**	**315**	**307**
Public and publicly guaranteed	165	188	111	114	2,246	617	315	307
Official creditors	90	160	63	84	2,207	506	231	187
Multilateral	43	44	54	56	51	53	59	75
of which: IBRD	12	13	7	12	8	3	6	2
IDA	0	0	0	0	0	0	0	0
Bilateral	48	116	9	28	2,156	453	173	112
Private creditors	75	27	48	30	39	111	83	120
of which: Bonds	0	0	0	0	0	50	44	23
Commercial banks	26	27	28	10	6	22	24	39
Private nonguaranteed	0	0	0	0	0	0	0	0
of which: Bonds	0	0	0	0	0	0	0	0
Interest payments	**217**	**124**	**52**	**36**	**377**	**224**	**144**	**133**
Public and publicly guaranteed	217	124	52	36	377	224	144	133
Official creditors	174	118	46	32	372	139	53	34
Multilateral	26	42	21	21	21	19	20	11
of which: IBRD	8	5	1	2	1	1	1	0
IDA	0	0	0	0	0	0	0	0
Bilateral	148	75	24	11	350	120	33	23
Private creditors	44	7	7	4	5	85	91	99
of which: Bonds	0	0	0	0	0	80	75	74
Commercial banks	26	7	5	3	2	4	14	25
Private nonguaranteed	0	0	0	0	0	0	0	0
of which: Bonds	0	0	0	0	0	0	0	0
8. Debt stock-flow reconciliation								
Total change in external debt stocks	189	-83	-183	310	-1,342	-672	-43	201
Net flows on external debt	14	-363	-58	-11	-1,066	-641	-60	240
9. Debt restructurings								
Total amount rescheduled	472	637	407	0	0	0	0	0
Total amount forgiven	41	0	0	0	89	9	0	0
Debt buyback	0	0	0	0	2,100	428	44	0

10. Contractual obligations on outstanding long-term external debt

	2011	2012	2013	2014	2015	2016	2017	2018
Official creditors								
Principal	186	128	96	92	114	114	120	119
Interest	27	23	22	22	22	20	18	16
Private creditors								
Principal	119	180	180	155	151	140	988	75
Interest	97	103	101	96	91	85	81	6

Notes:

Data on long-term public and publicly guaranteed debt before 2008 are World Bank staff estimates based on reports provided by the country and include the effects of Paris Club debt buyback agreement signed in 2007.

GAMBIA, THE

(US$ million, unless otherwise indicated)

	1995	2000	2005	2006	2007	2008	2009	2010
1. Summary external debt data								
External debt stocks	**426.1**	**483.4**	**659.8**	**710.1**	**692.0**	**365.1**	**459.6**	**470.2**
Long-term external debt	385.5	438.0	616.5	674.4	664.0	336.8	387.6	394.8
Public and publicly guaranteed	385.5	438.0	616.5	674.4	664.0	336.8	387.6	394.8
Private nonguaranteed	0.0	0.0	0.0	0.0	0.0	0.0	0.0	0.0
Use of IMF credit	25.8	18.1	20.8	17.8	6.3	12.3	28.6	31.1
Short-term external debt	14.8	27.3	22.4	17.9	21.6	15.9	43.4	44.2
interest arrears on long-term	0.7	0.0	1.4	0.9	0.6	1.9	2.4	2.2
Memorandum items								
Principal arrears on long-term	2.2	2.1	19.3	21.8	15.0	13.9	20.3	38.2
Long-term public sector debt	385.3	438.0	616.5	674.4	664.0	336.8	387.6	394.8
Long-term private sector debt	0.2	0.0	0.0	0.0	0.0	0.0	0.0	0.0
Public & publicly guaranteed commitments	40.3	24.5	53.8	28.6	47.3	59.3	29.8	5.0
External debt flows								
Disbursements	23.0	29.7	54.3	51.4	46.0	43.6	49.3	46.9
Long-term external debt	23.0	20.7	54.3	51.4	39.9	37.3	33.5	43.9
IMF purchases	0.0	9.1	0.0	0.0	6.1	6.3	15.8	3.0
Principal repayments	21.7	14.3	18.1	20.8	23.7	10.3	11.3	12.5
Long-term external debt	15.5	12.7	16.1	16.8	20.1	10.3	11.3	12.5
IMF repurchases	6.2	1.6	2.0	4.0	3.7	0.0	0.0	0.0
Net flows	-7.6	20.6	33.2	26.6	26.2	26.3	64.9	35.4
Long-term external debt	7.5	8.0	38.3	34.7	19.8	27.0	22.2	31.4
Short-term external debt	-8.8	5.2	-3.0	-4.0	4.0	-7.0	27.0	1.0
Interest payments	6.3	7.3	10.4	9.2	9.9	6.8	7.5	7.1
Long-term external debt	5.2	6.0	9.4	8.3	8.8	5.8	7.0	6.6
IMF charges	0.2	0.1	0.1	0.1	0.1	0.1	0.1	0.0
Short-term external debt	0.9	1.2	0.9	0.9	1.0	0.9	0.4	0.5
2. Other non-debt resource inflows								
Foreign direct investment	7.8	..	53.7	82.2	78.1	78.6	39.4	37.4
Portfolio equity	..	..	..	..	..	..	..	..
3. Currency composition of public and publicly guaranteed debt (%)								
Euro	..	..	3.5	3.3	3.6	5.2	5.0	5.9
Japanese yen	0.0	0.0	0.0	0.0	0.0	0.0	0.0	0.0
Pound sterling	6.3	4.8	2.7	2.4	2.3	0.0	0.0	0.0
Swiss franc	0.2	0.0	0.0	0.0	0.0	0.0	0.0	0.0
U.S.dollars	43.5	51.2	55.2	54.2	48.0	50.8	46.6	47.1
4. Average terms of new commitments								
Official creditors								
Interest (%)	3.5	1.7	2.8	0.2	2.4	1.9	0.6	0.2
Maturity (years)	21.3	27.4	30.1	29.2	25.2	25.0	24.1	25.0
Grace period (years)	6.2	6.8	7.6	8.6	7.6	6.2	6.4	1.4
Private creditors								
Interest (%)	0.0	0.0	0.0	0.0	4.7	0.0	0.0	0.0
Maturity (years)	0.0	0.0	0.0	0.0	12.4	0.0	0.0	0.0
Grace period (years)	0.0	0.0	0.0	0.0	2.4	0.0	0.0	0.0
5. Major economic aggregates								
Gross national income (GNI)	377.1	400.4	417.8	459.7	596.7	776.0	690.3	742.9
Exports of goods, services & income	181.0	..	189.8	205.5	271.2	335.8	290.0	270.0
Worker remit. & comp. of employees	..	..	59.3	63.8	55.7	64.8	79.8	115.7
Imports of goods, services & income	241.4	..	305.0	358.7	419.8	407.4	362.3	330.3
Profit remittances on FDI	..	..	26.9	32.9	38.4	42.8	11.7	11.5
Current account balance	-8.2	..	-43.4	-65.6	-58.4	10.9	63.0	52.4
International reserves	106.1	109.4	98.3	120.6	142.8	116.5	224.2	201.6
6. Ratios								
External debt stocks to exports (%)	235.4	..	347.7	345.6	255.1	108.7	158.4	174.1
External debt stocks to GNI (%)	113.0	120.7	157.9	154.5	116.0	47.0	66.6	63.3
Debt service to exports (%)	15.5	..	15.0	14.6	12.4	5.1	6.5	7.2
Short-term to external debt stocks (%)	3.5	5.7	3.4	2.5	3.1	4.4	9.4	9.4
Multilateral to external debt stocks (%)	76.6	71.1	76.1	78.0	78.9	59.3	58.5	56.7
Reserves to external debt stocks (%)	24.9	22.6	14.9	17.0	20.6	31.9	48.8	42.9
Reserves to imports (months)	5.3	..	3.9	4.0	4.1	3.4	7.4	7.3

GAMBIA, THE

(US$ million, unless otherwise indicated)

	1995	2000	2005	2006	2007	2008	2009	2010
7. Long-term external debt								
Debt outstanding and disbursed	**385.5**	**438.0**	**616.5**	**674.4**	**664.0**	**336.8**	**387.6**	**394.8**
Public and publicly guaranteed	385.5	438.0	616.5	674.4	664.0	336.8	387.6	394.8
Official creditors	385.2	437.0	616.5	674.4	664.0	334.3	384.2	385.2
Multilateral	326.2	343.8	502.3	553.6	545.9	216.6	268.7	266.7
of which: IBRD	0.0	0.0	0.0	0.0	0.0	0.0	0.0	0.0
IDA	161.6	170.7	244.9	263.5	218.9	61.9	64.3	65.0
Bilateral	59.0	93.2	114.2	120.8	118.1	117.7	115.5	118.5
Private creditors	0.2	1.0	0.0	0.0	0.0	2.5	3.4	9.6
of which: Bonds	0.0	0.0	0.0	0.0	0.0	0.0	0.0	0.0
Commercial banks	0.0	0.9	0.0	0.0	0.0	2.5	3.4	9.6
Private nonguaranteed	0.0	0.0	0.0	0.0	0.0	0.0	0.0	0.0
of which: Bonds	0.0	0.0	0.0	0.0	0.0	0.0	0.0	0.0
Disbursements	**23.0**	**20.7**	**54.3**	**51.4**	**39.9**	**37.3**	**33.5**	**43.9**
Public and publicly guaranteed	23.0	20.7	54.3	51.4	39.9	37.3	33.5	43.9
Official creditors	23.0	20.7	54.3	51.4	39.9	35.8	32.7	37.4
Multilateral	19.0	17.1	47.1	41.3	31.1	31.3	29.5	24.4
of which: IBRD	0.0	0.0	0.0	0.0	0.0	0.0	0.0	0.0
IDA	11.6	7.7	18.9	11.7	1.1	2.4	2.4	2.2
Bilateral	4.0	3.6	7.2	10.1	8.7	4.5	3.3	13.1
Private creditors	0.0	0.0	0.0	0.0	0.0	1.5	0.8	6.4
of which: Bonds	0.0	0.0	0.0	0.0	0.0	0.0	0.0	0.0
Commercial banks	0.0	0.0	0.0	0.0	0.0	1.5	0.8	6.4
Private nonguaranteed	0.0	0.0	0.0	0.0	0.0	0.0	0.0	0.0
of which: Bonds	0.0	0.0	0.0	0.0	0.0	0.0	0.0	0.0
Principal repayments	**15.5**	**12.7**	**16.1**	**16.8**	**20.1**	**10.3**	**11.3**	**12.5**
Public and publicly guaranteed	15.5	12.7	16.1	16.8	20.1	10.3	11.3	12.5
Official creditors	15.1	12.3	15.8	16.8	20.1	10.3	11.3	12.5
Multilateral	6.7	7.9	10.1	11.2	14.4	6.3	7.1	5.9
of which: IBRD	0.0	0.0	0.0	0.0	0.0	0.0	0.0	0.0
IDA	0.8	2.3	3.3	4.3	5.0	0.1	0.3	0.3
Bilateral	8.5	4.4	5.7	5.6	5.6	4.0	4.3	6.5
Private creditors	0.4	0.4	0.3	0.0	0.0	0.0	0.0	0.0
of which: Bonds	0.0	0.0	0.0	0.0	0.0	0.0	0.0	0.0
Commercial banks	0.0	0.3	0.3	0.0	0.0	0.0	0.0	0.0
Private nonguaranteed	0.0	0.0	0.0	0.0	0.0	0.0	0.0	0.0
of which: Bonds	0.0	0.0	0.0	0.0	0.0	0.0	0.0	0.0
Interest payments	**5.2**	**6.0**	**9.4**	**8.3**	**8.8**	**5.8**	**7.0**	**6.6**
Public and publicly guaranteed	5.2	6.0	9.4	8.3	8.8	5.8	7.0	6.6
Official creditors	5.2	5.9	9.4	8.3	8.8	5.8	7.0	6.6
Multilateral	3.5	3.6	5.2	5.0	5.1	3.0	4.4	3.5
of which: IBRD	0.0	0.0	0.0	0.0	0.0	0.0	0.0	0.0
IDA	1.2	1.2	1.9	2.0	2.0	0.5	0.5	0.5
Bilateral	1.7	2.3	4.2	3.3	3.7	2.8	2.7	3.1
Private creditors	0.0	0.1	0.0	0.0	0.0	0.0	0.0	0.0
of which: Bonds	0.0	0.0	0.0	0.0	0.0	0.0	0.0	0.0
Commercial banks	0.0	0.1	0.0	0.0	0.0	0.0	0.0	0.0
Private nonguaranteed	0.0	0.0	0.0	0.0	0.0	0.0	0.0	0.0
of which: Bonds	0.0	0.0	0.0	0.0	0.0	0.0	0.0	0.0
8. Debt stock-flow reconciliation								
Total change in external debt stocks	3.1	18.7	-13.4	50.3	-18.1	-326.9	94.5	10.6
Net flows on external debt	-7.6	20.6	33.2	26.6	26.2	26.3	64.9	35.4
9. Debt restructurings								
Total amount rescheduled	0.0	0.0	0.0	0.0	0.0	7.4	24.0	20.8
Total amount forgiven	0.0	0.0	0.7	0.2	14.4	228.4	0.0	0.0
Debt buyback	0.0	0.0	0.0	0.0	0.0	0.0	0.0	0.0

10. Contractual obligations on outstanding long-term external debt

	2011	2012	2013	2014	2015	2016	2017	2018
Official creditors								
Principal	20.9	21.6	23.1	25.6	28.0	26.4	26.3	25.7
Interest	6.0	6.1	6.0	5.8	5.5	5.1	4.7	4.3
Private creditors								
Principal	2.2	2.2	2.2	2.2	2.2	2.2	2.2	2.2
Interest	0.3	0.3	0.3	0.2	0.2	0.1	0.1	0.1

Notes:

Data on long-term public and publicly guaranteed debt for 2009 have been revised based on reports provided by the country.

GEORGIA

(US$ million, unless otherwise indicated)

	1995	2000	2005	2006	2007	2008	2009	2010
1. Summary external debt data								
External debt stocks	**1,240**	**1,638**	**1,909**	**2,297**	**2,610**	**7,352**	**8,270**	**9,238**
Long-term external debt	1,039	1,316	1,626	1,625	1,784	5,943	6,676	7,224
Public and publicly guaranteed	1,039	1,274	1,494	1,466	1,544	2,914	3,470	4,081
Private nonguaranteed	0	42	132	159	241	3,029	3,207	3,143
Use of IMF credit	116	278	232	236	252	460	786	1,050
Short-term external debt	85	44	50	436	574	948	808	963
interest arrears on long-term	61	1	11	7	7	7	7	7
Memorandum items								
Principal arrears on long-term	211	179	151	69	32	28	28	28
Long-term public sector debt	1,039	1,264	1,493	1,466	1,544	2,914	3,470	4,081
Long-term private sector debt	0	52	133	159	241	3,029	3,207	3,143
Public & publicly guaranteed commitments	91	72	84	104	55	812	781	964
External debt flows								
Disbursements	174	65	187	216	235	1,149	1,488	1,487
Long-term external debt	98	65	146	175	193	893	1,147	1,190
IMF purchases	76	0	41	41	43	256	341	297
Principal repayments	0	68	157	234	143	458	502	532
Long-term external debt	0	42	103	185	103	423	474	510
IMF repurchases	0	26	54	49	40	35	28	22
Net flows	-272	33	-30	372	231	1,065	846	1,111
Long-term external debt	98	23	43	-10	89	470	673	680
Short-term external debt	-446	36	-60	389	138	374	-140	156
Interest payments	20	49	30	39	49	252	280	281
Long-term external debt	17	43	27	31	31	223	248	245
IMF charges	3	5	1	1	1	2	7	12
Short-term external debt	0	1	2	7	17	27	25	25
2. Other non-debt resource inflows								
Foreign direct investment	..	131	453	1,170	1,750	1,564	658	814
Portfolio equity	..	0	3	143	34	118	13	-20
3. Currency composition of public and publicly guaranteed debt (%)								
Euro	..	..	20.2	15.5	17.4	9.2	8.0	8.1
Japanese yen	0.0	0.2	2.7	3.0	3.1	2.0	1.6	1.4
Pound sterling	0.0	0.0	0.0	0.0	0.0	0.0	0.0	0.0
Swiss franc	0.4	0.2	0.2	0.0	0.0	0.0	0.0	0.0
U.S.dollars	75.3	82.3	72.7	76.2	72.1	81.3	80.0	80.4
4. Average terms of new commitments								
Official creditors								
Interest (%)	1.5	1.1	0.8	1.4	0.8	1.3	1.0	2.3
Maturity (years)	32.3	32.0	40.3	34.8	26.9	25.4	30.9	20.0
Grace period (years)	9.6	8.9	10.7	8.8	10.2	8.7	7.8	5.4
Private creditors								
Interest (%)	0.0	0.0	0.0	0.0	0.0	7.5	0.0	9.9
Maturity (years)	0.0	0.0	0.0	0.0	0.0	5.0	0.0	5.0
Grace period (years)	0.0	0.0	0.0	0.0	0.0	5.0	0.0	5.0
5. Major economic aggregates								
Gross national income (GNI)	2,574	3,175	6,473	7,909	10,210	12,642	10,679	11,484
Exports of goods, services & income	..	844	2,451	2,893	3,664	4,183	3,630	4,480
Worker remit. & comp. of employees	..	274	346	485	695	732	714	806
Imports of goods, services & income	..	1,248	3,520	4,592	6,363	8,159	5,808	6,909
Profit remittances on FDI	..	0	116	94	298	361	263	471
Current account balance	..	-269	-710	-1,176	-2,009	-2,916	-1,210	-1,333
International reserves	199	116	479	931	1,361	1,480	2,110	2,264
6. Ratios								
External debt stocks to exports (%)	..	194.1	77.9	79.4	71.2	175.8	227.8	206.2
External debt stocks to GNI (%)	48.2	51.6	29.5	29.0	25.6	58.2	77.4	80.4
Debt service to exports (%)	..	13.9	7.6	9.4	5.2	17.0	21.5	18.1
Short-term to external debt stocks (%)	6.9	2.7	2.6	19.0	22.0	12.9	9.8	10.4
Multilateral to external debt stocks (%)	19.7	29.2	42.9	39.4	38.9	16.2	18.6	19.5
Reserves to external debt stocks (%)	16.0	7.1	25.1	40.5	52.2	20.1	25.5	24.5
Reserves to imports (months)	..	1.1	1.6	2.4	2.6	2.2	4.4	3.9

GEORGIA

(US$ million, unless otherwise indicated)

	1995	2000	2005	2006	2007	2008	2009	2010
7. Long-term external debt								
Debt outstanding and disbursed	**1,039**	**1,316**	**1,626**	**1,625**	**1,784**	**5,943**	**6,676**	**7,224**
Public and publicly guaranteed	1,039	1,274	1,494	1,466	1,544	2,914	3,470	4,081
Official creditors	939	1,272	1,492	1,464	1,542	1,720	2,095	2,390
Multilateral	245	478	819	904	1,015	1,190	1,535	1,802
of which: IBRD	0	0	0	0	0	0	100	173
IDA	84	347	679	785	885	989	1,153	1,186
Bilateral	694	794	673	560	527	530	560	588
Private creditors	100	2	2	2	2	1,194	1,375	1,691
of which: Bonds	0	0	0	0	0	500	500	750
Commercial banks	0	0	0	0	0	692	874	940
Private nonguaranteed	0	42	132	159	241	3,029	3,207	3,143
of which: Bonds	0	0	0	0	0	0	0	0
Disbursements	**98**	**65**	**146**	**175**	**193**	**893**	**1,147**	**1,190**
Public and publicly guaranteed	98	37	76	119	100	725	678	815
Official creditors	98	37	76	119	100	225	427	401
Multilateral	96	25	60	88	82	202	385	346
of which: IBRD	0	0	0	0	0	0	100	73
IDA	85	18	54	76	72	121	168	67
Bilateral	2	13	16	31	18	23	42	55
Private creditors	0	0	0	0	0	500	250	414
of which: Bonds	0	0	0	0	0	500	0	250
Commercial banks	0	0	0	0	0	0	250	164
Private nonguaranteed	0	28	69	56	93	168	469	375
of which: Bonds	0	0	0	0	0	0	0	0
Principal repayments	**0**	**42**	**103**	**185**	**103**	**423**	**474**	**510**
Public and publicly guaranteed	0	41	80	166	86	110	140	169
Official creditors	0	41	80	165	85	40	70	71
Multilateral	0	5	10	47	15	19	52	52
of which: IBRD	0	0	0	0	0	0	0	0
IDA	0	0	2	4	7	10	12	15
Bilateral	0	35	70	119	71	21	18	19
Private creditors	0	0	0	0	0	70	70	97
of which: Bonds	0	0	0	0	0	0	0	0
Commercial banks	0	0	0	0	0	69	69	97
Private nonguaranteed	0	2	23	19	17	314	334	342
of which: Bonds	0	0	0	0	0	0	0	0
Interest payments	**17**	**43**	**27**	**31**	**31**	**223**	**248**	**245**
Public and publicly guaranteed	17	42	23	24	23	52	74	84
Official creditors	17	42	23	24	23	25	29	37
Multilateral	0	8	11	11	10	13	13	12
of which: IBRD	0	0	0	0	0	0	1	1
IDA	0	3	6	6	6	7	7	8
Bilateral	17	34	12	13	13	12	16	25
Private creditors	0	0	0	0	0	27	45	47
of which: Bonds	0	0	0	0	0	19	38	38
Commercial banks	0	0	0	0	0	8	8	10
Private nonguaranteed	0	1	4	6	8	171	174	160
of which: Bonds	0	0	0	0	0	0	0	0
8. Debt stock-flow reconciliation								
Total change in external debt stocks	-210	-16	-156	388	313	4,742	919	967
Net flows on external debt	-272	33	-30	372	231	1,065	846	1,111
9. Debt restructurings								
Total amount rescheduled	0	0	57	44	0	0	0	0
Total amount forgiven	0	0	0	109	2	0	0	0
Debt buyback	0	0	0	0	0	0	0	0

10. Contractual obligations on outstanding long-term external debt

	2011	2012	2013	2014	2015	2016	2017	2018
Official creditors								
Principal	51	51	60	81	99	107	119	138
Interest	34	37	39	39	38	37	35	34
Private creditors								
Principal	509	533	1,029	526	765	477	477	498
Interest	242	219	176	134	110	63	41	17

Notes:

Data on long-term public and publicly guaranteed debt and long-term private nonguaranteed debt from 2008 to 2010 are World Bank staff estimates based on reports provided by the country.

GHANA

(US$ million, unless otherwise indicated)

	1995	2000	2005	2006	2007	2008	2009	2010
1. Summary external debt data								
External debt stocks	**5,495**	**6,116**	**6,780**	**3,320**	**4,855**	**5,382**	**6,331**	**8,368**
Long-term external debt	4,227	5,251	5,776	2,019	3,424	3,873	4,737	5,727
Public and publicly guaranteed	4,200	4,994	5,776	2,019	3,424	3,873	4,737	5,727
Private nonguaranteed	27	257	0	0	0	0	0	0
Use of IMF credit	648	293	417	159	167	162	271	392
Short-term external debt	620	572	587	1,143	1,264	1,347	1,323	2,249
interest arrears on long-term	26	10	9	19	9	9	41	13
Memorandum items								
Principal arrears on long-term	86	25	19	40	25	23	27	37
Long-term public sector debt	4,200	4,994	5,776	2,019	3,424	3,873	4,737	5,727
Long-term private sector debt	27	257	0	0	0	0	0	0
Public & publicly guaranteed commitments	620	453	352	571	1,404	2,652	1,227	2,900
External debt flows								
Disbursements	570	397	516	635	1,413	598	1,022	1,280
Long-term external debt	528	362	477	519	1,413	598	918	1,155
IMF purchases	42	35	39	116	0	0	104	124
Principal repayments	292	254	186	153	97	85	101	120
Long-term external debt	184	217	155	153	97	85	101	120
IMF repurchases	108	37	32	0	0	0	0	0
Net flows	349	7	220	1,029	1,446	596	865	2,114
Long-term external debt	344	144	322	366	1,315	513	817	1,036
Short-term external debt	71	-136	-109	546	131	83	-56	954
Interest payments	95	134	96	84	82	145	131	200
Long-term external debt	57	95	73	55	49	112	99	144
IMF charges	10	1	2	0	1	1	1	0
Short-term external debt	28	38	21	29	32	32	31	56
2. Other non-debt resource inflows								
Foreign direct investment	107	166	145	636	855	1,220	1,685	2,527
Portfolio equity	0	0	0	0	0	0	0	0
3. Currency composition of public and publicly guaranteed debt (%)								
Euro	..	..	3.1	10.6	9.7	10.7	12.8	13.3
Japanese yen	14.0	16.2	0.0	0.0	0.0	0.0	0.0	0.0
Pound sterling	5.2	2.1	0.0	0.1	0.0	0.0	0.0	0.0
Swiss franc	0.3	0.1	0.0	0.1	0.1	0.1	0.0	0.0
U.S.dollars	59.9	67.6	78.8	55.2	64.3	62.9	60.6	60.1
4. Average terms of new commitments								
Official creditors								
Interest (%)	1.5	1.4	0.8	1.0	1.3	1.9	1.2	1.3
Maturity (years)	34.8	34.7	43.0	35.0	25.9	22.6	28.1	27.5
Grace period (years)	9.4	8.9	10.3	8.4	6.2	5.6	7.4	7.6
Private creditors								
Interest (%)	6.4	6.2	0.8	3.0	8.5	4.7	2.7	1.9
Maturity (years)	6.6	10.2	40.2	11.6	10.1	10.7	14.0	18.4
Grace period (years)	1.3	2.7	10.7	2.1	10.0	2.6	2.4	5.3
5. Major economic aggregates								
Gross national income (GNI)	6,324	4,831	10,590	20,261	24,494	28,268	25,871	30,776
Exports of goods, services & income	1,596	2,456	3,952	5,183	6,088	7,156	7,711	9,490
Worker remit. & comp. of employees	17	32	99	105	117	126	114	136
Imports of goods, services & income	2,262	3,474	6,851	8,474	10,283	12,911	11,387	14,513
Profit remittances on FDI	17	17	94	92	135	172	241	396
Current account balance	-144	-387	-1,105	-1,043	-2,151	-3,543	-1,598	-2,700
International reserves	804	309	1,897	2,269	..	..	..	..
6. Ratios								
External debt stocks to exports (%)	344.4	249.0	171.6	64.1	79.7	75.2	82.1	88.2
External debt stocks to GNI (%)	86.9	126.6	64.0	16.4	19.8	19.0	24.5	27.2
Debt service to exports (%)	24.2	15.8	7.1	4.6	2.9	3.2	3.0	3.4
Short-term to external debt stocks (%)	11.3	9.4	8.7	34.4	26.0	25.0	20.9	26.9
Multilateral to external debt stocks (%)	54.3	59.9	74.4	37.2	31.7	34.3	34.8	31.3
Reserves to external debt stocks (%)	14.6	5.1	28.0	68.3	..	..	..	..
Reserves to imports (months)	4.3	1.1	3.3	3.2	..	..	..	..

(US$ million, unless otherwise indicated)

	1995	2000	2005	2006	2007	2008	2009	2010
7. Long-term external debt								
Debt outstanding and disbursed	**4,227**	**5,251**	**5,776**	**2,019**	**3,424**	**3,873**	**4,737**	**5,727**
Public and publicly guaranteed	4,200	4,994	5,776	2,019	3,424	3,873	4,737	5,727
Official creditors	3,847	4,703	5,361	1,583	2,165	2,561	3,206	3,980
Multilateral	2,982	3,663	5,045	1,234	1,538	1,843	2,203	2,620
of which: IBRD	59	9	0	0	0	0	0	0
IDA	2,375	3,130	4,234	815	1,087	1,330	1,581	1,868
Bilateral	865	1,039	316	349	627	718	1,002	1,360
Private creditors	352	292	415	435	1,259	1,311	1,531	1,747
of which: Bonds	0	0	0	0	750	750	750	750
Commercial banks	97	57	264	287	321	334	567	796
Private nonguaranteed	27	257	0	0	0	0	0	0
of which: Bonds	0	250	0	0	0	0	0	0
Disbursements	**528**	**362**	**477**	**519**	**1,413**	**598**	**918**	**1,155**
Public and publicly guaranteed	528	362	477	519	1,413	598	918	1,155
Official creditors	414	340	425	479	567	485	658	844
Multilateral	284	223	404	335	274	355	353	446
of which: IBRD	0	0	0	0	0	0	0	0
IDA	242	204	305	266	231	257	241	308
Bilateral	130	117	21	143	293	130	305	398
Private creditors	115	22	51	40	846	113	259	311
of which: Bonds	0	0	0	0	750	0	0	0
Commercial banks	64	14	47	29	44	58	254	296
Private nonguaranteed	0	0	0	0	0	0	0	0
of which: Bonds	0	0	0	0	0	0	0	0
Principal repayments	**184**	**217**	**155**	**153**	**97**	**85**	**101**	**120**
Public and publicly guaranteed	179	214	155	153	97	85	101	120
Official creditors	108	141	117	115	50	45	44	59
Multilateral	73	68	42	43	29	22	18	19
of which: IBRD	15	8	2	0	0	0	0	0
IDA	8	25	15	8	1	1	2	3
Bilateral	34	74	75	73	21	23	26	40
Private creditors	72	73	38	37	47	40	57	60
of which: Bonds	0	0	0	0	0	0	0	0
Commercial banks	2	27	18	21	29	33	34	41
Private nonguaranteed	5	3	0	0	0	0	0	0
of which: Bonds	0	0	0	0	0	0	0	0
Interest payments	**57**	**95**	**73**	**55**	**49**	**112**	**99**	**144**
Public and publicly guaranteed	55	80	73	55	49	112	99	144
Official creditors	50	64	55	39	29	28	43	58
Multilateral	40	39	42	29	17	18	18	20
of which: IBRD	6	1	0	0	0	0	0	0
IDA	17	22	31	18	8	9	10	12
Bilateral	10	26	13	9	12	11	25	38
Private creditors	5	16	17	16	21	84	56	86
of which: Bonds	0	0	0	0	0	64	32	64
Commercial banks	0	4	11	11	15	14	16	17
Private nonguaranteed	2	14	0	0	0	0	0	0
of which: Bonds	0	14	0	0	0	0	0	0
8. Debt stock-flow reconciliation								
Total change in external debt stocks	394	-304	-284	-3,460	1,535	527	949	2,038
Net flows on external debt	349	7	220	1,029	1,446	596	865	2,114
9. Debt restructurings								
Total amount rescheduled	0	0	0	7	0	0	0	0
Total amount forgiven	0	0	94	4,649	0	15	0	0
Debt buyback	0	0	0	0	0	0	0	0

10. Contractual obligations on outstanding long-term external debt

	2011	2012	2013	2014	2015	2016	2017	2018
Official creditors								
Principal	279	320	314	302	311	205	212	224
Interest	61	66	68	66	63	60	57	53
Private creditors								
Principal	111	150	147	148	143	185	980	224
Interest	101	117	118	117	114	111	107	38

Notes:

Long-term private nonguaranteed debt data only cover Bonds. Ghana was granted debt relief effective in 2006 under MDRI.

GRENADA

(US$ million, unless otherwise indicated)

	1995	2000	2005	2006	2007	2008	2009	2010
1. Summary external debt data								
External debt stocks	**127.0**	**201.4**	**405.9**	**499.1**	**537.2**	**553.8**	**558.6**	**576.0**
Long-term external debt	112.4	179.8	391.3	454.8	480.5	480.6	497.2	494.8
Public and publicly guaranteed	112.4	179.8	391.3	454.8	480.5	480.6	497.2	494.8
Private nonguaranteed	0.0	0.0	0.0	0.0	0.0	0.0	0.0	0.0
Use of IMF credit	0.0	0.0	8.4	9.5	7.7	13.0	23.0	29.1
Short-term external debt	14.6	21.6	6.3	34.8	49.0	60.2	38.3	52.1
interest arrears on long-term	6.6	4.5	4.3	5.8	12.0	11.2	13.3	25.1
Memorandum items								
Principal arrears on long-term	20.8	10.6	9.5	10.5	13.4	21.1	26.4	27.6
Long-term public sector debt	112.4	179.8	391.3	454.8	480.5	480.6	497.2	494.8
Long-term private sector debt	0.0	0.0	0.0	0.0	0.0	0.0	0.0	0.0
Public & publicly guaranteed commitments	17.0	97.4	22.5	35.4	32.8	22.3	24.0	17.3
External debt flows								
Disbursements	4.9	77.6	38.5	35.0	24.3	39.1	37.6	27.5
Long-term external debt	4.9	77.6	38.5	32.7	24.3	30.5	25.6	21.1
IMF purchases	0.0	0.0	0.0	2.3	0.0	8.5	12.0	6.4
Principal repayments	5.6	10.1	5.6	7.4	8.4	10.8	11.3	14.3
Long-term external debt	5.6	10.1	5.6	5.8	6.2	7.9	9.1	14.3
IMF repurchases	0.0	0.0	0.0	1.6	2.2	2.9	2.3	0.0
Net flows	-1.7	63.4	-28.1	54.6	23.8	40.3	2.2	15.2
Long-term external debt	-0.8	67.5	32.9	27.0	18.1	22.7	16.5	6.8
Short-term external debt	-1.0	-4.1	-61.0	27.0	8.0	12.0	-24.0	2.0
Interest payments	2.3	4.4	4.9	8.0	10.2	9.7	11.7	11.2
Long-term external debt	1.7	3.4	3.3	6.8	8.6	8.3	11.1	10.9
IMF charges	0.0	0.0	0.3	0.4	0.4	0.2	0.1	0.0
Short-term external debt	0.5	1.0	1.3	0.8	1.3	1.3	0.5	0.3
2. Other non-debt resource inflows								
Foreign direct investment	20.0	37.4	70.2	89.8	156.6	142.2	102.6	63.6
Portfolio equity	..	..	..	..	..	..	..	..
3. Currency composition of public and publicly guaranteed debt (%)								
Euro	..	..	0.4	0.3	0.3	0.3	0.3	0.3
Japanese yen	0.0	0.0	0.0	0.0	0.0	0.0	0.0	0.0
Pound sterling	33.7	6.3	0.2	0.0	0.0	0.7	0.7	0.6
Swiss franc	0.0	0.0	0.0	0.0	0.0	0.0	0.0	0.0
U.S.dollars	59.7	78.7	91.3	92.4	92.2	91.0	90.4	91.0
4. Average terms of new commitments								
Official creditors								
Interest (%)	2.6	3.8	2.8	1.8	2.6	2.6	2.6	3.1
Maturity (years)	28.2	24.4	26.9	30.7	27.5	19.5	25.7	21.6
Grace period (years)	5.6	7.2	5.3	9.7	7.5	3.3	6.8	5.9
Private creditors								
Interest (%)	0.0	5.0	0.0	5.3	0.0	0.0	0.0	0.0
Maturity (years)	0.0	12.5	0.0	5.1	0.0	0.0	0.0	0.0
Grace period (years)	0.0	7.2	0.0	3.1	0.0	0.0	0.0	0.0
5. Major economic aggregates								
Gross national income (GNI)	262.9	395.8	525.6	535.6	567.3	632.6	578.0	583.3
Exports of goods, services & income	128.7	240.8	160.3	175.6	202.6	197.9	183.8	178.0
Worker remit. & comp. of employees	37.8	46.4	51.6	53.9	54.8	55.4	53.4	54.5
Imports of goods, services & income	187.6	349.0	435.9	444.5	493.1	509.5	435.4	440.5
Profit remittances on FDI	12.6	27.8	22.7	22.0	35.7	35.5	55.4	35.4
Current account balance	-41.8	-88.1	-193.3	-226.7	-264.3	-274.5	-214.0	-218.2
International reserves	36.7	57.7	94.3	100.0	110.6	105.3	129.1	119.2
6. Ratios								
External debt stocks to exports (%)	98.7	83.6	253.2	284.3	265.1	279.9	304.0	323.6
External debt stocks to GNI (%)	48.3	50.9	77.2	93.2	94.7	87.5	96.6	98.7
Debt service to exports (%)	6.1	6.0	6.6	8.8	9.2	10.4	12.5	14.3
Short-term to external debt stocks (%)	11.5	10.7	1.6	7.0	9.1	10.9	6.9	9.0
Multilateral to external debt stocks (%)	39.6	31.4	27.3	25.7	28.2	31.1	33.3	33.0
Reserves to external debt stocks (%)	28.9	28.6	23.2	20.0	20.6	19.0	23.1	20.7
Reserves to imports (months)	2.4	2.0	2.6	2.7	2.7	2.5	3.6	3.2

GRENADA

(US$ million, unless otherwise indicated)

	1995	2000	2005	2006	2007	2008	2009	2010
7. Long-term external debt								
Debt outstanding and disbursed	**112.4**	**179.8**	**391.3**	**454.8**	**480.5**	**480.6**	**497.2**	**494.8**
Public and publicly guaranteed	112.4	179.8	391.3	454.8	480.5	480.6	497.2	494.8
Official creditors	104.7	116.8	172.4	206.0	232.6	260.7	277.3	279.2
Multilateral	50.3	63.3	110.9	128.5	151.3	172.5	185.7	189.8
of which: IBRD	0.0	2.2	10.1	9.0	12.0	11.5	10.8	14.2
IDA	7.3	9.6	22.9	27.8	34.8	36.6	39.4	44.0
Bilateral	54.4	53.5	61.4	77.5	81.3	88.2	91.6	89.4
Private creditors	7.7	63.0	218.9	248.7	247.9	219.9	219.9	215.6
of which: Bonds	0.0	26.6	214.3	239.4	239.4	210.3	210.3	210.3
Commercial banks	0.3	32.2	2.4	8.8	8.3	8.3	8.3	4.0
Private nonguaranteed	0.0	0.0	0.0	0.0	0.0	0.0	0.0	0.0
of which: Bonds	0.0	0.0	0.0	0.0	0.0	0.0	0.0	0.0
Disbursements	**4.9**	**77.6**	**38.5**	**32.7**	**24.3**	**30.5**	**25.6**	**21.1**
Public and publicly guaranteed	4.9	77.6	38.5	32.7	24.3	30.5	25.6	21.1
Official creditors	4.9	19.8	38.5	25.5	24.3	30.5	25.6	21.1
Multilateral	3.4	11.7	22.7	20.5	24.3	27.8	20.1	20.4
of which: IBRD	0.0	1.9	2.8	0.1	4.3	0.9	0.7	5.1
IDA	0.0	0.8	3.6	4.0	6.0	2.5	2.9	5.6
Bilateral	1.5	8.1	15.8	5.0	0.0	2.7	5.5	0.7
Private creditors	0.0	57.8	0.0	7.3	0.0	0.0	0.0	0.0
of which: Bonds	0.0	26.6	0.0	0.0	0.0	0.0	0.0	0.0
Commercial banks	0.0	30.0	0.0	7.3	0.0	0.0	0.0	0.0
Private nonguaranteed	0.0	0.0	0.0	0.0	0.0	0.0	0.0	0.0
of which: Bonds	0.0	0.0	0.0	0.0	0.0	0.0	0.0	0.0
Principal repayments	**5.6**	**10.1**	**5.6**	**5.8**	**6.2**	**7.9**	**9.1**	**14.3**
Public and publicly guaranteed	5.6	10.1	5.6	5.8	6.2	7.9	9.1	14.3
Official creditors	3.9	6.3	5.3	5.8	6.2	7.9	9.1	9.9
Multilateral	2.8	3.2	3.7	4.4	4.4	6.2	7.2	6.8
of which: IBRD	0.0	0.0	0.6	1.1	1.2	1.4	1.5	1.7
IDA	0.1	0.1	0.2	0.3	0.3	0.4	0.3	0.3
Bilateral	1.1	3.2	1.5	1.4	1.8	1.7	1.9	3.1
Private creditors	1.8	3.7	0.4	0.0	0.0	0.0	0.0	4.4
of which: Bonds	0.0	0.0	0.0	0.0	0.0	0.0	0.0	0.0
Commercial banks	0.2	2.4	0.4	0.0	0.0	0.0	0.0	4.4
Private nonguaranteed	0.0	0.0	0.0	0.0	0.0	0.0	0.0	0.0
of which: Bonds	0.0	0.0	0.0	0.0	0.0	0.0	0.0	0.0
Interest payments	**1.7**	**3.4**	**3.3**	**6.8**	**8.6**	**8.3**	**11.1**	**10.9**
Public and publicly guaranteed	1.7	3.4	3.3	6.8	8.6	8.3	11.1	10.9
Official creditors	1.6	2.3	3.3	4.5	5.6	5.6	5.8	5.7
Multilateral	1.3	1.1	2.6	3.8	3.9	4.3	4.6	4.2
of which: IBRD	0.0	0.0	0.4	0.5	0.5	0.6	0.5	0.4
IDA	0.1	0.1	0.2	0.2	0.2	0.3	0.3	0.3
Bilateral	0.2	1.3	0.7	0.7	1.6	1.3	1.2	1.5
Private creditors	0.2	1.1	0.0	2.3	3.0	2.6	5.4	5.2
of which: Bonds	0.0	0.0	0.0	2.3	2.3	2.1	5.1	5.1
Commercial banks	0.1	1.1	0.0	0.0	0.7	0.6	0.2	0.1
Private nonguaranteed	0.0	0.0	0.0	0.0	0.0	0.0	0.0	0.0
of which: Bonds	0.0	0.0	0.0	0.0	0.0	0.0	0.0	0.0
8. Debt stock-flow reconciliation								
Total change in external debt stocks	-2.0	65.6	-26.0	93.2	38.1	16.6	4.8	17.4
Net flows on external debt	-1.7	63.4	-28.1	54.6	23.8	40.3	2.2	15.2
9. Debt restructurings								
Total amount rescheduled	0.0	0.0	208.7	13.2	1.5	1.4	0.0	0.0
Total amount forgiven	0.6	0.0	0.0	0.0	0.0	0.0	0.0	0.0
Debt buyback	0.0	0.0	0.0	0.0	0.0	0.0	0.0	0.0

10. Contractual obligations on outstanding long-term external debt

	2011	2012	2013	2014	2015	2016	2017	2018
Official creditors								
Principal	18.0	15.2	28.6	12.5	14.6	13.9	13.9	13.4
Interest	6.5	6.4	6.2	5.6	5.3	4.9	4.5	4.2
Private creditors								
Principal	2.9	5.6	0.0	0.0	0.0	0.0	0.0	0.0
Interest	11.9	21.1	21.0	28.1	28.1	37.4	37.4	39.7

GUATEMALA

(US$ million, unless otherwise indicated)

	1995	2000	2005	2006	2007	2008	2009	2010
1. Summary external debt data								
External debt stocks	**3,282**	**3,853**	**10,981**	**12,308**	**14,570**	**14,771**	**13,764**	**14,340**
Long-term external debt	2,470	2,681	9,528	10,834	12,566	12,620	12,538	12,745
Public and publicly guaranteed	2,328	2,540	3,687	3,921	4,189	4,352	4,894	5,527
Private nonguaranteed	142	142	5,841	6,913	8,377	8,268	7,644	7,218
Use of IMF credit	0	0	0	0	0	0	0	0
Short-term external debt	811	1,172	1,453	1,474	2,004	2,151	1,226	1,595
interest arrears on long-term	219	317	414	0	0	0	0	0
Memorandum items								
Principal arrears on long-term	257	224	131	0	0	0	0	0
Long-term public sector debt	2,328	2,540	3,687	3,921	4,189	4,352	4,894	5,527
Long-term private sector debt	142	142	5,841	6,913	8,377	8,268	7,644	7,218
Public & publicly guaranteed commitments	99	87	82	755	398	508	1,532	275
External debt flows								
Disbursements	200	210	2,184	2,240	2,738	1,037	934	1,442
Long-term external debt	200	210	2,184	2,240	2,738	1,037	934	1,442
IMF purchases	0	0	0	0	0	0	0	0
Principal repayments	213	188	705	831	1,034	1,009	1,019	913
Long-term external debt	213	188	705	831	1,034	1,009	1,019	913
IMF repurchases	0	0	0	0	0	0	0	0
Net flows	140	56	1,316	1,844	2,234	175	-1,010	898
Long-term external debt	-13	22	1,479	1,409	1,704	28	-85	529
Short-term external debt	153	34	-163	435	530	147	-925	369
Interest payments	145	202	550	634	739	747	665	674
Long-term external debt	113	152	497	575	668	672	622	618
IMF charges	0	0	0	0	0	0	0	0
Short-term external debt	32	50	53	59	70	75	43	56
2. Other non-debt resource inflows								
Foreign direct investment	75	230	509	592	745	754	600	687
Portfolio equity	..	..	..	..	..	..	..	..
3. Currency composition of public and publicly guaranteed debt (%)								
Euro	..	..	2.5	2.3	2.1	1.9	1.7	1.3
Japanese yen	2.5	2.9	3.5	3.3	3.1	3.7	3.5	3.8
Pound sterling	0.0	0.0	0.0	0.0	0.0	0.0	0.0	0.0
Swiss franc	0.5	0.2	0.0	0.0	0.0	0.0	0.0	0.0
U.S.dollars	54.8	75.0	85.7	86.9	88.0	88.6	90.1	91.2
4. Average terms of new commitments								
Official creditors								
Interest (%)	4.2	7.2	5.4	5.6	5.9	4.3	1.6	3.7
Maturity (years)	30.9	19.2	25.8	23.0	19.4	20.1	23.2	28.2
Grace period (years)	7.9	4.7	5.1	4.1	3.9	4.0	6.3	4.8
Private creditors								
Interest (%)	0.0	0.0	0.0	0.0	0.0	0.0	0.0	0.0
Maturity (years)	0.0	0.0	0.0	0.0	0.0	0.0	0.0	0.0
Grace period (years)	0.0	0.0	0.0	0.0	0.0	0.0	0.0	0.0
5. Major economic aggregates								
Gross national income (GNI)	14,498	19,065	26,726	29,551	33,270	38,199	36,569	39,990
Exports of goods, services & income	2,870	4,077	7,069	8,036	9,270	10,264	9,572	11,070
Worker remit. & comp. of employees	358	596	3,067	3,700	4,236	4,460	4,019	4,229
Imports of goods, services & income	3,933	5,991	11,886	13,828	15,910	17,052	14,190	16,716
Profit remittances on FDI	95	248	370	608	819	886	951	997
Current account balance	-572	-1,050	-1,241	-1,524	-1,786	-1,681	8	-826
International reserves	783	1,806	3,777	4,055	4,315	4,654	5,205	5,949
6. Ratios								
External debt stocks to exports (%)	114.3	94.5	155.4	153.2	157.2	143.9	143.8	129.5
External debt stocks to GNI (%)	22.6	20.2	41.1	41.6	43.8	38.7	37.6	35.9
Debt service to exports (%)	12.5	9.6	17.8	18.2	19.1	17.1	17.6	14.3
Short-term to external debt stocks (%)	24.7	30.4	13.2	12.0	13.8	14.6	8.9	11.1
Multilateral to external debt stocks (%)	30.4	38.0	18.3	19.7	19.7	20.5	26.0	29.4
Reserves to external debt stocks (%)	23.9	46.9	34.4	32.9	29.6	31.5	37.8	41.5
Reserves to imports (months)	2.4	3.6	3.8	3.5	3.3	3.3	4.4	4.3

GUATEMALA

(US$ million, unless otherwise indicated)

	1995	2000	2005	2006	2007	2008	2009	2010
7. Long-term external debt								
Debt outstanding and disbursed	**2,470**	**2,681**	**9,528**	**10,834**	**12,566**	**12,620**	**12,538**	**12,745**
Public and publicly guaranteed	2,328	2,540	3,687	3,921	4,189	4,352	4,894	5,527
Official creditors	1,787	2,098	2,451	2,815	3,233	3,397	3,939	4,572
Multilateral	998	1,462	2,011	2,429	2,872	3,032	3,583	4,213
of which: IBRD	158	296	479	642	740	806	1,112	1,372
IDA	0	0	0	0	0	0	0	0
Bilateral	789	635	440	386	362	366	356	359
Private creditors	541	442	1,237	1,105	955	955	955	955
of which: Bonds	264	245	1,105	1,105	955	955	955	955
Commercial banks	61	0	0	0	0	0	0	0
Private nonguaranteed	142	142	5,841	6,913	8,377	8,268	7,644	7,218
of which: Bonds	0	0	50	50	50	55	5	5
Disbursements	**200**	**210**	**2,184**	**2,240**	**2,738**	**1,037**	**934**	**1,442**
Public and publicly guaranteed	200	210	144	581	599	396	807	879
Official creditors	128	210	144	581	599	396	807	879
Multilateral	87	157	131	572	594	386	783	858
of which: IBRD	13	51	34	199	136	133	379	335
IDA	0	0	0	0	0	0	0	0
Bilateral	41	53	13	9	6	10	24	21
Private creditors	73	0	0	0	0	0	0	0
of which: Bonds	59	0	0	0	0	0	0	0
Commercial banks	2	0	0	0	0	0	0	0
Private nonguaranteed	0	0	2,041	1,659	2,139	641	127	563
of which: Bonds	0	0	0	0	0	5	0	0
Principal repayments	**213**	**188**	**705**	**831**	**1,034**	**1,009**	**1,019**	**913**
Public and publicly guaranteed	194	168	199	244	359	259	268	263
Official creditors	151	136	199	234	209	259	268	263
Multilateral	92	78	145	163	163	224	233	227
of which: IBRD	40	13	33	36	38	67	72	75
IDA	0	0	0	0	0	0	0	0
Bilateral	59	58	54	71	46	35	35	36
Private creditors	43	32	1	11	150	0	0	0
of which: Bonds	15	31	0	0	150	0	0	0
Commercial banks	17	0	0	0	0	0	0	0
Private nonguaranteed	19	20	506	587	675	750	751	651
of which: Bonds	0	0	0	0	0	0	30	0
Interest payments	**113**	**152**	**497**	**575**	**668**	**672**	**622**	**618**
Public and publicly guaranteed	108	133	203	227	249	256	257	283
Official creditors	80	110	102	127	148	168	169	195
Multilateral	52	84	87	114	137	158	160	187
of which: IBRD	14	21	19	28	37	40	41	51
IDA	0	0	0	0	0	0	0	0
Bilateral	29	26	15	13	11	10	9	8
Private creditors	28	23	101	101	101	88	88	88
of which: Bonds	23	22	101	101	101	88	88	88
Commercial banks	3	0	0	0	0	0	0	0
Private nonguaranteed	5	19	294	348	420	416	365	335
of which: Bonds	0	0	5	5	5	5	0	0
8. Debt stock-flow reconciliation								
Total change in external debt stocks	175	72	1,265	1,326	2,262	202	-1,007	575
Net flows on external debt	140	56	1,316	1,844	2,234	175	-1,010	898
9. Debt restructurings								
Total amount rescheduled	0	0	0	0	0	0	0	0
Total amount forgiven	0	0	0	538	0	0	0	0
Debt buyback	0	0	0	0	0	0	0	0

10. Contractual obligations on outstanding long-term external debt

	2011	2012	2013	2014	2015	2016	2017	2018
Official creditors								
Principal	287	277	283	313	317	318	323	327
Interest	118	112	105	98	91	84	77	69
Private creditors								
Principal	2,187	1,664	1,306	810	592	493	395	391
Interest	336	198	152	115	87	64	46	37

Notes:

Data on long-term private nonguaranteed debt data are World Bank staff estimates.

GUINEA

(US$ million, unless otherwise indicated)

	1995	2000	2005	2006	2007	2008	2009	2010
1. Summary external debt data								
External debt stocks	**3,248**	**3,066**	**2,898**	**3,046**	**3,143**	**3,094**	**2,916**	**2,923**
Long-term external debt	2,991	2,655	2,727	2,822	2,939	2,831	2,819	2,752
Public and publicly guaranteed	2,991	2,655	2,727	2,822	2,939	2,831	2,819	2,752
Private nonguaranteed	0	0	0	0	0	0	0	0
Use of IMF credit	94	113	87	72	65	71	59	48
Short-term external debt	164	299	84	152	139	192	38	123
interest arrears on long-term	85	82	84	90	95	36	36	55
Memorandum items								
Principal arrears on long-term	372	322	306	311	271	126	127	201
Long-term public sector debt	2,991	2,655	2,727	2,822	2,939	2,831	2,819	2,752
Long-term private sector debt	0	0	0	0	0	0	0	0
Public & publicly guaranteed commitments	215	76	39	9	1	0	0	0
External debt flows								
Disbursements	200	75	91	73	89	94	49	36
Long-term external debt	169	75	91	73	78	67	49	36
IMF purchases	31	0	0	0	11	28	0	0
Principal repayments	128	100	116	106	106	103	95	63
Long-term external debt	120	92	91	86	85	84	82	53
IMF repurchases	9	8	26	19	21	20	13	10
Net flows	99	-37	-25	29	-36	103	-200	39
Long-term external debt	50	-17	1	-14	-7	-17	-33	-16
Short-term external debt	27	-12	0	62	-18	112	-154	66
Interest payments	49	57	47	50	50	37	33	24
Long-term external debt	44	41	46	46	49	34	32	23
IMF charges	0	1	1	0	0	0	0	0
Short-term external debt	5	15	0	4	1	3	0	1
2. Other non-debt resource inflows								
Foreign direct investment	1	10	105	125	386	382	50	101
Portfolio equity	..	..	..	..	..	..	..	..
3. Currency composition of public and publicly guaranteed debt (%)								
Euro	..	..	9.8	11.0	12.1	11.7	12.5	11.7
Japanese yen	3.5	3.1	2.0	1.7	1.6	1.9	1.7	1.7
Pound sterling	0.8	0.4	0.2	0.2	0.1	0.0	0.0	0.0
Swiss franc	0.3	0.2	0.2	0.2	0.2	0.3	0.3	0.3
U.S.dollars	48.4	60.5	63.8	63.1	63.3	66.0	65.3	65.4
4. Average terms of new commitments								
Official creditors								
Interest (%)	2.0	1.3	0.5	0.8	0.8	0.0	0.0	0.0
Maturity (years)	25.9	38.1	34.4	23.4	49.9	0.0	0.0	0.0
Grace period (years)	8.5	9.1	8.4	9.2	10.4	0.0	0.0	0.0
Private creditors								
Interest (%)	2.7	0.0	0.0	0.0	0.0	0.0	0.0	0.0
Maturity (years)	3.5	0.0	0.0	0.0	0.0	0.0	0.0	0.0
Grace period (years)	0.1	0.0	0.0	0.0	0.0	0.0	0.0	0.0
5. Major economic aggregates								
Gross national income (GNI)	3,609	3,035	2,658	2,496	3,819	3,321	3,692	4,231
Exports of goods, services & income	713	758	933	1,098	1,313	1,455	1,144	1,549
Worker remit. & comp. of employees	1	1	42	54	151	72	64	60
Imports of goods, services & income	1,109	973	1,083	1,298	1,637	1,911	1,581	1,892
Profit remittances on FDI	23	8	..	..	54	14	88	0
Current account balance	-216	-140	-160	-221	-455	-438	-403	-327
International reserves	87	168	97	..	..	..	..	..
6. Ratios								
External debt stocks to exports (%)	455.5	404.7	310.8	277.5	239.4	212.7	254.8	188.8
External debt stocks to GNI (%)	90.0	101.0	109.0	122.1	82.3	93.2	79.0	69.1
Debt service to exports (%)	24.9	20.7	17.5	14.2	11.9	9.7	11.1	5.6
Short-term to external debt stocks (%)	5.0	9.7	2.9	5.0	4.4	6.2	1.3	4.2
Multilateral to external debt stocks (%)	45.0	52.7	60.3	59.1	59.4	59.7	62.7	61.5
Reserves to external debt stocks (%)	2.7	5.5	3.4	..	..	..	..	..
Reserves to imports (months)	0.9	2.1	1.1	..	..	..	..	..

GUINEA

(US$ million, unless otherwise indicated)

	1995	2000	2005	2006	2007	2008	2009	2010
7. Long-term external debt								
Debt outstanding and disbursed	**2,991**	**2,655**	**2,727**	**2,822**	**2,939**	**2,831**	**2,819**	**2,752**
Public and publicly guaranteed	2,991	2,655	2,727	2,822	2,939	2,831	2,819	2,752
Official creditors	2,908	2,626	2,693	2,785	2,895	2,801	2,784	2,716
Multilateral	1,460	1,615	1,747	1,800	1,866	1,848	1,827	1,798
of which: IBRD	0	0	0	0	0	0	0	0
IDA	847	982	1,205	1,259	1,305	1,288	1,269	1,248
Bilateral	1,448	1,011	947	985	1,029	953	957	918
Private creditors	82	29	33	37	44	30	35	37
of which: Bonds	0	0	0	0	0	0	0	0
Commercial banks	25	0	5	8	15	18	23	25
Private nonguaranteed	0	0	0	0	0	0	0	0
of which: Bonds	0	0	0	0	0	0	0	0
Disbursements	**169**	**75**	**91**	**73**	**78**	**67**	**49**	**36**
Public and publicly guaranteed	169	75	91	73	78	67	49	36
Official creditors	169	75	89	70	72	63	45	33
Multilateral	161	70	41	33	41	45	16	19
of which: IBRD	0	0	0	0	0	0	0	0
IDA	59	29	32	22	21	22	0	0
Bilateral	8	5	48	37	32	18	29	13
Private creditors	0	0	2	3	6	4	4	4
of which: Bonds	0	0	0	0	0	0	0	0
Commercial banks	0	0	2	3	6	4	4	4
Private nonguaranteed	0	0	0	0	0	0	0	0
of which: Bonds	0	0	0	0	0	0	0	0
Principal repayments	**120**	**92**	**91**	**86**	**85**	**84**	**82**	**53**
Public and publicly guaranteed	120	92	91	86	85	84	82	53
Official creditors	105	92	91	86	85	84	82	53
Multilateral	35	51	49	46	46	58	58	30
of which: IBRD	0	0	0	0	0	0	0	0
IDA	2	11	9	10	12	25	27	0
Bilateral	70	40	42	40	39	25	23	23
Private creditors	15	0	0	0	0	0	0	0
of which: Bonds	0	0	0	0	0	0	0	0
Commercial banks	0	0	0	0	0	0	0	0
Private nonguaranteed	0	0	0	0	0	0	0	0
of which: Bonds	0	0	0	0	0	0	0	0
Interest payments	**44**	**41**	**46**	**46**	**49**	**34**	**32**	**23**
Public and publicly guaranteed	44	41	46	46	49	34	32	23
Official creditors	43	41	44	43	44	28	25	17
Multilateral	15	24	20	18	18	18	14	6
of which: IBRD	0	0	0	0	0	0	0	0
IDA	6	7	9	8	9	10	7	0
Bilateral	28	17	24	25	26	10	10	11
Private creditors	1	0	2	3	5	6	8	6
of which: Bonds	0	0	0	0	0	0	0	0
Commercial banks	0	0	2	3	5	6	8	6
Private nonguaranteed	0	0	0	0	0	0	0	0
of which: Bonds	0	0	0	0	0	0	0	0
8. Debt stock-flow reconciliation								
Total change in external debt stocks	136	-122	-238	148	97	-49	-178	7
Net flows on external debt	99	-37	-25	29	-36	103	-200	39
9. Debt restructurings								
Total amount rescheduled	130	0	0	0	41	86	17	13
Total amount forgiven	61	0	13	14	23	177	25	24
Debt buyback	0	0	0	0	0	0	0	0

10. Contractual obligations on outstanding long-term external debt

	2011	2012	2013	2014	2015	2016	2017	2018
Official creditors								
Principal	113	114	113	117	129	122	114	114
Interest	40	38	36	34	31	28	26	24
Private creditors								
Principal	0	0	0	0	0	0	0	0
Interest	2	2	2	2	2	2	2	2

Notes:

Data on long-term public and publicly guaranteed debt for 2010 are World Bank staff estimates. Data include the effects of Paris Club debt restructuring agreement signed in 2008. Data for 2007 and 2008 include the effects of Enhanced HIPC Initiative, in the amount of $14,757 thousand and $5,738 thousand respectively.

GUINEA-BISSAU

(US$ million, unless otherwise indicated)

	1995	2000	2005	2006	2007	2008	2009	2010
1. Summary external debt data								
External debt stocks	**895**	**947**	**1,013**	**1,036**	**1,080**	**1,086**	**1,118**	**1,095**
Long-term external debt	794	822	881	902	925	931	950	963
Public and publicly guaranteed	794	822	881	902	925	931	950	963
Private nonguaranteed	0	0	0	0	0	0	0	0
Use of IMF credit	6	25	12	8	5	9	10	4
Short-term external debt	95	100	121	126	149	146	158	128
interest arrears on long-term	89	87	119	126	142	144	151	127
Memorandum items								
Principal arrears on long-term	251	219	256	252	245	270	318	266
Long-term public sector debt	794	822	881	902	925	931	950	963
Long-term private sector debt	0	0	0	0	0	0	0	0
Public & publicly guaranteed commitments	22	27	9	0	0	0	0	0
External debt flows								
Disbursements	23	22	14	9	15	12	6	19
Long-term external debt	21	14	14	9	15	6	4	3
IMF purchases	2	9	0	0	0	6	3	16
Principal repayments	9	3	4	7	7	6	6	14
Long-term external debt	8	3	1	3	4	4	5	6
IMF repurchases	1	0	3	4	3	2	2	8
Net flows	13	29	9	0	16	0	5	-1
Long-term external debt	13	11	13	6	12	2	-1	-3
Short-term external debt	-1	10	-1	-2	7	-5	5	-6
Interest payments	6	2	2	3	3	4	4	3
Long-term external debt	6	2	2	3	3	3	4	3
IMF charges	0	0	0	0	0	0	0	0
Short-term external debt	0	0	0	0	0	0	0	0
2. Other non-debt resource inflows								
Foreign direct investment	0	1	9	18	19	5	14	9
Portfolio equity	..	..	..	..	0	..	..	..
3. Currency composition of public and publicly guaranteed debt (%)								
Euro	..	..	10.4	11.1	12.1	11.4	11.6	9.5
Japanese yen	0.0	0.0	0.0	0.0	0.0	0.0	0.0	0.0
Pound sterling	0.0	0.0	0.0	0.0	0.0	0.0	0.0	0.0
Swiss franc	6.6	11.0	12.6	5.1	5.4	5.6	5.7	4.8
U.S.dollars	38.3	34.0	46.7	52.3	50.0	50.6	50.9	54.6
4. Average terms of new commitments								
Official creditors								
Interest (%)	0.8	0.9	0.8	0.0	0.0	0.0	0.0	0.0
Maturity (years)	39.8	37.9	45.5	0.0	0.0	0.0	0.0	0.0
Grace period (years)	10.3	10.1	10.3	0.0	0.0	0.0	0.0	0.0
Private creditors								
Interest (%)	0.0	0.0	0.0	0.0	0.0	0.0	0.0	0.0
Maturity (years)	0.0	0.0	0.0	0.0	0.0	0.0	0.0	0.0
Grace period (years)	0.0	0.0	0.0	0.0	0.0	0.0	0.0	0.0
5. Major economic aggregates								
Gross national income (GNI)	236	203	561	569	680	833	824	877
Exports of goods, services & income	30	..	95	78	141	172	..	..
Worker remit. & comp. of employees	2	8	20	26	43	49	50	48
Imports of goods, services & income	110	..	157	176	246	299	..	..
Profit remittances on FDI	..	..	..	..	..	0	..	..
Current account balance	-35	..	-10	-40	-31	-29	..	..
International reserves	20	67	80	82	113	125	169	156
6. Ratios								
External debt stocks to exports (%)	3,024.9	..	1,063.7	1,330.8	766.6	630.8	..	..
External debt stocks to GNI (%)	379.4	466.5	180.6	182.0	158.8	130.3	135.6	124.8
Debt service to exports (%)	52.4	..	6.6	12.4	7.4	5.6	..	..
Short-term to external debt stocks (%)	10.6	10.6	11.9	12.2	13.8	13.5	14.1	11.7
Multilateral to external debt stocks (%)	41.3	41.9	45.1	46.4	47.3	46.8	45.3	44.9
Reserves to external debt stocks (%)	2.3	7.0	7.9	7.9	10.5	11.5	15.1	14.3
Reserves to imports (months)	2.2	..	6.1	5.6	5.5	5.0	..	..

GUINEA-BISSAU

(US$ million, unless otherwise indicated)

	1995	2000	2005	2006	2007	2008	2009	2010
7. Long-term external debt								
Debt outstanding and disbursed	**794**	**822**	**881**	**902**	**925**	**931**	**950**	**963**
Public and publicly guaranteed	794	822	881	902	925	931	950	963
Official creditors	763	822	881	902	925	931	950	963
Multilateral	370	397	457	481	511	508	507	492
of which: IBRD	0	0	0	0	0	0	0	0
IDA	210	228	284	297	315	309	304	289
Bilateral	393	425	424	421	414	423	443	471
Private creditors	31	0	0	0	0	0	0	0
of which: Bonds	0	0	0	0	0	0	0	0
Commercial banks	0	0	0	0	0	0	0	0
Private nonguaranteed	0	0	0	0	0	0	0	0
of which: Bonds	0	0	0	0	0	0	0	0
Disbursements	**21**	**14**	**14**	**9**	**15**	**6**	**4**	**3**
Public and publicly guaranteed	21	14	14	9	15	6	4	3
Official creditors	21	14	14	9	15	6	4	3
Multilateral	19	14	14	9	15	6	4	3
of which: IBRD	0	0	0	0	0	0	0	0
IDA	9	14	11	5	11	4	1	0
Bilateral	2	0	0	0	0	0	0	0
Private creditors	0	0	0	0	0	0	0	0
of which: Bonds	0	0	0	0	0	0	0	0
Commercial banks	0	0	0	0	0	0	0	0
Private nonguaranteed	0	0	0	0	0	0	0	0
of which: Bonds	0	0	0	0	0	0	0	0
Principal repayments	**8**	**3**	**1**	**3**	**4**	**4**	**5**	**6**
Public and publicly guaranteed	8	3	1	3	4	4	5	6
Official creditors	8	2	1	3	4	4	5	6
Multilateral	8	2	1	3	4	4	5	6
of which: IBRD	0	0	0	0	0	0	0	0
IDA	1	2	0	0	0	1	1	1
Bilateral	0	0	0	0	0	0	0	0
Private creditors	0	0	0	0	0	0	0	0
of which: Bonds	0	0	0	0	0	0	0	0
Commercial banks	0	0	0	0	0	0	0	0
Private nonguaranteed	0	0	0	0	0	0	0	0
of which: Bonds	0	0	0	0	0	0	0	0
Interest payments	**6**	**2**	**2**	**3**	**3**	**3**	**4**	**3**
Public and publicly guaranteed	6	2	2	3	3	3	4	3
Official creditors	6	2	2	3	3	3	4	3
Multilateral	4	2	2	3	3	3	4	3
of which: IBRD	0	0	0	0	0	0	0	0
IDA	2	2	1	2	2	2	2	2
Bilateral	1	0	0	0	0	0	0	0
Private creditors	0	0	0	0	0	0	0	0
of which: Bonds	0	0	0	0	0	0	0	0
Commercial banks	0	0	0	0	0	0	0	0
Private nonguaranteed	0	0	0	0	0	0	0	0
of which: Bonds	0	0	0	0	0	0	0	0
8. Debt stock-flow reconciliation								
Total change in external debt stocks	45	9	-92	23	44	6	32	-23
Net flows on external debt	13	29	9	0	16	0	5	-1
9. Debt restructurings								
Total amount rescheduled	14	0	0	0	0	0	0	117
Total amount forgiven	15	1	9	6	6	10	7	60
Debt buyback	0	0	0	0	0	0	0	0

10. Contractual obligations on outstanding long-term external debt

	2011	2012	2013	2014	2015	2016	2017	2018
Official creditors								
Principal	25	24	20	21	21	22	23	24
Interest	6	6	6	6	6	5	5	5
Private creditors								
Principal	0	0	0	0	0	0	0	0
Interest	0	0	0	0	0	0	0	0

Notes:

Data on long-term public and publicly guaranteed debt for 2010 are World Bank staff estimates, and include the effects of Paris Club debt restructuring agreement signed in 2010. Data for 2008, 2009, and 2010 include the effects of Enhanced HIPC Initiative, in the amount of $7,311 thousand, $7,383 thousand, and $7,793 thousand respectively.

GUYANA

(US$ million, unless otherwise indicated)

	1995	2000	2005	2006	2007	2008	2009	2010
1. Summary external debt data								
External debt stocks	**2,116**	**1,364**	**1,216**	**1,141**	**736**	**829**	**1,037**	**1,354**
Long-term external debt	1,794	1,128	1,043	923	584	676	783	888
Public and publicly guaranteed	1,794	1,124	1,041	923	584	676	781	888
Private nonguaranteed	0	4	2	0	0	0	2	0
Use of IMF credit	172	117	91	56	59	57	58	56
Short-term external debt	150	119	82	162	93	96	196	410
interest arrears on long-term	133	67	82	86	93	96	97	103
Memorandum items								
Principal arrears on long-term	114	65	66	76	75	75	78	82
Long-term public sector debt	1,794	1,124	1,041	923	584	676	781	888
Long-term private sector debt	0	4	2	0	0	0	2	0
Public & publicly guaranteed commitments	45	85	166	4	144	123	74	152
External debt flows								
Disbursements	59	73	131	136	101	139	105	124
Long-term external debt	45	64	104	109	101	139	105	124
IMF purchases	14	9	27	27	0	0	0	0
Principal repayments	74	39	24	15	16	16	8	17
Long-term external debt	50	23	16	15	16	16	8	16
IMF repurchases	24	17	8	0	0	0	0	1
Net flows	-8	21	76	197	9	123	196	315
Long-term external debt	-5	41	88	94	85	123	97	108
Short-term external debt	7	-13	-31	76	-76	0	99	208
Interest payments	35	30	11	16	12	11	12	14
Long-term external debt	31	26	10	14	9	10	11	11
IMF charges	3	1	0	0	0	0	0	0
Short-term external debt	1	3	1	2	2	0	1	3
2. Other non-debt resource inflows								
Foreign direct investment	74	67	77	102	152	168	144	188
Portfolio equity	..	..	..	..	..	..	..	..
3. Currency composition of public and publicly guaranteed debt (%)								
Euro	..	..	2.1	2.7	4.6	3.5	2.9	2.2
Japanese yen	0.2	0.0	0.0	0.0	0.0	0.0	0.0	0.0
Pound sterling	9.1	5.6	0.2	0.2	0.1	0.1	0.1	0.0
Swiss franc	0.1	0.0	0.0	0.0	0.0	0.0	0.0	0.0
U.S.dollars	64.9	69.3	74.3	70.7	86.5	88.9	90.2	90.3
4. Average terms of new commitments								
Official creditors								
Interest (%)	1.5	2.0	1.3	1.9	1.0	1.6	1.6	1.2
Maturity (years)	38.7	40.0	30.5	29.8	36.6	28.4	29.1	26.0
Grace period (years)	10.4	10.5	9.2	7.6	9.0	4.1	4.7	4.9
Private creditors								
Interest (%)	8.8	0.0	0.0	0.0	0.0	0.0	0.0	0.0
Maturity (years)	31.0	0.0	0.0	0.0	0.0	0.0	0.0	0.0
Grace period (years)	8.0	0.0	0.0	0.0	0.0	0.0	0.0	0.0
5. Major economic aggregates								
Gross national income (GNI)	567	661	804	1,502	2,027	2,251	2,325	2,561
Exports of goods, services & income	641	684	697	730	889	1,035	..	..
Worker remit. & comp. of employees	2	27	201	218	283	278	278	308
Imports of goods, services & income	838	813	960	1,127	1,288	1,556	..	..
Profit remittances on FDI	..	6	7	9	-7	0	..	..
Current account balance	-135	-82	-96	-181	-112	-192	-231	-239
International reserves	269	305	252	280	313	356	631	782
6. Ratios								
External debt stocks to exports (%)	329.9	199.5	174.5	156.3	82.7	80.1	..	..
External debt stocks to GNI (%)	373.1	206.6	151.2	76.0	36.3	36.8	44.6	52.8
Debt service to exports (%)	17.0	10.1	4.9	4.3	3.1	2.6	..	..
Short-term to external debt stocks (%)	7.1	8.7	6.7	14.2	12.7	11.6	18.9	30.3
Multilateral to external debt stocks (%)	30.2	43.9	70.0	63.1	49.9	46.0	43.2	37.1
Reserves to external debt stocks (%)	12.7	22.3	20.7	24.5	42.6	42.9	60.9	57.8
Reserves to imports (months)	3.9	4.5	3.1	3.0	2.9	2.7	..	..

GUYANA

(US$ million, unless otherwise indicated)

	1995	2000	2005	2006	2007	2008	2009	2010
7. Long-term external debt								
Debt outstanding and disbursed	**1,794**	**1,128**	**1,043**	**923**	**584**	**676**	**783**	**888**
Public and publicly guaranteed	1,794	1,124	1,041	923	584	676	781	888
Official creditors	1,709	1,079	1,033	915	575	655	760	867
Multilateral	639	599	851	720	367	381	448	502
of which: IBRD	35	8	0	0	0	0	0	0
IDA	203	180	226	9	10	10	10	9
Bilateral	1,070	480	182	194	209	274	312	365
Private creditors	86	45	9	8	8	21	21	21
of which: Bonds	29	27	0	0	0	0	0	0
Commercial banks	37	6	4	4	4	3	4	4
Private nonguaranteed	0	4	2	0	0	0	2	0
of which: Bonds	0	0	0	0	0	0	0	0
Disbursements	**45**	**64**	**104**	**109**	**101**	**139**	**105**	**124**
Public and publicly guaranteed	45	64	104	109	101	139	105	124
Official creditors	45	64	104	109	101	139	105	124
Multilateral	41	64	71	77	67	56	69	64
of which: IBRD	0	0	0	0	0	0	0	0
IDA	18	6	2	0	1	0	0	0
Bilateral	4	0	33	32	33	83	36	59
Private creditors	0	0	0	0	0	0	0	0
of which: Bonds	0	0	0	0	0	0	0	0
Commercial banks	0	0	0	0	0	0	0	0
Private nonguaranteed	0	0	0	0	0	0	0	0
of which: Bonds	0	0	0	0	0	0	0	0
Principal repayments	**50**	**23**	**16**	**15**	**16**	**16**	**8**	**16**
Public and publicly guaranteed	50	22	15	15	16	16	8	16
Official creditors	40	22	15	15	16	16	8	16
Multilateral	24	18	11	13	9	9	6	8
of which: IBRD	6	3	0	0	0	0	0	0
IDA	1	1	1	1	0	0	0	0
Bilateral	16	4	4	2	7	7	2	8
Private creditors	10	0	0	0	0	0	0	0
of which: Bonds	0	0	0	0	0	0	0	0
Commercial banks	2	0	0	0	0	0	0	0
Private nonguaranteed	0	0	0	0	0	0	0	0
of which: Bonds	0	0	0	0	0	0	0	0
Interest payments	**31**	**26**	**10**	**14**	**9**	**10**	**11**	**11**
Public and publicly guaranteed	31	26	10	14	9	10	10	11
Official creditors	30	26	10	14	9	10	10	11
Multilateral	18	10	10	12	6	8	8	8
of which: IBRD	3	1	0	0	0	0	0	0
IDA	1	1	2	1	0	0	0	0
Bilateral	12	16	0	3	3	3	3	3
Private creditors	1	0	0	0	0	0	0	0
of which: Bonds	0	0	0	0	0	0	0	0
Commercial banks	1	0	0	0	0	0	0	0
Private nonguaranteed	0	0	0	0	0	0	0	0
of which: Bonds	0	0	0	0	0	0	0	0
8. Debt stock-flow reconciliation								
Total change in external debt stocks	67	-48	-147	-75	-406	93	208	317
Net flows on external debt	-8	21	76	197	9	123	196	315
9. Debt restructurings								
Total amount rescheduled	1	0	79	0	0	0	0	0
Total amount forgiven	0	14	175	298	429	13	0	0
Debt buyback	0	0	0	0	0	0	0	0

10. Contractual obligations on outstanding long-term external debt

	2011	2012	2013	2014	2015	2016	2017	2018
Official creditors								
Principal	24	26	31	34	40	43	46	47
Interest	14	15	14	14	13	13	12	11
Private creditors								
Principal	0	0	0	0	0	0	0	0
Interest	0	0	0	0	0	0	0	0

HAITI

(US$ million, unless otherwise indicated)

	1995	2000	2005	2006	2007	2008	2009	2010
1. Summary external debt data								
External debt stocks	**821.1**	**1172.7**	**1327.0**	**1504.7**	**1580.1**	**1950.9**	**1325.2**	**491.8**
Long-term external debt	765.7	1043.0	1277.9	1346.1	1524.6	1846.1	1158.8	479.0
Public and publicly guaranteed	765.7	1043.0	1277.9	1346.1	1524.6	1846.1	1158.8	479.0
Private nonguaranteed	0.0	0.0	0.0	0.0	0.0	0.0	0.0	0.0
Use of IMF credit	28.7	39.4	21.4	32.5	55.6	104.8	166.4	12.7
Short-term external debt	26.6	90.3	27.7	126.0	0.0	0.0	0.0	0.1
interest arrears on long-term	1.0	1.0	14.7	18.0	0.0	0.0	0.0	0.1
Memorandum items								
Principal arrears on long-term	2.1	2.4	21.8	27.4	0.0	0.0	0.0	0.4
Long-term public sector debt	765.7	1043.0	1277.9	1346.1	1524.6	1846.1	1158.8	479.0
Long-term private sector debt	0.0	0.0	0.0	0.0	0.0	0.0	0.0	0.0
Public & publicly guaranteed commitments	253.6	0.0	240.2	0.0	116.5	185.4	113.9	200.1
External debt flows								
Disbursements	128.3	50.7	92.8	98.3	150.9	406.2	272.5	410.9
Long-term external debt	103.5	50.7	77.5	83.4	97.0	355.8	212.0	286.1
IMF purchases	24.8	0.0	15.3	14.9	53.9	50.5	60.5	124.8
Principal repayments	65.7	23.9	38.2	38.1	56.5	34.3	29.6	122.5
Long-term external debt	33.7	18.1	33.6	33.7	23.3	34.3	26.5	122.5
IMF repurchases	32.0	5.7	4.5	4.4	33.2	0.0	3.1	0.0
Net flows	75.2	21.0	20.6	155.2	-13.6	372.0	242.9	288.5
Long-term external debt	69.8	32.5	43.9	49.7	73.7	321.5	185.5	163.7
Short-term external debt	12.6	-5.8	-34.0	95.0	-108.0	0.0	0.0	0.0
Interest payments	32.4	20.5	19.0	21.4	25.9	23.6	15.2	8.4
Long-term external debt	25.4	14.7	17.3	17.1	22.3	23.3	14.6	8.0
IMF charges	5.5	1.2	0.5	1.2	0.7	0.3	0.6	0.4
Short-term external debt	1.5	4.6	1.2	3.1	3.0	0.0	0.0	0.0
2. Other non-debt resource inflows								
Foreign direct investment	7.4	13.3	26.0	160.6	74.5	29.8	38.0	150.0
Portfolio equity	..	..	..	..	..	..	..	..
3. Currency composition of public and publicly guaranteed debt (%)								
Euro	..	..	3.4	3.6	5.7	5.0	4.1	9.2
Japanese yen	0.0	0.0	0.0	0.0	0.0	0.0	0.0	0.0
Pound sterling	0.0	0.0	0.0	0.0	0.0	0.0	0.0	0.0
Swiss franc	0.0	0.0	0.0	0.0	0.0	0.0	0.0	0.0
U.S.dollars	77.5	82.1	80.4	81.3	80.9	84.1	87.2	78.1
4. Average terms of new commitments								
Official creditors								
Interest (%)	1.2	0.0	1.0	0.0	1.8	1.0	1.0	1.0
Maturity (years)	39.9	0.0	39.4	0.0	34.0	25.0	24.9	25.0
Grace period (years)	10.4	0.0	10.3	0.0	8.2	3.0	3.0	3.0
Private creditors								
Interest (%)	0.0	0.0	0.0	0.0	0.0	0.0	0.0	0.0
Maturity (years)	0.0	0.0	0.0	0.0	0.0	0.0	0.0	0.0
Grace period (years)	0.0	0.0	0.0	0.0	0.0	0.0	0.0	0.0
5. Major economic aggregates								
Gross national income (GNI)	..	..	4227.9	4236.0	6126.1	6429.0	6491.3	6731.3
Exports of goods, services & income	192.4	503.7	605.1	707.8	801.0	861.0	963.9	836.2
Worker remit. & comp. of employees	..	578.0	986.2	1062.9	1222.1	1369.8	1375.5	1498.7
Imports of goods, services & income	832.3	1377.9	1887.9	2153.7	2404.1	2876.3	2831.2	4159.4
Profit remittances on FDI	3.8	..	..	..	..	..	..	..
Current account balance	-87.1	-114.2	7.0	-85.1	-85.8	-289.1	-232.1	..
International reserves	198.8	182.5	133.8	253.9	453.1	542.5	790.0	1336.9
6. Ratios								
External debt stocks to exports (%)	426.8	232.8	219.3	212.6	197.3	226.6	137.5	58.8
External debt stocks to GNI (%)	..	..	31.4	35.5	25.8	30.3	20.4	7.3
Debt service to exports (%)	51.0	8.8	9.4	8.4	10.3	6.7	4.6	15.7
Short-term to external debt stocks (%)	3.2	7.7	2.1	8.4	..	..	..	0.0
Multilateral to external debt stocks (%)	74.9	77.3	81.1	76.0	79.0	68.1	39.2	14.3
Reserves to external debt stocks (%)	24.2	15.6	10.1	16.9	28.7	27.8	59.6	271.8
Reserves to imports (months)	2.9	1.6	0.9	1.4	2.3	2.3	3.3	3.9

(US$ million, unless otherwise indicated)

	1995	2000	2005	2006	2007	2008	2009	2010
7. Long-term external debt								
Debt outstanding and disbursed	**765.7**	**1043.0**	**1277.9**	**1346.1**	**1524.6**	**1846.1**	**1158.8**	**479.0**
Public and publicly guaranteed	765.7	1043.0	1277.9	1346.1	1524.6	1846.1	1158.8	479.0
Official creditors	765.7	1043.0	1277.9	1346.1	1524.6	1846.1	1158.8	479.0
Multilateral	615.3	906.6	1075.7	1144.3	1248.3	1328.6	519.8	70.5
of which: IBRD	0.0	0.0	0.0	0.0	0.0	0.0	0.0	0.0
IDA	389.4	480.1	505.5	511.5	518.4	507.2	38.5	0.0
Bilateral	150.4	136.4	202.2	201.9	276.3	517.5	639.0	408.5
Private creditors	0.0	0.0	0.0	0.0	0.0	0.0	0.0	0.0
of which: Bonds	0.0	0.0	0.0	0.0	0.0	0.0	0.0	0.0
Commercial banks	0.0	0.0	0.0	0.0	0.0	0.0	0.0	0.0
Private nonguaranteed	0.0	0.0	0.0	0.0	0.0	0.0	0.0	0.0
of which: Bonds	0.0	0.0	0.0	0.0	0.0	0.0	0.0	0.0
Disbursements	**103.5**	**50.7**	**77.5**	**83.4**	**97.0**	**355.8**	**212.0**	**286.1**
Public and publicly guaranteed	103.5	50.7	77.5	83.4	97.0	355.8	212.0	286.1
Official creditors	103.5	50.7	77.5	83.4	97.0	355.8	212.0	286.1
Multilateral	102.7	50.6	77.5	83.4	97.0	120.6	98.1	83.5
of which: IBRD	0.0	0.0	0.0	0.0	0.0	0.0	0.0	0.0
IDA	49.1	8.0	8.6	8.6	0.0	0.0	0.0	0.0
Bilateral	0.7	0.1	0.0	0.0	0.0	235.2	113.9	202.7
Private creditors	0.0	0.0	0.0	0.0	0.0	0.0	0.0	0.0
of which: Bonds	0.0	0.0	0.0	0.0	0.0	0.0	0.0	0.0
Commercial banks	0.0	0.0	0.0	0.0	0.0	0.0	0.0	0.0
Private nonguaranteed	0.0	0.0	0.0	0.0	0.0	0.0	0.0	0.0
of which: Bonds	0.0	0.0	0.0	0.0	0.0	0.0	0.0	0.0
Principal repayments	**33.7**	**18.1**	**33.6**	**33.7**	**23.3**	**34.3**	**26.5**	**122.5**
Public and publicly guaranteed	33.7	18.1	33.6	33.7	23.3	34.3	26.5	122.5
Official creditors	33.7	18.1	33.6	33.7	23.3	34.3	26.5	122.5
Multilateral	30.4	14.3	28.7	30.8	18.0	29.2	21.7	41.2
of which: IBRD	0.0	0.0	0.0	0.0	0.0	0.0	0.0	0.0
IDA	9.7	6.5	13.8	12.5	6.7	15.8	11.0	35.9
Bilateral	3.3	3.8	5.0	2.9	5.3	5.0	4.8	81.3
Private creditors	0.0	0.0	0.0	0.0	0.0	0.0	0.0	0.0
of which: Bonds	0.0	0.0	0.0	0.0	0.0	0.0	0.0	0.0
Commercial banks	0.0	0.0	0.0	0.0	0.0	0.0	0.0	0.0
Private nonguaranteed	0.0	0.0	0.0	0.0	0.0	0.0	0.0	0.0
of which: Bonds	0.0	0.0	0.0	0.0	0.0	0.0	0.0	0.0
Interest payments	**25.4**	**14.7**	**17.3**	**17.1**	**22.3**	**23.3**	**14.6**	**8.0**
Public and publicly guaranteed	25.4	14.7	17.3	17.1	22.3	23.3	14.6	8.0
Official creditors	25.4	14.7	17.3	17.1	22.3	23.3	14.6	8.0
Multilateral	24.0	9.4	15.3	15.5	17.3	19.5	11.6	6.6
of which: IBRD	0.0	0.0	0.0	0.0	0.0	0.0	0.0	0.0
IDA	10.4	3.6	4.9	3.7	3.5	4.2	2.4	0.2
Bilateral	1.3	5.3	2.0	1.6	5.0	3.8	3.0	1.4
Private creditors	0.0	0.0	0.0	0.0	0.0	0.0	0.0	0.0
of which: Bonds	0.0	0.0	0.0	0.0	0.0	0.0	0.0	0.0
Commercial banks	0.0	0.0	0.0	0.0	0.0	0.0	0.0	0.0
Private nonguaranteed	0.0	0.0	0.0	0.0	0.0	0.0	0.0	0.0
of which: Bonds	0.0	0.0	0.0	0.0	0.0	0.0	0.0	0.0
8. Debt stock-flow reconciliation								
Total change in external debt stocks	85.9	-16.3	16.0	177.7	75.5	370.8	-625.7	-833.4
Net flows on external debt	75.2	21.0	20.6	155.2	-13.6	372.0	242.9	288.5
9. Debt restructurings								
Total amount rescheduled	107.7	0.0	0.0	0.0	93.0	12.1	98.9	3.3
Total amount forgiven	11.2	0.0	0.0	1.1	32.3	17.8	936.0	1116.6
Debt buyback	0.0	0.0	0.0	0.0	0.0	0.0	0.0	0.0

10. Contractual obligations on outstanding long-term external debt

	2011	2012	2013	2014	2015	2016	2017	2018
Official creditors								
Principal	10.2	10.5	19.1	19.6	19.5	20.8	22.2	22.5
Interest	10.1	11.2	11.2	11.0	10.8	10.6	10.3	10.0
Private creditors								
Principal	0.0	0.0	0.0	0.0	0.0	0.0	0.0	0.0
Interest	0.0	0.0	0.0	0.0	0.0	0.0	0.0	0.0

Notes:

Data include the effects of Paris Club debt restructuring agreement signed in 2006 and 2009. Data for 2008, 2009, and 2010 include the effects of MDRI and HIPC debt relief, in the amount of $814 thousand, and $451,744 thousand, and $51 thousand respectively. In addition, the country's fiscal year-end for external debt data is September 2010, but data for 2010 include the effects of MDRI relief in October 2010 of $482 million.

HONDURAS

(US$ million, unless otherwise indicated)

	1995	2000	2005	2006	2007	2008	2009	2010
1. Summary external debt data								
External debt stocks	**4,851**	**5,402**	**5,225**	**4,203**	**3,305**	**3,505**	**3,674**	**4,168**
Long-term external debt	4,370	4,813	4,645	3,666	2,615	2,957	3,325	3,740
Public and publicly guaranteed	4,247	4,253	4,137	3,031	1,991	2,301	2,445	2,798
Private nonguaranteed	123	560	509	635	624	657	880	942
Use of IMF credit	99	216	168	31	32	31	32	30
Short-term external debt	382	374	412	506	658	517	317	398
interest arrears on long-term	63	35	12	5	5	3	10	11
Memorandum items								
Principal arrears on long-term	197	72	47	25	22	32	30	37
Long-term public sector debt	4,223	4,233	4,137	3,031	1,991	2,301	2,445	2,798
Long-term private sector debt	147	580	509	635	624	657	880	942
Public & publicly guaranteed commitments	358	174	369	198	269	545	257	895
External debt flows								
Disbursements	379	368	496	357	385	649	703	873
Long-term external debt	349	347	481	342	385	649	703	873
IMF purchases	31	21	15	15	0	0	0	0
Principal repayments	352	261	280	203	234	277	341	453
Long-term external debt	308	256	264	203	234	277	341	451
IMF repurchases	44	5	15	0	0	0	0	2
Net flows	90	44	246	255	304	233	155	500
Long-term external debt	40	90	217	140	152	372	362	421
Short-term external debt	62	-63	30	101	152	-139	-207	80
Interest payments	226	131	105	131	114	91	73	64
Long-term external debt	203	107	83	102	81	76	68	60
IMF charges	5	4	1	0	0	0	0	0
Short-term external debt	18	20	21	29	33	14	5	4
2. Other non-debt resource inflows								
Foreign direct investment	50	382	600	669	928	929	523	797
Portfolio equity	0	0	..	..	..	..	..	..
3. Currency composition of public and publicly guaranteed debt (%)								
Euro	..	..	5.7	4.9	8.8	9.4	10.0	8.3
Japanese yen	9.2	7.9	0.5	0.0	0.0	0.0	0.0	0.0
Pound sterling	0.6	0.4	0.0	0.0	0.0	0.0	0.0	0.0
Swiss franc	1.4	0.9	0.1	0.2	0.1	0.1	0.1	0.1
U.S.dollars	48.9	65.7	72.5	65.8	68.2	69.2	69.1	73.4
4. Average terms of new commitments								
Official creditors								
Interest (%)	2.3	1.5	1.3	1.7	1.8	2.8	3.4	2.6
Maturity (years)	29.5	39.7	26.3	29.1	27.0	24.5	26.7	23.0
Grace period (years)	7.2	10.2	9.3	8.6	8.5	5.4	5.5	5.2
Private creditors								
Interest (%)	8.4	3.8	1.7	0.0	0.0	0.0	0.8	1.0
Maturity (years)	28.6	7.2	50.0	0.0	0.0	0.0	18.2	18.4
Grace period (years)	1.1	3.0	10.5	0.0	0.0	0.0	18.2	0.0
5. Major economic aggregates								
Gross national income (GNI)	3,649	6,951	9,300	10,376	11,993	13,546	13,827	14,802
Exports of goods, services & income	1,667	4,001	5,893	6,220	6,821	7,380	5,852	6,818
Worker remit. & comp. of employees	124	484	1,818	2,367	2,648	2,858	2,520	2,649
Imports of goods, services & income	2,111	5,047	8,092	9,074	10,609	12,142	9,006	10,533
Profit remittances on FDI	40	160	479	621	535	488	499	567
Current account balance	-201	-508	-304	-404	-1,116	-1,782	-515	-955
International reserves	270	1,319	2,338	2,642	2,546	2,492	2,110	2,701
6. Ratios								
External debt stocks to exports (%)	291.0	135.0	88.7	67.6	48.5	47.5	62.8	61.1
External debt stocks to GNI (%)	132.9	77.7	56.2	40.5	27.6	25.9	26.6	28.2
Debt service to exports (%)	34.7	9.8	6.5	5.4	5.1	5.0	7.1	7.6
Short-term to external debt stocks (%)	7.9	6.9	7.9	12.0	19.9	14.7	8.6	9.6
Multilateral to external debt stocks (%)	44.4	50.5	60.9	54.3	38.5	40.8	41.3	45.4
Reserves to external debt stocks (%)	5.6	24.4	44.7	62.9	77.0	71.1	57.4	64.8
Reserves to imports (months)	1.5	3.1	3.5	3.5	2.9	2.5	2.8	3.1

HONDURAS

(US$ million, unless otherwise indicated)

	1995	2000	2005	2006	2007	2008	2009	2010
7. Long-term external debt								
Debt outstanding and disbursed	**4,370**	**4,813**	**4,645**	**3,666**	**2,615**	**2,957**	**3,325**	**3,740**
Public and publicly guaranteed	4,247	4,253	4,137	3,031	1,991	2,301	2,445	2,798
Official creditors	3,882	4,150	4,082	2,979	1,953	2,264	2,358	2,714
Multilateral	2,153	2,728	3,183	2,282	1,273	1,431	1,516	1,891
of which: IBRD	443	151	0	0	0	0	0	0
IDA	386	838	1,353	349	401	449	502	602
Bilateral	1,729	1,423	899	696	680	833	842	823
Private creditors	364	102	55	53	39	37	87	84
of which: Bonds	139	0	0	0	0	0	50	50
Commercial banks	82	46	44	43	28	26	26	23
Private nonguaranteed	123	560	509	635	624	657	880	942
of which: Bonds	0	0	0	0	0	0	0	0
Disbursements	**349**	**347**	**481**	**342**	**385**	**649**	**703**	**873**
Public and publicly guaranteed	287	163	302	210	230	431	246	452
Official creditors	258	159	297	210	229	430	196	452
Multilateral	209	120	253	186	152	196	112	435
of which: IBRD	7	0	0	0	0	0	0	0
IDA	77	38	151	58	46	51	49	109
Bilateral	49	38	44	24	77	234	84	17
Private creditors	29	4	4	0	1	1	50	0
of which: Bonds	0	0	0	0	0	0	50	0
Commercial banks	3	1	4	0	0	0	0	0
Private nonguaranteed	62	184	179	133	155	218	457	421
of which: Bonds	0	0	0	0	0	0	0	0
Principal repayments	**308**	**256**	**264**	**203**	**234**	**277**	**341**	**451**
Public and publicly guaranteed	270	90	138	90	104	54	107	62
Official creditors	243	89	138	87	102	53	106	61
Multilateral	158	86	122	49	38	33	34	46
of which: IBRD	58	27	70	0	0	0	0	0
IDA	2	2	8	3	0	0	0	0
Bilateral	84	3	15	38	65	19	72	15
Private creditors	27	1	1	3	2	1	1	1
of which: Bonds	13	0	0	0	0	0	0	0
Commercial banks	6	1	1	1	1	1	1	1
Private nonguaranteed	39	166	126	112	130	223	234	390
of which: Bonds	0	0	0	0	0	0	0	0
Interest payments	**203**	**107**	**83**	**102**	**81**	**76**	**68**	**60**
Public and publicly guaranteed	199	75	63	65	53	49	41	46
Official creditors	179	75	63	65	52	49	41	46
Multilateral	103	66	50	46	35	35	31	36
of which: IBRD	38	15	3	0	0	0	0	0
IDA	3	6	10	6	3	3	3	4
Bilateral	75	9	13	19	18	14	10	10
Private creditors	20	0	0	0	0	0	0	0
of which: Bonds	7	0	0	0	0	0	0	0
Commercial banks	5	0	0	0	0	0	0	0
Private nonguaranteed	5	31	20	37	28	27	27	14
of which: Bonds	0	0	0	0	0	0	0	0
8. Debt stock-flow reconciliation								
Total change in external debt stocks	125	39	-839	-1,023	-898	200	168	494
Net flows on external debt	90	44	246	255	304	233	155	500
9. Debt restructurings								
Total amount rescheduled	25	413	58	10	31	0	0	0
Total amount forgiven	10	19	779	1,511	1,193	62	8	1
Debt buyback	0	0	0	0	0	0	0	0

10. Contractual obligations on outstanding long-term external debt

	2011	2012	2013	2014	2015	2016	2017	2018
Official creditors								
Principal	87	88	96	124	138	144	158	166
Interest	66	80	83	84	82	79	76	72
Private creditors								
Principal	255	180	162	95	75	57	47	38
Interest	42	31	21	16	11	8	5	3

Notes:

Data for 2007 include the effects of MDRI, in the amount of $8,697 thousand.

INDIA

(US$ million, unless otherwise indicated)

	1995	2000	2005	2006	2007	2008	2009	2010
1. Summary external debt data								
External debt stocks	**95,174**	**100,243**	**120,222**	**158,501**	**202,929**	**225,994**	**249,993**	**290,282**
Long-term external debt	87,709	96,781	111,406	133,404	166,836	182,173	203,390	233,834
Public and publicly guaranteed	81,091	81,195	54,726	60,043	69,855	76,248	85,211	106,205
Private nonguaranteed	6,618	15,586	56,680	73,361	96,980	105,925	118,180	127,629
Use of IMF credit	2,416	0	0	0	0	0	0	0
Short-term external debt	5,049	3,462	8,816	25,097	36,093	43,821	46,603	56,448
interest arrears on long-term	0	0	0	0	0	0	0	0
Memorandum items								
Principal arrears on long-term	0	0	0	0	0	0	0	0
Long-term public sector debt	80,631	80,709	54,598	59,934	69,760	76,091	85,041	106,000
Long-term private sector debt	7,078	16,072	56,808	73,470	97,076	106,082	118,349	127,834
Public & publicly guaranteed commitments	4,914	10,707	3,340	6,555	11,986	8,402	12,729	13,663
External debt flows								
Disbursements	7,147	10,556	19,380	32,443	64,496	38,690	26,631	43,420
Long-term external debt	7,147	10,556	19,380	32,443	64,496	38,690	26,631	43,420
IMF purchases	0	0	0	0	0	0	0	0
Principal repayments	8,676	6,728	19,384	12,412	32,097	23,685	10,985	14,708
Long-term external debt	6,949	6,702	19,384	12,412	32,097	23,685	10,985	14,708
IMF repurchases	1,727	25	0	0	0	0	0	0
Net flows	-745	3,358	1,949	36,312	43,395	22,734	18,427	38,557
Long-term external debt	197	3,854	-3	20,031	32,399	15,005	15,646	28,712
Short-term external debt	785	-471	1,952	16,281	10,996	7,728	2,782	9,845
Interest payments	4,931	4,193	4,509	4,947	7,270	7,279	5,518	5,373
Long-term external debt	4,363	4,007	4,196	4,524	5,488	5,716	4,939	4,672
IMF charges	183	1	0	0	0	0	0	0
Short-term external debt	385	185	314	424	1,782	1,563	579	700
2. Other non-debt resource inflows								
Foreign direct investment	2,144	3,584	7,606	20,336	25,483	43,406	35,596	24,159
Portfolio equity	1,590	2,481	12,151	9,509	32,863	-15,030	21,112	39,972
3. Currency composition of public and publicly guaranteed debt (%)								
Euro	..	..	7.4	7.0	6.4	5.4	4.9	3.7
Japanese yen	15.1	12.6	20.0	20.3	19.1	23.0	20.3	19.0
Pound sterling	4.7	3.8	3.7	3.1	2.5	2.1	1.7	1.3
Swiss franc	0.9	0.3	0.3	0.3	0.2	0.2	0.1	0.1
U.S.dollars	52.0	66.3	65.6	66.1	67.3	64.4	67.6	71.4
4. Average terms of new commitments								
Official creditors								
Interest (%)	3.5	5.5	2.9	3.1	3.5	2.0	1.0	0.8
Maturity (years)	26.7	24.0	24.6	27.5	24.4	26.4	27.6	31.3
Grace period (years)	8.3	6.6	6.9	5.0	6.2	5.3	6.5	8.4
Private creditors								
Interest (%)	5.7	4.3	4.6	3.9	6.6	4.4	3.6	2.3
Maturity (years)	5.9	5.1	5.1	5.0	9.9	8.7	3.4	6.5
Grace period (years)	4.8	4.8	4.3	3.9	3.9	2.5	2.5	3.6
5. Major economic aggregates								
Gross national income (GNI)	352,268	455,206	828,137	943,976	1,237,315	1,206,624	1,372,631	1,717,580
Exports of goods, services & income	39,499	62,453	160,348	201,697	253,362	321,322	274,989	358,876
Worker remit. & comp. of employees	6,223	12,883	22,125	28,334	37,217	49,977	49,468	54,035
Imports of goods, services & income	53,444	80,489	194,274	239,713	298,582	401,046	350,203	462,815
Profit remittances on FDI	0	0	5,244	7,738	10,910	11,989	12,278	13,385
Current account balance	-5,563	-4,601	-10,284	-9,299	-8,076	-30,972	-25,922	-51,781
International reserves	22,865	41,059	137,825	178,050	276,578	257,423	284,683	300,480
6. Ratios								
External debt stocks to exports (%)	241.0	160.5	75.0	78.6	80.1	70.3	90.9	80.9
External debt stocks to GNI (%)	27.0	22.0	14.5	16.8	16.4	18.7	18.2	16.9
Debt service to exports (%)	34.4	17.5	14.9	8.6	15.5	9.6	6.0	5.6
Short-term to external debt stocks (%)	5.3	3.5	7.3	15.8	17.8	19.4	18.6	19.4
Multilateral to external debt stocks (%)	31.6	30.4	26.2	21.7	18.3	17.5	16.9	16.0
Reserves to external debt stocks (%)	24.0	41.0	114.6	112.3	136.3	113.9	113.9	103.5
Reserves to imports (months)	5.1	6.1	8.5	8.9	11.1	7.7	9.8	7.8

(US$ million, unless otherwise indicated)

7. Long-term external debt

	1995	2000	2005	2006	2007	2008	2009	2010
Debt outstanding and disbursed	**87,709**	**96,781**	**111,406**	**133,404**	**166,836**	**182,173**	**203,390**	**233,834**
Public and publicly guaranteed	81,091	81,195	54,726	60,043	69,855	76,248	85,211	106,205
Official creditors	57,595	51,709	49,992	52,867	57,269	62,523	65,868	72,641
Multilateral	30,052	30,474	31,448	34,408	37,227	39,436	42,351	46,531
of which: IBRD	9,849	7,078	5,276	6,007	6,680	7,429	8,382	11,180
IDA	17,499	18,888	22,728	24,433	25,319	25,365	26,050	25,888
Bilateral	27,543	21,235	18,543	18,459	20,042	23,087	23,516	26,111
Private creditors	23,496	29,486	4,734	7,176	12,587	13,725	19,343	33,564
of which: Bonds	3,324	10,240	1,360	2,213	4,664	4,520	9,521	20,430
Commercial banks	13,465	18,082	3,214	4,825	7,668	8,916	9,561	12,868
Private nonguaranteed	6,618	15,586	56,680	73,361	96,980	105,925	118,180	127,629
of which: Bonds	1,020	1,515	5,761	10,254	15,327	14,732	15,326	13,633
Disbursements	**7,147**	**10,556**	**19,380**	**32,443**	**64,496**	**38,690**	**26,631**	**43,420**
Public and publicly guaranteed	5,968	10,256	6,630	8,378	16,010	18,802	10,380	24,351
Official creditors	2,842	3,260	3,824	3,723	4,663	5,895	5,956	8,570
Multilateral	1,942	2,371	2,811	2,732	3,184	3,701	4,157	6,237
of which: IBRD	589	706	863	979	1,003	1,122	1,408	3,334
IDA	729	1,054	1,290	1,005	802	961	1,263	1,067
Bilateral	900	888	1,013	991	1,479	2,195	1,798	2,334
Private creditors	3,125	6,996	2,805	4,655	11,347	12,907	4,425	15,781
of which: Bonds	85	5,520	1,714	2,452	7,389	11,507	1,765	11,050
Commercial banks	1,719	878	1,091	2,203	3,831	1,400	2,660	4,731
Private nonguaranteed	1,179	300	12,751	24,066	48,486	19,888	16,250	19,069
of which: Bonds	520	0	2,920	4,549	7,793	594	2,473	1,288
Principal repayments	**6,949**	**6,702**	**19,384**	**12,412**	**32,097**	**23,685**	**10,985**	**14,708**
Public and publicly guaranteed	6,793	6,454	12,469	4,796	8,842	13,447	5,331	5,190
Official creditors	3,885	3,493	2,689	2,588	2,380	2,989	2,906	3,169
Multilateral	1,513	1,740	951	1,155	1,200	1,347	1,476	1,661
of which: IBRD	943	994	210	259	346	390	455	539
IDA	226	367	607	653	700	764	799	835
Bilateral	2,372	1,754	1,738	1,433	1,180	1,642	1,429	1,508
Private creditors	2,908	2,960	9,781	2,208	6,462	10,458	2,425	2,021
of which: Bonds	320	0	8,457	1,597	5,313	9,468	588	148
Commercial banks	1,807	2,737	1,193	589	1,130	971	1,814	1,849
Private nonguaranteed	156	249	6,914	7,617	23,255	10,238	5,654	9,518
of which: Bonds	0	35	117	57	409	880	1,679	1,851
Interest payments	**4,363**	**4,007**	**4,196**	**4,524**	**5,488**	**5,716**	**4,939**	**4,672**
Public and publicly guaranteed	3,832	3,378	3,022	1,291	1,450	1,522	1,319	1,060
Official creditors	1,872	1,435	1,059	1,074	1,170	1,160	1,008	794
Multilateral	1,061	835	458	648	782	747	558	361
of which: IBRD	770	428	159	280	356	313	213	86
IDA	131	139	187	185	189	201	186	189
Bilateral	811	601	601	426	388	413	450	433
Private creditors	1,960	1,942	1,963	217	280	362	311	266
of which: Bonds	187	143	1,799	40	41	61	60	39
Commercial banks	1,265	1,737	155	172	233	294	244	221
Private nonguaranteed	531	630	1,174	3,233	4,038	4,194	3,620	3,612
of which: Bonds	56	224	141	217	330	278	290	421

8. Debt stock-flow reconciliation

	1995	2000	2005	2006	2007	2008	2009	2010
Total change in external debt stocks	-4,435	1,115	-2,365	38,279	44,428	23,066	23,999	40,289
Net flows on external debt	-745	3,358	1,949	36,312	43,395	22,734	18,427	38,557

9. Debt restructurings

	1995	2000	2005	2006	2007	2008	2009	2010
Total amount rescheduled	0	0	0	0	0	0	0	0
Total amount forgiven	0	0	0	0	0	0	0	0
Debt buyback	0	0	0	0	0	0	0	0

10. Contractual obligations on outstanding long-term external debt

	2011	2012	2013	2014	2015	2016	2017	2018
Official creditors								
Principal	5,164	5,376	5,703	5,924	5,990	5,874	5,882	5,680
Interest	1,103	1,090	1,041	977	901	822	742	662
Private creditors								
Principal	39,155	33,797	25,513	17,776	13,619	9,158	6,758	5,363
Interest	6,071	4,520	3,955	2,460	1,799	1,295	917	602

Notes:

External debt data prior to 2003 are mechanically adjusted from fiscal year to calendar year. Public and publicly guaranteed bonds include Foreign Institutional Investor debt (FII) as reported by the Reserve Bank of India. Short-term debt is based on reports provided by the country.

INDONESIA

(US$ million, unless otherwise indicated)

	1995	2000	2005	2006	2007	2008	2009	2010
1. Summary external debt data								
External debt stocks	**124,389**	**143,344**	**134,347**	**125,343**	**133,847**	**147,622**	**162,850**	**179,064**
Long-term external debt	98,422	110,818	117,506	115,359	118,399	127,134	138,801	147,809
Public and publicly guaranteed	65,299	69,649	74,242	70,536	72,015	79,751	85,967	91,024
Private nonguaranteed	33,123	41,169	43,264	44,822	46,384	47,383	52,834	56,785
Use of IMF credit	0	10,838	7,807	0	0	0	0	0
Short-term external debt	25,966	21,688	9,034	9,984	15,448	20,488	24,050	31,255
interest arrears on long-term	0	4,632	0	0	0	0	0	0
Memorandum items								
Principal arrears on long-term	0	3,000	148	0	0	0	0	0
Long-term public sector debt	65,299	69,649	74,242	70,536	72,015	79,751	85,967	91,024
Long-term private sector debt	33,123	41,169	43,264	44,822	46,384	47,383	52,834	56,785
Public & publicly guaranteed commitments	11,003	2,221	4,541	4,727	5,880	9,720	14,791	7,864
External debt flows								
Disbursements	13,633	6,774	13,879	18,472	18,270	22,928	31,424	31,214
Long-term external debt	13,633	5,651	13,879	18,472	18,270	22,928	31,424	31,214
IMF purchases	0	1,123	0	0	0	0	0	0
Principal repayments	10,198	9,268	16,891	24,463	18,811	16,703	20,419	23,963
Long-term external debt	10,198	9,268	15,746	16,426	18,811	16,703	20,419	23,963
IMF repurchases	0	0	1,145	8,037	0	0	0	0
Net flows	9,945	-1,967	-8,603	-5,041	4,923	11,265	14,566	14,456
Long-term external debt	3,435	-3,617	-1,868	2,046	-541	6,225	11,005	7,251
Short-term external debt	6,509	527	-5,590	950	5,464	5,040	3,561	7,205
Interest payments	6,220	7,356	3,337	3,817	5,113	4,671	4,459	5,335
Long-term external debt	4,936	5,673	2,933	3,416	4,996	4,461	4,301	4,944
IMF charges	0	526	313	292	0	0	0	0
Short-term external debt	1,284	1,157	91	109	117	210	159	391
2. Other non-debt resource inflows								
Foreign direct investment	4,346	-4,550	8,336	4,914	6,928	9,318	4,877	13,304
Portfolio equity	1,493	-1,021	-165	1,898	3,559	322	787	2,132
3. Currency composition of public and publicly guaranteed debt (%)								
Euro	..	..	13.3	14.4	14.7	11.6	10.0	8.0
Japanese yen	35.3	33.1	33.8	34.0	33.5	36.6	32.4	34.7
Pound sterling	0.8	1.2	2.2	2.0	1.8	1.1	1.0	0.8
Swiss franc	0.7	0.6	0.6	0.6	0.5	0.4	0.4	0.3
U.S.dollars	21.5	50.3	45.4	44.3	44.7	45.6	51.8	51.8
4. Average terms of new commitments								
Official creditors								
Interest (%)	5.1	2.9	3.9	3.9	2.8	1.9	1.7	1.0
Maturity (years)	21.4	24.5	23.5	25.7	25.0	20.4	22.2	22.2
Grace period (years)	5.8	6.8	6.1	6.7	7.5	6.9	5.5	7.8
Private creditors								
Interest (%)	6.8	6.6	6.9	7.2	6.4	6.9	9.6	4.6
Maturity (years)	12.4	7.7	14.7	20.9	27.4	18.0	8.0	9.9
Grace period (years)	3.8	4.4	12.9	18.3	26.6	17.4	7.7	9.4
5. Major economic aggregates								
Gross national income (GNI)	196,188	150,317	271,958	349,038	414,334	492,094	520,467	686,633
Exports of goods, services & income	54,229	73,079	102,260	117,635	133,971	158,444	134,722	176,730
Worker remit. & comp. of employees	651	1,190	5,420	5,722	6,174	6,794	6,793	6,916
Imports of goods, services & income	61,641	66,903	106,775	111,639	128,582	163,683	128,671	175,713
Profit remittances on FDI	718	3,574	9,525	9,637	10,813	10,675	8,848	12,436
Current account balance	-6,431	7,992	278	10,859	10,493	125	10,628	5,654
International reserves	14,908	29,353	34,731	42,597	56,936	51,641	66,119	96,211
6. Ratios								
External debt stocks to exports (%)	229.4	196.1	131.4	106.6	99.9	93.2	120.9	101.3
External debt stocks to GNI (%)	63.4	95.4	49.4	35.9	32.3	30.0	31.3	26.1
Debt service to exports (%)	30.3	22.7	19.8	24.0	17.9	13.5	18.5	16.6
Short-term to external debt stocks (%)	20.9	15.1	6.7	8.0	11.5	13.9	14.8	17.5
Multilateral to external debt stocks (%)	16.1	13.9	13.8	14.6	13.9	13.5	12.9	12.6
Reserves to external debt stocks (%)	12.0	20.5	25.9	34.0	42.5	35.0	40.6	53.7
Reserves to imports (months)	2.9	5.3	3.9	4.6	5.3	3.8	6.2	6.6

(US$ million, unless otherwise indicated)

	1995	2000	2005	2006	2007	2008	2009	2010
7. Long-term external debt								
Debt outstanding and disbursed	**98,422**	**110,818**	**117,506**	**115,359**	**118,399**	**127,134**	**138,801**	**147,809**
Public and publicly guaranteed	65,299	69,649	74,242	70,536	72,015	79,751	85,967	91,024
Official creditors	51,272	54,883	59,945	58,422	58,720	63,184	63,270	66,484
Multilateral	20,013	19,904	18,514	18,246	18,611	19,962	21,052	22,567
of which: IBRD	12,503	11,715	8,132	7,423	6,821	6,968	7,876	9,054
IDA	756	714	1,001	1,318	1,550	2,006	2,234	2,313
Bilateral	31,260	34,979	41,431	40,176	40,109	43,222	42,218	43,917
Private creditors	14,027	14,766	14,297	12,114	13,296	16,567	22,696	24,540
of which: Bonds	704	971	4,029	5,157	6,370	10,450	14,344	16,990
Commercial banks	7,178	10,489	8,062	5,090	5,168	4,640	5,810	5,313
Private nonguaranteed	33,123	41,169	43,264	44,822	46,384	47,383	52,834	56,785
of which: Bonds	3,420	6,337	5,878	6,222	4,668	4,678	5,897	5,788
Disbursements	**13,633**	**5,651**	**13,879**	**18,472**	**18,270**	**22,928**	**31,424**	**31,214**
Public and publicly guaranteed	6,670	3,301	5,012	7,121	6,030	9,062	12,729	11,224
Official creditors	4,254	3,038	2,578	3,798	3,756	4,599	6,142	6,560
Multilateral	1,777	1,750	1,667	1,876	2,134	2,842	3,020	3,186
of which: IBRD	1,045	1,051	585	696	767	1,398	2,044	2,078
IDA	0	59	67	315	219	494	244	142
Bilateral	2,477	1,288	911	1,922	1,622	1,758	3,122	3,375
Private creditors	2,416	263	2,434	3,323	2,273	4,462	6,587	4,663
of which: Bonds	605	0	2,095	1,930	1,425	4,080	3,893	2,545
Commercial banks	1,010	258	264	947	552	378	1,656	1,185
Private nonguaranteed	6,963	2,350	8,866	11,351	12,240	13,867	18,695	19,990
of which: Bonds	1,763	350	194	144	486	368	1,808	195
Principal repayments	**10,198**	**9,268**	**15,746**	**16,426**	**18,811**	**16,703**	**20,419**	**23,963**
Public and publicly guaranteed	5,715	3,868	6,232	6,925	8,062	6,482	7,051	5,833
Official creditors	3,127	1,586	3,539	5,365	6,781	5,729	6,122	5,202
Multilateral	1,289	1,116	1,957	1,976	1,971	1,920	1,910	1,819
of which: IBRD	955	761	1,390	1,403	1,369	1,252	1,135	900
IDA	20	26	27	27	27	27	31	32
Bilateral	1,838	470	1,583	3,389	4,810	3,809	4,212	3,383
Private creditors	2,589	2,282	2,692	1,560	1,281	753	929	632
of which: Bonds	0	0	310	252	212	0	0	0
Commercial banks	1,681	2,107	1,679	982	679	594	767	476
Private nonguaranteed	4,483	5,400	9,515	9,501	10,749	10,221	13,368	18,129
of which: Bonds	120	2,400	267	257	432	261	388	411
Interest payments	**4,936**	**5,673**	**2,933**	**3,416**	**4,996**	**4,461**	**4,301**	**4,944**
Public and publicly guaranteed	3,775	3,738	1,921	2,118	2,730	2,718	2,802	3,034
Official creditors	2,667	2,575	1,189	1,712	2,042	1,968	1,693	1,586
Multilateral	1,403	1,383	865	832	861	789	584	514
of which: IBRD	921	950	481	425	435	370	249	291
IDA	6	5	9	10	11	13	15	16
Bilateral	1,264	1,192	324	880	1,180	1,179	1,109	1,072
Private creditors	1,107	1,163	732	406	689	751	1,109	1,448
of which: Bonds	6	72	136	97	331	439	837	1,225
Commercial banks	676	871	510	195	251	220	187	148
Private nonguaranteed	1,161	1,935	1,012	1,298	2,266	1,743	1,499	1,910
of which: Bonds	139	735	113	184	202	89	31	81
8. Debt stock-flow reconciliation								
Total change in external debt stocks	16,580	-8,117	-2,770	-9,004	8,504	13,775	15,228	16,213
Net flows on external debt	9,945	-1,967	-8,603	-5,041	4,923	11,265	14,566	14,456
9. Debt restructurings								
Total amount rescheduled	0	2,461	2,608	0	0	0	0	0
Total amount forgiven	0	0	0	92	0	0	0	0
Debt buyback	0	0	0	0	0	0	0	0

10. Contractual obligations on outstanding long-term external debt

	2011	2012	2013	2014	2015	2016	2017	2018
Official creditors								
Principal	6,342	6,159	6,453	6,122	5,790	5,190	4,558	4,426
Interest	1,437	1,316	1,187	1,043	902	770	659	563
Private creditors								
Principal	12,301	9,216	10,832	10,281	6,032	3,275	2,718	6,950
Interest	3,711	3,360	3,199	2,887	2,199	1,882	1,632	1,949

Notes:

Debt data are revised significantly as previous publications included local currency external debt. Data on long-term private nonguaranteed debt data might include short-term debt data until 2005 and are revised based on reports provided by the country from 2006. Short-term debt is based on reports provided by the country since 2005.

IRAN, ISLAMIC REPUBLIC OF

(US$ million, unless otherwise indicated)

	1995	*2000*	*2005*	*2006*	*2007*	*2008*	*2009*	*2010*
1. Summary external debt data								
External debt stocks	**21,565**	**7,717**	**21,879**	**19,387**	**21,074**	**13,969**	**13,464**	**12,570**
Long-term external debt	15,116	4,709	10,521	11,128	11,174	8,934	7,553	6,411
Public and publicly guaranteed	15,116	4,709	10,521	11,128	11,174	8,934	7,553	6,411
Private nonguaranteed	0	0	0	0	0	0	0	0
Use of IMF credit	0	0	0	0	0	0	0	0
Short-term external debt	6,449	3,008	11,358	8,259	9,900	5,035	5,911	6,159
interest arrears on long-term	6	0	0	0	0	0	0	0
Memorandum items								
Principal arrears on long-term	48	0	0	0	0	0	0	0
Long-term public sector debt	15,031	4,689	10,512	11,121	11,168	8,931	7,543	6,398
Long-term private sector debt	84	20	10	7	6	3	9	13
Public & publicly guaranteed commitments	1,978	2,813	1,992	797	0	35	44	21
External debt flows								
Disbursements	979	1,469	2,751	1,724	1,142	978	531	295
Long-term external debt	979	1,469	2,751	1,724	1,142	978	531	295
IMF purchases	0	0	0	0	0	0	0	0
Principal repayments	4,120	2,345	1,734	1,718	2,009	2,161	2,092	1,595
Long-term external debt	4,120	2,345	1,734	1,718	2,009	2,161	2,092	1,595
IMF repurchases	0	0	0	0	0	0	0	0
Net flows	-227	-1,485	1,439	-3,093	774	-6,049	-685	-1,052
Long-term external debt	-3,141	-876	1,017	6	-867	-1,184	-1,561	-1,300
Short-term external debt	2,914	-609	422	-3,099	1,641	-4,865	876	248
Interest payments	1,602	572	1,099	1,033	946	616	485	371
Long-term external debt	1,107	391	419	509	572	502	278	139
IMF charges	0	0	0	0	0	0	0	0
Short-term external debt	494	180	680	524	374	114	207	232
2. Other non-debt resource inflows								
Foreign direct investment	17	39	3,136	1,647	1,670	1,615	3,016	3,617
Portfolio equity	0	0	..	..	..	..	..	..
3. Currency composition of public and publicly guaranteed debt (%)								
Euro	..	..	52.3	55.9	58.8	57.2	57.3	56.9
Japanese yen	4.9	9.4	8.1	6.8	6.9	7.3	7.4	7.5
Pound sterling	0.0	0.6	0.1	0.1	0.0	0.0	0.0	0.0
Swiss franc	0.6	3.9	4.4	3.6	3.4	2.7	2.4	2.3
U.S.dollars	71.5	68.3	34.9	33.4	30.7	32.6	32.7	33.1
4. Average terms of new commitments								
Official creditors								
Interest (%)	7.5	4.9	4.4	5.9	0.0	0.0	3.9	0.0
Maturity (years)	8.2	13.6	15.0	11.8	0.0	0.0	6.5	0.0
Grace period (years)	2.3	4.4	4.4	3.8	0.0	0.0	2.4	0.0
Private creditors								
Interest (%)	6.3	6.6	4.9	6.0	0.0	5.6	5.4	4.4
Maturity (years)	11.3	10.8	10.1	10.0	0.0	6.7	6.0	7.2
Grace period (years)	3.4	2.9	2.6	2.5	0.0	2.2	1.5	2.7
5. Major economic aggregates								
Gross national income (GNI)	90,172	101,335	188,503	219,296	283,000	335,654	328,593	..
Exports of goods, services & income	19,269	30,131	..	..	..	..	..	..
Worker remit. & comp. of employees	1,600	536	1,032	1,032	1,115	1,115	1,072	1,181
Imports of goods, services & income	15,907	18,107	..	..	..	..	..	..
Profit remittances on FDI	0	0	..	..	..	..	..	..
Current account balance	3,358	12,481	..	..	..	..	..	..
International reserves	..	..	..	..	..	..	..	..
6. Ratios								
External debt stocks to exports (%)	111.9	25.6	..	..	..	..	..	..
External debt stocks to GNI (%)	23.9	7.6	11.6	8.8	7.4	4.2	4.1	..
Debt service to exports (%)	29.7	9.7	..	..	..	..	..	..
Short-term to external debt stocks (%)	29.9	39.0	51.9	42.6	47.0	36.0	43.9	49.0
Multilateral to external debt stocks (%)	1.8	6.6	1.7	2.9	3.3	5.4	6.3	6.6
Reserves to external debt stocks (%)	..	..	..	..	..	..	..	..
Reserves to imports (months)	..	..	..	..	..	..	..	..

IRAN, ISLAMIC REPUBLIC OF

(US$ million, unless otherwise indicated)

	1995	2000	2005	2006	2007	2008	2009	2010
7. Long-term external debt								
Debt outstanding and disbursed	**15,116**	**4,709**	**10,521**	**11,128**	**11,174**	**8,934**	**7,553**	**6,411**
Public and publicly guaranteed	15,116	4,709	10,521	11,128	11,174	8,934	7,553	6,411
Official creditors	11,354	1,664	2,045	2,284	2,436	2,389	2,272	2,025
Multilateral	381	507	381	559	699	761	854	830
of which: IBRD	316	481	378	559	699	761	836	801
IDA	0	0	0	0	0	0	0	0
Bilateral	10,974	1,157	1,663	1,725	1,737	1,628	1,418	1,195
Private creditors	3,761	3,045	8,477	8,844	8,738	6,545	5,280	4,385
of which: Bonds	0	0	0	0	0	0	0	0
Commercial banks	5	1,043	4,042	4,536	4,800	3,820	3,165	2,723
Private nonguaranteed	0	0	0	0	0	0	0	0
of which: Bonds	0	0	0	0	0	0	0	0
Disbursements	**979**	**1,469**	**2,751**	**1,724**	**1,142**	**978**	**531**	**295**
Public and publicly guaranteed	979	1,469	2,751	1,724	1,142	978	531	295
Official creditors	393	477	673	508	338	295	228	101
Multilateral	123	120	258	248	212	144	178	85
of which: IBRD	85	114	247	248	212	144	159	72
IDA	0	0	0	0	0	0	0	0
Bilateral	270	357	415	261	125	152	50	16
Private creditors	586	993	2,078	1,216	805	682	303	193
of which: Bonds	0	0	0	0	0	0	0	0
Commercial banks	1	268	1,399	941	653	605	276	180
Private nonguaranteed	0	0	0	0	0	0	0	0
of which: Bonds	0	0	0	0	0	0	0	0
Principal repayments	**4,120**	**2,345**	**1,734**	**1,718**	**2,009**	**2,161**	**2,092**	**1,595**
Public and publicly guaranteed	4,120	2,345	1,734	1,718	2,009	2,161	2,092	1,595
Official creditors	3,497	1,785	329	275	302	331	381	317
Multilateral	41	108	155	75	73	66	84	11
of which: IBRD	6	70	145	66	73	66	84	8
IDA	0	0	0	0	0	0	0	0
Bilateral	3,456	1,677	174	199	229	264	297	306
Private creditors	622	561	1,405	1,443	1,707	1,831	1,710	1,277
of which: Bonds	0	0	0	0	0	0	0	0
Commercial banks	1	67	713	689	932	1,051	1,006	726
Private nonguaranteed	0	0	0	0	0	0	0	0
of which: Bonds	0	0	0	0	0	0	0	0
Interest payments	**1,107**	**391**	**419**	**509**	**572**	**502**	**278**	**139**
Public and publicly guaranteed	1,107	391	419	509	572	502	278	139
Official creditors	787	190	103	98	114	89	73	53
Multilateral	27	44	39	25	36	25	15	8
of which: IBRD	19	40	39	25	36	25	15	8
IDA	0	0	0	0	0	0	0	0
Bilateral	759	146	63	73	78	64	58	45
Private creditors	321	202	316	410	458	413	205	86
of which: Bonds	0	0	0	0	0	0	0	0
Commercial banks	0	82	155	220	264	237	122	51
Private nonguaranteed	0	0	0	0	0	0	0	0
of which: Bonds	0	0	0	0	0	0	0	0
8. Debt stock-flow reconciliation								
Total change in external debt stocks	-677	-1,629	941	-2,492	1,686	-7,105	-505	-894
Net flows on external debt	-227	-1,485	1,439	-3,093	774	-6,049	-685	-1,052
9. Debt restructurings								
Total amount rescheduled	3,178	0	0	0	0	0	0	0
Total amount forgiven	0	0	0	0	0	0	0	0
Debt buyback	0	0	0	0	0	0	0	0

10. Contractual obligations on outstanding long-term external debt

	2011	2012	2013	2014	2015	2016	2017	2018
Official creditors								
Principal	480	443	272	230	161	144	103	81
Interest	43	30	21	15	11	7	5	3
Private creditors								
Principal	1,600	1,230	845	544	348	200	80	7
Interest	66	43	26	14	7	2	1	0

Notes:

Fiscal year-end for external debt data is March.

JAMAICA

(US$ million, unless otherwise indicated)

	1995	2000	2005	2006	2007	2008	2009	2010
1. Summary external debt data								
External debt stocks	**4,581**	**4,724**	**6,531**	**8,059**	**10,422**	**10,331**	**10,987**	**13,865**
Long-term external debt	3,849	3,871	5,914	6,956	8,883	9,068	9,943	11,900
Public and publicly guaranteed	3,721	3,768	5,524	6,144	6,710	6,904	6,702	7,593
Private nonguaranteed	128	103	390	811	2,173	2,164	3,241	4,307
Use of IMF credit	240	60	0	0	0	0	0	785
Short-term external debt	492	793	617	1,103	1,539	1,263	1,044	1,180
interest arrears on long-term	102	150	225	261	284	267	229	219
Memorandum items								
Principal arrears on long-term	203	131	146	219	157	146	176	153
Long-term public sector debt	3,721	3,767	5,523	6,143	6,709	6,902	6,701	7,592
Long-term private sector debt	128	104	391	813	2,174	2,165	3,242	4,308
Public & publicly guaranteed commitments	234	1,066	1,123	886	809	760	989	1,346
External debt flows								
Disbursements	316	904	1,346	1,216	2,396	692	1,539	3,138
Long-term external debt	305	904	1,346	1,216	2,396	692	1,539	2,360
IMF purchases	11	0	0	0	0	0	0	778
Principal repayments	436	443	551	312	590	459	702	340
Long-term external debt	340	424	550	312	590	459	702	340
IMF repurchases	95	19	1	0	0	0	0	0
Net flows	-106	440	317	1,354	2,219	-26	656	2,944
Long-term external debt	-35	481	797	904	1,806	233	837	2,020
Short-term external debt	14	-21	-479	450	413	-259	-181	146
Interest payments	232	261	419	512	717	700	758	846
Long-term external debt	191	208	387	473	657	673	746	828
IMF charges	17	4	0	0	0	0	0	6
Short-term external debt	24	49	32	39	60	27	12	11
2. Other non-debt resource inflows								
Foreign direct investment	147	468	682	882	866	1,437	541	228
Portfolio equity	0	0	0	0	0	0	0	0
3. Currency composition of public and publicly guaranteed debt (%)								
Euro	..	..	17.9	20.4	22.2	20.3	17.2	14.8
Japanese yen	9.9	7.1	3.4	2.8	2.4	2.7	2.6	2.5
Pound sterling	4.1	2.0	1.5	1.4	1.2	0.5	0.6	0.5
Swiss franc	0.0	0.0	0.0	0.0	0.0	0.0	0.0	0.0
U.S.dollars	47.6	61.7	70.1	70.0	69.8	72.6	76.3	79.6
4. Average terms of new commitments								
Official creditors								
Interest (%)	5.6	6.1	4.1	1.4	3.2	4.1	3.7	1.4
Maturity (years)	21.6	19.8	22.0	18.6	19.8	23.3	16.5	20.4
Grace period (years)	4.7	5.4	5.7	16.9	5.1	5.7	4.2	5.2
Private creditors								
Interest (%)	6.3	11.0	8.2	7.9	7.7	7.5	2.9	0.0
Maturity (years)	8.9	6.0	12.8	20.6	27.2	10.8	11.2	0.0
Grace period (years)	2.1	4.2	10.6	15.3	23.0	8.2	1.4	0.0
5. Major economic aggregates								
Gross national income (GNI)	5,569	8,662	10,476	11,375	12,037	13,559	12,018	13,305
Exports of goods, services & income	3,541	3,782	4,322	5,161	5,590	6,027	4,273	4,248
Worker remit. & comp. of employees	653	892	1,784	1,946	2,144	2,181	1,912	2,011
Imports of goods, services & income	4,246	4,970	6,972	8,092	9,668	10,970	7,259	7,192
Profit remittances on FDI	230	290	454	376	533	376	232	127
Current account balance	-99	-367	-1,071	-1,183	-2,038	-2,793	-1,128	-934
International reserves	681	1,054	2,170	2,318	1,879	1,773	2,076	2,501
6. Ratios								
External debt stocks to exports (%)	129.4	124.9	151.1	156.2	186.4	171.4	257.1	326.4
External debt stocks to GNI (%)	82.3	54.5	62.3	70.8	86.6	76.2	91.4	104.2
Debt service to exports (%)	18.8	18.6	22.4	16.0	23.4	19.2	34.1	27.9
Short-term to external debt stocks (%)	10.7	16.8	9.4	13.7	14.8	12.2	9.5	8.5
Multilateral to external debt stocks (%)	26.9	25.8	20.4	16.1	12.1	12.9	13.8	16.9
Reserves to external debt stocks (%)	14.9	22.3	33.2	28.8	18.0	17.2	18.9	18.0
Reserves to imports (months)	1.9	2.5	3.7	3.4	2.3	1.9	3.4	4.2

(US$ million, unless otherwise indicated)

	1995	2000	2005	2006	2007	2008	2009	2010
7. Long-term external debt								
Debt outstanding and disbursed	**3,849**	**3,871**	**5,914**	**6,956**	**8,883**	**9,068**	**9,943**	**11,900**
Public and publicly guaranteed	3,721	3,768	5,524	6,144	6,710	6,904	6,702	7,593
Official creditors	3,363	2,449	2,124	2,157	2,258	2,271	2,406	3,259
Multilateral	1,234	1,218	1,333	1,298	1,260	1,336	1,520	2,348
of which: IBRD	595	415	410	387	360	327	398	579
IDA	0	0	0	0	0	0	0	0
Bilateral	2,129	1,231	791	859	998	935	886	912
Private creditors	358	1,320	3,400	3,988	4,452	4,633	4,296	4,334
of which: Bonds	25	1,004	3,043	3,568	4,050	4,218	3,890	3,786
Commercial banks	269	265	317	385	357	380	365	505
Private nonguaranteed	128	103	390	811	2,173	2,164	3,241	4,307
of which: Bonds	55	0	300	730	2,130	2,130	3,215	4,290
Disbursements	**305**	**904**	**1,346**	**1,216**	**2,396**	**692**	**1,539**	**2,360**
Public and publicly guaranteed	250	904	1,039	786	996	692	454	1,285
Official creditors	193	311	87	234	274	266	350	1,075
Multilateral	125	255	67	82	93	219	336	971
of which: IBRD	61	98	17	18	19	13	120	222
IDA	0	0	0	0	0	0	0	0
Bilateral	68	57	20	153	182	47	14	104
Private creditors	57	593	952	552	722	426	104	210
of which: Bonds	13	553	875	450	625	350	0	0
Commercial banks	42	24	75	97	80	76	94	198
Private nonguaranteed	55	0	307	430	1,400	0	1,085	1,075
of which: Bonds	0	0	300	430	1,400	0	1,085	1,075
Principal repayments	**340**	**424**	**550**	**312**	**590**	**459**	**702**	**340**
Public and publicly guaranteed	335	360	541	303	567	450	693	331
Official creditors	255	273	231	246	244	260	229	208
Multilateral	127	122	119	137	154	148	153	136
of which: IBRD	85	60	39	43	48	47	49	41
IDA	0	0	0	0	0	0	0	0
Bilateral	129	151	113	109	89	113	76	72
Private creditors	80	87	310	58	324	190	464	124
of which: Bonds	0	13	256	0	229	138	345	68
Commercial banks	73	47	44	44	85	44	113	48
Private nonguaranteed	5	64	9	9	22	9	9	9
of which: Bonds	0	55	0	0	0	0	0	0
Interest payments	**191**	**208**	**387**	**473**	**657**	**673**	**746**	**828**
Public and publicly guaranteed	181	195	361	422	472	480	521	488
Official creditors	158	120	84	91	90	80	95	100
Multilateral	83	65	63	67	69	62	59	51
of which: IBRD	47	22	19	22	22	19	15	12
IDA	0	0	0	0	0	0	0	0
Bilateral	75	55	21	24	21	18	36	49
Private creditors	23	75	277	332	382	400	426	388
of which: Bonds	2	50	265	325	373	392	404	375
Commercial banks	19	18	11	6	8	7	21	12
Private nonguaranteed	11	13	26	51	185	193	225	341
of which: Bonds	5	2	21	45	181	191	224	340
8. Debt stock-flow reconciliation								
Total change in external debt stocks	-29	798	80	1,528	2,363	-91	656	2,878
Net flows on external debt	-106	440	317	1,354	2,219	-26	656	2,944
9. Debt restructurings								
Total amount rescheduled	105	0	0	0	0	0	0	0
Total amount forgiven	0	4	2	3	2	6	0	5
Debt buyback	0	0	0	0	0	0	0	0

10. Contractual obligations on outstanding long-term external debt

	2011	2012	2013	2014	2015	2016	2017	2018
Official creditors								
Principal	224	230	225	184	237	262	252	237
Interest	70	66	62	57	53	48	43	38
Private creditors								
Principal	529	854	224	909	1,937	259	1,422	960
Interest	754	717	643	586	462	369	295	185

JORDAN

(US$ million, unless otherwise indicated)

	1995	2000	2005	2006	2007	2008	2009	2010
1. Summary external debt data								
External debt stocks	**7,661**	**7,355**	**7,696**	**8,055**	**8,371**	**6,580**	**6,615**	**7,822**
Long-term external debt	6,624	6,183	6,878	7,143	7,321	5,126	5,445	6,504
Public and publicly guaranteed	6,624	6,183	6,878	7,143	7,321	5,126	5,445	6,504
Private nonguaranteed	0	0	0	0	0	0	0	0
Use of IMF credit	251	462	236	158	88	28	12	8
Short-term external debt	785	710	582	754	962	1,426	1,158	1,310
interest arrears on long-term	67	102	0	1	0	0	0	1
Memorandum items								
Principal arrears on long-term	177	281	17	36	34	34	17	17
Long-term public sector debt	6,624	6,148	6,790	7,000	7,172	4,978	5,306	6,371
Long-term private sector debt	0	35	88	142	150	148	139	133
Public & publicly guaranteed commitments	1,259	384	337	159	220	427	915	1,226
External debt flows								
Disbursements	724	196	434	277	190	230	762	1,389
Long-term external debt	609	176	434	277	190	230	762	1,389
IMF purchases	115	20	0	0	0	0	0	0
Principal repayments	337	424	418	441	486	2,471	421	491
Long-term external debt	329	393	341	353	409	2,412	405	487
IMF repurchases	8	31	77	88	76	59	16	4
Net flows	484	-399	97	7	-87	-1,777	73	1,049
Long-term external debt	280	-217	93	-76	-220	-2,182	357	902
Short-term external debt	97	-171	81	171	209	464	-268	151
Interest payments	263	315	198	249	284	232	164	162
Long-term external debt	209	239	160	196	227	200	147	147
IMF charges	10	24	10	10	7	3	0	0
Short-term external debt	43	52	27	42	49	29	17	16
2. Other non-debt resource inflows								
Foreign direct investment	13	913	1,984	3,544	2,622	2,827	2,427	1,701
Portfolio equity	0	-17	169	144	346	521	-30	-20
3. Currency composition of public and publicly guaranteed debt (%)								
Euro	..	..	21.1	23.3	24.1	12.6	12.0	9.3
Japanese yen	25.6	27.5	20.1	18.3	17.8	29.9	25.9	22.6
Pound sterling	5.5	3.4	8.9	9.3	9.3	0.0	0.0	0.0
Swiss franc	0.5	0.4	1.1	0.7	0.7	0.3	0.3	0.2
U.S.dollars	28.9	29.3	26.4	25.9	25.3	24.8	31.1	37.1
4. Average terms of new commitments								
Official creditors								
Interest (%)	4.7	4.8	2.9	3.4	4.6	3.4	2.1	2.0
Maturity (years)	21.8	19.5	23.6	21.1	20.5	20.8	18.1	13.2
Grace period (years)	8.4	6.4	6.0	5.8	6.0	5.7	4.6	4.0
Private creditors								
Interest (%)	0.0	0.0	0.0	0.2	0.0	0.0	0.0	3.9
Maturity (years)	0.0	0.0	0.0	34.3	0.0	0.0	0.0	5.0
Grace period (years)	0.0	0.0	0.0	11.3	0.0	0.0	0.0	4.9
5. Major economic aggregates								
Gross national income (GNI)	6,449	8,561	12,925	16,098	18,449	23,392	25,696	28,081
Exports of goods, services & income	3,594	4,207	7,426	9,144	10,684	13,751	12,098	13,268
Worker remit. & comp. of employees	1,441	1,845	2,500	2,883	3,434	3,794	3,597	3,641
Imports of goods, services & income	5,297	6,363	12,314	13,810	16,421	19,869	17,024	18,521
Profit remittances on FDI	0	33	74	130	163	257	294	283
Current account balance	-259	27	-2,272	-1,726	-2,875	-2,037	-1,128	-1,311
International reserves	2,279	3,441	5,461	6,982	7,925	8,918	12,135	13,633
6. Ratios								
External debt stocks to exports (%)	213.1	174.8	103.6	88.1	78.4	47.9	54.7	59.0
External debt stocks to GNI (%)	118.8	85.9	59.5	50.0	45.4	28.1	25.7	27.9
Debt service to exports (%)	16.7	17.6	8.3	7.5	7.2	19.7	4.8	4.9
Short-term to external debt stocks (%)	10.2	9.7	7.6	9.4	11.5	21.7	17.5	16.7
Multilateral to external debt stocks (%)	15.5	23.2	24.8	24.3	23.7	29.7	35.7	32.3
Reserves to external debt stocks (%)	29.8	46.8	71.0	86.7	94.7	135.5	183.4	174.3
Reserves to imports (months)	5.2	6.5	5.3	6.1	5.8	5.4	8.6	8.8

(US$ million, unless otherwise indicated)

	1995	2000	2005	2006	2007	2008	2009	2010
7. Long-term external debt								
Debt outstanding and disbursed	**6,624**	**6,183**	**6,878**	**7,143**	**7,321**	**5,126**	**5,445**	**6,504**
Public and publicly guaranteed	6,624	6,183	6,878	7,143	7,321	5,126	5,445	6,504
Official creditors	4,583	5,190	6,438	6,714	6,910	4,777	5,101	5,420
Multilateral	1,185	1,706	1,905	1,961	1,986	1,956	2,361	2,528
of which: IBRD	736	798	925	897	868	835	1,074	1,008
IDA	69	57	45	42	39	37	34	32
Bilateral	3,397	3,484	4,533	4,754	4,924	2,821	2,740	2,892
Private creditors	2,041	993	440	429	411	350	344	1,084
of which: Bonds	801	636	190	188	186	184	181	914
Commercial banks	337	1	0	0	0	6	12	24
Private nonguaranteed	0	0	0	0	0	0	0	0
of which: Bonds	0	0	0	0	0	0	0	0
Disbursements	**609**	**176**	**434**	**277**	**190**	**230**	**762**	**1,389**
Public and publicly guaranteed	609	176	434	277	190	230	762	1,389
Official creditors	609	176	269	277	190	224	756	627
Multilateral	259	80	161	194	133	158	630	429
of which: IBRD	158	38	48	43	39	41	335	33
IDA	0	0	0	0	0	0	0	0
Bilateral	351	96	108	83	57	67	126	198
Private creditors	0	0	165	0	0	6	6	762
of which: Bonds	0	0	145	0	0	0	0	750
Commercial banks	0	0	0	0	0	6	6	12
Private nonguaranteed	0	0	0	0	0	0	0	0
of which: Bonds	0	0	0	0	0	0	0	0
Principal repayments	**329**	**393**	**341**	**353**	**409**	**2,412**	**405**	**487**
Public and publicly guaranteed	329	393	341	353	409	2,412	405	487
Official creditors	128	238	322	340	392	2,338	394	460
Multilateral	117	124	170	168	174	185	202	275
of which: IBRD	77	53	73	78	78	86	95	101
IDA	2	3	3	3	3	3	3	3
Bilateral	11	114	152	172	218	2,154	191	185
Private creditors	201	155	20	12	17	73	11	27
of which: Bonds	0	95	11	1	2	2	2	17
Commercial banks	135	19	0	0	0	0	0	0
Private nonguaranteed	0	0	0	0	0	0	0	0
of which: Bonds	0	0	0	0	0	0	0	0
Interest payments	**209**	**239**	**160**	**196**	**227**	**200**	**147**	**147**
Public and publicly guaranteed	209	239	160	196	227	200	147	147
Official creditors	116	158	153	179	209	182	131	121
Multilateral	63	91	76	90	97	88	77	68
of which: IBRD	48	53	33	45	50	38	28	14
IDA	1	0	0	0	0	0	0	0
Bilateral	53	67	77	89	112	94	54	54
Private creditors	94	80	7	18	18	19	16	25
of which: Bonds	41	46	4	12	12	12	12	23
Commercial banks	32	1	0	0	0	0	0	0
Private nonguaranteed	0	0	0	0	0	0	0	0
of which: Bonds	0	0	0	0	0	0	0	0
8. Debt stock-flow reconciliation								
Total change in external debt stocks	107	-728	-370	359	316	-1,791	35	1,207
Net flows on external debt	484	-399	97	7	-87	-1,777	73	1,049
9. Debt restructurings								
Total amount rescheduled	365	194	220	208	196	0	0	0
Total amount forgiven	322	63	0	0	0	246	0	0
Debt buyback	0	85	0	0	0	2,038	0	0

10. Contractual obligations on outstanding long-term external debt

	2011	2012	2013	2014	2015	2016	2017	2018
Official creditors								
Principal	611	549	509	497	472	422	397	383
Interest	136	127	115	104	92	81	71	62
Private creditors								
Principal	19	30	17	12	763	14	15	16
Interest	43	42	41	41	40	11	10	10

KAZAKHSTAN

(US$ million, unless otherwise indicated)

	1995	2000	2005	2006	2007	2008	2009	2010
1. Summary external debt data								
External debt stocks	**3,750**	**12,433**	**43,478**	**72,443**	**95,542**	**107,278**	**111,115**	**118,723**
Long-term external debt	2,937	11,472	35,327	61,569	84,388	96,958	102,439	109,686
Public and publicly guaranteed	2,834	3,623	2,177	2,136	1,698	1,915	2,487	3,842
Private nonguaranteed	103	7,849	33,150	59,433	82,690	95,043	99,952	105,844
Use of IMF credit	432	0	0	0	0	0	0	0
Short-term external debt	381	961	8,151	10,873	11,154	10,321	8,676	9,037
interest arrears on long-term	162	0	0	0	0	0	0	0
Memorandum items								
Principal arrears on long-term	0	0	0	0	0	0	0	0
Long-term public sector debt	2,834	3,619	2,157	2,130	1,698	1,915	2,487	3,842
Long-term private sector debt	103	7,852	33,170	59,439	82,690	95,043	99,952	105,844
Public & publicly guaranteed commitments	982	688	159	30	0	174	3,550	1,340
External debt flows								
Disbursements	881	3,057	17,237	37,916	44,750	40,925	30,524	50,133
Long-term external debt	740	3,057	17,237	37,916	44,750	40,925	30,524	50,133
IMF purchases	141	0	0	0	0	0	0	0
Principal repayments	105	2,595	11,450	12,172	23,596	29,035	20,103	42,789
Long-term external debt	105	2,153	11,450	12,172	23,596	29,035	20,103	42,789
IMF repurchases	0	442	0	0	0	0	0	0
Net flows	868	1,057	9,995	28,466	21,434	11,057	8,776	7,705
Long-term external debt	635	904	5,786	25,744	21,154	11,890	10,421	7,344
Short-term external debt	93	595	4,209	2,722	281	-833	-1,645	361
Interest payments	130	775	1,730	2,303	3,575	4,391	5,677	4,971
Long-term external debt	102	713	1,526	1,953	3,537	4,117	5,373	4,655
IMF charges	17	11	0	0	0	0	0	0
Short-term external debt	10	51	204	350	38	274	304	316
2. Other non-debt resource inflows								
Foreign direct investment	964	1,283	1,971	6,278	11,119	14,322	13,771	9,961
Portfolio equity	..	19	150	2,789	828	-1,280	38	96
3. Currency composition of public and publicly guaranteed debt (%)								
Euro	..	..	1.9	2.1	2.6	1.9	1.4	0.8
Japanese yen	8.9	13.8	32.6	34.9	46.7	52.5	40.1	24.5
Pound sterling	0.0	0.6	0.0	0.0	0.0	0.0	0.0	0.0
Swiss franc	0.0	0.0	0.0	0.0	0.0	0.0	0.0	0.0
U.S.dollars	6.9	61.2	53.9	53.5	46.8	42.1	55.9	73.2
4. Average terms of new commitments								
Official creditors								
Interest (%)	5.5	3.0	5.0	6.2	0.0	3.0	1.4	1.0
Maturity (years)	14.3	27.6	16.8	16.3	0.0	15.1	21.2	23.4
Grace period (years)	4.5	8.4	5.3	4.8	0.0	5.3	4.7	3.5
Private creditors								
Interest (%)	6.4	11.0	0.0	0.0	0.0	0.0	0.0	0.0
Maturity (years)	5.9	6.0	0.0	0.0	0.0	0.0	0.0	0.0
Grace period (years)	2.3	5.6	0.0	0.0	0.0	0.0	0.0	0.0
5. Major economic aggregates								
Gross national income (GNI)	20,229	17,038	51,427	71,512	91,766	113,926	102,471	125,913
Exports of goods, services & income	6,020	10,480	31,209	43,011	55,379	79,637	50,665	66,917
Worker remit. & comp. of employees	116	122	178	186	223	192	261	291
Imports of goods, services & income	6,292	10,362	31,852	43,803	61,541	72,327	54,342	62,164
Profit remittances on FDI	74	1,046	4,633	7,694	11,305	16,956	10,711	14,923
Current account balance	-213	366	-1,056	-1,999	-8,322	6,326	-4,359	4,319
International reserves	1,660	2,099	7,070	19,127	17,641	19,883	23,183	28,265
6. Ratios								
External debt stocks to exports (%)	62.3	118.6	139.3	168.4	172.5	134.7	219.3	177.4
External debt stocks to GNI (%)	18.5	73.0	84.5	101.3	104.1	94.2	108.4	94.3
Debt service to exports (%)	3.9	32.2	42.2	33.7	49.1	42.0	50.9	71.4
Short-term to external debt stocks (%)	10.2	7.7	18.7	15.0	11.7	9.6	7.8	7.6
Multilateral to external debt stocks (%)	10.4	11.9	2.0	1.1	0.7	0.7	1.2	2.3
Reserves to external debt stocks (%)	44.3	16.9	16.3	26.4	18.5	18.5	20.9	23.8
Reserves to imports (months)	3.2	2.4	2.7	5.2	3.4	3.3	5.1	5.5

KAZAKHSTAN

(US$ million, unless otherwise indicated)

	1995	2000	2005	2006	2007	2008	2009	2010
7. Long-term external debt								
Debt outstanding and disbursed	**2,937**	**11,472**	**35,327**	**61,569**	**84,388**	**96,958**	**102,439**	**109,686**
Public and publicly guaranteed	2,834	3,623	2,177	2,136	1,698	1,915	2,487	3,842
Official creditors	2,293	2,239	1,780	1,762	1,684	1,912	2,486	3,842
Multilateral	392	1,482	869	823	711	748	1,349	2,785
of which: IBRD	295	1,057	599	502	427	463	547	1,830
IDA	0	0	0	0	0	0	0	0
Bilateral	1,901	757	911	939	973	1,164	1,137	1,057
Private creditors	541	1,384	396	374	13	3	1	0
of which: Bonds	0	1,000	350	350	0	0	0	0
Commercial banks	17	263	46	24	13	3	1	0
Private nonguaranteed	103	7,849	33,150	59,433	82,690	95,043	99,952	105,844
of which: Bonds	0	100	7,550	13,814	24,623	24,125	22,097	21,044
Disbursements	**740**	**3,057**	**17,237**	**37,916**	**44,750**	**40,925**	**30,524**	**50,133**
Public and publicly guaranteed	671	623	197	177	160	145	717	1,519
Official creditors	421	168	197	177	160	145	717	1,519
Multilateral	171	95	80	106	112	95	659	1,497
of which: IBRD	107	50	37	29	67	65	115	1,320
IDA	0	0	0	0	0	0	0	0
Bilateral	250	73	117	71	48	51	58	22
Private creditors	249	455	0	0	0	0	0	0
of which: Bonds	0	350	0	0	0	0	0	0
Commercial banks	17	105	0	0	0	0	0	0
Private nonguaranteed	69	2,434	17,040	37,739	44,590	40,780	29,807	48,615
of which: Bonds	0	0	3,050	6,219	10,993	540	0	450
Principal repayments	**105**	**2,153**	**11,450**	**12,172**	**23,596**	**29,035**	**20,103**	**42,789**
Public and publicly guaranteed	95	216	1,090	222	640	131	131	278
Official creditors	27	133	1,018	200	279	120	130	278
Multilateral	0	31	921	160	226	58	59	61
of which: IBRD	0	20	658	130	143	28	32	37
IDA	0	0	0	0	0	0	0	0
Bilateral	27	102	97	40	53	62	71	217
Private creditors	68	83	72	22	361	11	2	1
of which: Bonds	0	0	0	0	350	0	0	0
Commercial banks	0	30	72	22	11	11	2	1
Private nonguaranteed	11	1,937	10,360	11,949	22,957	28,905	19,971	42,511
of which: Bonds	0	0	0	0	100	850	2,108	1,503
Interest payments	**102**	**713**	**1,526**	**1,953**	**3,537**	**4,117**	**5,373**	**4,655**
Public and publicly guaranteed	100	235	146	113	96	67	58	54
Official creditors	59	124	102	71	74	66	58	54
Multilateral	15	82	73	44	46	35	28	27
of which: IBRD	14	62	54	31	29	19	17	7
IDA	0	0	0	0	0	0	0	0
Bilateral	44	42	28	27	29	31	30	27
Private creditors	41	112	44	42	22	1	0	0
of which: Bonds	0	90	39	39	19	0	0	0
Commercial banks	0	14	5	3	2	1	0	0
Private nonguaranteed	1	477	1,380	1,839	3,441	4,051	5,315	4,601
of which: Bonds	0	11	543	834	1,510	1,802	1,706	1,525
8. Debt stock-flow reconciliation								
Total change in external debt stocks	961	6,304	10,662	28,964	23,099	11,736	3,837	7,608
Net flows on external debt	868	1,057	9,995	28,466	21,434	11,057	8,776	7,705
9. Debt restructurings								
Total amount rescheduled	0	0	0	0	0	0	0	0
Total amount forgiven	0	0	0	0	0	0	0	0
Debt buyback	0	0	0	0	0	0	0	0

10. Contractual obligations on outstanding long-term external debt

	2011	2012	2013	2014	2015	2016	2017	2018
Official creditors								
Principal	133	276	428	470	369	370	368	359
Interest	52	53	52	54	56	53	49	45
Private creditors								
Principal	26,883	19,282	10,193	14,991	11,450	9,159	12,126	16
Interest	2,528	1,910	1,473	1,076	778	488	255	107

Notes:

Long-term private nonguaranteed debt includes only registered private debt of the National Bank of Kazakhstan. Short-term debt is based on the National Bank data from 2000.

KENYA

(US$ million, unless otherwise indicated)

	1995	2000	2005	2006	2007	2008	2009	2010
1. Summary external debt data								
External debt stocks	**7,309**	**6,141**	**6,428**	**6,622**	**7,462**	**7,549**	**8,182**	**8,400**
Long-term external debt	6,302	5,216	5,770	5,867	6,229	6,387	6,720	6,978
Public and publicly guaranteed	5,857	5,041	5,770	5,867	6,229	6,387	6,720	6,978
Private nonguaranteed	445	175	0	0	0	0	0	0
Use of IMF credit	374	127	159	153	269	252	451	417
Short-term external debt	634	798	499	602	964	910	1,012	1,005
interest arrears on long-term	31	47	21	34	57	66	73	80
Memorandum items								
Principal arrears on long-term	6	142	141	334	308	271	276	242
Long-term public sector debt	5,857	5,041	5,770	5,867	6,229	6,387	6,720	6,978
Long-term private sector debt	445	175	0	0	0	0	0	0
Public & publicly guaranteed commitments	326	355	297	575	1,146	395	1,323	1,608
External debt flows								
Disbursements	677	377	242	126	456	350	747	530
Long-term external debt	677	333	168	126	341	350	538	530
IMF purchases	0	44	74	0	115	0	209	0
Principal repayments	605	449	447	334	345	298	275	284
Long-term external debt	566	407	439	320	335	287	257	258
IMF repurchases	39	42	7	14	10	11	18	26
Net flows	78	-31	-459	-118	450	-11	567	232
Long-term external debt	111	-74	-271	-194	6	63	281	272
Short-term external debt	6	41	-254	90	339	-63	95	-14
Interest payments	299	142	91	94	108	113	111	115
Long-term external debt	261	100	72	71	78	91	85	90
IMF charges	2	1	1	1	1	1	2	0
Short-term external debt	36	41	18	23	29	21	23	25
2. Other non-debt resource inflows								
Foreign direct investment	42	111	21	51	729	96	116	186
Portfolio equity	5	-6	3	2	0	5	3	33
3. Currency composition of public and publicly guaranteed debt (%)								
Euro	..	..	19.2	18.9	19.8	17.0	18.1	16.1
Japanese yen	18.6	20.1	18.6	18.6	17.4	20.0	17.9	18.4
Pound sterling	3.8	2.5	0.6	0.7	0.6	0.4	0.4	0.4
Swiss franc	4.2	1.4	0.1	0.1	0.1	0.1	0.1	0.1
U.S.dollars	35.8	49.8	49.3	48.8	48.2	46.7	45.3	43.7
4. Average terms of new commitments								
Official creditors								
Interest (%)	2.1	1.1	1.5	1.7	1.1	1.3	1.3	1.0
Maturity (years)	35.7	39.0	32.4	33.4	39.7	30.6	32.8	33.6
Grace period (years)	9.8	10.0	7.7	8.9	9.9	8.3	8.9	10.0
Private creditors								
Interest (%)	4.8	7.5	0.0	0.0	0.0	1.0	3.9	2.7
Maturity (years)	5.2	5.9	0.0	0.0	17.3	13.0	7.8	8.3
Grace period (years)	0.6	1.4	0.0	0.0	2.5	1.5	3.3	1.8
5. Major economic aggregates								
Gross national income (GNI)	8,726	12,562	18,732	22,540	27,216	30,134	29,311	31,264
Exports of goods, services & income	3,580	2,821	5,416	6,045	7,223	8,467	7,567	9,037
Worker remit. & comp. of employees	298	538	805	1,128	1,588	1,692	1,686	1,777
Imports of goods, services & income	6,195	3,941	6,921	8,341	10,364	12,781	11,514	13,835
Profit remittances on FDI	116	29	35	39	124	52	60	67
Current account balance	-1,578	-199	-252	-510	-1,032	-1,983	-1,689	-2,512
International reserves	384	898	1,799	2,416	3,355	2,879	3,850	4,321
6. Ratios								
External debt stocks to exports (%)	204.2	217.7	118.7	109.5	103.3	89.2	108.1	93.0
External debt stocks to GNI (%)	83.8	48.9	34.3	29.4	27.4	25.1	27.9	26.9
Debt service to exports (%)	25.3	20.9	9.9	7.1	6.3	4.9	5.1	4.4
Short-term to external debt stocks (%)	8.7	13.0	7.8	9.1	12.9	12.1	12.4	12.0
Multilateral to external debt stocks (%)	39.7	46.2	53.3	52.0	48.3	49.4	48.2	48.9
Reserves to external debt stocks (%)	5.3	14.6	28.0	36.5	45.0	38.1	47.0	51.4
Reserves to imports (months)	0.7	2.7	3.1	3.5	3.9	2.7	4.0	3.7

(US$ million, unless otherwise indicated)

	1995	2000	2005	2006	2007	2008	2009	2010
7. Long-term external debt								
Debt outstanding and disbursed	**6,302**	**5,216**	**5,770**	**5,867**	**6,229**	**6,387**	**6,720**	**6,978**
Public and publicly guaranteed	5,857	5,041	5,770	5,867	6,229	6,387	6,720	6,978
Official creditors	5,212	4,559	5,406	5,540	5,890	6,068	6,368	6,667
Multilateral	2,903	2,836	3,426	3,445	3,601	3,727	3,946	4,110
of which: IBRD	435	47	0	0	0	0	0	0
IDA	1,977	2,262	2,663	2,764	2,968	3,050	3,156	3,238
Bilateral	2,309	1,724	1,980	2,095	2,288	2,341	2,422	2,557
Private creditors	645	482	363	327	339	319	352	311
of which: Bonds	0	0	0	0	0	0	0	0
Commercial banks	510	436	292	252	260	238	243	202
Private nonguaranteed	445	175	0	0	0	0	0	0
of which: Bonds	0	0	0	0	0	0	0	0
Disbursements	**677**	**333**	**168**	**126**	**341**	**350**	**538**	**530**
Public and publicly guaranteed	677	333	168	126	341	350	538	530
Official creditors	545	248	140	125	341	343	510	518
Multilateral	219	196	64	76	225	256	290	335
of which: IBRD	0	0	0	0	0	0	0	0
IDA	159	170	34	41	159	178	164	220
Bilateral	326	52	76	48	116	87	220	184
Private creditors	132	85	28	1	0	7	27	12
of which: Bonds	0	0	0	0	0	0	0	0
Commercial banks	72	77	28	1	0	0	0	1
Private nonguaranteed	0	0	0	0	0	0	0	0
of which: Bonds	0	0	0	0	0	0	0	0
Principal repayments	**566**	**407**	**439**	**320**	**335**	**287**	**257**	**258**
Public and publicly guaranteed	481	362	429	320	335	287	257	258
Official creditors	271	241	356	258	324	272	254	255
Multilateral	150	112	327	220	224	106	107	111
of which: IBRD	100	40	1	0	0	0	0	0
IDA	9	29	54	60	66	75	81	88
Bilateral	120	129	28	38	100	166	147	143
Private creditors	210	121	74	62	11	15	3	4
of which: Bonds	0	0	0	0	0	0	0	0
Commercial banks	164	108	72	61	9	13	0	1
Private nonguaranteed	85	45	10	0	0	0	0	0
of which: Bonds	0	0	0	0	0	0	0	0
Interest payments	**261**	**100**	**72**	**71**	**78**	**91**	**85**	**90**
Public and publicly guaranteed	220	81	72	70	78	91	85	90
Official creditors	167	55	66	65	76	90	84	90
Multilateral	77	38	48	36	32	35	33	34
of which: IBRD	43	7	0	0	0	0	0	0
IDA	14	16	23	22	22	24	22	23
Bilateral	89	17	17	29	44	55	51	55
Private creditors	53	27	6	5	2	1	1	1
of which: Bonds	0	0	0	0	0	0	0	0
Commercial banks	45	23	6	4	1	1	0	0
Private nonguaranteed	41	19	0	0	0	0	0	0
of which: Bonds	0	0	0	0	0	0	0	0
8. Debt stock-flow reconciliation								
Total change in external debt stocks	185	-334	-489	195	840	87	633	218
Net flows on external debt	78	-31	-459	-118	450	-11	567	232
9. Debt restructurings								
Total amount rescheduled	0	122	127	192	0	0	0	0
Total amount forgiven	0	10	3	8	0	0	5	31
Debt buyback	0	0	0	0	0	0	0	0

10. Contractual obligations on outstanding long-term external debt

	2011	2012	2013	2014	2015	2016	2017	2018
Official creditors								
Principal	343	356	361	345	377	405	445	480
Interest	100	104	105	104	101	96	90	83
Private creditors								
Principal	11	12	13	13	9	8	8	6
Interest	1	1	1	1	1	0	0	0

KOSOVO

(US$ million, unless otherwise indicated)

	1995	2000	2005	2006	2007	2008	2009	2010
1. Summary external debt data								
External debt stocks	..	..	..	..	..	..	**358.5**	**342.2**
Long-term external debt	..	..	..	..	..	..	358.5	342.2
Public and publicly guaranteed	..	..	..	..	..	..	358.5	342.2
Private nonguaranteed	..	..	..	..	..	..	0.0	0.0
Use of IMF credit	..	..	..	..	..	..	0.0	0.0
Short-term external debt	..	..	..	..	..	..	0.0	0.0
interest arrears on long-term	..	..	..	..	..	..	0.0	0.0
Memorandum items								
Principal arrears on long-term	..	..	..	..	..	..	0.0	0.0
Long-term public sector debt	..	..	..	..	..	..	358.5	342.2
Long-term private sector debt	..	..	..	..	..	..	0.0	0.0
Public & publicly guaranteed commitments	..	..	..	..	..	..	0.0	0.0
External debt flows								
Disbursements	..	..	..	..	..	..	0.0	0.0
Long-term external debt	..	..	..	..	..	..	0.0	0.0
IMF purchases	..	..	..	..	..	..	0.0	0.0
Principal repayments	..	..	..	..	..	..	207.7	16.3
Long-term external debt	..	..	..	..	..	..	207.7	16.3
IMF repurchases	..	..	..	..	..	..	0.0	0.0
Net flows	..	..	..	..	..	..	-207.7	-16.3
Long-term external debt	..	..	..	..	..	..	-207.7	-16.3
Short-term external debt	..	..	..	..	..	..	0.0	0.0
Interest payments	..	..	..	..	..	..	22.5	4.8
Long-term external debt	..	..	..	..	..	..	22.5	4.8
IMF charges	..	..	..	..	..	..	0.0	0.0
Short-term external debt	..	..	..	..	..	..	0.0	0.0
2. Other non-debt resource inflows								
Foreign direct investment	..	..	133.8	369.8	603.2	536.8	408.1	413.4
Portfolio equity	..	..	0.0	0.0	0.0	0.0	0.0	0.0
3. Currency composition of public and publicly guaranteed debt (%)								
Euro	..	..	..	..	..	..	0.0	0.0
Japanese yen	..	..	..	..	..	..	0.0	0.0
Pound sterling	..	..	..	..	..	..	0.0	0.0
Swiss franc	..	..	..	..	..	..	0.0	0.0
U.S.dollars	..	..	..	..	..	..	100.0	100.0
4. Average terms of new commitments								
Official creditors								
Interest (%)	..	..	..	..	..	..	0.0	0.0
Maturity (years)	..	..	..	..	..	..	0.0	0.0
Grace period (years)	..	..	..	..	..	..	0.0	0.0
Private creditors								
Interest (%)	..	..	..	..	..	..	0.0	0.0
Maturity (years)	..	..	..	..	..	..	0.0	0.0
Grace period (years)	..	..	..	..	..	..	0.0	0.0
5. Major economic aggregates								
Gross national income (GNI)	..	..	..	4137.7	4977.5	5873.0	5566.8	5745.0
Exports of goods, services & income	..	..	625.8	789.4	1023.6	1175.3	1100.8	1343.1
Worker remit. & comp. of employees	..	..	705.2	773.8	922.1	1045.6	972.9	931.6
Imports of goods, services & income	..	..	1804.5	2025.4	2560.9	3259.9	3164.3	3381.7
Profit remittances on FDI	..	..	28.1	31.2	59.0	88.4	102.0	38.2
Current account balance	..	..	-307.7	-283.6	-484.6	-920.9	-843.6	-859.8
International reserves	..	..	..	..	951.7	892.1	830.2	846.4
6. Ratios								
External debt stocks to exports (%)	..	..	..	..	..	..	32.6	25.5
External debt stocks to GNI (%)	..	..	..	..	..	..	6.4	6.0
Debt service to exports (%)	..	..	..	..	..	..	20.9	1.6
Short-term to external debt stocks (%)	..	..	..	..	..	..	..	..
Multilateral to external debt stocks (%)	..	..	..	..	..	..	100.0	100.0
Reserves to external debt stocks (%)	..	..	..	..	..	..	231.6	247.3
Reserves to imports (months)	..	..	..	..	4.5	3.3	3.1	3.0

	1995	2000	2005	2006	2007	2008	2009	2010
7. Long-term external debt								
Debt outstanding and disbursed	**..**	**..**	**..**	**..**	**..**	**..**	**358.5**	**342.2**
Public and publicly guaranteed	..	..	..	..	..	..	358.5	342.2
Official creditors	..	..	..	..	..	..	358.5	342.2
Multilateral	..	..	..	..	..	..	358.5	342.2
of which: IBRD	..	..	..	..	..	..	358.5	342.2
IDA	..	..	..	..	..	..	0.0	0.0
Bilateral	..	..	..	..	..	..	0.0	0.0
Private creditors	..	..	..	..	..	..	0.0	0.0
of which: Bonds	..	..	..	..	..	..	0.0	0.0
Commercial banks	..	..	..	..	..	..	0.0	0.0
Private nonguaranteed	..	..	..	..	..	..	0.0	0.0
of which: Bonds	..	..	..	..	..	..	0.0	0.0
Disbursements	**..**	**..**	**..**	**..**	**..**	**..**	**0.0**	**0.0**
Public and publicly guaranteed	..	..	..	..	..	..	0.0	0.0
Official creditors	..	..	..	..	..	..	0.0	0.0
Multilateral	..	..	..	..	..	..	0.0	0.0
of which: IBRD	..	..	..	..	..	..	0.0	0.0
IDA	..	..	..	..	..	..	0.0	0.0
Bilateral	..	..	..	..	..	..	0.0	0.0
Private creditors	..	..	..	..	..	..	0.0	0.0
of which: Bonds	..	..	..	..	..	..	0.0	0.0
Commercial banks	..	..	..	..	..	..	0.0	0.0
Private nonguaranteed	..	..	..	..	..	..	0.0	0.0
of which: Bonds	..	..	..	..	..	..	0.0	0.0
Principal repayments	**..**	**..**	**..**	**..**	**..**	**..**	**207.7**	**16.3**
Public and publicly guaranteed	..	..	..	..	..	..	207.7	16.3
Official creditors	..	..	..	..	..	..	207.7	16.3
Multilateral	..	..	..	..	..	..	207.7	16.3
of which: IBRD	..	..	..	..	..	..	207.7	16.3
IDA	..	..	..	..	..	..	0.0	0.0
Bilateral	..	..	..	..	..	..	0.0	0.0
Private creditors	..	..	..	..	..	..	0.0	0.0
of which: Bonds	..	..	..	..	..	..	0.0	0.0
Commercial banks	..	..	..	..	..	..	0.0	0.0
Private nonguaranteed	..	..	..	..	..	..	0.0	0.0
of which: Bonds	..	..	..	..	..	..	0.0	0.0
Interest payments	**..**	**..**	..	..	..	..	**22.5**	**4.8**
Public and publicly guaranteed	..	..	..	..	..	..	22.5	4.8
Official creditors	..	..	..	..	..	..	22.5	4.8
Multilateral	..	..	..	..	..	..	22.5	4.8
of which: IBRD	..	..	..	..	..	..	22.5	4.8
IDA	..	..	..	..	..	..	0.0	0.0
Bilateral	..	..	..	..	..	..	0.0	0.0
Private creditors	..	..	..	..	..	..	0.0	0.0
of which: Bonds	..	..	..	..	..	..	0.0	0.0
Commercial banks	..	..	..	..	..	..	0.0	0.0
Private nonguaranteed	..	..	..	..	..	..	0.0	0.0
of which: Bonds	..	..	..	..	..	..	0.0	0.0
8. Debt stock-flow reconciliation								
Total change in external debt stocks	..	..	..	..	..	..	0.0	-16.3
Net flows on external debt	..	..	..	..	..	..	-207.7	-16.3
9. Debt restructurings								
Total amount rescheduled	..	..	..	..	..	..	0.0	0.0
Total amount forgiven	..	..	..	..	..	..	0.0	0.0
Debt buyback	..	..	..	..	..	..	0.0	0.0

10. Contractual obligations on outstanding long-term external debt

	2011	2012	2013	2014	2015	2016	2017	2018
Official creditors								
Principal	16.3	16.3	16.3	16.3	16.3	16.3	16.3	0.0
Interest	4.6	4.3	4.1	3.9	3.7	3.5	3.2	0.0
Private creditors								
Principal	0.0	0.0	0.0	0.0	0.0	0.0	0.0	0.0
Interest	0.0	0.0	0.0	0.0	0.0	0.0	0.0	0.0

Notes:

Kosovo became independent in 2008 and, data are reported starting from 2009.

KYRGYZ REPUBLIC

(US$ million, unless otherwise indicated)

	1995	2000	2005	2006	2007	2008	2009	2010
1. Summary external debt data								
External debt stocks	**609**	**1,827**	**2,136**	**2,471**	**2,747**	**3,498**	**3,986**	**3,984**
Long-term external debt	472	1,510	1,825	2,101	2,278	2,942	3,395	3,612
Public and publicly guaranteed	472	1,220	1,665	1,831	1,898	1,963	2,320	2,442
Private nonguaranteed	0	290	161	270	380	980	1,076	1,171
Use of IMF credit	124	188	178	163	150	165	167	177
Short-term external debt	13	129	132	206	319	391	424	195
interest arrears on long-term	11	10	3	5	7	6	2	12
Memorandum items								
Principal arrears on long-term	11	28	6	6	9	11	2	7
Long-term public sector debt	472	1,220	1,665	1,831	1,898	1,963	2,320	2,442
Long-term private sector debt	0	290	161	270	380	980	1,076	1,171
Public & publicly guaranteed commitments	164	201	86	16	46	96	609	156
External debt flows								
Disbursements	201	180	151	243	281	921	660	702
Long-term external debt	155	161	133	239	277	879	635	668
IMF purchases	46	19	18	4	4	42	26	34
Principal repayments	36	97	104	65	151	285	226	483
Long-term external debt	36	86	74	38	126	261	200	462
IMF repurchases	0	11	31	27	25	23	26	22
Net flows	165	152	-149	250	241	709	472	-20
Long-term external debt	119	75	59	202	151	617	435	206
Short-term external debt	0	69	-195	72	111	73	37	-238
Interest payments	24	76	35	31	38	51	43	73
Long-term external debt	20	69	21	19	23	42	37	69
IMF charges	4	2	1	1	1	1	1	0
Short-term external debt	0	5	13	11	15	8	5	4
2. Other non-debt resource inflows								
Foreign direct investment	96	-2	43	182	208	377	189	438
Portfolio equity	0	0	0	0	1	6	1	-18
3. Currency composition of public and publicly guaranteed debt (%)								
Euro	..	..	2.8	3.5	4.3	4.0	3.5	3.1
Japanese yen	14.3	15.0	13.5	12.5	12.7	15.5	13.0	14.0
Pound sterling	0.0	0.0	0.0	0.0	0.0	0.0	0.0	0.0
Swiss franc	1.3	0.0	0.0	0.0	0.0	0.0	0.0	0.0
U.S.dollars	51.4	67.9	69.5	67.0	68.0	65.3	69.2	68.9
4. Average terms of new commitments								
Official creditors								
Interest (%)	3.7	1.0	1.0	1.4	0.5	1.6	1.3	1.2
Maturity (years)	28.4	35.8	36.2	31.6	26.7	21.7	31.5	36.1
Grace period (years)	8.1	9.5	9.3	8.1	7.3	5.9	6.5	9.4
Private creditors								
Interest (%)	0.0	0.0	0.0	0.0	0.0	0.0	0.0	0.0
Maturity (years)	0.0	0.0	0.0	0.0	0.0	0.0	0.0	0.0
Grace period (years)	0.0	0.0	0.0	0.0	0.0	0.0	0.0	0.0
5. Major economic aggregates								
Gross national income (GNI)	1,626	1,288	2,372	2,786	3,750	4,938	4,500	4,466
Exports of goods, services & income	452	590	963	1,326	2,065	2,812	2,582	2,543
Worker remit. & comp. of employees	1	9	322	481	715	1,232	992	1,275
Imports of goods, services & income	765	753	1,501	2,342	3,313	4,990	3,892	4,319
Profit remittances on FDI	0	37	36	40	40	173	126	327
Current account balance	-235	-76	-37	-286	-227	-701	-102	-385
International reserves	134	262	612	817	1,177	1,225	1,584	1,720
6. Ratios								
External debt stocks to exports (%)	134.9	309.8	221.8	186.3	133.0	124.4	154.4	156.7
External debt stocks to GNI (%)	37.5	141.9	90.0	88.7	73.3	70.8	88.6	89.2
Debt service to exports (%)	13.3	29.4	14.4	7.2	9.2	11.9	10.4	21.9
Short-term to external debt stocks (%)	2.1	7.1	6.2	8.4	11.6	11.2	10.6	4.9
Multilateral to external debt stocks (%)	30.3	39.5	51.5	48.2	46.6	36.9	32.9	32.5
Reserves to external debt stocks (%)	21.9	14.3	28.7	33.1	42.8	35.0	39.7	43.2
Reserves to imports (months)	2.1	4.2	4.9	4.2	4.3	2.9	4.9	4.8

KYRGYZ REPUBLIC

(US$ million, unless otherwise indicated)

	1995	2000	2005	2006	2007	2008	2009	2010
7. Long-term external debt								
Debt outstanding and disbursed	**472**	**1,510**	**1,825**	**2,101**	**2,278**	**2,942**	**3,395**	**3,612**
Public and publicly guaranteed	472	1,220	1,665	1,831	1,898	1,963	2,320	2,442
Official creditors	472	1,184	1,665	1,831	1,898	1,963	2,320	2,442
Multilateral	184	722	1,099	1,190	1,280	1,290	1,310	1,296
of which: IBRD	0	0	0	0	0	0	0	0
IDA	141	377	565	612	651	655	656	649
Bilateral	288	461	566	641	618	672	1,010	1,146
Private creditors	0	37	0	0	0	0	0	0
of which: Bonds	0	0	0	0	0	0	0	0
Commercial banks	0	28	0	0	0	0	0	0
Private nonguaranteed	0	290	161	270	380	980	1,076	1,171
of which: Bonds	0	0	0	0	0	0	0	0
Disbursements	**155**	**161**	**133**	**239**	**277**	**879**	**635**	**668**
Public and publicly guaranteed	155	153	76	87	66	51	378	147
Official creditors	155	149	76	87	66	51	378	147
Multilateral	124	107	70	73	58	50	40	43
of which: IBRD	0	0	0	0	0	0	0	0
IDA	81	52	34	26	22	20	8	19
Bilateral	31	42	6	15	8	1	338	104
Private creditors	0	4	0	0	0	0	0	0
of which: Bonds	0	0	0	0	0	0	0	0
Commercial banks	0	0	0	0	0	0	0	0
Private nonguaranteed	0	8	57	152	211	828	257	521
of which: Bonds	0	0	0	0	0	0	0	0
Principal repayments	**36**	**86**	**74**	**38**	**126**	**261**	**200**	**462**
Public and publicly guaranteed	36	17	16	20	25	35	38	38
Official creditors	36	13	16	20	25	35	38	38
Multilateral	30	8	16	20	22	29	33	35
of which: IBRD	0	0	0	0	0	0	0	0
IDA	0	0	4	6	9	11	12	14
Bilateral	6	5	0	0	3	6	6	3
Private creditors	0	4	0	0	0	0	0	0
of which: Bonds	0	0	0	0	0	0	0	0
Commercial banks	0	2	0	0	0	0	0	0
Private nonguaranteed	0	69	57	18	102	226	161	424
of which: Bonds	0	0	0	0	0	0	0	0
Interest payments	**20**	**69**	**21**	**19**	**23**	**42**	**37**	**69**
Public and publicly guaranteed	20	23	12	15	16	17	19	23
Official creditors	20	20	12	15	16	17	19	23
Multilateral	3	11	12	12	12	13	12	12
of which: IBRD	0	0	0	0	0	0	0	0
IDA	1	3	5	5	5	5	5	5
Bilateral	17	10	0	2	4	4	7	11
Private creditors	0	2	0	0	0	0	0	0
of which: Bonds	0	0	0	0	0	0	0	0
Commercial banks	0	2	0	0	0	0	0	0
Private nonguaranteed	0	47	9	5	6	24	18	46
of which: Bonds	0	0	0	0	0	0	0	0
8. Debt stock-flow reconciliation								
Total change in external debt stocks	163	92	-296	335	276	751	488	-2
Net flows on external debt	165	152	-149	250	241	709	472	-20
9. Debt restructurings								
Total amount rescheduled	0	32	520	7	7	15	16	0
Total amount forgiven	0	0	17	0	8	0	0	0
Debt buyback	0	0	0	0	0	0	0	0

10. Contractual obligations on outstanding long-term external debt

	2011	2012	2013	2014	2015	2016	2017	2018
Official creditors								
Principal	58	59	64	73	89	100	106	114
Interest	36	37	36	36	35	34	33	33
Private creditors								
Principal	313	233	199	117	93	69	56	45
Interest	50	37	25	18	13	9	5	3

Notes:

Data on long-term private nonguaranteed debt from 2008 are World Bank staff estimates based on reports provided by the country.

LAO PEOPLE'S DEMOCRATIC REPUBLIC

(US$ million, unless otherwise indicated)

	1995	2000	2005	2006	2007	2008	2009	2010
1. Summary external debt data								
External debt stocks	**2,155**	**2,501**	**2,844**	**3,377**	**4,388**	**5,008**	**5,458**	**5,559**
Long-term external debt	2,091	2,459	2,815	3,350	4,362	4,987	5,442	5,549
Public and publicly guaranteed	2,091	2,459	1,989	2,259	2,515	2,720	2,818	2,939
Private nonguaranteed	0	0	825	1,090	1,847	2,267	2,625	2,610
Use of IMF credit	64	42	29	27	26	21	16	10
Short-term external debt	0	0	0	0	0	0	0	0
interest arrears on long-term	0	0	0	0	0	0	0	0
Memorandum items								
Principal arrears on long-term	0	1	0	0	0	0	0	0
Long-term public sector debt	2,091	2,459	1,989	2,259	2,515	2,720	2,818	2,939
Long-term private sector debt	0	0	825	1,090	1,847	2,267	2,625	2,610
Public & publicly guaranteed commitments	110	68	76	16	210	13	123	0
External debt flows								
Disbursements	110	77	472	491	1,058	756	599	233
Long-term external debt	92	77	472	491	1,058	756	599	233
IMF purchases	18	0	0	0	0	0	0	0
Principal repayments	19	31	85	134	135	147	151	226
Long-term external debt	17	23	79	130	132	143	146	221
IMF repurchases	2	8	6	3	3	4	6	6
Net flows	91	47	386	357	923	608	447	6
Long-term external debt	75	55	392	361	926	613	453	12
Short-term external debt	0	0	0	0	0	0	0	0
Interest payments	6	9	47	48	55	60	69	79
Long-term external debt	6	9	47	48	54	60	69	79
IMF charges	0	0	0	0	0	0	0	0
Short-term external debt	0	0	0	0	0	0	0	0
2. Other non-debt resource inflows								
Foreign direct investment	95	34	28	187	324	228	319	350
Portfolio equity	0	0	0	0	0	0	0	0
3. Currency composition of public and publicly guaranteed debt (%)								
Euro	..	..	0.0	0.0	0.0	0.0	0.0	0.0
Japanese yen	1.1	0.4	0.1	0.0	0.0	0.0	0.0	0.0
Pound sterling	0.0	0.0	0.0	0.0	0.0	0.0	0.0	0.0
Swiss franc	0.0	0.0	0.0	0.0	0.0	0.0	0.0	0.0
U.S.dollars	13.1	18.4	66.0	69.4	69.9	70.5	71.5	71.8
4. Average terms of new commitments								
Official creditors								
Interest (%)	2.5	1.4	3.6	1.4	1.3	1.1	1.5	0.0
Maturity (years)	37.1	31.6	27.9	24.9	26.1	29.1	20.4	0.0
Grace period (years)	9.7	8.1	6.2	8.7	9.6	8.0	6.0	0.0
Private creditors								
Interest (%)	0.0	0.0	0.0	0.0	0.0	0.0	0.0	0.0
Maturity (years)	0.0	0.0	0.0	0.0	0.0	0.0	0.0	0.0
Grace period (years)	0.0	0.0	0.0	0.0	0.0	0.0	0.0	0.0
5. Major economic aggregates								
Gross national income (GNI)	1,758	1,664	2,610	3,249	4,050	5,202	5,916	7,040
Exports of goods, services & income	415	513	762	1,122	1,244	1,526	1,486	..
Worker remit. & comp. of employees	22	1	1	4	6	18	38	41
Imports of goods, services & income	761	638	1,003	1,173	1,202	1,566	1,669	..
Profit remittances on FDI	6	0	25	23	48	26	43	..
Current account balance	-237	-8	-174	75	139	115	9	..
International reserves	99	144	309	462	708	877	919	1,105
6. Ratios								
External debt stocks to exports (%)	519.1	487.3	373.0	301.1	352.6	328.3	367.3	..
External debt stocks to GNI (%)	122.6	150.3	109.0	104.0	108.4	96.3	92.3	79.0
Debt service to exports (%)	6.1	7.8	17.4	16.2	15.2	13.6	14.8	..
Short-term to external debt stocks (%)	..	0.0	..	..	..	..	..	..
Multilateral to external debt stocks (%)	28.8	41.6	53.6	49.6	42.1	39.3	36.1	35.7
Reserves to external debt stocks (%)	4.6	5.7	10.9	13.7	16.1	17.5	16.8	19.9
Reserves to imports (months)	1.6	2.7	3.7	4.7	7.1	6.7	6.6	..

(US$ million, unless otherwise indicated)

	1995	2000	2005	2006	2007	2008	2009	2010
7. Long-term external debt								
Debt outstanding and disbursed	**2,091**	**2,459**	**2,815**	**3,350**	**4,362**	**4,987**	**5,442**	**5,549**
Public and publicly guaranteed	2,091	2,459	1,989	2,259	2,515	2,720	2,818	2,939
Official creditors	2,091	2,459	1,989	2,259	2,515	2,720	2,818	2,939
Multilateral	620	1,041	1,525	1,676	1,847	1,966	1,971	1,983
of which: IBRD	0	0	0	0	0	0	0	0
IDA	285	403	598	643	686	685	680	655
Bilateral	1,471	1,418	464	584	668	755	847	955
Private creditors	0	0	0	0	0	0	0	0
of which: Bonds	0	0	0	0	0	0	0	0
Commercial banks	0	0	0	0	0	0	0	0
Private nonguaranteed	0	0	825	1,090	1,847	2,267	2,625	2,610
of which: Bonds	0	0	0	0	0	0	0	0
Disbursements	**92**	**77**	**472**	**491**	**1,058**	**756**	**599**	**233**
Public and publicly guaranteed	92	77	150	125	201	174	152	89
Official creditors	92	77	150	125	201	174	152	89
Multilateral	92	73	113	111	114	84	50	25
of which: IBRD	0	0	0	0	0	0	0	0
IDA	28	20	35	26	27	17	4	3
Bilateral	0	4	37	14	87	90	102	64
Private creditors	0	0	0	0	0	0	0	0
of which: Bonds	0	0	0	0	0	0	0	0
Commercial banks	0	0	0	0	0	0	0	0
Private nonguaranteed	0	0	321	366	857	581	447	144
of which: Bonds	0	0	0	0	0	0	0	0
Principal repayments	**17**	**23**	**79**	**130**	**132**	**143**	**146**	**221**
Public and publicly guaranteed	17	23	39	29	33	43	57	62
Official creditors	17	23	39	29	33	43	57	62
Multilateral	4	9	22	25	30	40	47	56
of which: IBRD	0	0	0	0	0	0	0	0
IDA	1	4	9	9	11	13	14	15
Bilateral	14	14	17	5	3	3	10	6
Private creditors	0	0	0	0	0	0	0	0
of which: Bonds	0	0	0	0	0	0	0	0
Commercial banks	0	0	0	0	0	0	0	0
Private nonguaranteed	0	0	40	101	100	100	89	159
of which: Bonds	0	0	0	0	0	0	0	0
Interest payments	**6**	**9**	**47**	**48**	**54**	**60**	**69**	**79**
Public and publicly guaranteed	6	9	14	20	18	23	25	29
Official creditors	6	9	14	20	18	23	25	29
Multilateral	5	9	14	15	16	18	18	18
of which: IBRD	0	0	0	0	0	0	0	0
IDA	2	3	5	5	5	5	5	5
Bilateral	1	0	0	5	2	5	7	10
Private creditors	0	0	0	0	0	0	0	0
of which: Bonds	0	0	0	0	0	0	0	0
Commercial banks	0	0	0	0	0	0	0	0
Private nonguaranteed	0	0	32	28	37	37	43	50
of which: Bonds	0	0	0	0	0	0	0	0
8. Debt stock-flow reconciliation								
Total change in external debt stocks	86	-31	228	533	1,011	620	450	101
Net flows on external debt	91	47	386	357	923	608	447	6
9. Debt restructurings								
Total amount rescheduled	0	0	0	0	0	0	0	0
Total amount forgiven	0	0	0	0	0	0	0	0
Debt buyback	0	0	0	0	0	0	0	0

10. Contractual obligations on outstanding long-term external debt

	2011	2012	2013	2014	2015	2016	2017	2018
Official creditors								
Principal	98	105	110	115	116	121	136	140
Interest	32	32	31	30	29	28	29	28
Private creditors								
Principal	705	496	444	261	209	157	131	104
Interest	114	85	58	42	30	20	13	6

Notes:

Data on long-term public and publicly guaranteed debt are World Bank staff estimates based on reports provided by the country. Long-term private nonguaranteed debt data are World Bank staff estimates.

LATVIA

(US$ million, unless otherwise indicated)

	1995	2000	2005	2006	2007	2008	2009	2010
1. Summary external debt data								
External debt stocks	**463**	**4,855**	**14,240**	**22,496**	**39,040**	**41,847**	**41,822**	**39,555**
Long-term external debt	271	1,979	6,747	12,021	22,335	26,879	30,408	25,319
Public and publicly guaranteed	271	827	1,053	1,257	1,477	1,945	6,602	6,891
Private nonguaranteed	0	1,151	5,694	10,764	20,858	24,934	23,806	18,428
Use of IMF credit	160	35	0	0	0	825	1,119	1,513
Short-term external debt	31	2,842	7,493	10,476	16,705	14,144	10,295	12,723
interest arrears on long-term	0	0	0	0	0	0	0	0
Memorandum items								
Principal arrears on long-term	0	0	0	0	0	0	0	0
Long-term public sector debt	252	818	1,034	1,239	1,460	1,930	6,590	6,837
Long-term private sector debt	19	1,160	5,713	10,782	20,875	24,949	23,818	18,482
Public & publicly guaranteed commitments	116	98	211	3	11	1,325	4,739	2,665
External debt flows								
Disbursements	75	410	5,160	6,862	9,281	10,604	10,372	7,103
Long-term external debt	75	410	5,160	6,862	9,281	9,758	10,097	6,694
IMF purchases	0	0	0	0	0	846	275	410
Principal repayments	10	330	2,699	2,542	3,036	4,365	6,628	9,671
Long-term external debt	7	319	2,699	2,542	3,036	4,365	6,628	9,671
IMF repurchases	3	10	0	0	0	0	0	0
Net flows	90	848	2,246	7,303	12,474	3,678	-105	-139
Long-term external debt	68	91	2,461	4,320	6,245	5,393	3,469	-2,977
Short-term external debt	25	767	-215	2,983	6,229	-2,561	-3,849	2,428
Interest payments	24	270	535	723	1,547	1,755	946	876
Long-term external debt	14	107	155	274	756	1,152	772	686
IMF charges	9	2	0	0	0	0	17	33
Short-term external debt	1	161	380	449	791	603	156	156
2. Other non-debt resource inflows								
Foreign direct investment	180	413	714	1,664	2,316	1,357	94	369
Portfolio equity	0	-7	12	22	-12	-50	-8	9
3. Currency composition of public and publicly guaranteed debt (%)								
Euro	..	..	87.6	90.6	92.9	95.6	99.0	99.3
Japanese yen	26.2	4.7	0.0	0.0	0.0	0.0	0.0	0.0
Pound sterling	0.0	0.0	0.0	0.0	0.0	0.0	0.0	0.0
Swiss franc	0.0	0.6	0.2	0.2	0.1	0.1	0.0	0.0
U.S.dollars	45.0	20.0	11.7	8.9	6.8	4.2	1.0	0.7
4. Average terms of new commitments								
Official creditors								
Interest (%)	5.3	5.8	2.3	3.9	0.0	4.5	3.1	3.8
Maturity (years)	14.1	14.9	19.4	25.1	0.0	16.0	6.7	11.9
Grace period (years)	4.1	5.8	7.2	5.1	0.0	16.0	5.5	5.0
Private creditors								
Interest (%)	5.1	0.0	0.0	0.0	4.0	5.5	4.6	0.0
Maturity (years)	4.0	0.0	0.0	0.0	8.7	10.0	3.2	0.0
Grace period (years)	2.5	0.0	0.0	0.0	0.2	10.0	1.9	0.0
5. Major economic aggregates								
Gross national income (GNI)	5,259	7,814	15,839	19,347	27,842	33,338	27,851	24,073
Exports of goods, services & income	..	..	8,295	9,861	13,419	15,958	12,555	13,808
Worker remit. & comp. of employees	..	72	381	482	552	601	591	614
Imports of goods, services & income	2,246	4,010	10,884	14,862	20,223	21,219	11,155	14,055
Profit remittances on FDI	0	92	617	983	1,240	611	-1,462	129
Current account balance	-16	-371	-1,992	-4,522	-6,425	-4,492	2,284	731
International reserves	602	919	2,360	4,511	5,761	5,244	6,902	7,606
6. Ratios								
External debt stocks to exports (%)	..	..	171.7	228.1	290.9	262.2	333.1	286.5
External debt stocks to GNI (%)	8.8	62.1	89.9	116.3	140.2	125.5	150.2	164.3
Debt service to exports (%)	..	..	39.0	33.1	34.2	38.4	60.3	76.4
Short-term to external debt stocks (%)	6.7	58.5	52.6	46.6	42.8	33.8	24.6	32.2
Multilateral to external debt stocks (%)	30.1	11.2	2.2	1.9	1.4	1.8	10.7	13.3
Reserves to external debt stocks (%)	130.1	18.9	16.6	20.1	14.8	12.5	16.5	19.2
Reserves to imports (months)	3.2	2.8	2.6	3.6	3.4	3.0	7.4	6.5

LATVIA

(US$ million, unless otherwise indicated)

	1995	2000	2005	2006	2007	2008	2009	2010
7. Long-term external debt								
Debt outstanding and disbursed	**271**	**1,979**	**6,747**	**12,021**	**22,335**	**26,879**	**30,408**	**25,319**
Public and publicly guaranteed	271	827	1,053	1,257	1,477	1,945	6,602	6,891
Official creditors	200	591	338	462	582	764	4,503	5,256
Multilateral	139	543	311	433	550	734	4,473	5,246
of which: IBRD	55	242	111	100	85	61	327	421
IDA	0	0	0	0	0	0	0	0
Bilateral	61	49	27	29	32	30	30	11
Private creditors	71	236	715	795	895	1,181	2,099	1,635
of which: Bonds	39	209	708	790	883	1,113	1,152	1,069
Commercial banks	0	2	0	0	9	65	946	566
Private nonguaranteed	0	1,151	5,694	10,764	20,858	24,934	23,806	18,428
of which: Bonds	0	0	124	380	442	278	278	267
Disbursements	**75**	**410**	**5,160**	**6,862**	**9,281**	**9,758**	**10,097**	**6,694**
Public and publicly guaranteed	75	94	21	125	118	915	4,504	1,237
Official creditors	26	91	21	125	110	264	3,653	1,130
Multilateral	23	91	21	125	110	264	3,653	1,130
of which: IBRD	9	63	2	0	0	0	295	135
IDA	0	0	0	0	0	0	0	0
Bilateral	3	1	0	0	0	0	0	0
Private creditors	49	3	0	0	8	650	851	106
of which: Bonds	43	0	0	0	0	587	0	0
Commercial banks	0	0	0	0	8	63	851	106
Private nonguaranteed	0	316	5,139	6,737	9,162	8,843	5,593	5,457
of which: Bonds	0	0	125	246	0	0	0	0
Principal repayments	**7**	**319**	**2,699**	**2,542**	**3,036**	**4,365**	**6,628**	**9,671**
Public and publicly guaranteed	7	81	96	35	41	343	47	478
Official creditors	4	73	93	32	39	45	44	62
Multilateral	4	53	79	32	39	45	44	44
of which: IBRD	0	9	64	19	22	24	22	17
IDA	0	0	0	0	0	0	0	0
Bilateral	0	19	15	0	0	0	0	18
Private creditors	3	8	3	3	1	298	2	417
of which: Bonds	0	0	0	0	0	294	0	0
Commercial banks	0	1	0	0	0	2	1	416
Private nonguaranteed	0	239	2,603	2,507	2,995	4,022	6,582	9,192
of which: Bonds	0	30	0	6	0	139	139	0
Interest payments	**14**	**107**	**155**	**274**	**756**	**1,152**	**772**	**686**
Public and publicly guaranteed	14	50	50	51	60	73	111	178
Official creditors	13	34	15	16	22	29	33	111
Multilateral	9	31	14	15	20	28	32	110
of which: IBRD	3	12	7	5	5	4	5	8
IDA	0	0	0	0	0	0	0	0
Bilateral	4	3	1	1	1	2	1	1
Private creditors	1	16	35	35	38	44	79	67
of which: Bonds	0	15	35	35	38	41	54	52
Commercial banks	0	0	0	0	0	3	24	15
Private nonguaranteed	0	57	104	223	696	1,079	661	508
of which: Bonds	0	2	6	16	21	20	20	15
8. Debt stock-flow reconciliation								
Total change in external debt stocks	89	794	1,838	8,256	16,544	2,807	-25	-2,267
Net flows on external debt	90	848	2,246	7,303	12,474	3,678	-105	-139
9. Debt restructurings								
Total amount rescheduled	0	0	0	0	0	0	0	0
Total amount forgiven	0	0	0	0	0	0	0	0
Debt buyback	0	0	0	0	0	0	0	0

10. Contractual obligations on outstanding long-term external debt

	2011	2012	2013	2014	2015	2016	2017	2018
Official creditors								
Principal	52	33	68	1,425	1,942	507	496	492
Interest	180	215	243	240	203	170	155	139
Private creditors								
Principal	5,477	3,469	3,106	2,371	1,473	1,129	927	1,280
Interest	1,229	488	395	312	204	164	134	115

Notes:

Short-term figures have been revised from 2006 as per the country reports.

LEBANON

(US$ million, unless otherwise indicated)

	1995	2000	2005	2006	2007	2008	2009	2010
1. Summary external debt data								
External debt stocks	**2,974**	**10,244**	**23,327**	**25,112**	**25,636**	**24,321**	**24,500**	**24,293**
Long-term external debt	1,609	7,704	19,877	20,912	21,437	21,066	21,285	20,713
Public and publicly guaranteed	1,559	6,968	18,866	20,107	20,907	20,596	20,615	20,213
Private nonguaranteed	50	736	1,011	805	530	470	670	500
Use of IMF credit	0	0	0	0	80	117	119	98
Short-term external debt	1,365	2,541	3,450	4,200	4,118	3,138	3,096	3,482
interest arrears on long-term	10	0	0	0	0	0	0	0
Memorandum items								
Principal arrears on long-term	43	0	0	0	0	0	0	0
Long-term public sector debt	1,559	6,942	18,866	20,107	20,907	20,596	20,615	20,213
Long-term private sector debt	50	762	1,011	805	530	470	670	500
Public & publicly guaranteed commitments	1,553	2,188	2,991	3,808	3,329	2,598	2,964	1,925
External debt flows								
Disbursements	907	2,445	3,179	3,817	3,452	2,749	3,332	2,143
Long-term external debt	907	2,445	3,179	3,817	3,374	2,709	3,332	2,143
IMF purchases	0	0	0	0	78	40	0	0
Principal repayments	104	884	2,172	3,004	3,078	2,905	3,096	2,651
Long-term external debt	104	884	2,172	3,004	3,078	2,905	3,096	2,632
IMF repurchases	0	0	0	0	0	0	0	19
Net flows	829	1,900	486	1,563	291	-1,136	195	-122
Long-term external debt	803	1,561	1,007	813	296	-196	237	-489
Short-term external debt	26	339	-521	750	-82	-980	-42	386
Interest payments	121	607	1,462	1,516	1,646	1,603	1,616	1,605
Long-term external debt	55	475	1,287	1,316	1,430	1,442	1,475	1,454
IMF charges	0	0	0	0	2	3	2	1
Short-term external debt	67	132	175	200	213	157	139	150
2. Other non-debt resource inflows								
Foreign direct investment	..	..	2,624	2,675	3,376	4,333	4,804	4,955
Portfolio equity	..	..	1,436	551	791	466	929	-50
3. Currency composition of public and publicly guaranteed debt (%)								
Euro	..	..	9.0	9.9	9.8	9.7	9.1	8.3
Japanese yen	0.0	0.1	0.1	0.1	0.2	0.3	0.3	0.4
Pound sterling	0.1	0.0	0.0	0.0	0.0	0.0	0.0	0.0
Swiss franc	0.0	0.0	0.0	0.0	0.0	0.0	0.0	0.0
U.S.dollars	68.8	67.9	85.7	85.3	85.8	86.3	86.9	87.9
4. Average terms of new commitments								
Official creditors								
Interest (%)	5.4	7.5	4.6	3.8	4.5	4.0	2.4	0.0
Maturity (years)	18.7	14.7	19.0	27.0	18.7	16.4	29.0	0.0
Grace period (years)	4.4	5.2	4.1	9.7	7.1	4.2	7.0	0.0
Private creditors								
Interest (%)	8.8	9.1	7.4	7.6	6.1	8.9	7.9	6.0
Maturity (years)	7.9	4.9	5.7	10.3	7.5	5.8	6.8	9.7
Grace period (years)	4.6	4.7	5.4	10.2	4.9	5.8	6.8	9.7
5. Major economic aggregates								
Gross national income (GNI)	12,211	17,581	21,652	22,621	25,797	30,517	34,194	40,032
Exports of goods, services & income	..	..	15,242	17,250	19,914	25,548	23,645	22,229
Worker remit. & comp. of employees	..	..	4,924	5,202	5,769	7,181	7,558	5,114
Imports of goods, services & income	..	..	19,053	20,335	24,287	32,011	32,214	32,188
Profit remittances on FDI	..	..	95	96	64	121	95	208
Current account balance	..	..	-2,748	-1,116	-1,605	-4,103	-6,741	-9,415
International reserves	8,100	8,475	16,618	19,239	20,599	28,265	39,132	44,476
6. Ratios								
External debt stocks to exports (%)	..	..	153.0	145.6	128.7	95.2	103.6	109.3
External debt stocks to GNI (%)	24.4	58.3	107.7	111.0	99.4	79.7	71.7	60.7
Debt service to exports (%)	..	..	23.8	26.2	23.7	17.6	19.9	19.1
Short-term to external debt stocks (%)	45.9	24.8	14.8	16.7	16.1	12.9	12.6	14.3
Multilateral to external debt stocks (%)	6.9	8.7	5.1	5.2	5.6	5.5	5.5	5.4
Reserves to external debt stocks (%)	272.3	82.7	71.2	76.6	80.4	116.2	159.7	183.1
Reserves to imports (months)	..	..	10.5	11.4	10.2	10.6	14.6	16.6

LEBANON

(US$ million, unless otherwise indicated)

	1995	2000	2005	2006	2007	2008	2009	2010
7. Long-term external debt								
Debt outstanding and disbursed	**1,609**	**7,704**	**19,877**	**20,912**	**21,437**	**21,066**	**21,285**	**20,713**
Public and publicly guaranteed	1,559	6,968	18,866	20,107	20,907	20,596	20,615	20,213
Official creditors	436	1,290	2,172	2,312	2,437	2,432	2,356	2,226
Multilateral	206	890	1,193	1,304	1,438	1,349	1,339	1,320
of which: IBRD	113	248	360	314	437	368	318	321
IDA	0	0	0	0	0	0	0	0
Bilateral	230	400	979	1,008	999	1,082	1,017	906
Private creditors	1,123	5,677	16,694	17,796	18,470	18,165	18,259	17,987
of which: Bonds	700	5,260	16,142	17,253	17,707	17,490	17,704	17,422
Commercial banks	359	403	545	534	755	667	549	559
Private nonguaranteed	50	736	1,011	805	530	470	670	500
of which: Bonds	50	736	1,011	805	530	470	670	500
Disbursements	**907**	**2,445**	**3,179**	**3,817**	**3,374**	**2,709**	**3,332**	**2,143**
Public and publicly guaranteed	857	2,330	2,649	3,817	3,374	2,709	3,132	2,143
Official creditors	213	238	106	238	287	421	223	199
Multilateral	80	200	78	213	242	161	173	134
of which: IBRD	51	42	32	37	162	40	23	24
IDA	0	0	0	0	0	0	0	0
Bilateral	133	38	28	25	45	260	51	65
Private creditors	644	2,092	2,543	3,579	3,087	2,288	2,909	1,943
of which: Bonds	300	2,031	2,500	3,547	2,738	2,257	2,894	1,925
Commercial banks	340	61	43	29	349	30	15	17
Private nonguaranteed	50	115	530	0	0	0	200	0
of which: Bonds	50	115	530	0	0	0	200	0
Principal repayments	**104**	**884**	**2,172**	**3,004**	**3,078**	**2,905**	**3,096**	**2,632**
Public and publicly guaranteed	104	834	1,907	2,798	2,803	2,845	3,096	2,462
Official creditors	93	74	143	232	362	375	334	298
Multilateral	10	44	100	158	218	232	187	161
of which: IBRD	4	17	38	90	48	116	73	20
IDA	0	0	0	0	0	0	0	0
Bilateral	83	30	43	74	144	143	147	137
Private creditors	11	760	1,764	2,566	2,441	2,470	2,762	2,164
of which: Bonds	0	400	1,695	2,507	2,369	2,430	2,706	2,151
Commercial banks	9	358	68	58	71	39	55	12
Private nonguaranteed	0	50	265	206	275	60	0	170
of which: Bonds	0	50	265	206	275	60	0	170
Interest payments	**55**	**475**	**1,287**	**1,316**	**1,430**	**1,442**	**1,475**	**1,454**
Public and publicly guaranteed	55	418	1,197	1,242	1,373	1,402	1,431	1,403
Official creditors	19	57	92	87	101	105	88	100
Multilateral	11	44	49	49	60	57	44	63
of which: IBRD	7	14	15	18	19	20	11	4
IDA	0	0	0	0	0	0	0	0
Bilateral	8	14	42	38	42	48	43	37
Private creditors	35	361	1,106	1,155	1,271	1,297	1,344	1,303
of which: Bonds	20	300	1,087	1,144	1,252	1,279	1,328	1,289
Commercial banks	12	59	18	10	19	17	15	13
Private nonguaranteed	0	57	90	74	57	40	43	51
of which: Bonds	0	57	90	74	57	40	43	51
8. Debt stock-flow reconciliation								
Total change in external debt stocks	839	1,760	200	1,785	523	-1,314	179	-207
Net flows on external debt	829	1,900	486	1,563	291	-1,136	195	-122
9. Debt restructurings								
Total amount rescheduled	0	0	0	0	0	0	0	0
Total amount forgiven	0	0	0	0	0	0	0	0
Debt buyback	0	0	0	0	0	0	0	0

10. Contractual obligations on outstanding long-term external debt

	2011	2012	2013	2014	2015	2016	2017	2018
Official creditors								
Principal	535	484	314	312	257	237	226	190
Interest	95	90	81	74	65	57	48	39
Private creditors								
Principal	2,257	2,951	1,955	1,988	1,179	1,579	1,929	580
Interest	1,283	1,134	914	763	673	550	409	326

Notes:

Data on long-term private nonguaranteed debt only cover Bonds.

LESOTHO

(US$ million, unless otherwise indicated)

	1995	*2000*	*2005*	*2006*	*2007*	*2008*	*2009*	*2010*
1. Summary external debt data								
External debt stocks	**684.4**	**671.8**	**662.0**	**649.8**	**677.6**	**688.8**	**704.8**	**725.9**
Long-term external debt	642.0	656.7	618.9	613.5	642.2	659.2	680.6	697.7
Public and publicly guaranteed	642.0	656.7	618.9	613.5	642.2	659.2	680.6	697.7
Private nonguaranteed	0.0	0.0	0.0	0.0	0.0	0.0	0.0	0.0
Use of IMF credit	38.4	11.1	35.0	36.3	35.4	29.7	24.1	28.2
Short-term external debt	4.0	4.0	8.0	0.0	0.0	0.0	0.0	0.0
interest arrears on long-term	0.0	0.0	0.0	0.0	0.0	0.0	0.0	0.0
Memorandum items								
Principal arrears on long-term	0.0	0.0	0.0	0.0	0.0	0.0	0.0	0.0
Long-term public sector debt	641.3	656.4	618.9	613.5	642.2	659.2	680.6	697.7
Long-term private sector debt	0.7	0.3	0.0	0.0	0.0	0.0	0.0	0.0
Public & publicly guaranteed commitments	67.4	33.9	15.0	21.5	61.2	41.5	36.2	238.5
External debt flows								
Disbursements	70.4	69.4	21.1	28.6	38.3	45.8	37.4	52.7
Long-term external debt	70.4	69.4	21.1	28.6	38.3	45.8	37.4	40.8
IMF purchases	0.0	0.0	0.0	0.0	0.0	0.0	0.0	11.9
Principal repayments	24.7	38.3	65.3	36.1	33.8	29.5	30.6	27.1
Long-term external debt	22.0	33.2	65.3	35.6	31.1	24.5	24.6	19.6
IMF repurchases	2.7	5.2	0.0	0.5	2.7	5.0	5.9	7.5
Net flows	45.7	31.0	-43.2	-15.5	4.5	16.3	6.8	25.6
Long-term external debt	48.4	36.2	-44.2	-7.0	7.2	21.3	12.7	21.2
Short-term external debt	0.0	0.0	1.0	-8.0	0.0	0.0	0.0	0.0
Interest payments	16.1	23.2	14.2	9.6	64.5	8.0	7.6	7.5
Long-term external debt	15.7	22.9	13.7	9.2	64.3	7.8	7.4	7.5
IMF charges	0.2	0.0	0.2	0.2	0.2	0.2	0.1	0.0
Short-term external debt	0.2	0.2	0.3	0.2	0.0	0.0	0.0	0.0
2. Other non-debt resource inflows								
Foreign direct investment	275.3	32.4	69.1	58.5	104.5	110.0	100.9	117.0
Portfolio equity	..	..	0.0	1.3	0.0	0.0	0.0	0.0
3. Currency composition of public and publicly guaranteed debt (%)								
Euro	..	..	9.8	9.8	9.2	7.5	6.8	5.5
Japanese yen	0.0	0.0	0.0	0.0	0.0	0.0	0.0	0.0
Pound sterling	0.8	1.8	0.9	0.7	0.5	0.4	0.4	0.3
Swiss franc	0.0	1.9	0.2	0.0	0.0	0.0	0.0	0.0
U.S.dollars	22.1	26.9	39.3	41.8	43.2	43.8	43.6	45.3
4. Average terms of new commitments								
Official creditors								
Interest (%)	5.9	0.3	1.7	0.8	3.2	1.7	1.0	5.0
Maturity (years)	27.5	19.3	31.0	38.1	31.0	23.9	40.9	27.0
Grace period (years)	5.7	5.4	8.5	10.3	7.8	6.3	9.3	6.6
Private creditors								
Interest (%)	6.5	4.6	0.0	0.0	0.0	0.0	0.0	0.0
Maturity (years)	17.9	2.0	0.0	0.0	0.0	0.0	0.0	0.0
Grace period (years)	4.1	0.5	0.0	0.0	0.0	0.0	0.0	0.0
5. Major economic aggregates								
Gross national income (GNI)	1151.5	973.6	1856.0	1858.2	2008.5	2131.0	2267.8	2552.8
Exports of goods, services & income	670.6	542.5	1397.6	1477.1	1654.9	1695.8	1550.2	1778.1
Worker remit. & comp. of employees	410.5	478.1	603.5	586.0	625.1	596.2	623.0	745.9
Imports of goods, services & income	1203.8	832.8	1888.5	1970.8	2251.8	2244.8	2276.4	2860.8
Profit remittances on FDI	71.4	15.0	191.6	249.4	301.2	333.9	296.4	338.9
Current account balance	-323.0	-151.4	-16.9	82.6	98.5	143.7	-2.4	-421.4
International reserves	456.7	417.9	519.1	658.4	..	..	..	..
6. Ratios								
External debt stocks to exports (%)	102.1	123.8	47.4	44.0	40.9	40.6	45.5	40.8
External debt stocks to GNI (%)	59.4	69.0	35.7	35.0	33.7	32.3	31.1	28.4
Debt service to exports (%)	6.1	11.3	5.7	3.1	5.9	2.2	2.5	1.9
Short-term to external debt stocks (%)	0.6	0.6	1.2	..	..	..	0.0	..
Multilateral to external debt stocks (%)	68.2	70.8	78.3	84.4	86.8	87.1	86.1	85.8
Reserves to external debt stocks (%)	66.7	62.2	78.4	101.3	..	..	..	..
Reserves to imports (months)	4.6	6.0	3.3	4.0	..	..	..	..

LESOTHO

(US$ million, unless otherwise indicated)

	1995	2000	2005	2006	2007	2008	2009	2010
7. Long-term external debt								
Debt outstanding and disbursed	**642.0**	**656.7**	**618.9**	**613.5**	**642.2**	**659.2**	**680.6**	**697.7**
Public and publicly guaranteed	642.0	656.7	618.9	613.5	642.2	659.2	680.6	697.7
Official creditors	607.1	580.9	590.6	591.9	624.6	646.6	667.1	684.1
Multilateral	466.9	475.7	518.4	548.2	587.8	599.9	606.8	622.7
of which: IBRD	54.0	58.6	12.7	9.1	4.2	3.3	2.5	1.8
IDA	152.8	183.2	258.2	274.6	293.2	302.7	310.7	328.4
Bilateral	140.1	105.3	72.2	43.7	36.8	46.7	60.3	61.4
Private creditors	34.9	75.8	28.4	21.6	17.5	12.5	13.6	13.6
of which: Bonds	0.0	0.0	0.0	0.0	0.0	0.0	0.0	0.0
Commercial banks	22.8	74.5	27.6	20.8	16.8	11.9	13.0	13.2
Private nonguaranteed	0.0	0.0	0.0	0.0	0.0	0.0	0.0	0.0
of which: Bonds	0.0	0.0	0.0	0.0	0.0	0.0	0.0	0.0
Disbursements	**70.4**	**69.4**	**21.1**	**28.6**	**38.3**	**45.8**	**37.4**	**40.8**
Public and publicly guaranteed	70.4	69.4	21.1	28.6	38.3	45.8	37.4	40.8
Official creditors	54.5	67.4	21.1	28.5	38.3	45.8	37.4	40.8
Multilateral	41.1	21.2	17.1	28.1	37.6	29.5	21.6	37.4
of which: IBRD	11.2	9.9	0.1	0.0	0.0	0.0	0.0	0.0
IDA	8.8	7.8	13.1	10.8	14.0	17.2	12.8	29.4
Bilateral	13.4	46.2	3.9	0.4	0.6	16.3	15.7	3.4
Private creditors	16.0	2.0	0.0	0.0	0.0	0.0	0.0	0.0
of which: Bonds	0.0	0.0	0.0	0.0	0.0	0.0	0.0	0.0
Commercial banks	16.0	2.0	0.0	0.0	0.0	0.0	0.0	0.0
Private nonguaranteed	0.0	0.0	0.0	0.0	0.0	0.0	0.0	0.0
of which: Bonds	0.0	0.0	0.0	0.0	0.0	0.0	0.0	0.0
Principal repayments	**22.0**	**33.2**	**65.3**	**35.6**	**31.1**	**24.5**	**24.6**	**19.6**
Public and publicly guaranteed	22.0	33.2	65.3	35.6	31.1	24.5	24.6	19.6
Official creditors	17.8	26.4	32.0	27.5	25.8	21.3	23.9	19.3
Multilateral	14.1	14.1	19.7	19.4	22.0	17.8	21.0	16.5
of which: IBRD	0.0	3.9	3.6	3.6	3.6	1.0	0.7	0.7
IDA	1.3	2.5	5.0	5.3	6.0	6.3	6.9	7.2
Bilateral	3.7	12.2	12.3	8.2	3.8	3.5	2.9	2.8
Private creditors	4.2	6.8	33.3	8.1	5.3	3.2	0.7	0.3
of which: Bonds	0.0	0.0	0.0	0.0	0.0	0.0	0.0	0.0
Commercial banks	2.0	6.8	33.2	8.0	5.2	3.1	0.6	0.2
Private nonguaranteed	0.0	0.0	0.0	0.0	0.0	0.0	0.0	0.0
of which: Bonds	0.0	0.0	0.0	0.0	0.0	0.0	0.0	0.0
Interest payments	**15.7**	**22.9**	**13.7**	**9.2**	**64.3**	**7.8**	**7.4**	**7.5**
Public and publicly guaranteed	15.7	22.9	13.7	9.2	64.3	7.8	7.4	7.5
Official creditors	12.4	16.0	7.7	7.1	63.3	6.7	6.9	6.4
Multilateral	8.6	7.7	5.5	5.4	5.4	5.3	5.3	4.8
of which: IBRD	3.5	3.2	0.5	0.6	0.5	0.0	0.1	0.0
IDA	1.1	1.4	2.1	2.1	2.2	2.3	2.2	2.3
Bilateral	3.8	8.3	2.1	1.7	57.9	1.4	1.6	1.6
Private creditors	3.3	7.0	6.0	2.1	1.1	1.1	0.5	1.0
of which: Bonds	0.0	0.0	0.0	0.0	0.0	0.0	0.0	0.0
Commercial banks	3.0	7.0	6.0	2.0	1.0	1.1	0.5	1.0
Private nonguaranteed	0.0	0.0	0.0	0.0	0.0	0.0	0.0	0.0
of which: Bonds	0.0	0.0	0.0	0.0	0.0	0.0	0.0	0.0
8. Debt stock-flow reconciliation								
Total change in external debt stocks	61.8	-10.2	-104.7	-12.1	27.8	11.2	16.0	21.1
Net flows on external debt	45.7	31.0	-43.2	-15.5	4.5	16.3	6.8	25.6
9. Debt restructurings								
Total amount rescheduled	0.0	0.0	0.0	0.0	0.0	0.0	0.0	0.0
Total amount forgiven	0.0	0.0	0.0	18.3	5.9	1.4	0.0	0.0
Debt buyback	0.0	0.0	0.0	0.0	0.0	0.0	0.0	0.0

10. Contractual obligations on outstanding long-term external debt

	2011	2012	2013	2014	2015	2016	2017	2018
Official creditors								
Principal	25.4	27.0	29.0	29.3	28.0	37.4	38.6	38.8
Interest	7.5	11.5	14.2	15.9	16.7	17.0	16.5	15.9
Private creditors								
Principal	0.2	0.2	0.2	0.2	8.2	0.2	0.2	0.2
Interest	1.2	1.2	1.2	1.2	1.2	0.1	0.1	0.1

Notes:

Large interest payment was made during 2007 to a creditor country to settle a long standing claim.

LIBERIA

(US$ million, unless otherwise indicated)

	1995	*2000*	*2005*	*2006*	*2007*	*2008*	*2009*	*2010*
1. Summary external debt data								
External debt stocks	**2458.0**	**2792.1**	**3897.6**	**4114.1**	**3721.5**	**3128.1**	**1655.6**	**228.0**
Long-term external debt	1152.8	1104.0	1179.1	1203.8	1033.5	865.0	673.1	183.6
Public and publicly guaranteed	1152.8	1104.0	1179.1	1203.8	1033.5	865.0	673.1	183.6
Private nonguaranteed	0.0	0.0	0.0	0.0	0.0	0.0	0.0	0.0
Use of IMF credit	335.6	292.3	319.6	335.7	351.9	858.0	891.2	44.4
Short-term external debt	969.6	1395.8	2398.9	2574.6	2336.1	1405.1	91.3	0.0
interest arrears on long-term	925.6	1395.8	2398.9	2574.6	2336.1	1405.1	91.3	0.0
Memorandum items								
Principal arrears on long-term	958.5	1112.5	1284.1	1339.8	1267.9	424.1	250.4	78.6
Long-term public sector debt	1152.8	1104.0	1179.1	1203.8	1033.5	865.0	673.1	183.6
Long-term private sector debt	0.0	0.0	0.0	0.0	0.0	0.0	0.0	0.0
Public & publicly guaranteed commitments	0.0	0.0	0.0	5.0	0.0	0.0	0.0	10.0
External debt flows								
Disbursements	0.0	0.0	0.0	0.0	0.0	880.5	17.6	17.3
Long-term external debt	0.0	0.0	0.0	0.0	0.0	0.0	0.0	3.7
IMF purchases	0.0	0.0	0.0	0.0	0.0	880.5	17.6	13.6
Principal repayments	0.1	0.6	0.1	0.7	261.4	389.5	36.3	3.7
Long-term external debt	0.0	0.0	0.0	0.0	260.7	37.5	36.3	3.7
IMF repurchases	0.1	0.6	0.1	0.7	0.7	352.0	0.0	0.0
Net flows	-0.1	-0.6	-0.1	-0.7	-261.4	491.1	-18.6	13.5
Long-term external debt	0.0	0.0	0.0	0.0	-260.7	-37.5	-36.3	0.0
Short-term external debt	0.0	0.0	0.0	0.0	0.0	0.0	0.0	0.0
Interest payments	1.5	0.1	0.9	0.1	380.5	545.0	27.7	1.8
Long-term external debt	0.0	0.0	0.0	0.0	380.5	69.0	16.8	0.6
IMF charges	1.5	0.1	0.8	0.0	0.0	475.9	10.9	1.2
Short-term external debt	0.0	0.0	0.0	0.0	0.0	0.0	0.0	0.0
2. Other non-debt resource inflows								
Foreign direct investment	5.0	20.8	82.8	107.9	131.6	394.5	217.8	452.9
Portfolio equity	..	..	..	..	..	..	..	..
3. Currency composition of public and publicly guaranteed debt (%)								
Euro	..	..	11.6	12.7	16.5	2.4	2.6	0.0
Japanese yen	7.7	7.2	6.6	6.4	7.8	8.2	0.0	0.0
Pound sterling	1.2	1.2	1.2	1.2	0.9	0.8	1.0	0.0
Swiss franc	0.0	0.0	0.0	0.0	0.0	0.0	0.0	0.0
U.S.dollars	48.8	56.8	53.7	52.8	64.8	82.7	88.9	95.2
4. Average terms of new commitments								
Official creditors								
Interest (%)	0.0	0.0	0.0	0.0	0.0	0.0	0.0	0.8
Maturity (years)	0.0	0.0	0.0	25.1	0.0	0.0	0.0	39.5
Grace period (years)	0.0	0.0	0.0	15.0	0.0	0.0	0.0	10.0
Private creditors								
Interest (%)	0.0	0.0	0.0	0.0	0.0	0.0	0.0	0.0
Maturity (years)	0.0	0.0	0.0	0.0	0.0	0.0	0.0	0.0
Grace period (years)	0.0	0.0	0.0	0.0	0.0	0.0	0.0	0.0
5. Major economic aggregates								
Gross national income (GNI)	..	388.5	417.2	443.9	559.9	672.8	734.4	804.5
Exports of goods, services & income	..	..	354.7	509.5	562.2	781.0	472.2	430.9
Worker remit. & comp. of employees	..	..	31.9	78.8	62.0	58.1	25.1	26.7
Imports of goods, services & income	..	300.3	1317.7	1882.4	1924.2	2310.7	1850.0	1806.8
Profit remittances on FDI	..	..	7.1	14.0	14.7	22.5	5.8	0.1
Current account balance	..	-84.4	-183.5	-172.8	-223.2	-354.3	-277.2	-415.7
International reserves	28.1	0.3	25.4	72.0	119.4	160.9	372.5	..
6. Ratios								
External debt stocks to exports (%)	..	..	1098.8	807.5	661.9	400.5	350.6	52.9
External debt stocks to GNI (%)	..	718.7	934.2	926.8	664.7	464.9	225.4	28.3
Debt service to exports (%)	..	..	0.3	0.2	114.2	119.6	13.5	1.3
Short-term to external debt stocks (%)	39.4	50.0	61.5	62.6	62.8	44.9	5.5	..
Multilateral to external debt stocks (%)	18.4	14.2	11.3	10.9	5.2	5.0	9.3	27.7
Reserves to external debt stocks (%)	1.1	0.0	0.7	1.7	3.2	5.1	22.5	..
Reserves to imports (months)	..	0.0	0.2	0.5	0.7	0.8	2.4	..

LIBERIA

(US$ million, unless otherwise indicated)

	1995	*2000*	*2005*	*2006*	*2007*	*2008*	*2009*	*2010*
7. Long-term external debt								
Debt outstanding and disbursed	**1152.8**	**1104.0**	**1179.1**	**1203.8**	**1033.5**	**865.0**	**673.1**	**183.6**
Public and publicly guaranteed	1152.8	1104.0	1179.1	1203.8	1033.5	865.0	673.1	183.6
Official creditors	945.3	907.3	981.3	1005.2	831.0	669.8	652.6	183.6
Multilateral	453.3	395.3	440.1	447.9	192.2	157.9	154.5	63.1
of which: IBRD	160.9	129.8	145.6	146.6	0.0	0.0	0.0	0.0
IDA	108.1	100.1	105.9	108.9	76.6	72.0	69.0	0.0
Bilateral	492.0	511.9	541.2	557.2	638.7	511.9	498.1	120.5
Private creditors	207.5	196.8	197.7	198.7	202.5	195.2	20.5	0.0
of which: Bonds	0.0	0.0	0.0	0.0	0.0	0.0	0.0	0.0
Commercial banks	186.8	179.7	178.5	178.2	180.8	195.2	20.5	0.0
Private nonguaranteed	0.0	0.0	0.0	0.0	0.0	0.0	0.0	0.0
of which: Bonds	0.0	0.0	0.0	0.0	0.0	0.0	0.0	0.0
Disbursements	**0.0**	**0.0**	**0.0**	**0.0**	**0.0**	**0.0**	**0.0**	**3.7**
Public and publicly guaranteed	0.0	0.0	0.0	0.0	0.0	0.0	0.0	3.7
Official creditors	0.0	0.0	0.0	0.0	0.0	0.0	0.0	3.7
Multilateral	0.0	0.0	0.0	0.0	0.0	0.0	0.0	0.0
of which: IBRD	0.0	0.0	0.0	0.0	0.0	0.0	0.0	0.0
IDA	0.0	0.0	0.0	0.0	0.0	0.0	0.0	0.0
Bilateral	0.0	0.0	0.0	0.0	0.0	0.0	0.0	3.7
Private creditors	0.0	0.0	0.0	0.0	0.0	0.0	0.0	0.0
of which: Bonds	0.0	0.0	0.0	0.0	0.0	0.0	0.0	0.0
Commercial banks	0.0	0.0	0.0	0.0	0.0	0.0	0.0	0.0
Private nonguaranteed	0.0	0.0	0.0	0.0	0.0	0.0	0.0	0.0
of which: Bonds	0.0	0.0	0.0	0.0	0.0	0.0	0.0	0.0
Principal repayments	**0.0**	**0.0**	**0.0**	**0.0**	**260.7**	**37.5**	**36.3**	**3.7**
Public and publicly guaranteed	0.0	0.0	0.0	0.0	260.7	37.5	36.3	3.7
Official creditors	0.0	0.0	0.0	0.0	260.7	37.5	4.3	3.7
Multilateral	0.0	0.0	0.0	0.0	260.7	37.5	4.3	3.7
of which: IBRD	0.0	0.0	0.0	0.0	162.5	0.0	0.0	0.0
IDA	0.0	0.0	0.0	0.0	35.3	4.3	3.3	1.7
Bilateral	0.0	0.0	0.0	0.0	0.0	0.0	0.0	0.0
Private creditors	0.0	0.0	0.0	0.0	0.0	0.0	32.0	0.0
of which: Bonds	0.0	0.0	0.0	0.0	0.0	0.0	0.0	0.0
Commercial banks	0.0	0.0	0.0	0.0	0.0	0.0	32.0	0.0
Private nonguaranteed	0.0	0.0	0.0	0.0	0.0	0.0	0.0	0.0
of which: Bonds	0.0	0.0	0.0	0.0	0.0	0.0	0.0	0.0
Interest payments	**0.0**	**0.0**	**0.0**	**0.0**	**380.5**	**69.0**	**16.8**	**0.6**
Public and publicly guaranteed	0.0	0.0	0.0	0.0	380.5	69.0	16.8	0.6
Official creditors	0.0	0.0	0.0	0.0	380.5	69.0	11.8	0.6
Multilateral	0.0	0.0	0.0	0.0	380.5	69.0	11.8	0.6
of which: IBRD	0.0	0.0	0.0	0.0	292.3	0.0	0.0	0.0
IDA	0.0	0.0	0.0	0.0	17.7	1.0	0.5	0.3
Bilateral	0.0	0.0	0.0	0.0	0.0	0.0	0.0	0.0
Private creditors	0.0	0.0	0.0	0.0	0.0	0.0	5.0	0.0
of which: Bonds	0.0	0.0	0.0	0.0	0.0	0.0	0.0	0.0
Commercial banks	0.0	0.0	0.0	0.0	0.0	0.0	5.0	0.0
Private nonguaranteed	0.0	0.0	0.0	0.0	0.0	0.0	0.0	0.0
of which: Bonds	0.0	0.0	0.0	0.0	0.0	0.0	0.0	0.0
8. Debt stock-flow reconciliation								
Total change in external debt stocks	110.1	246.7	89.3	216.5	-392.5	-593.4	-1472.5	-1427.7
Net flows on external debt	-0.1	-0.6	-0.1	-0.7	-261.4	491.1	-18.6	13.5
9. Debt restructurings								
Total amount rescheduled	0.0	0.0	0.0	0.0	0.0	295.0	2.7	92.1
Total amount forgiven	0.0	0.0	0.0	0.0	0.0	637.0	1449.2	1506.7
Debt buyback	0.0	0.0	0.0	0.0	0.0	0.0	32.0	0.0

10. Contractual obligations on outstanding long-term external debt

	2011	*2012*	*2013*	*2014*	*2015*	*2016*	*2017*	*2018*
Official creditors								
Principal	6.7	7.9	7.9	7.9	7.1	6.2	5.8	4.5
Interest	1.4	1.3	1.2	1.1	0.9	0.8	0.8	0.7
Private creditors								
Principal	0.0	0.0	0.0	0.0	0.0	0.0	0.0	0.0
Interest	0.0	0.0	0.0	0.0	0.0	0.0	0.0	0.0

Notes:

Historical data for long-term public and publicly guaranteed debt are revised based on reports provided by the Ministry of Finance. Data include the effects of Paris Club rescheduling agreement signed in 2008 and 2010 and of MDRI, in the amount of $64,756 thousand in 2010.

LITHUANIA

(US$ million, unless otherwise indicated)

	1995	2000	2005	2006	2007	2008	2009	2010
1. Summary external debt data								
External debt stocks	**769**	**4,723**	**11,433**	**18,571**	**29,443**	**31,788**	**31,821**	**29,602**
Long-term external debt	459	3,417	6,108	12,865	21,680	23,614	25,871	24,133
Public and publicly guaranteed	430	2,206	2,001	4,588	5,879	5,347	9,072	11,664
Private nonguaranteed	29	1,211	4,107	8,277	15,800	18,267	16,800	12,468
Use of IMF credit	262	192	0	0	0	0	0	0
Short-term external debt	49	1,114	5,325	5,706	7,763	8,174	5,949	5,469
interest arrears on long-term	0	0	0	0	0	0	0	0
Memorandum items								
Principal arrears on long-term	0	0	0	0	0	0	0	0
Long-term public sector debt	424	2,128	1,978	4,575	5,871	5,343	9,072	11,664
Long-term private sector debt	34	1,290	4,130	8,290	15,809	18,271	16,800	12,468
Public & publicly guaranteed commitments	422	828	0	2,513	822	110	4,458	3,214
External debt flows								
Disbursements	219	1,165	2,863	9,400	14,462	11,074	7,332	7,021
Long-term external debt	157	1,165	2,863	9,400	14,462	11,074	7,332	7,021
IMF purchases	63	0	0	0	0	0	0	0
Principal repayments	12	826	2,277	3,737	7,715	8,342	5,689	8,014
Long-term external debt	12	799	2,252	3,737	7,715	8,342	5,689	8,014
IMF repurchases	0	27	25	0	0	0	0	0
Net flows	228	383	2,145	6,044	8,805	3,143	-582	-1,473
Long-term external debt	144	366	611	5,663	6,747	2,732	1,642	-993
Short-term external debt	20	44	1,559	381	2,057	411	-2,225	-480
Interest payments	31	281	323	436	748	1,042	765	807
Long-term external debt	17	215	173	275	529	797	586	669
IMF charges	12	11	0	0	0	0	0	0
Short-term external debt	2	55	150	161	219	245	178	138
2. Other non-debt resource inflows								
Foreign direct investment	73	379	1,032	1,840	2,017	2,070	126	622
Portfolio equity	6	122	130	72	-166	3	-2	37
3. Currency composition of public and publicly guaranteed debt (%)								
Euro	..	..	81.0	96.4	98.3	98.4	82.7	63.1
Japanese yen	9.8	2.9	0.0	0.0	0.0	0.0	0.0	0.0
Pound sterling	0.0	0.1	0.0	0.0	0.0	0.0	0.0	0.0
Swiss franc	3.2	0.0	0.0	0.0	0.0	0.0	0.0	0.0
U.S.dollars	34.4	32.9	17.8	3.2	1.5	1.4	17.2	36.9
4. Average terms of new commitments								
Official creditors								
Interest (%)	6.3	7.1	0.0	1.6	0.0	0.0	4.1	3.3
Maturity (years)	14.6	13.3	0.0	5.0	0.0	0.0	23.7	24.9
Grace period (years)	4.4	7.8	0.0	1.0	0.0	0.0	6.9	7.0
Private creditors								
Interest (%)	8.1	7.8	0.0	4.8	4.9	5.5	7.7	6.8
Maturity (years)	5.4	5.0	0.0	8.1	10.3	13.0	5.7	9.3
Grace period (years)	1.2	4.8	0.0	8.1	10.3	1.0	4.7	9.3
5. Major economic aggregates								
Gross national income (GNI)	7,892	11,240	25,339	29,270	37,491	45,665	37,544	35,687
Exports of goods, services & income	3,242	5,295	15,327	18,364	21,980	29,567	20,948	25,745
Worker remit. & comp. of employees	1	50	534	994	1,433	1,488	1,172	1,575
Imports of goods, services & income	3,966	6,212	17,820	22,307	28,836	37,004	20,948	26,912
Profit remittances on FDI	8	123	711	878	1,423	1,298	-944	499
Current account balance	-614	-675	-1,831	-3,218	-5,692	-6,356	1,648	667
International reserves	829	1,363	3,816	5,773	7,721	6,444	6,657	6,836
6. Ratios								
External debt stocks to exports (%)	23.7	89.2	74.6	101.1	133.9	107.5	151.9	115.0
External debt stocks to GNI (%)	9.8	42.0	45.1	63.4	78.5	69.6	84.8	83.0
Debt service to exports (%)	1.3	20.9	17.0	22.7	38.5	31.7	30.8	34.3
Short-term to external debt stocks (%)	6.4	23.6	46.6	30.7	26.4	25.7	18.7	18.5
Multilateral to external debt stocks (%)	21.1	9.5	2.7	1.7	0.8	0.7	3.9	5.4
Reserves to external debt stocks (%)	107.7	28.9	33.4	31.1	26.2	20.3	20.9	23.1
Reserves to imports (months)	2.5	2.6	2.6	3.1	3.2	2.1	3.8	3.0

(US$ million, unless otherwise indicated)

	1995	2000	2005	2006	2007	2008	2009	2010
7. Long-term external debt								
Debt outstanding and disbursed	**459**	**3,417**	**6,108**	**12,865**	**21,680**	**23,614**	**25,871**	**24,133**
Public and publicly guaranteed	430	2,206	2,001	4,588	5,879	5,347	9,072	11,664
Official creditors	317	670	472	319	244	212	1,251	1,612
Multilateral	163	447	308	312	239	210	1,251	1,612
of which: IBRD	62	253	86	81	24	27	23	20
IDA	0	0	0	0	0	0	0	0
Bilateral	154	223	164	7	5	2	0	0
Private creditors	113	1,537	1,529	4,269	5,635	5,135	7,820	10,053
of which: Bonds	0	1,130	1,416	4,214	5,594	5,114	7,816	10,052
Commercial banks	1	188	63	51	40	20	4	0
Private nonguaranteed	29	1,211	4,107	8,277	15,800	18,267	16,800	12,468
of which: Bonds	0	37	0	0	1,030	1,030	1,030	793
Disbursements	**157**	**1,165**	**2,863**	**9,400**	**14,462**	**11,074**	**7,332**	**7,021**
Public and publicly guaranteed	157	479	45	2,540	843	116	3,589	3,214
Official creditors	92	146	45	28	20	6	1,028	464
Multilateral	38	139	42	28	20	6	1,028	464
of which: IBRD	12	66	14	10	0	6	0	0
IDA	0	0	0	0	0	0	0	0
Bilateral	54	7	3	0	0	0	0	0
Private creditors	64	333	0	2,511	822	110	2,561	2,750
of which: Bonds	0	300	0	2,511	822	110	2,561	2,750
Commercial banks	1	31	0	0	0	0	0	0
Private nonguaranteed	0	686	2,818	6,860	13,620	10,958	3,742	3,806
of which: Bonds	0	37	0	0	1,030	0	0	0
Principal repayments	**12**	**799**	**2,252**	**3,737**	**7,715**	**8,342**	**5,689**	**8,014**
Public and publicly guaranteed	12	310	802	273	145	344	119	78
Official creditors	3	82	235	209	128	28	30	18
Multilateral	0	62	144	52	125	25	27	18
of which: IBRD	0	9	111	19	58	3	3	3
IDA	0	0	0	0	0	0	0	0
Bilateral	3	19	91	157	3	2	2	0
Private creditors	9	229	567	64	17	316	89	59
of which: Bonds	0	25	405	0	0	294	73	56
Commercial banks	0	146	112	16	15	21	16	4
Private nonguaranteed	0	489	1,451	3,464	7,570	7,999	5,570	7,936
of which: Bonds	0	0	0	0	0	0	0	237
Interest payments	**17**	**215**	**173**	**275**	**529**	**797**	**586**	**669**
Public and publicly guaranteed	17	136	106	161	156	252	273	506
Official creditors	13	35	36	24	15	11	8	43
Multilateral	9	26	26	14	14	11	8	43
of which: IBRD	4	15	15	4	3	1	1	0
IDA	0	0	0	0	0	0	0	0
Bilateral	4	9	10	10	0	0	0	0
Private creditors	4	100	70	137	142	241	265	463
of which: Bonds	0	63	55	131	139	239	264	463
Commercial banks	0	20	6	3	2	2	0	0
Private nonguaranteed	0	80	67	114	373	545	313	163
of which: Bonds	0	0	0	0	41	58	45	18
8. Debt stock-flow reconciliation								
Total change in external debt stocks	267	308	940	7,138	10,872	2,345	33	-2,219
Net flows on external debt	228	383	2,145	6,044	8,805	3,143	-582	-1,473
9. Debt restructurings								
Total amount rescheduled	0	0	0	0	0	0	0	0
Total amount forgiven	0	0	0	0	0	0	0	0
Debt buyback	0	0	0	0	0	0	0	0

10. Contractual obligations on outstanding long-term external debt

	2011	2012	2013	2014	2015	2016	2017	2018
Official creditors								
Principal	25	26	18	21	38	124	144	142
Interest	44	47	49	50	50	49	46	43
Private creditors								
Principal	3,138	3,586	3,366	2,336	2,484	2,041	1,733	1,279
Interest	1,124	989	787	649	472	376	288	218

Notes:

Short-term debt data are based on reports provided by the country.

MACEDONIA, FYR

(US$ million, unless otherwise indicated)

	1995	2000	2005	2006	2007	2008	2009	2010
1. Summary external debt data								
External debt stocks	**1,277**	**1,469**	**2,970**	**3,284**	**4,161**	**4,681**	**5,593**	**5,804**
Long-term external debt	1,078	1,333	2,108	2,362	2,564	3,013	3,695	3,750
Public and publicly guaranteed	788	1,206	1,637	1,556	1,520	1,574	1,874	1,865
Private nonguaranteed	289	127	471	805	1,044	1,438	1,821	1,885
Use of IMF credit	57	81	62	56	0	0	0	0
Short-term external debt	143	55	800	867	1,597	1,668	1,899	2,054
interest arrears on long-term	143	4	9	15	28	29	30	59
Memorandum items								
Principal arrears on long-term	216	19	36	49	108	118	107	168
Long-term public sector debt	785	1,201	1,635	1,555	1,519	1,574	1,873	1,865
Long-term private sector debt	293	132	473	807	1,044	1,439	1,821	1,885
Public & publicly guaranteed commitments	206	123	274	137	103	155	410	238
External debt flows								
Disbursements	112	155	333	401	538	789	1,012	576
Long-term external debt	75	151	318	401	538	789	1,012	576
IMF purchases	38	4	16	0	0	0	0	0
Principal repayments	20	93	182	439	542	293	375	455
Long-term external debt	19	74	171	430	485	293	375	455
IMF repurchases	1	19	11	10	57	0	0	0
Net flows	74	59	117	23	713	566	867	248
Long-term external debt	56	78	147	-29	52	496	637	121
Short-term external debt	-18	-3	-34	61	717	69	230	127
Interest payments	11	45	92	125	163	181	177	214
Long-term external debt	9	37	54	82	88	104	93	122
IMF charges	2	3	1	2	1	0	0	0
Short-term external debt	1	5	37	40	74	77	84	92
2. Other non-debt resource inflows								
Foreign direct investment	9	215	97	424	699	587	197	296
Portfolio equity	0	0	54	86	170	-49	-14	-4
3. Currency composition of public and publicly guaranteed debt (%)								
Euro	..	..	40.8	52.3	63.0	64.0	69.6	69.6
Japanese yen	6.5	0.4	0.2	0.5	1.4	3.0	3.6	5.4
Pound sterling	1.1	0.2	0.1	0.1	0.0	0.0	0.0	0.0
Swiss franc	0.9	2.4	0.6	0.5	0.1	0.0	0.0	0.0
U.S.dollars	49.7	71.8	56.6	44.8	34.3	31.8	25.8	24.1
4. Average terms of new commitments								
Official creditors								
Interest (%)	3.8	5.5	3.1	3.7	5.0	3.2	1.9	1.4
Maturity (years)	23.0	19.5	16.7	16.8	17.0	17.4	15.3	14.6
Grace period (years)	6.7	6.4	5.1	5.4	5.0	4.6	4.7	4.6
Private creditors								
Interest (%)	2.3	9.2	4.6	5.8	0.0	1.8	9.9	0.0
Maturity (years)	29.7	3.4	10.0	16.1	0.0	4.3	3.5	4.3
Grace period (years)	10.9	0.5	9.9	3.9	0.0	0.1	3.5	0.9
5. Major economic aggregates								
Gross national income (GNI)	4,410	3,541	5,756	6,359	7,775	9,719	9,194	8,920
Exports of goods, services & income	..	1,679	2,654	3,147	4,423	5,268	3,726	4,402
Worker remit. & comp. of employees	..	81	227	267	345	407	381	388
Imports of goods, services & income	..	2,386	3,865	4,413	6,412	7,961	5,926	6,467
Profit remittances on FDI	..	31	142	59	470	253	138	239
Current account balance	..	-98	-159	-29	-606	-1,236	-599	-262
International reserves	275	460	1,340	1,889	2,264	2,110	2,288	2,277
6. Ratios								
External debt stocks to exports (%)	..	87.5	111.9	104.4	94.1	88.9	150.1	131.8
External debt stocks to GNI (%)	29.0	41.5	51.6	51.7	53.5	48.2	60.8	65.1
Debt service to exports (%)	..	8.2	10.3	17.9	15.9	9.0	14.8	15.2
Short-term to external debt stocks (%)	11.2	3.7	26.9	26.4	38.4	35.6	33.9	35.4
Multilateral to external debt stocks (%)	22.6	38.8	30.8	31.3	25.0	22.4	19.3	19.2
Reserves to external debt stocks (%)	21.5	31.3	45.1	57.5	54.4	45.1	40.9	39.2
Reserves to imports (months)	..	2.3	4.2	5.1	4.2	3.2	4.6	4.2

(US$ million, unless otherwise indicated)

	1995	2000	2005	2006	2007	2008	2009	2010
7. Long-term external debt								
Debt outstanding and disbursed	**1,078**	**1,333**	**2,108**	**2,362**	**2,564**	**3,013**	**3,695**	**3,750**
Public and publicly guaranteed	788	1,206	1,637	1,556	1,520	1,574	1,874	1,865
Official creditors	605	921	1,202	1,298	1,239	1,277	1,321	1,354
Multilateral	288	570	914	1,028	1,040	1,047	1,081	1,112
of which: IBRD	97	116	244	259	193	237	271	315
IDA	84	249	364	383	394	386	382	367
Bilateral	317	352	288	270	199	230	240	242
Private creditors	184	284	435	258	281	297	552	512
of which: Bonds	0	0	177	198	221	209	468	434
Commercial banks	103	274	252	56	57	79	77	72
Private nonguaranteed	289	127	471	805	1,044	1,438	1,821	1,885
of which: Bonds	0	0	0	0	0	0	0	0
Disbursements	**75**	**151**	**318**	**401**	**538**	**789**	**1,012**	**576**
Public and publicly guaranteed	75	98	293	112	142	174	347	182
Official creditors	74	96	104	83	138	137	103	175
Multilateral	74	79	94	71	108	86	76	149
of which: IBRD	20	13	54	11	54	52	43	72
IDA	42	38	8	5	0	0	0	0
Bilateral	0	17	11	12	31	52	27	26
Private creditors	0	1	189	29	3	37	244	7
of which: Bonds	0	0	187	0	0	0	244	0
Commercial banks	0	0	2	28	3	30	0	7
Private nonguaranteed	0	54	25	289	396	615	665	394
of which: Bonds	0	0	0	0	0	0	0	0
Principal repayments	**19**	**74**	**171**	**430**	**485**	**293**	**375**	**455**
Public and publicly guaranteed	19	25	81	307	294	78	88	98
Official creditors	19	23	67	79	286	74	81	90
Multilateral	19	20	31	36	171	52	60	64
of which: IBRD	19	3	11	12	134	8	9	11
IDA	0	0	2	4	5	6	7	8
Bilateral	0	3	36	43	115	21	21	26
Private creditors	0	2	14	228	8	5	7	9
of which: Bonds	0	0	0	0	0	0	0	0
Commercial banks	0	2	14	227	6	4	5	7
Private nonguaranteed	0	49	90	123	191	215	287	357
of which: Bonds	0	0	0	0	0	0	0	0
Interest payments	**9**	**37**	**54**	**82**	**88**	**104**	**93**	**122**
Public and publicly guaranteed	9	30	41	52	51	54	47	56
Official creditors	9	20	32	37	38	41	33	21
Multilateral	9	19	20	23	29	33	26	15
of which: IBRD	8	7	7	10	11	10	8	3
IDA	0	2	3	3	3	3	3	3
Bilateral	0	1	12	13	9	8	6	7
Private creditors	0	10	9	15	12	14	15	35
of which: Bonds	0	0	0	9	10	10	10	32
Commercial banks	0	10	8	6	2	3	5	3
Private nonguaranteed	0	7	13	30	38	50	46	66
of which: Bonds	0	0	0	0	0	0	0	0
8. Debt stock-flow reconciliation								
Total change in external debt stocks	174	44	153	315	876	520	912	211
Net flows on external debt	74	59	117	23	713	566	867	248
9. Debt restructurings								
Total amount rescheduled	256	44	0	0	0	0	0	0
Total amount forgiven	0	0	0	0	0	0	0	0
Debt buyback	0	0	0	0	0	0	0	0

10. Contractual obligations on outstanding long-term external debt

	2011	2012	2013	2014	2015	2016	2017	2018
Official creditors								
Principal	119	113	117	122	120	110	102	89
Interest	22	20	18	16	14	12	10	8
Private creditors								
Principal	403	357	565	142	293	106	104	121
Interest	121	90	45	43	35	25	18	12

Notes:

Short-term debt is based on Central Bank data from 2004.

MADAGASCAR

(US$ million, unless otherwise indicated)

	1995	2000	2005	2006	2007	2008	2009	2010
1. Summary external debt data								
External debt stocks	**4,302**	**4,691**	**3,494**	**1,492**	**1,707**	**2,076**	**2,203**	**2,295**
Long-term external debt	3,687	4,286	3,182	1,242	1,411	1,721	1,841	1,984
Public and publicly guaranteed	3,687	4,286	3,182	1,242	1,411	1,717	1,836	1,981
Private nonguaranteed	0	0	0	0	0	4	4	3
Use of IMF credit	73	104	212	29	43	99	101	97
Short-term external debt	542	301	99	221	254	255	262	214
interest arrears on long-term	486	203	72	186	189	188	189	188
Memorandum items								
Principal arrears on long-term	1,194	665	218	223	195	196	196	195
Long-term public sector debt	3,555	4,164	3,136	1,238	1,407	1,714	1,835	1,979
Long-term private sector debt	133	122	46	4	3	7	6	4
Public & publicly guaranteed commitments	80	187	295	284	192	544	83	0
External debt flows								
Disbursements	90	200	265	291	273	404	126	211
Long-term external debt	90	150	249	280	261	345	126	211
IMF purchases	0	50	17	12	12	59	0	0
Principal repayments	38	79	48	36	9	20	34	39
Long-term external debt	24	74	38	36	9	20	34	37
IMF repurchases	15	5	10	0	0	0	0	2
Net flows	59	45	244	263	294	386	98	125
Long-term external debt	66	76	211	243	252	325	92	174
Short-term external debt	7	-76	27	8	30	2	6	-47
Interest payments	20	38	30	23	13	12	17	17
Long-term external debt	16	28	28	21	10	11	15	16
IMF charges	0	0	1	0	0	0	0	0
Short-term external debt	3	9	1	2	3	1	1	1
2. Other non-debt resource inflows								
Foreign direct investment	10	83	85	295	773	1,169	1,066	860
Portfolio equity	..	..	..	..	..	..	..	..
3. Currency composition of public and publicly guaranteed debt (%)								
Euro	..	..	2.3	5.8	3.0	2.3	2.4	2.5
Japanese yen	7.7	7.4	0.0	0.0	0.0	0.0	0.0	0.0
Pound sterling	0.1	0.1	0.0	0.0	0.0	0.0	0.0	0.0
Swiss franc	1.3	0.9	0.1	0.4	0.4	0.3	0.3	0.3
U.S.dollars	45.0	56.8	71.9	55.7	57.2	53.8	52.5	53.1
4. Average terms of new commitments								
Official creditors								
Interest (%)	1.1	0.8	0.8	0.8	1.1	1.2	1.0	0.0
Maturity (years)	36.8	40.1	37.8	43.5	33.5	29.4	36.1	0.0
Grace period (years)	9.6	10.2	9.8	10.1	9.0	6.5	6.7	0.0
Private creditors								
Interest (%)	0.0	0.0	1.0	0.0	0.0	4.3	0.0	0.0
Maturity (years)	0.0	0.0	30.8	0.0	0.0	4.3	0.0	0.0
Grace period (years)	0.0	0.0	11.3	0.0	0.0	0.3	0.0	0.0
5. Major economic aggregates								
Gross national income (GNI)	3,002	3,807	4,960	5,435	7,288	9,344	8,397	8,628
Exports of goods, services & income	756	1,210	1,356	1,698	2,342	2,614	1,982	2,185
Worker remit. & comp. of employees	14	11	11	..	..	..	..	..
Imports of goods, services & income	1,161	1,584	2,146	2,484	3,606	4,805	4,134	3,351
Profit remittances on FDI	3	4	38	..	..	..	..	..
Current account balance	-276	-260	-554	-537	-898	-1,726	-1,840	-730
International reserves	109	285	481	583	847	982	1,135	1,172
6. Ratios								
External debt stocks to exports (%)	568.9	387.6	257.7	87.8	72.9	79.4	111.2	105.1
External debt stocks to GNI (%)	143.3	123.2	70.4	27.4	23.4	22.2	26.2	26.6
Debt service to exports (%)	7.7	9.6	5.8	3.5	0.9	1.3	2.5	2.6
Short-term to external debt stocks (%)	12.6	6.4	2.8	14.8	14.9	12.3	11.9	9.3
Multilateral to external debt stocks (%)	39.3	39.0	81.3	59.6	64.0	66.4	65.7	66.9
Reserves to external debt stocks (%)	2.5	6.1	13.8	39.1	49.6	47.3	51.5	51.0
Reserves to imports (months)	1.1	2.2	2.7	2.8	2.8	2.5	3.3	4.2

(US$ million, unless otherwise indicated)

	1995	2000	2005	2006	2007	2008	2009	2010
7. Long-term external debt								
Debt outstanding and disbursed	**3,687**	**4,286**	**3,182**	**1,242**	**1,411**	**1,721**	**1,841**	**1,984**
Public and publicly guaranteed	3,687	4,286	3,182	1,242	1,411	1,717	1,836	1,981
Official creditors	3,603	4,247	3,173	1,236	1,404	1,710	1,829	1,973
Multilateral	1,690	1,828	2,839	888	1,093	1,378	1,447	1,536
of which: IBRD	12	0	0	0	0	0	0	0
IDA	1,110	1,378	2,298	636	865	1,066	1,105	1,161
Bilateral	1,913	2,419	334	347	311	332	382	437
Private creditors	84	39	9	6	6	7	7	7
of which: Bonds	0	0	0	0	0	0	0	0
Commercial banks	28	23	8	5	5	6	6	6
Private nonguaranteed	0	0	0	0	0	4	4	3
of which: Bonds	0	0	0	0	0	0	0	0
Disbursements	**90**	**150**	**249**	**280**	**261**	**345**	**126**	**211**
Public and publicly guaranteed	90	150	249	280	261	342	124	211
Official creditors	89	150	249	280	261	342	124	211
Multilateral	78	143	248	256	250	300	71	117
of which: IBRD	0	0	0	0	0	0	0	0
IDA	76	94	221	178	198	211	31	76
Bilateral	11	7	1	24	10	41	54	94
Private creditors	1	0	0	0	0	0	0	0
of which: Bonds	0	0	0	0	0	0	0	0
Commercial banks	0	0	0	0	0	0	0	0
Private nonguaranteed	0	0	0	0	0	3	2	0
of which: Bonds	0	0	0	0	0	0	0	0
Principal repayments	**24**	**74**	**38**	**36**	**9**	**20**	**34**	**37**
Public and publicly guaranteed	24	74	38	36	9	20	32	36
Official creditors	19	73	37	33	8	20	32	36
Multilateral	18	37	22	19	7	5	14	11
of which: IBRD	4	0	0	0	0	0	0	0
IDA	7	17	11	7	0	1	1	1
Bilateral	1	36	15	14	1	14	18	25
Private creditors	5	0	1	3	1	0	0	0
of which: Bonds	0	0	0	0	0	0	0	0
Commercial banks	1	0	1	3	0	0	0	0
Private nonguaranteed	0	0	0	0	0	1	1	1
of which: Bonds	0	0	0	0	0	0	0	0
Interest payments	**16**	**28**	**28**	**21**	**10**	**11**	**15**	**16**
Public and publicly guaranteed	16	28	28	21	10	11	15	16
Official creditors	15	28	28	21	10	11	15	16
Multilateral	12	17	22	16	9	10	12	12
of which: IBRD	1	0	0	0	0	0	0	0
IDA	8	10	17	11	6	7	8	8
Bilateral	4	11	6	5	1	1	3	4
Private creditors	1	0	0	0	0	0	0	0
of which: Bonds	0	0	0	0	0	0	0	0
Commercial banks	0	0	0	0	0	0	0	0
Private nonguaranteed	0	0	0	0	0	0	0	0
of which: Bonds	0	0	0	0	0	0	0	0
8. Debt stock-flow reconciliation								
Total change in external debt stocks	226	-53	-295	-2,002	216	368	128	92
Net flows on external debt	59	45	244	263	294	386	98	125
9. Debt restructurings								
Total amount rescheduled	0	0	26	11	1	0	0	0
Total amount forgiven	0	0	100	2,475	143	6	0	0
Debt buyback	0	0	0	0	0	0	0	0

10. Contractual obligations on outstanding long-term external debt

	2011	2012	2013	2014	2015	2016	2017	2018
Official creditors								
Principal	63	64	57	67	66	58	64	72
Interest	19	19	20	19	19	18	18	17
Private creditors								
Principal	1	1	1	0	0	0	1	1
Interest	0	0	0	0	0	0	0	0

Notes:

Madagascar was granted debt relief effective in 2006 under MDRI.

MALAWI

(US$ million, unless otherwise indicated)

	1995	2000	2005	2006	2007	2008	2009	2010
1. Summary external debt data								
External debt stocks	**2237.8**	**2704.9**	**3183.2**	**848.1**	**790.4**	**893.7**	**1033.3**	**921.6**
Long-term external debt	2078.3	2544.1	3061.8	764.6	759.5	769.0	839.4	714.6
Public and publicly guaranteed	2078.3	2544.1	3061.8	764.6	759.5	769.0	839.4	714.6
Private nonguaranteed	0.0	0.0	0.0	0.0	0.0	0.0	0.0	0.0
Use of IMF credit	116.0	82.5	75.2	19.5	31.0	124.7	126.9	146.0
Short-term external debt	43.5	78.3	46.2	64.0	0.0	0.0	67.0	61.0
interest arrears on long-term	1.4	36.7	34.2	0.0	0.0	0.0	0.0	0.0
Memorandum items								
Principal arrears on long-term	7.2	72.3	13.3	0.0	0.0	0.0	0.0	0.0
Long-term public sector debt	2075.2	2541.4	3061.8	764.6	759.5	769.0	839.4	714.6
Long-term private sector debt	3.1	2.7	0.0	0.0	0.0	0.0	0.0	0.0
Public & publicly guaranteed commitments	102.3	58.5	24.7	20.1	94.4	178.0	193.7	82.0
External debt flows								
Disbursements	226.7	127.0	96.5	108.4	79.1	162.5	107.1	99.9
Long-term external debt	215.1	118.6	88.5	94.0	68.9	65.6	107.1	78.8
IMF purchases	11.6	8.5	8.0	14.5	10.2	97.0	0.0	21.2
Principal repayments	75.3	41.8	52.3	48.8	19.8	16.7	20.1	11.1
Long-term external debt	65.5	32.7	37.8	31.6	19.8	16.7	20.1	11.1
IMF repurchases	9.9	9.1	14.5	17.1	0.0	0.0	0.0	0.0
Net flows	183.4	83.3	45.3	111.7	-4.6	145.8	154.0	82.9
Long-term external debt	149.6	85.8	50.8	62.3	49.2	48.9	87.0	67.7
Short-term external debt	32.1	-1.9	1.0	52.0	-64.0	0.0	67.0	-6.0
Interest payments	42.7	21.1	23.4	20.9	13.3	15.2	15.6	7.6
Long-term external debt	38.7	17.9	21.8	18.0	11.4	14.9	14.5	6.8
IMF charges	1.4	0.4	1.2	1.0	0.1	0.3	0.6	0.0
Short-term external debt	2.5	2.9	0.5	1.9	1.8	0.0	0.4	0.8
2. Other non-debt resource inflows								
Foreign direct investment	5.6	26.0	52.3	72.2	92.0	170.0	60.0	140.0
Portfolio equity	..	..	..	..	..	..	..	..
3. Currency composition of public and publicly guaranteed debt (%)								
Euro	..	..	3.3	8.5	5.0	3.5	3.2	2.6
Japanese yen	12.3	8.4	6.2	0.0	0.0	0.0	0.0	0.0
Pound sterling	9.0	6.2	4.8	0.0	0.0	0.0	0.0	0.0
Swiss franc	0.1	0.1	0.0	0.0	0.0	0.0	0.0	0.0
U.S.dollars	53.6	65.9	65.8	56.1	57.1	54.2	52.7	41.8
4. Average terms of new commitments								
Official creditors								
Interest (%)	1.0	0.8	1.4	0.8	1.7	1.2	1.4	0.8
Maturity (years)	38.6	44.7	41.4	34.6	37.1	35.4	30.6	36.1
Grace period (years)	9.6	10.1	8.9	10.7	9.7	12.7	7.3	9.4
Private creditors								
Interest (%)	0.0	0.0	0.0	0.0	0.0	0.0	0.0	0.0
Maturity (years)	0.0	0.0	0.0	0.0	0.0	0.0	0.0	0.0
Grace period (years)	0.0	0.0	0.0	0.0	0.0	0.0	0.0	0.0
5. Major economic aggregates								
Gross national income (GNI)	1350.1	1707.2	2713.7	3078.4	3436.7	4051.1	4655.8	4979.9
Exports of goods, services & income	473.3	470.7	562.8	604.8	873.1	923.1	990.2	..
Worker remit. & comp. of employees	0.5	0.7	..	..	..	..	..	..
Imports of goods, services & income	708.2	679.6	1309.6	1359.9	1418.0	1669.8	1820.3	..
Profit remittances on FDI	8.6	15.1	..	..	..	..	..	..
Current account balance	-78.0	-73.5	-702.2	-701.1	-718.5	-661.5	-767.2	-705.1
International reserves	115.0	246.5	165.5	141.9	227.3	253.9	163.3	..
6. Ratios								
External debt stocks to exports (%)	472.8	574.7	565.6	140.2	90.5	96.8	104.3	..
External debt stocks to GNI (%)	165.8	158.4	117.3	27.5	23.0	22.1	22.2	18.5
Debt service to exports (%)	24.9	13.4	13.4	11.5	3.8	3.5	3.6	..
Short-term to external debt stocks (%)	1.9	2.9	1.5	7.5	..	..	6.5	6.6
Multilateral to external debt stocks (%)	76.3	75.6	80.5	50.8	55.3	54.4	52.3	62.5
Reserves to external debt stocks (%)	5.1	9.1	5.2	16.7	28.8	28.4	15.8	..
Reserves to imports (months)	1.9	4.4	1.5	1.3	1.9	1.8	1.1	..

MALAWI

(US$ million, unless otherwise indicated)

	1995	2000	2005	2006	2007	2008	2009	2010
7. Long-term external debt								
Debt outstanding and disbursed	**2078.3**	**2544.1**	**3061.8**	**764.6**	**759.5**	**769.0**	**839.4**	**714.6**
Public and publicly guaranteed	2078.3	2544.1	3061.8	764.6	759.5	769.0	839.4	714.6
Official creditors	2049.9	2526.1	3043.4	757.0	752.2	763.4	833.6	714.6
Multilateral	1708.3	2044.4	2561.4	430.8	437.0	486.3	539.9	575.7
of which: IBRD	55.0	8.5	0.0	0.0	0.0	0.0	0.0	0.0
IDA	1251.3	1592.2	1940.4	156.9	177.6	187.7	212.8	242.6
Bilateral	341.6	481.8	482.1	326.2	315.2	277.1	293.7	138.9
Private creditors	28.4	17.9	18.4	7.6	7.3	5.6	5.8	0.0
of which: Bonds	0.0	0.0	0.0	0.0	0.0	0.0	0.0	0.0
Commercial banks	0.0	0.0	16.7	6.2	6.0	5.6	5.8	0.0
Private nonguaranteed	0.0	0.0	0.0	0.0	0.0	0.0	0.0	0.0
of which: Bonds	0.0	0.0	0.0	0.0	0.0	0.0	0.0	0.0
Disbursements	**215.1**	**118.6**	**88.5**	**94.0**	**68.9**	**65.6**	**107.1**	**78.8**
Public and publicly guaranteed	215.1	118.6	88.5	94.0	68.9	65.6	107.1	78.8
Official creditors	215.1	118.6	88.5	94.0	68.9	65.6	107.1	78.8
Multilateral	97.3	118.6	87.7	82.2	51.5	61.8	55.9	53.8
of which: IBRD	0.0	0.0	0.0	0.0	0.0	0.0	0.0	0.0
IDA	73.3	97.0	45.1	46.2	13.8	11.9	24.2	33.9
Bilateral	117.8	0.0	0.8	11.7	17.4	3.8	51.2	25.0
Private creditors	0.0	0.0	0.0	0.0	0.0	0.0	0.0	0.0
of which: Bonds	0.0	0.0	0.0	0.0	0.0	0.0	0.0	0.0
Commercial banks	0.0	0.0	0.0	0.0	0.0	0.0	0.0	0.0
Private nonguaranteed	0.0	0.0	0.0	0.0	0.0	0.0	0.0	0.0
of which: Bonds	0.0	0.0	0.0	0.0	0.0	0.0	0.0	0.0
Principal repayments	**65.5**	**32.7**	**37.8**	**31.6**	**19.8**	**16.7**	**20.1**	**11.1**
Public and publicly guaranteed	65.5	32.7	37.8	31.6	19.8	16.7	20.1	11.1
Official creditors	42.6	32.7	35.2	30.1	18.7	16.6	20.1	11.1
Multilateral	28.3	30.1	29.7	24.7	8.0	6.5	7.5	8.9
of which: IBRD	11.7	7.6	0.2	0.0	0.0	0.0	0.0	0.0
IDA	7.1	15.8	12.4	9.8	0.0	0.0	0.0	0.1
Bilateral	14.3	2.6	5.5	5.4	10.8	10.1	12.6	2.2
Private creditors	22.8	0.0	2.5	1.5	1.0	0.1	0.0	0.0
of which: Bonds	0.0	0.0	0.0	0.0	0.0	0.0	0.0	0.0
Commercial banks	10.5	0.0	2.4	1.4	0.9	0.0	0.0	0.0
Private nonguaranteed	0.0	0.0	0.0	0.0	0.0	0.0	0.0	0.0
of which: Bonds	0.0	0.0	0.0	0.0	0.0	0.0	0.0	0.0
Interest payments	**38.7**	**17.9**	**21.8**	**18.0**	**11.4**	**14.9**	**14.5**	**6.8**
Public and publicly guaranteed	38.7	17.9	21.8	18.0	11.4	14.9	14.5	6.8
Official creditors	35.2	17.9	21.6	17.8	11.3	14.8	14.4	6.8
Multilateral	25.2	17.2	20.1	16.6	3.8	4.1	4.1	4.8
of which: IBRD	6.5	1.0	0.0	0.0	0.0	0.0	0.0	0.0
IDA	9.3	11.7	14.2	9.7	0.6	0.8	0.9	1.2
Bilateral	10.0	0.6	1.5	1.2	7.5	10.7	10.3	2.0
Private creditors	3.6	0.0	0.2	0.2	0.1	0.1	0.1	0.0
of which: Bonds	0.0	0.0	0.0	0.0	0.0	0.0	0.0	0.0
Commercial banks	0.6	0.0	0.2	0.2	0.1	0.1	0.1	0.0
Private nonguaranteed	0.0	0.0	0.0	0.0	0.0	0.0	0.0	0.0
of which: Bonds	0.0	0.0	0.0	0.0	0.0	0.0	0.0	0.0
8. Debt stock-flow reconciliation								
Total change in external debt stocks	217.7	-36.4	-244.2	-2335.1	-57.6	103.3	139.6	-111.7
Net flows on external debt	183.4	83.3	45.3	111.7	-4.6	145.8	154.0	82.9
9. Debt restructurings								
Total amount rescheduled	0.0	0.0	1.0	179.7	24.0	0.0	10.6	0.0
Total amount forgiven	0.0	0.0	53.6	2512.0	56.1	16.3	1.1	1.3
Debt buyback	0.0	0.0	0.0	0.0	0.0	0.0	0.0	0.0

10. Contractual obligations on outstanding long-term external debt

	2011	2012	2013	2014	2015	2016	2017	2018
Official creditors								
Principal	18.1	19.0	21.7	26.0	29.4	29.0	28.0	29.4
Interest	9.1	9.9	10.3	10.4	10.3	10.0	9.6	9.2
Private creditors								
Principal	0.0	0.0	0.0	0.0	0.0	0.0	0.0	0.0
Interest	0.0	0.0	0.0	0.0	0.0	0.0	0.0	0.0

Notes:
Malawi was granted debt relief effective in 2006 under MDRI. Data include the effects of Paris Club restructuring agreement signed in 2006. Data for 2008, 2009, and 2010 include the effects of Enhanced HIPC Initiative, in the amount of $835 thousand, $1,070 thousand, and $1,275 thousand respectively.

MALAYSIA

(US$ million, unless otherwise indicated)

	1995	2000	2005	2006	2007	2008	2009	2010
1. Summary external debt data								
External debt stocks	**34,343**	**41,765**	**51,855**	**54,883**	**61,420**	**66,074**	**66,272**	**81,497**
Long-term external debt	27,069	37,192	38,679	43,080	38,320	43,274	42,578	46,421
Public and publicly guaranteed	16,023	19,125	22,324	22,456	18,294	21,356	21,245	25,795
Private nonguaranteed	11,046	18,067	16,356	20,624	20,026	21,918	21,332	20,626
Use of IMF credit	0	0	0	0	0	0	0	0
Short-term external debt	7,274	4,573	13,176	11,803	23,100	22,800	23,695	35,076
interest arrears on long-term	0	0	0	0	0	0	0	0
Memorandum items								
Principal arrears on long-term	0	0	0	0	0	0	0	0
Long-term public sector debt	16,023	19,026	22,305	22,444	18,290	21,356	16,745	21,295
Long-term private sector debt	11,046	18,166	16,374	20,635	20,030	21,918	25,832	25,126
Public & publicly guaranteed commitments	3,772	5,464	1,212	1,990	202	2,533	4,500	5,742
External debt flows								
Disbursements	8,503	5,921	6,050	7,038	5,037	5,180	8,339	14,720
Long-term external debt	8,503	5,921	6,050	7,038	5,037	5,180	8,339	14,720
IMF purchases	0	0	0	0	0	0	0	0
Principal repayments	4,450	4,146	7,192	5,269	7,819	6,258	9,793	11,349
Long-term external debt	4,450	4,146	7,192	5,269	7,819	6,258	9,793	11,349
IMF repurchases	0	0	0	0	0	0	0	0
Net flows	5,138	337	601	396	8,516	-1,378	-560	14,753
Long-term external debt	4,053	1,775	-1,142	1,769	-2,781	-1,078	-1,455	3,372
Short-term external debt	1,085	-1,439	1,744	-1,373	11,297	-300	895	11,381
Interest payments	1,591	2,287	2,183	2,347	2,602	2,521	2,264	1,935
Long-term external debt	1,150	2,021	1,858	1,867	2,009	2,044	1,683	1,638
IMF charges	0	0	0	0	0	0	0	0
Short-term external debt	441	266	325	480	594	476	581	297
2. Other non-debt resource inflows								
Foreign direct investment	4,178	3,788	3,966	6,076	8,590	7,376	1,387	9,509
Portfolio equity	0	0	-1,200	2,355	-669	-10,716	-449	..
3. Currency composition of public and publicly guaranteed debt (%)								
Euro	..	..	4.2	4.6	6.2	5.0	0.1	0.1
Japanese yen	34.6	27.7	22.4	19.7	21.0	20.8	15.9	12.4
Pound sterling	1.0	0.2	0.0	0.0	0.0	0.0	0.0	0.0
Swiss franc	3.1	0.0	0.0	0.0	0.0	0.0	0.0	0.0
U.S.dollars	48.5	63.1	71.2	74.0	71.1	73.1	83.3	87.3
4. Average terms of new commitments								
Official creditors								
Interest (%)	3.4	3.1	0.0	0.0	0.0	0.0	0.0	0.0
Maturity (years)	24.4	24.1	0.0	0.0	0.0	0.0	0.0	0.0
Grace period (years)	6.3	3.5	0.0	0.0	0.0	0.0	0.0	0.0
Private creditors								
Interest (%)	6.3	7.0	5.2	5.7	5.7	4.7	5.3	2.3
Maturity (years)	16.9	7.6	9.6	9.2	8.8	7.0	8.4	4.7
Grace period (years)	14.0	4.0	9.5	5.6	0.8	0.8	8.4	2.6
5. Major economic aggregates								
Gross national income (GNI)	84,689	86,182	131,531	151,811	182,577	214,731	188,934	229,960
Exports of goods, services & income	85,992	114,356	166,757	191,091	217,062	242,135	197,637	254,129
Worker remit. & comp. of employees	116	342	1,117	1,365	1,556	1,329	1,131	1,301
Imports of goods, services & income	93,618	103,944	142,299	160,331	182,624	197,959	160,256	218,485
Profit remittances on FDI	4,144	7,173	8,330	8,858	9,932	13,838	11,119	..
Current account balance	-8,644	8,488	19,980	26,200	29,770	38,914	31,801	28,565
International reserves	24,699	28,651	70,458	82,876	101,995	92,166	96,704	106,528
6. Ratios								
External debt stocks to exports (%)	39.9	36.5	31.1	28.7	28.3	27.3	33.5	32.1
External debt stocks to GNI (%)	40.6	48.5	39.4	36.2	33.6	30.8	35.1	35.4
Debt service to exports (%)	7.0	5.6	5.6	4.0	4.8	3.6	6.1	5.2
Short-term to external debt stocks (%)	21.2	11.0	25.4	21.5	37.6	34.5	35.8	43.0
Multilateral to external debt stocks (%)	4.8	3.1	1.8	1.5	0.8	0.6	0.5	0.3
Reserves to external debt stocks (%)	71.9	68.6	135.9	151.0	166.1	139.5	145.9	130.7
Reserves to imports (months)	3.2	3.3	5.9	6.2	6.7	5.6	7.2	5.9

MALAYSIA

(US$ million, unless otherwise indicated)

	1995	2000	2005	2006	2007	2008	2009	2010
7. Long-term external debt								
Debt outstanding and disbursed	**27,069**	**37,192**	**38,679**	**43,080**	**38,320**	**43,274**	**42,578**	**46,421**
Public and publicly guaranteed	16,023	19,125	22,324	22,456	18,294	21,356	21,245	25,795
Official creditors	5,489	4,950	6,542	6,605	4,374	5,164	4,092	3,750
Multilateral	1,644	1,314	936	798	471	399	303	237
of which: IBRD	1,059	812	533	437	135	85	39	0
IDA	0	0	0	0	0	0	0	0
Bilateral	3,845	3,637	5,606	5,807	3,903	4,765	3,789	3,513
Private creditors	10,533	14,175	15,782	15,850	13,920	16,192	17,154	22,045
of which: Bonds	6,062	9,836	12,521	12,702	11,660	11,661	13,198	15,575
Commercial banks	4,171	2,292	1,867	1,987	1,307	3,729	3,380	6,045
Private nonguaranteed	11,046	18,067	16,356	20,624	20,026	21,918	21,332	20,626
of which: Bonds	1,765	3,402	7,623	7,960	7,009	6,568	5,927	4,893
Disbursements	**8,503**	**5,921**	**6,050**	**7,038**	**5,037**	**5,180**	**8,339**	**14,720**
Public and publicly guaranteed	4,150	3,460	2,182	1,801	558	1,942	5,319	6,014
Official creditors	837	1,446	981	396	206	98	47	18
Multilateral	135	61	36	30	21	13	8	5
of which: IBRD	88	15	0	0	0	0	0	0
IDA	0	0	0	0	0	0	0	0
Bilateral	702	1,385	944	366	185	85	39	13
Private creditors	3,313	2,015	1,201	1,405	352	1,844	5,271	5,996
of which: Bonds	2,100	1,061	1,150	1,000	0	0	4,500	2,339
Commercial banks	1,205	672	51	405	352	1,844	771	3,658
Private nonguaranteed	4,353	2,461	3,868	5,237	4,479	3,238	3,020	8,706
of which: Bonds	480	361	1,615	620	0	0	0	400
Principal repayments	**4,450**	**4,146**	**7,192**	**5,269**	**7,819**	**6,258**	**9,793**	**11,349**
Public and publicly guaranteed	1,701	2,017	4,752	2,447	3,646	1,503	5,351	1,863
Official creditors	455	840	1,218	811	1,691	820	1,053	688
Multilateral	261	139	155	167	354	100	102	75
of which: IBRD	194	100	92	96	302	50	47	38
IDA	0	0	0	0	0	0	0	0
Bilateral	195	701	1,064	644	1,337	720	951	612
Private creditors	1,245	1,176	3,534	1,635	1,956	683	4,298	1,176
of which: Bonds	140	200	2,036	920	1,170	0	2,959	0
Commercial banks	420	864	1,256	484	556	436	1,119	992
Private nonguaranteed	2,749	2,129	2,440	2,822	4,172	4,755	4,442	9,486
of which: Bonds	0	715	237	337	1,000	250	1,398	715
Interest payments	**1,150**	**2,021**	**1,858**	**1,867**	**2,009**	**2,044**	**1,683**	**1,638**
Public and publicly guaranteed	805	1,159	1,208	1,177	1,166	991	813	955
Official creditors	284	259	314	228	202	129	124	97
Multilateral	128	98	47	40	32	20	15	10
of which: IBRD	83	66	33	27	19	8	4	2
IDA	0	0	0	0	0	0	0	0
Bilateral	155	160	267	188	170	109	109	87
Private creditors	522	900	894	949	964	862	689	857
of which: Bonds	251	599	746	782	795	735	589	702
Commercial banks	190	189	91	109	119	90	83	147
Private nonguaranteed	345	862	650	690	843	1,053	870	684
of which: Bonds	28	159	363	437	434	373	339	295
8. Debt stock-flow reconciliation								
Total change in external debt stocks	4,007	-21	-160	3,027	6,537	4,655	198	15,224
Net flows on external debt	5,138	337	601	396	8,516	-1,378	-560	14,753
9. Debt restructurings								
Total amount rescheduled	0	0	0	0	0	0	0	0
Total amount forgiven	0	0	0	0	0	0	0	0
Debt buyback	0	0	0	0	0	0	0	0

10. Contractual obligations on outstanding long-term external debt

	2011	2012	2013	2014	2015	2016	2017	2018
Official creditors								
Principal	627	594	341	314	253	228	198	176
Interest	82	68	55	46	38	31	25	19
Private creditors								
Principal	8,385	5,584	4,174	5,989	8,059	2,227	1,657	61
Interest	1,337	1,191	1,081	984	720	482	419	397

Notes:

Long-term public and publicly guaranteed, long-term private nonguaranteed debt and short-term debt for 2010 are World Bank staff estimates based on government statistics. Short-term debt data for 2010 are based on reports provided by the country.

MALDIVES

(US$ million, unless otherwise indicated)

	1995	2000	2005	2006	2007	2008	2009	2010
1. Summary external debt data								
External debt stocks	**155**	**206**	**461**	**683**	**1,038**	**1,140**	**1,164**	**1,229**
Long-term external debt	152	185	399	579	853	920	970	989
Public and publicly guaranteed	152	185	330	384	444	497	569	653
Private nonguaranteed	0	0	70	195	408	423	400	336
Use of IMF credit	0	0	6	6	6	4	9	16
Short-term external debt	3	21	56	98	179	216	186	224
interest arrears on long-term	0	0	0	0	0	2	1	3
Memorandum items								
Principal arrears on long-term	0	0	0	0	0	9	9	2
Long-term public sector debt	152	183	300	356	419	475	550	638
Long-term private sector debt	0	1	99	223	434	445	420	351
Public & publicly guaranteed commitments	29	38	74	144	71	194	114	127
External debt flows								
Disbursements	35	14	130	209	323	163	199	212
Long-term external debt	35	14	124	209	323	163	191	204
IMF purchases	0	0	6	0	0	0	8	8
Principal repayments	7	14	31	42	69	89	150	179
Long-term external debt	7	14	31	42	69	86	147	179
IMF repurchases	0	0	0	0	0	2	3	1
Net flows	30	-4	123	209	335	109	19	69
Long-term external debt	28	0	93	167	254	76	44	26
Short-term external debt	2	-3	24	42	81	35	-30	36
Interest payments	4	6	13	20	32	36	26	24
Long-term external debt	4	5	11	15	22	27	21	14
IMF charges	0	0	0	0	0	0	0	0
Short-term external debt	0	1	2	5	10	9	6	10
2. Other non-debt resource inflows								
Foreign direct investment	7	22	53	64	91	135	112	164
Portfolio equity	..	..	..	..	..	..	..	..
3. Currency composition of public and publicly guaranteed debt (%)								
Euro	..	..	8.6	14.7	20.5	22.3	18.7	18.3
Japanese yen	0.0	0.0	0.0	0.0	0.0	0.3	1.2	4.5
Pound sterling	0.0	0.2	0.0	0.0	0.0	0.0	0.0	0.0
Swiss franc	0.0	0.0	0.0	0.0	0.0	0.0	0.0	0.0
U.S.dollars	51.3	53.3	55.7	52.0	48.5	47.6	54.0	47.4
4. Average terms of new commitments								
Official creditors								
Interest (%)	2.5	2.5	1.1	3.6	4.1	0.9	2.5	1.6
Maturity (years)	34.8	34.7	30.5	19.5	20.1	12.9	23.6	23.3
Grace period (years)	10.1	9.3	7.4	4.5	5.2	4.0	5.8	6.5
Private creditors								
Interest (%)	7.9	6.6	6.6	8.4	6.9	0.0	2.1	0.0
Maturity (years)	6.0	8.4	7.8	10.3	8.3	0.0	11.2	0.0
Grace period (years)	1.7	1.1	1.6	1.5	1.8	0.0	1.7	0.0
5. Major economic aggregates								
Gross national income (GNI)	379	594	726	878	1,011	1,208	1,265	1,419
Exports of goods, services & income	322	468	495	793	899	1,063	834	953
Worker remit. & comp. of employees	2	2	2	3	3	3	4	4
Imports of goods, services & income	337	492	910	1,103	1,323	1,647	1,196	1,349
Profit remittances on FDI	20	34	31	41	45	36	26	31
Current account balance	-18	-51	-273	-302	-438	-647	-419	-463
International reserves	48	123	189	234	311	244	276	364
6. Ratios								
External debt stocks to exports (%)	48.0	44.1	93.2	86.2	115.5	107.2	139.6	128.8
External debt stocks to GNI (%)	40.9	34.7	63.6	77.8	102.7	94.3	92.1	86.6
Debt service to exports (%)	3.4	4.2	8.8	7.8	11.2	11.7	21.2	21.3
Short-term to external debt stocks (%)	1.9	10.4	12.2	14.4	17.2	18.9	15.9	18.2
Multilateral to external debt stocks (%)	57.0	57.6	37.9	31.9	25.3	24.5	24.8	25.4
Reserves to external debt stocks (%)	31.0	59.6	41.0	34.3	30.0	21.4	23.7	29.7
Reserves to imports (months)	1.7	3.0	2.5	2.6	2.8	1.8	2.8	3.2

(US$ million, unless otherwise indicated)

	1995	2000	2005	2006	2007	2008	2009	2010
7. Long-term external debt								
Debt outstanding and disbursed	**152**	**185**	**399**	**579**	**853**	**920**	**970**	**989**
Public and publicly guaranteed	152	185	330	384	444	497	569	653
Official creditors	143	155	280	321	360	383	472	548
Multilateral	88	119	175	218	262	279	288	311
of which: IBRD	0	0	0	0	0	0	0	0
IDA	36	46	64	70	77	79	84	99
Bilateral	54	36	105	103	98	104	183	236
Private creditors	9	30	50	63	84	114	97	105
of which: Bonds	0	0	0	0	0	0	0	0
Commercial banks	3	24	50	63	84	114	97	105
Private nonguaranteed	0	0	70	195	408	423	400	336
of which: Bonds	0	0	0	0	0	0	0	0
Disbursements	**35**	**14**	**124**	**209**	**323**	**163**	**191**	**204**
Public and publicly guaranteed	35	14	52	67	74	102	114	143
Official creditors	31	6	35	50	45	55	109	109
Multilateral	16	6	16	39	39	36	16	47
of which: IBRD	0	0	0	0	0	0	0	0
IDA	4	3	5	3	5	4	6	17
Bilateral	15	0	19	11	6	19	93	63
Private creditors	4	7	16	17	29	47	5	34
of which: Bonds	0	0	0	0	0	0	0	0
Commercial banks	2	6	16	17	29	47	5	34
Private nonguaranteed	0	0	72	142	249	60	78	61
of which: Bonds	0	0	0	0	0	0	0	0
Principal repayments	**7**	**14**	**31**	**42**	**69**	**86**	**147**	**179**
Public and publicly guaranteed	7	14	24	25	33	40	47	53
Official creditors	5	7	15	18	22	25	24	29
Multilateral	1	2	4	4	8	13	12	16
of which: IBRD	0	0	0	0	0	0	0	0
IDA	0	0	1	1	1	1	1	2
Bilateral	4	4	11	14	14	12	12	13
Private creditors	2	7	9	7	11	15	23	24
of which: Bonds	0	0	0	0	0	0	0	0
Commercial banks	1	6	8	7	11	15	23	24
Private nonguaranteed	0	0	7	16	36	46	100	125
of which: Bonds	0	0	0	0	0	0	0	0
Interest payments	**4**	**5**	**11**	**15**	**22**	**27**	**21**	**14**
Public and publicly guaranteed	4	5	9	11	13	14	13	10
Official creditors	3	3	7	8	9	9	8	6
Multilateral	1	1	2	2	4	5	4	3
of which: IBRD	0	0	0	0	0	0	0	0
IDA	0	0	1	1	1	1	1	1
Bilateral	2	1	5	6	5	4	3	3
Private creditors	1	2	2	3	4	5	5	4
of which: Bonds	0	0	0	0	0	0	0	0
Commercial banks	0	2	2	3	4	5	5	4
Private nonguaranteed	0	0	2	4	9	13	7	5
of which: Bonds	0	0	0	0	0	0	0	0
8. Debt stock-flow reconciliation								
Total change in external debt stocks	31	-13	92	222	355	102	24	64
Net flows on external debt	30	-4	123	209	335	109	19	69
9. Debt restructurings								
Total amount rescheduled	0	0	0	0	0	0	0	0
Total amount forgiven	0	0	0	0	0	0	0	0
Debt buyback	0	0	0	0	0	0	0	0

10. Contractual obligations on outstanding long-term external debt

	2011	2012	2013	2014	2015	2016	2017	2018
Official creditors								
Principal	115	56	35	34	31	37	31	30
Interest	7	7	7	7	7	7	6	6
Private creditors								
Principal	121	89	75	50	41	32	26	21
Interest	18	14	10	7	5	4	2	1

Notes:

Short-term debt data are World Bank staff estimates based on government statistics.

MALI

(US$ million, unless otherwise indicated)

	1995	2000	2005	2006	2007	2008	2009	2010
1. Summary external debt data								
External debt stocks	**2,958**	**2,960**	**3,201**	**1,591**	**1,826**	**2,031**	**2,071**	**2,326**
Long-term external debt	2,739	2,671	3,036	1,553	1,807	1,985	2,002	2,271
Public and publicly guaranteed	2,739	2,671	3,036	1,553	1,807	1,985	2,002	2,271
Private nonguaranteed	0	0	0	0	0	0	0	0
Use of IMF credit	147	176	109	8	13	40	44	49
Short-term external debt	72	114	55	30	6	7	25	6
interest arrears on long-term	28	42	6	6	6	7	1	0
Memorandum items								
Principal arrears on long-term	342	541	80	91	27	36	4	1
Long-term public sector debt	2,739	2,671	3,036	1,553	1,807	1,985	2,002	2,271
Long-term private sector debt	0	0	0	0	0	0	0	0
Public & publicly guaranteed commitments	163	245	440	337	436	302	533	502
External debt flows								
Disbursements	238	109	282	151	261	263	497	318
Long-term external debt	193	100	280	145	257	234	494	312
IMF purchases	45	9	2	6	4	28	3	6
Principal repayments	62	66	69	58	43	44	46	39
Long-term external debt	55	50	52	58	43	44	46	39
IMF repurchases	7	16	17	0	0	0	0	0
Net flows	200	-31	219	68	194	218	475	260
Long-term external debt	138	50	228	87	214	190	448	272
Short-term external debt	24	-73	5	-25	-24	0	24	-18
Interest payments	25	26	31	26	20	25	22	22
Long-term external debt	22	18	27	24	19	25	22	21
IMF charges	1	1	0	0	0	0	0	0
Short-term external debt	2	8	3	2	1	0	0	0
2. Other non-debt resource inflows								
Foreign direct investment	111	82	188	48	54	132	718	148
Portfolio equity	0	0	9	3	-6	-3	-3	..
3. Currency composition of public and publicly guaranteed debt (%)								
Euro	..	..	14.4	19.8	18.1	15.4	3.1	3.5
Japanese yen	2.3	2.9	2.1	3.8	3.3	3.5	0.0	0.0
Pound sterling	1.8	1.8	0.1	0.2	0.0	0.0	0.0	0.0
Swiss franc	2.1	1.5	1.6	3.4	0.0	0.0	0.0	0.0
U.S.dollars	22.5	33.9	45.2	29.8	32.0	31.6	34.1	36.7
4. Average terms of new commitments								
Official creditors								
Interest (%)	1.5	0.6	1.1	0.7	1.4	1.1	1.1	0.8
Maturity (years)	31.2	34.9	34.4	38.7	32.0	36.8	34.3	28.9
Grace period (years)	8.8	8.8	8.6	8.2	8.2	9.3	8.6	8.6
Private creditors								
Interest (%)	0.0	0.0	0.0	0.0	0.0	5.9	4.0	0.0
Maturity (years)	0.0	0.0	0.0	0.0	0.0	11.4	11.2	0.0
Grace period (years)	0.0	0.0	0.0	0.0	0.0	4.9	4.7	0.0
5. Major economic aggregates								
Gross national income (GNI)	2,419	2,392	5,099	5,524	7,146	8,425	8,603	8,909
Exports of goods, services & income	538	665	1,407	1,897	1,985	2,604	2,180	2,425
Worker remit. & comp. of employees	112	73	177	212	344	431	454	436
Imports of goods, services & income	1,040	1,046	2,072	2,441	2,966	4,126	3,321	3,588
Profit remittances on FDI	5	76	155	215	243	278	430	0
Current account balance	-284	-255	-438	-219	-581	-1,066	-655	-705
International reserves	323	382	854	970	1,087	1,072	1,604	1,344
6. Ratios								
External debt stocks to exports (%)	550.2	445.4	227.5	83.9	92.0	78.0	95.0	95.9
External debt stocks to GNI (%)	122.3	123.7	62.8	28.8	25.5	24.1	24.1	26.1
Debt service to exports (%)	16.1	14.0	7.1	4.5	3.2	2.7	3.1	2.5
Short-term to external debt stocks (%)	2.4	3.8	1.7	1.9	0.3	0.3	1.2	0.3
Multilateral to external debt stocks (%)	47.2	51.1	70.0	44.2	52.8	56.5	75.6	76.9
Reserves to external debt stocks (%)	10.9	12.9	26.7	60.9	59.5	52.8	77.5	57.8
Reserves to imports (months)	3.7	4.4	4.9	4.8	4.4	3.1	5.8	4.5

(US$ million, unless otherwise indicated)

	1995	2000	2005	2006	2007	2008	2009	2010
7. Long-term external debt								
Debt outstanding and disbursed	**2,739**	**2,671**	**3,036**	**1,553**	**1,807**	**1,985**	**2,002**	**2,271**
Public and publicly guaranteed	2,739	2,671	3,036	1,553	1,807	1,985	2,002	2,271
Official creditors	2,737	2,671	3,032	1,546	1,800	1,979	1,995	2,266
Multilateral	1,397	1,513	2,241	703	964	1,148	1,565	1,790
of which: IBRD	0	0	0	0	0	0	0	0
IDA	863	957	1,424	297	452	534	698	840
Bilateral	1,340	1,158	791	843	836	831	430	476
Private creditors	2	0	5	7	7	5	7	5
of which: Bonds	0	0	0	0	0	0	0	0
Commercial banks	2	0	5	7	7	5	7	5
Private nonguaranteed	0	0	0	0	0	0	0	0
of which: Bonds	0	0	0	0	0	0	0	0
Disbursements	**193**	**100**	**280**	**145**	**257**	**234**	**494**	**312**
Public and publicly guaranteed	193	100	280	145	257	234	494	312
Official creditors	193	100	277	144	257	234	491	312
Multilateral	146	85	211	109	190	221	384	260
of which: IBRD	0	0	0	0	0	0	0	0
IDA	85	49	111	49	139	88	160	153
Bilateral	47	14	66	35	67	13	107	51
Private creditors	0	0	3	1	0	0	3	0
of which: Bonds	0	0	0	0	0	0	0	0
Commercial banks	0	0	3	1	0	0	3	0
Private nonguaranteed	0	0	0	0	0	0	0	0
of which: Bonds	0	0	0	0	0	0	0	0
Principal repayments	**55**	**50**	**52**	**58**	**43**	**44**	**46**	**39**
Public and publicly guaranteed	55	50	52	58	43	44	46	39
Official creditors	55	50	52	58	42	43	45	38
Multilateral	23	26	34	39	21	25	32	30
of which: IBRD	0	0	0	0	0	0	0	0
IDA	6	7	9	5	0	0	1	2
Bilateral	32	24	19	20	22	18	13	8
Private creditors	0	0	0	0	1	1	1	1
of which: Bonds	0	0	0	0	0	0	0	0
Commercial banks	0	0	0	0	1	1	1	1
Private nonguaranteed	0	0	0	0	0	0	0	0
of which: Bonds	0	0	0	0	0	0	0	0
Interest payments	**22**	**18**	**27**	**24**	**19**	**25**	**22**	**21**
Public and publicly guaranteed	22	18	27	24	19	25	22	21
Official creditors	22	18	27	23	19	24	21	21
Multilateral	12	12	21	16	11	13	15	15
of which: IBRD	0	0	0	0	0	0	0	0
IDA	6	7	11	7	3	4	4	5
Bilateral	10	5	6	7	8	11	6	6
Private creditors	0	0	0	1	0	0	0	0
of which: Bonds	0	0	0	0	0	0	0	0
Commercial banks	0	0	0	1	0	0	0	0
Private nonguaranteed	0	0	0	0	0	0	0	0
of which: Bonds	0	0	0	0	0	0	0	0
8. Debt stock-flow reconciliation								
Total change in external debt stocks	264	-236	-64	-1,609	234	206	39	256
Net flows on external debt	200	-31	219	68	194	218	475	260
9. Debt restructurings								
Total amount rescheduled	0	0	0	0	0	0	0	0
Total amount forgiven	0	34	33	1,898	105	9	498	0
Debt buyback	0	45	0	0	0	0	0	0

10. Contractual obligations on outstanding long-term external debt

	2011	2012	2013	2014	2015	2016	2017	2018
Official creditors								
Principal	91	96	97	100	110	108	116	136
Interest	27	29	31	31	31	30	29	28
Private creditors								
Principal	4	4	1	1	1	0	0	0
Interest	0	0	0	0	0	0	0	0

Notes:
Mali was granted debt relief effective in 2006 under MDRI. The data for Principal Arrears on long-term have been revised since 2001.

MAURITANIA

(US$ million, unless otherwise indicated)

	1995	2000	2005	2006	2007	2008	2009	2010
1. Summary external debt data								
External debt stocks	**2,396**	**2,378**	**2,308**	**1,618**	**1,704**	**1,986**	**2,048**	**2,461**
Long-term external debt	2,127	2,029	2,072	1,389	1,437	1,669	1,840	2,174
Public and publicly guaranteed	2,127	2,029	2,072	1,389	1,437	1,669	1,840	2,174
Private nonguaranteed	0	0	0	0	0	0	0	0
Use of IMF credit	100	98	69	0	13	16	16	50
Short-term external debt	169	251	167	229	254	301	192	237
interest arrears on long-term	79	112	109	130	128	135	134	76
Memorandum items								
Principal arrears on long-term	174	337	213	223	218	252	212	134
Long-term public sector debt	2,127	2,029	2,072	1,389	1,437	1,669	1,840	2,174
Long-term private sector debt	0	0	0	0	0	0	0	0
Public & publicly guaranteed commitments	114	106	395	158	307	326	692	470
External debt flows								
Disbursements	133	123	143	175	197	297	263	446
Long-term external debt	111	115	143	175	185	294	263	412
IMF purchases	22	8	0	0	13	3	0	34
Principal repayments	79	52	42	66	93	38	53	76
Long-term external debt	70	46	33	44	93	38	53	76
IMF repurchases	9	6	10	23	0	0	0	0
Net flows	68	62	92	149	131	300	102	473
Long-term external debt	42	69	111	131	92	257	210	336
Short-term external debt	14	-9	-9	41	27	40	-108	103
Interest payments	38	31	23	25	28	26	24	33
Long-term external debt	32	20	20	20	23	21	23	31
IMF charges	0	1	0	0	0	0	0	0
Short-term external debt	5	11	3	5	5	4	1	1
2. Other non-debt resource inflows								
Foreign direct investment	7	40	814	106	138	338	-38	14
Portfolio equity	0	0	..	..	..	..	..	..
3. Currency composition of public and publicly guaranteed debt (%)								
Euro	..	..	2.2	5.3	8.3	9.4	8.2	6.8
Japanese yen	3.1	3.6	0.1	0.1	0.1	0.1	0.0	0.0
Pound sterling	0.5	0.4	0.0	0.0	0.0	0.0	0.0	0.0
Swiss franc	0.0	0.0	0.1	0.1	0.1	0.1	0.0	0.0
U.S.dollars	34.0	40.9	49.3	32.1	35.9	37.7	38.9	44.3
4. Average terms of new commitments								
Official creditors								
Interest (%)	1.1	1.9	3.3	1.5	2.6	2.8	6.1	2.2
Maturity (years)	34.7	28.5	21.8	30.5	27.3	25.6	15.1	21.9
Grace period (years)	9.7	7.5	5.4	8.4	5.6	6.2	4.2	5.8
Private creditors								
Interest (%)	0.0	0.0	5.8	0.0	0.0	0.0	0.0	0.0
Maturity (years)	0.0	0.0	9.8	0.0	0.0	0.0	0.0	0.0
Grace period (years)	0.0	0.0	1.8	0.0	0.0	0.0	0.0	0.0
5. Major economic aggregates								
Gross national income (GNI)	1,366	1,092	1,922	2,334	2,828	3,619	3,079	3,672
Exports of goods, services & income	506	..	..	1,573	1,627	2,056	1,614	..
Worker remit. & comp. of employees	5	..	..	..	..	..	..	..
Imports of goods, services & income	559	..	..	1,778	2,286	2,810	2,136	..
Profit remittances on FDI	4	..	..	..	..	..	..	..
Current account balance	22	..	..	159	144	197	-386	..
International reserves	90	49	70	194	207	199	238	288
6. Ratios								
External debt stocks to exports (%)	473.9	..	..	102.9	104.7	96.6	126.9	..
External debt stocks to GNI (%)	175.3	217.8	120.1	69.3	60.2	54.9	66.5	67.0
Debt service to exports (%)	23.1	..	..	5.8	7.4	3.1	4.8	..
Short-term to external debt stocks (%)	7.1	10.6	7.2	14.1	14.9	15.1	9.4	9.6
Multilateral to external debt stocks (%)	38.6	41.8	61.2	45.1	47.0	46.4	53.8	54.9
Reserves to external debt stocks (%)	3.8	2.1	3.0	12.0	12.2	10.0	11.6	11.7
Reserves to imports (months)	1.9	..	..	1.3	1.1	0.8	1.3	..

MAURITANIA

(US$ million, unless otherwise indicated)

	1995	2000	2005	2006	2007	2008	2009	2010
7. Long-term external debt								
Debt outstanding and disbursed	**2,127**	**2,029**	**2,072**	**1,389**	**1,437**	**1,669**	**1,840**	**2,174**
Public and publicly guaranteed	2,127	2,029	2,072	1,389	1,437	1,669	1,840	2,174
Official creditors	2,119	2,009	2,048	1,368	1,417	1,655	1,827	2,173
Multilateral	926	994	1,413	730	800	922	1,103	1,350
of which: IBRD	11	0	0	0	0	0	0	0
IDA	336	449	677	130	203	243	282	316
Bilateral	1,193	1,016	635	638	616	734	725	823
Private creditors	8	19	23	22	20	14	12	1
of which: Bonds	0	0	0	0	0	0	0	0
Commercial banks	0	0	23	22	20	14	12	1
Private nonguaranteed	0	0	0	0	0	0	0	0
of which: Bonds	0	0	0	0	0	0	0	0
Disbursements	**111**	**115**	**143**	**175**	**185**	**294**	**263**	**412**
Public and publicly guaranteed	111	115	143	175	185	294	263	412
Official creditors	111	115	128	175	185	294	263	412
Multilateral	88	106	109	169	134	159	209	306
of which: IBRD	0	0	0	0	0	0	0	0
IDA	30	57	42	47	66	43	38	39
Bilateral	24	9	19	6	51	135	54	106
Private creditors	0	0	15	0	0	0	0	0
of which: Bonds	0	0	0	0	0	0	0	0
Commercial banks	0	0	15	0	0	0	0	0
Private nonguaranteed	0	0	0	0	0	0	0	0
of which: Bonds	0	0	0	0	0	0	0	0
Principal repayments	**70**	**46**	**33**	**44**	**93**	**38**	**53**	**76**
Public and publicly guaranteed	70	46	33	44	93	38	53	76
Official creditors	69	43	31	42	92	31	52	65
Multilateral	35	34	17	39	86	25	31	56
of which: IBRD	2	2	0	0	0	0	0	0
IDA	2	1	2	1	0	0	0	1
Bilateral	34	9	14	3	6	7	21	9
Private creditors	0	2	1	2	1	6	1	11
of which: Bonds	0	0	0	0	0	0	0	0
Commercial banks	0	0	1	2	1	6	1	11
Private nonguaranteed	0	0	0	0	0	0	0	0
of which: Bonds	0	0	0	0	0	0	0	0
Interest payments	**32**	**20**	**20**	**20**	**23**	**21**	**23**	**31**
Public and publicly guaranteed	32	20	20	20	23	21	23	31
Official creditors	32	18	19	19	22	21	23	31
Multilateral	15	14	15	16	17	14	13	18
of which: IBRD	1	0	0	0	0	0	0	0
IDA	2	2	6	3	2	2	2	2
Bilateral	17	5	4	3	5	7	10	12
Private creditors	0	2	1	1	1	0	0	1
of which: Bonds	0	0	0	0	0	0	0	0
Commercial banks	0	0	1	1	1	0	0	1
Private nonguaranteed	0	0	0	0	0	0	0	0
of which: Bonds	0	0	0	0	0	0	0	0
8. Debt stock-flow reconciliation								
Total change in external debt stocks	136	-155	-15	-690	86	281	62	414
Net flows on external debt	68	62	92	149	131	300	102	473
9. Debt restructurings								
Total amount rescheduled	65	11	10	0	0	0	0	116
Total amount forgiven	15	53	25	905	67	38	2	175
Debt buyback	0	0	0	0	0	0	0	0

10. Contractual obligations on outstanding long-term external debt

	2011	2012	2013	2014	2015	2016	2017	2018
Official creditors								
Principal	82	119	156	169	168	191	191	195
Interest	58	74	81	80	76	71	65	59
Private creditors								
Principal	1	0	0	0	0	0	0	0
Interest	0	0	0	0	0	0	0	0

Notes:

Mauritania was granted debt relief effective in 2006 under MDRI.

MAURITIUS

(US$ million, unless otherwise indicated)

	1995	2000	2005	2006	2007	2008	2009	2010
1. Summary external debt data								
External debt stocks	**1,415**	**946**	**782**	**629**	**668**	**632**	**826**	**1,076**
Long-term external debt	1,414	946	782	629	668	632	818	1,072
Public and publicly guaranteed	1,147	828	716	580	605	583	737	972
Private nonguaranteed	267	118	66	49	62	49	81	100
Use of IMF credit	0	0	0	0	0	0	0	0
Short-term external debt	1	..	..	..	..	..	8	3
interest arrears on long-term	1	0	0	0	0	0	0	0
Memorandum items								
Principal arrears on long-term	0	0	0	0	0	0	0	0
Long-term public sector debt	1,147	828	716	580	605	583	737	972
Long-term private sector debt	267	118	66	49	62	49	81	100
Public & publicly guaranteed commitments	566	101	62	56	150	114	1,260	266
External debt flows								
Disbursements	409	128	138	39	118	114	285	388
Long-term external debt	409	128	138	39	118	114	285	388
IMF purchases	0	0	0	0	0	0	0	0
Principal repayments	154	401	197	226	126	138	108	113
Long-term external debt	154	401	197	226	126	138	108	113
IMF repurchases	0	0	0	0	0	0	0	0
Net flows	255	-273	-59	-187	-8	-24	177	270
Long-term external debt	255	-273	-59	-187	-8	-24	177	275
Short-term external debt	..	..	..	..	..	..	..	-4
Interest payments	56	52	30	29	26	23	21	17
Long-term external debt	56	52	30	29	26	23	20	17
IMF charges	0	0	0	0	0	0	0	0
Short-term external debt	0	0	0	0	0	0	1	0
2. Other non-debt resource inflows								
Foreign direct investment	19	266	42	107	341	378	257	431
Portfolio equity	22	-4	36	35	50	34	206	-40
3. Currency composition of public and publicly guaranteed debt (%)								
Euro	..	..	49.1	53.3	51.8	46.5	40.8	32.0
Japanese yen	1.2	2.6	5.5	6.1	6.4	8.3	6.0	4.8
Pound sterling	1.7	1.6	1.5	1.7	1.5	1.5	1.1	0.8
Swiss franc	0.2	0.3	0.2	0.2	0.2	0.1	0.0	0.0
U.S.dollars	42.3	45.9	24.6	20.3	21.4	24.5	31.9	31.1
4. Average terms of new commitments								
Official creditors								
Interest (%)	5.1	3.9	2.6	5.0	4.1	4.0	1.1	1.3
Maturity (years)	17.5	15.7	14.2	17.2	18.7	15.6	18.2	18.5
Grace period (years)	5.5	4.7	4.8	5.8	5.3	5.5	5.1	5.3
Private creditors								
Interest (%)	6.3	7.5	2.5	0.0	0.0	0.0	2.8	0.0
Maturity (years)	6.1	1.9	1.0	0.0	0.0	0.0	11.3	0.0
Grace period (years)	4.3	1.9	0.0	0.0	0.0	0.0	1.8	0.0
5. Major economic aggregates								
Gross national income (GNI)	4,021	4,553	6,276	6,559	8,016	9,813	8,891	9,798
Exports of goods, services & income	2,402	2,671	3,899	4,374	5,259	5,748	4,635	5,413
Worker remit. & comp. of employees	132	177	215	215	215	215	211	226
Imports of goods, services & income	2,525	2,772	4,284	5,050	5,818	6,948	5,514	6,396
Profit remittances on FDI	16	8	34	88	90	163	195	92
Current account balance	-22	-37	-324	-604	-434	-976	-655	-800
International reserves	887	914	1,372	1,309	1,832	1,796	2,316	2,619
6. Ratios								
External debt stocks to exports (%)	58.9	35.4	20.1	14.4	12.7	11.0	17.8	19.9
External debt stocks to GNI (%)	35.2	20.8	12.5	9.6	8.3	6.4	9.3	11.0
Debt service to exports (%)	8.7	16.9	5.8	5.8	2.9	2.8	2.8	2.4
Short-term to external debt stocks (%)	0.1	..	..	..	..	..	0.9	0.3
Multilateral to external debt stocks (%)	19.1	22.8	32.0	35.2	38.0	42.7	45.6	46.5
Reserves to external debt stocks (%)	62.7	96.6	175.3	208.1	274.3	284.2	280.4	243.4
Reserves to imports (months)	4.2	4.0	3.8	3.1	3.8	3.1	5.0	4.9

(US$ million, unless otherwise indicated)

	1995	2000	2005	2006	2007	2008	2009	2010
7. Long-term external debt								
Debt outstanding and disbursed	**1,414**	**946**	**782**	**629**	**668**	**632**	**818**	**1,072**
Public and publicly guaranteed	1,147	828	716	580	605	583	737	972
Official creditors	663	494	504	440	497	500	652	884
Multilateral	270	216	250	221	253	270	377	501
of which: IBRD	140	86	68	61	81	103	204	197
IDA	17	13	10	10	9	9	8	7
Bilateral	393	278	253	219	243	230	275	383
Private creditors	484	334	213	140	109	83	85	88
of which: Bonds	150	0	0	0	0	0	0	0
Commercial banks	315	324	162	108	79	59	65	73
Private nonguaranteed	267	118	66	49	62	49	81	100
of which: Bonds	0	0	0	0	0	0	0	0
Disbursements	**409**	**128**	**138**	**39**	**118**	**114**	**285**	**388**
Public and publicly guaranteed	353	119	126	28	89	86	217	319
Official creditors	39	43	62	28	89	86	197	292
Multilateral	18	17	31	14	47	48	129	158
of which: IBRD	11	4	2	1	31	30	109	3
IDA	0	0	0	0	0	0	0	0
Bilateral	21	26	31	14	41	38	68	133
Private creditors	313	76	64	0	0	0	19	27
of which: Bonds	150	0	0	0	0	0	0	0
Commercial banks	159	76	61	0	0	0	19	27
Private nonguaranteed	56	9	11	11	29	28	69	69
of which: Bonds	0	0	0	0	0	0	0	0
Principal repayments	**154**	**401**	**197**	**226**	**126**	**138**	**108**	**113**
Public and publicly guaranteed	94	385	176	203	105	104	71	64
Official creditors	60	55	87	115	61	83	51	44
Multilateral	33	34	31	52	26	26	25	22
of which: IBRD	23	18	9	8	11	9	8	6
IDA	1	1	1	1	1	1	1	1
Bilateral	27	21	56	62	35	56	26	23
Private creditors	33	330	89	89	44	21	20	20
of which: Bonds	0	150	0	0	0	0	0	0
Commercial banks	22	146	81	67	38	16	15	15
Private nonguaranteed	60	16	21	23	21	35	37	49
of which: Bonds	0	0	0	0	0	0	0	0
Interest payments	**56**	**52**	**30**	**29**	**26**	**23**	**20**	**17**
Public and publicly guaranteed	50	51	30	29	26	23	20	16
Official creditors	35	23	19	19	18	18	16	15
Multilateral	16	9	7	9	9	9	7	5
of which: IBRD	11	5	2	3	4	4	3	3
IDA	0	0	0	0	0	0	0	0
Bilateral	19	14	13	10	9	9	9	9
Private creditors	14	29	10	10	8	5	3	2
of which: Bonds	0	5	0	0	0	0	0	0
Commercial banks	12	22	8	8	6	4	2	2
Private nonguaranteed	6	1	0	0	1	0	1	1
of which: Bonds	0	0	0	0	0	0	0	0
8. Debt stock-flow reconciliation								
Total change in external debt stocks	317	-325	-142	-153	39	-36	194	250
Net flows on external debt	255	-273	-59	-187	-8	-24	177	270
9. Debt restructurings								
Total amount rescheduled	0	0	0	0	0	0	0	0
Total amount forgiven	0	0	0	0	0	0	0	0
Debt buyback	0	0	0	0	0	0	0	0

10. Contractual obligations on outstanding long-term external debt

	2011	2012	2013	2014	2015	2016	2017	2018
Official creditors								
Principal	63	68	65	97	159	169	164	161
Interest	20	23	24	25	24	22	20	17
Private creditors								
Principal	48	34	32	19	15	11	10	9
Interest	7	5	3	3	2	1	1	1

Notes:

Long-term private nonguaranteed debt data and short-term debt data from 2009 are based on reports provided by the country. Historical private nonguaranteed debt data are World Bank staff estimates. Short-term debt data before 2009 are excluded since BIS data include debt liabilities of offshore centers located in the country.

MEXICO

(US$ million, unless otherwise indicated)

	1995	2000	2005	2006	2007	2008	2009	2010
1. Summary external debt data								
External debt stocks	**165,379**	**150,901**	**165,841**	**161,192**	**178,611**	**187,137**	**171,485**	**200,081**
Long-term external debt	112,250	131,969	143,640	134,934	151,249	158,732	143,895	161,068
Public and publicly guaranteed	93,902	81,488	108,482	96,029	105,376	113,950	99,374	111,467
Private nonguaranteed	18,348	50,481	35,158	38,905	45,872	44,782	44,521	49,600
Use of IMF credit	15,828	0	0	0	0	0	0	0
Short-term external debt	37,300	18,932	22,201	26,258	27,362	28,405	27,590	39,013
interest arrears on long-term	0	0	0	0	0	0	0	0
Memorandum items								
Principal arrears on long-term	0	0	0	0	0	0	0	0
Long-term public sector debt	93,471	81,210	108,448	96,022	105,374	113,950	99,374	111,467
Long-term private sector debt	18,779	50,758	35,192	38,912	45,875	44,782	44,521	49,600
Public & publicly guaranteed commitments	24,610	10,828	14,933	14,974	16,663	24,384	23,318	28,741
External debt flows								
Disbursements	42,966	34,024	25,948	29,483	33,335	33,704	32,005	39,706
Long-term external debt	29,678	32,830	25,948	29,483	33,335	33,704	32,005	39,706
IMF purchases	13,288	1,194	0	0	0	0	0	0
Principal repayments	15,309	44,451	25,098	42,434	24,285	23,568	22,315	21,680
Long-term external debt	14,165	38,958	25,098	42,434	24,285	23,568	22,315	21,680
IMF repurchases	1,144	5,493	0	0	0	0	0	0
Net flows	25,635	-15,557	2,739	-8,894	10,154	11,178	8,875	29,449
Long-term external debt	15,513	-6,128	850	-12,951	9,050	10,135	9,690	18,026
Short-term external debt	-2,022	-5,130	1,889	4,057	1,104	1,043	-815	11,423
Interest payments	10,801	14,059	10,571	11,343	12,234	9,458	8,436	9,536
Long-term external debt	7,645	12,014	8,624	9,677	10,218	8,551	7,710	7,090
IMF charges	545	153	0	0	0	0	0	0
Short-term external debt	2,611	1,892	1,947	1,665	2,016	907	726	2,446
2. Other non-debt resource inflows								
Foreign direct investment	9,526	18,110	24,122	20,052	29,734	26,295	15,334	18,679
Portfolio equity	519	447	3,353	2,805	-482	-3,503	4,169	641
3. Currency composition of public and publicly guaranteed debt (%)								
Euro	..	..	1.1	1.3	1.1	1.0	7.4	6.4
Japanese yen	8.3	7.6	1.8	1.0	0.8	0.9	4.6	6.1
Pound sterling	0.7	0.2	0.1	0.1	0.1	0.0	1.2	1.1
Swiss franc	0.4	0.0	0.2	0.2	0.2	0.1	0.5	0.6
U.S.dollars	65.2	85.0	95.7	96.9	97.4	97.8	86.2	85.8
4. Average terms of new commitments								
Official creditors								
Interest (%)	9.1	5.4	4.0	5.9	7.4	3.1	1.3	0.9
Maturity (years)	9.3	14.8	20.4	13.7	13.0	19.5	18.0	16.8
Grace period (years)	2.9	4.8	4.7	4.4	4.3	7.9	9.9	11.3
Private creditors								
Interest (%)	6.2	8.4	6.5	5.5	6.6	6.6	5.5	4.2
Maturity (years)	3.6	9.4	14.5	11.1	16.6	17.4	9.5	15.4
Grace period (years)	2.5	9.1	7.9	7.6	11.5	9.7	8.6	14.1
5. Major economic aggregates								
Gross national income (GNI)	273,409	566,409	834,030	933,395	1,016,935	1,079,005	867,973	1,025,199
Exports of goods, services & income	93,034	185,853	235,409	272,390	297,114	316,949	249,740	319,198
Worker remit. & comp. of employees	4,368	7,525	22,742	26,543	26,871	26,035	22,014	22,048
Imports of goods, services & income	98,571	211,589	262,626	302,826	332,360	358,750	277,623	346,329
Profit remittances on FDI	4,259	6,076	7,107	10,173	11,609	10,091	7,891	6,576
Current account balance	-1,576	-18,743	-5,080	-4,487	-8,851	-16,339	-6,352	-5,626
International reserves	17,046	35,577	74,110	76,329	87,208	95,300	99,889	120,584
6. Ratios								
External debt stocks to exports (%)	177.8	81.2	70.4	59.2	60.1	59.0	68.7	62.7
External debt stocks to GNI (%)	60.5	26.6	19.9	17.3	17.6	17.3	19.8	19.5
Debt service to exports (%)	28.1	31.5	15.2	19.7	12.3	10.4	12.3	9.8
Short-term to external debt stocks (%)	22.6	12.5	13.4	16.3	15.3	15.2	16.1	19.5
Multilateral to external debt stocks (%)	11.3	11.4	9.9	5.1	5.1	5.7	10.0	10.6
Reserves to external debt stocks (%)	10.3	23.6	44.7	47.4	48.8	50.9	58.2	60.3
Reserves to imports (months)	2.1	2.0	3.4	3.0	3.1	3.2	4.3	4.2

MEXICO

(US$ million, unless otherwise indicated)

	1995	2000	2005	2006	2007	2008	2009	2010
7. Long-term external debt								
Debt outstanding and disbursed	**112,250**	**131,969**	**143,640**	**134,934**	**151,249**	**158,732**	**143,895**	**161,068**
Public and publicly guaranteed	93,902	81,488	108,482	96,029	105,376	113,950	99,374	111,467
Official creditors	38,997	20,850	18,770	10,263	11,009	12,417	21,212	25,655
Multilateral	18,636	17,238	16,478	8,210	9,114	10,648	17,232	21,112
of which: IBRD	13,823	11,444	8,881	4,211	4,540	5,867	10,143	12,462
IDA	0	0	0	0	0	0	0	0
Bilateral	20,361	3,612	2,292	2,053	1,894	1,769	3,980	4,542
Private creditors	54,904	60,639	89,712	85,766	94,368	101,534	78,161	85,813
of which: Bonds	45,287	52,754	68,548	64,025	69,217	78,240	58,890	63,519
Commercial banks	5,302	5,281	20,272	20,940	24,414	22,590	17,552	19,530
Private nonguaranteed	18,348	50,481	35,158	38,905	45,872	44,782	44,521	49,600
of which: Bonds	13,026	20,644	19,442	19,389	22,680	19,958	21,525	29,970
Disbursements	**29,678**	**32,830**	**25,948**	**29,483**	**33,335**	**33,704**	**32,005**	**39,706**
Public and publicly guaranteed	23,399	11,483	15,143	14,977	15,625	24,746	21,926	26,862
Official creditors	13,426	2,855	2,309	2,365	2,165	2,761	8,719	5,721
Multilateral	2,663	2,534	1,946	2,108	1,739	2,613	7,571	4,247
of which: IBRD	1,732	1,748	997	1,429	671	1,940	4,882	2,449
IDA	0	0	0	0	0	0	0	0
Bilateral	10,763	322	363	257	426	147	1,148	1,474
Private creditors	9,973	8,628	12,833	12,612	13,459	21,985	13,206	21,141
of which: Bonds	7,059	7,368	10,096	8,069	11,746	18,224	10,897	11,984
Commercial banks	1,699	1,096	2,665	4,439	1,591	3,665	1,728	7,125
Private nonguaranteed	6,279	21,346	10,806	14,506	17,710	8,958	10,079	12,844
of which: Bonds	843	3,346	6,669	4,506	5,826	931	5,067	11,298
Principal repayments	**14,165**	**38,958**	**25,098**	**42,434**	**24,285**	**23,568**	**22,315**	**21,680**
Public and publicly guaranteed	9,136	16,328	15,682	31,570	13,541	13,834	11,869	13,938
Official creditors	3,072	3,377	2,527	10,948	1,539	1,459	1,792	1,676
Multilateral	1,714	1,816	1,982	10,420	901	1,120	1,110	667
of which: IBRD	1,411	1,330	1,379	6,100	342	596	669	194
IDA	0	0	0	0	0	0	0	0
Bilateral	1,358	1,561	545	527	638	339	682	1,009
Private creditors	6,064	12,950	13,155	20,623	12,001	12,374	10,077	12,263
of which: Bonds	3,534	9,256	9,989	15,003	10,307	9,649	4,965	7,118
Commercial banks	1,623	2,870	2,983	5,414	1,482	2,542	4,296	4,132
Private nonguaranteed	5,029	22,630	9,416	10,864	10,744	9,735	10,416	7,742
of which: Bonds	610	3,552	2,645	4,703	2,536	3,247	3,500	2,826
Interest payments	**7,645**	**12,014**	**8,624**	**9,677**	**10,218**	**8,551**	**7,710**	**7,090**
Public and publicly guaranteed	6,239	7,763	6,758	6,412	6,435	5,752	4,937	4,604
Official creditors	2,659	1,553	847	912	513	458	551	628
Multilateral	1,291	1,275	769	832	433	394	459	531
of which: IBRD	961	890	437	461	232	200	247	246
IDA	0	0	0	0	0	0	0	0
Bilateral	1,368	278	78	80	80	64	92	97
Private creditors	3,579	6,210	5,912	5,500	5,922	5,294	4,386	3,976
of which: Bonds	2,906	4,739	5,474	5,047	5,532	4,957	3,774	3,671
Commercial banks	346	877	404	414	355	309	562	280
Private nonguaranteed	1,407	4,251	1,866	3,266	3,783	2,799	2,773	2,486
of which: Bonds	1,054	1,620	957	1,621	1,694	1,310	1,583	1,379
8. Debt stock-flow reconciliation								
Total change in external debt stocks	26,833	-15,837	3,557	-4,648	17,418	8,526	-15,652	28,596
Net flows on external debt	25,635	-15,557	2,739	-8,894	10,154	11,178	8,875	29,449
9. Debt restructurings								
Total amount rescheduled	0	0	0	0	0	0	0	0
Total amount forgiven	293	478	0	0	0	0	0	0
Debt buyback	13	6,644	0	0	0	0	0	1,746

10. Contractual obligations on outstanding long-term external debt

	2011	2012	2013	2014	2015	2016	2017	2018
Official creditors								
Principal	1,975	1,531	1,485	1,433	1,375	1,361	1,245	1,708
Interest	379	341	307	272	238	212	189	166
Private creditors								
Principal	13,884	13,033	16,899	10,750	11,202	5,763	11,125	1,998
Interest	7,933	7,005	5,954	5,063	4,495	4,107	3,524	3,092

Notes:

Short-term debt for 2010 is based on reports provided by the country.

MOLDOVA

(US$ million, unless otherwise indicated)

	1995	2000	2005	2006	2007	2008	2009	2010
1. Summary external debt data								
External debt stocks	**695**	**1,690**	**2,051**	**2,437**	**3,173**	**3,461**	**3,557**	**4,615**
Long-term external debt	459	1,047	1,238	1,454	1,935	2,006	1,986	2,723
Public and publicly guaranteed	450	850	698	736	777	791	784	817
Private nonguaranteed	9	197	540	718	1,158	1,214	1,203	1,906
Use of IMF credit	230	154	95	141	160	166	154	327
Short-term external debt	6	489	718	842	1,079	1,289	1,417	1,564
interest arrears on long-term	5	22	56	15	21	22	38	37
Memorandum items								
Principal arrears on long-term	42	33	78	72	92	97	173	172
Long-term public sector debt	450	839	698	736	777	791	784	817
Long-term private sector debt	9	208	540	718	1,158	1,214	1,203	1,906
Public & publicly guaranteed commitments	169	20	24	40	96	30	70	183
External debt flows								
Disbursements	230	176	237	415	621	511	271	642
Long-term external debt	166	164	237	351	588	475	271	459
IMF purchases	64	12	0	64	33	36	0	183
Principal repayments	41	82	184	258	239	414	316	307
Long-term external debt	41	57	163	234	217	389	301	299
IMF repurchases	0	25	22	24	22	25	15	8
Net flows	189	560	157	322	613	305	67	483
Long-term external debt	124	107	75	117	371	86	-30	161
Short-term external debt	0	465	104	165	231	208	113	148
Interest payments	29	68	66	76	99	87	70	80
Long-term external debt	19	46	42	38	50	56	52	47
IMF charges	10	8	3	3	2	1	1	0
Short-term external debt	0	14	21	35	47	29	16	32
2. Other non-debt resource inflows								
Foreign direct investment	26	128	191	240	534	713	128	194
Portfolio equity	-1	3	1	2	2	11	2	6
3. Currency composition of public and publicly guaranteed debt (%)								
Euro	..	..	7.6	8.1	8.8	8.9	10.5	9.5
Japanese yen	8.4	3.4	3.3	3.0	2.9	3.4	3.0	2.9
Pound sterling	0.0	0.0	0.0	0.0	0.0	0.0	0.0	0.0
Swiss franc	0.0	0.0	0.0	0.0	0.0	0.0	0.0	0.0
U.S.dollars	22.8	67.1	68.9	69.2	69.0	67.8	66.6	69.4
4. Average terms of new commitments								
Official creditors								
Interest (%)	6.8	0.4	1.5	0.8	3.0	0.8	1.2	1.8
Maturity (years)	10.4	39.7	29.2	39.4	23.8	39.6	26.6	15.8
Grace period (years)	3.3	10.2	7.4	10.1	6.2	10.1	8.4	5.3
Private creditors								
Interest (%)	7.0	5.9	0.0	0.0	0.0	0.0	0.0	0.0
Maturity (years)	6.0	3.2	0.0	0.0	0.0	0.0	0.0	0.0
Grace period (years)	1.5	3.2	0.0	0.0	0.0	0.0	0.0	0.0
5. Major economic aggregates								
Gross national income (GNI)	1,724	1,310	3,347	3,809	4,819	6,653	5,743	6,280
Exports of goods, services & income	898	780	2,043	2,132	2,709	3,388	2,586	3,021
Worker remit. & comp. of employees	1	179	920	1,182	1,498	1,897	1,211	1,370
Imports of goods, services & income	1,038	1,089	2,844	3,335	4,615	6,014	4,276	4,850
Profit remittances on FDI	0	3	45	108	182	152	156	155
Current account balance	-85	-98	-226	-388	-674	-987	-469	-523
International reserves	257	222	597	775	1,334	1,672	1,480	1,718
6. Ratios								
External debt stocks to exports (%)	77.4	216.5	100.4	114.3	117.1	102.1	137.6	152.7
External debt stocks to GNI (%)	40.3	129.0	61.3	64.0	65.9	52.0	61.9	73.5
Debt service to exports (%)	7.9	19.2	12.2	15.7	12.5	14.8	14.9	12.8
Short-term to external debt stocks (%)	0.9	28.9	35.0	34.6	34.0	37.2	39.8	33.9
Multilateral to external debt stocks (%)	31.1	23.9	19.9	17.7	14.9	14.3	14.5	12.0
Reserves to external debt stocks (%)	37.0	13.2	29.1	31.8	42.0	48.3	41.6	37.2
Reserves to imports (months)	3.0	2.5	2.5	2.8	3.5	3.3	4.2	4.2

MOLDOVA

(US$ million, unless otherwise indicated)

	1995	2000	2005	2006	2007	2008	2009	2010
7. Long-term external debt								
Debt outstanding and disbursed	**459**	**1,047**	**1,238**	**1,454**	**1,935**	**2,006**	**1,986**	**2,723**
Public and publicly guaranteed	450	850	698	736	777	791	784	817
Official creditors	430	743	664	711	759	781	780	814
Multilateral	216	403	409	430	473	495	514	556
of which: IBRD	152	191	161	151	141	129	110	93
IDA	0	103	209	242	292	311	332	386
Bilateral	214	340	255	280	286	286	266	258
Private creditors	19	107	34	25	18	11	4	3
of which: Bonds	0	75	25	19	13	6	0	0
Commercial banks	4	12	7	6	5	4	4	3
Private nonguaranteed	9	197	540	718	1,158	1,214	1,203	1,906
of which: Bonds	0	0	0	0	0	0	0	0
Disbursements	**166**	**164**	**237**	**351**	**588**	**475**	**271**	**459**
Public and publicly guaranteed	159	54	26	31	47	43	41	89
Official creditors	139	52	26	31	47	43	41	89
Multilateral	81	50	25	29	47	43	41	74
of which: IBRD	50	6	0	0	0	0	0	0
IDA	0	30	24	23	39	24	21	64
Bilateral	58	1	1	3	1	0	0	15
Private creditors	19	2	0	0	0	0	0	0
of which: Bonds	0	0	0	0	0	0	0	0
Commercial banks	4	0	0	0	0	0	0	0
Private nonguaranteed	7	110	211	320	541	432	230	370
of which: Bonds	0	0	0	0	0	0	0	0
Principal repayments	**41**	**57**	**163**	**234**	**217**	**389**	**301**	**299**
Public and publicly guaranteed	39	30	42	53	41	42	53	48
Official creditors	39	27	35	45	34	35	46	47
Multilateral	35	21	35	23	21	22	25	25
of which: IBRD	0	5	13	14	15	17	18	18
IDA	0	0	0	0	1	2	3	4
Bilateral	4	5	0	22	13	13	22	22
Private creditors	0	3	7	8	7	6	7	1
of which: Bonds	0	0	6	6	6	6	6	0
Commercial banks	0	0	1	1	1	0	1	1
Private nonguaranteed	2	28	120	181	176	347	248	251
of which: Bonds	0	0	0	0	0	0	0	0
Interest payments	**19**	**46**	**42**	**38**	**50**	**56**	**52**	**47**
Public and publicly guaranteed	19	39	22	17	18	16	20	14
Official creditors	19	28	20	15	16	15	19	14
Multilateral	11	18	10	11	12	11	8	5
of which: IBRD	8	11	6	7	8	7	4	1
IDA	0	1	2	2	2	2	2	2
Bilateral	8	10	10	3	4	5	12	9
Private creditors	0	11	2	3	2	1	1	0
of which: Bonds	0	7	2	2	2	1	0	0
Commercial banks	0	0	0	0	0	0	0	0
Private nonguaranteed	0	7	20	21	33	39	32	33
of which: Bonds	0	0	0	0	0	0	0	0
8. Debt stock-flow reconciliation								
Total change in external debt stocks	193	672	108	386	736	287	96	1,058
Net flows on external debt	189	560	157	322	613	305	67	483
9. Debt restructurings								
Total amount rescheduled	0	246	0	88	32	31	0	0
Total amount forgiven	0	0	0	0	0	0	0	0
Debt buyback	0	0	0	0	0	0	0	0

10. Contractual obligations on outstanding long-term external debt

	2011	2012	2013	2014	2015	2016	2017	2018
Official creditors								
Principal	81	59	63	61	54	41	42	39
Interest	16	15	17	15	13	12	11	9
Private creditors								
Principal	553	346	205	226	184	31	22	52
Interest	72	39	27	48	33	10	3	8

Notes:

Data on long-term private nonguaranteed debt for 2010 are revised based on reports provided by the country. Short-term debt data are World Bank staff estimates based on government statistics.

MONGOLIA

(US$ million, unless otherwise indicated)

	1995	2000	2005	2006	2007	2008	2009	2010
1. Summary external debt data								
External debt stocks	**531**	**896**	**1,327**	**1,440**	**1,682**	**1,833**	**2,143**	**2,444**
Long-term external debt	472	833	1,267	1,363	1,581	1,705	1,889	2,016
Public and publicly guaranteed	472	833	1,267	1,361	1,576	1,657	1,821	1,795
Private nonguaranteed	0	0	0	3	5	48	68	221
Use of IMF credit	47	50	35	31	26	20	182	198
Short-term external debt	12	13	25	46	75	108	72	230
interest arrears on long-term	0	2	0	0	0	0	0	0
Memorandum items								
Principal arrears on long-term	4	17	21	25	26	26	10	11
Long-term public sector debt	451	832	1,267	1,361	1,576	1,657	1,821	1,795
Long-term private sector debt	22	1	0	3	5	48	68	221
Public & publicly guaranteed commitments	250	102	72	55	170	304	179	78
External debt flows								
Disbursements	101	83	91	92	167	121	411	270
Long-term external debt	101	75	91	92	167	121	246	246
IMF purchases	0	8	0	0	0	0	166	23
Principal repayments	42	28	23	31	37	46	79	144
Long-term external debt	32	22	17	25	30	41	73	139
IMF repurchases	9	6	6	6	7	5	7	5
Net flows	67	45	-73	82	160	108	296	284
Long-term external debt	68	53	74	67	137	80	173	107
Short-term external debt	8	-9	-142	21	29	33	-36	158
Interest payments	10	10	20	17	19	35	31	28
Long-term external debt	9	9	15	15	15	30	29	24
IMF charges	1	0	0	0	0	0	1	2
Short-term external debt	0	1	5	2	3	5	1	2
2. Other non-debt resource inflows								
Foreign direct investment	10	54	185	344	373	845	624	1,455
Portfolio equity	..	..	..	..	1	13	4	680
3. Currency composition of public and publicly guaranteed debt (%)								
Euro	..	..	7.6	8.4	9.1	8.5	8.4	8.2
Japanese yen	26.5	25.0	21.4	19.6	17.6	21.3	20.3	22.6
Pound sterling	0.0	0.0	0.0	0.0	0.0	0.0	0.0	0.0
Swiss franc	2.3	0.7	0.6	0.6	0.6	0.6	0.5	0.6
U.S.dollars	38.1	35.8	44.5	45.2	46.7	43.7	43.7	39.9
4. Average terms of new commitments								
Official creditors								
Interest (%)	2.2	1.2	1.1	1.0	0.9	1.0	0.7	0.8
Maturity (years)	35.3	31.9	31.5	32.5	33.9	39.3	31.0	39.1
Grace period (years)	10.1	9.3	7.9	8.5	11.1	9.8	9.7	10.1
Private creditors								
Interest (%)	0.0	0.0	0.0	0.0	8.6	0.0	8.0	0.0
Maturity (years)	0.0	0.0	0.0	0.0	3.0	0.0	3.0	0.0
Grace period (years)	0.0	0.0	0.0	0.0	3.0	0.0	3.0	0.0
5. Major economic aggregates								
Gross national income (GNI)	1,425	1,132	2,472	3,353	4,137	5,450	4,388	5,522
Exports of goods, services & income	511	627	1,494	2,048	2,586	3,045	2,324	3,423
Worker remit. & comp. of employees	..	12	180	181	178	225	200	277
Imports of goods, services & income	550	791	1,635	2,042	2,627	3,956	2,852	4,497
Profit remittances on FDI	18	9	41	145	126	109	121	465
Current account balance	39	-70	84	222	172	-690	-342	-887
International reserves	158	202	333	720	1,002	657	1,327	2,288
6. Ratios								
External debt stocks to exports (%)	103.8	143.1	88.8	70.3	65.0	60.2	92.2	71.4
External debt stocks to GNI (%)	37.2	79.2	53.7	42.9	40.6	33.6	48.8	44.3
Debt service to exports (%)	10.2	6.2	2.9	2.4	2.1	2.7	4.7	5.0
Short-term to external debt stocks (%)	2.2	1.4	1.9	3.2	4.5	5.9	3.4	9.4
Multilateral to external debt stocks (%)	32.0	51.5	59.3	59.3	56.2	52.6	49.9	43.9
Reserves to external debt stocks (%)	29.7	22.5	25.1	50.0	59.6	35.8	61.9	93.6
Reserves to imports (months)	3.4	3.1	2.4	4.2	4.6	2.0	5.6	6.1

(US$ million, unless otherwise indicated)

	1995	2000	2005	2006	2007	2008	2009	2010
7. Long-term external debt								
Debt outstanding and disbursed	**472**	**833**	**1,267**	**1,363**	**1,581**	**1,705**	**1,889**	**2,016**
Public and publicly guaranteed	472	833	1,267	1,361	1,576	1,657	1,821	1,795
Official creditors	404	831	1,266	1,348	1,487	1,571	1,737	1,788
Multilateral	170	462	787	854	944	964	1,069	1,073
of which: IBRD	0	0	0	0	0	0	0	0
IDA	59	137	277	301	331	338	392	403
Bilateral	234	369	479	494	543	606	668	716
Private creditors	68	3	0	13	89	86	84	7
of which: Bonds	0	0	0	0	75	75	75	0
Commercial banks	15	1	0	0	0	0	0	0
Private nonguaranteed	0	0	0	3	5	48	68	221
of which: Bonds	0	0	0	0	0	0	0	0
Disbursements	**101**	**75**	**91**	**92**	**167**	**121**	**246**	**246**
Public and publicly guaranteed	101	75	91	89	165	75	219	76
Official creditors	95	75	91	71	87	75	219	76
Multilateral	58	47	48	49	52	43	113	39
of which: IBRD	0	0	0	0	0	0	0	0
IDA	8	14	14	13	20	13	55	22
Bilateral	37	28	43	22	35	32	106	37
Private creditors	6	0	0	18	79	0	0	0
of which: Bonds	0	0	0	0	75	0	0	0
Commercial banks	0	0	0	0	0	0	0	0
Private nonguaranteed	0	0	0	2	2	47	27	170
of which: Bonds	0	0	0	0	0	0	0	0
Principal repayments	**32**	**22**	**17**	**25**	**30**	**41**	**73**	**139**
Public and publicly guaranteed	32	22	17	25	30	40	64	121
Official creditors	13	19	17	20	28	37	62	44
Multilateral	0	0	6	8	11	15	17	19
of which: IBRD	0	0	0	0	0	0	0	0
IDA	0	0	2	2	3	4	4	4
Bilateral	13	19	11	12	17	22	44	25
Private creditors	19	3	0	5	3	3	2	77
of which: Bonds	0	0	0	0	0	0	0	75
Commercial banks	5	0	0	0	0	0	0	0
Private nonguaranteed	0	0	0	0	0	1	8	18
of which: Bonds	0	0	0	0	0	0	0	0
Interest payments	**9**	**9**	**15**	**15**	**15**	**30**	**29**	**24**
Public and publicly guaranteed	9	9	15	15	15	24	26	20
Official creditors	5	9	15	15	15	18	19	19
Multilateral	1	4	7	8	8	9	9	10
of which: IBRD	0	0	0	0	0	0	0	0
IDA	0	1	2	2	2	3	2	3
Bilateral	4	5	8	7	7	9	10	9
Private creditors	4	0	0	0	0	7	7	1
of which: Bonds	0	0	0	0	0	6	6	1
Commercial banks	1	0	0	0	0	0	0	0
Private nonguaranteed	0	0	0	0	0	6	4	4
of which: Bonds	0	0	0	0	0	0	0	0
8. Debt stock-flow reconciliation								
Total change in external debt stocks	66	-18	-191	114	241	151	310	301
Net flows on external debt	67	45	-73	82	160	108	296	284
9. Debt restructurings								
Total amount rescheduled	0	0	0	3	0	0	0	0
Total amount forgiven	0	0	0	17	0	0	0	0
Debt buyback	0	0	0	0	0	0	0	0

10. Contractual obligations on outstanding long-term external debt

	2011	2012	2013	2014	2015	2016	2017	2018
Official creditors								
Principal	63	68	68	71	75	76	75	89
Interest	24	25	25	25	24	25	24	23
Private creditors								
Principal	27	40	41	27	50	47	1	0
Interest	6	5	4	3	2	1	0	0

Notes:

Long-term private nonguaranteed debt data only cover European Bank for Reconstruction and Development.

MONTENEGRO

(US$ million, unless otherwise indicated)

	1995	2000	2005	2006	2007	2008	2009	2010
1. Summary external debt data								
External debt stocks	..	..	..	**841**	**1,263**	**1,466**	**2,315**	**1,554**
Long-term external debt	..	..	..	841	858	864	1,108	1,368
Public and publicly guaranteed	..	..	..	829	848	855	1,093	1,350
Private nonguaranteed	..	..	..	12	10	9	15	19
Use of IMF credit	..	..	..	0	0	0	0	0
Short-term external debt	..	..	..	..	405	602	1,207	186
interest arrears on long-term	..	..	..	..	0	0	0	0
Memorandum items								
Principal arrears on long-term	..	..	..	0	0	0	0	0
Long-term public sector debt	..	..	..	829	848	855	1,093	1,350
Long-term private sector debt	..	..	..	12	10	9	15	19
Public & publicly guaranteed commitments	..	..	..	64	193	43	395	271
External debt flows								
Disbursements	..	..	..	88	78	64	249	388
Long-term external debt	..	..	..	88	78	64	249	388
IMF purchases	..	..	..	0	0	0	0	0
Principal repayments	..	..	..	13	109	28	31	61
Long-term external debt	..	..	..	13	109	28	31	61
IMF repurchases	..	..	..	0	0	0	0	0
Net flows	..	..	..	75	-32	233	823	-695
Long-term external debt	..	..	..	75	-32	36	218	326
Short-term external debt	..	..	..	..	..	197	605	-1,021
Interest payments	..	..	..	28	50	40	40	38
Long-term external debt	..	..	..	28	35	28	28	34
IMF charges	..	..	..	0	0	0	0	0
Short-term external debt	..	..	..	0	15	12	12	4
2. Other non-debt resource inflows								
Foreign direct investment	..	..	..	..	934	960	1,527	760
Portfolio equity	..	..	..	..	5	-6	-5	-8
3. Currency composition of public and publicly guaranteed debt (%)								
Euro	..	..	..	44.4	51.0	51.3	59.8	69.1
Japanese yen	..	..	..	0.0	0.0	0.0	0.0	0.0
Pound sterling	..	..	..	0.1	0.1	0.0	0.0	0.0
Swiss franc	..	..	..	1.8	3.9	4.0	3.3	2.9
U.S.dollars	..	..	..	50.6	41.4	39.3	32.4	24.0
4. Average terms of new commitments								
Official creditors								
Interest (%)	..	..	..	1.2	2.4	2.3	1.7	1.1
Maturity (years)	..	..	..	14.7	15.7	9.2	14.4	9.8
Grace period (years)	..	..	..	3.8	5.3	3.2	2.4	4.3
Private creditors								
Interest (%)	..	..	..	4.0	2.0	0.0	7.8	7.9
Maturity (years)	..	..	..	5.6	13.1	0.0	5.0	5.1
Grace period (years)	..	..	..	1.1	3.6	0.0	0.6	5.1
5. Major economic aggregates								
Gross national income (GNI)	..	..	..	2,735	3,690	4,587	4,149	3,976
Exports of goods, services & income	..	..	..	..	1,727	2,007	1,583	1,681
Worker remit. & comp. of employees	..	..	..	..	196	298	302	301
Imports of goods, services & income	..	..	..	..	3,283	4,433	2,947	2,864
Profit remittances on FDI	..	..	..	..	16	43	90	100
Current account balance	..	..	..	..	-1,475	-2,320	-1,245	-1,031
International reserves	..	..	..	457	689	436	573	556
6. Ratios								
External debt stocks to exports (%)	..	..	..	..	73.1	73.1	146.2	92.5
External debt stocks to GNI (%)	..	..	..	30.8	34.2	32.0	55.8	39.1
Debt service to exports (%)	..	..	..	..	9.2	3.4	4.5	5.9
Short-term to external debt stocks (%)	..	..	..	..	32.1	41.1	52.1	12.0
Multilateral to external debt stocks (%)	..	..	..	64.6	43.6	38.2	25.5	35.8
Reserves to external debt stocks (%)	..	..	..	54.4	54.5	29.7	24.7	35.8
Reserves to imports (months)	..	..	..	..	2.5	1.2	2.3	2.3

MONTENEGRO

(US$ million, unless otherwise indicated)

	1995	2000	2005	2006	2007	2008	2009	2010
7. Long-term external debt								
Debt outstanding and disbursed	..	..	..	**841**	**858**	**864**	**1,108**	**1,368**
Public and publicly guaranteed	..	..	..	829	848	855	1,093	1,350
Official creditors	..	..	..	810	832	840	893	837
Multilateral	..	..	..	543	550	560	591	556
of which: IBRD	..	..	..	345	283	269	261	236
IDA	..	..	..	47	56	71	75	79
Bilateral	..	..	..	266	281	281	302	281
Private creditors	..	..	..	19	17	15	201	512
of which: Bonds	..	..	..	0	0	0	0	267
Commercial banks	..	..	..	19	17	15	201	245
Private nonguaranteed	..	..	..	12	10	9	15	19
of which: Bonds	..	..	..	0	0	0	0	0
Disbursements	..	..	..	**88**	**78**	**64**	**249**	**388**
Public and publicly guaranteed	..	..	..	86	77	60	242	375
Official creditors	..	..	..	82	77	60	61	27
Multilateral	..	..	..	40	49	37	41	12
of which: IBRD	..	..	..	0	0	0	3	5
IDA	..	..	..	14	7	15	4	3
Bilateral	..	..	..	43	28	23	20	15
Private creditors	..	..	..	3	0	0	181	348
of which: Bonds	..	..	..	0	0	0	0	265
Commercial banks	..	..	..	3	0	0	181	83
Private nonguaranteed	..	..	..	2	1	4	7	12
of which: Bonds	..	..	..	0	0	0	0	0
Principal repayments	..	..	..	**13**	**109**	**28**	**31**	**61**
Public and publicly guaranteed	..	..	..	12	105	25	29	60
Official creditors	..	..	..	12	105	24	28	33
Multilateral	..	..	..	8	98	14	20	16
of which: IBRD	..	..	..	8	96	10	12	10
IDA	..	..	..	0	0	0	0	0
Bilateral	..	..	..	4	6	10	8	17
Private creditors	..	..	..	0	1	1	1	27
of which: Bonds	..	..	..	0	0	0	0	0
Commercial banks	..	..	..	0	1	1	1	27
Private nonguaranteed	..	..	..	0	4	3	2	2
of which: Bonds	..	..	..	0	0	0	0	0
Interest payments	..	..	..	**28**	**35**	**28**	**28**	**34**
Public and publicly guaranteed	..	..	..	28	34	27	28	33
Official creditors	..	..	..	27	34	27	26	20
Multilateral	..	..	..	21	28	22	19	14
of which: IBRD	..	..	..	16	22	15	10	5
IDA	..	..	..	0	0	0	1	1
Bilateral	..	..	..	6	6	5	7	6
Private creditors	..	..	..	1	1	0	2	13
of which: Bonds	..	..	..	0	0	0	0	0
Commercial banks	..	..	..	1	1	0	2	13
Private nonguaranteed	..	..	..	0	1	0	0	1
of which: Bonds	..	..	..	0	0	0	0	0
8. Debt stock-flow reconciliation								
Total change in external debt stocks	..	..	..	453	422	204	849	-760
Net flows on external debt	..	..	..	75	-32	233	823	-695
9. Debt restructurings								
Total amount rescheduled	..	..	..	39	0	0	0	0
Total amount forgiven	..	..	..	0	205	0	0	0
Debt buyback	..	..	..	0	0	0	0	0

10. Contractual obligations on outstanding long-term external debt

	2011	2012	2013	2014	2015	2016	2017	2018
Official creditors								
Principal	55	64	73	81	84	82	80	84
Interest	16	16	15	15	14	12	11	10
Private creditors								
Principal	54	57	57	48	284	5	4	4
Interest	36	32	28	24	22	1	0	0

Notes:

Long-term private nonguaranteed debt data only cover European Bank for Reconstruction and Development. Montenegro became independent in 2006 and started to report data in 2007.

MOROCCO

(US$ million, unless otherwise indicated)

	1995	2000	2005	2006	2007	2008	2009	2010
1. Summary external debt data								
External debt stocks	**23,771**	**20,674**	**16,174**	**17,815**	**20,543**	**20,825**	**23,751**	**25,403**
Long-term external debt	23,521	19,101	15,492	16,083	18,624	19,194	21,572	23,603
Public and publicly guaranteed	23,190	17,239	12,441	13,496	15,650	16,538	19,218	21,015
Private nonguaranteed	331	1,862	3,051	2,588	2,975	2,656	2,354	2,589
Use of IMF credit	52	0	0	0	0	0	0	0
Short-term external debt	198	1,573	682	1,732	1,919	1,631	2,179	1,800
interest arrears on long-term	92	122	0	0	0	0	0	0
Memorandum items								
Principal arrears on long-term	138	535	3	4	2	1	0	0
Long-term public sector debt	22,944	17,077	12,381	13,425	15,565	16,446	19,134	20,933
Long-term private sector debt	577	2,023	3,111	2,659	3,059	2,748	2,438	2,670
Public & publicly guaranteed commitments	2,583	535	2,277	2,842	3,888	1,421	3,309	6,667
External debt flows								
Disbursements	2,309	1,638	2,456	2,426	3,976	4,554	4,551	4,970
Long-term external debt	2,309	1,638	2,456	2,426	3,976	4,554	4,551	4,970
IMF purchases	0	0	0	0	0	0	0	0
Principal repayments	2,368	1,631	2,138	2,784	3,325	3,451	2,709	2,436
Long-term external debt	2,268	1,631	2,138	2,784	3,325	3,451	2,709	2,436
IMF repurchases	100	0	0	0	0	0	0	0
Net flows	-81	-448	832	692	838	814	2,390	2,155
Long-term external debt	41	7	318	-358	651	1,102	1,842	2,534
Short-term external debt	-22	-455	514	1,050	187	-288	548	-379
Interest payments	1,391	1,075	590	616	694	752	702	875
Long-term external debt	1,360	948	569	540	590	709	678	850
IMF charges	7	0	0	0	0	0	0	0
Short-term external debt	24	127	22	76	104	43	24	26
2. Other non-debt resource inflows								
Foreign direct investment	92	221	1,620	2,366	2,807	2,466	1,970	1,241
Portfolio equity	20	18	64	-298	-64	148	-4	132
3. Currency composition of public and publicly guaranteed debt (%)								
Euro	..	..	43.4	47.2	54.6	53.0	54.5	55.4
Japanese yen	3.8	3.3	5.1	5.0	4.7	6.1	5.9	6.8
Pound sterling	0.2	0.1	0.0	0.0	0.0	0.0	0.0	0.0
Swiss franc	0.1	0.1	0.1	0.1	0.0	0.0	0.0	0.0
U.S.dollars	27.2	37.6	23.8	19.6	12.6	11.9	10.4	10.3
4. Average terms of new commitments								
Official creditors								
Interest (%)	4.4	3.4	3.1	3.7	3.9	4.3	2.7	2.2
Maturity (years)	19.8	25.1	19.5	23.0	19.6	19.8	20.2	20.5
Grace period (years)	5.4	6.4	5.5	6.5	5.7	5.0	5.0	5.7
Private creditors								
Interest (%)	7.1	5.6	3.6	4.0	5.2	5.3	4.1	3.5
Maturity (years)	9.7	7.7	11.7	14.7	10.3	10.3	12.2	19.0
Grace period (years)	1.5	1.0	1.2	3.0	8.4	0.8	0.4	10.3
5. Major economic aggregates								
Gross national income (GNI)	31,668	36,053	58,760	64,703	74,246	87,411	89,489	90,246
Exports of goods, services & income	9,296	10,729	19,477	22,465	28,272	34,806	27,306	30,997
Worker remit. & comp. of employees	1,970	2,161	4,590	5,451	6,730	6,895	6,270	6,423
Imports of goods, services & income	12,812	13,686	23,811	27,383	36,098	48,102	39,728	42,193
Profit remittances on FDI	100	268	594	674	730	835	1,753	1,445
Current account balance	-1,186	-475	1,041	1,411	-122	-4,528	-4,971	-3,925
International reserves	3,874	5,017	16,551	20,791	24,714	22,720	23,568	23,609
6. Ratios								
External debt stocks to exports (%)	255.7	192.7	83.0	79.3	72.7	59.8	87.0	82.0
External debt stocks to GNI (%)	75.1	57.3	27.5	27.5	27.7	23.8	26.5	28.1
Debt service to exports (%)	40.4	25.2	14.0	15.1	14.2	12.1	12.5	10.7
Short-term to external debt stocks (%)	0.8	7.6	4.2	9.7	9.3	7.8	9.2	7.1
Multilateral to external debt stocks (%)	29.1	29.5	36.3	37.2	38.4	41.2	42.2	40.0
Reserves to external debt stocks (%)	16.3	24.3	102.3	116.7	120.3	109.1	99.2	92.9
Reserves to imports (months)	3.6	4.4	8.3	9.1	8.2	5.7	7.1	6.7

(US$ million, unless otherwise indicated)

	1995	2000	2005	2006	2007	2008	2009	2010
7. Long-term external debt								
Debt outstanding and disbursed	**23,521**	**19,101**	**15,492**	**16,083**	**18,624**	**19,194**	**21,572**	**23,603**
Public and publicly guaranteed	23,190	17,239	12,441	13,496	15,650	16,538	19,218	21,015
Official creditors	16,875	12,754	10,118	11,196	13,084	14,543	16,713	17,234
Multilateral	6,913	6,091	5,874	6,635	7,894	8,576	10,020	10,149
of which: IBRD	3,966	2,837	2,258	2,267	2,578	2,540	2,543	2,468
IDA	33	27	20	18	17	16	14	13
Bilateral	9,962	6,663	4,244	4,562	5,190	5,967	6,694	7,085
Private creditors	6,315	4,485	2,323	2,300	2,566	1,994	2,504	3,780
of which: Bonds	0	152	472	527	589	0	0	1,336
Commercial banks	4,234	3,300	1,466	1,470	1,745	1,749	2,259	2,251
Private nonguaranteed	331	1,862	3,051	2,588	2,975	2,656	2,354	2,589
of which: Bonds	0	0	0	0	0	0	0	0
Disbursements	**2,309**	**1,638**	**2,456**	**2,426**	**3,976**	**4,554**	**4,551**	**4,970**
Public and publicly guaranteed	2,206	980	1,658	1,850	2,714	3,093	3,468	3,854
Official creditors	1,521	631	1,562	1,531	1,810	2,800	2,868	2,229
Multilateral	1,008	466	1,134	1,030	1,125	1,533	1,828	1,246
of which: IBRD	426	138	262	176	418	242	241	271
IDA	0	0	0	0	0	0	0	0
Bilateral	513	166	427	501	685	1,267	1,040	983
Private creditors	686	349	97	320	904	292	600	1,625
of which: Bonds	0	0	0	0	0	0	0	1,327
Commercial banks	224	143	74	313	903	222	567	297
Private nonguaranteed	103	658	798	575	1,262	1,461	1,083	1,116
of which: Bonds	0	0	0	0	0	0	0	0
Principal repayments	**2,268**	**1,631**	**2,138**	**2,784**	**3,325**	**3,451**	**2,709**	**2,436**
Public and publicly guaranteed	2,238	1,592	1,881	1,558	1,861	1,795	1,138	1,282
Official creditors	1,638	926	1,303	1,063	990	1,043	966	1,099
Multilateral	625	550	689	591	525	592	532	620
of which: IBRD	348	307	309	330	294	262	238	202
IDA	1	1	1	1	1	1	1	1
Bilateral	1,012	376	613	472	464	450	434	479
Private creditors	600	666	578	495	872	753	172	184
of which: Bonds	0	30	41	0	0	589	0	0
Commercial banks	112	350	372	372	777	119	131	148
Private nonguaranteed	30	39	258	1,226	1,464	1,656	1,572	1,154
of which: Bonds	0	0	0	0	0	0	0	0
Interest payments	**1,360**	**948**	**569**	**540**	**590**	**709**	**678**	**850**
Public and publicly guaranteed	1,358	877	501	472	555	655	612	819
Official creditors	923	548	388	360	443	535	523	731
Multilateral	466	363	230	235	300	364	340	295
of which: IBRD	282	190	87	88	104	125	93	52
IDA	0	0	0	0	0	0	0	0
Bilateral	457	185	157	126	143	171	183	436
Private creditors	436	329	113	112	112	120	89	88
of which: Bonds	0	14	25	25	27	29	0	0
Commercial banks	259	228	65	70	72	80	80	78
Private nonguaranteed	2	71	68	67	34	54	66	31
of which: Bonds	0	0	0	0	0	0	0	0
8. Debt stock-flow reconciliation								
Total change in external debt stocks	798	-2,262	-709	1,641	2,728	281	2,926	1,652
Net flows on external debt	-81	-448	832	692	838	814	2,390	2,155
9. Debt restructurings								
Total amount rescheduled	0	0	0	0	0	0	0	0
Total amount forgiven	0	117	0	0	0	0	0	0
Debt buyback	0	0	0	0	0	0	0	0

10. Contractual obligations on outstanding long-term external debt

	2011	2012	2013	2014	2015	2016	2017	2018
Official creditors								
Principal	1,564	1,716	1,615	1,610	1,576	1,589	1,619	1,592
Interest	514	523	513	494	465	431	392	351
Private creditors								
Principal	431	463	541	525	531	540	1,208	527
Interest	228	237	232	220	205	190	157	124

MOZAMBIQUE
(US$ million, unless otherwise indicated)

	1995	2000	2005	2006	2007	2008	2009	2010
1. Summary external debt data								
External debt stocks	**7,409**	**7,205**	**4,153**	**2,649**	**2,908**	**3,392**	**4,046**	**4,124**
Long-term external debt	6,930	6,410	3,383	2,061	2,376	2,797	3,241	2,960
Public and publicly guaranteed	5,161	4,693	3,383	2,061	2,376	2,797	3,241	2,960
Private nonguaranteed	1,769	1,717	0	0	0	0	0	0
Use of IMF credit	202	219	157	10	15	15	171	190
Short-term external debt	277	576	613	578	516	581	634	975
interest arrears on long-term	248	411	525	496	387	450	467	878
Memorandum items								
Principal arrears on long-term	1,039	714	464	471	418	430	441	226
Long-term public sector debt	5,161	4,693	3,383	2,061	2,376	2,797	3,241	2,960
Long-term private sector debt	1,769	1,717	0	0	0	0	0	0
Public & publicly guaranteed commitments	150	237	170	331	410	649	474	718
External debt flows								
Disbursements	267	190	334	351	343	414	605	378
Long-term external debt	267	131	329	346	338	414	452	356
IMF purchases	0	60	5	5	5	0	153	22
Principal repayments	85	64	55	16	10	14	15	40
Long-term external debt	71	64	39	16	10	14	15	40
IMF repurchases	14	0	15	0	0	0	0	0
Net flows	193	62	315	329	380	402	626	268
Long-term external debt	196	67	290	330	328	400	437	316
Short-term external debt	11	-64	36	-6	47	2	36	-70
Interest payments	77	32	24	22	19	23	29	50
Long-term external debt	75	20	22	19	14	19	23	47
IMF charges	1	1	0	0	0	0	0	0
Short-term external debt	1	11	2	2	4	4	5	3
2. Other non-debt resource inflows								
Foreign direct investment	45	139	108	154	427	592	881	789
Portfolio equity	0	0	0	0	0	0	0	0
3. Currency composition of public and publicly guaranteed debt (%)								
Euro	..	..	3.4	6.0	6.5	6.7	6.8	9.5
Japanese yen	1.8	1.8	1.2	2.0	2.0	2.1	1.0	0.9
Pound sterling	2.1	2.1	0.0	0.0	0.0	0.0	0.0	0.0
Swiss franc	0.0	0.0	0.0	0.0	0.0	0.0	0.0	0.0
U.S.dollars	60.0	68.7	68.7	62.6	58.3	57.4	54.9	44.2
4. Average terms of new commitments								
Official creditors								
Interest (%)	0.9	0.8	0.7	0.7	0.8	1.1	1.3	0.7
Maturity (years)	36.8	46.6	38.1	42.2	37.5	36.4	33.5	41.9
Grace period (years)	9.3	12.9	10.1	9.6	9.7	13.1	8.2	10.2
Private creditors								
Interest (%)	0.0	0.0	0.0	4.9	5.7	0.0	0.0	1.2
Maturity (years)	0.0	0.0	0.0	11.2	11.5	0.0	12.8	32.3
Grace period (years)	0.0	0.0	0.0	1.7	2.0	0.0	2.8	13.3
5. Major economic aggregates								
Gross national income (GNI)	2,069	4,017	6,219	6,472	7,445	9,263	9,696	9,421
Exports of goods, services & income	470	769	2,186	2,927	3,064	3,375	2,629	3,052
Worker remit. & comp. of employees	59	37	57	80	99	116	111	132
Imports of goods, services & income	1,254	1,763	3,350	4,201	4,452	5,407	4,564	4,624
Profit remittances on FDI	..	0	284	471	554	544	84	70
Current account balance	-445	-764	-761	-773	-785	-1,179	-1,171	-913
International reserves	195	742	1,103	1,216	1,524	1,661	2,181	2,265
6. Ratios								
External debt stocks to exports (%)	1,575.0	937.3	190.0	90.5	94.9	100.5	153.9	135.1
External debt stocks to GNI (%)	358.2	179.3	66.8	40.9	39.1	36.6	41.7	43.8
Debt service to exports (%)	34.5	12.5	3.6	1.3	0.9	1.1	1.6	2.9
Short-term to external debt stocks (%)	3.7	8.0	14.8	21.8	17.7	17.1	15.7	23.6
Multilateral to external debt stocks (%)	17.2	15.4	56.4	38.3	46.4	49.9	49.3	53.5
Reserves to external debt stocks (%)	2.6	10.3	26.6	45.9	52.4	48.9	53.9	54.9
Reserves to imports (months)	1.9	5.1	4.0	3.5	4.1	3.7	5.7	5.9

MOZAMBIQUE

(US$ million, unless otherwise indicated)

	1995	2000	2005	2006	2007	2008	2009	2010
7. Long-term external debt								
Debt outstanding and disbursed	**6,930**	**6,410**	**3,383**	**2,061**	**2,376**	**2,797**	**3,241**	**2,960**
Public and publicly guaranteed	5,161	4,693	3,383	2,061	2,376	2,797	3,241	2,960
Official creditors	5,115	4,682	3,381	2,060	2,368	2,790	3,213	2,862
Multilateral	1,277	1,106	2,341	1,014	1,349	1,693	1,996	2,205
of which: IBRD	0	0	0	0	0	0	0	0
IDA	890	760	1,575	655	902	1,149	1,356	1,491
Bilateral	3,838	3,576	1,040	1,045	1,018	1,097	1,217	657
Private creditors	46	11	2	2	9	7	28	98
of which: Bonds	0	0	0	0	0	0	0	0
Commercial banks	7	0	0	0	0	0	0	51
Private nonguaranteed	1,769	1,717	0	0	0	0	0	0
of which: Bonds	0	0	0	0	0	0	0	0
Disbursements	**267**	**131**	**329**	**346**	**338**	**414**	**452**	**356**
Public and publicly guaranteed	231	131	329	346	338	414	452	356
Official creditors	231	131	329	346	332	412	429	277
Multilateral	219	128	327	341	319	358	295	252
of which: IBRD	0	0	0	0	0	0	0	0
IDA	160	97	227	223	212	255	199	163
Bilateral	11	3	3	5	13	55	134	26
Private creditors	0	0	0	0	6	2	23	79
of which: Bonds	0	0	0	0	0	0	0	0
Commercial banks	0	0	0	0	0	0	0	51
Private nonguaranteed	36	0	0	0	0	0	0	0
of which: Bonds	0	0	0	0	0	0	0	0
Principal repayments	**71**	**64**	**39**	**16**	**10**	**14**	**15**	**40**
Public and publicly guaranteed	67	34	18	16	10	14	15	40
Official creditors	58	33	18	16	10	11	12	32
Multilateral	13	18	12	11	5	7	8	14
of which: IBRD	0	0	0	0	0	0	0	0
IDA	0	2	5	3	0	0	2	5
Bilateral	45	15	7	5	4	4	4	18
Private creditors	9	1	0	0	0	3	3	8
of which: Bonds	0	0	0	0	0	0	0	0
Commercial banks	0	1	0	0	0	0	0	0
Private nonguaranteed	3	30	21	0	0	0	0	0
of which: Bonds	0	0	0	0	0	0	0	0
Interest payments	**75**	**20**	**22**	**19**	**14**	**19**	**23**	**47**
Public and publicly guaranteed	74	20	22	19	14	19	23	47
Official creditors	71	20	22	19	14	19	23	47
Multilateral	12	9	18	15	10	15	19	22
of which: IBRD	0	0	0	0	0	0	0	0
IDA	6	4	12	9	6	8	9	10
Bilateral	59	11	4	4	4	4	4	24
Private creditors	3	0	0	0	0	0	0	0
of which: Bonds	0	0	0	0	0	0	0	0
Commercial banks	0	0	0	0	0	0	0	0
Private nonguaranteed	1	0	0	0	0	0	0	0
of which: Bonds	0	0	0	0	0	0	0	0
8. Debt stock-flow reconciliation								
Total change in external debt stocks	187	34	-318	-1,504	259	485	653	78
Net flows on external debt	193	62	315	329	380	402	626	268
9. Debt restructurings								
Total amount rescheduled	66	0	0	0	14	0	0	0
Total amount forgiven	323	113	29	1,892	139	3	0	656
Debt buyback	0	0	0	0	0	0	0	0

10. Contractual obligations on outstanding long-term external debt

	2011	2012	2013	2014	2015	2016	2017	2018
Official creditors								
Principal	47	46	50	70	69	75	89	96
Interest	29	30	31	32	32	31	30	29
Private creditors								
Principal	6	7	7	7	7	7	6	5
Interest	3	4	5	4	4	4	4	3

Notes:

Mozambique was granted debt relief effective in 2006 under MDRI.

MYANMAR

(US$ million, unless otherwise indicated)

	1995	*2000*	*2005*	*2006*	*2007*	*2008*	*2009*	*2010*
1. Summary external debt data								
External debt stocks	**5,771**	**5,975**	**7,014**	**7,264**	**8,241**	**8,002**	**8,186**	**6,352**
Long-term external debt	5,378	5,287	5,515	5,609	6,221	6,121	6,320	4,395
Public and publicly guaranteed	5,378	5,287	5,515	5,609	6,221	6,121	6,320	4,395
Private nonguaranteed	0	0	0	0	0	0	0	0
Use of IMF credit	0	0	0	0	0	0	0	0
Short-term external debt	393	688	1,498	1,656	2,021	1,881	1,866	1,956
interest arrears on long-term	352	490	759	806	958	950	1,009	1,116
Memorandum items								
Principal arrears on long-term	1,359	1,784	2,914	3,128	3,757	3,840	4,147	4,562
Long-term public sector debt	5,271	5,193	5,414	5,508	6,102	6,000	6,193	4,367
Long-term private sector debt	107	94	101	101	118	121	127	28
Public & publicly guaranteed commitments	118	0	0	0	0	0	0	0
External debt flows								
Disbursements	86	14	1	0	1	1	0	1
Long-term external debt	86	14	1	0	1	1	0	1
IMF purchases	0	0	0	0	0	0	0	0
Principal repayments	180	22	25	9	11	10	9	651
Long-term external debt	180	22	25	9	11	10	9	651
IMF repurchases	0	0	0	0	0	0	0	0
Net flows	-74	33	-36	102	203	-142	-83	-668
Long-term external debt	-95	-7	-24	-9	-10	-10	-9	-651
Short-term external debt	20	41	-12	111	213	-132	-74	-17
Interest payments	70	14	46	55	42	23	20	36
Long-term external debt	68	2	1	1	2	2	2	20
IMF charges	0	0	0	0	0	0	0	0
Short-term external debt	2	12	44	54	40	21	18	16
2. Other non-debt resource inflows								
Foreign direct investment	280	258	237	279	258	283	323	756
Portfolio equity	..	..	..	..	..	..	..	..
3. Currency composition of public and publicly guaranteed debt (%)								
Euro	..	..	11.0	11.9	12.6	10.6	10.3	13.1
Japanese yen	52.3	44.9	45.4	44.5	47.2	48.9	49.8	41.6
Pound sterling	1.3	1.2	1.4	1.5	1.4	1.0	1.1	1.6
Swiss franc	0.0	0.0	0.0	0.0	0.0	0.0	0.0	0.0
U.S.dollars	22.6	35.4	33.5	33.3	30.3	30.6	29.9	31.3
4. Average terms of new commitments								
Official creditors								
Interest (%)	2.8	0.0	0.0	0.0	0.0	0.0	0.0	0.0
Maturity (years)	33.0	0.0	0.0	0.0	0.0	0.0	0.0	0.0
Grace period (years)	24.4	0.0	0.0	0.0	0.0	0.0	0.0	0.0
Private creditors								
Interest (%)	0.8	0.0	0.0	0.0	0.0	0.0	0.0	0.0
Maturity (years)	6.4	0.0	0.0	0.0	0.0	0.0	0.0	0.0
Grace period (years)	1.8	0.0	0.0	0.0	0.0	0.0	0.0	0.0
5. Major economic aggregates								
Gross national income (GNI)	..	..	..	..	..	..	..	..
Exports of goods, services & income	1,323	2,175	4,102	4,932	..	..	..	..
Worker remit. & comp. of employees	81	104	131	116	116	116	116	133
Imports of goods, services & income	2,146	2,662	3,689	4,252	..	..	..	..
Profit remittances on FDI	..	137	1,402	1,317	..	..	..	..
Current account balance	-261	-212	588	802	..	..	..	..
International reserves	651	286	889	1,383	..	..	..	..
6. Ratios								
External debt stocks to exports (%)	436.3	274.7	171.0	147.3	..	..	..	..
External debt stocks to GNI (%)	..	..	..	..	..	..	..	..
Debt service to exports (%)	18.9	1.7	1.7	1.3	..	..	..	..
Short-term to external debt stocks (%)	6.8	11.5	21.4	22.8	24.5	23.5	22.8	30.8
Multilateral to external debt stocks (%)	23.1	19.2	17.5	17.2	15.7	16.4	16.4	22.3
Reserves to external debt stocks (%)	11.3	4.8	12.7	19.0	..	..	..	..
Reserves to imports (months)	3.6	1.3	2.9	3.9	..	..	..	..

(US$ million, unless otherwise indicated)

	1995	2000	2005	2006	2007	2008	2009	2010
7. Long-term external debt								
Debt outstanding and disbursed	**5,378**	**5,287**	**5,515**	**5,609**	**6,221**	**6,121**	**6,320**	**4,395**
Public and publicly guaranteed	5,378	5,287	5,515	5,609	6,221	6,121	6,320	4,395
Official creditors	5,011	4,262	4,568	4,646	5,218	5,155	5,345	3,989
Multilateral	1,331	1,148	1,228	1,253	1,290	1,311	1,341	1,415
of which: IBRD	0	0	0	0	0	0	0	0
IDA	777	684	752	776	793	770	777	799
Bilateral	3,680	3,114	3,340	3,393	3,928	3,845	4,004	2,574
Private creditors	367	1,026	947	963	1,002	966	976	406
of which: Bonds	0	0	0	0	0	0	0	0
Commercial banks	0	546	546	546	546	546	546	0
Private nonguaranteed	0	0	0	0	0	0	0	0
of which: Bonds	0	0	0	0	0	0	0	0
Disbursements	**86**	**14**	**1**	**0**	**1**	**1**	**0**	**1**
Public and publicly guaranteed	86	14	1	0	1	1	0	1
Official creditors	17	12	1	0	1	1	0	1
Multilateral	0	1	0	0	0	0	0	0
of which: IBRD	0	0	0	0	0	0	0	0
IDA	0	0	0	0	0	0	0	0
Bilateral	16	11	1	0	1	0	0	1
Private creditors	69	3	0	0	0	0	0	0
of which: Bonds	0	0	0	0	0	0	0	0
Commercial banks	0	0	0	0	0	0	0	0
Private nonguaranteed	0	0	0	0	0	0	0	0
of which: Bonds	0	0	0	0	0	0	0	0
Principal repayments	**180**	**22**	**25**	**9**	**11**	**10**	**9**	**651**
Public and publicly guaranteed	180	22	25	9	11	10	9	651
Official creditors	147	2	8	8	11	10	9	105
Multilateral	25	2	2	2	2	1	1	1
of which: IBRD	0	0	0	0	0	0	0	0
IDA	9	0	0	0	0	0	0	0
Bilateral	122	0	6	6	9	9	8	104
Private creditors	34	20	17	1	1	0	0	546
of which: Bonds	0	0	0	0	0	0	0	0
Commercial banks	0	0	0	0	0	0	0	546
Private nonguaranteed	0	0	0	0	0	0	0	0
of which: Bonds	0	0	0	0	0	0	0	0
Interest payments	**68**	**2**	**1**	**1**	**2**	**2**	**2**	**20**
Public and publicly guaranteed	68	2	1	1	2	2	2	20
Official creditors	66	0	1	1	2	2	2	10
Multilateral	13	0	0	0	0	0	0	0
of which: IBRD	0	0	0	0	0	0	0	0
IDA	6	0	0	0	0	0	0	0
Bilateral	53	0	1	1	2	2	2	10
Private creditors	2	2	0	0	0	0	0	10
of which: Bonds	0	0	0	0	0	0	0	0
Commercial banks	0	0	0	0	0	0	0	10
Private nonguaranteed	0	0	0	0	0	0	0	0
of which: Bonds	0	0	0	0	0	0	0	0
8. Debt stock-flow reconciliation								
Total change in external debt stocks	-785	-29	-469	250	977	-240	184	-1,834
Net flows on external debt	-74	33	-36	102	203	-142	-83	-668
9. Debt restructurings								
Total amount rescheduled	0	0	0	0	0	0	0	0
Total amount forgiven	0	0	0	0	0	0	0	0
Debt buyback	0	0	0	0	0	0	0	0

10. Contractual obligations on outstanding long-term external debt

	2011	2012	2013	2014	2015	2016	2017	2018
Official creditors								
Principal	186	175	159	138	123	82	110	100
Interest	20	17	15	13	11	9	8	8
Private creditors								
Principal	0	0	0	0	0	0	0	0
Interest	0	0	0	0	0	0	0	0

Notes:

Fiscal year-end for external debt data is March. Data on long-term public and publicly guaranteed debt are World Bank staff estimates based on the original terms of the loans.

NEPAL

(US$ million, unless otherwise indicated)

	1995	2000	2005	2006	2007	2008	2009	2010
1. Summary external debt data								
External debt stocks	**2,410**	**2,867**	**3,180**	**3,392**	**3,602**	**3,685**	**3,683**	**3,702**
Long-term external debt	2,339	2,826	3,112	3,268	3,468	3,551	3,563	3,527
Public and publicly guaranteed	2,339	2,826	3,112	3,268	3,468	3,551	3,563	3,527
Private nonguaranteed	0	0	0	0	0	0	0	0
Use of IMF credit	48	12	20	43	79	77	76	114
Short-term external debt	23	29	47	81	55	57	44	61
interest arrears on long-term	2	0	0	0	0	0	0	0
Memorandum items								
Principal arrears on long-term	8	0	0	0	0	0	0	0
Long-term public sector debt	2,338	2,826	3,112	3,268	3,468	3,551	3,563	3,527
Long-term private sector debt	0	0	0	0	0	0	0	0
Public & publicly guaranteed commitments	89	86	195	166	131	84	183	432
External debt flows								
Disbursements	164	154	192	184	175	103	127	177
Long-term external debt	164	154	192	163	141	103	127	134
IMF purchases	0	0	0	21	33	0	0	44
Principal repayments	53	71	85	105	113	127	143	154
Long-term external debt	45	67	85	105	113	127	140	149
IMF repurchases	8	4	0	0	0	0	2	4
Net flows	71	69	118	113	36	-21	-29	41
Long-term external debt	119	87	107	58	29	-23	-14	-16
Short-term external debt	-40	-14	11	34	-26	2	-13	17
Interest payments	32	31	32	34	35	35	34	33
Long-term external debt	29	28	30	30	30	34	32	33
IMF charges	0	0	0	0	0	0	0	0
Short-term external debt	2	3	2	4	4	1	1	1
2. Other non-debt resource inflows								
Foreign direct investment	..	0	2	-7	6	1	38	88
Portfolio equity	0	0	..	..	..	..	..	..
3. Currency composition of public and publicly guaranteed debt (%)								
Euro	..	..	2.1	2.1	2.1	1.7	1.6	1.4
Japanese yen	11.3	9.2	8.9	7.7	7.1	8.0	7.1	7.3
Pound sterling	0.1	0.1	0.1	0.1	0.1	0.0	0.0	0.0
Swiss franc	0.0	0.0	0.0	0.0	0.0	0.0	0.0	0.0
U.S.dollars	44.0	38.6	43.6	44.2	43.5	42.5	42.3	41.9
4. Average terms of new commitments								
Official creditors								
Interest (%)	3.5	1.4	1.1	1.3	1.9	0.6	0.8	1.2
Maturity (years)	29.8	31.4	34.6	24.6	25.2	30.7	37.1	31.4
Grace period (years)	7.9	8.1	8.7	8.1	6.3	9.8	9.8	8.2
Private creditors								
Interest (%)	0.0	0.0	0.0	0.0	3.0	0.0	0.0	0.0
Maturity (years)	0.0	0.0	0.0	0.0	27.0	0.0	0.0	0.0
Grace period (years)	0.0	0.0	0.0	0.0	8.0	0.0	0.0	0.0
5. Major economic aggregates								
Gross national income (GNI)	4,407	5,514	8,153	9,144	10,383	12,695	13,050	15,823
Exports of goods, services & income	1,072	1,354	1,423	1,393	1,661	1,946	1,753	1,784
Worker remit. & comp. of employees	57	111	1,212	1,453	1,734	2,727	2,986	3,468
Imports of goods, services & income	1,659	1,825	2,803	3,030	3,743	4,456	5,160	6,004
Profit remittances on FDI	0	0	57	56	54	44	9	50
Current account balance	-356	-131	153	150	6	733	18	-128
International reserves	646	987	1,565	..	..	..	..	..
6. Ratios								
External debt stocks to exports (%)	224.7	211.7	223.4	243.6	216.9	189.4	210.1	207.6
External debt stocks to GNI (%)	54.7	52.0	39.0	37.1	34.7	29.0	28.2	23.4
Debt service to exports (%)	7.9	7.5	8.2	9.9	8.9	8.3	10.1	10.5
Short-term to external debt stocks (%)	0.9	1.0	1.5	2.4	1.5	1.5	1.2	1.6
Multilateral to external debt stocks (%)	81.0	85.7	86.1	86.0	86.8	86.5	87.2	85.1
Reserves to external debt stocks (%)	26.8	34.4	49.2	..	..	..	..	..
Reserves to imports (months)	4.7	6.5	6.7	..	..	..	..	..

(US$ million, unless otherwise indicated)

	1995	2000	2005	2006	2007	2008	2009	2010
7. Long-term external debt								
Debt outstanding and disbursed	**2,339**	**2,826**	**3,112**	**3,268**	**3,468**	**3,551**	**3,563**	**3,527**
Public and publicly guaranteed	2,339	2,826	3,112	3,268	3,468	3,551	3,563	3,527
Official creditors	2,282	2,821	3,108	3,264	3,464	3,547	3,559	3,524
Multilateral	1,952	2,457	2,737	2,918	3,126	3,187	3,211	3,150
of which: IBRD	0	0	0	0	0	0	0	0
IDA	1,023	1,132	1,396	1,468	1,524	1,507	1,483	1,426
Bilateral	329	364	370	346	338	360	349	374
Private creditors	57	5	5	5	5	4	4	3
of which: Bonds	0	0	0	0	0	0	0	0
Commercial banks	0	0	0	0	0	0	0	0
Private nonguaranteed	0	0	0	0	0	0	0	0
of which: Bonds	0	0	0	0	0	0	0	0
Disbursements	**164**	**154**	**192**	**163**	**141**	**103**	**127**	**134**
Public and publicly guaranteed	164	154	192	163	141	103	127	134
Official creditors	164	154	192	163	141	103	127	134
Multilateral	151	142	86	157	135	102	104	103
of which: IBRD	0	0	0	0	0	0	0	0
IDA	82	49	33	43	35	31	7	11
Bilateral	13	11	106	6	6	2	23	31
Private creditors	0	0	0	0	0	0	0	0
of which: Bonds	0	0	0	0	0	0	0	0
Commercial banks	0	0	0	0	0	0	0	0
Private nonguaranteed	0	0	0	0	0	0	0	0
of which: Bonds	0	0	0	0	0	0	0	0
Principal repayments	**45**	**67**	**85**	**105**	**113**	**127**	**140**	**149**
Public and publicly guaranteed	45	67	85	105	113	127	140	149
Official creditors	40	59	85	104	112	126	140	149
Multilateral	24	37	61	68	81	93	106	114
of which: IBRD	0	0	0	0	0	0	0	0
IDA	7	16	30	31	34	39	41	43
Bilateral	16	22	24	36	32	33	34	35
Private creditors	5	7	1	0	1	1	1	0
of which: Bonds	0	0	0	0	0	0	0	0
Commercial banks	0	0	0	0	0	0	0	0
Private nonguaranteed	0	0	0	0	0	0	0	0
of which: Bonds	0	0	0	0	0	0	0	0
Interest payments	**29**	**28**	**30**	**30**	**30**	**34**	**32**	**33**
Public and publicly guaranteed	29	28	30	30	30	34	32	33
Official creditors	24	27	30	30	30	34	32	32
Multilateral	17	22	26	25	26	29	28	28
of which: IBRD	0	0	0	0	0	0	0	0
IDA	7	8	12	11	11	12	11	11
Bilateral	8	5	4	5	4	4	4	4
Private creditors	5	1	0	0	0	0	0	0
of which: Bonds	0	0	0	0	0	0	0	0
Commercial banks	0	0	0	0	0	0	0	0
Private nonguaranteed	0	0	0	0	0	0	0	0
of which: Bonds	0	0	0	0	0	0	0	0
8. Debt stock-flow reconciliation								
Total change in external debt stocks	89	-152	-177	213	210	83	-2	19
Net flows on external debt	71	69	118	113	36	-21	-29	41
9. Debt restructurings								
Total amount rescheduled	0	0	0	0	0	0	0	0
Total amount forgiven	0	0	0	0	0	0	0	0
Debt buyback	0	0	0	0	0	0	0	0

10. Contractual obligations on outstanding long-term external debt

	2011	2012	2013	2014	2015	2016	2017	2018
Official creditors								
Principal	159	163	169	173	180	181	185	188
Interest	44	44	44	43	42	40	40	38
Private creditors								
Principal	1	1	1	1	1	0	0	0
Interest	0	0	0	0	0	0	0	0

NICARAGUA

(US$ million, unless otherwise indicated)

	1995	2000	2005	2006	2007	2008	2009	2010
1. Summary external debt data								
External debt stocks	**10,396**	**6,742**	**4,931**	**4,114**	**3,701**	**4,232**	**4,672**	**4,786**
Long-term external debt	8,572	5,661	4,190	3,434	2,813	3,402	3,806	3,922
Public and publicly guaranteed	8,572	5,380	3,899	3,201	2,151	2,234	2,488	2,668
Private nonguaranteed	0	281	292	232	662	1,168	1,318	1,255
Use of IMF credit	39	169	201	63	85	111	150	167
Short-term external debt	1,785	912	540	617	803	719	716	697
interest arrears on long-term	1,475	791	364	438	467	472	484	495
Memorandum items								
Principal arrears on long-term	3,230	900	550	558	482	465	458	456
Long-term public sector debt	8,572	5,416	3,817	3,188	2,137	2,222	2,475	2,655
Long-term private sector debt	0	246	374	245	676	1,180	1,331	1,267
Public & publicly guaranteed commitments	361	185	160	566	81	283	252	335
External debt flows								
Disbursements	277	537	287	312	940	975	803	583
Long-term external debt	277	511	287	250	922	946	766	563
IMF purchases	0	27	0	61	18	29	37	20
Principal repayments	203	189	118	107	329	308	386	415
Long-term external debt	190	183	110	107	329	308	386	415
IMF repurchases	13	5	9	0	0	0	0	0
Net flows	88	351	211	208	768	577	401	138
Long-term external debt	87	327	177	143	593	637	380	149
Short-term external debt	13	3	43	3	157	-89	-15	-30
Interest payments	85	98	53	58	77	107	131	106
Long-term external debt	76	91	45	50	64	97	122	99
IMF charges	1	1	0	0	0	0	1	0
Short-term external debt	8	7	8	8	13	9	8	7
2. Other non-debt resource inflows								
Foreign direct investment	89	267	241	287	382	626	434	508
Portfolio equity	0	0	..	..	..	..	..	..
3. Currency composition of public and publicly guaranteed debt (%)								
Euro	..	..	0.5	1.3	3.8	4.1	4.7	5.1
Japanese yen	1.3	2.3	0.0	0.0	0.0	0.0	0.0	0.0
Pound sterling	0.0	0.0	0.0	0.0	0.0	0.0	0.0	0.0
Swiss franc	0.0	0.0	0.1	0.1	0.0	0.0	0.0	0.0
U.S.dollars	72.9	71.1	81.1	76.4	84.7	84.6	84.4	84.7
4. Average terms of new commitments								
Official creditors								
Interest (%)	2.3	1.6	1.3	3.0	1.8	2.7	4.1	2.0
Maturity (years)	32.2	36.9	33.2	27.4	26.0	32.2	33.6	28.6
Grace period (years)	8.4	9.6	9.1	7.8	6.9	11.4	6.4	5.9
Private creditors								
Interest (%)	7.4	0.7	0.0	0.0	0.0	0.0	0.0	0.0
Maturity (years)	9.0	39.9	0.0	0.0	0.0	0.0	0.0	0.0
Grace period (years)	1.0	10.5	0.0	0.0	0.0	0.0	0.0	0.0
5. Major economic aggregates								
Gross national income (GNI)	2,821	3,735	4,723	5,103	5,565	6,152	5,960	6,223
Exports of goods, services & income	669	1,133	1,985	2,319	2,608	3,013	2,891	3,637
Worker remit. & comp. of employees	75	320	616	698	740	818	768	823
Imports of goods, services & income	1,529	2,385	3,626	4,161	4,906	5,724	4,838	5,773
Profit remittances on FDI	29	69	82	85	93	113	121	135
Current account balance	-722	-842	-784	-838	-1,224	-1,570	-828	-963
International reserves	142	492	728	922	1,103	1,141	1,573	1,799
6. Ratios								
External debt stocks to exports (%)	1,554.6	595.3	248.4	177.4	141.9	140.4	161.6	131.6
External debt stocks to GNI (%)	368.6	180.5	104.4	80.6	66.5	68.8	78.4	76.9
Debt service to exports (%)	43.1	25.3	8.6	7.1	15.6	13.8	17.9	14.3
Short-term to external debt stocks (%)	17.2	13.5	11.0	15.0	21.7	17.0	15.3	14.6
Multilateral to external debt stocks (%)	14.1	31.6	56.7	50.4	30.0	28.6	30.8	34.2
Reserves to external debt stocks (%)	1.4	7.3	14.8	22.4	29.8	27.0	33.7	37.6
Reserves to imports (months)	1.1	2.5	2.4	2.7	2.7	2.4	3.9	3.7

NICARAGUA

(US$ million, unless otherwise indicated)

	1995	2000	2005	2006	2007	2008	2009	2010
7. Long-term external debt								
Debt outstanding and disbursed	**8,572**	**5,661**	**4,190**	**3,434**	**2,813**	**3,402**	**3,806**	**3,922**
Public and publicly guaranteed	8,572	5,380	3,899	3,201	2,151	2,234	2,488	2,668
Official creditors	7,562	5,164	3,826	3,129	2,146	2,231	2,484	2,664
Multilateral	1,464	2,127	2,797	2,074	1,111	1,208	1,439	1,637
of which: IBRD	65	5	0	0	0	0	0	0
IDA	276	654	1,136	256	321	347	418	447
Bilateral	6,098	3,037	1,029	1,054	1,035	1,022	1,045	1,028
Private creditors	1,010	216	72	73	5	4	4	3
of which: Bonds	524	0	0	0	0	0	0	0
Commercial banks	383	188	55	55	0	0	0	0
Private nonguaranteed	0	281	292	232	662	1,168	1,318	1,255
of which: Bonds	0	0	0	0	0	0	0	0
Disbursements	**277**	**511**	**287**	**250**	**922**	**946**	**766**	**563**
Public and publicly guaranteed	277	226	226	250	368	183	291	267
Official creditors	258	220	226	250	368	183	291	267
Multilateral	177	172	215	220	329	128	246	235
of which: IBRD	0	0	0	0	0	0	0	0
IDA	18	87	63	61	53	28	67	37
Bilateral	80	48	11	30	39	55	45	32
Private creditors	20	6	0	0	0	0	0	0
of which: Bonds	0	0	0	0	0	0	0	0
Commercial banks	20	5	0	0	0	0	0	0
Private nonguaranteed	0	285	61	0	554	763	475	297
of which: Bonds	0	0	0	0	0	0	0	0
Principal repayments	**190**	**183**	**110**	**107**	**329**	**308**	**386**	**415**
Public and publicly guaranteed	190	70	63	48	214	51	61	55
Official creditors	89	61	63	48	197	51	61	55
Multilateral	47	36	21	27	169	21	25	20
of which: IBRD	15	5	0	0	0	0	0	0
IDA	1	2	0	0	0	0	0	0
Bilateral	42	26	41	21	28	30	36	35
Private creditors	101	8	0	0	17	0	0	0
of which: Bonds	0	0	0	0	0	0	0	0
Commercial banks	96	5	0	0	17	0	0	0
Private nonguaranteed	0	114	47	59	115	257	325	360
of which: Bonds	0	0	0	0	0	0	0	0
Interest payments	**76**	**91**	**45**	**50**	**64**	**97**	**122**	**99**
Public and publicly guaranteed	76	78	44	48	45	39	37	33
Official creditors	72	76	44	48	45	39	37	33
Multilateral	33	64	27	32	27	23	24	24
of which: IBRD	6	1	0	0	0	0	0	0
IDA	2	5	7	4	2	3	3	3
Bilateral	39	12	17	16	18	15	13	9
Private creditors	3	3	0	0	0	0	0	0
of which: Bonds	0	0	0	0	0	0	0	0
Commercial banks	3	2	0	0	0	0	0	0
Private nonguaranteed	0	12	2	2	19	59	85	66
of which: Bonds	0	0	0	0	0	0	0	0
8. Debt stock-flow reconciliation								
Total change in external debt stocks	-1,606	-45	-85	-817	-413	531	440	115
Net flows on external debt	88	351	211	208	768	577	401	138
9. Debt restructurings								
Total amount rescheduled	263	149	1	2	0	0	22	0
Total amount forgiven	2,273	35	167	1,230	1,276	56	16	10
Debt buyback	89	0	0	0	17	0	0	0

10. Contractual obligations on outstanding long-term external debt

	2011	2012	2013	2014	2015	2016	2017	2018
Official creditors								
Principal	87	90	92	94	103	111	119	122
Interest	44	45	46	46	45	43	40	38
Private creditors								
Principal	336	238	212	126	101	75	63	50
Interest	55	40	28	20	14	10	6	3

Notes:

Nicaragua was granted debt relief effective in 2006 under MDRI.

NIGER

(US$ million, unless otherwise indicated)

	1995	2000	2005	2006	2007	2008	2009	2010
1. Summary external debt data								
External debt stocks	**1,604**	**1,708**	**2,017**	**829**	**1,148**	**1,002**	**1,103**	**1,127**
Long-term external debt	1,480	1,563	1,849	755	847	858	915	972
Public and publicly guaranteed	1,347	1,495	1,817	729	827	845	909	972
Private nonguaranteed	133	68	33	26	20	13	7	0
Use of IMF credit	52	74	128	27	40	51	57	61
Short-term external debt	72	72	41	47	261	93	131	94
interest arrears on long-term	53	60	38	38	38	19	17	26
Memorandum items								
Principal arrears on long-term	74	97	52	46	49	66	55	111
Long-term public sector debt	1,347	1,495	1,817	729	827	845	909	972
Long-term private sector debt	133	68	33	26	20	13	7	0
Public & publicly guaranteed commitments	8	64	131	188	54	135	191	187
External debt flows								
Disbursements	28	87	152	126	92	109	108	95
Long-term external debt	28	76	135	117	80	98	103	90
IMF purchases	0	11	17	9	12	12	5	5
Principal repayments	41	16	27	160	17	18	36	18
Long-term external debt	31	14	22	46	17	18	36	18
IMF repurchases	10	2	5	114	0	0	0	0
Net flows	-9	52	122	-28	289	-58	112	31
Long-term external debt	-3	62	113	71	63	79	67	72
Short-term external debt	4	-20	-3	6	214	-149	40	-46
Interest payments	15	10	13	11	15	11	10	9
Long-term external debt	13	8	13	10	9	7	8	8
IMF charges	1	0	0	0	0	0	0	0
Short-term external debt	1	2	0	0	6	4	1	1
2. Other non-debt resource inflows								
Foreign direct investment	7	8	44	51	129	340	739	947
Portfolio equity	..	0	1	0	0	1	..	..
3. Currency composition of public and publicly guaranteed debt (%)								
Euro	..	..	11.1	1.2	0.5	0.5	0.8	1.1
Japanese yen	4.4	1.7	0.0	0.0	0.0	0.0	0.0	0.0
Pound sterling	1.0	1.2	0.0	0.0	0.0	0.0	0.0	0.0
Swiss franc	0.3	0.0	0.0	0.0	0.0	0.0	0.0	0.0
U.S.dollars	36.8	46.7	57.6	47.5	47.2	47.0	46.1	47.3
4. Average terms of new commitments								
Official creditors								
Interest (%)	0.6	0.7	0.9	0.8	1.6	1.4	1.2	1.5
Maturity (years)	33.5	36.5	34.9	36.7	28.4	34.0	32.5	33.0
Grace period (years)	8.4	9.4	8.8	9.5	7.9	9.1	9.5	9.5
Private creditors								
Interest (%)	0.0	0.0	0.0	0.0	0.0	0.0	0.0	0.0
Maturity (years)	0.0	0.0	0.0	0.0	0.0	0.0	0.0	0.0
Grace period (years)	0.0	0.0	0.0	0.0	0.0	0.0	0.0	0.0
5. Major economic aggregates								
Gross national income (GNI)	1,830	1,782	3,397	3,645	4,290	5,351	5,204	5,493
Exports of goods, services & income	327	334	602	641	807	1,124	..	..
Worker remit. & comp. of employees	8	14	66	78	79	94	94	88
Imports of goods, services & income	510	485	1,095	1,118	1,344	2,006	..	..
Profit remittances on FDI	4	2	21	13	28	23	..	..
Current account balance	-152	-104	-312	-314	-351	-651	..	..
International reserves	95	81	251	371	593	705	656	760
6. Ratios								
External debt stocks to exports (%)	490.3	512.0	335.0	129.4	142.2	89.1	..	..
External debt stocks to GNI (%)	87.6	95.9	59.4	22.7	26.8	18.7	21.2	20.5
Debt service to exports (%)	17.1	7.8	6.7	26.6	4.0	2.6	..	..
Short-term to external debt stocks (%)	4.5	4.2	2.0	5.7	22.8	9.3	11.8	8.4
Multilateral to external debt stocks (%)	55.0	60.3	78.9	62.5	53.4	62.4	61.1	63.9
Reserves to external debt stocks (%)	5.9	4.8	12.4	44.8	51.7	70.4	59.4	67.5
Reserves to imports (months)	2.2	2.0	2.7	4.0	5.3	4.2	..	..

NIGER

(US$ million, unless otherwise indicated)

	1995	2000	2005	2006	2007	2008	2009	2010
7. Long-term external debt								
Debt outstanding and disbursed	**1,480**	**1,563**	**1,849**	**755**	**847**	**858**	**915**	**972**
Public and publicly guaranteed	1,347	1,495	1,817	729	827	845	909	972
Official creditors	1,347	1,495	1,817	729	827	845	909	972
Multilateral	882	1,030	1,592	518	613	625	674	720
of which: IBRD	0	0	0	0	0	0	0	0
IDA	598	723	1,080	189	235	248	266	275
Bilateral	465	465	225	211	214	220	235	251
Private creditors	0	0	0	0	0	0	0	0
of which: Bonds	0	0	0	0	0	0	0	0
Commercial banks	0	0	0	0	0	0	0	0
Private nonguaranteed	133	68	33	26	20	13	7	0
of which: Bonds	0	0	0	0	0	0	0	0
Disbursements	**28**	**76**	**135**	**117**	**80**	**98**	**103**	**90**
Public and publicly guaranteed	28	76	135	117	80	98	103	90
Official creditors	28	76	135	117	80	98	103	90
Multilateral	28	76	133	111	80	79	88	75
of which: IBRD	0	0	0	0	0	0	0	0
IDA	24	68	65	55	37	15	16	14
Bilateral	0	0	2	6	0	18	15	15
Private creditors	0	0	0	0	0	0	0	0
of which: Bonds	0	0	0	0	0	0	0	0
Commercial banks	0	0	0	0	0	0	0	0
Private nonguaranteed	0	0	0	0	0	0	0	0
of which: Bonds	0	0	0	0	0	0	0	0
Principal repayments	**31**	**14**	**22**	**46**	**17**	**18**	**36**	**18**
Public and publicly guaranteed	7	12	15	39	10	12	29	11
Official creditors	7	12	15	39	10	12	29	11
Multilateral	7	10	13	26	10	11	27	11
of which: IBRD	0	0	0	0	0	0	0	0
IDA	3	8	1	1	0	0	0	0
Bilateral	0	2	2	13	0	1	2	0
Private creditors	0	0	0	0	0	0	0	0
of which: Bonds	0	0	0	0	0	0	0	0
Commercial banks	0	0	0	0	0	0	0	0
Private nonguaranteed	24	2	7	7	7	7	7	7
of which: Bonds	0	0	0	0	0	0	0	0
Interest payments	**13**	**8**	**13**	**10**	**9**	**7**	**8**	**8**
Public and publicly guaranteed	7	8	11	8	8	6	8	8
Official creditors	7	8	11	8	8	6	8	8
Multilateral	7	7	11	8	7	5	7	7
of which: IBRD	0	0	0	0	0	0	0	0
IDA	5	6	6	4	2	1	2	2
Bilateral	0	1	0	1	1	1	1	1
Private creditors	0	0	0	0	0	0	0	0
of which: Bonds	0	0	0	0	0	0	0	0
Commercial banks	0	0	0	0	0	0	0	0
Private nonguaranteed	6	0	2	2	2	1	0	0
of which: Bonds	0	0	0	0	0	0	0	0
8. Debt stock-flow reconciliation								
Total change in external debt stocks	62	5	2	-1,189	319	-146	101	24
Net flows on external debt	-9	52	122	-28	289	-58	112	31
9. Debt restructurings								
Total amount rescheduled	5	28	0	0	0	0	6	0
Total amount forgiven	4	0	28	1,206	1	42	0	0
Debt buyback	0	0	0	0	0	0	0	0

10. Contractual obligations on outstanding long-term external debt

	2011	2012	2013	2014	2015	2016	2017	2018
Official creditors								
Principal	44	50	30	31	37	41	43	42
Interest	10	11	12	13	13	13	13	13
Private creditors								
Principal	0	0	0	0	0	0	0	0
Interest	0	0	0	0	0	0	0	0

Notes:

Niger was granted debt relief effective in 2006 under MDRI.

NIGERIA

(US$ million, unless otherwise indicated)

	1995	2000	2005	2006	2007	2008	2009	2010
1. Summary external debt data								
External debt stocks	**34,092**	**31,355**	**22,060**	**7,693**	**8,531**	**11,334**	**7,713**	**7,883**
Long-term external debt	28,441	30,235	20,224	3,803	3,587	3,878	4,199	4,686
Public and publicly guaranteed	28,140	30,020	20,224	3,803	3,587	3,878	4,199	4,686
Private nonguaranteed	301	215	0	0	0	0	0	0
Use of IMF credit	0	0	0	0	0	0	0	0
Short-term external debt	5,651	1,120	1,836	3,890	4,944	7,456	3,514	3,197
interest arrears on long-term	4,717	44	3	0	0	0	0	0
Memorandum items								
Principal arrears on long-term	8,102	117	3	0	0	0	0	0
Long-term public sector debt	28,077	29,964	20,195	3,779	3,568	3,864	4,192	4,686
Long-term private sector debt	365	271	29	24	19	14	7	0
Public & publicly guaranteed commitments	0	86	706	507	777	986	985	1,595
External debt flows								
Disbursements	433	153	379	777	532	409	519	1,051
Long-term external debt	433	153	379	777	532	409	519	1,051
IMF purchases	0	0	0	0	0	0	0	0
Principal repayments	918	1,091	3,862	6,441	914	338	339	246
Long-term external debt	918	1,091	3,862	6,441	914	338	339	246
IMF repurchases	0	0	0	0	0	0	0	0
Net flows	-559	-696	-3,001	-3,607	672	2,583	-3,762	488
Long-term external debt	-486	-937	-3,483	-5,664	-382	71	180	805
Short-term external debt	-73	241	482	2,057	1,054	2,512	-3,942	-317
Interest payments	915	754	5,000	373	329	236	153	103
Long-term external debt	859	690	4,937	259	86	87	84	59
IMF charges	0	0	0	0	0	0	0	0
Short-term external debt	56	64	64	114	243	149	69	44
2. Other non-debt resource inflows								
Foreign direct investment	1,079	1,140	4,983	4,854	6,035	8,197	8,555	6,049
Portfolio equity	..	..	751	1,769	1,447	-954	487	2,161
3. Currency composition of public and publicly guaranteed debt (%)								
Euro	..	..	36.2	4.0	3.1	2.9	4.8	3.9
Japanese yen	12.6	2.3	9.9	0.0	0.0	0.0	0.0	0.0
Pound sterling	9.9	1.5	17.2	0.3	0.2	0.2	0.1	0.1
Swiss franc	0.6	0.0	1.9	0.0	0.0	0.0	0.0	0.0
U.S.dollars	29.6	85.1	27.3	59.8	59.0	61.9	59.1	61.7
4. Average terms of new commitments								
Official creditors								
Interest (%)	0.0	1.0	0.7	1.6	0.8	0.8	0.8	1.7
Maturity (years)	0.0	32.9	37.6	28.2	40.7	40.2	39.5	28.1
Grace period (years)	0.0	9.7	10.3	7.1	10.1	9.8	10.0	8.2
Private creditors								
Interest (%)	0.0	0.0	0.0	0.0	6.0	0.0	0.0	0.0
Maturity (years)	0.0	0.0	0.0	0.0	10.4	0.0	0.0	0.0
Grace period (years)	0.0	0.0	0.0	0.0	3.0	0.0	0.0	0.0
5. Major economic aggregates								
Gross national income (GNI)	25,888	40,256	98,881	141,275	154,068	194,690	158,437	176,769
Exports of goods, services & income	12,443	21,183	57,149	61,109	70,046	90,345	59,274	77,756
Worker remit. & comp. of employees	804	1,392	3,329	5,435	9,221	9,980	9,585	10,045
Imports of goods, services & income	15,820	15,383	35,773	42,389	60,948	81,632	64,815	95,373
Profit remittances on FDI	1,330	2,279	2,603	5,768	13,056	17,000	15,042	19,121
Current account balance	-2,578	7,427	36,529	36,518	27,643	28,079	13,153	2,476
International reserves	1,709	10,099	28,632	42,735	51,907	53,599	45,510	35,885
6. Ratios								
External debt stocks to exports (%)	274.0	148.0	38.6	12.6	12.2	12.5	13.0	10.1
External debt stocks to GNI (%)	131.7	77.9	22.3	5.4	5.5	5.8	4.9	4.5
Debt service to exports (%)	14.7	8.7	15.5	11.2	1.8	0.6	0.8	0.4
Short-term to external debt stocks (%)	16.6	3.6	8.3	50.6	58.0	65.8	45.6	40.6
Multilateral to external debt stocks (%)	14.5	10.5	11.5	34.9	34.0	26.5	45.4	54.6
Reserves to external debt stocks (%)	5.0	32.2	129.8	555.5	608.5	472.9	590.0	455.2
Reserves to imports (months)	1.3	7.9	9.6	12.1	10.2	7.9	8.4	4.5

(US$ million, unless otherwise indicated)

	1995	2000	2005	2006	2007	2008	2009	2010
7. Long-term external debt								
Debt outstanding and disbursed	**28,441**	**30,235**	**20,224**	**3,803**	**3,587**	**3,878**	**4,199**	**4,686**
Public and publicly guaranteed	28,140	30,020	20,224	3,803	3,587	3,878	4,199	4,686
Official creditors	20,492	26,574	18,015	2,962	3,260	3,549	3,991	4,593
Multilateral	4,944	3,302	2,536	2,687	2,904	3,000	3,499	4,304
of which: IBRD	3,221	1,625	722	534	381	211	113	43
IDA	268	644	1,136	1,541	1,929	2,243	2,739	3,662
Bilateral	15,548	23,272	15,479	275	356	549	492	289
Private creditors	7,648	3,446	2,209	841	326	328	208	92
of which: Bonds	2,051	2,051	1,442	0	0	0	0	0
Commercial banks	0	0	37	59	78	101	83	0
Private nonguaranteed	301	215	0	0	0	0	0	0
of which: Bonds	0	0	0	0	0	0	0	0
Disbursements	**433**	**153**	**379**	**777**	**532**	**409**	**519**	**1,051**
Public and publicly guaranteed	433	153	379	777	532	409	519	1,051
Official creditors	433	153	345	502	468	385	519	1,051
Multilateral	433	153	286	377	386	383	519	1,031
of which: IBRD	189	31	0	0	0	0	0	0
IDA	86	55	265	362	335	353	497	1,000
Bilateral	0	0	59	125	82	2	0	20
Private creditors	0	0	34	274	64	24	0	0
of which: Bonds	0	0	0	0	0	0	0	0
Commercial banks	0	0	26	33	18	24	0	0
Private nonguaranteed	0	0	0	0	0	0	0	0
of which: Bonds	0	0	0	0	0	0	0	0
Principal repayments	**918**	**1,091**	**3,862**	**6,441**	**914**	**338**	**339**	**246**
Public and publicly guaranteed	908	1,056	3,862	6,441	914	338	339	246
Official creditors	470	914	3,684	4,801	319	317	284	213
Multilateral	470	404	367	339	306	293	211	164
of which: IBRD	392	273	224	211	176	189	96	71
IDA	1	4	19	19	20	20	21	24
Bilateral	0	510	3,317	4,461	12	24	72	49
Private creditors	438	142	179	1,640	596	21	55	33
of which: Bonds	0	0	0	1,442	0	0	0	0
Commercial banks	0	0	3	1	0	0	18	0
Private nonguaranteed	10	35	0	0	0	0	0	0
of which: Bonds	0	0	0	0	0	0	0	0
Interest payments	**859**	**690**	**4,937**	**259**	**86**	**87**	**84**	**59**
Public and publicly guaranteed	840	673	4,937	259	86	87	84	59
Official creditors	323	516	4,717	91	80	83	71	53
Multilateral	323	190	97	86	74	62	47	41
of which: IBRD	266	103	39	33	25	17	8	2
IDA	2	5	12	14	15	17	17	23
Bilateral	0	326	4,620	5	7	21	24	12
Private creditors	516	157	220	168	6	4	14	6
of which: Bonds	128	128	170	143	0	0	0	0
Commercial banks	0	0	3	0	0	0	6	0
Private nonguaranteed	19	18	0	0	0	0	0	0
of which: Bonds	0	0	0	0	0	0	0	0
8. Debt stock-flow reconciliation								
Total change in external debt stocks	1,000	2,227	-15,707	-14,367	838	2,803	-3,621	169
Net flows on external debt	-559	-696	-3,001	-3,607	672	2,583	-3,762	488
9. Debt restructurings								
Total amount rescheduled	0	20,920	0	1	0	0	0	0
Total amount forgiven	95	0	7,284	10,891	0	0	0	0
Debt buyback	0	0	0	0	0	0	0	0

10. Contractual obligations on outstanding long-term external debt

	2011	2012	2013	2014	2015	2016	2017	2018
Official creditors								
Principal	191	170	166	148	96	109	129	225
Interest	65	68	71	72	74	75	75	74
Private creditors								
Principal	46	46	0	0	0	0	0	0
Interest	4	2	0	0	0	0	0	0

Notes:

Long-term private nonguaranteed debt data has been revised from 2007 based on reports provided by the country.

PAKISTAN

(US$ million, unless otherwise indicated)

	1995	2000	2005	2006	2007	2008	2009	2010
1. Summary external debt data								
External debt stocks	**30,169**	**32,732**	**33,566**	**36,711**	**41,531**	**49,057**	**54,588**	**56,773**
Long-term external debt	25,321	29,684	30,844	33,926	37,922	43,336	45,627	45,746
Public and publicly guaranteed	23,727	27,124	29,880	33,019	36,728	40,152	42,362	43,202
Private nonguaranteed	1,593	2,560	964	907	1,193	3,184	3,265	2,544
Use of IMF credit	1,613	1,529	1,492	1,462	1,381	4,352	7,495	8,736
Short-term external debt	3,235	1,519	1,230	1,322	2,228	1,370	1,466	2,291
interest arrears on long-term	0	0	0	0	0	0	0	0
Memorandum items								
Principal arrears on long-term	0	0	0	0	0	0	0	0
Long-term public sector debt	23,634	26,946	29,866	33,005	36,714	40,137	42,348	43,189
Long-term private sector debt	1,687	2,738	978	921	1,207	3,198	3,278	2,557
Public & publicly guaranteed commitments	2,257	865	4,523	3,415	3,668	4,019	5,372	3,459
External debt flows								
Disbursements	3,288	1,838	2,827	3,667	3,725	6,796	7,728	3,646
Long-term external debt	3,086	1,644	2,827	3,667	3,725	3,596	4,413	2,012
IMF purchases	202	195	0	0	0	3,201	3,315	1,634
Principal repayments	2,013	1,870	1,698	1,439	1,531	1,941	2,472	3,273
Long-term external debt	1,837	1,587	1,461	1,332	1,379	1,761	2,241	3,008
IMF repurchases	176	282	237	107	152	180	231	265
Net flows	2,572	-343	1,114	2,320	3,100	3,997	5,352	1,199
Long-term external debt	1,249	56	1,366	2,335	2,346	1,834	2,173	-996
Short-term external debt	1,297	-311	-15	92	906	-858	96	825
Interest payments	1,203	985	737	867	1,113	1,077	1,023	1,066
Long-term external debt	955	857	668	803	992	1,026	905	869
IMF charges	45	49	13	11	9	7	67	127
Short-term external debt	202	78	56	54	111	43	51	69
2. Other non-debt resource inflows								
Foreign direct investment	723	308	2,201	4,273	5,590	5,438	2,338	2,016
Portfolio equity	10	35	451	1,152	1,276	-270	-37	524
3. Currency composition of public and publicly guaranteed debt (%)								
Euro	..	..	12.1	12.0	11.7	10.1	9.8	8.9
Japanese yen	15.2	16.9	17.5	16.0	15.4	17.8	16.9	18.8
Pound sterling	0.8	0.7	0.4	0.3	0.3	0.2	0.2	0.1
Swiss franc	0.3	0.3	0.2	0.2	0.2	0.2	0.2	0.2
U.S.dollars	31.3	41.6	41.7	44.5	44.3	44.0	46.2	44.6
4. Average terms of new commitments								
Official creditors								
Interest (%)	5.0	6.2	1.8	4.0	3.0	2.2	1.6	2.3
Maturity (years)	18.7	12.8	26.9	21.2	28.9	22.9	23.2	22.0
Grace period (years)	5.5	3.1	8.2	6.1	7.8	5.9	6.8	7.3
Private creditors								
Interest (%)	7.0	8.0	4.7	7.4	6.7	0.0	0.0	0.0
Maturity (years)	4.4	5.3	6.3	17.5	9.0	0.0	0.0	0.0
Grace period (years)	0.9	1.0	4.1	17.5	8.8	0.0	0.0	0.0
5. Major economic aggregates								
Gross national income (GNI)	61,092	73,025	111,867	130,007	145,773	167,234	166,370	181,599
Exports of goods, services & income	10,400	10,237	19,768	21,419	23,312	26,762	22,937	28,554
Worker remit. & comp. of employees	1,712	1,075	4,280	5,121	5,998	7,039	8,717	9,690
Imports of goods, services & income	16,311	14,484	32,453	39,110	42,683	53,552	39,389	43,826
Profit remittances on FDI	300	429	1,871	2,580	2,974	3,203	2,548	2,131
Current account balance	-3,349	-85	-3,606	-6,750	-8,286	-15,655	-3,993	-1,490
International reserves	2,528	2,087	11,109	12,878	15,798	9,024	13,606	17,256
6. Ratios								
External debt stocks to exports (%)	290.1	319.7	169.8	171.4	178.2	183.3	238.0	198.8
External debt stocks to GNI (%)	49.4	44.8	30.0	28.2	28.5	29.3	32.8	31.3
Debt service to exports (%)	30.9	27.9	12.3	10.8	11.3	11.3	15.2	15.2
Short-term to external debt stocks (%)	10.7	4.6	3.7	3.6	5.4	2.8	2.7	4.0
Multilateral to external debt stocks (%)	40.4	41.2	47.5	48.1	48.1	45.1	43.4	43.4
Reserves to external debt stocks (%)	8.4	6.4	33.1	35.1	38.0	18.4	24.9	30.4
Reserves to imports (months)	1.9	1.7	4.1	4.0	4.4	2.0	4.1	4.7

PAKISTAN

(US$ million, unless otherwise indicated)

	1995	2000	2005	2006	2007	2008	2009	2010
7. Long-term external debt								
Debt outstanding and disbursed	**25,321**	**29,684**	**30,844**	**33,926**	**37,922**	**43,336**	**45,627**	**45,746**
Public and publicly guaranteed	23,727	27,124	29,880	33,019	36,728	40,152	42,362	43,202
Official creditors	22,631	25,074	28,698	30,778	33,734	37,066	39,857	41,403
Multilateral	12,179	13,491	15,942	17,665	19,978	22,109	23,667	24,614
of which: IBRD	3,082	3,093	2,238	2,143	2,086	1,946	1,769	1,688
IDA	3,321	3,828	6,865	7,871	9,075	9,053	10,075	10,118
Bilateral	10,452	11,583	12,756	13,113	13,757	14,957	16,190	16,789
Private creditors	1,097	2,051	1,182	2,241	2,994	3,086	2,505	1,799
of which: Bonds	150	623	1,100	1,900	2,650	2,650	2,150	1,550
Commercial banks	371	1,099	30	7	4	125	75	0
Private nonguaranteed	1,593	2,560	964	907	1,193	3,184	3,265	2,544
of which: Bonds	45	45	600	850	850	850	850	250
Disbursements	**3,086**	**1,644**	**2,827**	**3,667**	**3,725**	**3,596**	**4,413**	**2,012**
Public and publicly guaranteed	2,331	1,527	2,227	3,417	3,195	2,684	3,732	1,857
Official creditors	2,199	1,522	1,615	2,334	2,435	2,557	3,731	1,856
Multilateral	1,167	1,043	1,523	2,124	2,195	2,164	2,508	1,378
of which: IBRD	271	159	217	155	175	54	89	61
IDA	255	141	628	854	1,001	187	1,177	371
Bilateral	1,032	479	92	211	240	393	1,224	477
Private creditors	132	4	612	1,082	760	127	1	1
of which: Bonds	0	0	600	800	750	0	0	0
Commercial banks	87	0	0	0	0	125	0	0
Private nonguaranteed	755	117	600	250	530	912	681	155
of which: Bonds	0	0	600	250	0	0	0	0
Principal repayments	**1,837**	**1,587**	**1,461**	**1,332**	**1,379**	**1,761**	**2,241**	**3,008**
Public and publicly guaranteed	1,497	1,143	1,134	1,089	1,107	1,305	1,635	2,132
Official creditors	1,267	1,105	991	1,065	1,101	1,270	1,053	1,425
Multilateral	559	829	771	824	727	1,041	925	939
of which: IBRD	219	227	312	284	284	297	253	188
IDA	35	64	115	165	134	149	188	166
Bilateral	708	276	220	241	374	229	128	486
Private creditors	230	37	143	23	7	35	582	707
of which: Bonds	0	0	108	0	0	0	500	600
Commercial banks	138	30	15	23	3	3	50	75
Private nonguaranteed	340	445	327	243	272	456	606	876
of which: Bonds	0	0	0	0	0	0	0	600
Interest payments	**955**	**857**	**668**	**803**	**992**	**1,026**	**905**	**869**
Public and publicly guaranteed	825	641	591	724	861	879	800	780
Official creditors	759	527	541	611	687	682	631	648
Multilateral	445	383	229	258	310	318	278	215
of which: IBRD	217	182	92	107	114	88	53	18
IDA	24	29	52	56	64	77	75	81
Bilateral	313	144	312	354	377	364	353	433
Private creditors	66	114	50	112	174	197	169	131
of which: Bonds	9	61	47	110	171	184	156	120
Commercial banks	32	38	2	3	0	5	5	4
Private nonguaranteed	130	217	76	79	132	147	105	90
of which: Bonds	2	2	3	52	67	60	50	30
8. Debt stock-flow reconciliation								
Total change in external debt stocks	2,845	-1,109	-2,316	3,144	4,820	7,526	5,530	2,185
Net flows on external debt	2,572	-343	1,114	2,320	3,100	3,997	5,352	1,199
9. Debt restructurings								
Total amount rescheduled	0	918	0	0	0	0	0	0
Total amount forgiven	0	0	0	0	1	5	0	0
Debt buyback	0	0	0	0	0	0	0	0

10. Contractual obligations on outstanding long-term external debt

	2011	2012	2013	2014	2015	2016	2017	2018
Official creditors								
Principal	1,717	2,338	1,798	1,873	1,962	1,990	2,359	2,462
Interest	701	701	688	673	651	634	606	570
Private creditors								
Principal	671	488	692	281	217	645	865	92
Interest	242	213	177	151	138	110	60	29

Notes:

Data on long-term private nonguaranteed debt for 2010 are World Bank staff estimates based on the State Bank of Pakistan data.

PANAMA

(US$ million, unless otherwise indicated)

	1995	2000	2005	2006	2007	2008	2009	2010
1. Summary external debt data								
External debt stocks	**6,098**	**6,567**	**8,653**	**9,479**	**9,328**	**9,573**	**11,267**	**11,412**
Long-term external debt	3,781	6,476	8,629	9,464	9,323	9,573	11,267	11,412
Public and publicly guaranteed	3,781	5,696	6,887	7,770	8,262	8,462	10,131	10,421
Private nonguaranteed	0	780	1,742	1,694	1,061	1,111	1,136	991
Use of IMF credit	111	90	24	15	5	0	0	0
Short-term external debt	2,207	1	0	0	0	0	0	0
interest arrears on long-term	1,608	1	0	0	0	0	0	0
Memorandum items								
Principal arrears on long-term	1,996	1	0	0	0	0	0	0
Long-term public sector debt	3,781	5,696	6,887	7,770	8,262	8,462	10,131	10,421
Long-term private sector debt	0	780	1,742	1,694	1,061	1,111	1,136	991
Public & publicly guaranteed commitments	116	478	1,265	2,699	350	827	1,732	362
External debt flows								
Disbursements	112	724	1,595	3,029	679	704	1,890	446
Long-term external debt	99	724	1,595	3,029	679	704	1,890	446
IMF purchases	13	0	0	0	0	0	0	0
Principal repayments	172	462	1,412	2,226	181	916	190	320
Long-term external debt	133	410	1,403	2,216	171	910	190	320
IMF repurchases	39	52	10	10	10	5	0	0
Net flows	-925	262	182	804	498	-211	1,700	126
Long-term external debt	-34	314	192	814	509	-206	1,700	126
Short-term external debt	-866	0	0	0	0	0	0	0
Interest payments	144	424	619	780	664	690	716	757
Long-term external debt	101	418	618	779	663	690	716	757
IMF charges	7	7	1	1	1	0	0	0
Short-term external debt	36	0	0	0	0	0	0	0
2. Other non-debt resource inflows								
Foreign direct investment	223	624	918	2,557	1,777	2,196	1,773	2,363
Portfolio equity	0	..	..	..	..	..	..	..
3. Currency composition of public and publicly guaranteed debt (%)								
Euro	..	..	0.0	0.0	0.0	0.0	0.0	0.0
Japanese yen	10.4	1.8	1.0	0.8	0.7	0.8	0.9	2.0
Pound sterling	0.4	0.1	0.0	0.0	0.0	0.0	0.0	0.0
Swiss franc	0.1	0.0	0.0	0.0	0.0	0.0	0.0	0.0
U.S.dollars	70.8	91.9	96.2	97.1	97.6	97.9	98.3	97.4
4. Average terms of new commitments								
Official creditors								
Interest (%)	6.9	5.8	4.7	5.7	3.3	4.2	2.1	1.3
Maturity (years)	21.2	22.8	19.9	17.9	21.6	20.3	21.4	19.0
Grace period (years)	4.6	4.6	5.1	4.0	5.8	4.7	3.5	4.3
Private creditors								
Interest (%)	3.3	10.4	7.3	4.0	0.0	1.2	3.8	0.0
Maturity (years)	14.7	19.0	22.2	21.4	0.0	11.1	10.0	0.0
Grace period (years)	3.1	19.0	22.2	21.4	0.0	7.8	9.5	0.0
5. Major economic aggregates								
Gross national income (GNI)	7,542	11,007	14,340	15,879	18,488	21,432	22,620	24,916
Exports of goods, services & income	9,254	9,408	11,661	13,879	16,156	18,004	18,157	18,948
Worker remit. & comp. of employees	112	16	130	157	180	196	175	231
Imports of goods, services & income	9,878	10,258	12,925	14,579	17,816	20,964	18,411	22,092
Profit remittances on FDI	396	562	1,048	1,197	1,521	1,748	1,397	1,815
Current account balance	-471	-673	-1,022	-448	-1,407	-2,722	-44	-2,953
International reserves	781	723	1,211	1,335	1,935	2,424	3,028	2,714
6. Ratios								
External debt stocks to exports (%)	65.9	69.8	74.2	68.3	57.7	53.2	62.1	60.2
External debt stocks to GNI (%)	80.9	59.7	60.3	59.7	50.5	44.7	49.8	45.8
Debt service to exports (%)	3.4	9.4	17.4	21.7	5.2	8.9	5.0	5.7
Short-term to external debt stocks (%)	36.2	0.0	..	..	..	..	..	..
Multilateral to external debt stocks (%)	10.0	15.5	12.8	12.3	13.1	14.0	14.4	15.9
Reserves to external debt stocks (%)	12.8	11.0	14.0	14.1	20.7	25.3	26.9	23.8
Reserves to imports (months)	0.9	0.8	1.1	1.1	1.3	1.4	2.0	1.5

PANAMA

(US$ million, unless otherwise indicated)

	1995	2000	2005	2006	2007	2008	2009	2010
7. Long-term external debt								
Debt outstanding and disbursed	**3,781**	**6,476**	**8,629**	**9,464**	**9,323**	**9,573**	**11,267**	**11,412**
Public and publicly guaranteed	3,781	5,696	6,887	7,770	8,262	8,462	10,131	10,421
Official creditors	1,262	1,285	1,304	1,348	1,407	1,529	1,833	2,127
Multilateral	612	1,020	1,110	1,166	1,225	1,337	1,626	1,814
of which: IBRD	175	283	212	185	216	271	435	420
IDA	0	0	0	0	0	0	0	0
Bilateral	650	265	194	182	182	192	207	314
Private creditors	2,519	4,411	5,583	6,422	6,855	6,933	8,298	8,293
of which: Bonds	3	4,141	5,505	6,360	6,810	6,748	8,071	8,071
Commercial banks	2,475	267	78	62	45	186	227	223
Private nonguaranteed	0	780	1,742	1,694	1,061	1,111	1,136	991
of which: Bonds	0	266	635	581	1,061	1,061	1,061	911
Disbursements	**99**	**724**	**1,595**	**3,029**	**679**	**704**	**1,890**	**446**
Public and publicly guaranteed	99	486	1,325	2,461	199	654	1,865	441
Official creditors	95	97	94	183	199	254	461	441
Multilateral	93	88	91	182	188	241	426	334
of which: IBRD	3	22	9	15	74	99	203	24
IDA	0	0	0	0	0	0	0	0
Bilateral	2	10	3	1	11	13	35	107
Private creditors	5	388	1,231	2,278	0	400	1,404	0
of which: Bonds	0	370	1,230	2,276	0	235	1,323	0
Commercial banks	5	17	1	1	0	165	81	0
Private nonguaranteed	0	238	270	569	480	50	25	5
of which: Bonds	0	0	150	300	480	0	0	0
Principal repayments	**133**	**410**	**1,403**	**2,216**	**171**	**910**	**190**	**320**
Public and publicly guaranteed	133	385	1,151	1,584	171	910	190	170
Official creditors	116	108	139	145	154	160	154	165
Multilateral	84	57	126	133	139	143	134	146
of which: IBRD	43	24	39	41	43	45	39	38
IDA	0	0	0	0	0	0	0	0
Bilateral	32	52	12	12	14	17	20	20
Private creditors	17	277	1,013	1,439	17	750	36	5
of which: Bonds	0	120	995	1,422	0	742	0	0
Commercial banks	4	156	17	18	17	9	36	5
Private nonguaranteed	0	25	251	632	0	0	0	150
of which: Bonds	0	0	0	369	0	0	0	150
Interest payments	**101**	**418**	**618**	**779**	**663**	**690**	**716**	**757**
Public and publicly guaranteed	101	365	531	690	601	626	628	670
Official creditors	59	79	59	62	70	71	72	75
Multilateral	39	68	54	58	66	66	67	71
of which: IBRD	15	21	12	11	13	13	16	17
IDA	0	0	0	0	0	0	0	0
Bilateral	20	10	5	5	5	5	5	4
Private creditors	42	286	471	628	530	555	556	595
of which: Bonds	0	264	467	624	527	550	546	592
Commercial banks	37	22	4	4	3	5	11	3
Private nonguaranteed	0	53	87	88	63	64	88	87
of which: Bonds	0	24	44	46	63	63	83	83
8. Debt stock-flow reconciliation								
Total change in external debt stocks	-800	-262	266	826	-151	245	1,694	145
Net flows on external debt	-925	262	182	804	498	-211	1,700	126
9. Debt restructurings								
Total amount rescheduled	5	0	0	0	0	0	0	0
Total amount forgiven	0	477	0	0	0	7	0	0
Debt buyback	0	120	0	203	0	21	0	0

10. Contractual obligations on outstanding long-term external debt

	2011	2012	2013	2014	2015	2016	2017	2018
Official creditors								
Principal	185	183	190	203	198	204	192	175
Interest	53	50	47	43	39	34	30	26
Private creditors								
Principal	343	1,116	33	245	1,509	336	36	21
Interest	564	502	444	443	475	401	400	399

Notes:

Long-term private nonguaranteed debt data only cover Bonds. Short-term debt data are excluded since BIS data include debt liabilities of offshore centers located in the country. BIS short-term debt data for 2008, 2009, and 2010 are $16.7 billion, and $16.3 billion, and $19.5 billion respectively.

PAPUA NEW GUINEA

(US$ million, unless otherwise indicated)

	1995	2000	2005	2006	2007	2008	2009	2010
1. Summary external debt data								
External debt stocks	**2,506**	**2,292**	**1,880**	**1,826**	**1,430**	**1,418**	**1,573**	**5,822**
Long-term external debt	2,378	2,204	1,648	1,659	1,339	1,409	1,452	5,430
Public and publicly guaranteed	1,668	1,454	1,262	1,208	1,126	1,064	1,037	1,030
Private nonguaranteed	711	750	387	451	213	345	415	4,400
Use of IMF credit	50	39	0	0	0	0	0	0
Short-term external debt	78	49	232	167	91	9	121	392
interest arrears on long-term	0	0	0	0	0	0	0	0
Memorandum items								
Principal arrears on long-term	0	0	0	0	0	0	0	0
Long-term public sector debt	1,667	1,440	1,262	1,208	1,126	1,064	1,037	1,030
Long-term private sector debt	711	764	387	451	213	345	415	4,400
Public & publicly guaranteed commitments	175	319	0	53	37	133	122	278
External debt flows								
Disbursements	240	293	335	267	615	951	516	3,153
Long-term external debt	189	254	335	267	615	951	516	3,153
IMF purchases	51	38	0	0	0	0	0	0
Principal repayments	509	215	244	270	947	933	514	759
Long-term external debt	493	196	183	270	947	933	514	759
IMF repurchases	16	19	61	0	0	0	0	0
Net flows	-291	30	214	-68	-408	-64	114	2,665
Long-term external debt	-304	59	152	-3	-332	18	2	2,394
Short-term external debt	-21	-48	123	-65	-76	-82	112	271
Interest payments	117	90	63	56	60	42	29	53
Long-term external debt	111	85	54	46	55	40	28	50
IMF charges	1	1	1	0	0	0	0	0
Short-term external debt	5	4	9	10	5	2	1	3
2. Other non-debt resource inflows								
Foreign direct investment	455	96	38	13	102	-30	423	30
Portfolio equity	..	..	..	..	..	..	..	..
3. Currency composition of public and publicly guaranteed debt (%)								
Euro	..	..	3.8	4.2	4.6	4.3	4.3	3.8
Japanese yen	21.3	30.1	29.8	29.0	30.0	29.4	27.5	28.5
Pound sterling	0.6	0.8	0.0	0.0	0.0	0.0	0.0	0.0
Swiss franc	0.0	0.0	0.1	0.1	0.1	0.1	0.0	0.0
U.S.dollars	19.4	21.3	33.8	36.9	36.3	38.6	39.4	39.3
4. Average terms of new commitments								
Official creditors								
Interest (%)	5.2	6.5	0.0	4.4	0.8	2.1	1.7	0.8
Maturity (years)	10.6	17.3	0.0	26.1	34.7	28.2	32.1	34.7
Grace period (years)	4.4	5.1	0.0	5.2	10.2	6.7	8.5	8.9
Private creditors								
Interest (%)	0.0	6.2	0.0	0.0	0.0	0.0	0.0	0.0
Maturity (years)	0.0	5.3	0.0	0.0	0.0	0.0	0.0	0.0
Grace period (years)	0.0	2.5	0.0	0.0	0.0	0.0	0.0	0.0
5. Major economic aggregates								
Gross national income (GNI)	4,370	3,303	4,531	4,931	6,261	7,931	7,855	9,262
Exports of goods, services & income	3,014	2,369	3,649	4,597	5,205	6,259	4,626	6,278
Worker remit. & comp. of employees	16	7	7	4	8	15	12	15
Imports of goods, services & income	2,415	2,013	3,368	4,462	5,399	5,713	5,474	7,135
Profit remittances on FDI	409	198	511	815	674	611	537	..
Current account balance	674	351	539	333	56	708	-672	-662
International reserves	267	304	750	1,441	2,106	2,008	2,629	3,122
6. Ratios								
External debt stocks to exports (%)	83.1	96.8	51.5	39.7	27.5	22.6	34.0	92.7
External debt stocks to GNI (%)	57.3	69.4	41.5	37.0	22.8	17.9	20.0	62.9
Debt service to exports (%)	20.8	12.9	8.4	7.1	19.4	15.6	11.7	12.9
Short-term to external debt stocks (%)	3.1	2.2	12.3	9.1	6.4	0.6	7.7	6.7
Multilateral to external debt stocks (%)	37.4	36.1	44.4	44.6	52.4	50.8	46.0	12.2
Reserves to external debt stocks (%)	10.6	13.3	39.9	78.9	147.2	141.7	167.2	53.6
Reserves to imports (months)	1.3	1.8	2.7	3.9	4.7	4.2	5.8	5.3

PAPUA NEW GUINEA

(US$ million, unless otherwise indicated)

	1995	2000	2005	2006	2007	2008	2009	2010
7. Long-term external debt								
Debt outstanding and disbursed	**2,378**	**2,204**	**1,648**	**1,659**	**1,339**	**1,409**	**1,452**	**5,430**
Public and publicly guaranteed	1,668	1,454	1,262	1,208	1,126	1,064	1,037	1,030
Official creditors	1,441	1,394	1,210	1,163	1,085	1,020	1,000	997
Multilateral	938	826	835	815	750	721	724	712
of which: IBRD	299	244	249	246	183	158	149	139
IDA	108	92	78	76	73	71	82	86
Bilateral	503	567	375	348	335	299	276	285
Private creditors	227	60	51	45	42	44	36	33
of which: Bonds	0	0	0	0	0	0	0	0
Commercial banks	157	54	8	4	4	4	3	3
Private nonguaranteed	711	750	387	451	213	345	415	4,400
of which: Bonds	0	0	0	0	0	0	0	0
Disbursements	**189**	**254**	**335**	**267**	**615**	**951**	**516**	**3,153**
Public and publicly guaranteed	135	219	45	51	40	26	33	37
Official creditors	122	206	44	48	39	26	33	37
Multilateral	55	67	41	48	39	26	33	37
of which: IBRD	34	43	20	19	12	4	2	1
IDA	0	0	0	0	0	2	14	8
Bilateral	67	139	3	0	0	0	0	0
Private creditors	13	13	1	4	0	0	0	0
of which: Bonds	0	0	0	0	0	0	0	0
Commercial banks	13	13	0	0	0	0	0	0
Private nonguaranteed	54	35	290	216	575	925	483	3,116
of which: Bonds	0	0	0	0	0	0	0	0
Principal repayments	**493**	**196**	**183**	**270**	**947**	**933**	**514**	**759**
Public and publicly guaranteed	204	115	114	120	172	164	63	68
Official creditors	82	96	93	111	166	157	56	61
Multilateral	47	53	48	83	137	60	36	39
of which: IBRD	27	29	23	24	78	30	11	11
IDA	2	3	4	4	4	4	4	4
Bilateral	35	44	45	28	30	97	20	22
Private creditors	122	19	21	9	6	6	7	7
of which: Bonds	32	0	0	0	0	0	0	0
Commercial banks	63	10	15	4	0	0	0	0
Private nonguaranteed	289	80	69	150	775	769	451	691
of which: Bonds	0	0	0	0	0	0	0	0
Interest payments	**111**	**85**	**54**	**46**	**55**	**40**	**28**	**50**
Public and publicly guaranteed	82	54	38	38	39	32	21	16
Official creditors	63	50	36	37	38	31	20	16
Multilateral	44	31	22	26	28	20	13	9
of which: IBRD	22	15	10	13	15	9	4	1
IDA	1	1	1	1	1	1	1	1
Bilateral	19	18	14	11	10	11	7	7
Private creditors	19	5	2	1	1	1	1	1
of which: Bonds	2	0	0	0	0	0	0	0
Commercial banks	9	3	1	0	0	0	0	0
Private nonguaranteed	29	31	16	8	16	8	7	33
of which: Bonds	0	0	0	0	0	0	0	0
8. Debt stock-flow reconciliation								
Total change in external debt stocks	-287	-352	96	-54	-396	-13	155	4,249
Net flows on external debt	-291	30	214	-68	-408	-64	114	2,665
9. Debt restructurings								
Total amount rescheduled	0	0	0	0	0	0	0	0
Total amount forgiven	0	0	0	0	0	0	0	0
Debt buyback	0	0	0	0	0	0	0	0

10. Contractual obligations on outstanding long-term external debt

	2011	2012	2013	2014	2015	2016	2017	2018
Official creditors								
Principal	114	69	72	72	74	75	77	85
Interest	20	19	18	18	17	16	15	14
Private creditors								
Principal	785	248	123	154	918	540	747	459
Interest	58	57	73	71	66	52	47	30

Notes:

Long-term private nonguaranteed debt data for 2010 reported by country include a huge loan for about US$ 2.6 billion.

PARAGUAY

(US$ million, unless otherwise indicated)

	1995	2000	2005	2006	2007	2008	2009	2010
1. Summary external debt data								
External debt stocks	**2,572**	**3,088**	**3,227**	**3,421**	**3,568**	**4,159**	**3,984**	**4,938**
Long-term external debt	1,788	2,508	2,714	2,710	2,765	3,013	3,232	3,791
Public and publicly guaranteed	1,450	2,058	2,264	2,233	2,194	2,262	2,260	2,369
Private nonguaranteed	338	450	450	477	572	751	972	1,421
Use of IMF credit	0	0	0	0	0	0	0	0
Short-term external debt	784	580	513	711	803	1,146	752	1,147
interest arrears on long-term	7	11	0	0	0	0	0	0
Memorandum items								
Principal arrears on long-term	60	55	8	8	8	7	7	16
Long-term public sector debt	1,450	2,058	2,264	2,233	2,194	2,262	2,260	2,369
Long-term private sector debt	338	450	450	477	572	751	972	1,421
Public & publicly guaranteed commitments	363	125	99	530	43	171	411	279
External debt flows								
Disbursements	224	192	210	244	206	376	489	826
Long-term external debt	224	192	210	244	206	376	489	826
IMF purchases	0	0	0	0	0	0	0	0
Principal repayments	159	204	332	269	258	296	308	320
Long-term external debt	159	204	332	269	258	296	308	320
IMF repurchases	0	0	0	0	0	0	0	0
Net flows	261	-185	-274	174	39	423	-213	901
Long-term external debt	65	-13	-121	-24	-53	80	181	506
Short-term external debt	196	-173	-153	198	92	343	-394	395
Interest payments	135	148	144	152	166	165	134	143
Long-term external debt	93	115	115	121	135	136	122	131
IMF charges	0	0	0	0	0	0	0	0
Short-term external debt	42	33	29	31	30	29	12	12
2. Other non-debt resource inflows								
Foreign direct investment	103	104	54	173	206	279	205	427
Portfolio equity	..	..	..	..	..	..	..	..
3. Currency composition of public and publicly guaranteed debt (%)								
Euro	..	..	2.6	2.6	2.8	2.8	2.6	2.0
Japanese yen	22.7	15.0	13.4	13.7	14.0	18.6	19.3	19.3
Pound sterling	0.3	0.1	0.0	0.0	0.0	0.0	0.0	0.0
Swiss franc	0.1	0.1	0.0	0.0	0.0	0.0	0.0	0.0
U.S.dollars	28.7	60.0	68.4	68.8	68.9	66.1	67.5	70.2
4. Average terms of new commitments								
Official creditors								
Interest (%)	5.5	6.4	4.5	3.9	5.3	3.6	2.8	1.9
Maturity (years)	19.3	21.8	16.4	29.4	23.0	27.5	25.7	20.2
Grace period (years)	5.6	3.0	4.7	8.0	9.9	6.1	6.5	3.6
Private creditors								
Interest (%)	8.0	0.0	0.0	0.0	0.0	0.0	0.0	0.0
Maturity (years)	9.8	0.0	0.0	0.0	0.0	0.0	0.0	0.0
Grace period (years)	2.3	0.0	0.0	0.0	0.0	0.0	0.0	0.0
5. Major economic aggregates								
Gross national income (GNI)	8,176	7,094	7,415	9,184	12,060	16,659	13,954	19,497
Exports of goods, services & income	5,075	3,185	4,213	5,497	6,951	9,338	7,548	10,165
Worker remit. & comp. of employees	287	278	269	463	484	588	609	673
Imports of goods, services & income	5,363	3,524	4,421	5,795	7,140	10,056	8,024	11,283
Profit remittances on FDI	62	84	158	271	365	505	554	650
Current account balance	-92	-163	16	128	184	-304	43	-596
International reserves	1,106	772	1,297	1,702	2,461	2,863	3,862	4,167
6. Ratios								
External debt stocks to exports (%)	50.7	96.9	76.6	62.2	51.3	44.5	52.8	48.6
External debt stocks to GNI (%)	31.5	43.5	43.5	37.3	29.6	25.0	28.5	25.3
Debt service to exports (%)	5.8	11.1	11.3	7.6	6.1	4.9	5.9	4.6
Short-term to external debt stocks (%)	30.5	18.8	15.9	20.8	22.5	27.6	18.9	23.2
Multilateral to external debt stocks (%)	30.2	36.9	39.1	37.6	36.3	31.1	33.9	30.3
Reserves to external debt stocks (%)	43.0	25.0	40.2	49.8	69.0	68.8	96.9	84.4
Reserves to imports (months)	2.5	2.6	3.5	3.5	4.1	3.4	5.8	4.4

(US$ million, unless otherwise indicated)

	1995	2000	2005	2006	2007	2008	2009	2010
7. Long-term external debt								
Debt outstanding and disbursed	**1,788**	**2,508**	**2,714**	**2,710**	**2,765**	**3,013**	**3,232**	**3,791**
Public and publicly guaranteed	1,450	2,058	2,264	2,233	2,194	2,262	2,260	2,369
Official creditors	1,318	1,609	1,843	1,852	1,841	1,939	1,978	2,110
Multilateral	778	1,141	1,260	1,286	1,296	1,294	1,352	1,496
of which: IBRD	154	201	223	234	227	214	281	257
IDA	36	28	21	19	18	16	15	13
Bilateral	540	469	583	566	545	644	625	613
Private creditors	133	449	421	381	352	323	282	260
of which: Bonds	0	0	0	0	0	0	0	0
Commercial banks	56	424	403	374	345	316	275	253
Private nonguaranteed	338	450	450	477	572	751	972	1,421
of which: Bonds	0	0	0	0	0	0	0	0
Disbursements	**224**	**192**	**210**	**244**	**206**	**376**	**489**	**826**
Public and publicly guaranteed	216	192	144	154	111	196	248	303
Official creditors	204	192	141	154	111	196	248	303
Multilateral	129	166	75	111	101	108	181	290
of which: IBRD	26	47	17	32	13	9	101	8
IDA	0	0	0	0	0	0	0	0
Bilateral	75	26	66	44	10	89	67	13
Private creditors	11	0	3	0	0	0	0	0
of which: Bonds	0	0	0	0	0	0	0	0
Commercial banks	11	0	3	0	0	0	0	0
Private nonguaranteed	8	0	66	90	95	180	241	523
of which: Bonds	0	0	0	0	0	0	0	0
Principal repayments	**159**	**204**	**332**	**269**	**258**	**296**	**308**	**320**
Public and publicly guaranteed	157	111	205	209	206	237	262	246
Official creditors	123	105	176	169	177	208	221	224
Multilateral	76	61	108	105	127	140	141	148
of which: IBRD	41	19	25	26	27	30	33	33
IDA	1	1	1	1	1	1	1	1
Bilateral	47	43	68	64	50	68	80	76
Private creditors	34	7	29	40	29	29	41	22
of which: Bonds	0	0	0	0	0	0	0	0
Commercial banks	10	4	18	30	29	29	41	22
Private nonguaranteed	2	93	126	60	52	59	46	75
of which: Bonds	0	0	0	0	0	0	0	0
Interest payments	**93**	**115**	**115**	**121**	**135**	**136**	**122**	**131**
Public and publicly guaranteed	87	99	94	97	104	96	97	65
Official creditors	71	69	77	75	80	78	83	63
Multilateral	41	51	53	53	57	56	48	47
of which: IBRD	15	11	10	12	13	13	7	6
IDA	0	0	0	0	0	0	0	0
Bilateral	30	18	24	22	23	21	35	16
Private creditors	16	30	17	22	24	18	14	2
of which: Bonds	0	0	0	0	0	0	0	0
Commercial banks	2	29	16	21	24	18	14	2
Private nonguaranteed	6	16	21	24	31	40	25	66
of which: Bonds	0	0	0	0	0	0	0	0
8. Debt stock-flow reconciliation								
Total change in external debt stocks	469	-294	-379	194	147	591	-175	954
Net flows on external debt	261	-185	-274	174	39	423	-213	901
9. Debt restructurings								
Total amount rescheduled	0	0	0	0	0	0	0	0
Total amount forgiven	0	0	0	0	0	2	0	0
Debt buyback	0	0	0	0	0	0	0	0

10. Contractual obligations on outstanding long-term external debt

	2011	2012	2013	2014	2015	2016	2017	2018
Official creditors								
Principal	215	207	178	164	185	186	185	182
Interest	57	52	47	44	41	37	33	30
Private creditors								
Principal	405	296	277	174	146	111	97	84
Interest	77	58	42	30	21	15	10	6

PERU

(US$ million, unless otherwise indicated)

	1995	*2000*	*2005*	*2006*	*2007*	*2008*	*2009*	*2010*
1. Summary external debt data								
External debt stocks	**30,842**	**28,632**	**29,352**	**29,133**	**32,073**	**34,559**	**36,393**	**36,271**
Long-term external debt	20,228	24,145	26,083	26,101	26,739	29,138	31,662	30,216
Public and publicly guaranteed	18,940	19,208	22,511	22,161	19,832	19,394	20,800	20,027
Private nonguaranteed	1,288	4,938	3,572	3,940	6,907	9,744	10,862	10,189
Use of IMF credit	955	558	57	20	0	0	0	0
Short-term external debt	9,659	3,928	3,212	3,012	5,334	5,420	4,731	6,055
interest arrears on long-term	4,584	14	4	17	17	22	1	1
Memorandum items								
Principal arrears on long-term	4,150	29	2	33	8	10	1	1
Long-term public sector debt	18,934	17,937	21,613	21,341	19,020	18,689	20,210	19,559
Long-term private sector debt	1,294	6,209	4,470	4,760	7,719	10,449	11,453	10,657
Public & publicly guaranteed commitments	930	1,263	2,191	704	3,018	1,343	4,036	3,832
External debt flows								
Disbursements	880	2,066	3,721	2,002	7,149	4,630	4,772	8,296
Long-term external debt	880	2,066	3,721	2,002	7,149	4,630	4,772	8,296
IMF purchases	0	0	0	0	0	0	0	0
Principal repayments	521	1,139	4,227	1,564	6,765	3,263	2,220	4,059
Long-term external debt	521	997	4,187	1,525	6,745	3,263	2,220	4,059
IMF repurchases	0	141	40	39	20	0	0	0
Net flows	3,148	289	-44	225	2,705	1,449	1,883	5,561
Long-term external debt	359	1,069	-466	477	404	1,367	2,552	4,237
Short-term external debt	2,789	-638	461	-213	2,322	81	-668	1,324
Interest payments	722	1,432	1,838	1,997	2,286	1,996	2,141	2,726
Long-term external debt	485	1,172	1,717	1,849	2,109	1,807	1,976	2,550
IMF charges	52	33	3	2	0	0	0	0
Short-term external debt	184	227	118	146	176	189	166	176
2. Other non-debt resource inflows								
Foreign direct investment	2,557	810	2,579	3,467	5,491	6,924	5,576	7,328
Portfolio equity	171	123	769	-45	70	85	47	87
3. Currency composition of public and publicly guaranteed debt (%)								
Euro	..	..	7.0	7.7	8.2	11.1	7.2	4.4
Japanese yen	14.6	13.8	9.1	8.9	10.2	13.6	12.1	9.9
Pound sterling	1.2	0.4	0.1	0.1	0.0	0.0	0.0	0.0
Swiss franc	1.2	0.5	0.1	0.0	0.0	0.0	0.0	0.0
U.S.dollars	41.9	73.8	80.5	80.3	78.7	72.7	77.8	83.5
4. Average terms of new commitments								
Official creditors								
Interest (%)	6.2	5.8	5.0	5.2	5.5	3.2	1.3	1.7
Maturity (years)	17.4	22.0	16.4	17.2	16.6	18.7	19.5	15.6
Grace period (years)	4.6	5.0	7.0	6.5	5.6	7.1	9.4	6.4
Private creditors								
Interest (%)	0.0	9.0	7.7	0.0	7.5	0.0	7.2	7.4
Maturity (years)	0.0	5.0	22.0	0.0	21.8	0.0	13.0	30.8
Grace period (years)	0.0	0.1	22.0	0.0	20.6	0.0	13.0	30.8
5. Major economic aggregates								
Gross national income (GNI)	51,140	51,878	74,141	84,519	98,879	119,942	122,566	147,315
Exports of goods, services & income	7,197	9,247	20,282	27,540	32,833	36,504	32,040	40,696
Worker remit. & comp. of employees	599	718	1,440	1,837	2,131	2,444	2,409	2,534
Imports of goods, services & income	12,653	11,794	20,906	26,853	33,880	44,765	34,717	46,037
Profit remittances on FDI	834	344	4,030	6,741	7,788	8,346	7,173	9,478
Current account balance	-4,625	-1,546	1,148	2,872	1,460	-5,318	211	-2,315
International reserves	8,653	8,676	14,171	17,442	27,786	31,241	33,225	44,215
6. Ratios								
External debt stocks to exports (%)	428.6	309.6	144.7	105.8	97.7	94.7	113.6	89.1
External debt stocks to GNI (%)	60.3	55.2	39.6	34.5	32.4	28.8	29.7	24.6
Debt service to exports (%)	17.3	27.8	29.9	12.9	27.6	14.4	13.6	16.7
Short-term to external debt stocks (%)	31.3	13.7	10.9	10.3	16.6	15.7	13.0	16.7
Multilateral to external debt stocks (%)	12.0	19.2	26.9	26.8	24.7	23.1	23.0	21.7
Reserves to external debt stocks (%)	28.1	30.3	48.3	59.9	86.6	90.4	91.3	121.9
Reserves to imports (months)	8.2	8.8	8.1	7.8	9.8	8.4	11.5	11.5

PERU

(US$ million, unless otherwise indicated)

	1995	2000	2005	2006	2007	2008	2009	2010
7. Long-term external debt								
Debt outstanding and disbursed	**20,228**	**24,145**	**26,083**	**26,101**	**26,739**	**29,138**	**31,662**	**30,216**
Public and publicly guaranteed	18,940	19,208	22,511	22,161	19,832	19,394	20,800	20,027
Official creditors	15,238	14,377	13,805	13,479	11,293	12,338	11,740	10,573
Multilateral	3,716	5,511	7,885	7,810	7,922	7,988	8,377	7,854
of which: IBRD	1,729	2,590	2,816	2,633	2,649	2,712	2,846	2,965
IDA	0	0	0	0	0	0	0	0
Bilateral	11,522	8,866	5,920	5,669	3,371	4,350	3,362	2,719
Private creditors	3,702	4,830	8,706	8,682	8,539	7,056	9,061	9,454
of which: Bonds	0	3,727	8,390	8,390	8,270	6,879	8,911	9,311
Commercial banks	3,040	110	86	77	68	170	145	138
Private nonguaranteed	1,288	4,938	3,572	3,940	6,907	9,744	10,862	10,189
of which: Bonds	60	150	1,230	2,522	3,749	3,599	4,428	7,298
Disbursements	**880**	**2,066**	**3,721**	**2,002**	**7,149**	**4,630**	**4,772**	**8,296**
Public and publicly guaranteed	725	1,489	2,635	638	3,299	1,165	3,232	3,862
Official creditors	720	1,454	985	638	1,180	1,165	1,232	1,601
Multilateral	631	811	799	509	1,038	991	1,040	1,344
of which: IBRD	202	266	192	36	256	294	379	377
IDA	0	0	0	0	0	0	0	0
Bilateral	89	643	187	129	143	174	192	257
Private creditors	5	35	1,650	0	2,119	0	2,000	2,261
of which: Bonds	0	0	1,650	0	2,119	0	2,000	2,261
Commercial banks	0	34	0	0	0	0	0	0
Private nonguaranteed	155	577	1,086	1,364	3,849	3,466	1,539	4,434
of which: Bonds	0	0	1,080	1,292	1,227	0	878	2,871
Principal repayments	**521**	**997**	**4,187**	**1,525**	**6,745**	**3,263**	**2,220**	**4,059**
Public and publicly guaranteed	481	980	3,031	1,144	5,863	2,616	1,831	3,489
Official creditors	405	834	2,917	1,030	3,496	1,254	1,806	2,970
Multilateral	201	497	556	603	950	958	653	1,871
of which: IBRD	86	93	210	219	241	230	245	258
IDA	0	0	0	0	0	0	0	0
Bilateral	203	338	2,361	427	2,547	296	1,154	1,099
Private creditors	77	146	114	113	2,366	1,363	25	518
of which: Bonds	0	0	90	90	2,343	1,338	0	497
Commercial banks	28	130	11	9	9	23	23	21
Private nonguaranteed	40	17	1,156	381	882	647	389	570
of which: Bonds	0	0	0	0	0	150	50	0
Interest payments	**485**	**1,172**	**1,717**	**1,849**	**2,109**	**1,807**	**1,976**	**2,550**
Public and publicly guaranteed	414	1,103	1,403	1,389	1,512	1,184	1,084	1,096
Official creditors	395	915	807	724	818	571	451	346
Multilateral	245	382	354	434	483	408	314	251
of which: IBRD	118	189	105	137	150	136	107	62
IDA	0	0	0	0	0	0	0	0
Bilateral	150	533	453	290	335	163	137	95
Private creditors	19	188	596	665	694	613	632	750
of which: Bonds	0	179	568	637	669	603	623	742
Commercial banks	10	5	7	8	7	10	9	8
Private nonguaranteed	71	69	314	460	598	623	892	1,454
of which: Bonds	6	11	56	136	250	213	223	284
8. Debt stock-flow reconciliation								
Total change in external debt stocks	4,323	-515	-2,211	-219	2,940	2,486	1,835	-122
Net flows on external debt	3,148	289	-44	225	2,705	1,449	1,883	5,561
9. Debt restructurings								
Total amount rescheduled	919	1	21	0	0	0	30	0
Total amount forgiven	0	0	66	27	61	56	32	1,395
Debt buyback	0	0	0	0	2,343	838	0	497

10. Contractual obligations on outstanding long-term external debt

	2011	2012	2013	2014	2015	2016	2017	2018
Official creditors								
Principal	819	1,066	1,028	973	931	974	832	657
Interest	233	212	186	161	140	119	101	87
Private creditors								
Principal	563	1,075	726	797	746	1,155	1,130	1,240
Interest	1,240	1,202	1,166	1,129	1,070	985	939	885

Notes:

Data on long-term private nonguaranteed debt and short-term debt for 2010 are World Bank staff estimates based on reports provided by the country. Data for 2007 include Bond prepayment and prepayment to Paris Club creditors. Short-term debt data from 2007 are based on reports provided by the country.

PHILIPPINES

(US$ million, unless otherwise indicated)

	1995	*2000*	*2005*	*2006*	*2007*	*2008*	*2009*	*2010*
1. Summary external debt data								
External debt stocks	**39,379**	**58,304**	**61,658**	**60,412**	**66,040**	**64,995**	**63,116**	**72,337**
Long-term external debt	33,372	50,777	54,874	55,403	58,956	57,994	59,114	66,042
Public and publicly guaranteed	28,525	33,744	35,364	36,881	38,089	39,197	41,944	44,641
Private nonguaranteed	4,847	17,033	19,510	18,522	20,867	18,797	17,171	21,402
Use of IMF credit	728	2,032	389	0	0	0	0	0
Short-term external debt	5,279	5,495	6,395	5,009	7,084	7,001	4,002	6,295
interest arrears on long-term	0	0	0	0	0	0	0	0
Memorandum items								
Principal arrears on long-term	0	1	1	2	0	1	0	0
Long-term public sector debt	28,369	33,674	35,295	36,815	38,024	39,121	41,872	44,565
Long-term private sector debt	5,003	17,103	19,579	18,588	20,932	18,873	17,242	21,477
Public & publicly guaranteed commitments	2,594	5,353	3,776	4,124	2,521	3,442	7,787	8,934
External debt flows								
Disbursements	2,840	6,060	6,525	8,902	8,876	5,163	9,853	15,534
Long-term external debt	2,840	5,747	6,525	8,902	8,876	5,163	9,853	15,534
IMF purchases	0	313	0	0	0	0	0	0
Principal repayments	3,099	4,055	6,403	9,800	6,340	8,219	6,379	9,527
Long-term external debt	2,737	4,047	6,085	9,399	6,340	8,219	6,379	9,527
IMF repurchases	363	8	317	400	0	0	0	0
Net flows	-696	2,551	1,472	-2,284	4,611	-3,140	476	8,300
Long-term external debt	104	1,700	440	-498	2,536	-3,057	3,475	6,007
Short-term external debt	-437	546	1,349	-1,386	2,075	-83	-2,999	2,293
Interest payments	2,264	3,004	3,559	3,899	3,796	3,980	3,501	3,347
Long-term external debt	1,859	2,469	3,254	3,521	3,450	3,697	3,431	3,324
IMF charges	55	94	20	15	2	0	0	0
Short-term external debt	351	442	286	363	345	284	70	23
2. Other non-debt resource inflows								
Foreign direct investment	1,478	2,240	1,854	2,921	2,916	1,544	1,963	1,713
Portfolio equity	0	-202	1,465	2,525	3,178	-1,289	-1,096	481
3. Currency composition of public and publicly guaranteed debt (%)								
Euro	..	..	5.5	5.7	5.9	5.1	5.1	3.6
Japanese yen	39.2	38.2	34.7	32.4	33.2	38.4	33.7	36.0
Pound sterling	0.2	0.1	0.1	0.1	0.0	0.0	0.0	0.0
Swiss franc	0.3	0.1	0.2	0.2	0.2	0.1	0.1	0.1
U.S.dollars	27.3	42.2	49.5	53.0	52.9	49.8	55.8	56.2
4. Average terms of new commitments								
Official creditors								
Interest (%)	4.3	3.3	3.1	5.3	4.4	2.4	1.2	1.0
Maturity (years)	26.7	28.1	19.8	17.2	21.3	22.6	20.1	24.4
Grace period (years)	7.8	7.3	5.4	5.1	6.5	6.5	6.4	7.7
Private creditors								
Interest (%)	7.1	8.3	7.6	7.9	6.4	4.2	7.1	4.5
Maturity (years)	11.0	11.4	10.8	18.7	24.6	15.9	13.8	13.9
Grace period (years)	10.2	10.8	10.2	18.6	24.5	10.8	13.4	13.3
5. Major economic aggregates								
Gross national income (GNI)	76,450	80,996	102,768	120,950	148,461	173,708	168,141	199,897
Exports of goods, services & income	32,862	44,060	48,725	57,358	64,629	63,943	54,336	70,020
Worker remit. & comp. of employees	5,360	6,961	13,566	15,251	16,302	18,642	19,765	21,423
Imports of goods, services & income	35,722	51,928	58,136	65,214	71,670	75,563	61,257	78,150
Profit remittances on FDI	515	230	1,391	2,015	2,133	1,675	2,150	2,234
Current account balance	-1,980	-2,225	1,980	5,341	7,112	3,627	9,358	8,465
International reserves	7,781	15,074	18,474	22,963	33,740	37,498	44,206	62,326
6. Ratios								
External debt stocks to exports (%)	119.8	132.3	126.5	105.3	102.2	101.6	116.2	103.3
External debt stocks to GNI (%)	51.5	72.0	60.0	49.9	44.5	37.4	37.5	36.2
Debt service to exports (%)	16.3	16.0	20.4	23.9	15.7	19.1	18.2	18.4
Short-term to external debt stocks (%)	13.4	9.4	10.4	8.3	10.7	10.8	6.3	8.7
Multilateral to external debt stocks (%)	21.6	12.4	10.7	11.4	10.9	11.4	13.4	11.6
Reserves to external debt stocks (%)	19.8	25.9	30.0	38.0	51.1	57.7	70.0	86.2
Reserves to imports (months)	2.6	3.5	3.8	4.2	5.6	6.0	8.7	9.6

PHILIPPINES

(US$ million, unless otherwise indicated)

	1995	2000	2005	2006	2007	2008	2009	2010
7. Long-term external debt								
Debt outstanding and disbursed	**33,372**	**50,777**	**54,874**	**55,403**	**58,956**	**57,994**	**59,114**	**66,042**
Public and publicly guaranteed	28,525	33,744	35,364	36,881	38,089	39,197	41,944	44,641
Official creditors	22,626	19,890	18,580	18,623	19,586	21,601	22,067	23,198
Multilateral	8,490	7,207	6,620	6,874	7,219	7,414	8,449	8,372
of which: IBRD	5,002	3,627	2,885	2,690	2,726	2,533	2,488	2,567
IDA	183	207	197	196	195	187	181	171
Bilateral	14,137	12,683	11,960	11,749	12,367	14,186	13,618	14,826
Private creditors	5,899	13,855	16,784	18,258	18,503	17,597	19,877	21,443
of which: Bonds	4,666	10,466	14,290	16,386	16,904	16,144	18,627	20,221
Commercial banks	416	2,482	1,413	813	636	662	894	918
Private nonguaranteed	4,847	17,033	19,510	18,522	20,867	18,797	17,171	21,402
of which: Bonds	1,925	2,856	2,975	2,476	1,993	1,314	956	1,651
Disbursements	**2,840**	**5,747**	**6,525**	**8,902**	**8,876**	**5,163**	**9,853**	**15,534**
Public and publicly guaranteed	1,816	5,228	3,874	7,878	2,767	2,119	8,143	8,152
Official creditors	1,413	1,528	1,144	1,905	1,655	1,442	2,360	1,346
Multilateral	621	386	381	974	808	860	1,703	491
of which: IBRD	393	152	129	132	372	192	361	438
IDA	10	10	0	0	0	0	0	0
Bilateral	792	1,142	763	931	847	582	657	855
Private creditors	403	3,701	2,730	5,973	1,112	677	5,783	6,806
of which: Bonds	278	2,630	2,384	5,756	1,048	576	5,510	6,680
Commercial banks	102	997	221	165	36	100	272	122
Private nonguaranteed	1,024	519	2,651	1,024	6,109	3,044	1,710	7,382
of which: Bonds	864	5	250	0	0	0	0	1,012
Principal repayments	**2,737**	**4,047**	**6,085**	**9,399**	**6,340**	**8,219**	**6,379**	**9,527**
Public and publicly guaranteed	2,587	2,515	3,353	5,742	2,547	3,592	3,841	6,816
Official creditors	2,204	1,572	1,788	1,921	1,667	2,322	1,722	1,818
Multilateral	651	562	644	790	625	972	651	671
of which: IBRD	413	349	376	383	403	471	394	379
IDA	2	3	7	7	7	7	7	7
Bilateral	1,553	1,009	1,143	1,131	1,041	1,349	1,071	1,147
Private creditors	383	943	1,566	3,820	881	1,270	2,120	4,998
of which: Bonds	32	395	1,209	2,911	462	844	1,644	4,807
Commercial banks	76	474	265	831	252	94	53	108
Private nonguaranteed	150	1,533	2,732	3,658	3,792	4,627	2,537	2,711
of which: Bonds	0	445	333	604	558	572	339	174
Interest payments	**1,859**	**2,469**	**3,254**	**3,521**	**3,450**	**3,697**	**3,431**	**3,324**
Public and publicly guaranteed	1,707	1,882	2,409	2,736	2,527	2,865	2,840	2,977
Official creditors	1,320	841	584	583	614	612	542	498
Multilateral	604	414	258	280	333	310	248	196
of which: IBRD	376	223	124	141	160	143	112	81
IDA	1	2	2	1	1	1	1	1
Bilateral	716	427	326	303	280	301	294	301
Private creditors	387	1,041	1,825	2,153	1,913	2,253	2,298	2,479
of which: Bonds	287	880	1,725	2,033	1,841	2,198	2,257	2,441
Commercial banks	34	130	70	92	34	27	26	26
Private nonguaranteed	152	586	845	785	923	832	590	347
of which: Bonds	82	479	283	255	140	103	88	25
8. Debt stock-flow reconciliation								
Total change in external debt stocks	-878	-17	690	-1,246	5,628	-1,045	-1,879	9,221
Net flows on external debt	-696	2,551	1,472	-2,284	4,611	-3,140	476	8,300
9. Debt restructurings								
Total amount rescheduled	0	0	0	0	0	0	0	0
Total amount forgiven	0	0	0	0	0	0	0	0
Debt buyback	0	0	0	0	0	0	0	0

10. Contractual obligations on outstanding long-term external debt

	2011	2012	2013	2014	2015	2016	2017	2018
Official creditors								
Principal	2,092	2,009	2,177	1,961	1,653	1,607	1,556	1,524
Interest	464	423	385	348	317	287	258	229
Private creditors								
Principal	3,745	2,405	2,760	3,024	2,834	4,464	3,353	2,230
Interest	1,861	1,762	1,711	1,627	1,533	1,425	1,217	1,112

Notes:

Long-term private nonguaranteed debt includes the following monitored aggregate private-sector debt: unregistered debt, intercompany debt and capital leases.

Short-term debt is based on reports provided by the country.

ROMANIA

(US$ million, unless otherwise indicated)

	1995	2000	2005	2006	2007	2008	2009	2010
1. Summary external debt data								
External debt stocks	**6,832**	**11,160**	**38,861**	**53,935**	**84,162**	**102,487**	**118,008**	**121,505**
Long-term external debt	4,491	9,945	31,187	37,265	54,836	73,827	86,253	81,383
Public and publicly guaranteed	3,957	6,583	13,330	14,184	15,200	14,987	17,956	20,557
Private nonguaranteed	534	3,362	17,858	23,081	39,636	58,839	68,297	60,826
Use of IMF credit	1,038	453	261	104	0	0	9,544	15,092
Short-term external debt	1,303	763	7,413	16,567	29,326	28,660	22,210	25,029
interest arrears on long-term	0	12	13	6	6	2	1	1
Memorandum items								
Principal arrears on long-term	0	16	37	260	256	237	1	1
Long-term public sector debt	3,899	6,440	12,962	13,820	14,833	14,742	17,714	19,887
Long-term private sector debt	592	3,505	18,225	23,445	40,003	59,084	68,539	61,496
Public & publicly guaranteed commitments	1,641	2,864	2,897	2,594	985	3,335	8,472	1,838
External debt flows								
Disbursements	1,513	3,258	12,918	11,226	20,884	32,513	32,564	23,080
Long-term external debt	1,455	3,144	12,918	11,226	20,884	32,513	23,173	17,416
IMF purchases	57	114	0	0	0	0	9,391	5,664
Principal repayments	675	1,801	5,331	6,472	8,325	14,427	13,117	15,744
Long-term external debt	302	1,705	5,179	6,305	8,219	14,427	13,117	15,744
IMF repurchases	373	96	152	167	105	0	0	0
Net flows	1,174	1,843	10,619	13,915	25,319	17,424	12,998	10,155
Long-term external debt	1,153	1,439	7,739	4,922	12,665	18,086	10,056	1,672
Short-term external debt	337	386	3,032	9,161	12,760	-662	-6,449	2,819
Interest payments	321	698	1,587	2,176	3,243	3,696	3,178	2,801
Long-term external debt	206	632	1,248	1,404	1,956	2,904	2,737	2,158
IMF charges	69	24	13	10	3	0	77	301
Short-term external debt	47	42	326	762	1,284	792	364	342
2. Other non-debt resource inflows								
Foreign direct investment	419	1,037	6,482	11,393	9,925	13,883	4,846	3,453
Portfolio equity	0	58	229	301	746	23	7	4
3. Currency composition of public and publicly guaranteed debt (%)								
Euro	..	..	58.9	64.0	69.3	71.9	78.8	82.5
Japanese yen	2.7	5.3	3.2	3.5	3.4	4.5	3.6	3.9
Pound sterling	0.0	0.0	1.3	1.1	0.7	0.3	0.1	0.0
Swiss franc	1.8	0.9	0.7	0.6	0.5	0.4	0.2	0.1
U.S.dollars	34.4	42.5	26.9	22.8	18.9	17.3	13.3	10.5
4. Average terms of new commitments								
Official creditors								
Interest (%)	6.0	5.9	2.1	3.6	4.6	4.0	2.9	1.8
Maturity (years)	13.3	17.1	23.0	19.2	20.0	14.4	11.6	24.9
Grace period (years)	4.3	4.2	6.4	5.4	5.9	12.7	5.6	7.0
Private creditors								
Interest (%)	6.9	9.1	3.8	4.1	5.2	6.5	6.3	5.0
Maturity (years)	7.2	5.8	10.0	11.9	11.0	10.8	10.1	5.1
Grace period (years)	2.7	2.5	7.8	3.8	3.2	9.3	1.4	5.0
5. Major economic aggregates								
Gross national income (GNI)	35,236	36,768	98,008	119,825	169,088	199,261	164,073	159,027
Exports of goods, services & income	9,485	12,438	34,346	41,545	53,315	65,946	52,162	59,372
Worker remit. & comp. of employees	9	96	4,733	6,718	8,542	9,381	4,952	3,883
Imports of goods, services & income	11,628	14,653	47,298	60,454	83,013	98,549	64,825	70,374
Profit remittances on FDI	28	72	2,926	4,164	5,988	4,362	1,212	747
Current account balance	-1,774	-1,355	-8,504	-12,785	-23,080	-23,719	-6,955	-6,480
International reserves	2,624	3,396	21,601	30,206	39,974	39,768	44,383	48,048
6. Ratios								
External debt stocks to exports (%)	72.0	89.7	113.1	129.8	157.9	155.4	226.2	204.7
External debt stocks to GNI (%)	19.4	30.4	39.7	45.0	49.8	51.4	71.9	76.4
Debt service to exports (%)	10.5	20.1	20.1	20.8	21.7	27.5	31.2	31.2
Short-term to external debt stocks (%)	19.1	6.8	19.1	30.7	34.8	28.0	18.8	20.6
Multilateral to external debt stocks (%)	24.7	30.1	14.4	11.3	8.0	7.1	9.0	11.0
Reserves to external debt stocks (%)	38.4	30.4	55.6	56.0	47.5	38.8	37.6	39.5
Reserves to imports (months)	2.7	2.8	5.5	6.0	5.8	4.8	8.2	8.2

ROMANIA

(US$ million, unless otherwise indicated)

	1995	2000	2005	2006	2007	2008	2009	2010
7. Long-term external debt								
Debt outstanding and disbursed	**4,491**	**9,945**	**31,187**	**37,265**	**54,836**	**73,827**	**86,253**	**81,383**
Public and publicly guaranteed	3,957	6,583	13,330	14,184	15,200	14,987	17,956	20,557
Official creditors	2,998	4,149	6,152	6,674	7,301	8,006	11,271	14,233
Multilateral	1,685	3,364	5,602	6,092	6,709	7,295	10,579	13,373
of which: IBRD	844	1,898	2,448	2,481	2,604	2,572	2,995	2,830
IDA	0	0	0	0	0	0	0	0
Bilateral	1,312	785	550	583	592	710	692	860
Private creditors	959	2,434	7,177	7,510	7,899	6,982	6,686	6,324
of which: Bonds	0	736	2,123	2,371	2,650	2,714	2,809	1,670
Commercial banks	250	1,157	4,874	5,000	5,113	4,178	3,816	4,595
Private nonguaranteed	534	3,362	17,858	23,081	39,636	58,839	68,297	60,826
of which: Bonds	0	0	0	0	0	0	0	0
Disbursements	**1,455**	**3,144**	**12,918**	**11,226**	**20,884**	**32,513**	**23,173**	**17,416**
Public and publicly guaranteed	1,185	1,937	2,637	1,315	1,271	2,799	3,860	5,609
Official creditors	873	1,083	1,016	678	718	1,515	3,720	4,123
Multilateral	361	932	891	554	658	1,437	3,671	4,001
of which: IBRD	128	384	282	140	232	239	703	187
IDA	0	0	0	0	0	0	0	0
Bilateral	511	151	125	124	60	77	48	122
Private creditors	312	854	1,621	637	554	1,284	140	1,486
of which: Bonds	0	139	623	0	0	1,104	0	0
Commercial banks	165	674	958	620	527	175	140	1,468
Private nonguaranteed	271	1,207	10,281	9,911	19,613	29,715	19,313	11,807
of which: Bonds	0	0	0	0	0	0	0	0
Principal repayments	**302**	**1,705**	**5,179**	**6,305**	**8,219**	**14,427**	**13,117**	**15,744**
Public and publicly guaranteed	217	984	1,697	1,436	1,469	2,490	1,376	2,112
Official creditors	132	493	590	556	585	685	671	664
Multilateral	14	326	376	450	508	626	609	627
of which: IBRD	0	91	205	195	211	288	261	262
IDA	0	0	0	0	0	0	0	0
Bilateral	118	168	213	106	77	60	63	37
Private creditors	85	491	1,107	880	884	1,805	704	1,448
of which: Bonds	0	0	374	0	0	883	0	929
Commercial banks	13	328	646	813	844	875	635	503
Private nonguaranteed	86	721	3,482	4,868	6,750	11,937	11,741	13,632
of which: Bonds	0	75	0	0	0	0	0	0
Interest payments	**206**	**632**	**1,248**	**1,404**	**1,956**	**2,904**	**2,737**	**2,158**
Public and publicly guaranteed	179	439	677	707	803	876	705	596
Official creditors	124	269	229	272	316	345	322	293
Multilateral	70	207	206	252	299	328	305	276
of which: IBRD	53	104	88	111	132	130	95	51
IDA	0	0	0	0	0	0	0	0
Bilateral	54	62	23	20	17	17	17	17
Private creditors	56	171	443	435	487	531	383	303
of which: Bonds	0	45	184	131	171	199	156	145
Commercial banks	8	76	248	295	312	327	219	155
Private nonguaranteed	27	193	576	697	1,153	2,028	2,032	1,562
of which: Bonds	0	7	0	0	0	0	0	0
8. Debt stock-flow reconciliation								
Total change in external debt stocks	1,230	2,154	9,287	15,075	30,227	18,325	15,521	3,497
Net flows on external debt	1,174	1,843	10,619	13,915	25,319	17,424	12,998	10,155
9. Debt restructurings								
Total amount rescheduled	0	0	0	0	0	0	0	0
Total amount forgiven	0	0	19	0	0	0	5	0
Debt buyback	0	0	0	0	0	0	0	0

10. Contractual obligations on outstanding long-term external debt

	2011	2012	2013	2014	2015	2016	2017	2018
Official creditors								
Principal	781	891	972	1,583	2,510	2,005	2,019	1,832
Interest	408	441	453	449	401	346	291	237
Private creditors								
Principal	6,747	7,727	6,772	6,691	8,347	6,222	6,116	7,063
Interest	1,223	1,077	926	817	712	522	429	338

Notes:

Short-term debt is based on reports provided by the country.

RUSSIAN FEDERATION

(US$ million, unless otherwise indicated)

	1995	2000	2005	2006	2007	2008	2009	2010
1. Summary external debt data								
External debt stocks	**121,401**	**159,993**	**239,911**	**250,743**	**361,338**	**402,726**	**373,419**	**384,740**
Long-term external debt	101,582	132,751	212,780	210,142	289,337	347,925	341,116	345,983
Public and publicly guaranteed	101,582	110,989	86,877	107,442	148,737	141,725	148,116	162,924
Private nonguaranteed	0	21,762	125,903	102,700	140,600	206,200	193,000	183,059
Use of IMF credit	9,617	11,613	0	0	0	0	0	0
Short-term external debt	10,201	15,630	27,131	40,601	72,001	54,801	32,303	38,756
interest arrears on long-term	5,851	4,530	3,151	747	606	655	427	56
Memorandum items								
Principal arrears on long-term	22,417	7,368	2,064	506	39	115	0	0
Long-term public sector debt	101,582	110,989	86,877	107,442	148,737	141,725	148,116	162,924
Long-term private sector debt	0	21,762	125,903	102,700	140,600	206,200	193,000	183,059
Public & publicly guaranteed commitments	3,154	76	11,545	13,472	45,956	23,462	10,123	21,117
External debt flows								
Disbursements	8,536	1,387	55,068	49,795	96,278	108,173	42,090	51,406
Long-term external debt	3,083	1,387	55,068	49,795	96,278	108,173	42,090	51,406
IMF purchases	5,453	0	0	0	0	0	0	0
Principal repayments	3,273	6,221	32,475	37,396	24,111	44,579	38,944	44,197
Long-term external debt	3,273	3,333	29,086	37,396	24,111	44,579	38,944	44,197
IMF repurchases	0	2,888	3,389	0	0	0	0	0
Net flows	4,913	-2,835	23,227	28,273	103,708	46,345	-19,124	14,034
Long-term external debt	-190	-1,947	25,982	12,399	72,167	63,594	3,146	7,210
Short-term external debt	-350	2,000	634	15,874	31,541	-17,249	-22,270	6,824
Interest payments	2,885	5,604	9,446	12,890	16,135	22,570	18,144	17,652
Long-term external debt	2,591	4,284	8,569	11,599	13,771	20,715	17,605	17,229
IMF charges	294	691	27	0	0	0	0	0
Short-term external debt	0	630	850	1,291	2,364	1,855	539	423
2. Other non-debt resource inflows								
Foreign direct investment	2,065	2,714	12,886	29,701	55,073	75,002	36,500	42,868
Portfolio equity	47	150	-100	6,480	18,675	-15,005	3,369	-4,808
3. Currency composition of public and publicly guaranteed debt (%)								
Euro	..	..	10.2	3.8	2.9	3.9	4.1	3.5
Japanese yen	2.0	0.8	1.2	0.8	0.5	0.5	0.5	0.4
Pound sterling	0.8	0.1	0.0	0.0	0.0	0.0	0.0	0.0
Swiss franc	2.8	0.0	0.0	0.0	0.0	0.0	0.0	0.3
U.S.dollars	52.1	71.6	83.4	91.1	93.9	93.1	93.5	94.5
4. Average terms of new commitments								
Official creditors								
Interest (%)	7.0	7.3	4.4	0.0	3.5	0.0	0.6	0.0
Maturity (years)	16.7	16.8	17.3	6.3	11.1	0.0	13.3	0.0
Grace period (years)	5.6	5.3	4.8	3.3	3.3	0.0	3.8	0.0
Private creditors								
Interest (%)	7.0	7.1	5.2	6.1	5.8	5.4	5.5	4.2
Maturity (years)	14.4	9.1	4.0	4.7	6.5	5.7	5.6	6.4
Grace period (years)	2.5	2.1	1.6	3.2	4.3	3.9	5.3	5.7
5. Major economic aggregates								
Gross national income (GNI)	392,156	252,972	744,977	960,335	1,268,989	1,611,773	1,181,785	1,431,459
Exports of goods, services & income	97,265	119,350	286,244	364,409	441,054	584,560	378,166	482,121
Worker remit. & comp. of employees	2,502	1,275	3,012	3,344	4,713	6,033	5,359	5,264
Imports of goods, services & income	90,459	72,580	200,604	268,185	359,779	478,265	326,699	408,336
Profit remittances on FDI	197	887	19,483	34,601	43,195	62,290	37,472	48,189
Current account balance	6,963	46,839	84,602	94,686	77,768	103,530	48,605	70,599
International reserves	18,024	27,656	182,272	303,773	478,822	426,279	439,342	479,222
6. Ratios								
External debt stocks to exports (%)	124.8	134.1	83.8	68.8	81.9	68.9	98.7	79.8
External debt stocks to GNI (%)	31.0	63.2	32.2	26.1	28.5	25.0	31.6	26.9
Debt service to exports (%)	6.3	9.9	14.6	13.8	9.1	11.5	15.1	12.8
Short-term to external debt stocks (%)	8.4	9.8	11.3	16.2	19.9	13.6	8.7	10.1
Multilateral to external debt stocks (%)	1.6	4.4	2.3	2.2	1.4	1.1	1.0	0.8
Reserves to external debt stocks (%)	14.8	17.3	76.0	121.1	132.5	105.8	117.7	124.6
Reserves to imports (months)	2.4	4.6	10.9	13.6	16.0	10.7	16.1	14.1

RUSSIAN FEDERATION

(US$ million, unless otherwise indicated)

	1995	2000	2005	2006	2007	2008	2009	2010
7. Long-term external debt								
Debt outstanding and disbursed	**101,582**	**132,751**	**212,780**	**210,142**	**289,337**	**347,925**	**341,116**	**345,983**
Public and publicly guaranteed	101,582	110,989	86,877	107,442	148,737	141,725	148,116	162,924
Official creditors	57,449	70,851	34,723	11,220	9,677	8,396	7,333	6,389
Multilateral	1,985	7,040	5,627	5,451	5,099	4,477	3,724	3,042
of which: IBRD	1,524	6,844	5,091	4,759	4,292	3,851	3,211	2,618
IDA	0	0	0	0	0	0	0	0
Bilateral	55,464	63,811	29,096	5,769	4,579	3,919	3,609	3,347
Private creditors	44,133	40,138	52,154	96,223	139,059	133,329	140,783	156,535
of which: Bonds	1,115	36,368	40,244	44,146	60,619	67,238	70,117	82,643
Commercial banks	16,674	440	10,050	50,419	77,637	65,562	70,323	73,742
Private nonguaranteed	0	21,762	125,903	102,700	140,600	206,200	193,000	183,059
of which: Bonds	0	1,412	33,673	48,741	70,208	78,078	73,331	73,329
Disbursements	**3,083**	**1,387**	**55,068**	**49,795**	**96,278**	**108,173**	**42,090**	**51,406**
Public and publicly guaranteed	3,083	1,007	11,606	24,014	46,257	20,159	32,106	33,633
Official creditors	1,092	746	441	569	520	361	108	139
Multilateral	855	574	409	528	420	260	108	139
of which: IBRD	824	540	251	324	214	221	95	135
IDA	0	0	0	0	0	0	0	0
Bilateral	237	172	32	42	100	101	0	0
Private creditors	1,990	261	11,165	23,444	45,736	19,798	31,998	33,494
of which: Bonds	0	0	1,000	5,618	19,888	12,187	8,723	16,165
Commercial banks	20	0	10,050	17,826	25,848	7,611	23,275	17,328
Private nonguaranteed	0	380	43,462	25,781	50,021	88,014	9,984	17,774
of which: Bonds	0	75	14,620	16,192	26,395	14,333	2,286	11,976
Principal repayments	**3,273**	**3,333**	**29,086**	**37,396**	**24,111**	**44,579**	**38,944**	**44,197**
Public and publicly guaranteed	3,273	2,031	23,116	31,713	10,879	23,114	15,841	19,153
Official creditors	917	1,206	18,683	25,983	1,765	1,598	1,183	1,096
Multilateral	434	312	823	741	815	947	872	798
of which: IBRD	0	266	780	693	724	706	730	731
IDA	0	0	0	0	0	0	0	0
Bilateral	483	894	17,860	25,242	950	650	311	297
Private creditors	2,356	825	4,433	5,730	9,114	21,516	14,658	18,057
of which: Bonds	810	268	3,765	2,543	3,714	5,098	5,944	3,573
Commercial banks	51	19	0	2,900	4,679	16,110	8,526	14,284
Private nonguaranteed	0	1,302	5,971	5,683	13,232	21,465	23,103	25,044
of which: Bonds	0	825	822	1,475	6,065	6,020	7,033	9,669
Interest payments	**2,591**	**4,284**	**8,569**	**11,599**	**13,771**	**20,715**	**17,605**	**17,229**
Public and publicly guaranteed	2,591	3,207	5,221	5,279	4,730	6,264	5,421	5,803
Official creditors	1,245	1,227	2,339	1,735	453	333	182	62
Multilateral	132	431	201	276	301	234	135	36
of which: IBRD	57	412	184	243	262	202	121	30
IDA	0	0	0	0	0	0	0	0
Bilateral	1,113	796	2,137	1,458	152	99	47	26
Private creditors	1,346	1,979	2,882	3,545	4,277	5,931	5,239	5,741
of which: Bonds	140	1,845	2,804	2,857	3,356	4,372	4,657	4,896
Commercial banks	600	4	7	631	875	1,523	564	837
Private nonguaranteed	0	1,077	3,348	6,320	9,041	14,451	12,184	11,427
of which: Bonds	0	165	1,774	3,234	4,722	5,269	5,550	5,154
8. Debt stock-flow reconciliation								
Total change in external debt stocks	-374	-14,761	43,128	10,832	110,595	41,388	-29,307	11,321
Net flows on external debt	4,913	-2,835	23,227	28,273	103,708	46,345	-19,124	14,034
9. Debt restructurings								
Total amount rescheduled	7,166	26,526	0	1,170	0	0	0	0
Total amount forgiven	0	11,600	0	0	0	0	0	0
Debt buyback	0	0	0	0	0	0	0	0

10. Contractual obligations on outstanding long-term external debt

	2011	2012	2013	2014	2015	2016	2017	2018
Official creditors								
Principal	1,742	958	725	622	454	290	1,035	215
Interest	113	88	71	59	48	40	34	9
Private creditors								
Principal	62,304	45,111	46,455	38,271	32,049	20,390	29,696	23,277
Interest	14,346	12,430	10,625	8,760	7,112	5,824	4,932	3,547

Notes:

Data on long-term public and publicly guaranteed, long-term private nonguaranteed, and short-term debt for 2010 are World Bank staff estimates based on reports provided by the country.

RWANDA

(US$ million, unless otherwise indicated)

	1995	2000	2005	2006	2007	2008	2009	2010
1. Summary external debt data								
External debt stocks	**1029.0**	**1270.3**	**1508.9**	**413.0**	**584.6**	**662.8**	**748.9**	**794.6**
Long-term external debt	970.7	1146.6	1414.5	389.5	565.9	645.7	723.5	765.6
Public and publicly guaranteed	970.7	1146.6	1414.5	389.5	565.9	645.7	723.5	765.6
Private nonguaranteed	0.0	0.0	0.0	0.0	0.0	0.0	0.0	0.0
Use of IMF credit	26.3	85.8	77.0	4.3	8.1	11.4	15.2	14.9
Short-term external debt	32.0	37.9	17.4	19.2	10.6	5.7	10.1	14.1
interest arrears on long-term	17.5	16.2	13.4	12.2	10.6	0.7	0.1	0.1
Memorandum items								
Principal arrears on long-term	44.2	71.9	73.3	69.3	63.0	4.3	2.7	2.1
Long-term public sector debt	970.7	1146.6	1414.5	389.5	565.9	645.7	723.5	765.6
Long-term private sector debt	0.0	0.0	0.0	0.0	0.0	0.0	0.0	0.0
Public & publicly guaranteed commitments	50.0	55.0	73.0	17.9	386.6	0.0	52.1	138.3
External debt flows								
Disbursements	67.5	64.9	86.5	67.0	85.7	114.1	88.4	61.4
Long-term external debt	54.0	39.8	84.8	64.5	82.3	110.5	84.8	61.4
IMF purchases	13.5	25.1	1.7	2.5	3.5	3.6	3.6	0.0
Principal repayments	11.4	24.3	16.8	17.8	16.2	8.6	5.3	8.3
Long-term external debt	11.4	13.1	13.2	17.8	16.2	8.6	5.3	8.2
IMF repurchases	0.0	11.1	3.7	0.0	0.0	0.0	0.0	0.1
Net flows	52.6	24.3	66.6	52.3	62.6	110.5	88.1	57.0
Long-term external debt	42.6	26.7	71.6	46.7	66.1	101.9	79.5	53.1
Short-term external debt	-3.5	-16.4	-3.0	3.0	-7.0	5.0	5.0	4.0
Interest payments	8.9	11.4	10.8	8.2	6.7	5.7	6.0	6.2
Long-term external debt	8.3	8.5	10.2	7.9	6.5	5.5	5.8	6.0
IMF charges	0.1	1.4	0.4	0.0	0.0	0.1	0.1	0.0
Short-term external debt	0.5	1.5	0.2	0.3	0.2	0.1	0.1	0.2
2. Other non-debt resource inflows								
Foreign direct investment	2.2	8.3	8.0	11.2	67.1	103.4	118.7	42.3
Portfolio equity	..	..	..	..	..	..	..	..
3. Currency composition of public and publicly guaranteed debt (%)								
Euro	..	..	4.2	6.8	5.1	6.8	6.7	5.5
Japanese yen	1.3	0.4	0.0	0.0	0.0	0.0	0.0	0.0
Pound sterling	0.0	0.0	0.0	0.0	0.0	0.0	0.0	0.0
Swiss franc	0.0	0.0	0.0	0.0	0.0	0.0	0.0	0.0
U.S.dollars	45.6	58.5	63.8	54.4	44.4	41.9	41.2	40.1
4. Average terms of new commitments								
Official creditors								
Interest (%)	0.8	0.8	0.9	1.0	3.0	0.0	1.8	0.9
Maturity (years)	39.8	39.7	40.0	30.1	25.1	0.0	21.8	35.9
Grace period (years)	10.3	10.2	9.4	6.5	7.9	0.0	7.0	9.2
Private creditors								
Interest (%)	0.0	0.0	0.0	0.0	0.0	0.0	0.0	0.0
Maturity (years)	0.0	0.0	0.0	0.0	0.0	0.0	0.0	0.0
Grace period (years)	0.0	0.0	0.0	0.0	0.0	0.0	0.0	0.0
5. Major economic aggregates								
Gross national income (GNI)	1298.9	1719.6	2554.0	3082.5	3723.8	4677.2	5225.2	5581.8
Exports of goods, services & income	98.8	141.5	284.6	302.5	411.3	693.0	548.6	620.5
Worker remit. & comp. of employees	21.1	6.6	20.9	21.2	51.3	67.8	92.6	91.8
Imports of goods, services & income	391.3	451.7	702.8	778.3	971.4	1463.5	1531.2	1699.2
Profit remittances on FDI	1.5	3.1	4.7	3.9	9.3	15.4	4.7	0.0
Current account balance	57.5	-94.4	-52.1	-180.0	-146.6	-252.1	-378.6	-421.4
International reserves	99.1	190.6	405.8	439.7	552.8	596.3	742.7	812.8
6. Ratios								
External debt stocks to exports (%)	1041.4	897.7	530.1	136.5	142.1	95.6	136.5	128.1
External debt stocks to GNI (%)	79.2	73.9	59.1	13.4	15.7	14.2	14.3	14.2
Debt service to exports (%)	20.5	25.2	9.7	8.6	5.6	2.1	2.1	2.3
Short-term to external debt stocks (%)	3.1	3.0	1.2	4.6	1.8	0.9	1.4	1.8
Multilateral to external debt stocks (%)	79.1	78.5	90.0	81.2	79.9	84.8	82.2	80.5
Reserves to external debt stocks (%)	9.6	15.0	26.9	106.5	94.6	90.0	99.2	102.3
Reserves to imports (months)	3.0	5.1	6.9	6.8	6.8	4.9	5.8	5.7

RWANDA

(US$ million, unless otherwise indicated)

	1995	2000	2005	2006	2007	2008	2009	2010
7. Long-term external debt								
Debt outstanding and disbursed	**970.7**	**1146.6**	**1414.5**	**389.5**	**565.9**	**645.7**	**723.5**	**765.6**
Public and publicly guaranteed	970.7	1146.6	1414.5	389.5	565.9	645.7	723.5	765.6
Official creditors	970.7	1146.6	1414.5	389.5	565.9	645.7	723.5	765.6
Multilateral	813.7	996.6	1357.8	335.2	467.3	562.0	615.3	639.3
of which: IBRD	0.0	0.0	0.0	0.0	0.0	0.0	0.0	0.0
IDA	512.0	691.9	980.3	168.5	203.8	241.7	254.2	259.4
Bilateral	157.0	150.0	56.7	54.3	98.6	83.7	108.3	126.3
Private creditors	0.0	0.0	0.0	0.0	0.0	0.0	0.0	0.0
of which: Bonds	0.0	0.0	0.0	0.0	0.0	0.0	0.0	0.0
Commercial banks	0.0	0.0	0.0	0.0	0.0	0.0	0.0	0.0
Private nonguaranteed	0.0	0.0	0.0	0.0	0.0	0.0	0.0	0.0
of which: Bonds	0.0	0.0	0.0	0.0	0.0	0.0	0.0	0.0
Disbursements	**54.0**	**39.8**	**84.8**	**64.5**	**82.3**	**110.5**	**84.8**	**61.4**
Public and publicly guaranteed	54.0	39.8	84.8	64.5	82.3	110.5	84.8	61.4
Official creditors	54.0	39.8	84.8	64.5	82.3	110.5	84.8	61.4
Multilateral	54.0	39.8	84.8	64.5	70.9	101.4	58.5	43.1
of which: IBRD	0.0	0.0	0.0	0.0	0.0	0.0	0.0	0.0
IDA	34.8	37.2	46.8	37.0	27.6	40.5	10.5	9.8
Bilateral	0.0	0.0	0.0	0.0	11.4	9.1	26.4	18.3
Private creditors	0.0	0.0	0.0	0.0	0.0	0.0	0.0	0.0
of which: Bonds	0.0	0.0	0.0	0.0	0.0	0.0	0.0	0.0
Commercial banks	0.0	0.0	0.0	0.0	0.0	0.0	0.0	0.0
Private nonguaranteed	0.0	0.0	0.0	0.0	0.0	0.0	0.0	0.0
of which: Bonds	0.0	0.0	0.0	0.0	0.0	0.0	0.0	0.0
Principal repayments	**11.4**	**13.1**	**13.2**	**17.8**	**16.2**	**8.6**	**5.3**	**8.2**
Public and publicly guaranteed	11.4	13.1	13.2	17.8	16.2	8.6	5.3	8.2
Official creditors	11.4	13.1	13.2	17.8	16.2	8.6	5.3	8.2
Multilateral	11.2	10.8	8.2	12.6	10.9	8.2	4.9	7.0
of which: IBRD	0.0	0.0	0.0	0.0	0.0	0.0	0.0	0.0
IDA	5.8	6.3	0.2	0.0	0.0	0.0	0.0	0.5
Bilateral	0.2	2.3	5.0	5.1	5.2	0.4	0.4	1.2
Private creditors	0.0	0.0	0.0	0.0	0.0	0.0	0.0	0.0
of which: Bonds	0.0	0.0	0.0	0.0	0.0	0.0	0.0	0.0
Commercial banks	0.0	0.0	0.0	0.0	0.0	0.0	0.0	0.0
Private nonguaranteed	0.0	0.0	0.0	0.0	0.0	0.0	0.0	0.0
of which: Bonds	0.0	0.0	0.0	0.0	0.0	0.0	0.0	0.0
Interest payments	**8.3**	**8.5**	**10.2**	**7.9**	**6.5**	**5.5**	**5.8**	**6.0**
Public and publicly guaranteed	8.3	8.5	10.2	7.9	6.5	5.5	5.8	6.0
Official creditors	8.3	8.5	10.2	7.9	6.5	5.5	5.8	6.0
Multilateral	8.3	7.5	9.3	6.8	5.4	4.4	4.2	4.3
of which: IBRD	0.0	0.0	0.0	0.0	0.0	0.0	0.0	0.0
IDA	6.7	5.1	5.6	2.3	1.5	1.7	1.8	1.9
Bilateral	0.0	1.0	0.9	1.0	1.1	1.1	1.6	1.7
Private creditors	0.0	0.0	0.0	0.0	0.0	0.0	0.0	0.0
of which: Bonds	0.0	0.0	0.0	0.0	0.0	0.0	0.0	0.0
Commercial banks	0.0	0.0	0.0	0.0	0.0	0.0	0.0	0.0
Private nonguaranteed	0.0	0.0	0.0	0.0	0.0	0.0	0.0	0.0
of which: Bonds	0.0	0.0	0.0	0.0	0.0	0.0	0.0	0.0
8. Debt stock-flow reconciliation								
Total change in external debt stocks	76.7	-21.3	-145.7	-1095.9	171.6	78.2	86.1	45.6
Net flows on external debt	52.6	24.3	66.6	52.3	62.6	110.5	88.1	57.0
9. Debt restructurings								
Total amount rescheduled	6.1	6.8	8.0	14.0	0.1	0.0	0.0	0.0
Total amount forgiven	0.0	0.3	103.5	1215.5	0.6	29.5	4.6	4.2
Debt buyback	0.0	0.0	0.0	0.0	0.0	0.0	0.0	0.0

10. Contractual obligations on outstanding long-term external debt

	2011	2012	2013	2014	2015	2016	2017	2018
Official creditors								
Principal	16.0	18.3	20.4	27.2	33.0	33.9	34.3	34.8
Interest	8.5	9.3	9.8	10.1	10.1	9.9	9.6	9.2
Private creditors								
Principal	0.0	0.0	0.0	0.0	0.0	0.0	0.0	0.0
Interest	0.0	0.0	0.0	0.0	0.0	0.0	0.0	0.0

Notes:

Data on long-term public and publicly guaranteed have been revised from 2008 based on reports provided by the country.

SAMOA

(US$ million, unless otherwise indicated)

	1995	*2000*	*2005*	*2006*	*2007*	*2008*	*2009*	*2010*
1. Summary external debt data								
External debt stocks	**160.0**	**137.7**	**167.5**	**163.7**	**185.9**	**205.6**	**235.5**	**308.0**
Long-term external debt	160.0	137.7	167.5	163.7	185.9	205.6	226.4	299.1
Public and publicly guaranteed	160.0	137.7	167.5	163.7	185.9	205.6	226.4	299.1
Private nonguaranteed	0.0	0.0	0.0	0.0	0.0	0.0	0.0	0.0
Use of IMF credit	0.0	0.0	0.0	0.0	0.0	0.0	0.0	0.0
Short-term external debt	0.0	0.0	0.0	0.0	0.0	0.0	9.1	8.9
interest arrears on long-term	0.0	0.0	0.0	0.0	0.0	0.0	0.0	0.0
Memorandum items								
Principal arrears on long-term	0.0	0.0	0.0	0.0	0.0	0.0	0.0	0.0
Long-term public sector debt	160.0	137.7	167.5	163.7	185.9	205.6	226.4	299.1
Long-term private sector debt	0.0	0.0	0.0	0.0	0.0	0.0	0.0	0.0
Public & publicly guaranteed commitments	0.1	11.8	4.8	8.5	91.3	48.8	0.0	79.4
External debt flows								
Disbursements	6.8	6.7	10.4	7.3	17.8	25.5	34.1	78.9
Long-term external debt	6.8	6.7	10.4	7.3	17.8	25.5	25.2	78.9
IMF purchases	0.0	0.0	0.0	0.0	0.0	0.0	8.9	0.0
Principal repayments	3.0	4.2	4.3	4.9	5.3	6.0	6.0	7.2
Long-term external debt	3.0	4.2	4.3	4.9	5.3	6.0	6.0	7.2
IMF repurchases	0.0	0.0	0.0	0.0	0.0	0.0	0.0	0.0
Net flows	3.8	2.5	6.1	2.4	12.6	19.6	28.1	71.6
Long-term external debt	3.8	2.5	6.1	2.4	12.6	19.6	19.2	71.6
Short-term external debt	0.0	0.0	0.0	0.0	0.0	0.0	0.0	0.0
Interest payments	1.6	1.3	1.5	2.1	1.6	2.1	2.5	3.3
Long-term external debt	1.6	1.3	1.5	2.1	1.6	2.1	2.5	3.3
IMF charges	0.0	0.0	0.0	0.0	0.0	0.0	0.0	0.0
Short-term external debt	0.0	0.0	0.0	0.0	0.0	0.0	0.0	0.0
2. Other non-debt resource inflows								
Foreign direct investment	3.4	-1.5	-3.0	20.7	6.8	45.9	9.9	0.7
Portfolio equity	..	..	..	..	..	..	..	..
3. Currency composition of public and publicly guaranteed debt (%)								
Euro	..	..	1.7	1.7	1.4	0.9	0.8	0.4
Japanese yen	0.0	0.0	0.0	0.0	0.0	0.0	0.7	2.7
Pound sterling	0.0	0.0	0.0	0.0	0.0	0.0	0.0	0.0
Swiss franc	0.0	0.0	0.0	0.0	0.0	0.0	0.0	0.0
U.S.dollars	36.6	41.0	43.7	48.5	45.7	41.1	36.8	33.7
4. Average terms of new commitments								
Official creditors								
Interest (%)	0.0	1.1	3.8	1.4	1.1	0.8	0.0	1.4
Maturity (years)	20.5	35.1	19.6	31.4	28.8	22.9	0.0	29.1
Grace period (years)	8.5	9.0	5.1	7.9	8.5	5.9	0.0	8.0
Private creditors								
Interest (%)	0.0	0.0	0.0	0.0	0.0	0.0	0.0	0.0
Maturity (years)	0.0	0.0	0.0	0.0	0.0	0.0	0.0	0.0
Grace period (years)	0.0	0.0	0.0	0.0	0.0	0.0	0.0	0.0
5. Major economic aggregates								
Gross national income (GNI)	193.7	245.6	388.2	432.8	479.9	561.5	480.8	543.8
Exports of goods, services & income	69.1	..	131.3	149.7	190.0	193.8	181.5	201.7
Worker remit. & comp. of employees	41.0	45.0	109.9	108.0	119.8	135.0	131.4	143.4
Imports of goods, services & income	119.9	..	263.3	293.2	344.4	372.1	318.4	391.2
Profit remittances on FDI	..	..	7.7	13.8	37.9	50.5	27.4	17.5
Current account balance	9.3	..	-25.2	-47.8	-41.6	-53.5	-9.3	-57.9
International reserves	55.3	63.7	81.8	80.7	95.4	87.1	165.8	209.4
6. Ratios								
External debt stocks to exports (%)	231.6	..	127.5	109.4	97.8	106.1	129.8	152.7
External debt stocks to GNI (%)	82.6	56.1	43.1	37.8	38.7	36.6	49.0	56.6
Debt service to exports (%)	6.6	..	4.4	4.6	3.6	4.2	4.7	5.2
Short-term to external debt stocks (%)	..	..	..	..	..	..	..	..
Multilateral to external debt stocks (%)	93.1	93.9	92.6	99.8	95.1	85.6	76.5	71.2
Reserves to external debt stocks (%)	34.6	46.2	48.8	49.3	51.3	42.4	70.4	68.0
Reserves to imports (months)	5.5	..	3.7	3.3	3.3	2.8	6.3	6.4

(US$ million, unless otherwise indicated)

	1995	2000	2005	2006	2007	2008	2009	2010
7. Long-term external debt								
Debt outstanding and disbursed	**160.0**	**137.7**	**167.5**	**163.7**	**185.9**	**205.6**	**226.4**	**299.1**
Public and publicly guaranteed	160.0	137.7	167.5	163.7	185.9	205.6	226.4	299.1
Official creditors	160.0	137.7	167.5	163.7	185.9	205.6	226.4	299.1
Multilateral	149.1	129.3	155.0	163.4	176.8	176.0	180.1	219.2
of which: IBRD	0.0	0.0	0.0	0.0	0.0	0.0	0.0	0.0
IDA	44.7	47.3	64.2	69.3	77.7	79.0	79.9	99.3
Bilateral	11.0	8.4	12.5	0.3	9.1	29.6	46.3	79.9
Private creditors	0.0	0.0	0.0	0.0	0.0	0.0	0.0	0.0
of which: Bonds	0.0	0.0	0.0	0.0	0.0	0.0	0.0	0.0
Commercial banks	0.0	0.0	0.0	0.0	0.0	0.0	0.0	0.0
Private nonguaranteed	0.0	0.0	0.0	0.0	0.0	0.0	0.0	0.0
of which: Bonds	0.0	0.0	0.0	0.0	0.0	0.0	0.0	0.0
Disbursements	**6.8**	**6.7**	**10.4**	**7.3**	**17.8**	**25.5**	**25.2**	**78.9**
Public and publicly guaranteed	6.8	6.7	10.4	7.3	17.8	25.5	25.2	78.9
Official creditors	6.8	6.7	10.4	7.3	17.8	25.5	25.2	78.9
Multilateral	6.6	6.7	10.4	7.3	9.3	5.9	8.5	47.7
of which: IBRD	0.0	0.0	0.0	0.0	0.0	0.0	0.0	0.0
IDA	0.7	5.7	7.7	3.5	6.9	3.1	1.8	21.9
Bilateral	0.2	0.0	0.0	0.0	8.6	19.6	16.7	31.1
Private creditors	0.0	0.0	0.0	0.0	0.0	0.0	0.0	0.0
of which: Bonds	0.0	0.0	0.0	0.0	0.0	0.0	0.0	0.0
Commercial banks	0.0	0.0	0.0	0.0	0.0	0.0	0.0	0.0
Private nonguaranteed	0.0	0.0	0.0	0.0	0.0	0.0	0.0	0.0
of which: Bonds	0.0	0.0	0.0	0.0	0.0	0.0	0.0	0.0
Principal repayments	**3.0**	**4.2**	**4.3**	**4.9**	**5.3**	**6.0**	**6.0**	**7.2**
Public and publicly guaranteed	3.0	4.2	4.3	4.9	5.3	6.0	6.0	7.2
Official creditors	3.0	4.2	4.3	4.9	5.3	6.0	6.0	7.2
Multilateral	2.6	3.3	3.9	4.7	5.2	5.9	6.0	7.2
of which: IBRD	0.0	0.0	0.0	0.0	0.0	0.0	0.0	0.0
IDA	0.2	0.7	1.0	1.1	1.2	1.3	1.5	1.9
Bilateral	0.3	0.9	0.3	0.2	0.0	0.1	0.0	0.1
Private creditors	0.0	0.0	0.0	0.0	0.0	0.0	0.0	0.0
of which: Bonds	0.0	0.0	0.0	0.0	0.0	0.0	0.0	0.0
Commercial banks	0.0	0.0	0.0	0.0	0.0	0.0	0.0	0.0
Private nonguaranteed	0.0	0.0	0.0	0.0	0.0	0.0	0.0	0.0
of which: Bonds	0.0	0.0	0.0	0.0	0.0	0.0	0.0	0.0
Interest payments	**1.6**	**1.3**	**1.5**	**2.1**	**1.6**	**2.1**	**2.5**	**3.3**
Public and publicly guaranteed	1.6	1.3	1.5	2.1	1.6	2.1	2.5	3.3
Official creditors	1.6	1.3	1.5	2.1	1.6	2.1	2.5	3.3
Multilateral	1.5	1.2	1.5	2.1	1.6	1.8	1.7	1.7
of which: IBRD	0.0	0.0	0.0	0.0	0.0	0.0	0.0	0.0
IDA	0.3	0.3	0.6	0.5	0.6	0.6	0.6	0.6
Bilateral	0.1	0.0	0.0	0.0	0.0	0.3	0.8	1.6
Private creditors	0.0	0.0	0.0	0.0	0.0	0.0	0.0	0.0
of which: Bonds	0.0	0.0	0.0	0.0	0.0	0.0	0.0	0.0
Commercial banks	0.0	0.0	0.0	0.0	0.0	0.0	0.0	0.0
Private nonguaranteed	0.0	0.0	0.0	0.0	0.0	0.0	0.0	0.0
of which: Bonds	0.0	0.0	0.0	0.0	0.0	0.0	0.0	0.0
8. Debt stock-flow reconciliation								
Total change in external debt stocks	5.5	-8.7	-7.3	-3.7	22.2	19.7	29.9	72.5
Net flows on external debt	3.8	2.5	6.1	2.4	12.6	19.6	28.1	71.6
9. Debt restructurings								
Total amount rescheduled	0.0	0.0	0.0	0.0	0.0	0.0	0.0	0.0
Total amount forgiven	0.0	0.0	0.0	12.2	0.0	0.0	0.0	0.0
Debt buyback	0.0	0.0	0.0	0.0	0.0	0.0	0.0	0.0

10. Contractual obligations on outstanding long-term external debt

	2011	2012	2013	2014	2015	2016	2017	2018
Official creditors								
Principal	7.2	8.4	9.3	12.9	14.3	16.0	17.3	19.9
Interest	3.6	3.7	3.8	3.8	3.8	3.8	3.6	3.5
Private creditors								
Principal	0.0	0.0	0.0	0.0	0.0	0.0	0.0	0.0
Interest	0.0	0.0	0.0	0.0	0.0	0.0	0.0	0.0

Notes:

Short-term debt data are excluded since BIS data include debt liabilities of offshore centers located in the country. BIS short-term debt data for 2008, 2009, and 2010 are $1.1 billion, $1.2 billion, and $2.1 billion respectively.

SAO TOME AND PRINCIPE

(US$ million, unless otherwise indicated)

	1995	2000	2005	2006	2007	2008	2009	2010
1. Summary external debt data								
External debt stocks	**245.7**	**304.0**	**334.7**	**350.6**	**165.2**	**130.8**	**148.8**	**170.2**
Long-term external debt	231.8	278.3	317.1	331.4	143.5	108.7	125.0	145.3
Public and publicly guaranteed	231.8	278.3	317.1	331.4	143.5	108.7	125.0	145.3
Private nonguaranteed	0.0	0.0	0.0	0.0	0.0	0.0	0.0	0.0
Use of IMF credit	0.8	2.5	3.2	4.1	2.6	3.8	4.5	4.9
Short-term external debt	13.0	23.3	14.4	15.1	19.2	18.2	19.4	19.9
interest arrears on long-term	6.0	11.3	14.4	14.1	8.2	8.2	8.4	5.9
Memorandum items								
Principal arrears on long-term	27.2	47.7	55.8	69.6	71.6	66.0	63.9	67.7
Long-term public sector debt	231.8	278.3	317.1	331.4	143.5	108.7	120.0	140.3
Long-term private sector debt	0.0	0.0	0.0	0.0	0.0	0.0	5.0	5.0
Public & publicly guaranteed commitments	0.0	18.2	0.0	0.0	5.0	3.9	10.0	66.3
External debt flows								
Disbursements	13.0	11.9	6.1	3.9	5.5	6.6	19.4	20.3
Long-term external debt	13.0	9.4	5.4	2.7	4.2	5.2	18.8	19.8
IMF purchases	0.0	2.5	0.6	1.2	1.3	1.3	0.6	0.6
Principal repayments	1.1	2.2	4.6	5.1	5.0	1.7	1.7	1.2
Long-term external debt	0.8	2.2	4.4	4.6	4.2	1.7	1.7	1.2
IMF repurchases	0.2	0.0	0.1	0.6	0.8	0.0	0.0	0.0
Net flows	12.9	9.7	1.5	-0.2	10.5	3.9	18.7	22.1
Long-term external debt	12.2	7.2	1.0	-1.9	-0.1	3.5	17.1	18.6
Short-term external debt	1.0	0.0	0.0	1.0	10.0	-1.0	1.0	3.0
Interest payments	1.2	2.1	2.1	1.9	1.4	0.6	0.3	0.4
Long-term external debt	0.9	1.2	2.1	1.8	1.2	0.3	0.3	0.3
IMF charges	0.0	0.0	0.0	0.0	0.0	0.0	0.0	0.0
Short-term external debt	0.3	0.9	0.0	0.0	0.3	0.3	0.0	0.2
2. Other non-debt resource inflows								
Foreign direct investment	0.0	3.8	16.2	27.5	22.0	56.7	7.5	3.0
Portfolio equity	0.0	0.0	..	..	..	..	..	..
3. Currency composition of public and publicly guaranteed debt (%)								
Euro	..	..	6.2	6.6	3.8	4.5	3.8	14.9
Japanese yen	0.0	0.0	0.0	0.0	0.0	0.0	0.0	0.0
Pound sterling	0.0	0.0	0.0	0.0	0.0	0.0	0.0	0.0
Swiss franc	0.0	4.7	5.2	5.3	13.4	18.7	16.8	15.8
U.S.dollars	40.0	43.7	45.0	44.8	64.7	53.7	58.8	50.8
4. Average terms of new commitments								
Official creditors								
Interest (%)	0.0	0.9	0.0	0.0	4.6	0.8	0.0	1.9
Maturity (years)	0.0	39.4	0.0	0.0	20.0	22.8	29.8	29.9
Grace period (years)	0.0	10.1	0.0	0.0	8.0	7.0	5.8	9.9
Private creditors								
Interest (%)	0.0	0.0	0.0	0.0	0.0	0.0	0.0	0.0
Maturity (years)	0.0	0.0	0.0	0.0	0.0	0.0	0.0	0.0
Grace period (years)	0.0	0.0	0.0	0.0	0.0	0.0	0.0	0.0
5. Major economic aggregates								
Gross national income (GNI)	..	..	111.8	126.5	149.6	174.8	192.0	199.6
Exports of goods, services & income	..	16.8	17.9	22.3	20.3	19.4	21.3	24.7
Worker remit. & comp. of employees	..	0.5	1.5	1.6	2.0	3.0	2.0	2.0
Imports of goods, services & income	..	41.2	57.6	80.1	85.8	115.6	104.7	126.9
Profit remittances on FDI	0.0	0.0	..	..	..	..	..	..
Current account balance	..	-20.1	-36.2	-57.7	-64.3	-93.5	-78.8	-99.6
International reserves	5.1	11.6	26.7	34.2	39.3	..	..	..
6. Ratios								
External debt stocks to exports (%)	..	1806.6	1868.5	1574.6	814.8	672.4	699.0	688.9
External debt stocks to GNI (%)	..	..	299.3	277.1	110.4	74.8	77.5	85.3
Debt service to exports (%)	..	25.6	37.0	31.5	31.7	12.0	9.7	6.5
Short-term to external debt stocks (%)	5.3	7.7	4.3	4.3	11.6	13.9	13.0	11.7
Multilateral to external debt stocks (%)	61.9	55.7	59.0	57.9	22.8	27.4	24.7	21.9
Reserves to external debt stocks (%)	2.1	3.8	8.0	9.7	23.8	..	..	..
Reserves to imports (months)	..	3.4	5.6	5.1	5.5	..	..	..

(US$ million, unless otherwise indicated)

	1995	2000	2005	2006	2007	2008	2009	2010
7. Long-term external debt								
Debt outstanding and disbursed	**231.8**	**278.3**	**317.1**	**331.4**	**143.5**	**108.7**	**125.0**	**145.3**
Public and publicly guaranteed	231.8	278.3	317.1	331.4	143.5	108.7	125.0	145.3
Official creditors	231.8	278.3	317.1	331.4	143.5	108.7	125.0	145.3
Multilateral	152.0	169.3	197.4	203.2	37.7	35.9	36.7	37.3
of which: IBRD	0.0	0.0	0.0	0.0	0.0	0.0	0.0	0.0
IDA	53.6	58.9	72.4	76.4	10.7	13.3	14.4	14.2
Bilateral	79.9	109.0	119.7	128.3	105.8	72.9	88.3	108.0
Private creditors	0.0	0.0	0.0	0.0	0.0	0.0	0.0	0.0
of which: Bonds	0.0	0.0	0.0	0.0	0.0	0.0	0.0	0.0
Commercial banks	0.0	0.0	0.0	0.0	0.0	0.0	0.0	0.0
Private nonguaranteed	0.0	0.0	0.0	0.0	0.0	0.0	0.0	0.0
of which: Bonds	0.0	0.0	0.0	0.0	0.0	0.0	0.0	0.0
Disbursements	**13.0**	**9.4**	**5.4**	**2.7**	**4.2**	**5.2**	**18.8**	**19.8**
Public and publicly guaranteed	13.0	9.4	5.4	2.7	4.2	5.2	18.8	19.8
Official creditors	13.0	9.4	5.4	2.7	4.2	5.2	18.8	19.8
Multilateral	13.0	8.4	5.4	2.7	4.2	5.2	3.8	2.3
of which: IBRD	0.0	0.0	0.0	0.0	0.0	0.0	0.0	0.0
IDA	5.6	1.7	2.5	1.9	2.6	2.7	1.0	0.1
Bilateral	0.0	1.0	0.0	0.0	0.0	0.0	15.0	17.4
Private creditors	0.0	0.0	0.0	0.0	0.0	0.0	0.0	0.0
of which: Bonds	0.0	0.0	0.0	0.0	0.0	0.0	0.0	0.0
Commercial banks	0.0	0.0	0.0	0.0	0.0	0.0	0.0	0.0
Private nonguaranteed	0.0	0.0	0.0	0.0	0.0	0.0	0.0	0.0
of which: Bonds	0.0	0.0	0.0	0.0	0.0	0.0	0.0	0.0
Principal repayments	**0.8**	**2.2**	**4.4**	**4.6**	**4.2**	**1.7**	**1.7**	**1.2**
Public and publicly guaranteed	0.8	2.2	4.4	4.6	4.2	1.7	1.7	1.2
Official creditors	0.8	2.2	4.4	4.6	4.2	1.7	1.7	1.2
Multilateral	0.8	1.9	2.1	3.8	4.2	1.7	1.4	1.2
of which: IBRD	0.0	0.0	0.0	0.0	0.0	0.0	0.0	0.0
IDA	0.1	0.5	0.1	0.1	0.0	0.0	0.0	0.0
Bilateral	0.0	0.3	2.4	0.8	0.0	0.0	0.3	0.0
Private creditors	0.0	0.0	0.0	0.0	0.0	0.0	0.0	0.0
of which: Bonds	0.0	0.0	0.0	0.0	0.0	0.0	0.0	0.0
Commercial banks	0.0	0.0	0.0	0.0	0.0	0.0	0.0	0.0
Private nonguaranteed	0.0	0.0	0.0	0.0	0.0	0.0	0.0	0.0
of which: Bonds	0.0	0.0	0.0	0.0	0.0	0.0	0.0	0.0
Interest payments	**0.9**	**1.2**	**2.1**	**1.8**	**1.2**	**0.3**	**0.3**	**0.3**
Public and publicly guaranteed	0.9	1.2	2.1	1.8	1.2	0.3	0.3	0.3
Official creditors	0.9	1.2	2.1	1.8	1.2	0.3	0.3	0.3
Multilateral	0.8	1.2	1.4	1.5	1.2	0.3	0.3	0.3
of which: IBRD	0.0	0.0	0.0	0.0	0.0	0.0	0.0	0.0
IDA	0.3	0.5	0.5	0.4	0.1	0.1	0.1	0.1
Bilateral	0.1	0.0	0.7	0.3	0.0	0.0	0.0	0.0
Private creditors	0.0	0.0	0.0	0.0	0.0	0.0	0.0	0.0
of which: Bonds	0.0	0.0	0.0	0.0	0.0	0.0	0.0	0.0
Commercial banks	0.0	0.0	0.0	0.0	0.0	0.0	0.0	0.0
Private nonguaranteed	0.0	0.0	0.0	0.0	0.0	0.0	0.0	0.0
of which: Bonds	0.0	0.0	0.0	0.0	0.0	0.0	0.0	0.0
8. Debt stock-flow reconciliation								
Total change in external debt stocks	22.9	-16.9	-25.4	15.9	-185.4	-34.4	18.0	21.4
Net flows on external debt	12.9	9.7	1.5	-0.2	10.5	3.9	18.7	22.1
9. Debt restructurings								
Total amount rescheduled	30.3	7.2	0.0	0.0	0.0	0.0	0.0	0.0
Total amount forgiven	0.0	11.4	2.9	1.4	196.2	42.1	2.0	0.0
Debt buyback	0.0	0.0	0.0	0.0	0.0	0.0	0.0	0.0

10. Contractual obligations on outstanding long-term external debt

	2011	2012	2013	2014	2015	2016	2017	2018
Official creditors								
Principal	4.3	4.3	4.3	3.9	4.6	2.6	2.6	2.7
Interest	0.8	0.8	0.8	0.7	0.7	0.7	0.7	0.7
Private creditors								
Principal	0.0	0.0	0.0	0.0	0.0	0.0	0.0	0.0
Interest	0.0	0.0	0.0	0.0	0.0	0.0	0.0	0.0

Notes:

Data for 2010 include the effects of HIPC debt reliefs in the amount of $37 thousand.

SENEGAL

(US$ million, unless otherwise indicated)

	1995	2000	2005	2006	2007	2008	2009	2010
1. Summary external debt data								
External debt stocks	**3,916**	**3,622**	**3,831**	**1,905**	**2,553**	**2,820**	**3,499**	**3,677**
Long-term external debt	3,309	3,221	3,646	1,794	2,193	2,559	3,314	3,464
Public and publicly guaranteed	3,266	3,208	3,505	1,644	1,993	2,378	2,957	3,155
Private nonguaranteed	44	13	141	151	200	180	357	308
Use of IMF credit	347	255	148	26	27	64	167	213
Short-term external debt	260	146	36	84	332	197	18	0
interest arrears on long-term	9	1	0	0	0	0	0	0
Memorandum items								
Principal arrears on long-term	51	17	10	18	15	5	5	6
Long-term public sector debt	3,234	3,208	3,505	1,644	1,993	2,378	2,957	3,155
Long-term private sector debt	76	13	141	151	200	180	357	308
Public & publicly guaranteed commitments	333	241	327	534	294	567	774	309
External debt flows								
Disbursements	256	156	387	280	497	560	935	485
Long-term external debt	173	137	382	259	497	522	835	436
IMF purchases	83	19	5	20	0	38	100	49
Principal repayments	196	148	145	111	126	125	148	227
Long-term external debt	156	127	112	111	126	125	148	227
IMF repurchases	41	21	34	0	0	0	0	1
Net flows	87	-153	242	217	619	300	608	240
Long-term external debt	17	10	270	149	371	397	688	209
Short-term external debt	28	-161	0	48	248	-135	-179	-18
Interest payments	87	76	57	74	63	55	52	75
Long-term external debt	70	58	55	70	50	49	50	75
IMF charges	3	1	1	0	0	0	0	0
Short-term external debt	14	17	2	4	12	6	1	0
2. Other non-debt resource inflows								
Foreign direct investment	32	63	45	220	297	398	208	237
Portfolio equity	4	-2	-6	0	8	-93	..	..
3. Currency composition of public and publicly guaranteed debt (%)								
Euro	..	..	10.9	8.8	9.9	15.9	17.7	18.8
Japanese yen	3.6	3.5	2.7	5.2	0.0	0.2	0.2	0.2
Pound sterling	0.1	0.1	0.0	0.0	0.0	0.0	0.0	0.0
Swiss franc	0.5	0.2	0.0	0.0	0.0	0.0	0.0	0.0
U.S.dollars	35.8	45.0	59.4	40.2	40.9	36.9	39.5	38.3
4. Average terms of new commitments								
Official creditors								
Interest (%)	1.2	0.8	1.2	0.9	1.9	2.7	1.2	1.0
Maturity (years)	37.6	40.1	34.0	33.9	23.5	23.4	34.7	36.0
Grace period (years)	9.1	9.9	7.6	8.5	5.8	6.7	8.4	9.4
Private creditors								
Interest (%)	0.0	3.0	0.0	6.3	0.0	0.0	8.8	0.0
Maturity (years)	0.0	9.3	0.0	9.0	0.0	0.0	5.0	0.0
Grace period (years)	0.0	2.8	0.0	0.4	0.0	0.0	5.0	0.0
5. Major economic aggregates								
Gross national income (GNI)	4,724	4,601	8,546	9,290	11,238	13,163	12,747	12,900
Exports of goods, services & income	1,593	1,383	2,451	2,522	3,013	3,736	..	..
Worker remit. & comp. of employees	146	233	789	925	1,192	1,476	1,365	1,346
Imports of goods, services & income	2,033	1,929	3,880	4,220	5,614	7,304	..	..
Profit remittances on FDI	62	75	62	70	78	123	..	..
Current account balance	-244	-332	-676	-861	-1,312	-1,884	..	..
International reserves	272	388	1,186	1,334	1,660	1,602	2,123	2,047
6. Ratios								
External debt stocks to exports (%)	245.8	261.9	156.3	75.5	84.7	75.5	..	..
External debt stocks to GNI (%)	82.9	78.7	44.8	20.5	22.7	21.4	27.4	28.5
Debt service to exports (%)	17.8	16.2	8.3	7.3	6.3	4.8	..	..
Short-term to external debt stocks (%)	6.6	4.0	0.9	4.4	13.0	7.0	0.5	0.0
Multilateral to external debt stocks (%)	48.2	52.8	73.5	51.7	54.1	55.1	51.6	53.7
Reserves to external debt stocks (%)	6.9	10.7	31.0	70.1	65.0	56.8	60.7	55.7
Reserves to imports (months)	1.6	2.4	3.7	3.8	3.5	2.6	..	..

SENEGAL

(US$ million, unless otherwise indicated)

	1995	2000	2005	2006	2007	2008	2009	2010
7. Long-term external debt								
Debt outstanding and disbursed	**3,309**	**3,221**	**3,646**	**1,794**	**2,193**	**2,559**	**3,314**	**3,464**
Public and publicly guaranteed	3,266	3,208	3,505	1,644	1,993	2,378	2,957	3,155
Official creditors	3,194	3,203	3,496	1,632	1,986	2,374	2,755	2,955
Multilateral	1,889	1,913	2,816	985	1,382	1,553	1,806	1,976
of which: IBRD	35	1	0	0	0	0	0	0
IDA	1,126	1,330	2,045	495	652	780	921	1,017
Bilateral	1,305	1,291	680	648	604	821	949	979
Private creditors	72	5	9	11	7	4	202	200
of which: Bonds	0	0	0	0	0	0	200	200
Commercial banks	66	5	9	11	7	4	2	0
Private nonguaranteed	44	13	141	151	200	180	357	308
of which: Bonds	0	0	0	0	0	0	0	0
Disbursements	**173**	**137**	**382**	**259**	**497**	**522**	**835**	**436**
Public and publicly guaranteed	172	136	333	225	472	518	627	353
Official creditors	172	131	333	220	472	518	427	353
Multilateral	144	119	262	193	395	243	264	250
of which: IBRD	0	0	0	0	0	0	0	0
IDA	107	92	182	131	133	135	137	113
Bilateral	28	12	71	28	78	275	162	103
Private creditors	0	5	0	4	0	0	200	0
of which: Bonds	0	0	0	0	0	0	200	0
Commercial banks	0	5	0	4	0	0	0	0
Private nonguaranteed	1	1	49	35	24	4	208	83
of which: Bonds	0	0	0	0	0	0	0	0
Principal repayments	**156**	**127**	**112**	**111**	**126**	**125**	**148**	**227**
Public and publicly guaranteed	150	125	83	96	72	86	98	82
Official creditors	129	124	81	94	67	84	96	80
Multilateral	98	68	40	49	38	44	60	45
of which: IBRD	12	3	0	0	0	0	0	0
IDA	6	11	12	7	0	1	2	4
Bilateral	31	57	41	45	30	40	35	35
Private creditors	21	0	2	3	4	3	3	2
of which: Bonds	0	0	0	0	0	0	0	0
Commercial banks	12	0	2	3	4	3	3	2
Private nonguaranteed	5	3	29	14	54	39	49	144
of which: Bonds	0	0	0	0	0	0	0	0
Interest payments	**70**	**58**	**55**	**70**	**50**	**49**	**50**	**75**
Public and publicly guaranteed	69	58	45	61	34	36	41	64
Official creditors	65	58	44	60	33	36	41	46
Multilateral	38	26	31	49	25	23	22	22
of which: IBRD	3	0	0	0	0	0	0	0
IDA	8	8	16	10	5	5	6	7
Bilateral	27	32	13	11	9	12	19	24
Private creditors	3	0	1	1	1	0	0	18
of which: Bonds	0	0	0	0	0	0	0	18
Commercial banks	2	0	1	1	1	0	0	0
Private nonguaranteed	1	0	10	9	16	13	9	11
of which: Bonds	0	0	0	0	0	0	0	0

	1995	2000	2005	2006	2007	2008	2009	2010
8. Debt stock-flow reconciliation								
Total change in external debt stocks	218	-346	-75	-1,926	648	267	679	178
Net flows on external debt	87	-153	242	217	619	300	608	240

	1995	2000	2005	2006	2007	2008	2009	2010
9. Debt restructurings								
Total amount rescheduled	258	0	31	262	4	2	0	0
Total amount forgiven	27	24	49	2,442	146	3	0	23
Debt buyback	0	0	0	0	0	0	0	0

10. Contractual obligations on outstanding long-term external debt

	2011	2012	2013	2014	2015	2016	2017	2018
Official creditors								
Principal	162	173	176	135	145	152	156	157
Interest	46	44	42	39	38	37	35	33
Private creditors								
Principal	62	62	62	262	62	0	0	0
Interest	22	21	20	19	1	0	0	0

Notes:

Senegal was granted debt relief effective in 2006 under MDRI.

SERBIA

(US$ million, unless otherwise indicated)

	1995	2000	2005	2006	2007	2008	2009	2010
1. Summary external debt data								
External debt stocks	**10,785**	**11,499**	**16,078**	**19,801**	**26,122**	**30,406**	**33,111**	**32,222**
Long-term external debt	8,562	6,789	12,970	17,560	23,873	26,719	27,910	27,389
Public and publicly guaranteed	6,788	6,178	7,756	7,752	8,469	8,399	8,835	9,477
Private nonguaranteed	1,773	611	5,214	9,808	15,404	18,320	19,076	17,912
Use of IMF credit	84	152	866	0	0	0	1,601	2,034
Short-term external debt	2,139	4,558	2,242	2,241	2,249	3,687	3,600	2,798
interest arrears on long-term	1,396	3,668	728	584	703	704	712	352
Memorandum items								
Principal arrears on long-term	4,182	5,275	805	732	1,250	1,625	1,832	1,976
Long-term public sector debt	6,693	6,095	7,756	7,752	8,463	8,376	8,780	9,370
Long-term private sector debt	1,869	694	5,214	9,808	15,410	18,343	19,130	18,019
Public & publicly guaranteed commitments	0	71	350	668	511	433	2,510	2,232
External debt flows								
Disbursements	0	376	3,088	5,283	6,661	6,996	6,104	5,052
Long-term external debt	0	222	2,904	5,283	6,661	6,996	4,529	4,594
IMF purchases	0	154	185	0	0	0	1,575	458
Principal repayments	0	73	776	1,558	2,334	3,486	3,613	3,431
Long-term external debt	0	0	570	1,319	2,334	3,486	3,613	3,431
IMF repurchases	0	73	206	239	0	0	0	0
Net flows	120	51	2,827	3,868	4,216	4,948	2,396	1,178
Long-term external debt	0	222	2,334	3,964	4,328	3,511	916	1,163
Short-term external debt	120	-252	515	143	-112	1,437	-95	-442
Interest payments	47	47	456	589	898	1,249	1,032	873
Long-term external debt	0	0	367	504	840	1,136	916	759
IMF charges	0	29	32	6	0	0	7	21
Short-term external debt	47	18	57	79	59	113	110	93
2. Other non-debt resource inflows								
Foreign direct investment	45	52	2,051	4,968	3,432	2,996	1,936	1,340
Portfolio equity	..	..	..	..	772	-57	22	84
3. Currency composition of public and publicly guaranteed debt (%)								
Euro	..	..	32.3	35.5	37.8	37.6	42.4	46.6
Japanese yen	2.2	2.0	1.2	1.2	1.1	1.4	1.2	1.2
Pound sterling	0.7	0.5	0.2	0.2	0.1	0.1	0.1	0.1
Swiss franc	3.6	2.8	1.9	3.4	3.2	3.1	2.8	2.9
U.S.dollars	19.8	24.6	62.5	57.7	55.3	55.0	50.6	46.3
4. Average terms of new commitments								
Official creditors								
Interest (%)	0.0	0.4	1.7	4.1	5.0	3.7	1.3	2.3
Maturity (years)	0.0	23.2	17.6	16.6	18.6	22.0	20.9	15.1
Grace period (years)	0.0	7.8	6.6	3.8	6.3	6.6	5.9	4.0
Private creditors								
Interest (%)	0.0	7.8	0.0	4.1	0.0	5.0	0.0	4.9
Maturity (years)	0.0	6.4	0.0	7.1	0.0	2.0	0.0	5.3
Grace period (years)	0.0	1.9	0.0	7.1	0.0	2.0	0.0	1.4
5. Major economic aggregates								
Gross national income (GNI)	..	6,082	24,910	28,806	38,555	47,501	40,965	38,235
Exports of goods, services & income	..	..	..	..	12,579	15,792	12,544	13,933
Worker remit. & comp. of employees	..	..	..	..	3,064	2,710	3,936	3,351
Imports of goods, services & income	..	..	..	..	23,401	29,927	20,348	21,169
Profit remittances on FDI	..	..	..	..	596	890	451	552
Current account balance	..	..	..	..	-6,890	-10,395	-2,867	-2,819
International reserves	..	517	5,842	11,889	14,214	11,478	15,228	13,308
6. Ratios								
External debt stocks to exports (%)	..	..	..	..	207.7	192.5	264.0	231.3
External debt stocks to GNI (%)	..	189.1	64.5	68.7	67.8	64.0	80.8	84.3
Debt service to exports (%)	..	..	..	..	25.7	30.0	37.0	30.9
Short-term to external debt stocks (%)	19.8	39.6	13.9	11.3	8.6	12.1	10.9	8.7
Multilateral to external debt stocks (%)	12.2	12.5	22.1	20.0	17.2	15.0	13.3	15.0
Reserves to external debt stocks (%)	..	4.5	36.3	60.0	54.4	37.7	46.0	41.3
Reserves to imports (months)	..	..	..	..	7.3	4.6	9.0	7.5

SERBIA

(US$ million, unless otherwise indicated)

	1995	2000	2005	2006	2007	2008	2009	2010
7. Long-term external debt								
Debt outstanding and disbursed	**8,562**	**6,789**	**12,970**	**17,560**	**23,873**	**26,719**	**27,910**	**27,389**
Public and publicly guaranteed	6,788	6,178	7,756	7,752	8,469	8,399	8,835	9,477
Official creditors	4,588	4,243	6,679	6,622	7,289	7,223	7,660	8,144
Multilateral	1,311	1,440	3,559	3,958	4,504	4,554	4,404	4,848
of which: IBRD	1,252	1,097	2,147	2,127	2,326	2,276	1,783	1,818
IDA	0	0	486	553	625	655	676	681
Bilateral	3,277	2,803	3,119	2,664	2,786	2,669	3,256	3,296
Private creditors	2,200	1,935	1,077	1,129	1,180	1,175	1,175	1,332
of which: Bonds	0	0	0	0	0	0	0	0
Commercial banks	2,193	1,928	1,076	1,128	1,179	1,174	1,174	1,331
Private nonguaranteed	1,773	611	5,214	9,808	15,404	18,320	19,076	17,912
of which: Bonds	0	0	0	0	165	165	165	165
Disbursements	**0**	**222**	**2,904**	**5,283**	**6,661**	**6,996**	**4,529**	**4,594**
Public and publicly guaranteed	0	222	311	456	316	294	966	1,365
Official creditors	0	187	311	406	275	291	966	1,126
Multilateral	0	0	286	392	241	278	416	885
of which: IBRD	0	0	0	0	0	0	56	243
IDA	0	0	85	43	47	34	17	16
Bilateral	0	187	25	14	34	13	550	241
Private creditors	0	35	0	50	41	3	0	239
of which: Bonds	0	0	0	0	0	0	0	0
Commercial banks	0	0	0	50	41	3	0	239
Private nonguaranteed	0	0	2,593	4,828	6,345	6,703	3,562	3,230
of which: Bonds	0	0	0	0	165	0	0	0
Principal repayments	**0**	**0**	**570**	**1,319**	**2,334**	**3,486**	**3,613**	**3,431**
Public and publicly guaranteed	0	0	48	278	184	181	158	351
Official creditors	0	0	48	278	184	180	154	275
Multilateral	0	0	31	264	91	118	87	176
of which: IBRD	0	0	17	242	17	22	0	71
IDA	0	0	0	0	0	0	0	0
Bilateral	0	0	16	13	93	62	67	98
Private creditors	0	0	0	0	0	1	4	76
of which: Bonds	0	0	0	0	0	0	0	0
Commercial banks	0	0	0	0	0	1	4	76
Private nonguaranteed	0	0	522	1,041	2,149	3,305	3,454	3,081
of which: Bonds	0	0	0	0	0	0	0	0
Interest payments	**0**	**0**	**367**	**504**	**840**	**1,136**	**916**	**759**
Public and publicly guaranteed	0	0	237	264	415	354	348	321
Official creditors	0	0	194	219	369	328	303	241
Multilateral	0	0	134	143	174	186	175	113
of which: IBRD	0	0	99	106	112	96	98	44
IDA	0	0	4	4	5	5	5	5
Bilateral	0	0	60	76	195	142	128	128
Private creditors	0	0	44	45	46	26	45	80
of which: Bonds	0	0	0	0	0	0	0	0
Commercial banks	0	0	44	45	46	26	45	80
Private nonguaranteed	0	0	129	240	425	782	568	438
of which: Bonds	0	0	0	0	7	10	10	10
8. Debt stock-flow reconciliation								
Total change in external debt stocks	-315	599	1,604	3,722	6,322	4,284	2,705	-890
Net flows on external debt	120	51	2,827	3,868	4,216	4,948	2,396	1,178
9. Debt restructurings								
Total amount rescheduled	0	0	8	0	0	0	205	0
Total amount forgiven	0	0	59	610	14	0	0	0
Debt buyback	0	0	0	0	0	0	0	0

10. Contractual obligations on outstanding long-term external debt

	2011	2012	2013	2014	2015	2016	2017	2018
Official creditors								
Principal	403	503	622	688	756	797	751	789
Interest	200	211	212	208	198	186	171	156
Private creditors								
Principal	4,054	3,140	2,580	2,279	1,684	1,306	566	551
Interest	638	524	435	338	251	171	125	97

Notes:

Beginning 2006, the DRS data for Serbia exclude Montenegro. Short-term debt is based on Central Bank data.

SEYCHELLES

(US$ million, unless otherwise indicated)

	1995	2000	2005	2006	2007	2008	2009	2010
1. Summary external debt data								
External debt stocks	**198**	**304**	**671**	**1,097**	**1,410**	**1,501**	**1,723**	**1,510**
Long-term external debt	185	220	398	504	626	650	736	498
Public and publicly guaranteed	185	220	398	504	626	650	736	498
Private nonguaranteed	0	0	0	0	0	0	0	0
Use of IMF credit	0	0	0	0	0	9	19	31
Short-term external debt	13	84	273	593	784	842	968	980
interest arrears on long-term	2	5	57	48	60	78	110	24
Memorandum items								
Principal arrears on long-term	20	21	116	101	113	114	234	45
Long-term public sector debt	185	220	398	504	626	650	736	498
Long-term private sector debt	0	0	0	0	0	0	0	0
Public & publicly guaranteed commitments	9	32	56	248	141	104	40	25
External debt flows								
Disbursements	17	38	59	211	151	94	43	62
Long-term external debt	17	38	59	211	151	84	34	49
IMF purchases	0	0	0	0	0	10	9	13
Principal repayments	16	10	41	124	46	53	43	9
Long-term external debt	16	10	41	124	46	53	43	9
IMF repurchases	0	0	0	0	0	0	0	0
Net flows	-9	71	180	416	284	81	93	151
Long-term external debt	1	29	18	87	105	31	-10	40
Short-term external debt	-10	42	162	329	179	40	94	98
Interest payments	8	11	18	53	64	39	18	40
Long-term external debt	7	7	11	29	28	21	8	28
IMF charges	0	0	0	0	0	0	0	0
Short-term external debt	1	4	7	24	36	18	10	12
2. Other non-debt resource inflows								
Foreign direct investment	46	24	86	146	249	241	275	369
Portfolio equity	0	0	..	..	..	..	..	..
3. Currency composition of public and publicly guaranteed debt (%)								
Euro	..	..	13.7	12.9	23.1	20.0	29.7	22.6
Japanese yen	0.0	2.1	1.8	1.2	1.0	1.2	1.0	0.0
Pound sterling	7.8	6.5	4.2	3.7	2.8	2.0	3.5	2.2
Swiss franc	6.0	4.5	2.9	2.5	2.0	2.1	1.9	0.0
U.S.dollars	14.1	35.6	55.3	67.7	61.5	65.8	55.4	60.4
4. Average terms of new commitments								
Official creditors								
Interest (%)	4.3	3.3	2.0	4.9	4.2	2.0	1.4	2.4
Maturity (years)	18.2	12.3	14.4	14.0	11.2	13.8	21.4	25.2
Grace period (years)	4.7	2.4	4.8	3.8	5.0	3.0	6.7	10.2
Private creditors								
Interest (%)	0.0	4.4	6.1	9.1	2.8	5.1	7.1	2.5
Maturity (years)	0.0	9.2	5.9	5.1	3.4	2.8	5.1	18.4
Grace period (years)	0.0	2.5	0.9	4.6	2.1	0.4	0.2	6.9
5. Major economic aggregates								
Gross national income (GNI)	489	583	844	924	955	836	702	855
Exports of goods, services & income	345	492	729	861	874	979	841	845
Worker remit. & comp. of employees	1	3	12	13	11	8	12	11
Imports of goods, services & income	350	545	935	1,038	1,187	1,449	1,152	1,354
Profit remittances on FDI	14	8	20	25	29	46	48	52
Current account balance	1	-43	-174	-134	-264	-407	-253	-484
International reserves	27	44	56	113	41	64	191	236
6. Ratios								
External debt stocks to exports (%)	57.4	61.7	92.0	127.5	161.4	153.3	204.9	178.7
External debt stocks to GNI (%)	40.5	52.1	79.5	118.7	147.7	179.5	245.5	176.7
Debt service to exports (%)	6.9	4.2	8.0	20.6	12.6	9.4	7.3	5.7
Short-term to external debt stocks (%)	6.6	27.7	40.7	54.1	55.6	56.1	56.2	64.9
Multilateral to external debt stocks (%)	31.9	19.0	10.7	3.8	3.6	2.9	2.6	4.9
Reserves to external debt stocks (%)	13.7	14.4	8.4	10.3	2.9	4.3	11.1	15.6
Reserves to imports (months)	0.9	1.0	0.7	1.3	0.4	0.5	2.0	2.1

SEYCHELLES

(US$ million, unless otherwise indicated)

	1995	2000	2005	2006	2007	2008	2009	2010
7. Long-term external debt								
Debt outstanding and disbursed	**185**	**220**	**398**	**504**	**626**	**650**	**736**	**498**
Public and publicly guaranteed	185	220	398	504	626	650	736	498
Official creditors	149	159	224	207	210	196	300	248
Multilateral	63	58	72	42	51	44	45	74
of which: IBRD	5	3	2	0	0	0	0	17
IDA	0	0	0	0	0	0	0	0
Bilateral	85	101	152	165	159	152	255	174
Private creditors	36	61	175	297	416	453	436	250
of which: Bonds	0	0	0	200	311	305	307	169
Commercial banks	22	50	86	73	85	135	115	67
Private nonguaranteed	0	0	0	0	0	0	0	0
of which: Bonds	0	0	0	0	0	0	0	0
Disbursements	**17**	**38**	**59**	**211**	**151**	**84**	**34**	**49**
Public and publicly guaranteed	17	38	59	211	151	84	34	49
Official creditors	17	19	8	6	11	4	25	33
Multilateral	9	7	5	3	11	0	16	33
of which: IBRD	1	0	0	0	0	0	0	18
IDA	0	0	0	0	0	0	0	0
Bilateral	7	12	3	3	0	4	9	0
Private creditors	0	19	51	204	140	80	9	16
of which: Bonds	0	0	0	200	105	0	0	0
Commercial banks	0	19	48	4	35	80	9	16
Private nonguaranteed	0	0	0	0	0	0	0	0
of which: Bonds	0	0	0	0	0	0	0	0
Principal repayments	**16**	**10**	**41**	**124**	**46**	**53**	**43**	**9**
Public and publicly guaranteed	16	10	41	124	46	53	43	9
Official creditors	7	5	11	42	20	15	18	6
Multilateral	4	2	2	36	4	6	16	3
of which: IBRD	1	1	1	2	0	0	0	0
IDA	0	0	0	0	0	0	0	0
Bilateral	3	3	9	6	16	8	2	3
Private creditors	9	5	30	82	26	38	25	3
of which: Bonds	0	0	0	0	0	2	0	0
Commercial banks	5	2	14	17	23	31	25	3
Private nonguaranteed	0	0	0	0	0	0	0	0
of which: Bonds	0	0	0	0	0	0	0	0
Interest payments	**7**	**7**	**11**	**29**	**28**	**21**	**8**	**28**
Public and publicly guaranteed	7	7	11	29	28	21	8	28
Official creditors	5	2	3	22	3	4	4	2
Multilateral	4	1	1	20	2	2	2	1
of which: IBRD	0	0	0	0	0	0	0	0
IDA	0	0	0	0	0	0	0	0
Bilateral	1	1	2	2	1	1	2	1
Private creditors	2	5	8	7	25	18	4	26
of which: Bonds	0	0	0	0	19	10	0	20
Commercial banks	1	4	4	2	5	7	4	5
Private nonguaranteed	0	0	0	0	0	0	0	0
of which: Bonds	0	0	0	0	0	0	0	0
8. Debt stock-flow reconciliation								
Total change in external debt stocks	-2	52	227	426	312	92	221	-213
Net flows on external debt	-9	71	180	416	284	81	93	151
9. Debt restructurings								
Total amount rescheduled	0	0	26	7	0	4	103	243
Total amount forgiven	0	0	7	0	0	0	8	192
Debt buyback	0	0	0	0	0	0	0	0

10. Contractual obligations on outstanding long-term external debt

	2011	2012	2013	2014	2015	2016	2017	2018
Official creditors								
Principal	14	14	17	21	17	17	16	15
Interest	3	2	2	2	2	2	1	1
Private creditors								
Principal	3	6	8	8	8	17	25	22
Interest	6	6	6	6	6	6	5	5

SIERRA LEONE

(US$ million, unless otherwise indicated)

	1995	*2000*	*2005*	*2006*	*2007*	*2008*	*2009*	*2010*
1. Summary external debt data								
External debt stocks	**1219.6**	**1189.8**	**1750.8**	**1473.9**	**523.6**	**607.1**	**701.0**	**778.0**
Long-term external debt	1027.7	972.8	1538.2	1428.4	482.1	544.9	604.8	660.9
Public and publicly guaranteed	1027.7	972.8	1538.2	1428.4	482.1	544.9	604.8	660.9
Private nonguaranteed	0.0	0.0	0.0	0.0	0.0	0.0	0.0	0.0
Use of IMF credit	164.9	173.6	192.1	34.8	36.5	53.2	73.2	113.0
Short-term external debt	26.9	43.5	20.6	10.7	5.1	9.0	23.0	4.1
interest arrears on long-term	6.9	36.3	10.6	10.7	0.1	0.0	0.0	0.1
Memorandum items								
Principal arrears on long-term	107.6	66.0	246.4	249.6	220.0	219.7	219.5	219.5
Long-term public sector debt	943.6	972.8	1538.2	1428.4	482.1	544.9	604.8	660.9
Long-term private sector debt	84.1	0.0	0.0	0.0	0.0	0.0	0.0	0.0
Public & publicly guaranteed commitments	47.7	65.0	42.6	48.2	64.9	67.2	92.1	95.6
External debt flows								
Disbursements	114.8	90.3	71.4	40.3	31.4	87.0	81.0	109.3
Long-term external debt	95.0	76.6	50.7	26.9	31.4	68.9	62.2	66.5
IMF purchases	19.8	13.7	20.7	13.4	0.0	18.0	18.8	42.8
Principal repayments	60.1	34.9	7.3	12.3	5.1	2.4	3.4	7.0
Long-term external debt	56.6	9.6	4.8	7.8	5.1	2.4	3.4	4.9
IMF repurchases	3.5	25.2	2.4	4.5	0.0	0.0	0.0	2.1
Net flows	54.7	56.8	54.2	18.0	31.4	88.5	91.6	83.3
Long-term external debt	38.4	66.9	45.9	19.1	26.4	66.5	58.8	61.6
Short-term external debt	0.0	1.4	-10.0	-10.0	5.0	4.0	14.0	-19.0
Interest payments	22.0	11.8	10.3	11.3	4.7	3.3	4.5	4.1
Long-term external debt	19.8	8.9	9.1	10.4	4.4	2.9	3.7	4.0
IMF charges	0.8	2.5	0.9	1.0	0.2	0.2	0.3	0.0
Short-term external debt	1.4	0.4	0.4	0.0	0.1	0.2	0.5	0.1
2. Other non-debt resource inflows								
Foreign direct investment	7.3	39.0	83.2	58.8	96.6	57.6	74.3	86.6
Portfolio equity	0.0	0.0	..	..	..	..	5.6	..
3. Currency composition of public and publicly guaranteed debt (%)								
Euro	..	..	10.4	8.8	5.2	3.9	3.2	2.4
Japanese yen	7.6	7.1	7.4	7.9	0.0	0.0	0.0	0.0
Pound sterling	0.5	0.6	0.3	0.3	0.0	0.0	0.0	0.0
Swiss franc	2.9	2.2	1.5	1.8	0.1	0.0	0.0	0.0
U.S.dollars	41.0	44.9	55.0	53.0	68.3	64.5	63.9	64.3
4. Average terms of new commitments								
Official creditors								
Interest (%)	0.6	0.8	1.0	1.2	1.1	1.0	1.4	0.8
Maturity (years)	32.6	39.8	34.1	25.5	21.8	31.9	29.7	32.5
Grace period (years)	7.8	10.3	8.5	8.4	5.5	9.2	8.9	8.6
Private creditors								
Interest (%)	0.0	0.0	0.0	0.0	0.0	0.0	0.0	0.0
Maturity (years)	0.0	0.0	0.0	0.0	0.0	0.0	0.0	0.0
Grace period (years)	0.0	0.0	0.0	0.0	0.0	0.0	0.0	0.0
5. Major economic aggregates								
Gross national income (GNI)	818.5	616.1	1176.0	1364.2	1629.1	1915.7	1856.4	1905.0
Exports of goods, services & income	129.0	62.5	267.2	316.7	377.5	352.6	339.8	432.6
Worker remit. & comp. of employees	23.7	7.1	2.4	15.6	42.0	27.5	46.8	57.5
Imports of goods, services & income	290.3	262.4	509.3	489.0	641.0	689.1	681.3	937.7
Profit remittances on FDI	11.3	1.8	41.2	27.3	121.8	76.0	39.0	46.2
Current account balance	-118.1	-112.3	-104.9	-95.0	-160.1	-225.4	-193.8	-320.1
International reserves	34.6	49.2	170.5	183.9	216.6	220.2	405.0	409.0
6. Ratios								
External debt stocks to exports (%)	945.2	1904.6	655.3	465.4	138.7	172.2	206.3	179.9
External debt stocks to GNI (%)	149.0	193.1	148.9	108.0	32.1	31.7	37.8	40.8
Debt service to exports (%)	63.6	74.8	6.6	7.5	2.6	1.6	2.3	2.6
Short-term to external debt stocks (%)	2.2	3.7	1.2	0.7	1.0	1.5	3.3	0.5
Multilateral to external debt stocks (%)	35.6	48.4	49.3	57.8	42.5	45.0	46.0	47.7
Reserves to external debt stocks (%)	2.8	4.1	9.7	12.5	41.4	36.3	57.8	52.6
Reserves to imports (months)	1.4	2.3	4.0	4.5	4.1	3.8	7.1	5.2

SIERRA LEONE

(US$ million, unless otherwise indicated)

	1995	2000	2005	2006	2007	2008	2009	2010
7. Long-term external debt								
Debt outstanding and disbursed	**1027.7**	**972.8**	**1538.2**	**1428.4**	**482.1**	**544.9**	**604.8**	**660.9**
Public and publicly guaranteed	1027.7	972.8	1538.2	1428.4	482.1	544.9	604.8	660.9
Official creditors	935.5	967.5	1325.5	1217.2	271.0	333.8	393.7	449.8
Multilateral	433.6	576.0	863.6	852.1	222.7	273.0	322.3	371.2
of which: IBRD	2.9	0.0	0.0	0.0	0.0	0.0	0.0	0.0
IDA	231.3	353.7	558.6	533.5	83.6	108.4	124.3	154.6
Bilateral	501.9	391.5	461.9	365.1	48.3	60.8	71.4	78.5
Private creditors	92.2	5.3	212.7	211.2	211.1	211.1	211.1	211.1
of which: Bonds	0.0	0.0	0.0	0.0	0.0	0.0	0.0	0.0
Commercial banks	0.0	0.0	211.1	211.1	211.1	211.1	211.1	211.1
Private nonguaranteed	0.0	0.0	0.0	0.0	0.0	0.0	0.0	0.0
of which: Bonds	0.0	0.0	0.0	0.0	0.0	0.0	0.0	0.0
Disbursements	**95.0**	**76.6**	**50.7**	**26.9**	**31.4**	**68.9**	**62.2**	**66.5**
Public and publicly guaranteed	95.0	76.6	50.7	26.9	31.4	68.9	62.2	66.5
Official creditors	95.0	76.6	50.7	26.9	31.4	68.9	62.2	66.5
Multilateral	87.3	74.4	49.5	25.5	27.5	55.6	51.0	59.4
of which: IBRD	0.0	0.0	0.0	0.0	0.0	0.0	0.0	0.0
IDA	44.0	70.1	18.7	16.3	14.2	25.7	15.1	32.1
Bilateral	7.7	2.2	1.3	1.4	3.9	13.4	11.2	7.1
Private creditors	0.0	0.0	0.0	0.0	0.0	0.0	0.0	0.0
of which: Bonds	0.0	0.0	0.0	0.0	0.0	0.0	0.0	0.0
Commercial banks	0.0	0.0	0.0	0.0	0.0	0.0	0.0	0.0
Private nonguaranteed	0.0	0.0	0.0	0.0	0.0	0.0	0.0	0.0
of which: Bonds	0.0	0.0	0.0	0.0	0.0	0.0	0.0	0.0
Principal repayments	**56.6**	**9.6**	**4.8**	**7.8**	**5.1**	**2.4**	**3.4**	**4.9**
Public and publicly guaranteed	56.6	9.6	4.8	7.8	5.1	2.4	3.4	4.9
Official creditors	28.2	9.6	4.8	7.8	5.1	2.4	3.4	4.9
Multilateral	3.5	7.5	1.8	5.0	2.5	1.3	2.0	3.9
of which: IBRD	0.5	0.3	0.0	0.0	0.0	0.0	0.0	0.0
IDA	1.6	1.8	0.2	0.4	0.0	0.0	0.0	0.0
Bilateral	24.7	2.2	3.1	2.8	2.5	1.2	1.3	1.0
Private creditors	28.4	0.0	0.0	0.0	0.0	0.0	0.0	0.0
of which: Bonds	0.0	0.0	0.0	0.0	0.0	0.0	0.0	0.0
Commercial banks	28.4	0.0	0.0	0.0	0.0	0.0	0.0	0.0
Private nonguaranteed	0.0	0.0	0.0	0.0	0.0	0.0	0.0	0.0
of which: Bonds	0.0	0.0	0.0	0.0	0.0	0.0	0.0	0.0
Interest payments	**19.8**	**8.9**	**9.1**	**10.4**	**4.4**	**2.9**	**3.7**	**4.0**
Public and publicly guaranteed	19.8	8.9	9.1	10.4	4.4	2.9	3.7	4.0
Official creditors	19.8	8.9	9.1	10.4	4.4	2.9	3.7	4.0
Multilateral	2.9	3.5	5.9	6.5	2.8	2.2	2.6	2.8
of which: IBRD	0.3	0.0	0.0	0.0	0.0	0.0	0.0	0.0
IDA	1.6	2.3	3.5	3.5	0.6	0.7	0.8	0.9
Bilateral	16.9	5.4	3.1	3.9	1.6	0.7	1.1	1.1
Private creditors	0.0	0.0	0.0	0.0	0.0	0.0	0.0	0.0
of which: Bonds	0.0	0.0	0.0	0.0	0.0	0.0	0.0	0.0
Commercial banks	0.0	0.0	0.0	0.0	0.0	0.0	0.0	0.0
Private nonguaranteed	0.0	0.0	0.0	0.0	0.0	0.0	0.0	0.0
of which: Bonds	0.0	0.0	0.0	0.0	0.0	0.0	0.0	0.0
8. Debt stock-flow reconciliation								
Total change in external debt stocks	-309.6	-70.8	123.2	-276.9	-950.3	83.4	93.9	77.0
Net flows on external debt	54.7	56.8	54.2	18.0	31.4	88.5	91.6	83.3
9. Debt restructurings								
Total amount rescheduled	29.3	0.4	4.7	4.6	8.8	8.1	11.6	0.0
Total amount forgiven	329.4	0.0	34.2	256.2	958.7	7.0	3.6	3.5
Debt buyback	29.4	0.0	0.0	0.0	0.0	0.0	0.0	0.0

10. Contractual obligations on outstanding long-term external debt

	2011	2012	2013	2014	2015	2016	2017	2018
Official creditors								
Principal	14.2	16.4	15.2	17.6	20.8	22.2	37.1	34.1
Interest	5.2	6.0	6.2	6.3	6.3	6.1	5.7	5.1
Private creditors								
Principal	0.0	0.0	0.0	0.0	0.0	0.0	0.0	0.0
Interest	0.0	0.0	0.0	0.0	0.0	0.0	0.0	0.0

Notes:

Data on public and publicly guaranteed debt owed to commercial banks are revised from 2005. Data include the effects of Paris Club debt restructuring agreement signed in 2007. Data for 2007 include the effects of MDRI and HIPC debt relief, in the amount of $526 million.

SOLOMON ISLANDS

(US$ million, unless otherwise indicated)

	1995	2000	2005	2006	2007	2008	2009	2010
1. Summary external debt data								
External debt stocks	**158.7**	**155.4**	**166.5**	**173.5**	**177.3**	**165.9**	**155.9**	**215.5**
Long-term external debt	149.1	152.1	151.2	157.9	173.9	162.8	154.4	201.9
Public and publicly guaranteed	100.3	120.7	144.2	150.9	148.1	137.1	132.9	125.3
Private nonguaranteed	48.8	31.5	7.0	7.0	25.9	25.8	21.5	76.6
Use of IMF credit	0.0	0.0	0.0	0.0	0.0	0.0	0.0	9.6
Short-term external debt	9.7	3.2	15.3	15.6	3.4	3.1	1.5	4.0
interest arrears on long-term	8.4	1.8	12.3	13.6	3.4	3.1	1.5	4.0
Memorandum items								
Principal arrears on long-term	11.4	3.3	11.4	13.7	13.0	9.4	8.9	9.1
Long-term public sector debt	100.3	120.7	144.2	150.9	148.1	137.1	132.9	125.3
Long-term private sector debt	48.8	31.5	7.0	7.0	25.9	25.8	21.5	76.6
Public & publicly guaranteed commitments	12.3	4.0	0.4	0.6	0.0	0.0	0.0	0.0
External debt flows								
Disbursements	11.8	3.4	5.7	5.1	24.5	1.1	13.7	46.4
Long-term external debt	11.8	3.4	5.7	5.1	24.5	1.1	13.7	36.8
IMF purchases	0.0	0.0	0.0	0.0	0.0	0.0	0.0	9.5
Principal repayments	6.5	6.2	10.0	2.8	10.7	10.8	7.6	17.5
Long-term external debt	6.5	6.2	10.0	2.8	10.7	10.8	7.6	17.5
IMF repurchases	0.0	0.0	0.0	0.0	0.0	0.0	0.0	0.0
Net flows	4.5	-4.4	-2.3	1.2	11.8	-9.7	6.1	28.9
Long-term external debt	5.3	-2.9	-4.3	2.2	13.8	-9.7	6.1	19.4
Short-term external debt	-0.8	-1.5	2.0	-1.0	-2.0	0.0	0.0	0.0
Interest payments	1.6	2.9	4.0	1.5	3.3	4.3	2.4	3.2
Long-term external debt	1.5	2.7	3.9	1.3	3.2	4.3	2.4	3.2
IMF charges	0.0	0.0	0.0	0.0	0.0	0.0	0.0	0.0
Short-term external debt	0.1	0.1	0.1	0.2	0.1	0.0	0.0	0.0
2. Other non-debt resource inflows								
Foreign direct investment	2.0	13.0	18.6	34.1	64.4	94.9	117.6	237.8
Portfolio equity	0.0	0.0	..	..	..	..	..	..
3. Currency composition of public and publicly guaranteed debt (%)								
Euro	..	..	7.1	7.6	9.2	7.2	7.3	5.1
Japanese yen	3.8	3.4	2.8	2.6	0.0	0.0	0.0	0.0
Pound sterling	6.4	2.9	0.0	0.0	0.0	0.0	0.0	0.0
Swiss franc	0.0	0.0	0.0	0.0	0.0	0.0	0.0	0.0
U.S.dollars	53.9	67.1	73.7	73.9	75.4	78.0	77.7	79.2
4. Average terms of new commitments								
Official creditors								
Interest (%)	3.4	0.8	0.0	0.0	0.0	0.0	3.5	0.0
Maturity (years)	18.9	40.0	0.0	0.0	0.0	0.0	24.5	0.0
Grace period (years)	3.6	10.5	0.0	0.0	0.0	0.0	3.5	0.0
Private creditors								
Interest (%)	7.8	0.0	5.0	0.0	0.0	0.0	0.0	0.0
Maturity (years)	10.2	0.0	5.1	4.0	0.0	0.0	0.0	0.0
Grace period (years)	0.7	0.0	0.0	0.6	0.0	0.0	0.0	0.0
5. Major economic aggregates								
Gross national income (GNI)	320.7	435.5	415.5	460.9	549.7	551.5	473.1	554.7
Exports of goods, services & income	211.3	128.8	154.9	179.6	237.7	289.7	248.8	349.1
Worker remit. & comp. of employees	..	4.3	7.2	1.9	2.1	1.7	2.4	2.9
Imports of goods, services & income	239.4	176.4	250.1	294.9	411.4	524.0	476.2	676.9
Profit remittances on FDI	6.8	8.3	5.3	23.6	41.0	103.5	125.4	..
Current account balance	8.3	-41.0	-90.2	-42.7	-80.9	-124.4	-120.8	-196.6
International reserves	15.9	32.0	95.4	104.4	119.1	89.5	146.0	265.8
6. Ratios								
External debt stocks to exports (%)	75.1	120.6	107.5	96.6	74.6	57.3	62.7	61.7
External debt stocks to GNI (%)	49.5	35.7	40.1	37.6	32.3	30.1	33.0	38.8
Debt service to exports (%)	3.8	7.1	9.1	2.4	5.9	5.2	4.0	5.9
Short-term to external debt stocks (%)	6.1	2.1	9.2	9.0	1.9	1.8	1.0	1.9
Multilateral to external debt stocks (%)	50.1	64.6	64.3	65.6	68.6	68.5	71.5	49.0
Reserves to external debt stocks (%)	10.0	20.6	57.3	60.2	67.1	54.0	93.6	123.4
Reserves to imports (months)	0.8	2.2	4.6	4.2	3.5	2.1	3.7	4.7

(US$ million, unless otherwise indicated)

	1995	2000	2005	2006	2007	2008	2009	2010
7. Long-term external debt								
Debt outstanding and disbursed	**149.1**	**152.1**	**151.2**	**157.9**	**173.9**	**162.8**	**154.4**	**201.9**
Public and publicly guaranteed	100.3	120.7	144.2	150.9	148.1	137.1	132.9	125.3
Official creditors	95.1	117.3	143.8	149.9	147.5	136.6	132.7	125.2
Multilateral	79.5	100.4	107.0	113.7	121.7	113.7	111.5	105.6
of which: IBRD	0.0	0.0	0.0	0.0	0.0	0.0	0.0	0.0
IDA	25.9	38.4	43.4	44.9	45.8	44.5	43.7	41.7
Bilateral	15.6	16.9	36.8	36.2	25.8	23.0	21.2	19.6
Private creditors	5.2	3.4	0.4	1.0	0.6	0.4	0.2	0.1
of which: Bonds	0.0	0.0	0.0	0.0	0.0	0.0	0.0	0.0
Commercial banks	0.0	0.0	0.0	0.0	0.0	0.0	0.0	0.0
Private nonguaranteed	48.8	31.5	7.0	7.0	25.9	25.8	21.5	76.6
of which: Bonds	0.0	0.0	0.0	0.0	0.0	0.0	0.0	0.0
Disbursements	**11.8**	**3.4**	**5.7**	**5.1**	**24.5**	**1.1**	**13.7**	**36.8**
Public and publicly guaranteed	9.1	3.4	5.7	5.1	4.5	0.1	0.0	0.0
Official creditors	4.8	3.4	5.3	4.4	4.5	0.1	0.0	0.0
Multilateral	4.8	1.4	5.3	4.4	4.5	0.1	0.0	0.0
of which: IBRD	0.0	0.0	0.0	0.0	0.0	0.0	0.0	0.0
IDA	3.2	0.6	0.9	0.3	0.0	0.0	0.0	0.0
Bilateral	0.0	2.0	0.0	0.0	0.0	0.0	0.0	0.0
Private creditors	4.2	0.0	0.4	0.6	0.0	0.0	0.0	0.0
of which: Bonds	0.0	0.0	0.0	0.0	0.0	0.0	0.0	0.0
Commercial banks	0.0	0.0	0.0	0.0	0.0	0.0	0.0	0.0
Private nonguaranteed	2.8	0.0	0.0	0.0	20.0	1.0	13.7	36.8
of which: Bonds	0.0	0.0	0.0	0.0	0.0	0.0	0.0	0.0
Principal repayments	**6.5**	**6.2**	**10.0**	**2.8**	**10.7**	**10.8**	**7.6**	**17.5**
Public and publicly guaranteed	1.8	2.7	5.8	2.8	8.3	10.8	6.5	8.6
Official creditors	1.3	2.7	3.2	2.8	7.9	10.7	6.3	8.4
Multilateral	0.6	1.1	2.0	2.1	2.6	7.8	4.6	6.8
of which: IBRD	0.0	0.0	0.0	0.0	0.0	0.0	0.0	0.0
IDA	0.1	0.2	0.8	0.9	1.0	1.0	1.1	1.2
Bilateral	0.7	1.6	1.2	0.6	5.3	2.8	1.7	1.6
Private creditors	0.5	0.0	2.6	0.1	0.4	0.1	0.2	0.2
of which: Bonds	0.0	0.0	0.0	0.0	0.0	0.0	0.0	0.0
Commercial banks	0.0	0.0	0.0	0.0	0.0	0.0	0.0	0.0
Private nonguaranteed	4.7	3.5	4.2	0.0	2.4	0.0	1.1	8.9
of which: Bonds	0.0	0.0	0.0	0.0	0.0	0.0	0.0	0.0
Interest payments	**1.5**	**2.7**	**3.9**	**1.3**	**3.2**	**4.3**	**2.4**	**3.2**
Public and publicly guaranteed	0.9	0.8	1.7	1.3	3.2	4.3	1.8	1.7
Official creditors	0.8	0.8	1.7	1.3	3.2	4.3	1.8	1.7
Multilateral	0.5	0.7	0.8	0.8	0.9	2.8	1.0	1.0
of which: IBRD	0.0	0.0	0.0	0.0	0.0	0.0	0.0	0.0
IDA	0.2	0.3	0.3	0.3	0.3	0.4	0.3	0.3
Bilateral	0.3	0.1	0.9	0.4	2.3	1.5	0.8	0.7
Private creditors	0.1	0.0	0.0	0.0	0.0	0.0	0.0	0.0
of which: Bonds	0.0	0.0	0.0	0.0	0.0	0.0	0.0	0.0
Commercial banks	0.0	0.0	0.0	0.0	0.0	0.0	0.0	0.0
Private nonguaranteed	0.6	1.9	2.3	0.0	0.0	0.0	0.5	1.5
of which: Bonds	0.0	0.0	0.0	0.0	0.0	0.0	0.0	0.0
8. Debt stock-flow reconciliation								
Total change in external debt stocks	3.8	-9.6	-10.6	7.1	3.8	-11.4	-10.0	59.6
Net flows on external debt	4.5	-4.4	-2.3	1.2	11.8	-9.7	6.1	28.9
9. Debt restructurings								
Total amount rescheduled	0.0	7.8	0.0	0.0	0.0	0.0	0.0	0.0
Total amount forgiven	6.3	0.0	8.1	0.0	4.9	0.0	0.0	0.0
Debt buyback	0.0	0.0	0.0	0.0	0.0	0.0	0.0	0.0

10. Contractual obligations on outstanding long-term external debt

	2011	2012	2013	2014	2015	2016	2017	2018
Official creditors								
Principal	7.5	7.4	6.9	6.9	6.4	6.4	6.2	5.8
Interest	1.8	1.7	1.6	1.5	1.4	1.3	1.2	1.1
Private creditors								
Principal	6.8	6.8	6.8	6.8	6.8	6.8	6.8	6.8
Interest	0.3	0.3	0.2	0.2	0.2	0.2	0.1	0.1

SOMALIA

(US$ million, unless otherwise indicated)

	1995	2000	2005	2006	2007	2008	2009	2010
1. Summary external debt data								
External debt stocks	**2,670**	**2,548**	**2,730**	**2,814**	**2,919**	**2,922**	**2,944**	**2,942**
Long-term external debt	1,961	1,825	1,882	1,923	1,979	1,983	1,987	1,990
Public and publicly guaranteed	1,961	1,825	1,882	1,923	1,979	1,983	1,987	1,990
Private nonguaranteed	0	0	0	0	0	0	0	0
Use of IMF credit	166	146	160	168	177	173	176	172
Short-term external debt	543	577	689	723	763	766	781	780
interest arrears on long-term	512	555	689	723	763	766	781	780
Memorandum items								
Principal arrears on long-term	1,120	1,218	1,423	1,481	1,554	1,580	1,614	1,646
Long-term public sector debt	1,961	1,825	1,882	1,923	1,979	1,983	1,987	1,990
Long-term private sector debt	0	0	0	0	0	0	0	0
Public & publicly guaranteed commitments	0	0	0	0	0	0	0	0
External debt flows								
Disbursements	0	0	0	0	0	0	0	0
Long-term external debt	0	0	0	0	0	0	0	0
IMF purchases	0	0	0	0	0	0	0	0
Principal repayments	0	0	0	0	0	0	0	0
Long-term external debt	0	0	0	0	0	0	0	0
IMF repurchases	0	0	0	0	0	0	0	0
Net flows	0	-7	0	0	0	0	0	0
Long-term external debt	0	0	0	0	0	0	0	0
Short-term external debt	0	-7	0	0	0	0	0	0
Interest payments	1	0	0	0	0	2	0	0
Long-term external debt	0	0	0	0	0	0	0	0
IMF charges	1	0	0	0	0	2	0	0
Short-term external debt	0	0	0	0	0	0	0	0
2. Other non-debt resource inflows								
Foreign direct investment	1	0	24	96	141	87	108	112
Portfolio equity	..	..	..	..	..	..	..	..
3. Currency composition of public and publicly guaranteed debt (%)								
Euro	..	..	5.6	6.1	6.6	6.3	6.5	6.0
Japanese yen	3.1	3.0	2.8	2.7	2.8	3.5	3.4	3.8
Pound sterling	0.1	0.1	0.1	0.2	0.2	0.1	0.1	0.1
Swiss franc	0.0	0.0	0.0	0.0	0.0	0.0	0.0	0.0
U.S.dollars	50.2	52.0	51.8	51.4	50.6	50.4	50.4	50.0
4. Average terms of new commitments								
Official creditors								
Interest (%)	0.0	0.0	0.0	0.0	0.0	0.0	0.0	0.0
Maturity (years)	0.0	0.0	0.0	0.0	0.0	0.0	0.0	0.0
Grace period (years)	0.0	0.0	0.0	0.0	0.0	0.0	0.0	0.0
Private creditors								
Interest (%)	0.0	0.0	0.0	0.0	0.0	0.0	0.0	0.0
Maturity (years)	0.0	0.0	0.0	0.0	0.0	0.0	0.0	0.0
Grace period (years)	0.0	0.0	0.0	0.0	0.0	0.0	0.0	0.0
5. Major economic aggregates								
Gross national income (GNI)	..	..	..	..	..	..	..	..
Exports of goods, services & income	..	..	..	..	..	..	..	..
Worker remit. & comp. of employees	..	..	..	..	..	..	..	..
Imports of goods, services & income	..	..	..	..	..	..	..	..
Profit remittances on FDI	..	..	..	..	..	..	..	..
Current account balance	..	..	..	..	..	..	..	..
International reserves	..	..	..	..	..	..	..	..
6. Ratios								
External debt stocks to exports (%)	..	..	..	..	..	..	..	..
External debt stocks to GNI (%)	..	..	..	..	..	..	..	..
Debt service to exports (%)	..	..	..	..	..	..	..	..
Short-term to external debt stocks (%)	20.3	22.6	25.2	25.7	26.1	26.2	26.5	26.5
Multilateral to external debt stocks (%)	29.4	27.8	27.7	27.7	27.7	27.5	27.4	27.2
Reserves to external debt stocks (%)	..	..	..	..	..	..	..	..
Reserves to imports (months)	..	..	..	..	..	..	..	..

SOMALIA

(US$ million, unless otherwise indicated)

	1995	2000	2005	2006	2007	2008	2009	2010
7. Long-term external debt								
Debt outstanding and disbursed	**1,961**	**1,825**	**1,882**	**1,923**	**1,979**	**1,983**	**1,987**	**1,990**
Public and publicly guaranteed	1,961	1,825	1,882	1,923	1,979	1,983	1,987	1,990
Official creditors	1,924	1,792	1,846	1,886	1,940	1,946	1,950	1,954
Multilateral	786	709	755	779	808	803	805	801
of which: IBRD	0	0	0	0	0	0	0	0
IDA	432	396	422	435	448	446	448	443
Bilateral	1,138	1,083	1,091	1,107	1,132	1,143	1,145	1,153
Private creditors	37	33	35	37	38	37	38	37
of which: Bonds	0	0	0	0	0	0	0	0
Commercial banks	0	0	0	0	0	0	0	0
Private nonguaranteed	0	0	0	0	0	0	0	0
of which: Bonds	0	0	0	0	0	0	0	0
Disbursements	**0**	**0**	**0**	**0**	**0**	**0**	**0**	**0**
Public and publicly guaranteed	0	0	0	0	0	0	0	0
Official creditors	0	0	0	0	0	0	0	0
Multilateral	0	0	0	0	0	0	0	0
of which: IBRD	0	0	0	0	0	0	0	0
IDA	0	0	0	0	0	0	0	0
Bilateral	0	0	0	0	0	0	0	0
Private creditors	0	0	0	0	0	0	0	0
of which: Bonds	0	0	0	0	0	0	0	0
Commercial banks	0	0	0	0	0	0	0	0
Private nonguaranteed	0	0	0	0	0	0	0	0
of which: Bonds	0	0	0	0	0	0	0	0
Principal repayments	**0**	**0**	**0**	**0**	**0**	**0**	**0**	**0**
Public and publicly guaranteed	0	0	0	0	0	0	0	0
Official creditors	0	0	0	0	0	0	0	0
Multilateral	0	0	0	0	0	0	0	0
of which: IBRD	0	0	0	0	0	0	0	0
IDA	0	0	0	0	0	0	0	0
Bilateral	0	0	0	0	0	0	0	0
Private creditors	0	0	0	0	0	0	0	0
of which: Bonds	0	0	0	0	0	0	0	0
Commercial banks	0	0	0	0	0	0	0	0
Private nonguaranteed	0	0	0	0	0	0	0	0
of which: Bonds	0	0	0	0	0	0	0	0
Interest payments	**0**	**0**	**0**	**0**	**0**	**0**	**0**	**0**
Public and publicly guaranteed	0	0	0	0	0	0	0	0
Official creditors	0	0	0	0	0	0	0	0
Multilateral	0	0	0	0	0	0	0	0
of which: IBRD	0	0	0	0	0	0	0	0
IDA	0	0	0	0	0	0	0	0
Bilateral	0	0	0	0	0	0	0	0
Private creditors	0	0	0	0	0	0	0	0
of which: Bonds	0	0	0	0	0	0	0	0
Commercial banks	0	0	0	0	0	0	0	0
Private nonguaranteed	0	0	0	0	0	0	0	0
of which: Bonds	0	0	0	0	0	0	0	0
8. Debt stock-flow reconciliation								
Total change in external debt stocks	54	-45	-98	84	104	3	22	-1
Net flows on external debt	0	-7	0	0	0	0	0	0
9. Debt restructurings								
Total amount rescheduled	0	0	0	0	0	0	0	0
Total amount forgiven	0	0	0	0	0	0	0	0
Debt buyback	0	0	0	0	0	0	0	0

10. Contractual obligations on outstanding long-term external debt

	2011	2012	2013	2014	2015	2016	2017	2018
Official creditors								
Principal	35	33	32	34	29	28	28	26
Interest	6	6	5	5	5	4	4	4
Private creditors								
Principal	0	0	0	0	0	0	0	0
Interest	0	0	0	0	0	0	0	0

Notes:

Data on long-term public and publicly guaranteed debt are World Bank staff estimates based on the original terms of the loans.

SOUTH AFRICA

(US$ million, unless otherwise indicated)

	1995	2000	2005	2006	2007	2008	2009	2010
1. Summary external debt data								
External debt stocks	**25,358**	**24,861**	**31,070**	**35,523**	**43,610**	**42,551**	**42,466**	**45,165**
Long-term external debt	14,772	15,308	21,360	20,263	27,052	24,614	29,192	32,860
Public and publicly guaranteed	9,837	9,088	15,633	13,914	14,101	13,781	15,428	17,753
Private nonguaranteed	4,935	6,220	5,727	6,349	12,951	10,833	13,764	15,107
Use of IMF credit	913	0	0	0	0	0	0	0
Short-term external debt	9,673	9,553	9,710	15,260	16,558	17,937	13,274	12,305
interest arrears on long-term	0	0	0	0	0	0	0	0
Memorandum items								
Principal arrears on long-term	0	0	0	0	0	0	0	0
Long-term public sector debt	9,837	8,054	15,633	13,914	14,101	13,781	15,428	17,753
Long-term private sector debt	4,935	7,254	5,727	6,349	12,951	10,833	13,764	15,107
Public & publicly guaranteed commitments	3,225	2,223	2,270	1,876	1,870	1,216	7,578	6,614
External debt flows								
Disbursements	3,549	3,611	5,641	4,877	8,727	1,871	4,339	5,698
Long-term external debt	3,549	3,611	5,641	4,877	8,727	1,871	4,339	5,698
IMF purchases	0	0	0	0	0	0	0	0
Principal repayments	2,070	2,609	2,034	3,831	3,353	2,789	2,127	2,608
Long-term external debt	2,070	2,609	2,034	3,831	3,353	2,789	2,127	2,608
IMF repurchases	0	0	0	0	0	0	0	0
Net flows	3,412	-260	5,408	6,597	6,672	461	-2,451	2,121
Long-term external debt	1,478	1,002	3,607	1,047	5,374	-918	2,212	3,090
Short-term external debt	1,934	-1,262	1,801	5,550	1,298	1,379	-4,663	-969
Interest payments	1,320	1,252	1,198	1,639	1,911	1,769	1,615	2,476
Long-term external debt	855	743	846	1,183	1,330	1,251	1,146	2,092
IMF charges	50	0	0	0	0	0	0	0
Short-term external debt	415	509	352	456	581	517	468	384
2. Other non-debt resource inflows								
Foreign direct investment	1,248	969	6,522	-184	5,737	9,645	5,354	1,565
Portfolio equity	2,914	4,169	7,230	14,959	8,670	-4,707	9,364	5,826
3. Currency composition of public and publicly guaranteed debt (%)								
Euro	..	..	13.3	30.9	26.7	20.6	19.1	15.4
Japanese yen	3.0	3.8	0.0	0.0	0.0	0.0	0.0	0.0
Pound sterling	0.0	0.0	0.0	0.0	0.0	0.0	0.0	0.0
Swiss franc	0.0	0.0	0.0	0.0	0.0	0.0	0.0	0.0
U.S.dollars	90.6	92.0	85.0	67.1	71.4	77.7	79.6	80.4
4. Average terms of new commitments								
Official creditors								
Interest (%)	0.0	5.9	0.0	0.0	0.0	0.0	1.2	0.8
Maturity (years)	0.0	12.3	0.0	0.0	0.0	0.0	19.7	28.1
Grace period (years)	0.0	4.0	0.0	0.0	0.0	0.0	5.2	7.1
Private creditors								
Interest (%)	5.4	6.1	3.9	6.5	6.8	3.4	6.9	4.1
Maturity (years)	14.3	9.8	6.4	8.9	10.1	2.8	10.0	9.1
Grace period (years)	1.8	2.3	2.9	8.9	9.9	0.8	10.0	7.2
5. Major economic aggregates								
Gross national income (GNI)	148,238	129,704	242,122	255,872	276,401	266,336	276,439	356,475
Exports of goods, services & income	35,538	39,507	72,202	84,117	97,135	104,867	82,551	104,355
Worker remit. & comp. of employees	105	344	658	734	834	823	902	1,119
Imports of goods, services & income	37,386	38,771	78,267	95,499	114,803	122,618	91,193	112,194
Profit remittances on FDI	535	2,329	4,320	4,843	8,666	8,031	5,279	6,165
Current account balance	-2,493	-191	-8,518	-13,745	-20,018	-20,083	-11,327	-10,117
International reserves	4,464	7,702	20,624	25,593	32,919	34,070	39,603	43,820
6. Ratios								
External debt stocks to exports (%)	71.4	62.9	43.0	42.2	44.9	40.6	51.4	43.3
External debt stocks to GNI (%)	17.1	19.2	12.8	13.9	15.8	16.0	15.4	12.7
Debt service to exports (%)	9.5	9.8	4.5	6.5	5.4	4.3	4.5	4.9
Short-term to external debt stocks (%)	38.1	38.4	31.3	43.0	38.0	42.2	31.3	27.2
Multilateral to external debt stocks (%)	..	0.6	0.9	0.9	0.7	0.6	0.5	2.5
Reserves to external debt stocks (%)	17.6	31.0	66.4	72.0	75.5	80.1	93.3	97.0
Reserves to imports (months)	1.4	2.4	3.2	3.2	3.4	3.3	5.2	4.7

(US$ million, unless otherwise indicated)

	1995	2000	2005	2006	2007	2008	2009	2010
7. Long-term external debt								
Debt outstanding and disbursed	**14,772**	**15,308**	**21,360**	**20,263**	**27,052**	**24,614**	**29,192**	**32,860**
Public and publicly guaranteed	9,837	9,088	15,633	13,914	14,101	13,781	15,428	17,753
Official creditors	0	145	286	316	291	259	227	1,139
Multilateral	0	145	286	316	291	259	227	1,139
of which: IBRD	0	3	31	29	27	26	21	384
IDA	0	0	0	0	0	0	0	0
Bilateral	0	0	0	0	0	0	0	0
Private creditors	9,837	8,943	15,347	13,598	13,810	13,522	15,201	16,614
of which: Bonds	2,454	4,749	7,132	6,791	7,593	7,429	9,279	11,065
Commercial banks	3,978	1,973	7,271	6,009	5,563	5,585	5,559	5,331
Private nonguaranteed	4,935	6,220	5,727	6,349	12,951	10,833	13,764	15,107
of which: Bonds	350	1,110	1,307	1,484	6,715	6,017	6,049	5,471
Disbursements	**3,549**	**3,611**	**5,641**	**4,877**	**8,727**	**1,871**	**4,339**	**5,698**
Public and publicly guaranteed	3,199	1,597	2,678	2,075	1,870	1,219	2,332	3,777
Official creditors	0	91	58	49	0	3	32	913
Multilateral	0	91	58	49	0	3	32	913
of which: IBRD	0	3	9	0	0	3	0	371
IDA	0	0	0	0	0	0	0	0
Bilateral	0	0	0	0	0	0	0	0
Private creditors	3,199	1,506	2,620	2,026	1,870	1,216	2,300	2,864
of which: Bonds	391	765	0	1,876	1,670	0	2,000	2,000
Commercial banks	830	420	2,620	150	200	1,216	300	864
Private nonguaranteed	350	2,014	2,963	2,802	6,857	652	2,007	1,921
of which: Bonds	350	712	1,307	0	5,587	0	0	0
Principal repayments	**2,070**	**2,609**	**2,034**	**3,831**	**3,353**	**2,789**	**2,127**	**2,608**
Public and publicly guaranteed	1,168	1,627	1,780	1,729	1,855	1,465	1,419	1,278
Official creditors	0	0	27	26	26	26	38	40
Multilateral	0	0	27	26	26	26	38	40
of which: IBRD	0	0	1	2	3	3	5	8
IDA	0	0	0	0	0	0	0	0
Bilateral	0	0	0	0	0	0	0	0
Private creditors	1,168	1,627	1,753	1,703	1,829	1,439	1,381	1,238
of which: Bonds	10	284	0	300	1,222	0	250	0
Commercial banks	719	949	1,608	1,257	462	1,294	986	1,093
Private nonguaranteed	902	982	254	2,102	1,498	1,324	708	1,330
of which: Bonds	0	0	0	0	1,390	698	0	578
Interest payments	**855**	**743**	**846**	**1,183**	**1,330**	**1,251**	**1,146**	**2,092**
Public and publicly guaranteed	597	546	635	886	917	821	686	716
Official creditors	0	1	12	15	18	16	10	20
Multilateral	0	1	12	15	18	16	10	20
of which: IBRD	0	0	1	1	1	1	1	10
IDA	0	0	0	0	0	0	0	0
Bilateral	0	0	0	0	0	0	0	0
Private creditors	597	545	623	871	899	804	676	696
of which: Bonds	188	275	347	409	520	523	542	631
Commercial banks	245	130	212	408	333	244	105	45
Private nonguaranteed	258	196	212	297	413	431	460	1,377
of which: Bonds	0	27	61	89	132	241	241	1,027
8. Debt stock-flow reconciliation								
Total change in external debt stocks	3,687	954	3,958	4,453	8,087	-1,059	-85	2,698
Net flows on external debt	3,412	-260	5,408	6,597	6,672	461	-2,451	2,121
9. Debt restructurings								
Total amount rescheduled	0	0	0	0	0	0	0	0
Total amount forgiven	0	0	0	0	0	0	0	0
Debt buyback	0	0	0	0	1,222	0	0	0

10. Contractual obligations on outstanding long-term external debt

	2011	2012	2013	2014	2015	2016	2017	2018
Official creditors								
Principal	42	37	26	23	209	209	374	374
Interest	9	16	23	29	33	35	35	34
Private creditors								
Principal	4,328	6,326	5,509	4,179	1,941	2,081	1,386	528
Interest	2,069	1,889	1,493	1,078	822	642	501	438

Notes:

Data on long-term public and publicly guaranteed, long-term private nonguaranteed, and short-term debt for 2010 are World Bank staff estimates based on aggregate information provided by the authority.

SRI LANKA

(US$ million, unless otherwise indicated)

	1995	*2000*	*2005*	*2006*	*2007*	*2008*	*2009*	*2010*
1. Summary external debt data								
External debt stocks	**8,395**	**9,087**	**11,372**	**11,887**	**14,369**	**15,615**	**17,213**	**20,452**
Long-term external debt	7,264	8,242	9,999	10,788	12,474	13,346	14,618	17,368
Public and publicly guaranteed	7,175	7,874	9,611	10,295	11,835	12,612	13,652	16,449
Private nonguaranteed	90	368	388	493	639	734	967	919
Use of IMF credit	595	161	381	244	251	169	721	1,311
Short-term external debt	535	685	992	855	1,643	2,100	1,873	1,773
interest arrears on long-term	35	112	0	0	11	13	24	28
Memorandum items								
Principal arrears on long-term	42	216	0	0	9	12	71	81
Long-term public sector debt	7,055	7,766	9,611	10,295	11,835	12,612	13,652	16,449
Long-term private sector debt	210	476	388	493	639	734	967	919
Public & publicly guaranteed commitments	406	448	938	1,208	2,190	1,975	2,447	4,178
External debt flows								
Disbursements	671	732	1,082	1,049	1,698	1,238	2,846	3,715
Long-term external debt	671	732	929	1,049	1,698	1,238	2,209	3,084
IMF purchases	0	0	153	0	0	0	638	631
Principal repayments	280	539	266	661	540	882	1,064	750
Long-term external debt	246	453	228	507	535	804	967	716
IMF repurchases	34	86	38	154	5	78	97	34
Net flows	385	-25	1,160	251	1,935	811	1,545	2,861
Long-term external debt	425	279	701	542	1,163	434	1,242	2,368
Short-term external debt	-6	-218	344	-137	777	455	-238	-104
Interest payments	172	248	154	267	297	349	353	695
Long-term external debt	145	213	106	208	218	286	325	661
IMF charges	3	1	11	13	11	8	3	10
Short-term external debt	24	34	37	46	69	56	25	23
2. Other non-debt resource inflows								
Foreign direct investment	56	173	272	480	603	752	404	478
Portfolio equity	..	..	-216	-304	-322	-488	-382	-1,049
3. Currency composition of public and publicly guaranteed debt (%)								
Euro	..	..	7.8	9.1	9.5	9.2	9.3	7.9
Japanese yen	28.6	30.0	30.4	29.0	26.2	31.4	29.4	28.2
Pound sterling	1.8	0.5	0.1	0.1	0.1	0.1	0.0	0.0
Swiss franc	0.4	0.2	0.0	0.0	0.0	0.0	0.0	0.0
U.S.dollars	35.9	38.4	40.8	41.1	44.3	40.4	42.7	47.7
4. Average terms of new commitments								
Official creditors								
Interest (%)	3.3	2.4	1.6	3.0	3.3	2.1	2.5	1.9
Maturity (years)	29.7	32.0	28.1	24.3	23.5	21.0	20.7	21.7
Grace period (years)	8.3	8.5	7.4	7.0	7.0	7.6	5.5	6.3
Private creditors								
Interest (%)	4.8	6.6	5.4	4.8	7.4	3.1	7.2	5.7
Maturity (years)	11.3	10.4	8.4	7.5	5.9	9.9	5.6	10.1
Grace period (years)	1.9	1.3	3.0	3.3	4.0	3.4	5.1	8.9
5. Major economic aggregates								
Gross national income (GNI)	12,860	16,016	24,107	27,879	31,998	39,746	41,583	48,916
Exports of goods, services & income	4,840	6,527	7,963	8,819	9,864	10,338	9,099	11,099
Worker remit. & comp. of employees	809	1,166	1,991	2,185	2,527	2,947	3,363	4,155
Imports of goods, services & income	6,342	8,554	10,441	12,321	13,575	16,889	12,318	16,178
Profit remittances on FDI	72	109	115	362	349	470	230	386
Current account balance	-770	-1,044	-650	-1,498	-1,401	-3,885	-215	-1,418
International reserves	2,112	1,131	2,735	2,832	3,518	2,617	5,354	7,195
6. Ratios								
External debt stocks to exports (%)	173.4	139.2	142.8	134.8	145.7	151.0	189.2	184.3
External debt stocks to GNI (%)	65.3	56.7	47.2	42.6	44.9	39.3	41.4	41.8
Debt service to exports (%)	9.3	12.1	5.3	10.5	8.5	11.9	15.6	13.0
Short-term to external debt stocks (%)	6.4	7.5	8.7	7.2	11.4	13.4	10.9	8.7
Multilateral to external debt stocks (%)	34.0	37.6	40.0	41.6	37.3	35.6	34.1	29.7
Reserves to external debt stocks (%)	25.2	12.5	24.1	23.8	24.5	16.8	31.1	35.2
Reserves to imports (months)	4.0	1.6	3.1	2.8	3.1	1.9	5.2	5.3

(US$ million, unless otherwise indicated)

	1995	2000	2005	2006	2007	2008	2009	2010
7. Long-term external debt								
Debt outstanding and disbursed	**7,264**	**8,242**	**9,999**	**10,788**	**12,474**	**13,346**	**14,618**	**17,368**
Public and publicly guaranteed	7,175	7,874	9,611	10,295	11,835	12,612	13,652	16,449
Official creditors	6,493	6,934	8,983	9,583	10,373	11,286	11,934	13,602
Multilateral	2,858	3,412	4,554	4,945	5,362	5,559	5,875	6,079
of which: IBRD	49	13	0	0	0	0	0	0
IDA	1,463	1,610	2,095	2,245	2,357	2,381	2,487	2,531
Bilateral	3,635	3,522	4,429	4,638	5,011	5,726	6,059	7,524
Private creditors	681	940	627	712	1,462	1,327	1,718	2,847
of which: Bonds	0	65	65	65	565	500	1,000	2,000
Commercial banks	324	356	442	558	799	731	647	776
Private nonguaranteed	90	368	388	493	639	734	967	919
of which: Bonds	0	0	100	100	100	100	0	0
Disbursements	**671**	**732**	**929**	**1,049**	**1,698**	**1,238**	**2,209**	**3,084**
Public and publicly guaranteed	671	563	818	918	1,524	1,083	1,822	2,987
Official creditors	469	348	670	767	754	789	1,160	1,804
Multilateral	197	123	347	328	266	374	424	468
of which: IBRD	0	0	0	0	0	0	0	0
IDA	106	47	113	100	74	95	147	142
Bilateral	272	225	322	439	488	415	736	1,336
Private creditors	201	215	149	151	769	293	662	1,183
of which: Bonds	0	0	0	0	500	0	500	1,000
Commercial banks	92	42	138	148	268	290	155	183
Private nonguaranteed	0	169	111	131	174	156	387	97
of which: Bonds	0	0	0	0	0	0	0	0
Principal repayments	**246**	**453**	**228**	**507**	**535**	**804**	**967**	**716**
Public and publicly guaranteed	244	439	209	481	507	743	812	571
Official creditors	148	216	123	400	450	519	555	507
Multilateral	26	50	84	100	114	146	163	174
of which: IBRD	7	5	1	0	0	0	0	0
IDA	8	18	40	43	49	55	56	59
Bilateral	122	167	40	300	336	373	393	333
Private creditors	96	223	86	82	57	224	257	64
of which: Bonds	0	50	0	0	0	65	0	0
Commercial banks	54	94	53	45	49	151	250	56
Private nonguaranteed	2	14	19	26	28	61	154	145
of which: Bonds	0	0	0	0	0	0	100	0
Interest payments	**145**	**213**	**106**	**208**	**218**	**286**	**325**	**661**
Public and publicly guaranteed	144	178	84	184	191	251	285	641
Official creditors	112	125	65	156	164	178	227	354
Multilateral	29	32	46	58	57	65	58	101
of which: IBRD	5	1	0	0	0	0	0	0
IDA	11	12	17	17	17	19	17	18
Bilateral	84	93	19	99	108	113	170	254
Private creditors	32	54	19	28	27	73	58	287
of which: Bonds	0	6	4	5	0	46	43	72
Commercial banks	19	28	12	19	26	25	14	25
Private nonguaranteed	1	35	22	24	26	35	40	20
of which: Bonds	0	0	7	7	7	7	7	0
8. Debt stock-flow reconciliation								
Total change in external debt stocks	435	-713	330	515	2,482	1,246	1,598	3,239
Net flows on external debt	385	-25	1,160	251	1,935	811	1,545	2,861
9. Debt restructurings								
Total amount rescheduled	0	0	265	0	0	0	0	0
Total amount forgiven	7	9	2	0	1	8	0	0
Debt buyback	0	0	0	0	0	0	0	0

10. Contractual obligations on outstanding long-term external debt

	2011	2012	2013	2014	2015	2016	2017	2018
Official creditors								
Principal	687	731	801	911	1,014	1,072	1,086	1,093
Interest	241	257	264	260	250	236	221	207
Private creditors								
Principal	314	773	275	194	678	150	130	143
Interest	210	197	143	133	107	82	77	72

ST. KITTS AND NEVIS

(US$ million, unless otherwise indicated)

	1995	2000	2005	2006	2007	2008	2009	2010
1. Summary external debt data								
External debt stocks	**55.4**	**155.9**	**293.0**	**289.2**	**271.9**	**245.8**	**227.1**	**202.7**
Long-term external debt	54.2	153.0	290.3	285.2	269.7	244.4	222.9	198.1
Public and publicly guaranteed	54.2	153.0	290.3	285.2	269.7	244.4	222.9	198.1
Private nonguaranteed	0.0	0.0	0.0	0.0	0.0	0.0	0.0	0.0
Use of IMF credit	0.0	2.1	0.0	0.0	0.0	0.0	3.5	3.4
Short-term external debt	1.2	0.8	2.7	4.0	2.3	1.3	0.8	1.2
interest arrears on long-term	1.2	0.8	2.7	4.0	2.3	1.3	0.8	1.2
Memorandum items								
Principal arrears on long-term	0.7	0.4	1.5	1.3	0.6	10.0	11.7	2.7
Long-term public sector debt	52.9	153.0	290.3	285.2	269.7	244.4	222.9	198.1
Long-term private sector debt	1.3	0.0	0.0	0.0	0.0	0.0	0.0	0.0
Public & publicly guaranteed commitments	11.4	32.4	22.9	16.6	8.4	0.1	0.4	4.4
External debt flows								
Disbursements	5.6	31.9	6.9	22.0	11.7	5.0	9.0	7.1
Long-term external debt	5.6	31.9	6.9	22.0	11.7	5.0	5.6	7.1
IMF purchases	0.0	0.0	0.0	0.0	0.0	0.0	3.4	0.0
Principal repayments	4.8	12.4	28.1	28.1	28.6	29.8	27.2	31.4
Long-term external debt	4.8	12.4	28.1	28.1	28.6	29.8	27.2	31.4
IMF repurchases	0.0	0.0	0.0	0.0	0.0	0.0	0.0	0.0
Net flows	0.9	19.6	-21.2	-6.1	-17.0	-24.7	-18.2	-24.3
Long-term external debt	0.9	19.6	-21.2	-6.1	-17.0	-24.7	-21.6	-24.3
Short-term external debt	0.0	0.0	0.0	0.0	0.0	0.0	0.0	0.0
Interest payments	1.9	7.2	20.5	19.3	19.3	16.6	14.5	13.4
Long-term external debt	1.9	7.1	20.5	19.3	19.3	16.6	14.5	13.3
IMF charges	0.0	0.1	0.0	0.0	0.0	0.0	0.0	0.0
Short-term external debt	0.0	0.0	0.0	0.0	0.0	0.0	0.0	0.0
2. Other non-debt resource inflows								
Foreign direct investment	20.5	96.2	93.0	110.4	134.5	177.9	130.8	128.0
Portfolio equity	..	..	..	..	..	..	..	..
3. Currency composition of public and publicly guaranteed debt (%)								
Euro	..	..	1.5	2.3	2.5	2.3	2.4	2.4
Japanese yen	0.0	0.0	0.0	0.0	0.0	0.0	0.0	0.0
Pound sterling	7.4	1.5	0.1	0.1	0.1	0.1	0.1	0.1
Swiss franc	0.0	0.0	0.0	0.0	0.0	0.0	0.0	0.0
U.S.dollars	51.4	79.7	84.8	84.7	84.5	85.5	85.5	85.5
4. Average terms of new commitments								
Official creditors								
Interest (%)	3.7	4.8	2.0	5.1	6.4	2.0	2.0	2.3
Maturity (years)	19.1	16.5	20.9	20.2	19.5	22.0	15.5	18.1
Grace period (years)	5.2	4.5	4.1	3.6	4.8	5.0	2.2	7.0
Private creditors								
Interest (%)	0.0	7.0	0.0	2.5	0.0	0.0	0.0	2.5
Maturity (years)	0.0	9.7	0.0	8.0	0.0	0.0	0.0	8.0
Grace period (years)	0.0	1.1	0.0	2.0	0.0	0.0	0.0	2.0
5. Major economic aggregates								
Gross national income (GNI)	219.8	296.1	403.6	454.8	481.4	559.6	493.0	507.4
Exports of goods, services & income	125.3	155.5	237.3	249.0	245.4	240.1	196.1	192.7
Worker remit. & comp. of employees	20.2	27.1	33.5	36.4	40.3	44.5	43.5	43.9
Imports of goods, services & income	189.9	284.4	325.9	366.3	385.9	448.4	394.5	331.7
Profit remittances on FDI	14.4	21.2	20.3	20.2	24.0	23.4	20.3	19.3
Current account balance	-45.5	-66.2	-64.7	-85.1	-111.3	-175.2	-152.7	-96.0
International reserves	33.5	45.2	71.6	88.7	95.8	110.4	136.4	168.9
6. Ratios								
External debt stocks to exports (%)	44.2	100.3	123.5	116.1	110.8	102.4	115.8	105.2
External debt stocks to GNI (%)	25.2	52.7	72.6	63.6	56.5	43.9	46.1	40.0
Debt service to exports (%)	5.3	12.6	20.5	19.0	19.5	19.3	21.3	23.2
Short-term to external debt stocks (%)	2.2	0.5	0.9	1.4	0.8	0.5	0.4	0.6
Multilateral to external debt stocks (%)	53.4	34.5	33.8	36.3	39.4	42.3	44.7	48.8
Reserves to external debt stocks (%)	60.4	29.0	24.4	30.7	35.2	44.9	60.1	83.3
Reserves to imports (months)	2.1	1.9	2.6	2.9	3.0	3.0	4.1	6.1

(US$ million, unless otherwise indicated)

	1995	2000	2005	2006	2007	2008	2009	2010
7. Long-term external debt								
Debt outstanding and disbursed	**54.2**	**153.0**	**290.3**	**285.2**	**269.7**	**244.4**	**222.9**	**198.1**
Public and publicly guaranteed	54.2	153.0	290.3	285.2	269.7	244.4	222.9	198.1
Official creditors	48.6	102.6	156.0	164.4	162.0	151.6	141.8	132.6
Multilateral	29.6	53.8	99.0	104.9	107.1	104.0	101.6	98.9
of which: IBRD	1.1	4.5	13.0	13.2	13.3	13.2	12.4	9.8
IDA	1.6	1.4	1.4	1.4	1.4	1.4	1.4	1.3
Bilateral	19.0	48.8	57.0	59.5	54.8	47.6	40.3	33.8
Private creditors	5.6	50.4	134.4	120.8	107.7	92.9	81.0	65.5
of which: Bonds	0.0	0.0	29.1	29.1	29.1	29.1	29.1	24.1
Commercial banks	0.0	43.2	104.7	91.7	78.7	63.8	51.9	41.4
Private nonguaranteed	0.0	0.0	0.0	0.0	0.0	0.0	0.0	0.0
of which: Bonds	0.0	0.0	0.0	0.0	0.0	0.0	0.0	0.0
Disbursements	**5.6**	**31.9**	**6.9**	**22.0**	**11.7**	**5.0**	**5.6**	**7.1**
Public and publicly guaranteed	5.6	31.9	6.9	22.0	11.7	5.0	5.6	7.1
Official creditors	5.0	7.7	6.9	21.4	11.7	5.0	5.6	7.0
Multilateral	3.8	7.2	6.9	10.2	8.5	5.0	5.6	7.0
of which: IBRD	0.3	1.1	0.8	1.4	2.4	2.6	1.7	0.0
IDA	0.0	0.0	0.0	0.0	0.0	0.0	0.0	0.0
Bilateral	1.3	0.5	0.0	11.2	3.2	0.0	0.0	0.0
Private creditors	0.6	24.2	0.0	0.6	0.0	0.0	0.0	0.1
of which: Bonds	0.0	0.0	0.0	0.0	0.0	0.0	0.0	0.0
Commercial banks	0.0	24.2	0.0	0.6	0.0	0.0	0.0	0.1
Private nonguaranteed	0.0	0.0	0.0	0.0	0.0	0.0	0.0	0.0
of which: Bonds	0.0	0.0	0.0	0.0	0.0	0.0	0.0	0.0
Principal repayments	**4.8**	**12.4**	**28.1**	**28.1**	**28.6**	**29.8**	**27.2**	**31.4**
Public and publicly guaranteed	4.8	12.4	28.1	28.1	28.6	29.8	27.2	31.4
Official creditors	3.3	4.7	12.9	13.9	15.6	14.9	15.4	15.8
Multilateral	1.5	2.1	4.3	5.1	7.3	7.7	8.3	9.3
of which: IBRD	0.0	0.1	1.0	1.3	2.2	2.7	2.5	2.6
IDA	0.0	0.0	0.0	0.0	0.0	0.0	0.0	0.0
Bilateral	1.8	2.7	8.6	8.7	8.3	7.2	7.1	6.6
Private creditors	1.5	7.6	15.2	14.2	13.1	14.9	11.9	15.6
of which: Bonds	0.0	0.0	0.0	0.0	0.0	0.0	0.0	5.0
Commercial banks	0.0	4.2	13.9	13.6	13.1	14.9	11.9	10.6
Private nonguaranteed	0.0	0.0	0.0	0.0	0.0	0.0	0.0	0.0
of which: Bonds	0.0	0.0	0.0	0.0	0.0	0.0	0.0	0.0
Interest payments	**1.9**	**7.1**	**20.5**	**19.3**	**19.3**	**16.6**	**14.5**	**13.3**
Public and publicly guaranteed	1.9	7.1	20.5	19.3	19.3	16.6	14.5	13.3
Official creditors	1.5	4.1	7.6	7.7	8.7	7.0	6.3	5.3
Multilateral	1.0	2.0	3.7	4.1	4.9	3.9	3.8	3.5
of which: IBRD	0.1	0.3	0.7	0.7	0.8	0.6	0.4	0.2
IDA	0.0	0.0	0.0	0.0	0.0	0.0	0.0	0.0
Bilateral	0.5	2.2	3.9	3.6	3.7	3.1	2.5	1.8
Private creditors	0.4	3.0	12.9	11.5	10.7	9.6	8.2	8.0
of which: Bonds	0.0	0.0	2.2	2.4	2.4	2.4	1.8	2.6
Commercial banks	0.0	2.3	10.5	9.1	8.3	7.2	6.4	5.4
Private nonguaranteed	0.0	0.0	0.0	0.0	0.0	0.0	0.0	0.0
of which: Bonds	0.0	0.0	0.0	0.0	0.0	0.0	0.0	0.0
8. Debt stock-flow reconciliation								
Total change in external debt stocks	-0.8	19.8	-22.8	-3.8	-17.3	-26.2	-18.6	-24.4
Net flows on external debt	0.9	19.6	-21.2	-6.1	-17.0	-24.7	-18.2	-24.3
9. Debt restructurings								
Total amount rescheduled	0.0	0.0	0.0	0.0	0.0	0.0	0.0	0.0
Total amount forgiven	0.0	0.0	0.0	0.0	0.0	0.0	0.0	0.0
Debt buyback	0.0	0.0	0.0	0.0	0.0	0.0	0.0	0.0

10. Contractual obligations on outstanding long-term external debt

	2011	2012	2013	2014	2015	2016	2017	2018
Official creditors								
Principal	20.2	19.6	14.4	11.3	11.0	10.4	9.4	8.0
Interest	3.6	2.9	2.3	2.0	1.7	1.5	1.3	1.2
Private creditors								
Principal	17.5	20.5	22.0	2.7	2.3	1.2	0.5	0.5
Interest	5.1	3.0	1.9	0.8	0.6	0.5	0.4	0.3

Notes:

Data on long-term public and publicly-guaranteed debt for 2010 are provided by the country.

ST. LUCIA

(US$ million, unless otherwise indicated)

	1995	2000	2005	2006	2007	2008	2009	2010
1. Summary external debt data								
External debt stocks	**128.3**	**221.3**	**411.0**	**363.7**	**469.2**	**827.1**	**369.3**	**463.6**
Long-term external debt	111.3	153.5	235.0	246.7	295.8	312.2	295.9	285.9
Public and publicly guaranteed	111.3	153.5	235.0	246.7	295.8	312.2	295.9	285.9
Private nonguaranteed	0.0	0.0	0.0	0.0	0.0	0.0	0.0	0.0
Use of IMF credit	0.0	0.0	0.0	0.0	0.0	0.0	10.8	10.6
Short-term external debt	16.9	67.8	176.0	117.0	173.3	514.9	62.6	167.1
interest arrears on long-term	0.0	0.0	0.0	0.0	0.3	0.9	2.6	5.1
Memorandum items								
Principal arrears on long-term	0.0	0.0	0.0	0.0	0.4	0.0	2.1	3.5
Long-term public sector debt	111.3	153.5	235.0	246.7	295.8	312.2	295.9	285.9
Long-term private sector debt	0.0	0.0	0.0	0.0	0.0	0.0	0.0	0.0
Public & publicly guaranteed commitments	50.4	65.3	8.2	4.4	9.8	5.4	12.6	12.0
External debt flows								
Disbursements	11.5	48.7	11.7	25.8	24.1	11.5	21.0	21.3
Long-term external debt	11.5	48.7	11.7	25.8	24.1	11.5	10.4	21.3
IMF purchases	0.0	0.0	0.0	0.0	0.0	0.0	10.6	0.0
Principal repayments	6.2	20.9	14.2	17.8	26.4	32.4	27.3	29.6
Long-term external debt	6.2	20.9	14.2	17.8	26.4	32.4	27.3	29.6
IMF repurchases	0.0	0.0	0.0	0.0	0.0	0.0	0.0	0.0
Net flows	12.3	40.3	64.5	-51.1	53.8	320.1	-460.2	93.8
Long-term external debt	5.4	27.8	-2.5	7.9	-2.2	-20.9	-16.9	-8.2
Short-term external debt	6.9	12.5	67.0	-59.0	56.0	341.0	-454.0	102.0
Interest payments	5.7	9.2	17.5	15.9	20.3	25.3	14.8	13.7
Long-term external debt	4.8	6.4	12.8	12.2	14.8	15.0	13.3	9.6
IMF charges	0.0	0.0	0.0	0.0	0.0	0.0	0.0	0.0
Short-term external debt	0.9	2.8	4.8	3.7	5.5	10.3	1.5	4.1
2. Other non-debt resource inflows								
Foreign direct investment	33.0	53.7	78.2	233.9	271.9	161.2	146.4	121.1
Portfolio equity	..	..	..	..	..	..	..	..
3. Currency composition of public and publicly guaranteed debt (%)								
Euro	..	..	6.7	7.0	8.2	6.1	5.9	4.9
Japanese yen	2.4	0.3	0.0	0.0	0.0	0.0	0.0	0.0
Pound sterling	13.7	2.1	0.2	0.0	0.0	0.0	0.0	0.0
Swiss franc	0.5	0.0	0.0	0.0	0.0	0.0	0.0	0.0
U.S.dollars	53.4	55.0	68.5	65.1	67.0	70.7	69.5	70.1
4. Average terms of new commitments								
Official creditors								
Interest (%)	4.7	6.0	2.5	0.0	0.8	0.8	3.4	1.1
Maturity (years)	24.8	22.7	24.9	0.0	34.6	34.3	14.0	32.9
Grace period (years)	7.1	5.5	7.8	0.0	10.1	9.8	0.8	8.4
Private creditors								
Interest (%)	0.0	8.7	0.0	7.2	0.0	0.0	7.2	0.0
Maturity (years)	0.0	13.2	0.0	10.3	0.0	0.0	6.0	0.0
Grace period (years)	0.0	13.2	0.0	10.3	0.0	0.0	6.0	0.0
5. Major economic aggregates								
Gross national income (GNI)	521.2	662.9	785.5	876.4	889.9	907.0	872.8	857.8
Exports of goods, services & income	385.4	380.6	533.0	451.8	469.5	537.5	560.3	611.4
Worker remit. & comp. of employees	23.1	26.4	29.5	30.3	31.1	31.5	30.5	31.4
Imports of goods, services & income	437.5	484.4	675.5	772.8	827.8	900.5	706.1	776.5
Profit remittances on FDI	35.3	31.4	51.1	34.0	45.1	52.5	35.3	25.7
Current account balance	-33.1	-78.8	-129.5	-309.0	-344.7	-346.8	-133.4	-150.5
International reserves	63.1	78.8	116.4	134.5	153.7	142.8	174.8	206.3
6. Ratios								
External debt stocks to exports (%)	33.3	58.1	77.1	80.5	99.9	153.9	65.9	75.8
External debt stocks to GNI (%)	24.6	33.4	52.3	41.5	52.7	91.2	42.3	54.0
Debt service to exports (%)	3.1	7.9	6.0	7.5	9.9	10.7	7.5	7.1
Short-term to external debt stocks (%)	13.2	30.6	42.8	32.2	36.9	62.3	16.9	36.0
Multilateral to external debt stocks (%)	61.6	45.0	34.2	41.6	35.3	24.4	53.3	43.6
Reserves to external debt stocks (%)	49.2	35.6	28.3	37.0	32.8	17.3	47.3	44.5
Reserves to imports (months)	1.7	2.0	2.1	2.1	2.2	1.9	3.0	3.2

(US$ million, unless otherwise indicated)

	1995	2000	2005	2006	2007	2008	2009	2010
7. Long-term external debt								
Debt outstanding and disbursed	**111.3**	**153.5**	**235.0**	**246.7**	**295.8**	**312.2**	**295.9**	**285.9**
Public and publicly guaranteed	111.3	153.5	235.0	246.7	295.8	312.2	295.9	285.9
Official creditors	111.3	120.7	160.9	174.3	197.2	228.5	220.8	222.7
Multilateral	79.0	99.5	140.5	151.4	165.5	201.4	196.7	202.0
of which: IBRD	2.1	6.0	10.3	10.0	17.8	18.2	19.2	20.8
IDA	7.9	11.6	27.2	40.7	46.2	49.2	50.0	59.5
Bilateral	32.3	21.3	20.4	23.0	31.8	27.1	24.1	20.7
Private creditors	0.0	32.8	74.0	72.4	98.6	83.6	75.1	63.3
of which: Bonds	0.0	0.0	0.0	4.4	4.4	4.4	7.8	7.8
Commercial banks	0.0	32.8	74.0	68.0	94.2	79.2	67.3	55.4
Private nonguaranteed	0.0	0.0	0.0	0.0	0.0	0.0	0.0	0.0
of which: Bonds	0.0	0.0	0.0	0.0	0.0	0.0	0.0	0.0
Disbursements	**11.5**	**48.7**	**11.7**	**25.8**	**24.1**	**11.5**	**10.4**	**21.3**
Public and publicly guaranteed	11.5	48.7	11.7	25.8	24.1	11.5	10.4	21.3
Official creditors	11.5	16.8	11.7	21.3	24.1	11.5	7.0	21.3
Multilateral	10.8	15.7	7.4	17.2	18.2	8.9	7.0	19.9
of which: IBRD	0.7	0.9	1.1	0.7	9.6	2.6	3.8	4.5
IDA	2.1	0.7	3.5	12.2	4.1	3.9	0.9	10.8
Bilateral	0.8	1.1	4.4	4.1	5.9	2.7	0.0	1.5
Private creditors	0.0	31.9	0.0	4.4	0.0	0.0	3.4	0.0
of which: Bonds	0.0	0.0	0.0	4.4	0.0	0.0	3.4	0.0
Commercial banks	0.0	31.9	0.0	0.0	0.0	0.0	0.0	0.0
Private nonguaranteed	0.0	0.0	0.0	0.0	0.0	0.0	0.0	0.0
of which: Bonds	0.0	0.0	0.0	0.0	0.0	0.0	0.0	0.0
Principal repayments	**6.2**	**20.9**	**14.2**	**17.8**	**26.4**	**32.4**	**27.3**	**29.6**
Public and publicly guaranteed	6.2	20.9	14.2	17.8	26.4	32.4	27.3	29.6
Official creditors	6.2	11.7	9.5	11.8	14.5	17.5	15.4	17.7
Multilateral	4.2	6.6	7.0	8.4	9.3	11.4	12.0	13.9
of which: IBRD	0.1	0.5	1.0	1.1	1.8	2.3	2.7	2.8
IDA	0.0	0.1	0.3	0.4	0.4	0.4	0.5	0.6
Bilateral	2.0	5.1	2.5	3.4	5.2	6.1	3.4	3.7
Private creditors	0.0	9.2	4.7	6.0	11.9	15.0	11.9	11.9
of which: Bonds	0.0	0.0	0.0	0.0	0.0	0.0	0.0	0.0
Commercial banks	0.0	9.2	4.7	6.0	11.9	15.0	11.9	11.9
Private nonguaranteed	0.0	0.0	0.0	0.0	0.0	0.0	0.0	0.0
of which: Bonds	0.0	0.0	0.0	0.0	0.0	0.0	0.0	0.0
Interest payments	**4.8**	**6.4**	**12.8**	**12.2**	**14.8**	**15.0**	**13.3**	**9.6**
Public and publicly guaranteed	4.8	6.4	12.8	12.2	14.8	15.0	13.3	9.6
Official creditors	4.8	5.2	6.3	6.0	6.1	8.1	7.2	6.4
Multilateral	3.0	4.0	5.4	5.1	4.8	7.0	6.2	5.5
of which: IBRD	0.1	0.3	0.5	0.5	0.7	0.9	0.9	0.7
IDA	0.0	0.1	0.2	0.3	0.3	0.4	0.4	0.4
Bilateral	1.8	1.2	0.9	0.9	1.3	1.1	1.0	0.9
Private creditors	0.0	1.2	6.5	6.2	8.7	6.9	6.1	3.2
of which: Bonds	0.0	0.0	0.0	0.2	0.3	0.3	0.3	0.6
Commercial banks	0.0	1.2	6.5	6.0	8.4	6.6	5.8	2.7
Private nonguaranteed	0.0	0.0	0.0	0.0	0.0	0.0	0.0	0.0
of which: Bonds	0.0	0.0	0.0	0.0	0.0	0.0	0.0	0.0
8. Debt stock-flow reconciliation								
Total change in external debt stocks	14.7	37.0	59.3	-47.2	105.4	357.9	-457.8	94.3
Net flows on external debt	12.3	40.3	64.5	-51.1	53.8	320.1	-460.2	93.8
9. Debt restructurings								
Total amount rescheduled	0.0	0.0	0.0	0.0	0.0	67.5	0.0	0.2
Total amount forgiven	0.0	0.0	0.0	0.0	0.0	0.0	0.0	0.0
Debt buyback	0.0	0.0	0.0	0.0	0.0	0.0	0.0	0.0

10. Contractual obligations on outstanding long-term external debt

	2011	2012	2013	2014	2015	2016	2017	2018
Official creditors								
Principal	20.8	18.0	15.6	14.9	14.2	14.2	14.0	13.7
Interest	3.4	3.1	2.8	2.6	2.3	2.1	1.8	1.6
Private creditors								
Principal	10.6	10.6	7.5	1.1	28.0	5.2	0.2	0.0
Interest	4.9	4.1	3.3	2.9	1.8	0.2	0.0	0.0

ST. VINCENT AND THE GRENADINES

(US$ million, unless otherwise indicated)

	1995	2000	2005	2006	2007	2008	2009	2010
1. Summary external debt data								
External debt stocks	**118.3**	**194.6**	**252.1**	**243.0**	**201.4**	**204.0**	**209.6**	**261.1**
Long-term external debt	91.3	163.3	247.8	242.5	199.8	203.9	203.2	255.3
Public and publicly guaranteed	91.3	163.3	247.8	242.5	199.8	203.9	203.2	255.3
Private nonguaranteed	0.0	0.0	0.0	0.0	0.0	0.0	0.0	0.0
Use of IMF credit	0.0	0.0	0.0	0.0	0.0	0.0	5.9	5.8
Short-term external debt	27.0	31.4	4.3	0.5	1.6	0.2	0.5	0.0
interest arrears on long-term	0.1	0.4	4.3	0.5	1.6	0.2	0.5	0.0
Memorandum items								
Principal arrears on long-term	0.6	0.9	3.0	0.3	0.3	0.3	0.8	0.2
Long-term public sector debt	91.3	163.3	247.8	242.5	199.8	203.9	203.2	255.3
Long-term private sector debt	0.0	0.0	0.0	0.0	0.0	0.0	0.0	0.0
Public & publicly guaranteed commitments	12.6	1.0	66.4	0.0	0.7	16.0	35.4	59.3
External debt flows								
Disbursements	3.3	8.5	42.4	14.1	15.4	23.4	26.0	76.2
Long-term external debt	3.3	8.5	42.4	14.1	15.4	23.4	20.2	76.2
IMF purchases	0.0	0.0	0.0	0.0	0.0	0.0	5.8	0.0
Principal repayments	4.5	6.1	15.5	22.1	18.3	18.7	21.4	22.9
Long-term external debt	4.5	6.1	15.5	22.1	18.3	18.7	21.4	22.9
IMF repurchases	0.0	0.0	0.0	0.0	0.0	0.0	0.0	0.0
Net flows	3.0	1.6	26.9	-8.0	-2.9	4.7	4.6	53.3
Long-term external debt	-1.2	2.4	26.9	-8.0	-2.9	4.7	-1.1	53.3
Short-term external debt	4.2	-0.8	0.0	0.0	0.0	0.0	0.0	0.0
Interest payments	4.1	7.0	8.2	11.2	9.5	10.7	9.8	8.7
Long-term external debt	2.6	5.1	8.2	11.2	9.5	10.7	9.7	8.7
IMF charges	0.0	0.0	0.0	0.0	0.0	0.0	0.0	0.0
Short-term external debt	1.5	1.9	0.0	0.0	0.0	0.0	0.0	0.0
2. Other non-debt resource inflows								
Foreign direct investment	30.6	37.7	40.1	109.1	130.5	159.2	106.1	99.7
Portfolio equity	..	..	..	..	..	..	..	..
3. Currency composition of public and publicly guaranteed debt (%)								
Euro	..	..	5.4	5.8	7.5	6.3	5.6	3.2
Japanese yen	0.1	0.0	0.0	0.0	0.0	0.0	0.0	0.0
Pound sterling	5.4	2.9	0.1	0.1	0.1	0.1	0.1	0.1
Swiss franc	1.4	0.3	0.0	0.0	0.0	0.0	0.0	0.0
U.S.dollars	68.2	82.2	73.8	75.0	71.2	75.0	77.7	85.3
4. Average terms of new commitments								
Official creditors								
Interest (%)	3.5	2.5	4.7	0.0	0.8	0.0	2.8	2.5
Maturity (years)	19.9	30.1	18.4	0.0	34.8	0.0	21.5	20.3
Grace period (years)	4.2	10.3	4.6	0.0	10.3	0.0	5.6	4.7
Private creditors								
Interest (%)	0.0	0.0	7.0	0.0	0.0	8.5	0.0	0.0
Maturity (years)	0.0	0.0	10.0	0.0	0.0	10.0	0.0	0.0
Grace period (years)	0.0	0.0	0.5	0.0	0.0	0.5	0.0	0.0
5. Major economic aggregates								
Gross national income (GNI)	254.8	316.9	418.8	473.7	533.3	559.2	561.8	539.3
Exports of goods, services & income	140.3	182.6	208.9	225.6	225.6	220.3	202.8	193.1
Worker remit. & comp. of employees	17.2	22.5	26.5	29.7	33.1	31.1	30.1	30.6
Imports of goods, services & income	190.0	222.8	329.2	365.1	439.6	463.8	414.0	412.2
Profit remittances on FDI	11.1	12.7	22.1	23.0	19.6	18.1	12.4	10.1
Current account balance	-40.2	-23.9	-102.2	-119.4	-193.9	-230.3	-199.8	-206.0
International reserves	29.8	55.2	69.5	78.7	87.0	83.7	87.8	112.7
6. Ratios								
External debt stocks to exports (%)	84.3	106.6	120.7	107.7	89.3	92.6	103.3	135.2
External debt stocks to GNI (%)	46.4	61.4	60.2	51.3	37.8	36.5	37.3	48.4
Debt service to exports (%)	6.1	7.2	11.3	14.8	12.3	13.4	15.3	16.4
Short-term to external debt stocks (%)	22.8	16.1	1.7	0.2	0.8	0.1	0.2	0.0
Multilateral to external debt stocks (%)	49.3	34.0	32.9	38.5	52.6	52.8	57.7	72.2
Reserves to external debt stocks (%)	25.2	28.4	27.6	32.4	43.2	41.0	41.9	43.2
Reserves to imports (months)	1.9	3.0	2.5	2.6	2.4	2.2	2.5	3.3

ST. VINCENT AND THE GRENADINES

(US$ million, unless otherwise indicated)

	1995	2000	2005	2006	2007	2008	2009	2010
7. Long-term external debt								
Debt outstanding and disbursed	**91.3**	**163.3**	**247.8**	**242.5**	**199.8**	**203.9**	**203.2**	**255.3**
Public and publicly guaranteed	91.3	163.3	247.8	242.5	199.8	203.9	203.2	255.3
Official creditors	86.5	104.8	114.8	124.1	135.1	133.3	143.3	206.6
Multilateral	58.4	66.2	82.9	93.4	105.9	107.8	121.0	188.4
of which: IBRD	0.4	0.1	0.9	3.4	3.2	3.0	3.3	5.2
IDA	8.1	7.0	15.3	16.5	18.2	19.3	20.4	21.3
Bilateral	28.2	38.6	31.9	30.6	29.2	25.5	22.4	18.2
Private creditors	4.8	58.5	133.0	118.4	64.7	70.6	59.8	48.7
of which: Bonds	0.0	0.0	0.0	0.0	0.0	0.0	0.0	0.0
Commercial banks	4.8	0.6	59.9	53.5	47.2	56.1	48.2	40.3
Private nonguaranteed	0.0	0.0	0.0	0.0	0.0	0.0	0.0	0.0
of which: Bonds	0.0	0.0	0.0	0.0	0.0	0.0	0.0	0.0
Disbursements	**3.3**	**8.5**	**42.4**	**14.1**	**15.4**	**23.4**	**20.2**	**76.2**
Public and publicly guaranteed	3.3	8.5	42.4	14.1	15.4	23.4	20.2	76.2
Official creditors	3.3	8.5	12.4	14.1	15.4	7.4	20.2	76.2
Multilateral	1.7	5.7	11.5	13.7	15.4	7.3	20.2	76.2
of which: IBRD	0.0	0.0	0.0	2.5	0.0	0.1	0.7	2.3
IDA	0.0	0.0	3.3	0.8	1.3	1.6	1.3	1.6
Bilateral	1.5	2.8	0.8	0.4	0.0	0.1	0.0	0.0
Private creditors	0.1	0.0	30.0	0.0	0.0	16.0	0.0	0.0
of which: Bonds	0.0	0.0	0.0	0.0	0.0	0.0	0.0	0.0
Commercial banks	0.1	0.0	30.0	0.0	0.0	16.0	0.0	0.0
Private nonguaranteed	0.0	0.0	0.0	0.0	0.0	0.0	0.0	0.0
of which: Bonds	0.0	0.0	0.0	0.0	0.0	0.0	0.0	0.0
Principal repayments	**4.5**	**6.1**	**15.5**	**22.1**	**18.3**	**18.7**	**21.4**	**22.9**
Public and publicly guaranteed	4.5	6.1	15.5	22.1	18.3	18.7	21.4	22.9
Official creditors	4.5	5.7	7.7	7.5	7.1	8.6	10.6	11.8
Multilateral	3.4	3.7	4.9	4.8	4.3	5.2	7.4	8.1
of which: IBRD	0.1	0.0	0.0	0.0	0.2	0.3	0.4	0.4
IDA	0.1	0.1	0.3	0.3	0.3	0.3	0.4	0.4
Bilateral	1.1	2.0	2.8	2.7	2.7	3.4	3.2	3.7
Private creditors	0.0	0.4	7.7	14.6	11.3	10.1	10.7	11.1
of which: Bonds	0.0	0.0	0.0	0.0	0.0	0.0	0.0	0.0
Commercial banks	0.0	0.4	0.2	6.4	6.3	7.1	7.9	7.9
Private nonguaranteed	0.0	0.0	0.0	0.0	0.0	0.0	0.0	0.0
of which: Bonds	0.0	0.0	0.0	0.0	0.0	0.0	0.0	0.0
Interest payments	**2.6**	**5.1**	**8.2**	**11.2**	**9.5**	**10.7**	**9.7**	**8.7**
Public and publicly guaranteed	2.6	5.1	8.2	11.2	9.5	10.7	9.7	8.7
Official creditors	2.4	3.3	3.5	3.7	3.6	5.6	4.4	4.4
Multilateral	1.7	2.1	2.4	2.8	2.8	4.0	3.6	3.8
of which: IBRD	0.0	0.0	0.1	0.1	0.2	0.2	0.2	0.2
IDA	0.1	0.1	0.1	0.1	0.1	0.1	0.1	0.1
Bilateral	0.7	1.2	1.0	1.0	0.8	1.7	0.7	0.6
Private creditors	0.3	1.8	4.7	7.5	5.9	5.1	5.4	4.3
of which: Bonds	0.0	0.0	0.0	0.0	0.0	0.0	0.0	0.0
Commercial banks	0.3	0.1	2.1	4.1	3.7	3.8	4.0	3.5
Private nonguaranteed	0.0	0.0	0.0	0.0	0.0	0.0	0.0	0.0
of which: Bonds	0.0	0.0	0.0	0.0	0.0	0.0	0.0	0.0
8. Debt stock-flow reconciliation								
Total change in external debt stocks	4.1	1.3	24.0	-9.2	-41.6	2.7	5.5	51.5
Net flows on external debt	3.0	1.6	26.9	-8.0	-2.9	4.7	4.6	53.3
9. Debt restructurings								
Total amount rescheduled	0.0	0.0	0.0	0.0	0.0	0.0	0.0	0.0
Total amount forgiven	0.0	0.0	0.0	0.0	42.9	0.0	0.0	0.0
Debt buyback	0.0	0.0	0.0	0.0	0.0	0.0	0.0	0.0

10. Contractual obligations on outstanding long-term external debt

	2011	2012	2013	2014	2015	2016	2017	2018
Official creditors								
Principal	16.0	14.9	13.9	12.4	15.0	15.6	14.8	14.2
Interest	4.5	4.6	4.4	4.1	3.8	3.5	3.1	2.7
Private creditors								
Principal	11.0	11.0	10.5	7.6	4.6	1.6	1.6	0.8
Interest	3.3	2.5	1.8	1.1	0.6	0.3	0.2	0.0

Notes:

Short-term debt data are excluded since BIS data include debt liabilities of offshore centers located in the country. BIS short-term debt data for 2008, 2009, and 2010 are $447 million, $474 million, and $479 million respectively.

SUDAN

(US$ million, unless otherwise indicated)

	1995	2000	2005	2006	2007	2008	2009	2010
1. Summary external debt data								
External debt stocks	**17,602**	**15,983**	**17,474**	**18,412**	**19,468**	**20,106**	**20,746**	**21,846**
Long-term external debt	10,275	10,647	11,232	11,922	12,738	13,120	13,707	14,444
Public and publicly guaranteed	9,779	10,151	11,232	11,922	12,738	13,120	13,707	14,444
Private nonguaranteed	496	496	0	0	0	0	0	0
Use of IMF credit	960	625	518	518	482	406	403	390
Short-term external debt	6,367	4,711	5,724	5,972	6,248	6,580	6,637	7,012
interest arrears on long-term	5,736	4,441	5,313	5,636	5,974	6,104	6,420	6,658
Memorandum items								
Principal arrears on long-term	7,635	7,246	7,666	8,017	8,272	8,113	8,227	8,380
Long-term public sector debt	10,275	10,647	11,232	11,922	12,738	13,120	13,707	14,444
Long-term private sector debt	0	0	0	0	0	0	0	0
Public & publicly guaranteed commitments	0	343	358	606	285	1,036	1,104	847
External debt flows								
Disbursements	51	861	387	549	717	673	971	935
Long-term external debt	51	861	387	549	717	673	971	935
IMF purchases	0	0	0	0	0	0	0	0
Principal repayments	54	197	319	236	276	284	373	403
Long-term external debt	15	143	291	209	216	219	362	397
IMF repurchases	39	54	28	27	60	66	11	6
Net flows	0	625	77	238	379	591	339	669
Long-term external debt	36	718	96	339	501	454	609	538
Short-term external debt	3	-39	9	-75	-62	202	-259	137
Interest payments	15	48	79	64	95	84	118	89
Long-term external debt	2	42	67	54	87	68	111	83
IMF charges	13	0	0	0	0	0	0	0
Short-term external debt	0	5	12	10	8	15	7	5
2. Other non-debt resource inflows								
Foreign direct investment	12	392	2,305	3,534	2,426	2,601	2,662	2,894
Portfolio equity	0	0	..	-35	-17	0	0	..
3. Currency composition of public and publicly guaranteed debt (%)								
Euro	..	..	8.5	8.8	9.7	9.6	9.6	9.3
Japanese yen	2.9	2.0	1.3	1.2	0.7	0.9	0.6	0.7
Pound sterling	3.4	3.3	3.0	3.2	3.0	2.3	2.4	2.2
Swiss franc	19.6	12.2	13.8	14.0	14.2	14.6	14.4	15.0
U.S.dollars	47.6	60.3	53.6	52.0	50.3	49.1	50.5	50.8
4. Average terms of new commitments								
Official creditors								
Interest (%)	0.0	1.7	3.1	3.9	2.2	2.9	3.1	2.8
Maturity (years)	0.0	24.8	16.4	13.5	19.8	20.5	12.5	20.3
Grace period (years)	0.0	4.7	4.8	4.1	5.1	5.5	3.1	4.0
Private creditors								
Interest (%)	0.0	0.0	0.0	0.0	0.0	0.0	0.0	0.0
Maturity (years)	0.0	0.0	0.0	0.0	0.0	0.0	0.0	0.0
Grace period (years)	0.0	0.0	0.0	0.0	0.0	0.0	0.0	0.0
5. Major economic aggregates								
Gross national income (GNI)	12,920	11,303	26,052	34,081	42,631	53,132	50,018	55,939
Exports of goods, services & income	683	1,839	4,982	5,993	9,447	12,207	8,900	11,796
Worker remit. & comp. of employees	346	641	1,016	1,179	1,769	3,100	2,135	1,974
Imports of goods, services & income	1,243	2,594	9,196	12,008	13,098	13,905	14,145	15,092
Profit remittances on FDI	0	0	1,399	2,093	2,404	2,971	3,035	3,320
Current account balance	-500	-518	-2,768	-4,811	-3,268	-1,314	-4,232	-1,165
International reserves	163	138	1,869	1,660	1,378	1,399	1,094	..
6. Ratios								
External debt stocks to exports (%)	2,577.5	869.3	350.7	307.2	206.1	164.7	233.1	185.2
External debt stocks to GNI (%)	136.2	141.4	67.1	54.0	45.7	37.8	41.5	39.1
Debt service to exports (%)	10.1	13.3	8.0	5.0	3.9	3.0	5.5	4.2
Short-term to external debt stocks (%)	36.2	29.5	32.8	32.4	32.1	32.7	32.0	32.1
Multilateral to external debt stocks (%)	12.1	12.3	14.8	15.2	16.1	16.3	16.0	15.3
Reserves to external debt stocks (%)	0.9	0.9	10.7	9.0	7.1	7.0	5.3	..
Reserves to imports (months)	1.6	0.6	2.4	1.7	1.3	1.2	0.9	..

(US$ million, unless otherwise indicated)

	1995	2000	2005	2006	2007	2008	2009	2010
7. Long-term external debt								
Debt outstanding and disbursed	**10,275**	**10,647**	**11,232**	**11,922**	**12,738**	**13,120**	**13,707**	**14,444**
Public and publicly guaranteed	9,779	10,151	11,232	11,922	12,738	13,120	13,707	14,444
Official creditors	7,921	8,393	9,145	9,722	10,405	10,730	11,258	11,815
Multilateral	2,133	1,968	2,580	2,790	3,130	3,280	3,320	3,342
of which: IBRD	6	1	0	0	0	0	0	0
IDA	1,272	1,167	1,234	1,271	1,307	1,300	1,306	1,290
Bilateral	5,787	6,425	6,565	6,933	7,275	7,450	7,938	8,474
Private creditors	1,859	1,758	2,087	2,200	2,333	2,390	2,449	2,629
of which: Bonds	0	0	0	0	0	0	0	0
Commercial banks	1,855	1,296	1,584	1,696	1,829	1,887	1,945	2,125
Private nonguaranteed	496	496	0	0	0	0	0	0
of which: Bonds	0	0	0	0	0	0	0	0
Disbursements	**51**	**861**	**387**	**549**	**717**	**673**	**971**	**935**
Public and publicly guaranteed	51	861	387	549	717	673	971	935
Official creditors	51	318	387	549	717	673	971	935
Multilateral	51	171	138	150	214	184	127	133
of which: IBRD	0	0	0	0	0	0	0	0
IDA	0	0	0	0	0	0	0	0
Bilateral	0	146	249	398	503	489	844	802
Private creditors	0	543	0	0	0	0	0	0
of which: Bonds	0	0	0	0	0	0	0	0
Commercial banks	0	87	0	0	0	0	0	0
Private nonguaranteed	0	0	0	0	0	0	0	0
of which: Bonds	0	0	0	0	0	0	0	0
Principal repayments	**15**	**143**	**291**	**209**	**216**	**219**	**362**	**397**
Public and publicly guaranteed	15	143	291	209	216	219	362	397
Official creditors	15	143	291	209	216	219	362	397
Multilateral	15	32	27	15	37	29	73	67
of which: IBRD	0	2	0	0	0	0	0	0
IDA	0	2	1	2	0	1	0	0
Bilateral	0	111	264	194	179	189	290	330
Private creditors	0	0	0	0	0	0	0	0
of which: Bonds	0	0	0	0	0	0	0	0
Commercial banks	0	0	0	0	0	0	0	0
Private nonguaranteed	0	0	0	0	0	0	0	0
of which: Bonds	0	0	0	0	0	0	0	0
Interest payments	**2**	**42**	**67**	**54**	**87**	**68**	**111**	**83**
Public and publicly guaranteed	2	42	67	54	87	68	111	83
Official creditors	2	42	67	54	87	68	111	83
Multilateral	2	16	23	12	42	35	45	32
of which: IBRD	0	0	0	0	0	0	0	0
IDA	0	2	1	1	0	2	0	0
Bilateral	0	26	43	42	45	33	67	51
Private creditors	0	0	0	0	0	0	0	0
of which: Bonds	0	0	0	0	0	0	0	0
Commercial banks	0	0	0	0	0	0	0	0
Private nonguaranteed	0	0	0	0	0	0	0	0
of which: Bonds	0	0	0	0	0	0	0	0
8. Debt stock-flow reconciliation								
Total change in external debt stocks	684	-122	-769	938	1,056	638	640	1,100
Net flows on external debt	0	625	77	238	379	591	339	669
9. Debt restructurings								
Total amount rescheduled	0	8	0	0	0	0	0	259
Total amount forgiven	0	0	15	0	52	108	52	0
Debt buyback	0	0	0	0	0	0	0	0

10. Contractual obligations on outstanding long-term external debt

	2011	2012	2013	2014	2015	2016	2017	2018
Official creditors								
Principal	1,014	968	649	672	606	498	455	429
Interest	175	157	144	142	134	121	115	106
Private creditors								
Principal	0	0	0	0	0	0	0	0
Interest	0	0	0	0	0	0	0	0

Notes:

Data on long-term public and publicly guaranteed debt exclude penalty interest.

SWAZILAND

(US$ million, unless otherwise indicated)

	1995	2000	2005	2006	2007	2008	2009	2010
1. Summary external debt data								
External debt stocks	**249.5**	**264.8**	**442.3**	**413.8**	**404.1**	**370.0**	**417.8**	**615.8**
Long-term external debt	238.3	262.9	362.2	364.7	368.6	355.0	390.8	385.2
Public and publicly guaranteed	238.3	262.9	362.2	364.7	368.6	355.0	390.8	385.2
Private nonguaranteed	0.0	0.0	0.0	0.0	0.0	0.0	0.0	0.0
Use of IMF credit	0.0	0.0	0.0	0.0	0.0	0.0	0.0	0.0
Short-term external debt	11.1	1.8	80.1	49.1	35.5	15.0	27.0	230.7
interest arrears on long-term	0.5	0.0	15.1	18.1	5.5	15.0	25.0	35.7
Memorandum items								
Principal arrears on long-term	4.0	0.2	7.1	10.6	6.2	11.5	22.3	29.6
Long-term public sector debt	238.3	262.9	362.2	364.7	368.6	355.0	390.8	385.2
Long-term private sector debt	0.0	0.0	0.0	0.0	0.0	0.0	0.0	0.0
Public & publicly guaranteed commitments	29.0	0.7	0.0	6.6	0.0	0.1	24.2	0.1
External debt flows								
Disbursements	8.1	15.8	51.1	22.9	12.4	56.6	33.2	8.0
Long-term external debt	8.1	15.8	51.1	22.9	12.4	56.6	33.2	8.0
IMF purchases	0.0	0.0	0.0	0.0	0.0	0.0	0.0	0.0
Principal repayments	13.5	12.4	18.1	17.4	22.4	33.5	28.4	26.9
Long-term external debt	13.5	12.4	18.1	17.4	22.4	33.5	28.4	26.9
IMF repurchases	0.0	0.0	0.0	0.0	0.0	0.0	0.0	0.0
Net flows	-1.1	-47.5	54.1	-28.5	-11.0	-6.9	6.8	174.1
Long-term external debt	-5.4	3.4	33.1	5.5	-10.0	23.1	4.8	-18.9
Short-term external debt	4.3	-50.9	21.0	-34.0	-1.0	-30.0	2.0	193.0
Interest payments	4.6	18.2	16.4	18.1	24.8	19.1	15.8	14.2
Long-term external debt	4.1	16.1	13.6	15.1	23.4	18.8	15.8	13.0
IMF charges	0.0	0.0	0.0	0.0	0.0	0.0	0.0	0.0
Short-term external debt	0.4	2.1	2.8	3.1	1.4	0.4	0.0	1.3
2. Other non-debt resource inflows								
Foreign direct investment	51.8	90.7	-45.9	121.0	37.5	105.7	65.7	92.7
Portfolio equity	0.8	1.4	0.8	5.5	1.0	43.9	-6.6	..
3. Currency composition of public and publicly guaranteed debt (%)								
Euro	..	..	11.5	11.7	12.2	18.3	17.6	15.6
Japanese yen	0.0	0.0	0.0	0.0	0.0	0.0	0.0	0.0
Pound sterling	4.6	1.0	0.2	0.1	0.0	0.0	0.0	0.0
Swiss franc	0.0	0.0	0.0	0.0	0.0	0.0	0.0	0.0
U.S.dollars	8.2	10.4	16.5	15.6	14.5	14.1	15.6	15.0
4. Average terms of new commitments								
Official creditors								
Interest (%)	7.1	3.0	0.0	2.5	0.0	2.8	3.0	4.0
Maturity (years)	19.5	40.2	0.0	21.8	0.0	41.4	27.6	19.9
Grace period (years)	5.0	27.2	0.0	4.3	0.0	10.8	4.8	5.4
Private creditors								
Interest (%)	0.0	0.0	0.0	0.0	0.0	0.0	0.0	0.0
Maturity (years)	0.0	0.0	0.0	0.0	0.0	0.0	0.0	0.0
Grace period (years)	0.0	0.0	0.0	0.0	0.0	0.0	0.0	0.0
5. Major economic aggregates								
Gross national income (GNI)	1779.5	1523.8	2702.3	2683.7	2990.9	2829.5	2708.1	3586.2
Exports of goods, services & income	1182.2	1376.4	2190.4	2187.8	2480.3	2091.2	2150.9	..
Worker remit. & comp. of employees	82.6	56.9	95.4	98.6	100.5	89.6	93.5	109.0
Imports of goods, services & income	1355.9	1522.9	2390.5	2515.9	2739.8	2532.3	2757.1	..
Profit remittances on FDI	68.0	65.9	44.0	167.0	160.0	252.7	352.5	..
Current account balance	-29.7	-45.9	-102.6	-196.6	-65.5	-231.2	-414.3	..
International reserves	298.2	351.8	243.9	372.5	774.2	751.9	958.9	756.3
6. Ratios								
External debt stocks to exports (%)	21.1	19.2	20.2	18.9	16.3	17.7	19.4	..
External debt stocks to GNI (%)	14.0	17.4	16.4	15.4	13.5	13.1	15.4	17.2
Debt service to exports (%)	1.5	2.2	1.6	1.6	1.9	2.5	2.1	..
Short-term to external debt stocks (%)	4.5	0.7	18.1	11.9	8.8	4.1	6.5	37.5
Multilateral to external debt stocks (%)	48.2	56.6	54.1	59.5	62.3	65.1	61.0	38.9
Reserves to external debt stocks (%)	119.5	132.9	55.1	90.0	191.6	203.2	229.5	122.8
Reserves to imports (months)	2.6	2.8	1.2	1.8	3.4	3.6	4.2	..

SWAZILAND

(US$ million, unless otherwise indicated)

	1995	2000	2005	2006	2007	2008	2009	2010
7. Long-term external debt								
Debt outstanding and disbursed	**238.3**	**262.9**	**362.2**	**364.7**	**368.6**	**355.0**	**390.8**	**385.2**
Public and publicly guaranteed	238.3	262.9	362.2	364.7	368.6	355.0	390.8	385.2
Official creditors	238.1	243.1	338.5	343.2	346.6	338.9	370.5	362.6
Multilateral	120.3	149.9	239.3	246.1	251.7	240.9	254.7	239.8
of which: IBRD	19.2	9.0	23.6	22.4	20.1	14.2	7.6	2.4
IDA	5.9	4.7	3.4	3.2	2.9	2.7	2.4	2.2
Bilateral	117.8	93.2	99.1	97.1	94.9	98.0	115.8	122.8
Private creditors	0.3	19.8	23.7	21.5	22.0	16.1	20.3	22.6
of which: Bonds	0.0	0.0	0.0	0.0	0.0	0.0	0.0	0.0
Commercial banks	0.0	19.8	23.7	21.5	22.0	16.1	20.3	22.6
Private nonguaranteed	0.0	0.0	0.0	0.0	0.0	0.0	0.0	0.0
of which: Bonds	0.0	0.0	0.0	0.0	0.0	0.0	0.0	0.0
Disbursements	**8.1**	**15.8**	**51.1**	**22.9**	**12.4**	**56.6**	**33.2**	**8.0**
Public and publicly guaranteed	8.1	15.8	51.1	22.9	12.4	56.6	33.2	8.0
Official creditors	8.1	15.8	51.1	22.9	12.4	56.6	33.2	8.0
Multilateral	7.2	15.8	32.0	19.3	11.9	39.6	20.7	4.3
of which: IBRD	0.0	0.7	1.5	0.0	0.0	0.0	0.0	0.0
IDA	0.0	0.0	0.0	0.0	0.0	0.0	0.0	0.0
Bilateral	1.0	0.0	19.2	3.7	0.5	17.0	12.5	3.8
Private creditors	0.0	0.0	0.0	0.0	0.0	0.0	0.0	0.0
of which: Bonds	0.0	0.0	0.0	0.0	0.0	0.0	0.0	0.0
Commercial banks	0.0	0.0	0.0	0.0	0.0	0.0	0.0	0.0
Private nonguaranteed	0.0	0.0	0.0	0.0	0.0	0.0	0.0	0.0
of which: Bonds	0.0	0.0	0.0	0.0	0.0	0.0	0.0	0.0
Principal repayments	**13.5**	**12.4**	**18.1**	**17.4**	**22.4**	**33.5**	**28.4**	**26.9**
Public and publicly guaranteed	13.5	12.4	18.1	17.4	22.4	33.5	28.4	26.9
Official creditors	13.2	12.4	18.1	17.4	22.4	33.5	28.4	26.9
Multilateral	8.2	8.1	12.6	12.2	14.7	26.1	24.9	24.1
of which: IBRD	3.5	0.9	1.5	1.2	2.3	5.9	6.6	5.2
IDA	0.3	0.3	0.3	0.3	0.3	0.2	0.3	0.3
Bilateral	5.0	4.3	5.5	5.2	7.7	7.4	3.5	2.8
Private creditors	0.3	0.0	0.0	0.0	0.0	0.0	0.0	0.0
of which: Bonds	0.0	0.0	0.0	0.0	0.0	0.0	0.0	0.0
Commercial banks	0.0	0.0	0.0	0.0	0.0	0.0	0.0	0.0
Private nonguaranteed	0.0	0.0	0.0	0.0	0.0	0.0	0.0	0.0
of which: Bonds	0.0	0.0	0.0	0.0	0.0	0.0	0.0	0.0
Interest payments	**4.1**	**16.1**	**13.6**	**15.1**	**23.4**	**18.8**	**15.8**	**13.0**
Public and publicly guaranteed	4.1	16.1	13.6	15.1	23.4	18.8	15.8	13.0
Official creditors	4.1	10.2	10.5	12.0	20.5	16.3	14.6	13.0
Multilateral	3.1	5.2	9.1	10.7	12.6	13.0	11.7	11.4
of which: IBRD	1.2	0.8	1.0	1.0	1.0	0.8	0.6	0.3
IDA	0.0	0.0	0.0	0.0	0.0	0.0	0.0	0.0
Bilateral	0.9	5.0	1.4	1.4	7.9	3.3	2.9	1.6
Private creditors	0.1	5.9	3.2	3.0	2.9	2.5	1.2	0.0
of which: Bonds	0.0	0.0	0.0	0.0	0.0	0.0	0.0	0.0
Commercial banks	0.0	5.9	3.2	3.0	2.9	2.5	1.2	0.0
Private nonguaranteed	0.0	0.0	0.0	0.0	0.0	0.0	0.0	0.0
of which: Bonds	0.0	0.0	0.0	0.0	0.0	0.0	0.0	0.0
8. Debt stock-flow reconciliation								
Total change in external debt stocks	8.8	-68.0	19.0	-28.5	-9.7	-34.1	47.8	198.0
Net flows on external debt	-1.1	-47.5	54.1	-28.5	-11.0	-6.9	6.8	174.1
9. Debt restructurings								
Total amount rescheduled	0.0	0.0	0.0	0.0	0.0	0.0	0.0	0.0
Total amount forgiven	0.0	0.0	0.0	0.0	0.0	0.0	0.0	0.0
Debt buyback	0.0	0.0	0.0	0.0	0.0	0.0	0.0	0.0

10. Contractual obligations on outstanding long-term external debt

	2011	2012	2013	2014	2015	2016	2017	2018
Official creditors								
Principal	34.4	32.2	30.9	30.0	28.2	25.0	22.2	21.7
Interest	11.2	10.5	9.5	8.4	7.3	6.4	5.7	5.1
Private creditors								
Principal	0.0	0.0	0.0	0.0	0.0	0.0	0.0	0.0
Interest	3.1	3.1	3.1	3.1	3.1	3.1	3.1	3.1

SYRIAN ARAB REPUBLIC

(US$ million, unless otherwise indicated)

	1995	*2000*	*2005*	*2006*	*2007*	*2008*	*2009*	*2010*
1. Summary external debt data								
External debt stocks	**21,897**	**22,156**	**5,513**	**5,457**	**5,515**	**5,191**	**5,112**	**4,729**
Long-term external debt	16,955	16,464	5,007	4,867	4,866	4,611	4,356	4,171
Public and publicly guaranteed	16,955	16,464	5,007	4,867	4,866	4,611	4,356	4,171
Private nonguaranteed	0	0	0	0	0	0	0	0
Use of IMF credit	0	0	0	0	0	0	0	0
Short-term external debt	4,942	5,692	506	589	649	581	756	558
interest arrears on long-term	2,013	2,372	193	196	142	145	206	217
Memorandum items								
Principal arrears on long-term	5,743	8,828	265	270	213	220	226	232
Long-term public sector debt	16,954	16,464	5,007	4,867	4,866	4,611	4,356	4,171
Long-term private sector debt	0	0	0	0	0	0	0	0
Public & publicly guaranteed commitments	0	69	476	330	270	684	576	497
External debt flows								
Disbursements	297	18	170	181	372	249	278	286
Long-term external debt	297	18	170	181	372	249	278	286
IMF purchases	0	0	0	0	0	0	0	0
Principal repayments	69	239	439	688	545	552	489	497
Long-term external debt	69	239	439	688	545	552	489	497
IMF repurchases	0	0	0	0	0	0	0	0
Net flows	540	-826	-376	-427	-58	-374	-97	-420
Long-term external debt	229	-221	-269	-507	-172	-303	-211	-211
Short-term external debt	311	-605	-107	80	114	-71	114	-209
Interest payments	213	247	126	132	135	140	141	133
Long-term external debt	74	127	110	112	110	118	116	110
IMF charges	0	0	0	0	0	0	0	0
Short-term external debt	139	120	16	20	25	22	25	23
2. Other non-debt resource inflows								
Foreign direct investment	100	270	500	659	1,242	1,467	2,570	1,381
Portfolio equity	0	0	..	..	..	..	..	..
3. Currency composition of public and publicly guaranteed debt (%)								
Euro	..	..	12.1	14.0	19.8	20.3	24.0	25.4
Japanese yen	3.9	4.9	9.8	14.3	13.3	16.0	14.9	15.9
Pound sterling	1.0	0.6	0.0	0.0	0.0	0.0	0.0	0.0
Swiss franc	0.0	0.0	0.0	0.0	0.0	0.0	0.0	0.0
U.S.dollars	81.8	84.1	49.3	42.8	37.4	34.2	31.9	29.3
4. Average terms of new commitments								
Official creditors								
Interest (%)	0.0	1.0	4.8	1.6	2.0	1.6	1.9	0.0
Maturity (years)	0.0	25.3	18.6	20.1	19.2	19.3	26.8	19.2
Grace period (years)	0.0	5.3	4.3	8.5	4.6	6.0	7.2	4.0
Private creditors								
Interest (%)	0.0	0.0	0.0	0.0	0.0	0.0	0.0	0.0
Maturity (years)	0.0	0.0	0.0	0.0	0.0	0.0	0.0	0.0
Grace period (years)	0.0	0.0	0.0	0.0	0.0	0.0	0.0	0.0
5. Major economic aggregates								
Gross national income (GNI)	11,591	18,446	27,685	32,400	39,715	51,433	52,828	57,982
Exports of goods, services & income	6,201	7,190	11,907	13,597	16,212	19,914	16,026	..
Worker remit. & comp. of employees	339	180	823	795	1,150	1,400	1,550	1,646
Imports of goods, services & income	6,545	6,614	12,359	13,242	16,573	20,998	18,250	..
Profit remittances on FDI	0	0	1,220	1,165	1,085	1,527	1,301	..
Current account balance	263	1,061	299	920	459	66	-1,161	..
International reserves	448	355	17,774	16,997	17,707	17,784	18,300	20,632
6. Ratios								
External debt stocks to exports (%)	353.1	308.1	46.3	40.1	34.0	26.1	31.9	..
External debt stocks to GNI (%)	188.9	120.1	19.9	16.8	13.9	10.1	9.7	8.2
Debt service to exports (%)	4.5	6.8	4.7	6.0	4.2	3.5	3.9	..
Short-term to external debt stocks (%)	22.6	25.7	9.2	10.8	11.8	11.2	14.8	11.8
Multilateral to external debt stocks (%)	4.8	2.6	18.1	20.0	25.5	27.3	30.0	33.6
Reserves to external debt stocks (%)	2.0	1.6	322.4	311.5	321.1	342.6	358.0	436.3
Reserves to imports (months)	0.8	0.6	17.3	15.4	12.8	10.2	12.0	..

(US$ million, unless otherwise indicated)

	1995	2000	2005	2006	2007	2008	2009	2010
7. Long-term external debt								
Debt outstanding and disbursed	**16,955**	**16,464**	**5,007**	**4,867**	**4,866**	**4,611**	**4,356**	**4,171**
Public and publicly guaranteed	16,955	16,464	5,007	4,867	4,866	4,611	4,356	4,171
Official creditors	15,719	15,502	5,007	4,867	4,866	4,611	4,356	4,171
Multilateral	1,051	576	997	1,091	1,404	1,418	1,533	1,591
of which: IBRD	428	25	0	0	0	0	0	0
IDA	44	30	22	21	19	18	16	15
Bilateral	14,668	14,926	4,010	3,776	3,461	3,193	2,824	2,580
Private creditors	1,236	962	0	0	0	0	0	0
of which: Bonds	0	0	0	0	0	0	0	0
Commercial banks	0	0	0	0	0	0	0	0
Private nonguaranteed	0	0	0	0	0	0	0	0
of which: Bonds	0	0	0	0	0	0	0	0
Disbursements	**297**	**18**	**170**	**181**	**372**	**249**	**278**	**286**
Public and publicly guaranteed	297	18	170	181	372	249	278	286
Official creditors	297	18	170	181	372	249	278	286
Multilateral	123	12	111	148	319	170	229	237
of which: IBRD	0	0	0	0	0	0	0	0
IDA	0	0	0	0	0	0	0	0
Bilateral	174	6	59	33	53	79	49	50
Private creditors	0	0	0	0	0	0	0	0
of which: Bonds	0	0	0	0	0	0	0	0
Commercial banks	0	0	0	0	0	0	0	0
Private nonguaranteed	0	0	0	0	0	0	0	0
of which: Bonds	0	0	0	0	0	0	0	0
Principal repayments	**69**	**239**	**439**	**688**	**545**	**552**	**489**	**497**
Public and publicly guaranteed	69	239	439	688	545	552	489	497
Official creditors	68	224	428	688	545	552	489	497
Multilateral	42	66	79	90	102	112	116	138
of which: IBRD	13	14	0	0	0	0	0	0
IDA	0	1	1	1	1	1	1	1
Bilateral	26	158	349	598	443	439	373	359
Private creditors	1	16	11	0	0	0	0	0
of which: Bonds	0	0	0	0	0	0	0	0
Commercial banks	0	0	0	0	0	0	0	0
Private nonguaranteed	0	0	0	0	0	0	0	0
of which: Bonds	0	0	0	0	0	0	0	0
Interest payments	**74**	**127**	**110**	**112**	**110**	**118**	**116**	**110**
Public and publicly guaranteed	74	127	110	112	110	118	116	110
Official creditors	74	126	110	112	110	118	116	110
Multilateral	37	82	41	44	47	56	58	59
of which: IBRD	12	57	0	0	0	0	0	0
IDA	0	0	0	0	0	0	0	0
Bilateral	37	44	68	68	63	62	58	51
Private creditors	0	1	0	0	0	0	0	0
of which: Bonds	0	0	0	0	0	0	0	0
Commercial banks	0	0	0	0	0	0	0	0
Private nonguaranteed	0	0	0	0	0	0	0	0
of which: Bonds	0	0	0	0	0	0	0	0
8. Debt stock-flow reconciliation								
Total change in external debt stocks	863	-730	-13,455	-56	58	-324	-79	-383
Net flows on external debt	540	-826	-376	-427	-58	-374	-97	-420
9. Debt restructurings								
Total amount rescheduled	0	566	1,650	0	41	0	0	0
Total amount forgiven	0	0	12,595	0	77	45	28	0
Debt buyback	0	0	0	0	0	0	0	0

10. Contractual obligations on outstanding long-term external debt

	2011	2012	2013	2014	2015	2016	2017	2018
Official creditors								
Principal	595	611	617	603	510	415	379	376
Interest	110	113	112	106	101	91	82	73
Private creditors								
Principal	0	0	0	0	0	0	0	0
Interest	0	0	0	0	0	0	0	0

TAJIKISTAN

(US$ million, unless otherwise indicated)

	1995	2000	2005	2006	2007	2008	2009	2010
1. Summary external debt data								
External debt stocks	**634**	**1,034**	**1,006**	**950**	**1,222**	**2,376**	**2,549**	**2,955**
Long-term external debt	590	846	852	876	1,103	2,271	2,434	2,733
Public and publicly guaranteed	590	755	826	840	1,063	1,374	1,606	1,806
Private nonguaranteed	0	91	26	37	40	897	827	927
Use of IMF credit	0	111	127	44	46	15	41	101
Short-term external debt	43	77	27	29	72	90	74	122
interest arrears on long-term	43	45	2	0	0	0	0	0
Memorandum items								
Principal arrears on long-term	142	121	23	1	0	0	0	364
Long-term public sector debt	590	755	821	837	1,063	1,374	1,606	1,806
Long-term private sector debt	0	91	31	39	40	897	827	927
Public & publicly guaranteed commitments	0	53	87	640	160	105	130	312
External debt flows								
Disbursements	28	62	137	164	266	387	562	951
Long-term external debt	28	37	108	149	266	387	521	892
IMF purchases	0	25	29	14	0	0	40	60
Principal repayments	0	37	56	39	41	97	426	628
Long-term external debt	0	28	42	39	41	66	411	628
IMF repurchases	0	10	14	0	0	31	15	0
Net flows	28	-4	24	128	268	307	120	370
Long-term external debt	28	9	66	110	225	321	110	263
Short-term external debt	0	-29	-58	4	43	18	-16	47
Interest payments	0	25	13	25	21	31	42	55
Long-term external debt	0	21	10	23	20	28	41	54
IMF charges	0	2	1	0	0	0	0	0
Short-term external debt	0	2	2	1	1	2	1	1
2. Other non-debt resource inflows								
Foreign direct investment	10	24	54	339	360	376	16	16
Portfolio equity	..	..	..	..	..	..	..	..
3. Currency composition of public and publicly guaranteed debt (%)								
Euro	..	..	6.1	5.3	3.9	2.8	2.8	2.6
Japanese yen	0.0	0.0	0.0	0.0	0.0	0.0	0.0	0.0
Pound sterling	0.0	0.0	0.0	0.0	0.0	0.0	0.0	0.0
Swiss franc	0.0	0.0	0.0	0.0	0.0	0.0	0.0	0.0
U.S.dollars	97.0	97.9	86.3	85.7	86.2	86.3	82.9	81.5
4. Average terms of new commitments								
Official creditors								
Interest (%)	0.0	3.8	0.7	2.0	1.5	1.4	2.0	1.7
Maturity (years)	0.0	26.4	29.5	20.7	30.5	31.1	20.9	20.6
Grace period (years)	0.0	6.7	7.8	5.3	7.9	11.6	5.5	5.4
Private creditors								
Interest (%)	0.0	0.0	0.0	0.0	0.0	0.0	0.0	0.0
Maturity (years)	0.0	0.0	0.0	0.0	0.0	0.0	0.0	0.0
Grace period (years)	0.0	0.0	0.0	0.0	0.0	0.0	0.0	0.0
5. Major economic aggregates								
Gross national income (GNI)	1,183	824	2,234	2,729	3,634	5,108	4,907	5,570
Exports of goods, services & income	..	..	1,264	1,658	1,728	1,776	1,225	1,526
Worker remit. & comp. of employees	..	..	467	1,019	1,691	2,544	1,748	2,254
Imports of goods, services & income	..	..	1,733	2,425	3,780	4,227	3,140	3,422
Profit remittances on FDI	..	..	2	46	26	4	5	9
Current account balance	..	..	-19	-21	-495	48	-180	-383
International reserves	..	94	189	204	..	..	..	..
6. Ratios								
External debt stocks to exports (%)	..	..	79.6	57.3	70.7	133.8	208.0	193.6
External debt stocks to GNI (%)	53.6	125.4	45.0	34.8	33.6	46.5	51.9	53.1
Debt service to exports (%)	..	..	5.5	3.9	3.6	7.2	38.2	44.8
Short-term to external debt stocks (%)	6.8	7.5	2.7	3.1	5.9	3.8	2.9	4.1
Multilateral to external debt stocks (%)	..	18.0	51.6	63.3	54.6	30.9	32.5	32.0
Reserves to external debt stocks (%)	..	9.1	18.8	21.5	..	..	..	..
Reserves to imports (months)	..	..	1.3	1.0	..	..	..	..

TAJIKISTAN

(US$ million, unless otherwise indicated)

	1995	2000	2005	2006	2007	2008	2009	2010
7. Long-term external debt								
Debt outstanding and disbursed	**590**	**846**	**852**	**876**	**1,103**	**2,271**	**2,434**	**2,733**
Public and publicly guaranteed	590	755	826	840	1,063	1,374	1,606	1,806
Official creditors	522	704	817	837	1,063	1,374	1,606	1,806
Multilateral	0	186	519	602	667	733	830	945
of which: IBRD	0	0	0	0	0	0	0	0
IDA	0	143	308	339	360	365	373	377
Bilateral	522	518	298	235	396	641	777	861
Private creditors	68	51	8	3	0	0	0	0
of which: Bonds	0	0	0	0	0	0	0	0
Commercial banks	68	51	0	0	0	0	0	0
Private nonguaranteed	0	91	26	37	40	897	827	927
of which: Bonds	0	0	0	0	0	0	0	0
Disbursements	**28**	**37**	**108**	**149**	**266**	**387**	**521**	**892**
Public and publicly guaranteed	28	36	105	133	250	356	211	249
Official creditors	28	36	105	133	250	356	211	249
Multilateral	0	36	73	64	52	69	103	144
of which: IBRD	0	0	0	0	0	0	0	0
IDA	0	23	35	16	8	10	9	15
Bilateral	28	0	32	69	198	287	108	104
Private creditors	0	0	0	0	0	0	0	0
of which: Bonds	0	0	0	0	0	0	0	0
Commercial banks	0	0	0	0	0	0	0	0
Private nonguaranteed	0	1	3	16	16	31	310	643
of which: Bonds	0	0	0	0	0	0	0	0
Principal repayments	**0**	**28**	**42**	**39**	**41**	**66**	**411**	**628**
Public and publicly guaranteed	0	15	37	34	29	52	35	35
Official creditors	0	15	37	30	29	52	35	35
Multilateral	0	0	14	11	12	10	14	15
of which: IBRD	0	0	0	0	0	0	0	0
IDA	0	0	0	0	1	2	4	4
Bilateral	0	15	22	19	17	42	20	20
Private creditors	0	0	0	3	0	0	0	0
of which: Bonds	0	0	0	0	0	0	0	0
Commercial banks	0	0	0	0	0	0	0	0
Private nonguaranteed	0	12	5	6	12	15	376	593
of which: Bonds	0	0	0	0	0	0	0	0
Interest payments	**0**	**21**	**10**	**23**	**20**	**28**	**41**	**54**
Public and publicly guaranteed	0	7	9	21	18	26	24	23
Official creditors	0	4	9	19	18	26	24	23
Multilateral	0	1	6	13	11	13	9	8
of which: IBRD	0	0	0	0	0	0	0	0
IDA	0	1	2	3	3	3	3	3
Bilateral	0	3	3	7	7	12	15	15
Private creditors	0	4	0	2	0	0	0	0
of which: Bonds	0	0	0	0	0	0	0	0
Commercial banks	0	4	0	0	0	0	0	0
Private nonguaranteed	0	14	1	2	2	3	17	31
of which: Bonds	0	0	0	0	0	0	0	0
8. Debt stock-flow reconciliation								
Total change in external debt stocks	53	-241	-33	-56	272	1,154	173	406
Net flows on external debt	28	-4	24	128	268	307	120	370
9. Debt restructurings								
Total amount rescheduled	0	0	0	0	0	0	0	0
Total amount forgiven	0	2	0	102	0	0	0	0
Debt buyback	0	0	0	0	0	0	0	0

10. Contractual obligations on outstanding long-term external debt

	2011	2012	2013	2014	2015	2016	2017	2018
Official creditors								
Principal	89	85	90	93	94	107	108	110
Interest	28	29	28	28	27	26	24	23
Private creditors								
Principal	153	115	99	54	42	32	26	21
Interest	51	37	27	19	13	9	6	3

TANZANIA

(US$ million, unless otherwise indicated)

	1995	*2000*	*2005*	*2006*	*2007*	*2008*	*2009*	*2010*
1. Summary external debt data								
External debt stocks	**7,365**	**7,142**	**8,355**	**4,049**	**5,008**	**5,964**	**7,324**	**8,664**
Long-term external debt	6,204	5,969	7,006	3,035	3,925	4,600	5,654	6,795
Public and publicly guaranteed	6,204	5,969	6,446	2,452	3,181	3,711	4,638	5,572
Private nonguaranteed	0	0	560	583	744	889	1,016	1,224
Use of IMF credit	197	324	342	13	18	17	329	354
Short-term external debt	964	849	1,006	1,001	1,065	1,346	1,341	1,515
interest arrears on long-term	904	647	615	595	628	763	836	909
Memorandum items								
Principal arrears on long-term	1,494	695	655	405	430	497	521	491
Long-term public sector debt	6,106	5,917	6,446	2,452	3,181	3,711	4,638	5,572
Long-term private sector debt	98	52	560	583	744	889	1,016	1,224
Public & publicly guaranteed commitments	141	391	617	840	858	824	823	2,033
External debt flows								
Disbursements	261	264	474	577	654	523	1,372	1,260
Long-term external debt	261	211	466	573	649	523	1,065	1,229
IMF purchases	0	53	8	4	4	0	307	30
Principal repayments	141	104	77	36	20	22	105	132
Long-term external debt	122	94	31	36	20	22	105	131
IMF repurchases	19	10	46	0	0	0	0	0
Net flows	98	205	459	557	665	647	1,188	1,229
Long-term external debt	139	118	435	538	630	501	960	1,098
Short-term external debt	-22	44	62	15	31	146	-78	101
Interest payments	85	63	54	51	44	42	59	67
Long-term external debt	80	51	44	39	26	27	45	51
IMF charges	1	2	1	0	0	0	1	0
Short-term external debt	4	10	9	12	19	15	13	16
2. Other non-debt resource inflows								
Foreign direct investment	120	463	936	403	582	400	415	433
Portfolio equity	0	0	3	3	3	3	3	3
3. Currency composition of public and publicly guaranteed debt (%)								
Euro	..	..	2.9	7.5	6.6	5.6	4.6	3.5
Japanese yen	10.9	7.9	7.0	4.9	4.0	4.3	3.4	4.7
Pound sterling	10.2	8.9	4.8	0.7	0.1	0.1	0.1	0.1
Swiss franc	0.1	0.0	0.0	0.0	0.0	0.0	0.0	0.0
U.S.dollars	38.8	51.9	54.1	46.3	40.1	41.2	44.5	48.3
4. Average terms of new commitments								
Official creditors								
Interest (%)	1.7	0.9	1.2	0.8	0.7	0.7	0.8	0.7
Maturity (years)	22.3	38.2	37.1	41.0	41.3	42.5	37.5	38.7
Grace period (years)	7.4	9.8	9.3	10.1	10.1	10.3	9.9	10.7
Private creditors								
Interest (%)	1.9	0.0	0.0	0.0	4.7	0.0	3.9	0.0
Maturity (years)	3.7	1.0	0.0	0.0	11.1	0.0	3.0	0.0
Grace period (years)	1.6	1.0	0.0	0.0	1.6	0.0	3.0	0.0
5. Major economic aggregates								
Gross national income (GNI)	5,126	10,066	14,114	14,331	16,839	20,731	21,385	23,012
Exports of goods, services & income	1,297	1,341	3,056	3,523	4,182	5,688	5,274	6,552
Worker remit. & comp. of employees	1	8	19	15	14	19	23	25
Imports of goods, services & income	2,281	2,230	4,656	5,246	6,683	8,972	7,905	9,354
Profit remittances on FDI	2	13	319	25	309	205	184	187
Current account balance	-590	-499	-1,105	-1,134	-1,849	-2,675	-1,934	-1,978
International reserves	270	974	2,049	2,259	2,886	2,863	3,470	3,905
6. Ratios								
External debt stocks to exports (%)	567.9	532.6	273.4	114.9	119.7	104.8	138.9	132.2
External debt stocks to GNI (%)	143.7	70.9	59.2	28.3	29.7	28.8	34.2	37.7
Debt service to exports (%)	17.4	12.4	4.3	2.5	1.5	1.1	3.1	3.0
Short-term to external debt stocks (%)	13.1	11.9	12.0	24.7	21.3	22.6	18.3	17.5
Multilateral to external debt stocks (%)	37.9	45.7	58.3	36.7	43.6	44.9	48.8	50.6
Reserves to external debt stocks (%)	3.7	13.6	24.5	55.8	57.6	48.0	47.4	45.1
Reserves to imports (months)	1.4	5.2	5.3	5.2	5.2	3.8	5.3	5.0

TANZANIA

(US$ million, unless otherwise indicated)

	1995	2000	2005	2006	2007	2008	2009	2010
7. Long-term external debt								
Debt outstanding and disbursed	**6,204**	**5,969**	**7,006**	**3,035**	**3,925**	**4,600**	**5,654**	**6,795**
Public and publicly guaranteed	6,204	5,969	6,446	2,452	3,181	3,711	4,638	5,572
Official creditors	5,798	5,776	6,341	2,358	3,079	3,613	4,521	5,459
Multilateral	2,791	3,267	4,868	1,484	2,182	2,677	3,573	4,382
of which: IBRD	87	11	0	0	0	0	0	0
IDA	2,182	2,593	3,861	1,056	1,585	1,971	2,598	3,248
Bilateral	3,008	2,508	1,472	873	897	936	948	1,077
Private creditors	406	194	105	95	102	98	118	113
of which: Bonds	0	0	0	0	0	0	0	0
Commercial banks	75	81	66	54	60	57	59	55
Private nonguaranteed	0	0	560	583	744	889	1,016	1,224
of which: Bonds	0	0	0	0	0	0	0	0
Disbursements	**261**	**211**	**466**	**573**	**649**	**523**	**1,065**	**1,229**
Public and publicly guaranteed	261	211	466	573	649	523	919	1,013
Official creditors	220	206	447	560	646	523	889	996
Multilateral	187	187	444	494	627	523	884	835
of which: IBRD	0	0	0	0	0	0	0	0
IDA	160	142	275	416	475	394	608	653
Bilateral	33	19	3	66	19	0	5	161
Private creditors	40	5	19	13	3	0	30	17
of which: Bonds	0	0	0	0	0	0	0	0
Commercial banks	5	5	19	13	3	0	0	17
Private nonguaranteed	0	0	0	0	0	0	146	216
of which: Bonds	0	0	0	0	0	0	0	0
Principal repayments	**122**	**94**	**31**	**36**	**20**	**22**	**105**	**131**
Public and publicly guaranteed	122	94	31	36	20	13	26	52
Official creditors	100	77	31	33	19	13	13	35
Multilateral	78	29	26	27	13	13	13	17
of which: IBRD	34	4	0	0	0	0	0	0
IDA	12	9	15	7	1	1	1	3
Bilateral	21	47	5	7	6	0	0	18
Private creditors	22	17	0	2	1	0	13	17
of which: Bonds	0	0	0	0	0	0	0	0
Commercial banks	0	0	0	2	1	0	0	17
Private nonguaranteed	0	0	0	0	0	9	79	79
of which: Bonds	0	0	0	0	0	0	0	0
Interest payments	**80**	**51**	**44**	**39**	**26**	**27**	**45**	**51**
Public and publicly guaranteed	80	51	42	37	23	21	27	34
Official creditors	77	49	42	35	22	21	24	31
Multilateral	56	23	38	29	17	21	24	29
of which: IBRD	8	1	0	0	0	0	0	0
IDA	16	15	30	19	10	13	15	20
Bilateral	20	26	4	7	6	0	1	2
Private creditors	3	2	0	2	1	0	3	3
of which: Bonds	0	0	0	0	0	0	0	0
Commercial banks	0	0	0	2	1	0	0	2
Private nonguaranteed	0	0	2	2	2	6	18	17
of which: Bonds	0	0	0	0	0	0	0	0
8. Debt stock-flow reconciliation								
Total change in external debt stocks	144	-717	-223	-4,306	959	956	1,360	1,340
Net flows on external debt	98	205	459	557	665	647	1,188	1,229
9. Debt restructurings								
Total amount rescheduled	0	342	0	0	0	0	0	0
Total amount forgiven	140	588	296	5,202	13	22	5	47
Debt buyback	0	0	0	0	0	0	0	0

10. Contractual obligations on outstanding long-term external debt

	2011	2012	2013	2014	2015	2016	2017	2018
Official creditors								
Principal	104	104	76	87	108	132	159	182
Interest	48	51	53	54	55	54	53	52
Private creditors								
Principal	6	385	291	174	140	106	86	68
Interest	2	29	19	14	10	6	4	2

Notes:

Data on long-term public and publicly guaranteed debt include debt liabilities of Zanzibar. Data on long-term private nonguaranteed debt are World Bank staff estimates from 2004 to 2007. Data on long-term private nonguaranteed debt are reported by Central Bank from 2008. Tanzania was granted debt relief effective in 2006 under MDRI.

THAILAND

(US$ million, unless otherwise indicated)

	1995	2000	2005	2006	2007	2008	2009	2010
1. Summary external debt data								
External debt stocks	**100,039**	**79,720**	**46,362**	**45,901**	**45,306**	**49,839**	**57,886**	**71,263**
Long-term external debt	55,944	61,778	30,348	28,089	27,011	30,649	30,877	32,791
Public and publicly guaranteed	16,826	29,463	14,673	12,551	10,863	11,588	11,188	11,357
Private nonguaranteed	39,117	32,316	15,675	15,538	16,148	19,061	19,689	21,434
Use of IMF credit	0	3,062	0	0	0	0	0	0
Short-term external debt	44,095	14,880	16,014	17,812	18,295	19,189	27,010	38,471
interest arrears on long-term	0	0	0	0	0	4	8	2
Memorandum items								
Principal arrears on long-term	0	0	0	0	0	0	0	0
Long-term public sector debt	16,826	29,463	14,673	12,551	10,863	11,588	11,188	11,357
Long-term private sector debt	39,117	32,316	15,675	15,538	16,148	19,061	19,689	21,434
Public & publicly guaranteed commitments	2,930	1,337	2,166	500	511	2,663	923	1,122
External debt flows								
Disbursements	10,715	4,031	16,133	13,725	18,130	13,049	9,043	10,565
Long-term external debt	10,715	4,031	16,133	13,725	18,130	13,049	9,043	10,565
IMF purchases	0	0	0	0	0	0	0	0
Principal repayments	4,398	9,142	16,553	12,834	20,475	15,226	10,911	9,661
Long-term external debt	4,398	8,945	16,553	12,834	20,475	15,226	10,911	9,661
IMF repurchases	0	198	0	0	0	0	0	0
Net flows	21,233	-13,649	4,106	2,689	-1,862	-1,288	5,948	12,373
Long-term external debt	6,317	-4,913	-420	891	-2,345	-2,178	-1,868	905
Short-term external debt	14,916	-8,538	4,526	1,798	483	890	7,816	11,468
Interest payments	4,189	4,849	1,624	1,919	1,748	1,780	1,515	1,627
Long-term external debt	2,646	3,776	1,121	1,158	959	1,285	1,220	1,201
IMF charges	0	168	0	0	0	0	0	0
Short-term external debt	1,543	905	503	761	789	495	296	426
2. Other non-debt resource inflows								
Foreign direct investment	2,068	3,366	8,055	9,453	11,324	8,531	4,976	6,306
Portfolio equity	2,253	900	5,121	5,242	4,268	-3,802	1,334	3,430
3. Currency composition of public and publicly guaranteed debt (%)								
Euro	..	..	2.0	2.2	2.5	2.0	1.9	1.6
Japanese yen	47.7	46.3	53.6	56.1	58.6	56.2	59.7	63.1
Pound sterling	0.2	0.1	0.1	0.1	0.1	0.0	0.0	0.0
Swiss franc	0.9	0.0	0.0	0.0	0.0	0.0	0.0	0.0
U.S.dollars	27.2	46.3	42.9	40.9	38.0	41.0	38.1	35.1
4. Average terms of new commitments								
Official creditors								
Interest (%)	4.4	1.5	1.6	0.0	2.0	1.0	1.0	1.3
Maturity (years)	23.5	38.1	17.5	0.0	17.2	24.7	24.1	21.9
Grace period (years)	6.4	8.2	6.9	0.0	5.2	6.7	6.6	6.4
Private creditors								
Interest (%)	6.6	1.5	4.3	5.4	5.4	3.4	3.7	1.1
Maturity (years)	8.9	7.5	10.5	5.9	9.9	6.4	9.1	4.9
Grace period (years)	4.3	3.5	9.1	2.3	9.9	3.5	1.1	4.9
5. Major economic aggregates								
Gross national income (GNI)	165,281	120,809	167,799	198,726	237,961	262,864	253,428	305,087
Exports of goods, services & income	74,093	85,997	133,171	157,417	188,929	216,708	186,533	233,681
Worker remit. & comp. of employees	1,695	1,697	1,187	1,333	1,635	1,898	1,637	1,764
Imports of goods, services & income	88,161	77,269	143,821	158,468	177,190	219,263	169,156	223,731
Profit remittances on FDI	0	0	4,501	4,031	5,798	4,142	3,402	3,403
Current account balance	-13,582	9,313	-7,647	2,316	15,678	2,211	21,861	14,754
International reserves	36,939	32,665	52,076	67,008	87,472	111,009	138,419	172,028
6. Ratios								
External debt stocks to exports (%)	135.0	92.7	34.8	29.2	24.0	23.0	31.0	30.5
External debt stocks to GNI (%)	60.5	66.0	27.6	23.1	19.0	19.0	22.8	23.4
Debt service to exports (%)	11.6	16.3	13.6	9.4	11.8	7.8	6.7	4.8
Short-term to external debt stocks (%)	44.1	18.7	34.5	38.8	40.4	38.5	46.7	54.0
Multilateral to external debt stocks (%)	3.2	6.7	1.8	1.4	0.6	0.5	0.4	0.3
Reserves to external debt stocks (%)	36.9	41.0	112.3	146.0	193.1	222.7	239.1	241.4
Reserves to imports (months)	5.0	5.1	4.3	5.1	5.9	6.1	9.8	9.2

THAILAND

(US$ million, unless otherwise indicated)

	1995	2000	2005	2006	2007	2008	2009	2010
7. Long-term external debt								
Debt outstanding and disbursed	**55,944**	**61,778**	**30,348**	**28,089**	**27,011**	**30,649**	**30,877**	**32,791**
Public and publicly guaranteed	16,826	29,463	14,673	12,551	10,863	11,588	11,188	11,357
Official creditors	11,187	20,820	7,862	7,023	6,297	6,947	6,468	6,843
Multilateral	3,206	5,330	819	632	288	264	208	187
of which: IBRD	1,805	2,940	386	336	63	65	74	73
IDA	102	90	73	69	66	62	59	56
Bilateral	7,981	15,489	7,043	6,391	6,009	6,683	6,259	6,656
Private creditors	5,639	8,643	6,811	5,528	4,566	4,641	4,720	4,515
of which: Bonds	1,574	2,630	4,236	3,046	2,566	1,954	1,754	1,954
Commercial banks	3,045	5,116	2,077	2,067	1,673	2,446	2,818	2,472
Private nonguaranteed	39,117	32,316	15,675	15,538	16,148	19,061	19,689	21,434
of which: Bonds	7,375	8,414	4,385	3,535	3,281	3,181	3,040	4,570
Disbursements	**10,715**	**4,031**	**16,133**	**13,725**	**18,130**	**13,049**	**9,043**	**10,565**
Public and publicly guaranteed	2,758	3,031	1,871	926	564	1,598	866	510
Official creditors	1,417	2,156	434	426	274	74	76	160
Multilateral	358	751	43	36	2	2	13	5
of which: IBRD	146	456	30	31	2	2	13	5
IDA	0	0	0	0	0	0	0	0
Bilateral	1,059	1,405	391	389	272	73	63	155
Private creditors	1,341	876	1,436	500	290	1,524	790	350
of which: Bonds	242	0	936	200	290	524	0	350
Commercial banks	1,088	455	300	300	0	1,000	790	0
Private nonguaranteed	7,956	1,000	14,262	12,799	17,566	11,451	8,177	10,055
of which: Bonds	2,080	0	1,300	735	475	0	0	1,900
Principal repayments	**4,398**	**8,945**	**16,553**	**12,834**	**20,475**	**15,226**	**10,911**	**9,661**
Public and publicly guaranteed	1,888	3,010	2,798	2,800	1,988	2,531	1,188	1,168
Official creditors	925	1,666	2,321	1,211	1,272	1,008	468	534
Multilateral	360	753	528	224	351	30	69	27
of which: IBRD	201	181	128	81	275	0	4	7
IDA	2	3	3	3	3	3	3	3
Bilateral	566	912	1,793	987	921	978	399	507
Private creditors	962	1,344	477	1,589	716	1,522	720	634
of which: Bonds	199	174	172	1,308	219	1,192	200	150
Commercial banks	430	1,072	261	179	397	227	428	423
Private nonguaranteed	2,510	5,935	13,755	10,034	18,488	12,696	9,723	8,493
of which: Bonds	0	1,044	908	1,585	729	100	141	370
Interest payments	**2,646**	**3,776**	**1,121**	**1,158**	**959**	**1,285**	**1,220**	**1,201**
Public and publicly guaranteed	874	1,577	484	499	397	450	365	356
Official creditors	521	1,008	234	188	155	120	112	113
Multilateral	218	350	54	36	26	9	6	2
of which: IBRD	135	178	29	21	16	3	2	1
IDA	1	1	1	1	1	0	0	0
Bilateral	302	658	180	153	129	111	106	110
Private creditors	353	569	250	311	242	330	253	243
of which: Bonds	97	193	158	188	125	107	60	61
Commercial banks	195	353	77	106	103	212	189	179
Private nonguaranteed	1,772	2,199	637	658	562	836	855	845
of which: Bonds	222	476	286	268	275	244	251	234
8. Debt stock-flow reconciliation								
Total change in external debt stocks	34,505	-17,050	-3,072	-461	-595	4,532	8,048	13,376
Net flows on external debt	21,233	-13,649	4,106	2,689	-1,862	-1,288	5,948	12,373
9. Debt restructurings								
Total amount rescheduled	0	0	0	0	0	0	0	0
Total amount forgiven	0	0	0	0	0	0	0	0
Debt buyback	0	0	0	0	0	0	0	0

10. Contractual obligations on outstanding long-term external debt

	2011	2012	2013	2014	2015	2016	2017	2018
Official creditors								
Principal	482	427	449	452	510	542	550	537
Interest	124	125	122	118	111	103	94	84
Private creditors								
Principal	6,151	3,999	3,371	2,344	3,191	873	1,324	526
Interest	534	428	351	297	229	173	149	127

Notes:

Short-term debt data from 2007 are based on reports provided by the country.

TOGO

(US$ million, unless otherwise indicated)

	1995	2000	2005	2006	2007	2008	2009	2010
1. Summary external debt data								
External debt stocks	**1,476**	**1,430**	**1,673**	**1,777**	**1,957**	**1,627**	**1,633**	**1,728**
Long-term external debt	1,286	1,228	1,440	1,541	1,642	1,469	1,494	1,534
Public and publicly guaranteed	1,286	1,228	1,440	1,541	1,642	1,469	1,494	1,534
Private nonguaranteed	0	0	0	0	0	0	0	0
Use of IMF credit	105	70	14	8	2	48	91	133
Short-term external debt	85	132	220	227	313	110	48	61
interest arrears on long-term	27	63	168	208	237	26	31	32
Memorandum items								
Principal arrears on long-term	64	62	308	365	431	47	41	49
Long-term public sector debt	1,286	1,228	1,440	1,541	1,642	1,469	1,494	1,534
Long-term private sector debt	0	0	0	0	0	0	0	0
Public & publicly guaranteed commitments	69	0	26	51	20	0	212	40
External debt flows								
Disbursements	59	24	10	48	3	52	76	128
Long-term external debt	26	24	10	48	3	2	35	84
IMF purchases	33	0	0	0	0	49	41	44
Principal repayments	18	19	19	22	11	142	41	26
Long-term external debt	7	10	8	16	4	141	41	26
IMF repurchases	11	9	11	6	7	2	0	0
Net flows	39	-44	17	-7	49	-83	-33	113
Long-term external debt	19	14	2	32	-1	-138	-7	58
Short-term external debt	-2	-49	26	-33	57	8	-67	12
Interest payments	11	10	2	4	4	54	14	9
Long-term external debt	8	5	0	2	1	51	13	8
IMF charges	1	0	0	0	0	0	0	0
Short-term external debt	3	5	1	2	2	3	0	1
2. Other non-debt resource inflows								
Foreign direct investment	26	42	77	77	49	24	49	41
Portfolio equity	0	6	16	10	6	1	2	..
3. Currency composition of public and publicly guaranteed debt (%)								
Euro	..	..	18.4	19.2	20.1	14.8	14.8	13.1
Japanese yen	3.3	6.2	5.0	4.6	4.5	4.1	4.0	4.2
Pound sterling	1.7	1.6	1.2	1.3	1.2	0.1	0.1	0.1
Swiss franc	10.9	7.8	9.3	9.3	9.5	4.4	4.3	4.6
U.S.dollars	47.4	52.6	49.8	48.4	47.0	58.7	56.7	54.4
4. Average terms of new commitments								
Official creditors								
Interest (%)	0.7	0.0	1.7	1.3	1.0	0.0	1.9	2.2
Maturity (years)	37.6	0.0	25.8	20.9	20.1	0.0	21.8	23.3
Grace period (years)	9.9	0.0	6.2	5.0	0.6	0.0	8.1	7.5
Private creditors								
Interest (%)	0.0	0.0	0.0	0.0	0.0	0.0	0.0	0.0
Maturity (years)	0.0	0.0	0.0	0.0	0.0	0.0	0.0	0.0
Grace period (years)	0.0	0.0	0.0	0.0	0.0	0.0	0.0	0.0
5. Major economic aggregates								
Gross national income (GNI)	1,265	1,300	1,831	1,995	2,198	2,804	2,812	2,826
Exports of goods, services & income	473	457	857	879	974	1,217	1,265	..
Worker remit. & comp. of employees	15	34	193	232	284	337	335	333
Imports of goods, services & income	713	664	1,249	1,299	1,469	1,760	1,777	..
Profit remittances on FDI	1	17	47	55	44	49	42	..
Current account balance	-122	-140	-204	-176	-216	-219	-177	..
International reserves	130	141	192	375	438	582	703	715
6. Ratios								
External debt stocks to exports (%)	311.7	313.1	195.2	202.2	200.9	133.7	129.1	..
External debt stocks to GNI (%)	116.7	110.0	91.4	89.1	89.0	58.0	58.1	61.1
Debt service to exports (%)	6.2	6.5	2.4	3.0	1.5	16.1	4.4	..
Short-term to external debt stocks (%)	5.8	9.3	13.1	12.8	16.0	6.8	3.0	3.5
Multilateral to external debt stocks (%)	48.3	53.6	52.6	53.0	50.8	52.0	50.6	48.4
Reserves to external debt stocks (%)	8.8	9.9	11.4	21.1	22.4	35.8	43.1	41.4
Reserves to imports (months)	2.2	2.5	1.8	3.5	3.6	4.0	4.7	..

TOGO

(US$ million, unless otherwise indicated)

	1995	2000	2005	2006	2007	2008	2009	2010
7. Long-term external debt								
Debt outstanding and disbursed	**1,286**	**1,228**	**1,440**	**1,541**	**1,642**	**1,469**	**1,494**	**1,534**
Public and publicly guaranteed	1,286	1,228	1,440	1,541	1,642	1,469	1,494	1,534
Official creditors	1,235	1,228	1,440	1,541	1,642	1,469	1,494	1,534
Multilateral	713	766	880	942	994	846	827	837
of which: IBRD	0	0	0	0	0	0	0	0
IDA	541	604	667	696	723	604	586	554
Bilateral	522	461	560	599	648	623	667	697
Private creditors	52	0	0	0	0	0	0	0
of which: Bonds	0	0	0	0	0	0	0	0
Commercial banks	52	0	0	0	0	0	0	0
Private nonguaranteed	0	0	0	0	0	0	0	0
of which: Bonds	0	0	0	0	0	0	0	0
Disbursements	**26**	**24**	**10**	**48**	**3**	**2**	**35**	**84**
Public and publicly guaranteed	26	24	10	48	3	2	35	84
Official creditors	26	24	10	48	3	2	35	84
Multilateral	26	21	10	25	3	2	12	47
of which: IBRD	0	0	0	0	0	0	0	0
IDA	20	15	0	0	0	0	0	0
Bilateral	0	4	0	23	0	0	23	37
Private creditors	0	0	0	0	0	0	0	0
of which: Bonds	0	0	0	0	0	0	0	0
Commercial banks	0	0	0	0	0	0	0	0
Private nonguaranteed	0	0	0	0	0	0	0	0
of which: Bonds	0	0	0	0	0	0	0	0
Principal repayments	**7**	**10**	**8**	**16**	**4**	**141**	**41**	**26**
Public and publicly guaranteed	7	10	8	16	4	141	41	26
Official creditors	7	10	8	16	4	141	41	26
Multilateral	6	9	1	2	3	140	41	26
of which: IBRD	0	0	0	0	0	0	0	0
IDA	3	5	0	0	0	117	22	22
Bilateral	1	2	7	14	2	1	0	0
Private creditors	0	0	0	0	0	0	0	0
of which: Bonds	0	0	0	0	0	0	0	0
Commercial banks	0	0	0	0	0	0	0	0
Private nonguaranteed	0	0	0	0	0	0	0	0
of which: Bonds	0	0	0	0	0	0	0	0
Interest payments	**8**	**5**	**0**	**2**	**1**	**51**	**13**	**8**
Public and publicly guaranteed	8	5	0	2	1	51	13	8
Official creditors	8	5	0	2	1	51	13	8
Multilateral	5	5	0	0	1	51	12	7
of which: IBRD	0	0	0	0	0	0	0	0
IDA	4	3	0	0	0	40	5	4
Bilateral	3	0	0	1	1	0	1	1
Private creditors	0	0	0	0	0	0	0	0
of which: Bonds	0	0	0	0	0	0	0	0
Commercial banks	0	0	0	0	0	0	0	0
Private nonguaranteed	0	0	0	0	0	0	0	0
of which: Bonds	0	0	0	0	0	0	0	0
8. Debt stock-flow reconciliation								
Total change in external debt stocks	20	-94	-151	104	180	-329	6	95
Net flows on external debt	39	-44	17	-7	49	-83	-33	113
9. Debt restructurings								
Total amount rescheduled	133	0	0	0	0	274	35	30
Total amount forgiven	107	0	0	0	0	319	12	10
Debt buyback	0	0	0	0	0	0	0	0

10. Contractual obligations on outstanding long-term external debt

	2011	2012	2013	2014	2015	2016	2017	2018
Official creditors								
Principal	56	58	61	71	70	74	75	74
Interest	26	26	26	25	24	23	21	20
Private creditors								
Principal	0	0	0	0	0	0	0	0
Interest	0	0	0	0	0	0	0	0

Notes:

Data on long-term public and publicly guaranteed debt include the effects of Paris Club debt restructuring agreement signed in 2008, 2009, and 2010. Only partial implementation is included because of the late agreement date in 2010.

TONGA

(US$ million, unless otherwise indicated)

	1995	2000	2005	2006	2007	2008	2009	2010
1. Summary external debt data								
External debt stocks	**62.8**	**65.2**	**79.6**	**81.7**	**86.5**	**88.8**	**104.6**	**143.5**
Long-term external debt	62.8	65.0	79.5	81.6	86.5	88.8	104.6	143.5
Public and publicly guaranteed	62.8	65.0	79.5	81.6	86.5	88.8	104.6	143.5
Private nonguaranteed	0.0	0.0	0.0	0.0	0.0	0.0	0.0	0.0
Use of IMF credit	0.0	0.0	0.0	0.0	0.0	0.0	0.0	0.0
Short-term external debt	0.0	0.2	0.1	0.1	0.0	0.0	0.0	0.0
interest arrears on long-term	0.0	0.2	0.1	0.1	0.0	0.0	0.0	0.0
Memorandum items								
Principal arrears on long-term	0.0	0.4	0.6	1.3	0.8	0.4	0.7	0.0
Long-term public sector debt	62.8	65.0	79.5	81.6	86.5	88.8	104.6	143.5
Long-term private sector debt	0.0	0.0	0.0	0.0	0.0	0.0	0.0	0.0
Public & publicly guaranteed commitments	12.0	0.0	1.0	0.0	57.9	0.0	0.9	43.1
External debt flows								
Disbursements	6.2	5.4	4.5	2.8	4.5	8.5	17.4	40.9
Long-term external debt	6.2	5.4	4.5	2.8	4.5	8.5	17.4	40.9
IMF purchases	0.0	0.0	0.0	0.0	0.0	0.0	0.0	0.0
Principal repayments	2.4	3.7	3.7	3.2	3.6	3.7	2.4	2.7
Long-term external debt	2.4	3.7	3.7	3.2	3.6	3.7	2.4	2.7
IMF repurchases	0.0	0.0	0.0	0.0	0.0	0.0	0.0	0.0
Net flows	3.8	1.8	0.9	-0.4	0.9	4.8	14.9	38.2
Long-term external debt	3.8	1.8	0.9	-0.4	0.9	4.8	14.9	38.2
Short-term external debt	0.0	0.0	0.0	0.0	0.0	0.0	0.0	0.0
Interest payments	0.7	0.9	1.2	0.8	1.1	1.7	1.4	2.3
Long-term external debt	0.7	0.9	1.2	0.8	1.1	1.7	1.4	2.3
IMF charges	0.0	0.0	0.0	0.0	0.0	0.0	0.0	0.0
Short-term external debt	0.0	0.0	0.0	0.0	0.0	0.0	0.0	0.0
2. Other non-debt resource inflows								
Foreign direct investment	..	4.8	7.2	10.1	27.7	4.2	0.0	16.2
Portfolio equity	..	..	..	..	..	..	..	..
3. Currency composition of public and publicly guaranteed debt (%)								
Euro	..	..	7.3	5.8	3.6	0.1	0.1	0.0
Japanese yen	0.0	0.0	0.0	0.0	0.0	0.0	0.0	0.0
Pound sterling	1.6	0.2	0.0	0.0	0.0	0.0	0.0	0.0
Swiss franc	0.0	0.0	0.0	0.0	0.0	0.0	0.0	0.0
U.S.dollars	10.7	4.8	28.0	31.2	35.1	33.8	30.3	21.4
4. Average terms of new commitments								
Official creditors								
Interest (%)	4.5	0.0	0.8	0.0	2.0	0.0	0.0	2.0
Maturity (years)	35.9	0.0	39.9	0.0	20.8	0.0	0.0	20.2
Grace period (years)	8.9	0.0	10.4	0.0	5.8	0.0	0.0	5.2
Private creditors								
Interest (%)	0.0	0.0	0.0	0.0	0.0	0.0	3.7	0.0
Maturity (years)	0.0	0.0	0.0	0.0	0.0	0.0	10.1	11.5
Grace period (years)	0.0	0.0	0.0	0.0	0.0	0.0	0.0	0.0
5. Major economic aggregates								
Gross national income (GNI)	206.2	191.0	259.6	300.1	312.2	355.5	332.6	361.7
Exports of goods, services & income	..	..	59.5	44.2	51.1	60.1	53.6	54.9
Worker remit. & comp. of employees	..	..	68.9	78.9	101.3	94.3	71.5	84.6
Imports of goods, services & income	..	..	157.3	158.1	181.3	222.4	194.4	160.3
Profit remittances on FDI	..	..	..	0.0	0.0	0.0	0.0	..
Current account balance	..	..	-21.3	-31.1	-19.4	-66.0	-54.2	..
International reserves	28.7	24.6	46.9	48.0	65.2	69.8	95.7	104.5
6. Ratios								
External debt stocks to exports (%)	..	..	133.9	184.7	169.2	147.9	195.1	261.4
External debt stocks to GNI (%)	30.5	34.2	30.7	27.2	27.7	25.0	31.4	39.7
Debt service to exports (%)	..	..	8.2	9.1	9.2	9.1	7.2	9.1
Short-term to external debt stocks (%)	..	0.4	0.1	0.2	..	..	..	..
Multilateral to external debt stocks (%)	66.4	81.9	84.4	85.4	87.0	81.3	69.7	49.3
Reserves to external debt stocks (%)	45.7	37.8	58.9	58.7	75.4	78.5	91.5	72.8
Reserves to imports (months)	..	..	3.6	3.6	4.3	3.8	5.9	7.8

TONGA

(US$ million, unless otherwise indicated)

	1995	2000	2005	2006	2007	2008	2009	2010
7. Long-term external debt								
Debt outstanding and disbursed	**62.8**	**65.0**	**79.5**	**81.6**	**86.5**	**88.8**	**104.6**	**143.5**
Public and publicly guaranteed	62.8	65.0	79.5	81.6	86.5	88.8	104.6	143.5
Official creditors	58.5	65.0	79.5	81.6	86.5	88.8	103.7	142.4
Multilateral	41.7	53.4	67.2	69.8	75.2	72.2	72.9	70.8
of which: IBRD	0.0	0.0	0.0	0.0	0.0	0.0	0.0	0.0
IDA	4.8	4.0	12.6	16.0	21.1	21.6	23.2	23.6
Bilateral	16.8	11.6	12.3	11.8	11.2	16.6	30.8	71.7
Private creditors	4.3	0.0	0.0	0.0	0.0	0.0	0.9	1.1
of which: Bonds	0.0	0.0	0.0	0.0	0.0	0.0	0.0	0.0
Commercial banks	0.0	0.0	0.0	0.0	0.0	0.0	0.0	0.3
Private nonguaranteed	0.0	0.0	0.0	0.0	0.0	0.0	0.0	0.0
of which: Bonds	0.0	0.0	0.0	0.0	0.0	0.0	0.0	0.0
Disbursements	**6.2**	**5.4**	**4.5**	**2.8**	**4.5**	**8.5**	**17.4**	**40.9**
Public and publicly guaranteed	6.2	5.4	4.5	2.8	4.5	8.5	17.4	40.9
Official creditors	6.2	5.4	4.5	2.8	4.5	8.5	16.5	40.7
Multilateral	6.2	3.0	4.5	2.8	4.5	0.7	1.6	1.0
of which: IBRD	0.0	0.0	0.0	0.0	0.0	0.0	0.0	0.0
IDA	0.2	0.0	4.5	2.8	4.5	0.7	1.6	1.0
Bilateral	0.0	2.4	0.0	0.0	0.0	7.8	15.0	39.7
Private creditors	0.0	0.0	0.0	0.0	0.0	0.0	0.8	0.2
of which: Bonds	0.0	0.0	0.0	0.0	0.0	0.0	0.0	0.0
Commercial banks	0.0	0.0	0.0	0.0	0.0	0.0	0.0	0.2
Private nonguaranteed	0.0	0.0	0.0	0.0	0.0	0.0	0.0	0.0
of which: Bonds	0.0	0.0	0.0	0.0	0.0	0.0	0.0	0.0
Principal repayments	**2.4**	**3.7**	**3.7**	**3.2**	**3.6**	**3.7**	**2.4**	**2.7**
Public and publicly guaranteed	2.4	3.7	3.7	3.2	3.6	3.7	2.4	2.7
Official creditors	2.4	2.4	3.7	3.2	3.6	3.7	2.4	2.6
Multilateral	0.8	1.0	2.6	2.0	2.1	2.3	1.5	2.0
of which: IBRD	0.0	0.0	0.0	0.0	0.0	0.0	0.0	0.0
IDA	0.0	0.1	0.1	0.1	0.1	0.1	0.1	0.2
Bilateral	1.7	1.4	1.1	1.2	1.4	1.5	0.8	0.6
Private creditors	0.0	1.3	0.0	0.0	0.0	0.0	0.0	0.1
of which: Bonds	0.0	0.0	0.0	0.0	0.0	0.0	0.0	0.0
Commercial banks	0.0	0.0	0.0	0.0	0.0	0.0	0.0	0.0
Private nonguaranteed	0.0	0.0	0.0	0.0	0.0	0.0	0.0	0.0
of which: Bonds	0.0	0.0	0.0	0.0	0.0	0.0	0.0	0.0
Interest payments	**0.7**	**0.9**	**1.2**	**0.8**	**1.1**	**1.7**	**1.4**	**2.3**
Public and publicly guaranteed	0.7	0.9	1.2	0.8	1.1	1.7	1.4	2.3
Official creditors	0.7	0.8	1.2	0.8	1.1	1.7	1.4	2.3
Multilateral	0.5	0.5	0.9	0.7	0.8	0.9	0.6	0.6
of which: IBRD	0.0	0.0	0.0	0.0	0.0	0.0	0.0	0.0
IDA	0.0	0.0	0.1	0.1	0.1	0.2	0.2	0.2
Bilateral	0.2	0.3	0.3	0.1	0.3	0.8	0.8	1.6
Private creditors	0.0	0.1	0.0	0.0	0.0	0.0	0.0	0.1
of which: Bonds	0.0	0.0	0.0	0.0	0.0	0.0	0.0	0.0
Commercial banks	0.0	0.0	0.0	0.0	0.0	0.0	0.0	0.0
Private nonguaranteed	0.0	0.0	0.0	0.0	0.0	0.0	0.0	0.0
of which: Bonds	0.0	0.0	0.0	0.0	0.0	0.0	0.0	0.0
8. Debt stock-flow reconciliation								
Total change in external debt stocks	5.2	-3.6	-5.3	2.1	4.8	2.4	15.8	38.9
Net flows on external debt	3.8	1.8	0.9	-0.4	0.9	4.8	14.9	38.2
9. Debt restructurings								
Total amount rescheduled	0.0	0.0	0.0	0.0	0.0	0.0	0.0	0.0
Total amount forgiven	0.0	0.0	0.0	0.0	0.0	1.7	0.0	0.0
Debt buyback	0.0	0.0	0.0	0.0	0.0	0.0	0.0	0.0

10. Contractual obligations on outstanding long-term external debt

	2011	2012	2013	2014	2015	2016	2017	2018
Official creditors								
Principal	4.4	4.5	6.7	7.8	10.6	10.6	10.6	10.2
Interest	2.9	3.0	3.0	3.0	2.9	2.8	2.6	2.4
Private creditors								
Principal	0.1	0.1	0.1	0.1	0.1	0.1	0.1	0.1
Interest	0.0	0.0	0.0	0.0	0.0	0.0	0.0	0.0

Notes:

Short-term debt data from 2005 and long-term private nonguaranteed debt data from 2009 are based on reports provided by the country.

TUNISIA

(US$ million, unless otherwise indicated)

	1995	2000	2005	2006	2007	2008	2009	2010
1. Summary external debt data								
External debt stocks	**10,818**	**11,307**	**17,875**	**18,634**	**20,441**	**20,773**	**21,711**	**21,584**
Long-term external debt	9,215	9,684	14,740	15,277	16,457	16,446	16,910	16,605
Public and publicly guaranteed	9,022	8,884	12,999	13,438	14,508	14,439	14,840	14,609
Private nonguaranteed	193	800	1,741	1,839	1,949	2,007	2,070	1,996
Use of IMF credit	293	32	0	0	0	0	0	0
Short-term external debt	1,310	1,590	3,135	3,357	3,984	4,327	4,801	4,979
interest arrears on long-term	0	0	0	0	0	0	0	0
Memorandum items								
Principal arrears on long-term	1	0	0	0	0	0	0	0
Long-term public sector debt	9,016	8,884	12,969	13,408	14,418	14,344	14,692	14,412
Long-term private sector debt	200	800	1,772	1,869	2,038	2,102	2,218	2,193
Public & publicly guaranteed commitments	1,949	1,412	1,738	1,175	992	1,497	1,511	812
External debt flows								
Disbursements	1,389	1,542	1,256	1,453	1,615	1,079	1,547	1,714
Long-term external debt	1,389	1,542	1,256	1,453	1,615	1,079	1,547	1,714
IMF purchases	0	0	0	0	0	0	0	0
Principal repayments	939	1,336	1,186	1,652	1,570	1,167	1,347	1,633
Long-term external debt	924	1,295	1,186	1,652	1,570	1,167	1,347	1,633
IMF repurchases	15	40	0	0	0	0	0	0
Net flows	654	259	-141	22	672	255	675	258
Long-term external debt	465	246	69	-200	45	-88	201	81
Short-term external debt	204	52	-210	222	627	343	474	177
Interest payments	541	570	848	881	926	845	758	716
Long-term external debt	486	489	686	686	742	744	700	647
IMF charges	17	3	0	0	0	0	0	0
Short-term external debt	38	78	162	195	184	101	58	68
2. Other non-debt resource inflows								
Foreign direct investment	264	752	723	3,270	1,532	2,638	1,595	1,401
Portfolio equity	12	-18	12	65	30	-39	-89	-26
3. Currency composition of public and publicly guaranteed debt (%)								
Euro	..	..	40.1	46.7	50.2	48.5	49.0	49.1
Japanese yen	13.5	21.6	17.4	14.4	15.4	19.5	18.5	18.2
Pound sterling	0.0	0.5	0.3	0.2	0.1	0.1	0.1	0.1
Swiss franc	0.2	0.7	0.5	0.4	0.3	0.3	0.3	0.2
U.S.dollars	17.5	30.0	20.3	17.7	14.3	12.8	12.5	12.0
4. Average terms of new commitments								
Official creditors								
Interest (%)	6.2	4.0	3.1	2.9	2.1	2.9	2.0	1.2
Maturity (years)	24.2	20.8	19.0	21.3	22.3	20.7	21.7	21.6
Grace period (years)	4.6	6.0	3.7	6.5	5.9	5.2	5.3	4.1
Private creditors								
Interest (%)	6.0	3.9	4.4	4.8	3.4	4.5	3.2	1.9
Maturity (years)	8.5	14.4	14.4	13.2	19.9	11.3	15.8	16.9
Grace period (years)	5.1	12.5	12.7	1.8	18.9	1.6	4.4	4.1
5. Major economic aggregates								
Gross national income (GNI)	17,174	18,526	27,309	29,553	33,625	38,471	41,240	42,242
Exports of goods, services & income	8,098	8,701	14,969	16,350	20,631	25,719	20,235	22,667
Worker remit. & comp. of employees	680	796	1,393	1,510	1,716	1,977	1,964	1,970
Imports of goods, services & income	9,646	10,347	16,580	18,412	23,167	29,352	23,420	26,706
Profit remittances on FDI	174	468	962	988	1,523	1,958	1,588	1,658
Current account balance	-774	-821	-299	-619	-917	-1,711	-1,234	-2,104
International reserves	1,689	1,871	4,548	6,912	8,032	9,039	11,294	9,764
6. Ratios								
External debt stocks to exports (%)	133.6	129.9	119.4	114.0	99.1	80.8	107.3	95.2
External debt stocks to GNI (%)	63.0	61.0	65.5	63.1	60.8	54.0	52.6	51.1
Debt service to exports (%)	18.3	21.9	13.6	15.5	12.1	7.8	10.4	10.4
Short-term to external debt stocks (%)	12.1	14.1	17.5	18.0	19.5	20.8	22.1	23.1
Multilateral to external debt stocks (%)	35.0	30.7	30.6	30.4	30.5	28.5	30.0	30.9
Reserves to external debt stocks (%)	15.6	16.6	25.4	37.1	39.3	43.5	52.0	45.2
Reserves to imports (months)	2.1	2.2	3.3	4.5	4.2	3.7	5.8	4.4

(US$ million, unless otherwise indicated)

	1995	2000	2005	2006	2007	2008	2009	2010
7. Long-term external debt								
Debt outstanding and disbursed	**9,215**	**9,684**	**14,740**	**15,277**	**16,457**	**16,446**	**16,910**	**16,605**
Public and publicly guaranteed	9,022	8,884	12,999	13,438	14,508	14,439	14,840	14,609
Official creditors	7,398	6,089	8,387	8,724	9,536	9,263	9,960	10,158
Multilateral	3,783	3,477	5,477	5,657	6,227	5,919	6,514	6,664
of which: IBRD	1,717	1,211	1,565	1,444	1,571	1,353	1,385	1,381
IDA	49	39	28	26	24	22	20	18
Bilateral	3,616	2,612	2,909	3,067	3,308	3,344	3,446	3,494
Private creditors	1,624	2,795	4,613	4,714	4,972	5,176	4,880	4,452
of which: Bonds	535	1,327	3,510	3,636	3,899	4,050	3,776	3,819
Commercial banks	236	786	817	847	900	998	994	570
Private nonguaranteed	193	800	1,741	1,839	1,949	2,007	2,070	1,996
of which: Bonds	0	0	0	0	0	0	0	0
Disbursements	**1,389**	**1,542**	**1,256**	**1,453**	**1,615**	**1,079**	**1,547**	**1,714**
Public and publicly guaranteed	1,359	1,242	1,126	1,283	1,426	909	1,367	1,540
Official creditors	611	709	843	963	1,103	831	1,314	1,504
Multilateral	467	428	606	673	846	550	943	1,094
of which: IBRD	138	136	177	112	161	70	184	234
IDA	0	0	0	0	0	0	0	0
Bilateral	145	281	236	290	256	282	370	411
Private creditors	747	533	283	320	324	77	54	36
of which: Bonds	588	0	249	251	255	0	0	0
Commercial banks	56	488	32	67	68	72	50	29
Private nonguaranteed	30	300	130	170	189	170	180	174
of which: Bonds	0	0	0	0	0	0	0	0
Principal repayments	**924**	**1,295**	**1,186**	**1,652**	**1,570**	**1,167**	**1,347**	**1,633**
Public and publicly guaranteed	889	1,263	1,128	1,580	1,491	1,055	1,230	1,385
Official creditors	639	661	868	1,152	1,094	952	832	873
Multilateral	363	408	533	843	783	635	502	546
of which: IBRD	203	150	232	366	169	273	152	157
IDA	2	2	2	2	2	2	2	2
Bilateral	276	253	336	309	310	317	330	327
Private creditors	250	602	260	429	397	102	399	512
of which: Bonds	0	371	136	301	250	0	313	0
Commercial banks	63	134	63	67	86	62	61	462
Private nonguaranteed	35	32	58	72	79	112	117	249
of which: Bonds	0	0	0	0	0	0	0	0
Interest payments	**486**	**489**	**686**	**686**	**742**	**744**	**700**	**647**
Public and publicly guaranteed	478	479	584	595	619	629	598	546
Official creditors	368	297	332	336	354	364	334	308
Multilateral	255	215	249	262	270	286	261	237
of which: IBRD	129	79	69	72	67	74	57	42
IDA	0	0	0	0	0	0	0	0
Bilateral	113	82	83	74	83	78	73	71
Private creditors	110	182	251	259	265	265	263	238
of which: Bonds	14	99	200	211	216	217	217	193
Commercial banks	18	37	36	35	38	39	40	39
Private nonguaranteed	8	10	102	91	123	115	102	102
of which: Bonds	0	0	0	0	0	0	0	0
8. Debt stock-flow reconciliation								
Total change in external debt stocks	1,205	-553	-1,627	759	1,807	332	939	-127
Net flows on external debt	654	259	-141	22	672	255	675	258
9. Debt restructurings								
Total amount rescheduled	0	0	0	0	0	0	0	0
Total amount forgiven	0	0	0	0	0	0	0	0
Debt buyback	0	0	0	0	0	0	0	0

10. Contractual obligations on outstanding long-term external debt

	2011	2012	2013	2014	2015	2016	2017	2018
Official creditors								
Principal	1,246	1,098	1,037	1,032	1,055	988	958	874
Interest	280	271	256	238	215	192	167	144
Private creditors								
Principal	1,437	1,112	847	260	211	168	413	106
Interest	310	223	165	135	124	114	104	88

Notes:

Long-term private nonguaranteed debt data for 2010 are World Bank staff estimates based on information provided by the government. Short-term debt is based on reports provided by the country.

TURKEY

(US$ million, unless otherwise indicated)

	1995	2000	2005	2006	2007	2008	2009	2010
1. Summary external debt data								
External debt stocks	**73,781**	**116,646**	**168,818**	**204,788**	**252,950**	**284,080**	**271,225**	**293,872**
Long-term external debt	57,396	83,558	115,889	151,403	202,656	222,452	213,555	210,123
Public and publicly guaranteed	50,317	55,730	64,470	69,827	82,455	83,764	87,083	93,088
Private nonguaranteed	7,079	27,828	51,418	81,576	120,201	138,687	126,472	117,035
Use of IMF credit	685	4,176	14,646	10,762	7,158	8,524	7,958	5,627
Short-term external debt	15,701	28,912	38,283	42,623	43,135	53,104	49,711	78,123
interest arrears on long-term	0	0	0	0	0	0	0	0
Memorandum items								
Principal arrears on long-term	0	0	0	0	0	0	0	0
Long-term public sector debt	50,131	55,713	64,299	69,616	81,973	82,706	85,810	91,707
Long-term private sector debt	7,265	27,846	51,589	81,787	120,683	139,745	127,746	118,415
Public & publicly guaranteed commitments	4,435	14,470	10,464	11,233	15,722	12,258	8,716	16,476
External debt flows								
Disbursements	6,980	26,414	40,595	58,813	72,829	68,553	39,605	46,499
Long-term external debt	6,638	22,955	38,135	55,872	71,682	64,999	39,605	46,499
IMF purchases	341	3,459	2,461	2,941	1,147	3,554	0	0
Principal repayments	7,020	13,831	31,279	31,002	36,681	42,066	50,013	47,187
Long-term external debt	7,020	13,744	23,499	23,510	31,517	40,099	49,307	45,016
IMF repurchases	0	87	7,780	7,493	5,164	1,967	706	2,171
Net flows	4,350	18,023	16,738	32,151	36,661	36,456	-13,801	27,724
Long-term external debt	-382	9,211	14,636	32,363	40,165	24,899	-9,702	1,483
Short-term external debt	4,391	5,440	7,422	4,340	512	9,969	-3,393	28,412
Interest payments	4,431	6,853	8,515	9,719	12,111	13,450	12,226	11,501
Long-term external debt	3,464	5,000	6,224	7,428	10,038	11,183	10,295	8,637
IMF charges	24	52	951	799	563	408	192	130
Short-term external debt	942	1,800	1,340	1,492	1,510	1,859	1,740	2,734
2. Other non-debt resource inflows								
Foreign direct investment	885	982	10,031	20,185	22,047	19,504	8,409	9,278
Portfolio equity	195	489	5,669	1,939	5,138	716	2,827	3,468
3. Currency composition of public and publicly guaranteed debt (%)								
Euro	..	..	23.4	25.1	26.8	27.3	29.5	31.1
Japanese yen	23.3	12.1	3.8	3.2	2.8	3.8	3.7	4.5
Pound sterling	0.9	0.8	0.1	0.0	0.0	0.0	0.0	0.0
Swiss franc	2.9	0.3	0.2	0.2	0.2	0.3	0.2	0.2
U.S.dollars	38.3	58.0	72.0	70.9	69.7	68.2	66.1	63.8
4. Average terms of new commitments								
Official creditors								
Interest (%)	5.4	6.5	2.8	4.5	4.4	3.9	2.5	1.5
Maturity (years)	17.7	14.6	24.6	16.2	18.2	22.0	18.2	20.5
Grace period (years)	5.7	4.8	6.7	6.2	6.9	6.8	7.1	9.9
Private creditors								
Interest (%)	6.3	8.6	6.1	6.4	6.5	6.9	6.7	4.7
Maturity (years)	4.5	11.3	13.1	11.5	14.7	13.2	9.0	16.6
Grace period (years)	2.7	8.5	12.1	10.0	13.0	10.9	8.6	12.7
5. Major economic aggregates								
Gross national income (GNI)	166,281	262,566	477,141	524,244	640,047	721,975	606,365	727,445
Exports of goods, services & income	38,070	53,189	108,782	123,637	150,811	182,932	148,466	159,736
Worker remit. & comp. of employees	3,327	4,560	887	1,146	1,248	1,476	970	874
Imports of goods, services & income	44,806	67,873	132,433	157,794	191,488	227,004	164,756	208,804
Profit remittances on FDI	312	279	1,051	1,182	2,213	2,940	2,914	3,044
Current account balance	-2,338	-9,920	-22,197	-32,249	-38,434	-41,959	-13,991	-47,739
International reserves	13,891	23,515	52,494	63,265	76,496	73,675	74,933	85,959
6. Ratios								
External debt stocks to exports (%)	193.8	219.3	155.2	165.6	167.7	155.3	182.7	184.0
External debt stocks to GNI (%)	44.4	44.4	35.4	39.1	39.5	39.3	44.7	40.4
Debt service to exports (%)	30.1	38.9	36.6	32.9	32.4	30.3	41.9	36.7
Short-term to external debt stocks (%)	21.3	24.8	22.7	20.8	17.1	18.7	18.3	26.6
Multilateral to external debt stocks (%)	12.1	4.9	4.5	4.3	4.8	4.9	6.2	6.7
Reserves to external debt stocks (%)	18.8	20.2	31.1	30.9	30.2	25.9	27.6	29.3
Reserves to imports (months)	3.7	4.2	4.8	4.8	4.8	3.9	5.5	4.9

(US$ million, unless otherwise indicated)

	1995	2000	2005	2006	2007	2008	2009	2010
7. Long-term external debt								
Debt outstanding and disbursed	**57,396**	**83,558**	**115,889**	**151,403**	**202,656**	**222,452**	**213,555**	**210,123**
Public and publicly guaranteed	50,317	55,730	64,470	69,827	82,455	83,764	87,083	93,088
Official creditors	17,324	12,537	12,435	13,469	17,083	19,713	23,128	26,504
Multilateral	8,962	5,684	7,622	8,758	12,074	13,819	16,842	19,780
of which: IBRD	4,939	3,634	5,829	6,854	7,541	8,046	9,769	11,563
IDA	130	101	71	65	59	54	48	42
Bilateral	8,362	6,853	4,813	4,711	5,009	5,894	6,285	6,724
Private creditors	32,993	43,193	52,035	56,358	65,372	64,051	63,956	66,584
of which: Bonds	13,646	21,766	30,434	34,390	41,888	41,343	43,058	46,276
Commercial banks	15,643	19,313	20,836	21,386	22,996	22,293	20,503	19,837
Private nonguaranteed	7,079	27,828	51,418	81,576	120,201	138,687	126,472	117,035
of which: Bonds	149	1,784	4,025	5,776	6,662	6,759	6,606	8,502
Disbursements	**6,638**	**22,955**	**38,135**	**55,872**	**71,682**	**64,999**	**39,605**	**46,499**
Public and publicly guaranteed	4,862	14,075	7,756	9,511	13,300	10,679	9,866	14,637
Official creditors	808	2,393	1,001	2,377	3,119	3,850	4,773	5,620
Multilateral	466	1,490	851	2,013	2,754	2,781	3,719	4,788
of which: IBRD	422	1,291	461	1,796	1,223	1,198	2,281	2,785
IDA	0	0	0	0	0	0	0	0
Bilateral	342	903	151	364	366	1,069	1,054	832
Private creditors	4,053	11,682	6,754	7,134	10,181	6,829	5,093	9,017
of which: Bonds	2,343	7,118	5,230	5,509	7,463	4,000	3,739	6,665
Commercial banks	1,256	4,207	1,520	1,624	2,698	2,764	1,275	2,180
Private nonguaranteed	1,777	8,881	30,379	46,362	58,382	54,320	29,739	31,862
of which: Bonds	0	454	3,125	1,727	950	150	150	2,300
Principal repayments	**7,020**	**13,744**	**23,499**	**23,510**	**31,517**	**40,099**	**49,307**	**45,016**
Public and publicly guaranteed	5,987	6,268	7,957	6,133	6,491	7,666	6,469	5,959
Official creditors	1,991	1,745	1,653	1,672	1,674	1,576	1,650	1,788
Multilateral	1,229	1,043	863	1,003	960	934	1,002	1,131
of which: IBRD	882	486	755	807	666	628	662	690
IDA	6	6	6	6	6	6	6	6
Bilateral	762	702	790	668	714	642	648	657
Private creditors	3,996	4,523	6,303	4,462	4,816	6,091	4,819	4,171
of which: Bonds	1,716	1,869	3,993	2,463	2,798	3,902	2,387	2,684
Commercial banks	1,579	1,782	2,028	1,801	1,891	2,053	2,333	1,393
Private nonguaranteed	1,033	7,476	15,543	17,376	25,026	32,433	42,838	39,057
of which: Bonds	0	0	1,150	0	200	0	350	320
Interest payments	**3,464**	**5,000**	**6,224**	**7,428**	**10,038**	**11,183**	**10,295**	**8,637**
Public and publicly guaranteed	3,126	3,467	4,636	4,590	5,437	5,327	4,945	4,684
Official creditors	977	659	596	531	661	703	651	488
Multilateral	656	374	448	407	531	577	522	371
of which: IBRD	396	237	248	329	389	360	304	166
IDA	1	1	1	1	0	0	0	0
Bilateral	321	285	148	125	130	126	129	117
Private creditors	2,149	2,807	4,040	4,059	4,776	4,624	4,294	4,197
of which: Bonds	1,074	1,598	2,938	2,862	3,507	3,488	3,324	3,417
Commercial banks	782	1,064	1,049	1,155	1,233	1,110	952	765
Private nonguaranteed	339	1,533	1,587	2,838	4,600	5,856	5,350	3,953
of which: Bonds	13	126	338	328	412	371	288	228
8. Debt stock-flow reconciliation								
Total change in external debt stocks	7,532	15,019	9,327	35,971	48,161	31,130	-12,856	22,648
Net flows on external debt	4,350	18,023	16,738	32,151	36,661	36,456	-13,801	27,724
9. Debt restructurings								
Total amount rescheduled	0	0	0	0	0	0	0	0
Total amount forgiven	0	0	0	0	0	0	0	0
Debt buyback	0	0	0	0	0	0	0	0

10. Contractual obligations on outstanding long-term external debt

	2011	2012	2013	2014	2015	2016	2017	2018
Official creditors								
Principal	1,890	1,994	2,176	2,323	2,434	2,920	3,084	1,855
Interest	610	623	619	597	562	506	447	373
Private creditors								
Principal	34,136	26,195	20,415	15,230	16,015	11,728	11,867	5,674
Interest	7,215	7,212	6,918	5,506	5,730	4,440	4,192	3,146

Notes:
Historical data are revised as data in previous publications included local currency debt data. Data on long-term public and publicly guaranteed debt include nonresident deposits made under the Dresdner Bank scheme, amounting to $10.2 billion at end-2010. Short-term debt data are based on government statistics.

TURKMENISTAN

(US$ million, unless otherwise indicated)

	1995	2000	2005	2006	2007	2008	2009	2010
1. Summary external debt data								
External debt stocks	**402.2**	**2518.3**	**1058.0**	**886.0**	**743.4**	**638.2**	**552.0**	**421.6**
Long-term external debt	384.9	2288.1	911.0	734.3	649.9	587.4	477.2	366.8
Public and publicly guaranteed	384.9	2271.3	877.8	730.5	648.2	586.8	463.3	359.5
Private nonguaranteed	0.0	16.7	33.1	3.9	1.8	0.6	13.9	7.4
Use of IMF credit	0.0	0.0	0.0	0.0	0.0	0.0	0.0	0.0
Short-term external debt	17.4	230.3	147.0	151.7	93.5	50.8	74.8	54.8
interest arrears on long-term	9.4	5.0	5.0	3.7	3.5	0.8	0.8	0.8
Memorandum items								
Principal arrears on long-term	130.2	148.1	16.9	1.4	1.7	1.7	1.7	1.7
Long-term public sector debt	384.9	2271.3	877.8	730.5	648.2	586.8	463.3	359.5
Long-term private sector debt	0.0	16.7	33.1	3.9	1.8	0.6	13.9	7.4
Public & publicly guaranteed commitments	290.5	4.7	22.0	50.2	65.7	0.0	0.0	0.0
External debt flows								
Disbursements	113.0	430.1	89.0	9.5	38.9	25.9	35.2	25.5
Long-term external debt	113.0	430.1	89.0	9.5	38.9	25.9	35.2	25.5
IMF purchases	0.0	0.0	0.0	0.0	0.0	0.0	0.0	0.0
Principal repayments	80.3	353.0	261.4	216.5	166.3	140.8	146.4	142.8
Long-term external debt	80.3	353.0	261.4	216.5	166.3	140.8	146.4	142.8
IMF repurchases	0.0	0.0	0.0	0.0	0.0	0.0	0.0	0.0
Net flows	-39.2	-1.6	-280.4	-200.9	-185.4	-154.9	-87.2	-137.4
Long-term external debt	32.8	77.1	-172.4	-206.9	-127.4	-114.9	-111.2	-117.4
Short-term external debt	-72.0	-78.8	-108.0	6.0	-58.0	-40.0	24.0	-20.0
Interest payments	24.1	115.2	45.9	38.3	33.9	28.9	18.6	11.5
Long-term external debt	22.1	101.9	39.1	33.2	29.8	26.7	17.6	10.8
IMF charges	0.0	0.0	0.0	0.0	0.0	0.0	0.0	0.0
Short-term external debt	2.0	13.2	6.8	5.1	4.0	2.2	1.0	0.8
2. Other non-debt resource inflows								
Foreign direct investment	233.0	131.0	418.2	730.9	856.0	1277.0	3867.0	2083.0
Portfolio equity	..	..	..	..	..	..	..	..
3. Currency composition of public and publicly guaranteed debt (%)								
Euro	..	..	31.8	35.9	35.6	30.9	32.5	29.1
Japanese yen	0.0	31.6	43.7	43.3	40.5	41.5	33.4	28.9
Pound sterling	0.0	0.0	0.0	0.0	0.0	0.0	0.0	0.0
Swiss franc	0.0	0.0	0.0	0.0	0.0	0.0	0.0	0.0
U.S.dollars	72.1	51.5	18.2	13.4	9.8	7.9	6.4	3.6
4. Average terms of new commitments								
Official creditors								
Interest (%)	4.4	4.0	1.4	3.2	3.0	0.0	0.0	0.0
Maturity (years)	13.4	10.2	13.8	20.1	20.0	0.0	0.0	0.0
Grace period (years)	2.8	3.7	6.0	4.6	3.5	0.0	0.0	0.0
Private creditors								
Interest (%)	6.5	0.0	0.0	0.0	0.0	0.0	0.0	0.0
Maturity (years)	7.4	0.0	0.0	0.0	0.0	0.0	0.0	0.0
Grace period (years)	1.9	0.0	0.0	0.0	0.0	0.0	0.0	0.0
5. Major economic aggregates								
Gross national income (GNI)	2500.6	2727.4	7541.4	9651.6	11917.2	15861.1	17177.8	19774.0
Exports of goods, services & income	..	..	..	..	..	..	..	..
Worker remit. & comp. of employees	..	..	..	..	..	..	..	..
Imports of goods, services & income	..	..	..	..	..	..	..	..
Profit remittances on FDI	..	..	..	..	..	..	..	..
Current account balance	..	..	..	..	..	..	..	..
International reserves	1168.0	..	..	..	..	..	..	..
6. Ratios								
External debt stocks to exports (%)	..	..	..	..	..	..	..	..
External debt stocks to GNI (%)	16.1	92.3	14.0	9.2	6.2	4.0	3.2	2.1
Debt service to exports (%)	..	..	..	..	..	..	..	..
Short-term to external debt stocks (%)	4.3	9.1	13.9	17.1	12.6	8.0	13.5	13.0
Multilateral to external debt stocks (%)	14.5	1.9	3.8	3.4	3.1	3.1	3.1	3.4
Reserves to external debt stocks (%)	290.4	..	..	..	..	..	..	..
Reserves to imports (months)	..	..	..	..	..	..	..	..

	1995	2000	2005	2006	2007	2008	2009	2010
7. Long-term external debt								
Debt outstanding and disbursed	**384.9**	**2288.1**	**911.0**	**734.3**	**649.9**	**587.4**	**477.2**	**366.8**
Public and publicly guaranteed	384.9	2271.3	877.8	730.5	648.2	586.8	463.3	359.5
Official creditors	218.8	838.6	685.9	575.2	523.4	500.2	409.5	341.6
Multilateral	58.2	48.3	40.4	30.1	23.0	20.1	17.4	14.4
of which: IBRD	0.9	28.0	29.1	21.0	15.4	14.2	12.8	11.4
IDA	0.0	0.0	0.0	0.0	0.0	0.0	0.0	0.0
Bilateral	160.6	790.3	645.4	545.1	500.4	480.2	392.1	327.2
Private creditors	166.0	1432.7	192.0	155.3	124.8	86.5	53.9	17.8
of which: Bonds	0.0	0.0	0.0	0.0	0.0	0.0	0.0	0.0
Commercial banks	0.0	240.5	125.4	109.1	90.2	63.5	42.3	17.8
Private nonguaranteed	0.0	16.7	33.1	3.9	1.8	0.6	13.9	7.4
of which: Bonds	0.0	0.0	0.0	0.0	0.0	0.0	0.0	0.0
Disbursements	**113.0**	**430.1**	**89.0**	**9.5**	**38.9**	**25.9**	**35.2**	**25.5**
Public and publicly guaranteed	113.0	420.9	24.9	9.1	38.9	25.6	22.4	17.9
Official creditors	32.3	292.6	24.9	9.1	38.9	25.6	22.4	17.9
Multilateral	1.0	29.3	0.5	0.0	0.0	0.0	0.0	0.0
of which: IBRD	1.0	20.1	0.0	0.0	0.0	0.0	0.0	0.0
IDA	0.0	0.0	0.0	0.0	0.0	0.0	0.0	0.0
Bilateral	31.4	263.3	24.4	9.1	38.9	25.6	22.4	17.9
Private creditors	80.7	128.3	0.0	0.0	0.0	0.0	0.0	0.0
of which: Bonds	0.0	0.0	0.0	0.0	0.0	0.0	0.0	0.0
Commercial banks	0.0	91.2	0.0	0.0	0.0	0.0	0.0	0.0
Private nonguaranteed	0.0	9.2	64.1	0.5	0.0	0.3	12.8	7.5
of which: Bonds	0.0	0.0	0.0	0.0	0.0	0.0	0.0	0.0
Principal repayments	**80.3**	**353.0**	**261.4**	**216.5**	**166.3**	**140.8**	**146.4**	**142.8**
Public and publicly guaranteed	80.3	347.4	189.1	188.0	164.3	139.3	146.4	129.8
Official creditors	19.6	44.0	112.6	140.5	124.6	104.3	112.4	96.7
Multilateral	0.0	4.7	4.6	10.9	7.5	2.8	2.8	2.9
of which: IBRD	0.0	0.5	1.8	8.2	5.6	1.2	1.3	1.4
IDA	0.0	0.0	0.0	0.0	0.0	0.0	0.0	0.0
Bilateral	19.6	39.3	108.0	129.6	117.2	101.5	109.6	93.8
Private creditors	60.7	303.4	76.5	47.5	39.7	35.0	34.0	33.1
of which: Bonds	0.0	0.0	0.0	0.0	0.0	0.0	0.0	0.0
Commercial banks	0.0	13.0	34.7	27.1	28.2	23.5	22.5	21.6
Private nonguaranteed	0.0	5.5	72.3	28.5	2.0	1.5	0.0	13.0
of which: Bonds	0.0	0.0	0.0	0.0	0.0	0.0	0.0	0.0
Interest payments	**22.1**	**101.9**	**39.1**	**33.2**	**29.8**	**26.7**	**17.6**	**10.8**
Public and publicly guaranteed	22.1	101.2	37.3	32.3	29.6	26.6	17.1	10.3
Official creditors	11.7	27.8	23.9	23.7	19.8	20.1	14.3	9.6
Multilateral	1.9	2.5	1.9	2.4	1.7	1.1	0.7	0.4
of which: IBRD	0.1	1.3	1.0	1.5	1.1	0.6	0.3	0.1
IDA	0.0	0.0	0.0	0.0	0.0	0.0	0.0	0.0
Bilateral	9.8	25.3	22.0	21.3	18.1	18.9	13.6	9.2
Private creditors	10.3	73.4	13.4	8.6	9.7	6.6	2.8	0.8
of which: Bonds	0.0	0.0	0.0	0.0	0.0	0.0	0.0	0.0
Commercial banks	0.0	8.5	5.9	5.1	6.9	4.9	2.3	0.7
Private nonguaranteed	0.0	0.7	1.8	0.9	0.3	0.1	0.4	0.4
of which: Bonds	0.0	0.0	0.0	0.0	0.0	0.0	0.0	0.0
8. Debt stock-flow reconciliation								
Total change in external debt stocks	-28.8	-118.0	-464.3	-172.0	-142.6	-105.2	-86.2	-130.4
Net flows on external debt	-39.2	-1.6	-280.4	-200.9	-185.4	-154.9	-87.2	-137.4
9. Debt restructurings								
Total amount rescheduled	0.0	48.0	0.0	0.0	0.0	0.0	0.0	0.0
Total amount forgiven	0.0	0.0	0.0	0.0	0.0	0.0	0.0	0.0
Debt buyback	0.0	0.0	0.0	0.0	0.0	0.0	0.0	0.0

10. Contractual obligations on outstanding long-term external debt

	2011	2012	2013	2014	2015	2016	2017	2018
Official creditors								
Principal	96.1	37.5	35.3	35.7	35.7	16.2	13.8	12.9
Interest	8.5	6.7	6.0	5.3	4.6	3.7	3.3	3.0
Private creditors								
Principal	19.8	1.9	1.8	1.2	0.6	0.0	0.0	0.0
Interest	0.5	0.1	0.1	0.0	0.0	0.0	0.0	0.0

Notes:

Data on long-term public and publicly guaranteed debt for 2010 are World Bank staff estimates. Long-term private nonguaranteed debt data only cover European Bank for Reconstruction and Development.

UGANDA

(US$ million, unless otherwise indicated)

	1995	2000	2005	2006	2007	2008	2009	2010
1. Summary external debt data								
External debt stocks	**3,609**	**3,497**	**4,395**	**1,232**	**1,582**	**2,221**	**2,465**	**2,994**
Long-term external debt	3,089	3,051	4,184	1,075	1,546	1,754	2,221	2,671
Public and publicly guaranteed	3,089	3,051	4,184	1,075	1,546	1,754	2,221	2,671
Private nonguaranteed	0	0	0	0	0	0	0	0
Use of IMF credit	417	316	131	9	9	9	9	9
Short-term external debt	103	129	79	148	26	458	235	314
interest arrears on long-term	69	58	29	27	26	26	26	26
Memorandum items								
Principal arrears on long-term	226	124	75	64	53	51	51	51
Long-term public sector debt	3,066	3,047	4,184	1,075	1,545	1,753	2,216	2,666
Long-term private sector debt	23	5	0	0	1	1	5	5
Public & publicly guaranteed commitments	95	145	382	166	686	621	783	908
External debt flows								
Disbursements	290	230	230	250	473	275	493	486
Long-term external debt	234	219	224	247	473	275	493	486
IMF purchases	56	12	6	3	0	0	0	0
Principal repayments	97	48	135	70	50	52	49	40
Long-term external debt	69	26	99	70	50	52	49	40
IMF repurchases	28	21	36	0	0	0	0	0
Net flows	189	177	85	251	303	655	221	525
Long-term external debt	165	192	125	177	424	223	444	446
Short-term external debt	-4	-6	-10	71	-121	432	-223	79
Interest payments	38	26	35	28	15	22	22	24
Long-term external debt	34	21	33	24	12	15	18	21
IMF charges	2	2	0	0	0	0	0	0
Short-term external debt	2	4	3	4	3	6	4	3
2. Other non-debt resource inflows								
Foreign direct investment	121	161	380	644	792	729	789	817
Portfolio equity	..	..	..	19	-23	13	131	-70
3. Currency composition of public and publicly guaranteed debt (%)								
Euro	..	..	2.8	14.2	10.3	7.5	5.1	3.4
Japanese yen	1.2	1.8	0.0	0.0	0.0	0.3	0.5	0.8
Pound sterling	2.1	0.6	0.0	0.0	0.0	0.0	0.0	0.0
Swiss franc	0.0	0.0	0.0	0.0	0.0	0.0	0.0	0.0
U.S.dollars	66.2	62.5	67.8	55.1	48.1	46.5	47.6	47.2
4. Average terms of new commitments								
Official creditors								
Interest (%)	0.9	0.8	0.8	0.8	0.8	0.7	0.9	0.6
Maturity (years)	39.2	40.0	45.7	39.3	41.1	40.7	41.8	40.2
Grace period (years)	10.0	7.9	10.2	9.8	9.9	9.9	9.0	11.1
Private creditors								
Interest (%)	0.0	7.5	0.0	0.0	0.0	0.0	0.0	0.0
Maturity (years)	0.0	8.2	0.0	0.0	0.0	0.0	0.0	0.0
Grace period (years)	0.0	2.8	0.0	0.0	0.0	0.0	0.0	0.0
5. Major economic aggregates								
Gross national income (GNI)	5,698	6,086	8,966	9,728	11,687	14,160	15,516	16,720
Exports of goods, services & income	682	716	1,591	1,785	2,466	3,137	3,335	3,494
Worker remit. & comp. of employees	..	238	322	411	452	724	778	915
Imports of goods, services & income	1,603	1,574	2,653	3,297	4,275	5,691	5,547	6,425
Profit remittances on FDI	60	19	202	249	262	250	164	192
Current account balance	-281	-359	-26	-396	-701	-1,314	-1,064	-1,740
International reserves	459	808	1,344	1,811	2,560	2,301	2,994	2,838
6. Ratios								
External debt stocks to exports (%)	529.2	488.2	276.3	69.0	64.2	70.8	73.9	85.7
External debt stocks to GNI (%)	63.3	57.5	49.0	12.7	13.5	15.7	15.9	17.9
Debt service to exports (%)	19.8	10.3	10.7	5.5	2.6	2.4	2.1	1.8
Short-term to external debt stocks (%)	2.8	3.7	1.8	12.0	1.7	20.6	9.5	10.5
Multilateral to external debt stocks (%)	61.8	75.3	89.5	69.0	84.4	70.2	81.8	80.7
Reserves to external debt stocks (%)	12.7	23.1	30.6	147.0	161.8	103.6	121.5	94.8
Reserves to imports (months)	3.4	6.2	6.1	6.6	7.2	4.9	6.5	5.3

UGANDA

(US$ million, unless otherwise indicated)

	1995	2000	2005	2006	2007	2008	2009	2010
7. Long-term external debt								
Debt outstanding and disbursed	**3,089**	**3,051**	**4,184**	**1,075**	**1,546**	**1,754**	**2,221**	**2,671**
Public and publicly guaranteed	3,089	3,051	4,184	1,075	1,546	1,754	2,221	2,671
Official creditors	3,002	3,027	4,182	1,073	1,545	1,753	2,220	2,671
Multilateral	2,232	2,634	3,932	850	1,335	1,560	2,017	2,416
of which: IBRD	0	0	0	0	0	0	0	0
IDA	1,792	2,115	3,141	436	840	1,004	1,379	1,682
Bilateral	770	393	250	223	210	193	203	255
Private creditors	87	24	2	2	1	0	0	0
of which: Bonds	4	4	0	0	0	0	0	0
Commercial banks	21	9	2	2	1	0	0	0
Private nonguaranteed	0	0	0	0	0	0	0	0
of which: Bonds	0	0	0	0	0	0	0	0
Disbursements	**234**	**219**	**224**	**247**	**473**	**275**	**493**	**486**
Public and publicly guaranteed	234	219	224	247	473	275	493	486
Official creditors	234	219	224	247	473	275	493	486
Multilateral	213	218	224	247	449	265	463	445
of which: IBRD	0	0	0	0	0	0	0	0
IDA	159	190	133	156	374	172	365	326
Bilateral	21	0	0	0	24	11	30	41
Private creditors	0	0	0	0	0	0	0	0
of which: Bonds	0	0	0	0	0	0	0	0
Commercial banks	0	0	0	0	0	0	0	0
Private nonguaranteed	0	0	0	0	0	0	0	0
of which: Bonds	0	0	0	0	0	0	0	0
Principal repayments	**69**	**26**	**99**	**70**	**50**	**52**	**49**	**40**
Public and publicly guaranteed	69	26	99	70	50	52	49	40
Official creditors	60	25	98	69	49	52	49	39
Multilateral	49	9	34	37	24	25	29	24
of which: IBRD	12	0	0	0	0	0	0	0
IDA	8	3	21	10	0	0	1	3
Bilateral	11	16	64	33	24	27	20	15
Private creditors	9	1	1	1	1	1	0	0
of which: Bonds	0	0	0	0	0	0	0	0
Commercial banks	7	1	1	1	1	1	0	0
Private nonguaranteed	0	0	0	0	0	0	0	0
of which: Bonds	0	0	0	0	0	0	0	0
Interest payments	**34**	**21**	**33**	**24**	**12**	**15**	**18**	**21**
Public and publicly guaranteed	34	21	33	24	12	15	18	21
Official creditors	32	20	32	24	12	15	18	21
Multilateral	22	10	31	23	11	13	16	19
of which: IBRD	1	0	0	0	0	0	0	0
IDA	13	6	24	14	5	7	9	11
Bilateral	10	11	2	1	1	2	2	2
Private creditors	2	0	0	0	0	0	0	0
of which: Bonds	0	0	0	0	0	0	0	0
Commercial banks	2	0	0	0	0	0	0	0
Private nonguaranteed	0	0	0	0	0	0	0	0
of which: Bonds	0	0	0	0	0	0	0	0
8. Debt stock-flow reconciliation								
Total change in external debt stocks	211	-1	-329	-3,163	350	639	244	529
Net flows on external debt	189	177	85	251	303	655	221	525
9. Debt restructurings								
Total amount rescheduled	172	35	154	10	0	0	0	25
Total amount forgiven	41	217	53	3,554	20	7	0	2
Debt buyback	0	0	0	0	0	0	0	0

10. Contractual obligations on outstanding long-term external debt

	2011	2012	2013	2014	2015	2016	2017	2018
Official creditors								
Principal	48	53	58	59	59	61	78	92
Interest	27	29	30	31	32	31	31	30
Private creditors								
Principal	0	0	0	0	0	0	0	0
Interest	0	0	0	0	0	0	0	0

UKRAINE

(US$ million, unless otherwise indicated)

	1995	2000	2005	2006	2007	2008	2009	2010
1. Summary external debt data								
External debt stocks	**8,429**	**12,185**	**32,488**	**51,221**	**77,481**	**96,696**	**103,435**	**116,808**
Long-term external debt	6,664	9,665	19,237	35,030	54,137	71,351	72,587	76,104
Public and publicly guaranteed	6,581	8,136	9,649	10,872	14,450	14,703	13,482	16,246
Private nonguaranteed	84	1,528	9,588	24,158	39,687	56,648	59,106	59,858
Use of IMF credit	1,542	2,073	1,188	830	431	4,709	10,974	14,245
Short-term external debt	223	447	12,063	15,361	22,914	20,636	19,873	26,459
interest arrears on long-term	35	183	110	150	199	335	650	866
Memorandum items								
Principal arrears on long-term	88	567	240	286	322	653	2,651	4,013
Long-term public sector debt	6,581	8,112	9,632	10,864	14,450	14,703	13,482	16,246
Long-term private sector debt	84	1,553	9,605	24,166	39,687	56,648	59,106	59,858
Public & publicly guaranteed commitments	673	157	2,063	2,219	4,328	1,000	1,079	3,745
External debt flows								
Disbursements	1,997	1,628	7,965	17,878	28,515	36,388	22,600	38,932
Long-term external debt	801	1,377	7,965	17,878	28,515	31,646	16,430	35,499
IMF purchases	1,196	251	0	0	0	4,742	6,170	3,433
Principal repayments	636	2,945	4,388	7,109	8,808	14,220	18,232	25,672
Long-term external debt	636	2,096	4,088	6,699	8,381	13,879	18,143	25,672
IMF repurchases	0	849	300	410	427	341	88	0
Net flows	1,337	-1,291	5,275	14,027	27,211	19,754	3,291	19,630
Long-term external debt	165	-719	3,877	11,180	20,134	17,767	-1,713	9,827
Short-term external debt	-24	26	1,698	3,258	7,504	-2,414	-1,078	6,370
Interest payments	501	708	1,425	2,199	3,097	3,712	4,591	4,429
Long-term external debt	447	572	981	1,671	2,400	3,266	4,200	3,835
IMF charges	42	122	50	53	39	14	135	241
Short-term external debt	12	14	393	475	659	433	256	353
2. Other non-debt resource inflows								
Foreign direct investment	267	595	7,808	5,604	9,891	10,913	4,816	6,495
Portfolio equity	0	146	82	322	715	388	105	290
3. Currency composition of public and publicly guaranteed debt (%)								
Euro	..	18.6	18.6	16.6	17.0	15.2	17.0	13.3
Japanese yen	0.0	2.0	1.2	3.6	2.7	3.1	3.6	0.9
Pound sterling	0.0	0.0	0.0	0.0	0.0	0.0	0.0	0.0
Swiss franc	0.0	0.0	0.0	5.8	4.7	4.9	0.0	0.0
U.S.dollars	63.3	53.2	69.9	65.9	70.3	72.3	75.6	83.5
4. Average terms of new commitments								
Official creditors								
Interest (%)	4.7	7.3	3.6	6.2	3.5	2.3	1.4	0.6
Maturity (years)	13.4	15.2	19.8	20.0	17.9	23.7	27.5	11.5
Grace period (years)	4.8	4.5	6.0	5.5	5.6	5.2	5.0	6.0
Private creditors								
Interest (%)	6.5	0.0	5.2	5.1	5.9	6.3	0.0	4.9
Maturity (years)	8.0	0.0	10.7	9.6	6.6	7.0	0.0	7.0
Grace period (years)	2.5	0.0	9.9	9.6	6.6	4.0	0.0	7.0
5. Major economic aggregates								
Gross national income (GNI)	47,438	30,320	85,157	106,031	140,602	178,815	114,788	135,987
Exports of goods, services & income	17,337	19,665	45,136	51,571	67,657	91,031	58,877	73,970
Worker remit. & comp. of employees	..	33	595	829	4,503	5,769	5,073	5,607
Imports of goods, services & income	18,961	19,032	45,450	56,361	76,468	106,921	63,270	79,829
Profit remittances on FDI	0	43	268	996	1,178	2,506	2,542	2,218
Current account balance	-1,152	1,481	2,531	-1,617	-5,272	-12,763	-1,732	-2,884
International reserves	1,069	1,477	19,388	22,360	32,484	31,543	26,501	34,571
6. Ratios								
External debt stocks to exports (%)	48.6	62.0	72.0	99.3	114.5	106.2	175.7	157.9
External debt stocks to GNI (%)	17.8	40.2	38.2	48.3	55.1	54.1	90.1	85.9
Debt service to exports (%)	6.6	18.6	12.9	18.0	17.6	19.7	38.8	40.7
Short-term to external debt stocks (%)	2.6	3.7	37.1	30.0	29.6	21.3	19.2	22.7
Multilateral to external debt stocks (%)	7.8	19.5	8.2	5.4	4.5	4.2	4.3	3.8
Reserves to external debt stocks (%)	12.7	12.1	59.7	43.7	41.9	32.6	25.6	29.6
Reserves to imports (months)	0.7	0.9	5.1	4.8	5.1	3.5	5.0	5.2

UKRAINE

(US$ million, unless otherwise indicated)

	1995	2000	2005	2006	2007	2008	2009	2010
7. Long-term external debt								
Debt outstanding and disbursed	**6,664**	**9,665**	**19,237**	**35,030**	**54,137**	**71,351**	**72,587**	**76,104**
Public and publicly guaranteed	6,581	8,136	9,649	10,872	14,450	14,703	13,482	16,246
Official creditors	4,346	5,000	5,021	4,899	5,365	5,793	6,026	5,789
Multilateral	659	2,372	2,666	2,780	3,449	4,099	4,480	4,392
of which: IBRD	491	1,991	2,429	2,362	2,309	3,022	3,294	3,212
IDA	0	0	0	0	0	0	0	0
Bilateral	3,687	2,628	2,355	2,119	1,916	1,694	1,547	1,397
Private creditors	2,235	3,136	4,628	5,973	9,085	8,910	7,455	10,456
of which: Bonds	1,200	2,379	2,250	3,686	7,035	7,105	5,907	9,148
Commercial banks	130	134	1,349	1,260	1,025	786	531	296
Private nonguaranteed	84	1,528	9,588	24,158	39,687	56,648	59,106	59,858
of which: Bonds	0	0	550	1,513	4,185	4,965	5,059	5,114
Disbursements	**801**	**1,377**	**7,965**	**17,878**	**28,515**	**31,646**	**16,430**	**35,499**
Public and publicly guaranteed	732	173	1,411	2,233	4,315	923	664	3,998
Official creditors	550	141	563	319	804	918	664	313
Multilateral	525	119	556	319	800	917	607	265
of which: IBRD	401	113	484	85	115	889	509	158
IDA	0	0	0	0	0	0	0	0
Bilateral	25	22	7	0	3	2	57	49
Private creditors	182	32	847	1,915	3,511	4	0	3,685
of which: Bonds	0	0	747	1,915	3,511	0	0	3,685
Commercial banks	0	14	100	0	0	4	0	0
Private nonguaranteed	69	1,204	6,554	15,645	24,200	30,723	15,766	31,500
of which: Bonds	0	0	450	962	2,800	1,230	789	1,730
Principal repayments	**636**	**2,096**	**4,088**	**6,699**	**8,381**	**13,879**	**18,143**	**25,672**
Public and publicly guaranteed	595	1,250	1,193	1,235	1,070	703	1,942	1,107
Official creditors	165	1,208	546	532	498	456	475	468
Multilateral	127	63	265	252	246	232	263	271
of which: IBRD	0	24	168	171	189	203	235	243
IDA	0	0	0	0	0	0	0	0
Bilateral	38	1,145	281	280	252	224	212	197
Private creditors	430	42	647	704	572	246	1,467	639
of which: Bonds	200	33	622	602	328	0	1,209	401
Commercial banks	2	2	0	95	241	242	255	235
Private nonguaranteed	40	845	2,895	5,463	7,310	13,176	16,202	24,565
of which: Bonds	0	0	0	0	129	450	695	1,925
Interest payments	**447**	**572**	**981**	**1,671**	**2,400**	**3,266**	**4,200**	**3,835**
Public and publicly guaranteed	440	500	508	564	690	635	696	469
Official creditors	306	148	130	176	185	163	168	111
Multilateral	13	139	87	135	149	135	148	98
of which: IBRD	8	118	76	121	134	118	78	34
IDA	0	0	0	0	0	0	0	0
Bilateral	293	8	43	41	36	28	20	14
Private creditors	134	352	379	388	505	472	528	357
of which: Bonds	87	344	172	158	293	295	392	251
Commercial banks	3	8	128	152	134	100	58	29
Private nonguaranteed	7	71	473	1,107	1,710	2,630	3,505	3,367
of which: Bonds	0	0	41	89	247	336	423	407
8. Debt stock-flow reconciliation								
Total change in external debt stocks	2,793	-1,764	3,137	18,733	26,260	19,214	6,739	13,374
Net flows on external debt	1,337	-1,291	5,275	14,027	27,211	19,754	3,291	19,630
9. Debt restructurings								
Total amount rescheduled	2,535	2,185	0	0	0	0	0	0
Total amount forgiven	0	0	0	0	0	0	0	0
Debt buyback	0	0	0	0	0	0	0	0

10. Contractual obligations on outstanding long-term external debt

	2011	2012	2013	2014	2015	2016	2017	2018
Official creditors								
Principal	587	581	590	465	491	488	488	479
Interest	84	71	59	51	46	41	36	31
Private creditors								
Principal	17,199	11,961	8,997	4,561	7,504	3,320	2,464	7,713
Interest	2,873	2,288	1,715	1,401	1,103	912	951	1,529

Notes:

Short-term debt is based on reports provided by the National Bank of Ukraine.

URUGUAY

(US$ million, unless otherwise indicated)

	1995	2000	2005	2006	2007	2008	2009	2010
1. Summary external debt data								
External debt stocks	**5,318**	**8,408**	**11,101**	**9,611**	**9,837**	**9,644**	**11,131**	**11,347**
Long-term external debt	3,960	5,873	8,061	8,872	8,929	8,827	10,007	9,797
Public and publicly guaranteed	3,833	5,551	7,736	8,552	8,642	8,640	9,927	9,704
Private nonguaranteed	127	322	325	319	287	187	80	93
Use of IMF credit	21	149	2,304	0	0	0	0	0
Short-term external debt	1,336	2,387	736	739	908	817	1,124	1,550
interest arrears on long-term	0	0	0	0	0	0	0	0
Memorandum items								
Principal arrears on long-term	0	0	0	0	0	0	0	0
Long-term public sector debt	3,831	5,550	7,736	8,552	8,642	8,640	9,927	9,704
Long-term private sector debt	130	322	325	319	287	187	80	93
Public & publicly guaranteed commitments	452	759	2,855	1,516	591	897	1,623	148
External debt flows								
Disbursements	661	928	1,626	1,791	544	682	1,575	417
Long-term external debt	661	928	1,329	1,493	544	682	1,575	417
IMF purchases	0	0	297	298	0	0	0	0
Principal repayments	484	666	1,276	4,937	540	913	534	700
Long-term external debt	474	666	807	2,267	540	913	534	700
IMF repurchases	10	0	469	2,670	0	0	0	0
Net flows	281	382	203	-3,143	173	-321	1,348	144
Long-term external debt	187	262	522	-774	4	-230	1,041	-282
Short-term external debt	104	120	-147	3	169	-91	307	426
Interest payments	379	544	629	723	659	499	446	670
Long-term external debt	298	413	434	580	609	462	395	599
IMF charges	2	8	115	106	5	0	0	0
Short-term external debt	80	123	80	37	45	37	51	71
2. Other non-debt resource inflows								
Foreign direct investment	157	269	847	1,493	1,329	1,809	1,262	1,627
Portfolio equity	0	5	-2	-27	2	-12	-12	-12
3. Currency composition of public and publicly guaranteed debt (%)								
Euro	..	..	8.5	7.3	7.3	5.6	5.0	4.7
Japanese yen	6.4	3.4	2.9	2.5	5.4	6.4	5.1	5.6
Pound sterling	1.9	1.0	0.1	0.0	0.0	0.0	0.0	0.0
Swiss franc	0.0	0.0	0.0	0.0	0.0	0.0	0.0	0.0
U.S.dollars	53.8	80.8	83.9	86.5	84.1	85.1	87.8	89.3
4. Average terms of new commitments								
Official creditors								
Interest (%)	3.9	7.2	4.6	5.4	5.6	3.7	2.2	1.4
Maturity (years)	14.9	14.8	17.7	21.2	16.3	11.7	17.0	19.1
Grace period (years)	5.5	5.2	5.3	4.9	6.4	3.1	7.2	6.4
Private creditors								
Interest (%)	7.0	7.8	8.0	7.6	2.2	8.0	8.6	2.3
Maturity (years)	7.2	7.7	15.3	30.0	10.0	8.3	15.0	19.3
Grace period (years)	3.3	7.2	15.0	30.0	10.0	7.8	13.0	8.1
5. Major economic aggregates								
Gross national income (GNI)	18,994	22,757	16,863	19,366	23,359	30,449	30,651	39,162
Exports of goods, services & income	3,911	4,441	5,648	6,529	7,818	10,130	9,070	11,020
Worker remit. & comp. of employees	..	..	77	89	96	108	101	103
Imports of goods, services & income	4,200	5,035	5,750	7,047	8,176	11,758	9,004	11,302
Profit remittances on FDI	54	99	228	261	531	663	401	730
Current account balance	-213	-566	42	-392	-220	-1,480	207	-160
International reserves	1,813	2,776	3,078	3,091	4,121	6,360	8,038	7,656
6. Ratios								
External debt stocks to exports (%)	136.0	189.3	196.5	147.2	125.8	95.2	122.7	103.0
External debt stocks to GNI (%)	28.0	36.9	65.8	49.6	42.1	31.7	36.3	29.0
Debt service to exports (%)	22.1	27.2	33.7	86.7	15.3	13.9	10.8	12.4
Short-term to external debt stocks (%)	25.1	28.4	6.6	7.7	9.2	8.5	10.1	13.7
Multilateral to external debt stocks (%)	23.7	22.9	27.9	26.4	25.7	30.4	32.8	30.8
Reserves to external debt stocks (%)	34.1	33.0	27.7	32.2	41.9	66.0	72.2	67.5
Reserves to imports (months)	5.2	6.6	6.4	5.3	6.0	6.5	10.7	8.1

(US$ million, unless otherwise indicated)

	1995	2000	2005	2006	2007	2008	2009	2010
7. Long-term external debt								
Debt outstanding and disbursed	**3,960**	**5,873**	**8,061**	**8,872**	**8,929**	**8,827**	**10,007**	**9,797**
Public and publicly guaranteed	3,833	5,551	7,736	8,552	8,642	8,640	9,927	9,704
Official creditors	1,588	2,228	3,244	2,714	2,702	3,092	3,790	3,611
Multilateral	1,259	1,926	3,097	2,533	2,529	2,936	3,653	3,495
of which: IBRD	513	552	816	653	666	713	1,099	1,055
IDA	0	0	0	0	0	0	0	0
Bilateral	329	302	146	181	173	157	137	117
Private creditors	2,245	3,323	4,492	5,838	5,940	5,547	6,138	6,093
of which: Bonds	1,963	2,774	4,201	5,789	5,896	5,464	6,071	6,021
Commercial banks	252	530	279	38	34	77	63	70
Private nonguaranteed	127	322	325	319	287	187	80	93
of which: Bonds	110	300	300	300	287	187	80	93
Disbursements	**661**	**928**	**1,329**	**1,493**	**544**	**682**	**1,575**	**417**
Public and publicly guaranteed	591	928	1,329	1,493	457	682	1,575	417
Official creditors	128	300	389	205	199	632	966	398
Multilateral	103	299	384	159	189	632	966	398
of which: IBRD	32	134	134	42	74	147	450	46
IDA	0	0	0	0	0	0	0	0
Bilateral	25	1	5	46	10	0	0	0
Private creditors	463	629	940	1,289	259	51	609	19
of which: Bonds	348	615	919	1,286	255	2	599	0
Commercial banks	111	1	21	3	4	48	11	19
Private nonguaranteed	70	0	0	0	87	0	0	0
of which: Bonds	70	0	0	0	87	0	0	0
Principal repayments	**474**	**666**	**807**	**2,267**	**540**	**913**	**534**	**700**
Public and publicly guaranteed	469	606	799	2,261	421	813	434	700
Official creditors	124	162	341	746	230	253	288	593
Multilateral	117	121	328	732	208	231	267	573
of which: IBRD	78	58	104	205	61	85	85	88
IDA	0	0	0	0	0	0	0	0
Bilateral	7	42	13	14	21	22	21	21
Private creditors	345	443	458	1,515	191	560	146	106
of which: Bonds	273	285	260	1,268	181	552	95	93
Commercial banks	66	154	196	245	9	5	49	11
Private nonguaranteed	5	60	8	5	119	100	100	0
of which: Bonds	0	47	0	0	100	100	100	0
Interest payments	**298**	**413**	**434**	**580**	**609**	**462**	**395**	**599**
Public and publicly guaranteed	293	381	406	553	583	449	384	592
Official creditors	124	147	152	152	145	129	126	152
Multilateral	91	134	149	149	140	124	122	149
of which: IBRD	40	42	34	41	38	31	28	15
IDA	0	0	0	0	0	0	0	0
Bilateral	33	13	3	3	5	5	4	3
Private creditors	169	233	255	401	438	320	258	440
of which: Bonds	151	182	242	391	436	318	254	437
Commercial banks	15	51	12	9	2	1	3	3
Private nonguaranteed	4	33	27	27	26	13	11	8
of which: Bonds	3	29	26	26	25	13	11	7
8. Debt stock-flow reconciliation								
Total change in external debt stocks	243	518	-604	-1,490	227	-193	1,488	216
Net flows on external debt	281	382	203	-3,143	173	-321	1,348	144
9. Debt restructurings								
Total amount rescheduled	0	0	0	0	0	0	0	0
Total amount forgiven	0	0	0	0	4	0	0	0
Debt buyback	0	0	0	955	178	542	1	0

10. Contractual obligations on outstanding long-term external debt

	2011	2012	2013	2014	2015	2016	2017	2018
Official creditors								
Principal	285	272	290	311	306	295	407	255
Interest	73	68	62	56	49	42	34	28
Private creditors								
Principal	278	44	37	26	162	305	760	25
Interest	447	438	436	433	426	400	377	354

Notes:

Long-term private nonguaranteed debt data only cover Bonds. Short-term debt data are based on reports provided by the Central Bank data.

UZBEKISTAN

(US$ million, unless otherwise indicated)

	1995	2000	2005	2006	2007	2008	2009	2010
1. Summary external debt data								
External debt stocks	**1,799**	**4,633**	**4,282**	**4,074**	**4,211**	**4,686**	**6,550**	**7,404**
Long-term external debt	1,430	4,224	4,170	3,916	4,013	4,465	6,386	7,167
Public and publicly guaranteed	1,415	3,762	3,619	3,289	3,134	3,144	3,246	3,426
Private nonguaranteed	15	462	551	627	879	1,321	3,141	3,741
Use of IMF credit	157	127	0	0	0	0	0	0
Short-term external debt	212	282	112	158	198	221	163	238
interest arrears on long-term	0	3	8	0	2	10	19	70
Memorandum items								
Principal arrears on long-term	0	17	35	0	37	34	56	92
Long-term public sector debt	1,288	3,605	3,577	3,276	3,115	3,138	3,241	3,423
Long-term private sector debt	142	618	592	640	898	1,327	3,145	3,744
Public & publicly guaranteed commitments	980	310	212	107	428	305	432	1,546
External debt flows								
Disbursements	791	769	400	349	661	1,012	2,633	1,183
Long-term external debt	630	769	400	349	661	1,012	2,633	1,183
IMF purchases	161	0	0	0	0	0	0	0
Principal repayments	149	648	642	677	649	711	717	471
Long-term external debt	149	583	623	677	649	711	717	471
IMF repurchases	0	65	18	0	0	0	0	0
Net flows	563	-223	-308	-274	50	316	1,849	737
Long-term external debt	481	186	-223	-328	12	301	1,916	713
Short-term external debt	-79	-344	-66	54	38	15	-67	24
Interest payments	95	237	145	173	175	149	123	124
Long-term external debt	80	206	141	170	168	141	120	118
IMF charges	3	9	0	0	0	0	0	0
Short-term external debt	13	23	4	3	7	8	2	6
2. Other non-debt resource inflows								
Foreign direct investment	-24	75	192	174	705	711	711	822
Portfolio equity	..	..	..	..	..	..	..	..
3. Currency composition of public and publicly guaranteed debt (%)								
Euro	..	..	17.9	17.8	17.6	14.5	12.6	10.4
Japanese yen	3.1	21.2	21.4	21.3	22.6	26.9	23.8	22.7
Pound sterling	0.0	0.0	0.0	0.0	0.0	0.0	0.0	0.0
Swiss franc	0.1	0.0	0.5	0.4	0.4	0.3	0.2	0.2
U.S.dollars	66.5	56.7	52.9	51.9	49.7	48.4	53.0	54.5
4. Average terms of new commitments								
Official creditors								
Interest (%)	5.2	6.0	1.9	2.9	2.8	2.3	1.3	1.4
Maturity (years)	18.1	18.4	25.8	22.2	20.9	24.9	26.6	24.7
Grace period (years)	5.1	4.4	7.3	6.7	6.0	6.0	6.9	6.7
Private creditors								
Interest (%)	7.1	7.3	0.0	4.3	4.7	4.8	3.6	2.6
Maturity (years)	9.1	6.4	0.0	6.6	5.4	6.1	12.9	7.7
Grace period (years)	2.5	1.4	0.0	1.1	0.9	1.6	3.4	1.9
5. Major economic aggregates								
Gross national income (GNI)	13,324	13,541	14,283	16,942	22,385	27,490	32,636	39,013
Exports of goods, services & income	..	..	..	..	..	..	..	..
Worker remit. & comp. of employees	..	..	..	..	..	..	..	..
Imports of goods, services & income	..	..	..	..	..	..	..	..
Profit remittances on FDI	..	..	..	..	..	..	..	..
Current account balance	..	..	..	..	..	..	..	..
International reserves	..	..	..	..	..	..	..	..
6. Ratios								
External debt stocks to exports (%)	..	..	..	..	..	..	..	..
External debt stocks to GNI (%)	13.5	34.2	30.0	24.0	18.8	17.0	20.1	19.0
Debt service to exports (%)	..	..	..	..	..	..	..	..
Short-term to external debt stocks (%)	11.8	6.1	2.6	3.9	4.7	4.7	2.5	3.2
Multilateral to external debt stocks (%)	13.7	9.8	18.5	20.3	20.6	19.6	16.3	15.9
Reserves to external debt stocks (%)	..	..	..	..	..	..	..	..
Reserves to imports (months)	..	..	..	..	..	..	..	..

UZBEKISTAN

(US$ million, unless otherwise indicated)

	1995	2000	2005	2006	2007	2008	2009	2010
7. Long-term external debt								
Debt outstanding and disbursed	**1,430**	**4,224**	**4,170**	**3,916**	**4,013**	**4,465**	**6,386**	**7,167**
Public and publicly guaranteed	1,415	3,762	3,619	3,289	3,134	3,144	3,246	3,426
Official creditors	1,023	2,117	2,445	2,393	2,458	2,664	2,912	3,173
Multilateral	246	454	791	826	868	920	1,065	1,175
of which: IBRD	157	217	299	316	317	313	284	259
IDA	0	0	11	26	43	55	83	114
Bilateral	777	1,663	1,653	1,567	1,590	1,744	1,847	1,998
Private creditors	393	1,645	1,175	896	676	480	333	252
of which: Bonds	0	0	0	0	0	0	0	0
Commercial banks	0	368	193	149	125	111	73	58
Private nonguaranteed	15	462	551	627	879	1,321	3,141	3,741
of which: Bonds	0	0	0	0	0	0	0	0
Disbursements	**630**	**769**	**400**	**349**	**661**	**1,012**	**2,633**	**1,183**
Public and publicly guaranteed	619	713	255	173	229	315	481	447
Official creditors	399	409	193	156	209	277	473	433
Multilateral	246	121	136	110	93	106	212	192
of which: IBRD	162	31	25	32	17	15	5	5
IDA	0	0	7	13	16	13	28	32
Bilateral	154	288	57	46	116	171	260	240
Private creditors	219	304	62	17	21	37	8	15
of which: Bonds	0	0	0	0	0	0	0	0
Commercial banks	0	59	34	10	20	37	1	15
Private nonguaranteed	12	56	145	177	432	697	2,152	736
of which: Bonds	0	0	0	0	0	0	0	0
Principal repayments	**149**	**583**	**623**	**677**	**649**	**711**	**717**	**471**
Public and publicly guaranteed	148	443	510	579	496	458	383	340
Official creditors	119	148	177	237	218	239	223	254
Multilateral	0	29	67	82	61	67	67	86
of which: IBRD	0	5	20	21	25	29	32	32
IDA	0	0	0	0	0	0	0	0
Bilateral	119	119	110	155	157	172	156	168
Private creditors	29	295	333	341	278	219	161	86
of which: Bonds	0	0	0	0	0	0	0	0
Commercial banks	0	72	49	62	51	47	40	27
Private nonguaranteed	1	140	113	99	153	253	333	131
of which: Bonds	0	0	0	0	0	0	0	0
Interest payments	**80**	**206**	**141**	**170**	**168**	**141**	**120**	**118**
Public and publicly guaranteed	79	182	117	146	141	114	82	62
Official creditors	52	75	63	93	96	84	70	59
Multilateral	4	26	32	42	47	43	34	22
of which: IBRD	2	12	12	15	18	18	15	11
IDA	0	0	0	0	0	0	0	1
Bilateral	47	49	31	51	49	41	36	37
Private creditors	27	108	53	52	45	30	12	4
of which: Bonds	0	0	0	0	0	0	0	0
Commercial banks	0	29	10	9	9	7	3	1
Private nonguaranteed	1	24	24	24	27	27	39	56
of which: Bonds	0	0	0	0	0	0	0	0
8. Debt stock-flow reconciliation								
Total change in external debt stocks	552	-307	-541	-208	137	475	1,864	855
Net flows on external debt	563	-223	-308	-274	50	316	1,849	737
9. Debt restructurings								
Total amount rescheduled	0	0	0	0	0	0	0	0
Total amount forgiven	0	0	0	0	0	0	0	0
Debt buyback	0	0	0	0	0	0	0	0

10. Contractual obligations on outstanding long-term external debt

	2011	2012	2013	2014	2015	2016	2017	2018
Official creditors								
Principal	262	257	261	291	289	251	241	242
Interest	74	73	70	67	62	57	53	49
Private creditors								
Principal	1,021	911	554	434	324	267	211	211
Interest	23	17	12	8	6	4	2	0

Notes:

Data on long-term private nonguaranteed debt for 2010 data are provided by the country.

VANUATU

(US$ million, unless otherwise indicated)

	1995	2000	2005	2006	2007	2008	2009	2010
1. Summary external debt data								
External debt stocks	**48.9**	**74.5**	**82.1**	**83.1**	**98.2**	**125.8**	**129.8**	**148.3**
Long-term external debt	43.9	73.1	71.9	72.0	78.1	89.7	98.8	99.3
Public and publicly guaranteed	43.9	73.1	71.9	72.0	78.1	89.7	98.8	99.3
Private nonguaranteed	0.0	0.0	0.0	0.0	0.0	0.0	0.0	0.0
Use of IMF credit	0.0	0.0	0.0	0.0	0.0	0.0	0.0	0.0
Short-term external debt	5.0	1.4	10.2	11.1	20.1	36.1	31.0	49.0
interest arrears on long-term	0.0	0.0	0.2	0.1	0.1	0.1	0.0	0.0
Memorandum items								
Principal arrears on long-term	0.0	0.0	0.8	0.5	0.6	0.6	0.0	0.0
Long-term public sector debt	43.9	73.1	71.9	72.0	78.1	89.7	98.8	99.3
Long-term private sector debt	0.0	0.0	0.0	0.0	0.0	0.0	0.0	0.0
Public & publicly guaranteed commitments	1.8	4.6	0.0	0.0	8.0	28.8	0.0	0.0
External debt flows								
Disbursements	3.2	14.2	0.0	0.0	3.9	10.1	11.7	0.0
Long-term external debt	3.2	14.2	0.0	0.0	3.9	10.1	11.7	0.0
IMF purchases	0.0	0.0	0.0	0.0	0.0	0.0	0.0	0.0
Principal repayments	0.8	0.9	1.1	2.2	2.1	2.5	3.5	3.6
Long-term external debt	0.8	0.9	1.1	2.2	2.1	2.5	3.5	3.6
IMF repurchases	0.0	0.0	0.0	0.0	0.0	0.0	0.0	0.0
Net flows	2.4	13.6	-28.1	-1.2	10.8	23.6	3.1	14.4
Long-term external debt	2.4	13.4	-1.1	-2.2	1.8	7.6	8.1	-3.6
Short-term external debt	0.0	0.3	-27.0	1.0	9.0	16.0	-5.0	18.0
Interest payments	0.8	1.0	1.5	1.4	1.7	2.0	2.1	2.3
Long-term external debt	0.5	0.6	0.7	1.0	0.9	1.1	1.4	1.4
IMF charges	0.0	0.0	0.0	0.0	0.0	0.0	0.0	0.0
Short-term external debt	0.3	0.3	0.8	0.5	0.8	0.8	0.7	0.9
2. Other non-debt resource inflows								
Foreign direct investment	31.0	20.3	13.3	43.4	34.2	43.9	32.1	38.9
Portfolio equity	0.0	0.0	..	..	..	..	..	..
3. Currency composition of public and publicly guaranteed debt (%)								
Euro	..	..	13.6	13.4	12.5	9.2	7.1	5.2
Japanese yen	0.0	0.0	0.0	0.0	0.0	0.0	0.0	0.0
Pound sterling	0.1	0.0	0.0	0.0	0.0	0.0	0.0	0.0
Swiss franc	0.0	0.0	0.0	0.0	0.0	0.0	0.0	0.0
U.S.dollars	43.3	56.8	54.0	54.1	51.3	47.1	41.6	42.3
4. Average terms of new commitments								
Official creditors								
Interest (%)	0.0	2.0	0.0	0.0	0.0	2.0	0.0	0.0
Maturity (years)	23.0	14.5	0.0	0.0	20.0	20.0	0.0	0.0
Grace period (years)	16.1	3.5	0.0	0.0	5.0	5.3	0.0	0.0
Private creditors								
Interest (%)	0.0	0.0	0.0	0.0	0.0	0.0	0.0	0.0
Maturity (years)	0.0	0.0	0.0	0.0	0.0	0.0	0.0	0.0
Grace period (years)	0.0	0.0	0.0	0.0	0.0	0.0	0.0	0.0
5. Major economic aggregates								
Gross national income (GNI)	216.8	267.8	380.4	428.3	516.9	613.2	593.8	708.6
Exports of goods, services & income	123.0	175.7	204.6	215.3	255.7	311.1	329.1	356.1
Worker remit. & comp. of employees	13.5	34.7	5.1	5.0	5.5	5.5	5.5	6.4
Imports of goods, services & income	164.5	178.8	258.6	270.7	313.2	391.4	396.8	419.9
Profit remittances on FDI	35.6	21.9	35.3	34.2	45.6	..	..	..
Current account balance	-18.2	5.0	-34.0	-30.1	-34.4	-40.2	-37.6	-38.3
International reserves	48.3	38.9	67.2	104.7	119.6	115.2	148.6	161.4
6. Ratios								
External debt stocks to exports (%)	39.8	42.4	40.1	38.6	38.4	40.5	39.4	41.6
External debt stocks to GNI (%)	22.6	27.8	21.6	19.4	19.0	20.5	21.9	20.9
Debt service to exports (%)	1.3	1.1	1.3	1.7	1.5	1.4	1.7	1.7
Short-term to external debt stocks (%)	10.2	1.9	12.4	13.4	20.5	28.7	23.9	33.0
Multilateral to external debt stocks (%)	63.7	86.1	82.1	81.1	70.5	56.4	52.8	46.4
Reserves to external debt stocks (%)	98.7	52.3	81.9	125.9	121.8	91.6	114.5	108.8
Reserves to imports (months)	3.5	2.6	3.1	4.6	4.6	3.5	4.5	4.6

(US$ million, unless otherwise indicated)

	1995	2000	2005	2006	2007	2008	2009	2010
7. Long-term external debt								
Debt outstanding and disbursed	**43.9**	**73.1**	**71.9**	**72.0**	**78.1**	**89.7**	**98.8**	**99.3**
Public and publicly guaranteed	43.9	73.1	71.9	72.0	78.1	89.7	98.8	99.3
Official creditors	43.5	73.1	71.9	72.0	78.1	89.7	98.8	99.3
Multilateral	31.2	64.1	67.4	67.4	69.3	71.0	68.6	68.8
of which: IBRD	0.0	0.0	0.0	0.0	0.0	0.0	0.0	0.0
IDA	13.2	12.9	12.9	13.2	13.4	12.9	12.4	11.7
Bilateral	12.3	8.9	4.5	4.6	8.8	18.7	30.2	30.5
Private creditors	0.4	0.0	0.0	0.0	0.0	0.0	0.0	0.0
of which: Bonds	0.0	0.0	0.0	0.0	0.0	0.0	0.0	0.0
Commercial banks	0.0	0.0	0.0	0.0	0.0	0.0	0.0	0.0
Private nonguaranteed	0.0	0.0	0.0	0.0	0.0	0.0	0.0	0.0
of which: Bonds	0.0	0.0	0.0	0.0	0.0	0.0	0.0	0.0
Disbursements	**3.2**	**14.2**	**0.0**	**0.0**	**3.9**	**10.1**	**11.7**	**0.0**
Public and publicly guaranteed	3.2	14.2	0.0	0.0	3.9	10.1	11.7	0.0
Official creditors	3.2	14.2	0.0	0.0	3.9	10.1	11.7	0.0
Multilateral	1.4	14.2	0.0	0.0	0.0	0.0	0.0	0.0
of which: IBRD	0.0	0.0	0.0	0.0	0.0	0.0	0.0	0.0
IDA	0.4	0.0	0.0	0.0	0.0	0.0	0.0	0.0
Bilateral	1.8	0.0	0.0	0.0	3.9	10.1	11.7	0.0
Private creditors	0.0	0.0	0.0	0.0	0.0	0.0	0.0	0.0
of which: Bonds	0.0	0.0	0.0	0.0	0.0	0.0	0.0	0.0
Commercial banks	0.0	0.0	0.0	0.0	0.0	0.0	0.0	0.0
Private nonguaranteed	0.0	0.0	0.0	0.0	0.0	0.0	0.0	0.0
of which: Bonds	0.0	0.0	0.0	0.0	0.0	0.0	0.0	0.0
Principal repayments	**0.8**	**0.9**	**1.1**	**2.2**	**2.1**	**2.5**	**3.5**	**3.6**
Public and publicly guaranteed	0.8	0.9	1.1	2.2	2.1	2.5	3.5	3.6
Official creditors	0.6	0.9	1.1	2.2	2.1	2.5	3.5	3.6
Multilateral	0.4	0.5	0.7	1.8	1.7	2.1	3.2	3.3
of which: IBRD	0.0	0.0	0.0	0.0	0.0	0.0	0.0	0.0
IDA	0.0	0.2	0.3	0.3	0.4	0.4	0.6	0.5
Bilateral	0.2	0.4	0.4	0.4	0.4	0.5	0.3	0.3
Private creditors	0.2	0.0	0.0	0.0	0.0	0.0	0.0	0.0
of which: Bonds	0.0	0.0	0.0	0.0	0.0	0.0	0.0	0.0
Commercial banks	0.0	0.0	0.0	0.0	0.0	0.0	0.0	0.0
Private nonguaranteed	0.0	0.0	0.0	0.0	0.0	0.0	0.0	0.0
of which: Bonds	0.0	0.0	0.0	0.0	0.0	0.0	0.0	0.0
Interest payments	**0.5**	**0.6**	**0.7**	**1.0**	**0.9**	**1.1**	**1.4**	**1.4**
Public and publicly guaranteed	0.5	0.6	0.7	1.0	0.9	1.1	1.4	1.4
Official creditors	0.5	0.6	0.7	1.0	0.9	1.1	1.4	1.4
Multilateral	0.3	0.5	0.6	0.9	0.7	0.8	0.8	0.9
of which: IBRD	0.0	0.0	0.0	0.0	0.0	0.0	0.0	0.0
IDA	0.1	0.1	0.1	0.1	0.1	0.1	0.1	0.1
Bilateral	0.2	0.1	0.1	0.1	0.2	0.4	0.6	0.6
Private creditors	0.0	0.0	0.0	0.0	0.0	0.0	0.0	0.0
of which: Bonds	0.0	0.0	0.0	0.0	0.0	0.0	0.0	0.0
Commercial banks	0.0	0.0	0.0	0.0	0.0	0.0	0.0	0.0
Private nonguaranteed	0.0	0.0	0.0	0.0	0.0	0.0	0.0	0.0
of which: Bonds	0.0	0.0	0.0	0.0	0.0	0.0	0.0	0.0
8. Debt stock-flow reconciliation								
Total change in external debt stocks	3.4	8.8	-38.6	1.0	15.1	27.6	4.0	18.5
Net flows on external debt	2.4	13.6	-28.1	-1.2	10.8	23.6	3.1	14.4
9. Debt restructurings								
Total amount rescheduled	0.0	0.0	0.0	0.0	0.0	0.0	0.0	0.0
Total amount forgiven	0.0	0.0	3.8	0.0	0.0	0.0	0.0	0.0
Debt buyback	0.0	0.0	0.0	0.0	0.0	0.0	0.0	0.0

10. Contractual obligations on outstanding long-term external debt

	2011	2012	2013	2014	2015	2016	2017	2018
Official creditors								
Principal	3.5	4.2	5.2	6.2	5.8	5.8	5.8	5.8
Interest	1.8	1.8	1.8	1.7	1.6	1.5	1.4	1.7
Private creditors								
Principal	0.0	0.0	0.0	0.0	0.0	0.0	0.0	0.0
Interest	0.0	0.0	0.0	0.0	0.0	0.0	0.0	0.0

Notes:

Data on long-term public and publicly guaranteed debt for 2010 are World Bank staff estimates.

VENEZUELA, REPUBLICA BOLIVARIANA de

(US$ million, unless otherwise indicated)

	1995	2000	2005	2006	2007	2008	2009	2010
1. Summary external debt data								
External debt stocks	**35,744**	**42,338**	**44,888**	**43,747**	**48,316**	**52,751**	**55,235**	**55,572**
Long-term external debt	30,442	33,950	34,780	31,899	30,497	33,185	38,493	40,146
Public and publicly guaranteed	28,428	27,817	31,078	27,165	27,537	29,875	35,183	37,086
Private nonguaranteed	2,013	6,132	3,702	4,734	2,960	3,310	3,310	3,060
Use of IMF credit	2,239	203	0	0	0	0	0	0
Short-term external debt	3,063	8,186	10,108	11,848	17,819	19,566	16,741	15,426
interest arrears on long-term	273	59	5	2	0	0	7	7
Memorandum items								
Principal arrears on long-term	1,022	79	8	0	0	0	0	0
Long-term public sector debt	27,854	27,368	31,026	27,121	27,520	29,865	35,178	37,084
Long-term private sector debt	2,588	6,581	3,754	4,778	2,977	3,320	3,316	3,062
Public & publicly guaranteed commitments	1,033	1,683	6,717	1,220	1,854	4,354	7,892	5,894
External debt flows								
Disbursements	1,829	2,342	7,246	1,751	2,053	5,490	6,068	4,317
Long-term external debt	1,829	2,342	7,246	1,751	2,053	5,490	6,068	4,317
IMF purchases	0	0	0	0	0	0	0	0
Principal repayments	2,739	3,428	2,804	6,513	2,285	2,748	812	2,623
Long-term external debt	2,278	2,921	2,804	6,513	2,285	2,748	812	2,623
IMF repurchases	462	507	0	0	0	0	0	0
Net flows	-1,558	1,614	6,714	-3,019	5,741	4,490	2,424	378
Long-term external debt	-448	-579	4,443	-4,762	-232	2,743	5,256	1,693
Short-term external debt	-648	2,700	2,271	1,743	5,973	1,747	-2,832	-1,315
Interest payments	2,433	2,931	2,931	3,336	3,600	3,333	3,170	3,462
Long-term external debt	2,097	2,435	2,656	2,850	2,584	2,858	2,765	3,088
IMF charges	142	28	0	0	0	0	0	0
Short-term external debt	193	467	275	486	1,016	474	406	374
2. Other non-debt resource inflows								
Foreign direct investment	985	4,701	2,602	-508	1,008	350	-3,105	-1,404
Portfolio equity	270	-574	28	41	66	3	121	8
3. Currency composition of public and publicly guaranteed debt (%)								
Euro	..	..	11.5	14.1	14.8	8.2	6.7	5.9
Japanese yen	4.2	1.9	0.5	0.7	1.0	1.0	0.8	0.4
Pound sterling	1.2	0.8	0.0	0.0	0.0	0.0	0.0	0.0
Swiss franc	0.7	0.4	0.0	0.1	0.1	0.1	0.0	0.0
U.S.dollars	68.9	83.3	83.6	80.8	81.5	88.7	91.0	92.6
4. Average terms of new commitments								
Official creditors								
Interest (%)	6.8	8.0	6.2	5.6	5.7	3.2	2.8	2.5
Maturity (years)	17.2	12.7	10.4	18.0	20.0	18.0	16.8	15.4
Grace period (years)	5.2	2.6	2.7	7.8	10.5	5.5	5.3	3.1
Private creditors								
Interest (%)	7.7	8.2	6.6	5.7	7.0	9.2	8.1	12.8
Maturity (years)	3.3	7.1	13.8	11.7	30.2	17.5	12.5	12.0
Grace period (years)	3.0	2.5	13.7	5.2	30.2	17.5	12.5	0.3
5. Major economic aggregates								
Gross national income (GNI)	72,946	115,760	143,314	182,434	229,002	311,828	323,481	387,566
Exports of goods, services & income	22,620	37,760	61,134	75,348	80,971	105,363	61,913	69,450
Worker remit. & comp. of employees	2	17	148	165	151	137	131	143
Imports of goods, services & income	20,715	25,737	35,955	48,808	62,477	67,363	53,029	54,513
Profit remittances on FDI	431	1,424	3,953	6,540	4,785	4,152	1,903	1,955
Current account balance	2,014	11,853	25,110	26,462	18,063	37,392	8,561	14,378
International reserves	10,715	15,899	29,803	36,715	33,759	43,065	34,318	29,665
6. Ratios								
External debt stocks to exports (%)	158.0	112.1	73.4	58.1	59.7	50.1	89.2	80.0
External debt stocks to GNI (%)	49.0	36.6	31.3	24.0	21.1	16.9	17.1	14.3
Debt service to exports (%)	22.9	16.8	9.4	13.1	7.3	5.8	6.4	8.8
Short-term to external debt stocks (%)	8.6	19.3	22.5	27.1	36.9	37.1	30.3	27.8
Multilateral to external debt stocks (%)	9.3	7.6	6.2	6.9	5.1	5.1	5.6	7.2
Reserves to external debt stocks (%)	30.0	37.6	66.4	83.9	69.9	81.6	62.1	53.4
Reserves to imports (months)	6.2	7.4	9.9	9.0	6.5	7.7	7.8	6.5

(US$ million, unless otherwise indicated)

	1995	2000	2005	2006	2007	2008	2009	2010
7. Long-term external debt								
Debt outstanding and disbursed	**30,442**	**33,950**	**34,780**	**31,899**	**30,497**	**33,185**	**38,493**	**40,146**
Public and publicly guaranteed	28,428	27,817	31,078	27,165	27,537	29,875	35,183	37,086
Official creditors	4,833	6,177	3,417	3,811	3,395	3,536	4,130	4,957
Multilateral	3,323	3,216	2,786	3,026	2,488	2,687	3,120	4,014
of which: IBRD	1,639	972	200	51	0	0	0	0
IDA	0	0	0	0	0	0	0	0
Bilateral	1,510	2,961	632	785	907	849	1,011	942
Private creditors	23,595	21,640	27,661	23,354	24,142	26,339	31,053	32,129
of which: Bonds	20,745	16,217	23,546	19,478	20,675	23,353	28,360	29,762
Commercial banks	1,233	3,490	3,172	2,855	2,584	2,345	2,205	2,012
Private nonguaranteed	2,013	6,132	3,702	4,734	2,960	3,310	3,310	3,060
of which: Bonds	114	3,880	3,670	4,734	2,960	3,310	3,310	3,060
Disbursements	**1,829**	**2,342**	**7,246**	**1,751**	**2,053**	**5,490**	**6,068**	**4,317**
Public and publicly guaranteed	1,749	2,342	7,246	1,651	2,053	4,840	6,068	4,317
Official creditors	610	786	402	1,110	535	645	1,035	1,294
Multilateral	284	402	173	831	325	556	735	1,234
of which: IBRD	47	50	13	9	0	0	0	0
IDA	0	0	0	0	0	0	0	0
Bilateral	326	385	229	279	210	88	300	60
Private creditors	1,139	1,556	6,844	541	1,518	4,196	5,033	3,023
of which: Bonds	349	462	6,143	0	1,250	4,000	4,992	3,000
Commercial banks	616	667	356	151	135	145	30	10
Private nonguaranteed	80	0	0	100	0	650	0	0
of which: Bonds	0	0	0	100	0	650	0	0
Principal repayments	**2,278**	**2,921**	**2,804**	**6,513**	**2,285**	**2,748**	**812**	**2,623**
Public and publicly guaranteed	1,775	2,265	2,117	5,935	2,011	2,448	812	2,373
Official creditors	375	613	738	737	991	526	449	478
Multilateral	202	356	530	608	873	376	299	339
of which: IBRD	116	208	106	159	50	0	0	0
IDA	0	0	0	0	0	0	0	0
Bilateral	173	257	208	129	118	150	150	139
Private creditors	1,400	1,652	1,379	5,198	1,020	1,922	363	1,896
of which: Bonds	817	1,119	646	4,292	209	1,299	0	1,609
Commercial banks	45	372	441	558	492	348	190	160
Private nonguaranteed	503	655	687	578	274	300	0	250
of which: Bonds	0	0	0	546	274	300	0	250
Interest payments	**2,097**	**2,435**	**2,656**	**2,850**	**2,584**	**2,858**	**2,765**	**3,088**
Public and publicly guaranteed	1,986	1,867	2,307	2,412	2,313	2,524	2,440	2,787
Official creditors	298	343	204	219	243	234	185	175
Multilateral	233	259	162	175	194	161	138	135
of which: IBRD	120	91	10	6	1	0	0	0
IDA	0	0	0	0	0	0	0	0
Bilateral	66	84	41	44	49	73	48	40
Private creditors	1,688	1,524	2,103	2,193	2,070	2,290	2,255	2,612
of which: Bonds	1,534	1,298	1,747	1,834	1,751	2,006	2,024	2,411
Commercial banks	65	176	297	288	264	241	210	194
Private nonguaranteed	111	568	349	439	271	334	324	301
of which: Bonds	10	304	296	392	271	274	281	269
8. Debt stock-flow reconciliation								
Total change in external debt stocks	-1,199	1,290	6,096	-1,140	4,569	4,435	2,484	337
Net flows on external debt	-1,558	1,614	6,714	-3,019	5,741	4,490	2,424	378
9. Debt restructurings								
Total amount rescheduled	0	0	0	0	0	0	0	0
Total amount forgiven	0	0	0	0	1	2	1	1
Debt buyback	0	0	419	4,292	177	4	0	1,490

10. Contractual obligations on outstanding long-term external debt

	2011	2012	2013	2014	2015	2016	2017	2018
Official creditors								
Principal	497	612	625	552	473	582	536	585
Interest	147	163	167	165	161	153	142	130
Private creditors								
Principal	2,404	819	1,737	1,922	1,453	2,086	79	2,262
Interest	3,005	2,866	2,803	2,623	2,409	2,283	2,215	2,181

Notes:

Long-term private nonguaranteed debt data only cover Bonds. Short-term debt is based on the Central Bank data from 1999 to 2010.

VIETNAM

(US$ million, unless otherwise indicated)

	1995	2000	2005	2006	2007	2008	2009	2010
1. Summary external debt data								
External debt stocks	**25,428**	**12,822**	**18,992**	**18,577**	**22,713**	**24,954**	**28,718**	**35,139**
Long-term external debt	21,778	11,583	16,215	15,969	17,919	20,554	23,447	28,145
Public and publicly guaranteed	21,778	11,583	16,215	15,969	17,919	20,554	23,447	28,145
Private nonguaranteed	0	0	0	0	0	0	0	0
Use of IMF credit	377	316	203	181	164	121	84	45
Short-term external debt	3,272	923	2,574	2,427	4,630	4,279	5,186	6,949
interest arrears on long-term	2,501	78	74	0	0	1	0	0
Memorandum items								
Principal arrears on long-term	8,915	1,378	1,346	0	0	0	0	0
Long-term public sector debt	21,778	11,583	16,215	15,969	17,919	20,554	23,447	28,145
Long-term private sector debt	0	0	0	0	0	0	0	0
Public & publicly guaranteed commitments	2,466	1,191	2,660	2,297	2,080	3,670	6,175	5,459
External debt flows								
Disbursements	730	1,271	2,047	1,228	1,945	1,878	3,891	4,437
Long-term external debt	639	1,271	2,047	1,228	1,945	1,878	3,891	4,437
IMF purchases	92	0	0	0	0	0	0	0
Principal repayments	225	958	533	509	637	755	781	851
Long-term external debt	225	937	480	476	612	716	743	813
IMF repurchases	0	21	54	33	25	39	38	38
Net flows	823	471	1,927	646	3,511	771	4,017	5,348
Long-term external debt	414	334	1,567	752	1,333	1,163	3,148	3,623
Short-term external debt	317	158	413	-73	2,203	-352	908	1,763
Interest payments	139	352	434	452	608	566	435	521
Long-term external debt	81	298	318	328	413	432	374	442
IMF charges	11	3	1	1	1	1	1	0
Short-term external debt	46	51	115	123	194	134	61	79
2. Other non-debt resource inflows								
Foreign direct investment	1,780	1,298	1,954	2,400	6,700	9,579	7,600	8,000
Portfolio equity	..	..	115	1,313	6,243	-578	128	2,383
3. Currency composition of public and publicly guaranteed debt (%)								
Euro	..	..	5.7	6.7	7.0	5.9	5.5	4.9
Japanese yen	5.6	23.5	26.2	29.2	30.8	37.3	35.5	36.0
Pound sterling	0.1	0.1	0.1	0.1	0.1	0.1	0.1	0.0
Swiss franc	0.0	0.1	0.0	0.0	0.0	0.0	0.0	0.0
U.S.dollars	8.4	43.3	44.8	42.4	40.7	37.0	39.2	41.2
4. Average terms of new commitments								
Official creditors								
Interest (%)	2.3	1.4	1.3	1.9	0.9	1.9	1.1	1.1
Maturity (years)	31.5	36.1	33.6	33.2	36.6	32.7	29.3	29.6
Grace period (years)	9.5	9.6	9.1	8.7	10.1	9.0	8.2	8.5
Private creditors								
Interest (%)	6.7	0.0	6.9	4.2	0.0	0.0	0.3	4.8
Maturity (years)	7.3	0.0	10.2	21.1	0.0	0.0	14.9	11.8
Grace period (years)	2.0	0.0	10.1	6.6	0.0	0.0	4.9	7.0
5. Major economic aggregates								
Gross national income (GNI)	20,510	30,726	51,873	59,507	68,937	87,351	91,826	96,322
Exports of goods, services & income	..	17,481	36,987	45,594	55,757	71,048	63,615	80,108
Worker remit. & comp. of employees	..	..	4,000	4,800	5,500	7,200	6,840	8,000
Imports of goods, services & income	..	18,107	40,927	49,807	69,140	89,182	76,671	92,280
Profit remittances on FDI	..	..	..	..	..	..	..	..
Current account balance	..	1,106	-560	-164	-6,953	-10,823	-6,608	-4,287
International reserves	1,324	3,417	9,051	13,384	23,479	23,890	16,447	12,467
6. Ratios								
External debt stocks to exports (%)	..	73.3	51.3	40.7	40.7	35.1	45.1	43.9
External debt stocks to GNI (%)	124.0	41.7	36.6	31.2	32.9	28.6	31.3	36.5
Debt service to exports (%)	..	7.5	2.6	2.1	2.2	1.9	1.9	1.7
Short-term to external debt stocks (%)	12.9	7.2	13.6	13.1	20.4	17.1	18.1	19.8
Multilateral to external debt stocks (%)	1.3	14.8	27.1	31.5	31.4	32.1	35.9	34.9
Reserves to external debt stocks (%)	5.2	26.6	47.7	72.0	103.4	95.7	57.3	35.5
Reserves to imports (months)	..	2.3	2.7	3.2	4.1	3.2	2.6	1.6

VIETNAM

(US$ million, unless otherwise indicated)

	1995	2000	2005	2006	2007	2008	2009	2010
7. Long-term external debt								
Debt outstanding and disbursed	**21,778**	**11,583**	**16,215**	**15,969**	**17,919**	**20,554**	**23,447**	**28,145**
Public and publicly guaranteed	21,778	11,583	16,215	15,969	17,919	20,554	23,447	28,145
Official creditors	20,450	8,680	14,258	14,093	16,117	18,789	21,643	25,255
Multilateral	325	1,895	5,144	5,860	7,122	7,999	10,309	12,262
of which: IBRD	0	0	0	0	0	0	0	700
IDA	231	1,113	3,187	3,663	4,549	5,074	6,270	7,010
Bilateral	20,126	6,785	9,114	8,233	8,995	10,789	11,334	12,993
Private creditors	1,328	2,903	1,957	1,876	1,802	1,766	1,805	2,890
of which: Bonds	0	560	1,171	1,130	1,089	1,059	1,038	2,020
Commercial banks	1,043	1,658	454	484	516	546	652	774
Private nonguaranteed	0	0	0	0	0	0	0	0
of which: Bonds	0	0	0	0	0	0	0	0
Disbursements	**639**	**1,271**	**2,047**	**1,228**	**1,945**	**1,878**	**3,891**	**4,437**
Public and publicly guaranteed	639	1,271	2,047	1,228	1,945	1,878	3,891	4,437
Official creditors	233	1,176	1,260	1,151	1,892	1,816	3,725	3,206
Multilateral	100	395	639	548	1,011	873	2,333	2,055
of which: IBRD	0	0	0	0	0	0	0	700
IDA	47	174	391	340	748	592	1,206	853
Bilateral	133	781	621	602	881	943	1,392	1,151
Private creditors	406	95	786	78	53	62	165	1,231
of which: Bonds	0	0	750	0	0	0	0	1,000
Commercial banks	389	9	36	78	53	62	165	231
Private nonguaranteed	0	0	0	0	0	0	0	0
of which: Bonds	0	0	0	0	0	0	0	0
Principal repayments	**225**	**937**	**480**	**476**	**612**	**716**	**743**	**813**
Public and publicly guaranteed	225	937	480	476	612	716	743	813
Official creditors	175	134	303	313	456	569	613	693
Multilateral	7	6	31	43	61	80	110	130
of which: IBRD	0	0	0	0	0	0	0	0
IDA	1	2	14	23	30	37	47	52
Bilateral	168	128	272	270	395	489	503	563
Private creditors	50	802	176	163	156	147	130	121
of which: Bonds	0	0	41	41	41	31	20	19
Commercial banks	0	617	58	55	44	58	62	75
Private nonguaranteed	0	0	0	0	0	0	0	0
of which: Bonds	0	0	0	0	0	0	0	0
Interest payments	**81**	**298**	**318**	**328**	**413**	**432**	**374**	**442**
Public and publicly guaranteed	81	298	318	328	413	432	374	442
Official creditors	50	77	256	233	299	319	286	327
Multilateral	2	14	52	55	64	71	81	106
of which: IBRD	0	0	0	0	0	0	0	5
IDA	2	7	30	33	34	38	40	47
Bilateral	47	63	204	178	235	245	204	221
Private creditors	32	220	62	95	114	113	88	114
of which: Bonds	0	23	22	57	72	71	63	96
Commercial banks	24	153	24	26	29	32	22	17
Private nonguaranteed	0	0	0	0	0	0	0	0
of which: Bonds	0	0	0	0	0	0	0	0
8. Debt stock-flow reconciliation								
Total change in external debt stocks	628	-10,387	1,052	-416	4,136	2,242	3,763	6,422
Net flows on external debt	823	471	1,927	646	3,511	771	4,017	5,348
9. Debt restructurings								
Total amount rescheduled	89	0	201	0	0	0	0	0
Total amount forgiven	32	10,395	3	0	0	0	0	0
Debt buyback	0	0	0	0	0	0	0	0

10. Contractual obligations on outstanding long-term external debt

	2011	2012	2013	2014	2015	2016	2017	2018
Official creditors								
Principal	906	913	1,237	1,324	1,204	1,325	1,305	1,408
Interest	423	437	440	433	417	403	388	370
Private creditors								
Principal	90	140	137	135	154	918	157	126
Interest	155	163	161	158	154	124	94	91

Notes:
Arrears were removed from 2006 based on reports provided by the country. Data does not include long-term private publicly guaranteed and non-guaranteed debt. World Bank staff is currently working with the country on private debt reporting.

YEMEN, REPUBLIC OF

(US$ million, unless otherwise indicated)

	1995	2000	2005	2006	2007	2008	2009	2010
1. Summary external debt data								
External debt stocks	**6,251**	**5,125**	**5,459**	**5,663**	**6,107**	**6,274**	**6,370**	**6,324**
Long-term external debt	5,562	4,109	4,814	5,099	5,524	5,696	5,875	5,933
Public and publicly guaranteed	5,562	4,109	4,814	5,099	5,524	5,696	5,875	5,933
Private nonguaranteed	0	0	0	0	0	0	0	0
Use of IMF credit	0	317	292	246	169	95	53	78
Short-term external debt	689	699	353	318	413	483	442	313
interest arrears on long-term	473	27	94	100	107	112	117	124
Memorandum items								
Principal arrears on long-term	2,408	297	193	143	151	160	165	173
Long-term public sector debt	5,562	4,109	4,814	5,099	5,524	5,696	5,875	5,933
Long-term private sector debt	0	0	0	0	0	0	0	0
Public & publicly guaranteed commitments	80	327	207	328	332	410	200	289
External debt flows								
Disbursements	124	137	265	353	390	285	332	340
Long-term external debt	124	137	265	353	390	285	332	287
IMF purchases	0	0	0	0	0	0	0	53
Principal repayments	65	153	150	161	199	206	184	182
Long-term external debt	65	81	94	101	113	134	140	155
IMF repurchases	0	71	56	60	87	71	44	27
Net flows	42	270	176	151	278	145	102	22
Long-term external debt	59	56	171	252	277	151	192	132
Short-term external debt	-17	285	61	-41	88	65	-46	-136
Interest payments	37	91	62	74	72	79	79	78
Long-term external debt	25	45	55	67	65	70	72	74
IMF charges	0	10	3	3	2	1	0	0
Short-term external debt	11	35	4	4	5	7	6	4
2. Other non-debt resource inflows								
Foreign direct investment	-218	6	-302	1,121	917	1,555	129	-329
Portfolio equity	0	0	0	0	0	0	0	0
3. Currency composition of public and publicly guaranteed debt (%)								
Euro	..	..	1.7	1.8	1.9	1.8	1.9	1.8
Japanese yen	6.1	7.7	6.4	5.9	5.5	6.2	5.8	5.1
Pound sterling	0.6	0.3	0.1	0.0	0.0	0.0	0.0	0.0
Swiss franc	0.3	0.0	0.0	0.0	0.0	0.0	0.0	0.0
U.S.dollars	21.6	68.2	67.3	65.2	61.8	59.5	58.8	57.3
4. Average terms of new commitments								
Official creditors								
Interest (%)	5.1	0.9	2.4	1.9	2.7	2.5	2.1	1.5
Maturity (years)	12.5	35.2	30.0	28.4	22.5	27.7	26.3	14.0
Grace period (years)	3.3	8.9	8.3	7.8	5.8	6.9	6.8	2.6
Private creditors								
Interest (%)	0.0	0.0	0.0	0.0	0.0	0.0	0.0	0.0
Maturity (years)	0.0	0.0	0.0	0.0	0.0	0.0	0.0	0.0
Grace period (years)	0.0	0.0	0.0	0.0	0.0	0.0	0.0	0.0
5. Major economic aggregates								
Gross national income (GNI)	3,678	8,834	15,125	17,847	20,306	24,779	24,894	..
Exports of goods, services & income	2,197	4,158	6,963	8,181	8,158	10,504	7,207	9,390
Worker remit. & comp. of employees	1,081	1,288	1,283	1,283	1,322	1,411	1,160	1,240
Imports of goods, services & income	3,069	4,221	7,745	9,332	11,092	13,918	11,287	12,890
Profit remittances on FDI	433	855	1,603	1,403	1,390	1,875	927	..
Current account balance	184	1,337	624	206	-1,508	-1,251	-2,565	-1,209
International reserves	638	2,914	6,141	7,543	7,757	8,155	6,990	5,939
6. Ratios								
External debt stocks to exports (%)	284.5	123.3	78.4	69.2	74.9	59.7	88.4	67.4
External debt stocks to GNI (%)	169.9	58.0	36.1	31.7	30.1	25.3	25.6	..
Debt service to exports (%)	4.6	5.9	3.0	2.9	3.3	2.7	3.6	2.8
Short-term to external debt stocks (%)	11.0	13.6	6.5	5.6	6.8	7.7	6.9	5.0
Multilateral to external debt stocks (%)	20.5	32.7	40.6	44.3	47.5	48.4	49.6	51.9
Reserves to external debt stocks (%)	10.2	56.9	112.5	133.2	127.0	130.0	109.7	93.9
Reserves to imports (months)	2.5	8.3	9.5	9.7	8.4	7.0	7.4	5.5

YEMEN, REPUBLIC OF

(US$ million, unless otherwise indicated)

	1995	2000	2005	2006	2007	2008	2009	2010
7. Long-term external debt								
Debt outstanding and disbursed	**5,562**	**4,109**	**4,814**	**5,099**	**5,524**	**5,696**	**5,875**	**5,933**
Public and publicly guaranteed	5,562	4,109	4,814	5,099	5,524	5,696	5,875	5,933
Official creditors	3,844	4,046	4,807	5,092	5,517	5,690	5,871	5,930
Multilateral	1,278	1,676	2,219	2,507	2,901	3,036	3,159	3,283
of which: IBRD	0	0	0	0	0	0	0	0
IDA	827	1,216	1,689	1,894	2,058	2,113	2,187	2,180
Bilateral	2,565	2,370	2,588	2,584	2,616	2,654	2,712	2,647
Private creditors	1,718	63	7	7	7	6	5	3
of which: Bonds	0	0	0	0	0	0	0	0
Commercial banks	80	53	7	7	7	6	5	3
Private nonguaranteed	0	0	0	0	0	0	0	0
of which: Bonds	0	0	0	0	0	0	0	0
Disbursements	**124**	**137**	**265**	**353**	**390**	**285**	**332**	**287**
Public and publicly guaranteed	124	137	265	353	390	285	332	287
Official creditors	124	137	265	353	390	285	332	287
Multilateral	109	111	217	262	345	241	212	246
of which: IBRD	0	0	0	0	0	0	0	0
IDA	42	65	129	160	122	108	101	73
Bilateral	15	27	49	91	45	44	120	41
Private creditors	0	0	0	0	0	0	0	0
of which: Bonds	0	0	0	0	0	0	0	0
Commercial banks	0	0	0	0	0	0	0	0
Private nonguaranteed	0	0	0	0	0	0	0	0
of which: Bonds	0	0	0	0	0	0	0	0
Principal repayments	**65**	**81**	**94**	**101**	**113**	**134**	**140**	**155**
Public and publicly guaranteed	65	81	94	101	113	134	140	155
Official creditors	63	81	94	101	112	133	139	154
Multilateral	53	60	58	61	66	78	84	97
of which: IBRD	0	0	0	0	0	0	0	0
IDA	8	14	27	31	34	38	42	45
Bilateral	10	20	36	39	46	55	55	56
Private creditors	2	0	0	0	1	1	1	1
of which: Bonds	0	0	0	0	0	0	0	0
Commercial banks	0	0	0	0	1	1	1	1
Private nonguaranteed	0	0	0	0	0	0	0	0
of which: Bonds	0	0	0	0	0	0	0	0
Interest payments	**25**	**45**	**55**	**67**	**65**	**70**	**72**	**74**
Public and publicly guaranteed	25	45	55	67	65	70	72	74
Official creditors	25	45	55	67	65	70	72	74
Multilateral	18	21	27	30	34	38	40	40
of which: IBRD	0	0	0	0	0	0	0	0
IDA	6	9	15	15	15	16	15	16
Bilateral	7	24	28	37	31	32	32	34
Private creditors	0	0	0	0	0	0	0	0
of which: Bonds	0	0	0	0	0	0	0	0
Commercial banks	0	0	0	0	0	0	0	0
Private nonguaranteed	0	0	0	0	0	0	0	0
of which: Bonds	0	0	0	0	0	0	0	0
8. Debt stock-flow reconciliation								
Total change in external debt stocks	97	-1,117	-112	203	444	167	96	-46
Net flows on external debt	42	270	176	151	278	145	102	22
9. Debt restructurings								
Total amount rescheduled	0	123	65	0	0	0	0	0
Total amount forgiven	0	9	116	123	8	20	0	93
Debt buyback	0	0	0	0	0	0	0	0

10. Contractual obligations on outstanding long-term external debt

	2011	2012	2013	2014	2015	2016	2017	2018
Official creditors								
Principal	233	249	271	291	292	301	299	307
Interest	87	91	90	88	85	81	75	69
Private creditors								
Principal	1	1	1	1	0	0	0	0
Interest	0	0	0	0	0	0	0	0

ZAMBIA

(US$ million, unless otherwise indicated)

	1995	2000	2005	2006	2007	2008	2009	2010
1. Summary external debt data								
External debt stocks	**6,958**	**5,722**	**5,373**	**2,273**	**2,749**	**2,974**	**3,039**	**3,689**
Long-term external debt	5,304	4,508	4,538	1,788	2,087	2,205	2,220	2,104
Public and publicly guaranteed	5,291	4,444	3,942	962	1,107	1,157	1,200	1,309
Private nonguaranteed	13	65	596	826	981	1,049	1,020	794
Use of IMF credit	1,239	1,138	591	41	87	96	345	395
Short-term external debt	415	76	244	443	575	674	474	1,191
interest arrears on long-term	177	33	90	140	149	152	154	167
Memorandum items								
Principal arrears on long-term	772	137	340	315	316	319	320	321
Long-term public sector debt	5,259	4,413	3,939	962	1,106	1,157	1,200	1,309
Long-term private sector debt	45	95	599	827	981	1,049	1,020	795
Public & publicly guaranteed commitments	382	330	58	139	144	133	175	779
External debt flows								
Disbursements	2,606	287	235	445	357	250	369	251
Long-term external debt	352	261	218	421	315	239	126	195
IMF purchases	2,253	26	16	24	42	11	244	56
Principal repayments	2,067	98	215	87	75	114	122	87
Long-term external debt	242	98	136	87	75	114	122	86
IMF repurchases	1,825	0	79	0	0	0	0	1
Net flows	435	159	84	507	405	232	45	868
Long-term external debt	110	163	82	334	240	125	4	109
Short-term external debt	-104	-30	65	149	123	96	-202	704
Interest payments	545	88	66	53	46	52	47	60
Long-term external debt	125	80	58	44	32	39	36	29
IMF charges	419	6	4	0	0	0	1	0
Short-term external debt	1	3	5	9	13	13	10	31
2. Other non-debt resource inflows								
Foreign direct investment	97	122	357	616	1,324	939	695	1,041
Portfolio equity	..	6	5	2	4	-6	-13	101
3. Currency composition of public and publicly guaranteed debt (%)								
Euro	..	..	5.9	20.4	18.2	14.8	13.3	10.6
Japanese yen	11.2	13.9	1.2	0.0	0.0	0.0	0.0	0.1
Pound sterling	7.7	3.9	5.1	0.7	0.5	0.3	0.4	0.3
Swiss franc	0.1	0.0	0.0	0.0	0.0	0.0	0.0	0.0
U.S.dollars	39.6	61.7	72.9	39.4	41.3	39.3	37.4	34.0
4. Average terms of new commitments								
Official creditors								
Interest (%)	1.5	0.8	0.8	1.2	1.3	0.8	0.6	1.7
Maturity (years)	37.3	39.6	35.8	29.5	31.5	46.3	34.1	23.5
Grace period (years)	10.3	10.1	8.2	8.0	7.7	10.3	9.1	7.0
Private creditors								
Interest (%)	10.5	0.0	0.0	0.0	0.0	3.0	0.0	0.0
Maturity (years)	9.2	0.0	0.0	0.0	0.0	3.9	0.0	0.0
Grace period (years)	2.9	0.0	0.0	0.0	0.0	0.0	0.0	0.0
5. Major economic aggregates								
Gross national income (GNI)	3,235	3,082	6,586	9,534	10,055	13,241	11,442	14,300
Exports of goods, services & income	..	891	2,533	4,190	4,818	5,291	4,564	7,734
Worker remit. & comp. of employees	..	..	53	58	59	68	41	44
Imports of goods, services & income	..	1,496	3,239	4,411	6,047	6,890	4,543	7,551
Profit remittances on FDI	..	..	461	1,107	1,474	1,346	265	1,832
Current account balance	..	-591	-600	141	-698	-1,039	537	615
International reserves	223	245	560	720	1,090	1,096	1,892	2,094
6. Ratios								
External debt stocks to exports (%)	..	642.0	212.1	54.2	57.1	56.2	66.6	47.7
External debt stocks to GNI (%)	215.1	185.7	81.6	23.8	27.3	22.5	26.6	25.8
Debt service to exports (%)	..	20.8	11.1	3.4	2.5	3.1	3.7	1.9
Short-term to external debt stocks (%)	6.0	1.3	4.5	19.5	20.9	22.6	15.6	32.3
Multilateral to external debt stocks (%)	30.5	42.0	58.2	29.8	27.7	27.5	28.7	25.0
Reserves to external debt stocks (%)	3.2	4.3	10.4	31.7	39.6	36.8	62.3	56.8
Reserves to imports (months)	..	2.0	2.1	2.0	2.2	1.9	5.0	3.3

ZAMBIA

(US$ million, unless otherwise indicated)

	1995	2000	2005	2006	2007	2008	2009	2010
7. Long-term external debt								
Debt outstanding and disbursed	**5,304**	**4,508**	**4,538**	**1,788**	**2,087**	**2,205**	**2,220**	**2,104**
Public and publicly guaranteed	5,291	4,444	3,942	962	1,107	1,157	1,200	1,309
Official creditors	5,080	4,412	3,646	914	1,059	1,108	1,158	1,276
Multilateral	2,120	2,403	3,125	678	762	818	871	924
of which: IBRD	163	25	0	0	0	0	0	0
IDA	1,270	1,823	2,488	260	323	371	407	430
Bilateral	2,960	2,009	521	236	297	290	287	353
Private creditors	210	31	295	48	48	48	42	33
of which: Bonds	0	0	0	0	0	0	0	0
Commercial banks	16	0	0	0	0	0	0	0
Private nonguaranteed	13	65	596	826	981	1,049	1,020	794
of which: Bonds	0	0	0	0	0	0	0	0
Disbursements	**352**	**261**	**218**	**421**	**315**	**239**	**126**	**195**
Public and publicly guaranteed	351	251	114	164	118	118	91	168
Official creditors	327	251	114	164	118	108	91	168
Multilateral	251	249	109	108	79	100	70	96
of which: IBRD	0	0	0	0	0	0	0	0
IDA	209	210	77	40	51	51	33	32
Bilateral	76	2	5	56	39	8	21	72
Private creditors	24	0	0	0	0	10	0	0
of which: Bonds	0	0	0	0	0	0	0	0
Commercial banks	8	0	0	0	0	0	0	0
Private nonguaranteed	1	10	105	257	197	121	35	27
of which: Bonds	0	0	0	0	0	0	0	0
Principal repayments	**242**	**98**	**136**	**87**	**75**	**114**	**122**	**86**
Public and publicly guaranteed	241	79	71	51	32	61	59	47
Official creditors	180	79	59	51	32	52	52	38
Multilateral	120	51	21	25	30	29	28	25
of which: IBRD	50	8	0	0	0	0	0	0
IDA	2	4	1	1	0	1	1	2
Bilateral	60	28	38	26	3	23	24	13
Private creditors	61	1	12	0	0	8	7	8
of which: Bonds	0	0	0	0	0	0	0	0
Commercial banks	2	0	0	0	0	0	0	0
Private nonguaranteed	1	18	66	36	43	53	63	40
of which: Bonds	0	0	0	0	0	0	0	0
Interest payments	**125**	**80**	**58**	**44**	**32**	**39**	**36**	**29**
Public and publicly guaranteed	125	76	29	21	9	14	13	11
Official creditors	116	76	29	21	9	14	13	11
Multilateral	65	33	25	17	8	9	8	8
of which: IBRD	15	3	0	0	0	0	0	0
IDA	9	13	16	8	2	3	3	3
Bilateral	51	42	4	4	2	5	5	3
Private creditors	9	0	0	0	0	0	0	0
of which: Bonds	0	0	0	0	0	0	0	0
Commercial banks	1	0	0	0	0	0	0	0
Private nonguaranteed	0	4	28	23	23	24	24	18
of which: Bonds	0	0	0	0	0	0	0	0
8. Debt stock-flow reconciliation								
Total change in external debt stocks	149	-137	-2,075	-3,100	476	225	64	650
Net flows on external debt	435	159	84	507	405	232	45	868
9. Debt restructurings								
Total amount rescheduled	20	169	58	9	51	0	0	0
Total amount forgiven	3	56	1,643	3,592	11	12	3	3
Debt buyback	0	0	0	0	0	0	0	0

10. Contractual obligations on outstanding long-term external debt

	2011	2012	2013	2014	2015	2016	2017	2018
Official creditors								
Principal	54	54	49	52	55	87	95	96
Interest	14	16	18	20	21	21	20	20
Private creditors								
Principal	152	106	95	56	45	34	28	23
Interest	35	26	18	13	9	6	4	2

Notes:

Zambia was granted debt relief effective in 2006 under MDRI. Data on long-term public and publicly guaranteed debt from 2007-2008 are World Bank staff estimates based on reports provided by the country. Data on long-term private nonguaranteed debt from 2007 are World Bank staff estimates.

ZIMBABWE

(US$ million, unless otherwise indicated)

	1995	2000	2005	2006	2007	2008	2009	2010
1. Summary external debt data								
External debt stocks	**4,989**	**3,807**	**4,113**	**4,495**	**5,198**	**5,076**	**4,801**	**5,016**
Long-term external debt	3,843	2,979	3,227	3,413	3,788	3,750	3,831	4,064
Public and publicly guaranteed	3,462	2,774	3,195	3,387	3,713	3,661	3,742	3,686
Private nonguaranteed	381	205	32	26	75	89	89	378
Use of IMF credit	461	281	111	113	118	114	116	110
Short-term external debt	685	547	776	970	1,292	1,212	854	843
interest arrears on long-term	3	34	419	481	589	621	707	706
Memorandum items								
Principal arrears on long-term	21	124	1,353	1,594	1,893	1,954	2,170	2,194
Long-term public sector debt	3,462	2,767	3,187	3,387	3,713	3,661	3,742	3,686
Long-term private sector debt	381	212	39	26	75	89	89	378
Public & publicly guaranteed commitments	218	50	11	201	0	0	0	0
External debt flows								
Disbursements	654	185	25	45	227	94	79	369
Long-term external debt	574	185	25	45	227	94	79	369
IMF purchases	80	0	0	0	0	0	0	0
Principal repayments	398	282	210	38	55	57	66	66
Long-term external debt	398	212	45	35	55	55	66	62
IMF repurchases	0	70	165	3	0	2	0	4
Net flows	442	-330	-224	138	386	-75	-431	293
Long-term external debt	176	-27	-20	10	173	39	13	307
Short-term external debt	187	-233	-40	132	214	-112	-444	-10
Interest payments	238	138	27	54	41	26	35	43
Long-term external debt	189	81	7	4	14	10	30	41
IMF charges	13	10	0	23	0	0	0	0
Short-term external debt	35	48	19	27	27	16	5	2
2. Other non-debt resource inflows								
Foreign direct investment	118	23	103	40	69	52	105	105
Portfolio equity	..	..	..	..	..	..	..	..
3. Currency composition of public and publicly guaranteed debt (%)								
Euro	..	..	32.0	33.6	34.2	32.7	33.4	31.9
Japanese yen	3.6	5.4	5.3	5.0	4.7	6.0	5.8	6.7
Pound sterling	6.7	5.5	5.9	6.3	5.9	4.4	4.8	4.7
Swiss franc	0.9	0.4	0.4	0.4	0.4	0.5	0.5	0.5
U.S.dollars	26.2	29.9	28.6	27.7	29.3	30.3	29.9	30.1
4. Average terms of new commitments								
Official creditors								
Interest (%)	3.0	4.8	3.0	6.1	0.0	0.0	0.0	0.9
Maturity (years)	23.3	12.9	15.0	4.1	0.0	0.0	0.0	24.5
Grace period (years)	6.8	3.6	4.5	0.5	0.0	0.0	0.0	7.0
Private creditors								
Interest (%)	6.1	13.9	6.5	0.0	0.0	0.0	0.0	0.0
Maturity (years)	8.8	9.8	5.5	0.0	0.0	0.0	0.0	0.0
Grace period (years)	1.6	4.1	0.9	0.0	0.0	0.0	0.0	0.0
5. Major economic aggregates								
Gross national income (GNI)	6,785	6,245	5,308	4,890	4,654	3,939	5,394	6,988
Exports of goods, services & income	..	..	..	..	..	..	..	..
Worker remit. & comp. of employees	..	..	..	..	..	..	..	..
Imports of goods, services & income	..	..	..	..	..	..	..	..
Profit remittances on FDI	..	..	..	..	..	..	..	..
Current account balance	..	..	-532	-356	-342	-762	..	..
International reserves	888	321	..	..	..	..	..	..
6. Ratios								
External debt stocks to exports (%)	..	..	..	..	..	..	..	..
External debt stocks to GNI (%)	73.5	61.0	77.5	91.9	111.7	128.9	89.0	71.8
Debt service to exports (%)	..	..	..	..	..	..	..	..
Short-term to external debt stocks (%)	13.7	14.4	18.9	21.6	24.9	23.9	17.8	16.8
Multilateral to external debt stocks (%)	29.9	35.5	36.1	34.4	31.0	31.6	33.7	31.8
Reserves to external debt stocks (%)	17.8	8.4	..	..	..	..	..	..
Reserves to imports (months)	..	..	..	..	..	..	..	..

ZIMBABWE

(US$ million, unless otherwise indicated)

	1995	2000	2005	2006	2007	2008	2009	2010
7. Long-term external debt								
Debt outstanding and disbursed	**3,843**	**2,979**	**3,227**	**3,413**	**3,788**	**3,750**	**3,831**	**4,064**
Public and publicly guaranteed	3,462	2,774	3,195	3,387	3,713	3,661	3,742	3,686
Official creditors	2,798	2,437	2,789	2,946	3,247	3,236	3,296	3,253
Multilateral	1,491	1,352	1,485	1,547	1,611	1,605	1,619	1,593
of which: IBRD	560	416	437	445	455	464	463	463
IDA	336	437	478	501	522	519	522	513
Bilateral	1,307	1,085	1,304	1,399	1,636	1,631	1,677	1,660
Private creditors	664	337	406	441	466	425	446	432
of which: Bonds	120	0	0	0	0	0	0	0
Commercial banks	162	198	264	287	306	264	279	267
Private nonguaranteed	381	205	32	26	75	89	89	378
of which: Bonds	0	0	0	0	0	0	0	0
Disbursements	**574**	**185**	**25**	**45**	**227**	**94**	**79**	**369**
Public and publicly guaranteed	345	139	25	28	160	28	13	20
Official creditors	232	125	17	23	160	13	13	19
Multilateral	125	44	7	2	0	0	0	0
of which: IBRD	32	19	0	0	0	0	0	0
IDA	15	8	0	0	0	0	0	0
Bilateral	106	81	10	21	160	13	13	19
Private creditors	114	15	8	5	0	14	0	0
of which: Bonds	0	0	0	0	0	0	0	0
Commercial banks	72	11	4	0	0	0	0	0
Private nonguaranteed	229	46	0	17	68	66	66	350
of which: Bonds	0	0	0	0	0	0	0	0
Principal repayments	**398**	**212**	**45**	**35**	**55**	**55**	**66**	**62**
Public and publicly guaranteed	307	147	31	13	36	3	0	1
Official creditors	166	114	21	11	36	3	0	1
Multilateral	77	77	5	2	2	3	0	0
of which: IBRD	47	46	2	0	0	0	0	0
IDA	1	0	0	0	0	0	0	0
Bilateral	89	37	16	9	33	0	0	1
Private creditors	142	33	10	2	0	0	0	0
of which: Bonds	30	0	0	0	0	0	0	0
Commercial banks	32	12	1	0	0	0	0	0
Private nonguaranteed	91	65	14	22	19	52	66	61
of which: Bonds	0	0	0	0	0	0	0	0
Interest payments	**189**	**81**	**7**	**4**	**14**	**10**	**30**	**41**
Public and publicly guaranteed	163	64	3	2	13	5	14	13
Official creditors	115	51	2	2	13	5	14	13
Multilateral	81	37	2	0	0	1	0	0
of which: IBRD	46	26	1	0	0	0	0	0
IDA	2	1	0	0	0	0	0	0
Bilateral	34	14	0	2	12	4	14	13
Private creditors	48	13	1	0	0	0	0	0
of which: Bonds	6	0	0	0	0	0	0	0
Commercial banks	11	5	0	0	0	0	0	0
Private nonguaranteed	26	17	4	2	1	5	16	28
of which: Bonds	0	0	0	0	0	0	0	0
8. Debt stock-flow reconciliation								
Total change in external debt stocks	503	-516	-548	383	703	-122	-275	215
Net flows on external debt	442	-330	-224	138	386	-75	-431	293
9. Debt restructurings								
Total amount rescheduled	0	0	0	0	0	0	0	0
Total amount forgiven	66	0	0	0	0	0	0	0
Debt buyback	0	0	0	0	0	0	0	0

10. Contractual obligations on outstanding long-term external debt

	2011	2012	2013	2014	2015	2016	2017	2018
Official creditors								
Principal	409	163	114	82	62	58	57	56
Interest	43	22	16	13	11	10	9	8
Private creditors								
Principal	39	39	39	39	38	38	38	38
Interest	9	8	7	7	6	5	4	3

About the Data

Data Sources

The principal sources of information for the tables in this volume are reports to the World Bank through the World Bank's Debtor Reporting System (DRS) from member countries that have received either International Bank for Reconstruction and Development (IBRD) loans or International Development Association (IDA) credits. The DRS has its origin in the World Bank's need to monitor and assess the financial position of its borrowers. Since 1951, borrowers have been required to provide statistics on their public external debt and private sector debt that benefits from a public guarantee. In its design, consistency, and continuity of coverage, the DRS is a unique resource. Reporting countries submit detailed reports on the annual status, transactions, and terms of the long-term external debt of public agencies and that of private ones guaranteed by a public agency in the debtor country. The DRS maintains these records on a loan-by-loan basis. In 1973, coverage of the DRS was expanded to include private sector nonguaranteed borrowing, but for this category of debt, data are provided by borrowers in aggregate rather than loan by loan.

Data submitted to the DRS are processed in the World Bank External Debt (WBXD) system, along with additional information received from the files of the African Development Bank, the Asian Development Bank, the Inter-American Development Bank (IDB), the International Monetary Fund (IMF), institutions of the World Bank Group (IBRD and IDA), and the European Bank for Reconstruction and Development (EBRD). The WBXD is an internal system of the World Bank. Among its outputs is the Global Development Finance (GDF) database, from which the tables in this publication, GDF CD-ROM and online database are produced.

Data on exports and imports (on a balance of payments basis), international reserves, current account balances, foreign direct investment (FDI), portfolio equity flows, and profit remittances of FDI are drawn mainly from the files of the IMF, supplemented by United Nations Conference on Trade and Development (UNCTAD) reports and country data. Balance of payments data are presented according to the fifth edition of the IMF's *Balance of Payments Manual* (BPM5). Official aid flows come from data collected and published by the Development Assistance Committee (DAC) of the Organisation for Economic Co-operation and Development (OECD). Short-term external debt data are as reported by debtor countries or are estimates based on the Bank for International Settlements (BIS) quarterly series of commercial banks' claims on developing countries. For some countries, estimates were prepared by pooling creditor and debtor information. Data on the gross national income of most developing countries are collected from national statistical organizations or central banks by visiting and resident World Bank missions.

Every effort has been made to ensure the accuracy and completeness of the external debt statistics. Coverage has been improved through the efforts of the reporting agencies and close collaboration between the Bank and our partners Commonwealth Secretariat (COMSEC) and UNCTAD, which provide debt recording and reporting systems across the globe, as well as through the work of the World Bank missions, which visit member countries to gather data and to provide technical assistance on debt issues.

Nevertheless, quality and coverage vary among debtors and may also vary for the same debtor from year to year. Data on long-term external debt reported by member countries are checked against, and supplemented by, data from several other sources. Among these sources are the statements and reports of several regional development banks, government lending agencies, and official government Web sites.

Methodology

Aggregations

Total debt stock and other aggregate measures are derived from the summation of loan-level data on stocks and flows after conversion to a common currency. Other tabulations are compiled using terms and conditions reported in the loan-level data, such as currency composition, cancellations, rescheduling of other liabilities into long-term public and publicly guaranteed external debt, and debt buybacks.

Aggregates for regional and income groups are based on the World Bank's operational classifications, which may differ from common geographic usage or income groups used by other organizations. Country classifications of DRS reporting countries in 2010 are shown in country groups in the back of the publication. The same classification is used for all historical data shown in Global Development Finance and the online database.

Currency Conversion

Data on external obligations are normally reported to the World Bank in the currency of repayment and are converted into a common currency (U.S. dollars) using official exchange rates published by the IMF.

Commitments, disbursements, and debt service payments (flows) are converted to U.S. dollars at the annual average exchange rate for the year. Debt outstanding (disbursed and undisbursed) at the end of a given year (stock) is converted at the exchange rate in effect at the end of the relevant year. Consequently, year-to-year changes in debt outstanding and disbursed may not be equal to net flows (disbursements less principal repayments); similarly, changes in debt outstanding (including undisbursed debt) may not equal commitments less repayments. Discrepancies will be particularly significant when exchange rates have moved sharply during the year. Projected debt service is converted to U.S. dollars at rates in effect at the end of December 2010.

Beginning with 1991, all ruble debt owed to the former Soviet Union has been converted at a rate of US$1 = 0.6 ruble, except in cases where a bilateral agreement specifying a different conversion rate is in place. Adoption of this methodology does not constitute an endorsement by the World Bank staff of the appropriateness or validity of the exchange rate used. This matter must be resolved bilaterally between the Russian Federation and its debtor countries.

Starting with the 1988–89 edition of World Debt Tables (the predecessor of GDF), all data pertaining to IBRD loans from 1985 onward are recorded at their current market value. Starting with the 1991–92 edition, all data pertaining to Asian Development Bank loans from 1989 onward are recorded at their current market value. Starting with the 1998 edition, all data pertaining to African Development Bank and African Development Fund loans from 1997 onward are recorded at their current market value.

Debt Stock and Flow Reconciliation

Because of currency conversions and the timing of transactions, there may be differences between the change in aggregate stocks from one period to the next and flows during the relevant period; changes in debt outstanding, including undisbursed amounts, will therefore differ from commitments less repayments.

Changes in the stock of debt from one period to the next can be attributed to five factors: the net flow of debt, the net change in interest arrears, the capitalization of interest, a reduction in debt resulting from debt forgiveness or other debt reduction mechanisms, and cross-currency valuation effects. Any residual difference in the change in stock not explained by one of those five factors may indicate inconsistencies in the reported data or specific phenomena prevailing in an individual country (for example, an incomplete historical series for all categories of debt). Starting in 1989, the GDF includes a debt stock reconciliation, but not all components are shown in the GDF print edition.

External Debt Restructuring

Starting in 1985, the WBXD includes information on restructuring of debt by official creditors in the context of the Paris Club, restructuring by commercial creditors, debt swap operations, buybacks, and bond exchanges. It attempts to capture accurately the effect of debt restructuring on both external debt stocks and external debt flows, consistent with the terms on which the restructuring takes place. In the compilation and presentation of external debt data, a distinction is made between cash flows and imputed flows. According to this criterion, restructured service payments and the shift in liabilities from one financial instrument to another as a result of debt restructuring are considered to be imputed flows. Both cash flows and imputed flows are recorded separately in WBXD.

The imputed flows and stock changes associated with debt restructuring are included in the GDF tables and online database to complement the cash-basis transactions recorded in the main body of the data. Such data encompass information on the debt stock and debt flows restructured each year, the amount of principal forgiven (interest forgiven is shown as a memorandum item), and the amount of external debt stock reduced either by forgiveness or by a debt buyback operation. Changes in creditors and debtors that result from debt restructuring are also reflected. For example, when insured commercial credits are rescheduled, the creditor classification shifts from private to official (bilateral), reflecting the assumption of the assets by the official credit insurance agencies in the creditor country. The GDF data will show a reduction in the external debt owed to the original private creditors equal or similar to the amount of debt restructured and a corresponding increase in the debt owed to the new official creditor. Similarly on the debtor side, when a government accepts responsibility for the payment of restructured debt previously owed by a private enterprise, the relevant change in the debtor category will be reflected. Likewise, if short-term external debt is restructured into a long-term obligation, the stock of short-term external debt will decline and the stock of long-term external debt will rise by the amount of short-term debt restructured. In the event of a debt swap of long-term external debt (external debt to equity, external debt for nature, or external debt for development), the face value of the external debt swapped will be recorded as a decline in long-term external debt stock, but no flow transaction (principal repayment) will be recorded.

Projections of Future Disbursements and Debt Service Payments

The WBXD system projects future disbursements and future debt service payments on the assumption that every existing loan commitment will be fully used and repaid in full.

Future Disbursements

Disbursement projections are made using one of the following methods:

- *Specific schedules.* Debtor countries are requested to submit a schedule of future disbursements, if available, at the time each new loan is first reported.
- *Standard schedules.* In the absence of specific schedules, the WBXD system projects the future disbursement schedule according to the undisbursed balance of each loan at the end of the most recent reporting period.

These projected schedules are based on profiles derived from the disbursement pattern of comparable loans that fully disbursed. Thirty different profiles have been compiled corresponding to each category of creditor and, in the case of official creditors, for concessional and nonconcessional loans. Each profile is derived by applying regression analysis techniques to a body of data on actual disbursements for each fully disbursed loan in the WBXD database. The profiles are periodically updated to take into account the evolving pattern of disbursements observed for fully disbursed loans.

Future principal payments are generated by the WBXD system according to the repayment terms of each loan. Principal repayments (amortization) are based on the amount of the loan commitment. If the amortization schedule follows a set pattern (for example, equal semiannual payments), the WBXD system calculates repayments automatically using the loan commitment amount, the first and final payment dates, and the frequency of the payments. If future payments are irregular, the WBXD system requires a schedule.

Future interest payments are generated by the WBXD system according to the disbursed and outstanding balance of the loan at the beginning of the period. Using the interest rate specified in the loan contract, the first and final interest payment dates, and the frequency of payments, the WBXD system calculates the stream of future interest payments due. If interest payments are irregular, the WBXD system requires a schedule.

Future debt service payments are the sum of future principal and interest payments due on existing commitments, including the undisbursed portion. They do not include debt service payments that may become due as a result of new loans contracted in subsequent years, nor do they take into account the effect of any change to future debt service obligations resulting from actions such as prepayment or rescheduling or from cancellations that occurred after the most recent year-end data reported to the DRS.

Both projected disbursements and future debt service payments are converted into U.S. dollars using end-December 2010 exchange rates. Likewise, future interest payments on loans with a variable interest rate (for example, loans from commercial banks tied to the London Interbank Offered Rate [LIBOR]) are based on the interest rate prevailing at end-December 2010.

Treatment of Arrears

The DRS collects information on arrears of both principal and interest. Principal in arrears is included in the amount of long-term external debt outstanding and is shown separately. Interest in arrears on long-term external debt and interest in arrears on the use of IMF credit are included as part of short-term external debt outstanding and are shown separately. Clearance of interest in arrears by repayment will be recorded as an interest payment in the relevant creditor category of the loan (or loans) on which the arrears were incurred, as a corresponding reduction in the level of short-term debt outstanding, and as a net reduction in interest arrears. Clearance of interest arrears through debt restructuring or forgiveness will be recorded as a reduction in the level of short-term debt outstanding and a net reduction in interest arrears. When interests are rescheduled, they will be capitalized: this change will be recorded as an increase in long-term debt outstanding equal to the amount of interest capitalized and the reduction in short-term debt outstanding noted previously.

External Debt and Its Components

This section describes the compilation of the major components of external debt included in the GDF tables and database and the relationship between them, as shown in figure 1. Information about general methods of compiling external debt data is discussed in the section titled "Methodology." For concise definitions, see the Glossary.

Total External Debt

Total external debt shown in the GDF is the sum of long-term external debt, short-term debt, and IMF credit. It represents the total debt owed to nonresident creditors and repayable in foreign currencies or in goods or services by public and private entities in the country. (Debt repayable in domestic currency is not included.)

Short-Term Debt

Short-term debt is defined as external debt with an original maturity of one year or less. The DRS requires debtor countries to report only on their long-term external debt. However, to gain a comprehensive picture of total external obligations, the World Bank encourages debtor countries to provide voluntarily information on their short-term external obligations.

By its nature, short-term external debt is difficult to monitor: loan-by-loan registration is normally impractical, and monitoring systems typically rely on information requested periodically by the central bank from the banking sector. The World Bank regards the debtor country as the authoritative source of information on its short-term debt. When such information is not made available from the debtor country, data from creditor sources may be used to get an indication of the magnitude of a country's short-term external debt. The most important source is the BIS quarterly series showing the maturity distribution of commercial banks' claims on developing countries. These data are reported on the basis of residual maturity, but an estimate of short-term external liabilities by original maturity can be derived by deducting from claims due in one year those that, 12 months earlier, had a maturity of between one and two years. However, not all commercial banks report to the BIS in a way that allows the full maturity distribution to be determined, and the BIS data include liabilities only to banks within

Figure 1. External Debt and Its Components

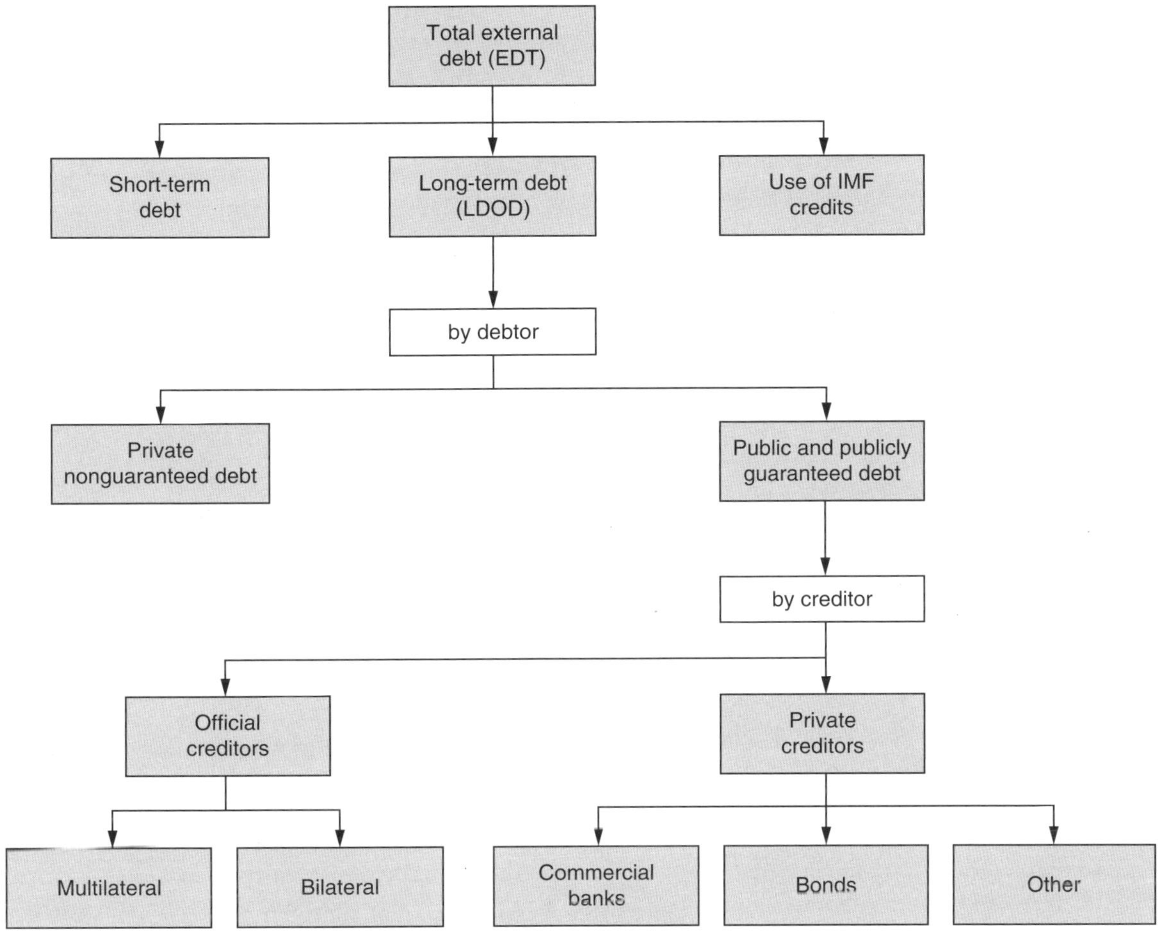

the BIS reporting area. Consequently, the results should be interpreted with caution.

The flow of short-term debt may be derived from the change in claims (stock) data in the BIS quarterly series over consecutive periods, but valuation adjustments resulting from exchange rate movements will affect the calculations, as will prepayment and refinancing of long-term maturities falling due. When short-term external debt has been rescheduled, lags in reporting and differences in the treatment of the rescheduled external debt by debtors and creditors may result in double counting.

The information on short-term debt shown in this publication comes primarily from either creditor or government sources. Unless otherwise specified in the country tables, the data for short-term debt are derived from the data provided by BIS on international bank lending, which are based on time remaining to original maturity. Interest in arrears on long-term external debt and interest in arrears on the use of IMF credit are added to short-term debt and are separately identified.

Use of IMF Credit

Data related to the operations of the IMF are provided by the IMF Treasurer's Department. They are converted from special drawing rights into dollars using end-of-period exchange rates for stocks and average-over-the-period exchange rates for flows. IMF trust fund operations under the Enhanced Structural Adjustment Facility, Extended Fund Facility, Poverty Reduction and Growth Facility, and Structural Adjustment Facility

(Enhanced Structural Adjustment Facility in 1999) are presented together with all of the IMF's special facilities (buffer stock, supplemental reserve, compensatory and contingency facilities, oil facilities, and other facilities).

Long-Term Debt

Long-term debt has an original maturity of more than one year. It comprises the obligations of both public and private debtors. Private nonguaranteed debt comprises the external obligations of private debtors that are not guaranteed for repayment by a public entity in the debtor country.

Public and publicly guaranteed debt comprises the external obligations of public debtors and has two components: (a) public debt, which is borrowing by the national government or agency, by a political subdivision or agency, or by autonomous public bodies, and (b) publicly guaranteed debt, which is borrowing by a private agency that is guaranteed for repayment by a public entity.

Private Nonguaranteed Debt

The DRS reporting requirements were expanded in 1973 to include long-term private nonguaranteed debt. Data are reported annually on an aggregate basis and include, for the reporting year, the total amount of disbursed and outstanding debt; the amount of disbursements, principal repayments, and interest payments; the principal and interest rescheduled; and the projected principal and interest payments for future years. The aggregate data are usually reported in U.S. dollars, and no information on the underlying currency composition is given.

DRS reporting countries recognize the importance of monitoring borrowing by their private sector, particularly when it constitutes a significant portion of total external debt, but many countries acknowledge the difficulty of this process. Detailed data are available only when countries have registration requirements for private nonguaranteed debt in place, most commonly in connection with exchange controls. When formal registration of private nonguaranteed debt is not mandatory, compilers must rely on balance of payments data and financial surveys.

The data on private nonguaranteed debt in this publication is as reported or as estimated for countries where this type of external debt is known to be significant. The estimation of private nonguaranteed debt is based on the national data on quarterly external debt statistics or IMF data. Flows are derived from the change in stock over consecutive periods and are adjusted for the effects of exchange rate movements (assuming the currency composition mirrors that of public and publicly guaranteed debt) and for any known debt restructuring. Principal repayments are estimated on the basis of the average maturity observed for loans to private sector borrowers in countries reporting to the DRS and on the basis of the stock of debt outstanding. Interest payments are estimated on the basis of the stock of debt outstanding and interest rates prevailing in international capital markets.

Balance of payments data provide a useful guideline in the estimation process: private nonguaranteed external debt may be derived as a residual between net long-term external borrowing recorded in the balance of payments and net longterm public and publicly guaranteed external debt reported to the DRS.

Public and Publicly Guaranteed Debt

Data related to public and publicly guaranteed debt are reported to the DRS on a loan-by-loan basis. The data provide annual information on the disbursed and outstanding balance and the undisbursed balance of each loan, the cumulative disbursements, the principal and interest paid and principal and interest restructured in the reporting year, and the stock of any outstanding payment's arrears of principal and interest. Detailed information on the terms and conditions of each loan is also reported. Public debt and publicly guaranteed debt are shown as a single line in this publication and then further disaggregated by creditor type and, in the case of private creditors, by type of credit instrument.

Official Creditors

Official creditors include multilateral and bilateral lenders. In general, official creditors provide loans (and, in some cases, provide grants) to public bodies, although in some cases they may lend to other entities with a public guarantee.

Multilateral creditors are international financial institutions such as the World Bank, regional development banks, and other multilateral and intergovernmental agencies whose lending is administered on a multilateral basis. Funds administered by an international financial organization on behalf of a single donor government constitute bilateral loans (or grants). For lending by a number of multilateral creditors, the data presented in this publication are taken from the creditors' records. Such creditors include the African Development Bank, the Asian Development Bank, the IDB, the IBRD, and the IDA. (IBRD and IDA are institutions of the World Bank.)

Bilateral creditors are governments and their agencies, including central banks, aid agencies, official export credit agencies, and autonomous agencies such as the U.S. Department of Agriculture or the Federal Home Loan Bank. Member countries of the OECD Development Assistance Committee and some other countries also report information on loans extended bilaterally or officially guaranteed to the Creditor Reporting System of the OECD.

Private Creditors

Private creditors include commercial banks, bondholders, and other private creditors. This line includes only publicly guaranteed creditors. Nonguaranteed private creditors are shown separately.

Bonds include publicly issued or privately placed bonds.

Commercial bank loans are loans from private banks and other private financial institutions.

Credits of other private creditors include credits from manufacturers, exporters, and other suppliers of goods, plus bank credits covered by a guarantee of an export credit agency. This line is included in the online database but is not shown in the published tables. It can be obtained as the difference between (a) credits of total private creditors and (b) bonds and commercial bank loans.

Sources of the Macroeconomic Indicators

The macroeconomic data are prepared by The World Bank from a variety of sources. Data on Workers' Remittances and Compensation of Employees are prepared by World Bank staff based on IMF balance of payments statistics. Data on Foreign Direct Investments are prepared by World Bank staff based on IMF balance of payments statistics and United Nations Conference on Trade and Development (UNCTAD) publication. Other macroeconomic data are from IMF balance of payments statistics.

Data on ***Foreign Direct Investments*** are gap filled with countries' balance of payments statistics for the following countries:

Ecuador
Malaysia
Papua New Guinea

Data on ***Exports of Goods, Services, and Income*** are gap filled with countries' balance of payments statistics for the following countries:

Algeria
Angola
Botswana
Cape Verde
Comoros (from 2005)
Democratic Republic of Congo (from 2005)
Dominican Republic
Ecuador
Egypt
Haiti
Madagascar (from 2006)
Malaysia
Mali
Mauritania (from 2006)
Papua New Guinea
Rwanda
São Tomé and Principe
Solomon Islands
Tonga
Vanuatu (from 2008)
Republic of Yemen

Data on ***Imports of Goods, Services, and Income*** are gap filled with countries' balance of payments statistics for the following countries:

Algeria
Angola
Botswana
Cape Verde
Comoros (from 2005)
Democratic Republic of Congo (from 2005)
Dominican Republic
Ecuador
Egypt
Haiti
Madagascar (from 2006)

Malaysia
Mali
Mauritania (from 2006)
Papua New Guinea
Rwanda
São Tomé and Principe
Solomon Islands
Tonga
Vanuatu (from 2008)
Republic of Yemen

Data for ***Current Account Balance*** are based on countries' balance of payments statistics for the following countries:

Algeria
Angola
Botswana
Comoros (from 2005)
Democratic Republic of Congo (from 2006)
Dominican Republic
Ecuador
Egypt
Guyana (from 2009)
Madagascar (from 2006)
Malawi (from 2005)
Malaysia
Mali
Mauritania (from 2006)
Papua New Guinea
Rwanda
São Tomé and Principe
Solomon Islands
Vanuatu (from 2008)
Republic of Yemen
Zimbabwe (from 2005)

Country Groups

Regional Groups

East Asia and Pacific

Cambodia (A)
China (P)
Fiji (A)
Indonesia (A)
Lao PDR (P)
Malaysia (E)
Mongolia (A)
Myanmar (E)
Papua New Guinea (A)
Philippines (A)
Samoa (A)
Solomon Islands (A)
Thailand (A)
Tonga (A)
Vanuatu (E)
Vietnam (P)

Europe and Central Asia

Albania (A)
Armenia (A)
Azerbaijan (A)
Belarus (A)
Bosnia and Herzegovina[a] (A)
Bulgaria (A)
Georgia (A)
Kazakhstan (A)
Kosovo (A)
Kyrgyz Republic (A)
Latvia (A)
Lithuania (A)
Macedonia, FYR (A)
Moldova (A)
Montenegro (A)
Romania (A)
Russian Federation (P)
Serbia[a/b] (A)
Tajikistan (A)
Turkey (A)
Turkmenistan (E)
Ukraine (A)
Uzbekistan (A)

Latin America and the Caribbean

Argentina (A)
Belize (A)
Bolivia (A)
Brazil (A)
Chile (A)
Colombia (A)
Costa Rica (A)
Dominica (A)
Dominican Republic (A)
Ecuador (A)
El Salvador (A)
Grenada (A)
Guatemala (A)
Guyana (A)
Haiti (A)
Honduras (A)
Jamaica (A)
Mexico (A)
Nicaragua (A)
Panama (A)
Paraguay (A)
Peru (A)
St. Kitts and Nevis (A)
St. Lucia (A)
St. Vincent and the Grenadines (A)
Uruguay (A)
Venezuela, RB (A)

Middle East and North Africa

Algeria (A)
Djibouti (A)
Egypt, Arab Rep. (A)
Iran, Islamic Rep. (A)
Jordan (A)
Lebanon (A)
Morocco (A)
Syrian Arab Republic (A)
Tunisia (A)
Yemen, Republic of (A)

South Asia

Afghanistan (A)
Bangladesh (A)
Bhutan (A)
India (A)
Maldives (A)
Nepal (A)
Pakistan (A)
Sri Lanka (A)

Sub-Saharan Africa

Angola (A)
Benin (A)
Botswana (A)
Burkina Faso (A)
Burundi (P)
Cameroon (A)
Cape Verde (A)
Central African Republic (P)
Chad (A)
Comoros (A)
Congo, Dem. Rep. (E)
Congo, Rep. (E)
Côte d'Ivoire (E)
Eritrea (E)
Ethiopia (A)
Gabon (A)
Gambia,The (A)
Ghana (A)
Guinea (E)
Guinea-Bissau (E)
Kenya (A)
Lesotho (A)
Liberia (A)
Madagascar (A)
Malawi (A)
Mali (A)
Mauritania (A)
Mauritius (A)
Mozambique (A)
Niger (A)
Nigeria (A)
Rwanda (A)
São Tomé and Principe (A)
Senegal (A)
Seychelles (A)
Sierra Leone (A)
Somalia (E)
South Africa (P)
Sudan (A)
Swaziland (A)
Tanzania (A)
Togo (A)
Uganda (A)
Zambia (P)
Zimbabwe (A)

Note: Letters in parenthesis indicate DRS reporters' status: (A) as reported, (P) preliminary, and (E) estimated. The status "as reported" indicates that the country was fully current in its reporting under the DRS and that World Bank staff are satisfied that the reported data give an adequate and fair representation of the country's total public debt. "Preliminary" data are based on reported or collected information, but because of incompleteness or other reasons, an element of staff estimation is included. "Estimated" data indicate that countries are not current in their reporting and that a significant element of staff estimation has been necessary in producing the data tables.

a. For Bosnia and Herzegovina, total debt before 1999, excluding IBRD and IMF obligations and short-term debt, is included under Serbia.
b. Data prior to 2006 include Montenegro.

Income Groups

Low-income countries

Afghanistan
Bangladesh
Benin
Burkina Faso
Burundi
Cambodia
Central African Republic
Chad
Comoros
Congo, Dem. Rep.
Eritrea
Ethiopia
Gambia, The
Guinea
Guinea-Bissau
Haiti
Kenya
Kyrgyz Republic
Liberia
Madagascar
Malawi
Mali
Mozambique
Myanmar
Nepal
Niger
Rwanda
Sierra Leone
Somalia
Tajikistan
Tanzania
Togo
Uganda
Zimbabwe

Middle-income countries

Albania
Algeria
Angola
Argentina
Armenia
Azerbaijan
Belarus
Belize
Bhutan
Bolivia
Bosnia and Herzegovina
Botswana
Brazil
Bulgaria
Cameroon
Cape Verde
Chile
China
Colombia
Congo, Rep.
Costa Rica
Côte d'Ivoire
Djibouti
Dominica
Dominican Republic
Ecuador
Egypt, Arab Rep.
El Salvador
Fiji
Gabon
Georgia
Ghana
Grenada
Guatemala
Guyana
Honduras
India
Indonesia
Iran, Islamic Rep.
Jamaica
Jordan
Kazakhstan
Kosovo
Lao PDR
Latvia
Lebanon
Lesotho
Lithuania
Macedonia, FYR
Malaysia
Maldives
Mauritania
Mauritius
Mexico
Moldova
Mongolia
Montenegro
Morocco
Nicaragua
Nigeria
Pakistan
Panama
Papua New Guinea
Paraguay
Peru
Philippines
Romania
Russian Federation
Samoa
São Tomé and Principe
Senegal
Serbia
Seychelles
Solomon Islands
South Africa
Sri Lanka
St. Kitts and Nevis
St. Lucia
St. Vincent and the Grenadines
Sudan
Swaziland
Syrian Arab Republic
Thailand
Tonga
Tunisia
Turkey
Turkmenistan
Ukraine
Uruguay
Uzbekistan
Vanuatu
Venezuela, RB
Vietnam
Yemen, Republic of
Zambia

Note: Low-income economies are those with a GNI per capita of $1,005 or less in 2010. Middle-income economies are those with a GNI per capita of more than $1,006 but less than $12,275. Lower-middle-income and upper-middle-income economies are separated at a GNI per capita of $3,976.

Glossary

Average terms of new commitments provide information on the average terms (interest rate, maturity, and grace period) of new commitments on public and publicly guaranteed external debt contracted with public and private creditors. Averages are weighted by the amounts of the loans.

Bilateral official creditors are official agencies that make loans on behalf of one government to another government or to public (and, in some cases, private) borrowers in another country.

Bonds are debt instruments issued by public and publicly guaranteed or private debtors with durations of one year or longer. Bonds usually give the holder the unconditional right to fixed money income or contractually determined, variable money income.

Commercial banks are private banks that provide loans and other financial services.

Commitments of public and publicly guaranteed debt constitute the total amount of new long-term loans to public sector borrowers or borrowers with a public sector guarantee extended by official and private lenders and for which contracts were signed in the year specified.

Contractual obligations on outstanding long-term external debt are the anticipated debt service payments on long-term external debt contracted up to December 31 of reporting year.

Currency composition of public and publicly guaranteed debt provides information on the share of loans outstanding and disbursed by currency of repayment. For major multilateral creditors, the currency composition of the relevant unit of account is also taken into account. The principal currencies in which the external debt of low- and middle-income countries is contracted (the euro, Japanese yen, pound sterling, Swiss franc, and U.S. dollar) are separately identified. Beginning in 2001, debt denominated in the currencies of the members in the euro area is included under the euro rather than the national currencies that previously prevailed.

Current account balance is the sum of net balances on trade in goods, services, and income and the net current transfers.

Debt buyback is the repurchase by a debtor of its own debt, either at a discount price or at par value. In the event of a buyback of long-term debt, the face value of the debt bought back will be recorded as a decline in stock outstanding of long-term debt, and the cash amount received by creditors will be recorded as a principal repayment. For example, if a country buys back long-term external debt of face value B at a price P, then long-term external debt will decline by B, and principal repayment will increase by P. The difference between the price at which the debt was bought back and the face value is recorded as a debt stock write-off (the related transactions are not separately indentified in the *Global Development Finance* (GDF) publication but are available in the CD-ROM and online database).

Debt forgiveness grants include both debts canceled by agreement between debtor and creditor and reductions in the net present value of official nonconcessional loans resulting from concessional rescheduling or refinancing. Data are recorded on a disbursement basis and include debt forgiveness from bilateral and multilateral creditors.

Debt outstanding and disbursed is the value at year's end of long-term external debt owed by public and publicly guaranteed debtors and private nonguaranteed debtors.

Debt restructurings are revisions to debt service obligations agreed on by creditors and debtors. Such agreements change the amount and timing of future principal and interest payments.

Debt service to exports is the ratio of the sum of principal repayments and interest paid on total long-term debt (public and publicly guaranteed debt and private nonguaranteed debt) to the value of exports of goods and services and receipts of income from abroad.

Debt stock-flow reconciliation shows the indicators that affect the change in debt stocks from one period to the next.

Disbursements are drawings during the year specified on loan commitments contracted by the borrower.

Exports of goods, services, and income constitute the total value of exports of goods and services, receipts of compensation of nonresident workers, and investment income from abroad.

External debt flows are debt-related transactions during the year specified. They include disbursements, principal repayments, and interest payments.

External debt stocks comprise public and publicly guaranteed long-term external debt, private nonguaranteed long-term external debt, use of IMF credit, and short-term external debt, including interest arrears on long-term debt. The relation between external debt stock and its components is illustrated on page 323 (figure 1).

External debt stocks to exports is the ratio of outstanding external debt to the value of exports of goods and services and receipts of income from abroad.

External debt stocks to GNI is the ratio of outstanding external debt to gross national income.

Foreign direct investment refers to direct investment flows in the reporting economy. It is the sum of equity capital, reinvestment earnings, and other capital. The term describes a category of international investment made by a resident entity in one economy (direct investor) with the objective of establishing a lasting interest in an enterprise resident in an economy other than that of the investor (direct investment enterprise). Ownership of 10 percent or more of the ordinary shares or voting stock is the criterion for determining the existence of a direct investment relationship.

Grace period is the time between the date on which a loan is committed and the date on which the first principal payment is due. The information presented in *Global Development Finance* is the average grace period on all public and publicly guaranteed debt committed during the specified period.

Grants are legally binding commitments that obligate a specific value of funds available for disbursement for which there is no payment requirement. They include debt forgiveness grants and grants from bilateral and multilateral agencies (such as the International Development Association).

Gross national income (GNI) is the sum of value added by all resident producers, plus any product taxes (less subsidies) not included in the valuation of output, plus net receipts of primary income compensation of employees and property income) from abroad. Yearly average exchange rates are used to convert GNI from local currency to U.S. dollars.

Heavily Indebted Poor Country (HIPC) Initiative is a program of the World Bank and the International Monetary Fund to provide debt relief to qualifying countries with unsustainable debt burdens.

Imports of goods, services, and income constitute the total value of goods and services imported and income payable to nonresidents.

Interest arrears on long-term debt are interest payments due but not paid, shown on a cumulative basis. Interest arrears are due and payable immediately and are therefore regarded as short-term obligations. Thus, an increase in interest arrears on long-term debt will be recorded as an increase in short-term debt. Interest in arrears on the use of IMF credit is also considered to be part of short-term external debt.

Interest payments are the amounts of interest paid in foreign currency, goods, or services in the year specified.

Interest rate is the interest rate applicable to a loan commitment as specified in the loan contract. The information presented in *Global Development Finance* is the average interest on all public and publicly guaranteed debt committed during the specified period.

International Bank for Reconstruction and Development (IBRD) is a multilateral official creditor. It is the nonconcessional lending arm of the World Bank Group.

International Development Association (IDA) is a multilateral official creditor. It is the concessional financing arm of the World Bank Group. The IDA also provides grant financing to qualified borrowers.

International Monetary Fund (IMF) charges are the amounts of interest paid in foreign currency in the year specified for transactions with the IMF.

International Monetary Fund (IMF) purchases are the total drawings on the general resources account of the IMF during the year specified, excluding drawings in the reserve tranche.

International Monetary Fund (IMF) repurchases are the amounts of principal (amortization) paid in foreign currency in the year specified for transactions with the IMF.

International reserves constitute the sum of a country's monetary authority's holdings of special drawing rights, its reserve position in the IMF, its holdings of foreign exchange, and its holdings of gold (valued at year-end London prices).

Long-term external debt is debt that has an original or extended maturity of more than one year and that is owed to nonresidents by residents of an economy and is repayable in foreign currency, goods, or services.

Long-term private sector debt is long-term debt owed by the private sector, whether publicly guaranteed or not.

Long-term public sector debt is long-term external debt owed by the public sector.

Maturity is the date on which the final principal repayment on a loan is due. It is the sum of the grace and repayment periods. The information presented in *Global Development Finance* is the average maturity on all public and publicly guaranteed debt committed during the specified period.

Multilateral Debt Relief Initiative (MDRI) is a program of the World Bank, the IMF, the Inter-American Development Bank, and the African Development Bank that provides additional debt relief to countries that have completed the HIPC process.

Multilateral official creditors are official agencies owned or governed by more than one country that provide loan financing. They include international financial institutions such as the World Bank, regional development banks, and other intergovernmental agencies.

Multilateral to external debt stocks is the ratio of the stock of debt owed to multilateral creditors to total external debt.

Net flows on external debt are disbursements on long-term external debt and IMF purchases minus principal repayments on long-term external debt and IMF repurchases. Up to 1984, this calculation included only long-term external debt and IMF flows. From 1985, the calculation includes the change in stock of short-term debt (excluding interest arrears on long-term external debt).

Official creditors are governments or other bilateral public entities, such as export-import agencies, development agencies, and multilateral financial institutions such as the World Bank and regional development banks.

Portfolio equity is the category of international investment that covers investment in equity securities. Equity securities include shares, stocks, participation, or similar documents (such as American Depositary Receipts) that usually denote ownership of equity.

Present value of debt outstanding is the nominal value of all future debt service obligations on existing debt discounted at prevailing market rates of interest. The interest rates used in this calculation are the Commercial Interest Reference Rates (CIRR) for each relevant currency compiled and published by the Organisation for Economic Cooperation and Development.

Principal arrears on long-term debt are principal repayments due but not paid on long-term external debt, shown on a cumulative basis.

Principal repayments are the amounts of principal (amortization) paid in foreign currency, goods, or services in the year specified with respect to long-term external debt.

Private creditors are bondholders, commercial banks, and other trade-related lenders.

Private nonguaranteed debt is debt owed by private sector borrowers to external creditors on loans that do not benefit from a public sector guarantee by the debtor country.

Profit remittances on FDI are payments of direct investment income (debit side), which consist of income on equity (dividends, branch profits, and reinvested earnings) and income on the intercompany debt (interest).

Public and publicly guaranteed debt outstanding and disbursed is the value of debt at year's end of public sector borrowers, or borrowers with a public sector guarantee, owed to official and private lenders.

Public and publicly guaranteed external debt comprises public debt (an external obligation of a public debtor, such as the national government or agency, a political subdivision or agency, or an autonomous public body) and publicly guaranteed external debt (an external obligation of a private debtor that is guaranteed for repayment by a public entity).

Reserves to external debt stocks is the ratio of international reserves to outstanding external debt.

Reserves to imports (months) is the ratio of international reserves to the value of imports of goods, services, and income in the year shown and is expressed in months:

$$\frac{\text{Reserves}}{\text{Imports/12}}$$

Short-term external debt has an original maturity of one year or less. Available data permit no distinction among public, publicly guaranteed, and private nonguaranteed short-term external debt.

Short-term to external debt stock ratio is the ratio of short-term external debt to total outstanding external debt.

Special Drawing Rights (SDRs) refer to an international reserve asset that was created by the IMF in 1969 to supplement its member countries' official reserves. The value of SDRs is based on a basket of four key international currencies: the U.S. dollar, the pound sterling, the Japanese yen, and the euro. In addition to playing a role as a supplementary reserve asset, SDRs serve as the unit of account for the IMF and some other international organizations.

Technical cooperation grants include (a) free-standing technical cooperation grants, which are intended to finance the transfer of technical and managerial skills or of technology for the purpose of building up general national capacity without reference to any specific investment projects, and (b) investment-related technical cooperation grants, which are aimed at strengthening the capacity to execute specific investment projects.

Total amount forgiven is the total amount of principal and interest due, principal and interest in arrears, and debt stock forgiven in the year specified.

Total amount rescheduled is the total amount of external debt rescheduled, including principal and interest due, principal and interest in arrears, charges, penalties, and debt stock in the year specified.

Total change in external debt stocks is the difference in the external debt stock between two consecutive years.

Use of IMF credit denotes members' drawings on the IMF other than amounts drawn against the country's reserve tranche position. Use of IMF credit includes purchases and drawings under Stand-By, Extended, Structural Adjustment, Enhanced Structural Adjustment, and Systemic Transformation Facility Arrangements as well as Trust Fund loans.

Worker remittances and compensation of employees constitute the sum of workers' remittances, compensation of employees, and migrants' transfers as defined in the IMF's *Balance of Payments Manual* (BPM5).

Users' Guide

The general cutoff date for all data in this publication is end-September 2011. The economic aggregates presented in the tables are prepared for the convenience of users. Although debt ratios can give useful information about developments in debt-servicing capacity, conclusions drawn from them will not be valid unless accompanied by careful economic evaluation.

The macroeconomic data provided are collected from national statistical organizations, but in some cases may be subject to considerable margin of error. The usual care must be taken in interpreting the ratios, particularly for the most recent years, because figures may be preliminary and subject to revision.

Country notes at the end of each country table summarize major events that have taken place in the country in recent years; describe the sources of information for short-term and private nonguaranteed external debt; and highlight main issues in data collection process. Unless otherwise specified in the country table, data on long-term public and publicly guaranteed external debt for 2010 are based on reports provided by the country.

Abbreviations

The following abbreviations are used in the principal ratios and indicator tables:

BIS	Bank for International Settlements
CIRR	Commercial Interest Reference Rates
COMSEC	Commonwealth Secretariat
CRS	Creditor Reporting System (of the OECD)
DAC	Development Assistance Committee (of the OECD)
DRS	Debtor Reporting System (of the World Bank)
FDI	Foreign Direct Investment
GNI	Gross National Income
HIPC	Highly Indebted Poor Country (Initiative of the World Bank and IMF)
IBRD	International Bank for Reconstruction and Development (of the World Bank)
IDA	International Development Association (of the World Bank)
IMF	International Monetary Fund
LIBOR	London Interbank Offered Rate
MDRI	Multilateral Debt Relief Initiative
ODA	Official Development Assistance
OECD	Organization for Economic Co-operation and Development
SDRs	Special drawing rights (of the IMF)
UNCTAD	United Nations Conference on Trade and Development
WBXD	World Bank External Debt System

Symbols

The following symbols have been used throughout:

0 or 0.0 means zero or small enough that the number would round to zero at the displayed number of decimal places.

.. means that data are not available or that aggregates cannot be calculated because of missing data in the years shown.

$ indicates current U.S. dollars unless otherwise specified.

ECO-AUDIT

Environmental Benefits Statement

The World Bank is committed to preserving endangered forests and natural resources. The Office of the Publisher has chosen to print ***Global Development Finance 2012*** on recycled paper with 30 percent postconsumer waste, in accordance with the recommended standards for paper usage set by the Green Press Initiative, a nonprofit program supporting publishers in using fiber that is not sourced from endangered forests. For more information, visit www.greenpressinitiative.org.

Saved:

- 14 trees
- 6 million Btu of total energy
- 1,362 lb. of net greenhouse gases
- 6,141 gal. of water
- 389 lb. of solid waste

green press INITIATIVE